The International Companion to Scottish Literature 1400–1650

INTERNATIONAL COMPANIONS TO SCOTTISH LITERATURE

Series Editors: Ian Brown and Thomas Owen Clancy

Titles in the series include:

International Companion to Lewis Grassic Gibbon
Edited by Scott Lyall
ISBN 978-1-908980-13-7

International Companion to Edwin Morgan
Edited by Alan Riach
ISBN 978-1-908980-14-4

International Companion to Scottish Poetry
Edited by Carla Sassi
ISBN 978-1-908980-15-1

International Companion to James Macpherson and The Poems of Ossian
Edited by Dafydd Moore
ISBN 978-1-908980-19-9

International Companion to John Galt
Edited by Gerard Carruthers and Colin Kidd
ISBN 978-1-908980-27-4

International Companion to Scottish Literature 1400–1650
Edited by Nicola Royan
ISBN 978-1-908980-23-6

The International Companion to Scottish Literature 1400–1650

Edited by Nicola Royan

Scottish Literature International

Published by
Scottish Literature International
Scottish Literature
7 University Gardens
University of Glasgow
Glasgow G12 8QH

Scottish Literature International is an imprint of
the Association for Scottish Literary Studies

www.asls.org.uk

ASLS is a registered charity no. SC006535

First published 2018

Text © ASLS and the individual contributors

All rights reserved. No part of this book may be
reproduced, stored in a retrieval system, or
transmitted in any form or means, electronic,
mechanical, photocopying, recording or otherwise,
without the prior permission of the
Association for Scottish Literary Studies.

A CIP catalogue for this title
is available from the British Library

ISBN 978-1-908980-23-6

Contents

Series Editors' Preface vii
Acknowledgements. ix
Abbreviations. xi

Introduction: Literatures of the Stewart Kingdom. 1
Nicola Royan

PART 1: LANGUAGE AND TRANSMISSION

1. The Languages of Scotland. 19
   Sara Pons-Sanz and Aonghas MacCoinnich
2. The Transmission of Older Scots Literature 38
   Sally Mapstone

PART 2: CULTURE AND IDENTITY

3. Expressions of Faith: Religious Writing. 60
   Sìm Innes and Steven Reid
4. The Purposes of Literature 79
   William Gillies and Kate McClune
5. Historiography in Highlands and Lowlands 100
   Ulrike Hogg and Martin MacGregor

PART 3: GENRE AND APPROACH

6. Lyric. 124
   Mícheál B. Ó Mainnín and Nicola Royan
7. Chivalric Literature 157
   Rhiannon Purdie and Katie Stevenson
8. Elegy and Commemorative Writing. 173
   Joanna Martin and Kate L. Mathis
9. Satire 200
   Tricia A. McElroy and Nicole Meier
10. Performance 217
    John J. McGavin and Dòmhnall Uilleam Stiùbhart
11. Translation 237
    Kaarina Hollo and Thomas Rutledge

Contents (continued)

Endnotes *267*
Further Reading *355*
Notes on Contributors *361*
Index *365*

Series Editors' Preface

Periodisation is a highly sensitive and tendentious process, often incorporating hidden assumptions about the historically significant events in the continuous process of making literature, or any other form of knowledge and understanding. With other members of the editorial team of *The Edinburgh History of Scottish Literature*, for example, we wrestled with possible boundaries before adopting 1707 and the Union of the Parliaments as a significant period break, when 1746, Culloden and its after-effects were much more significant for Scottish literature in Gaelic. In the first period volume published in this series, *Twentieth Century Scottish Literature*, we were as comfortable as we might be that that century – running into this one – might make a sensible period division, as would the forthcoming volume on the nineteenth century. Defining earlier periods offered more challenges. In the end we have adopted a process that is avowedly imprecise and fluid, driven by our desire to reflect so far as possible changes that affected literature in all of the relevant languages of Scotland of the given period.

Perhaps our choices will seem as arbitrary as that of 1707, a political more than cultural watershed, but we hope they offer food for fruitful discussion. A planned volume on early Scottish literature will conclude at around 1400, making the appearance of Barbour's *Bruce* with all it stands for a culmination of a long period of writing in many languages in what would become Scotland. For the period this volume deals with, we wished to avoid the vexed word 'renaissance' in the title: it means different things at different times, all equally valid, in the study of Scottish literature. So we use a time period to mark this volume, concluding with the year of defeat of the Scottish army by Cromwell at Dunbar, given what that meant in the ensuing years for Scottish culture and politics, let alone its literature. Behind this decision lay our view that 1650 was as good a year as any to mark the beginning of the process of thinking and writing that is called the Scottish Enlightenment. The period volume after this one will thus be concerned with the literature of the long eighteenth century. This has meant, for the present volume, that authors have spanned a number of sub-periods often thought as dividing marks in Scottish history and literature, in particular the religious changes attendant on the Scottish Reformation.

The complexity of the linguistic and literary communities of Scotland is further reflected, as in the volume on Scottish poetry edited by Carla Sassi, by encouragement to editors in all these periods to consider, where appropriate, joint chapters that look across linguistic communities. Such communities were not sealed from one another, but – as is demonstrated in several chapters of this volume – mutually interrelated. The strategies adopted for the earlier-period volumes of this series are, therefore, challenging and sometimes require very fresh thinking of editors and authors. Hence, we are more than usually immensely grateful to Nicola Royan and every contributor to this volume. Their work, we suggest, opens up new vistas in the understanding of Scottish literature of the period 1400–1650.

Ian Brown
Thomas Owen Clancy

Acknowledgements

This collection has been an extraordinarily long time in the gathering. As a result, an equal debt of gratitude is owed to the contributors and to the general editors of the series, Ian Brown and Thomas Clancy, and to the Association for Scottish Literary Studies. The contributors have revised chapters, answered queries, expressed interest, and had complete confidence that the volume would be published. The series editors have done the same, and also intervened at crucial moments to ensure that publication happened. Thomas, in particular, has spent several months chivvying and checking, to bring the project to fruition.

One of the distinguishing features of this collection has been to try to bring the different languages of Scottish writing together, specifically not to separate Gaelic and Latin into individual chapters, but rather to try to acknowledge the multilingual nature of Scottish writing. As a result, as editor I have learned a great deal, and I would like to thank the contributors for that, too. It has been a privilege to work with so many great scholars.

Every editor needs encouragement, and I have received that from colleagues at Nottingham, including Lynda Pratt, Thorlac Turville-Petre and Joanna Martin, and from colleagues in Scottish studies, in addition to the contributors, such as Theo van Heijnsbergen and Rod Lyall. The School of English, University of Nottingham, has also helped more materially, with a grant to support proofreading and indexing.

I have been working in Older Scots for some twenty-five years, and I owe an overwhelming debt to three groups of people: firstly, two Honours classes in Scottish Literature, University of Glasgow 1992 and 2001, whom I hope very much would have found this Companion to be precisely what they wanted; secondly, to the academic community, within and outwith Scotland, who are concerned with studying late medieval and early modern Scotland, its languages, its literatures, peoples and cultures, from whom I have learned how to be a scholar; and thirdly, to my family, who are prepared to show an interest in Older Scots just to humour me.

Abbreviations

ACMRS: Arizona Center for Medieval and Renaissance Studies.
AHSL: R. D. S. Jack (ed.), *History of Scottish Literature* vol 1: *Origins to 1660* (Aberdeen: AUP, 1988).
Aitken et al, *Bards and Makars*: Adam J. Aitken et al. (eds), *Bards and Makars: Scottish Language and Literature: Medieval and Renaissance* (Glasgow: University of Glasgow Press, 1977).
ASLS: Association for Scottish Literary Studies.
AUP: Aberdeen University Press.
Bawcutt and Riddy, *LSP*: Priscilla Bawcutt and Felicity Riddy (eds), *Longer Scottish Poems* vol. 1: 1375–1650 (Edinburgh: SAP, 1987).
Bawcutt, *Dunbar*: *The Poems of William Dunbar*, ed. P. Bawcutt, 2 vols (Glasgow: ASLS, 1998). Individual poems will be identified with B and number, as they appear in this edition.
Bawcutt and Hadley Williams, *Medieval Scottish Poetry*: P. Bawcutt and J. Hadley Williams (eds), *A Companion to Medieval Scottish Poetry* (Cambridge: D. S. Brewer, 2006).
BBIAS: *Bibliographical Bulletin of the International Arthurian Society*.
BDL: Book of the Dean of Lismore, Edinburgh, NLS, Adv.MS.72.1.37.
Boardman and Foran, *Barbour's Bruce*: Steve Boardman and Susan Foran (eds), *Barbour's Bruce and its Cultural Contexts: Politics, Chivalry and Literature in Late Medieval Scotland* (Woodbridge: D. S. Brewer, 2015).
Caie et al, *European Sun*: G. Caie, R. J. Lyall, S. Mapstone and K. Simpson (eds), *The European Sun: Proceedings of the Seventh International Conference on Medieval and Renaissance Scottish Language and Literature* (East Linton: Tuckwell Press, 2001).

Chron. Bower: Walter Bower, *Scotichronicon*, ed. D. E. R. Watt et al, 9 vols. (Aberdeen and Edinburgh: AUP and Mercat Press, 1989–98).

CUP: Cambridge University Press.

DOST: *Dictionary of the Older Scottish Tongue*, found at *Dictionary of the Scots Language*. 2004. Scottish Language Dictionaries Ltd. www.dsl.ac.uk.

DSL: *Dictionary of the Scots Language* 2004. Scottish Language Dictionaries Ltd. www.dsl.ac.uk.

EHSL: I. Brown, T. Clancy, S. Manning and M. Pittock (eds), *The Edinburgh History of Scottish Literature vol 1: From Columba to the Union (until 1707)* (Edinburgh: EUP, 2006).

EUP: Edinburgh University Press.

FMLS: *Forum for Modern Language Studies.*

Fox, *Henryson*: *The Poems of Robert Henryson*, ed. Denton Fox (Oxford: OUP, 1981).

Gillies, *Gaelic and Scotland*: William Gillies (ed.), *Gaelic and Scotland: Alba agus a' Ghàidhlig* (Edinburgh: EUP, 1989).

IR: *Innes Review.*

Hadley Williams, *Lyndsay*: Janet Hadley Williams (ed.), *Sir David Lyndsay: Selected Poems* (Glasgow: ASLS, 2001).

Hadley Williams and McClure, *Fresche Fontanis*: J. Hadley Williams and J. D. McClure (eds), *Fresche Fontanis: Proceedings of the 2008 Medieval and Renaissance Scottish Languages and Literatures Conference* (Newcastle: Cambridge Scholars, 2013).

Houwen et al, *Palace in the Wild*: L. A. J. R. Houwen, A. A. MacDonald and S. L. Mapstone (eds), *A Palace in the Wild: Essays on Vernacular Culture and Humanism in Late-Medieval and Renaissance Scotland* (Leuven: Peeters, 2000).

JEBS: *Journal of the Edinburgh Bibliographic Society.*

McClure and Spiller, *Bryght Lanternis*: J. Derrick McClure and Michael R. G. Spiller (eds), *Bryght Lanternis: Essays on the Language and Literature of Medieval and Renaissance Scotland* (Aberdeen: AUP, 1989).

MacDonald et al, *Renaissance in Scotland*: A. A. MacDonald, M. Lynch and I. B. Cowan (eds), *The Renaissance in Scotland: Studies in Literature, Religion, History and Culture* (Leiden: E. J. Brill, 1994).

Mapstone, *Dunbar*: Sally Mapstone (ed.), *William Dunbar, 'The Nobill Poyet': Essays in Honour of Priscilla Bawcutt* (East Linton: Tuckwell Press, 2001).
Mapstone, *Older Scottish Literature*: Sally Mapstone (ed.), *Older Scottish Literature* (Edinburgh: John Donald, 2005).
Mason, *Kingship and Commonweal*: Roger A. Mason, *Kingship and the Commonweal: Political Thought in Renaissance and Reformation Scotland* (East Linton: Tuckwell Press, 1998).
MIP: Medieval Institute Publications.
MUP: Manchester University Press.
NIMEV: Julia Boffey and A. S. G. Edwards (eds), *New Index of Middle English Verse* (London: British Library, 2004).
NLS: National Library of Scotland.
OED: Oxford English Dictionary (Oxford: OUP, 2017). www.oed.com.
OUP: Oxford University Press.
PBA: *Proceedings of the British Academy.*
PMLA: *Proceedings of the Modern Languages Association.*
RES: *Review of English Studies.*
RoSC: *Review of Scottish Culture.*
Royan, *Langage Cleir Illumynate*: N. Royan (ed.), *Langage Cleir Illumynate: Scottish Poetry from Barbour to Drummond, 1375–1630* (Amsterdam: Rodopi, 2007).
SAP: Scottish Academic Press.
ScotStud: *Scottish Studies.*
SGS: *Scottish Gaelic Studies.*
SGTS: Scottish Gaelic Text Society. Unless otherwise stated, place of publication for all Society publications is Edinburgh.
SHR: *Scottish Historical Review.*
SHS: Scottish History Society. Place of publication for all Society publications is Edinburgh.
SL: *Scottish Language.*
SLJ/SSR/SLR: *Scottish Literary Journal, Scottish Studies Review, Scottish Literary Review*, published by ASLS.
SSL: *Studies in Scottish Literature.*
STC: *A short-title catalogue of books printed in England, Scotland & Ireland and of English books printed abroad, 1475–1640*, first compiled by A. W. Pollard & G. R. Redgrave. Rev. edn. 3 vols (London: Bibliographical Society, 1976–1991).

ABBREVIATIONS

STS: Scottish Text Society. Place of publication for all Society publications is Edinburgh.

TGSI: *Transactions of the Gaelic Society of Inverness.*

Van Heijnsbergen et al, *Literature, Letters and Canonical*: Theo van Heijnsbergen and Nicola Royan (eds), *Literature, Letters and the Canonical in Early Modern Scotland* (East Linton: Tuckwell Press, 2002).

Watson, *Scottish Verse*: William J. Watson (ed.), *Scottish Verse from the Book of the Dean of Lismore* (Edinburgh: SGTS, 1937).

As far as possible, dates of birth and death are taken from the *Oxford Dictionary of National Biography.*

Introduction: Literatures of the Stewart Kingdom[1]

Nicola Royan

The definition of any literary period is always problematic, since cultural endeavour is generally untidy in its relationship to useful dates, events and even historical movements. While the title of this volume sidesteps the problem of labelling by its use of dates, most readers will interpret those dates as representing a meaningful and coherent literary period, as experienced in an agreed geographical location. While the dates are fixed, however, there are nevertheless changes and uncertainties. To begin with, the geographic extent of the Scottish kingdom changes during this period. By 1470, the northern isles, Orkney and Shetland, had become part of the kingdom through the marriage of James III (1452–1488) to Margaret of Denmark (1456/7–1486); after the suppression of the Lordship of the Isles by James IV (1473–1513), the Western Isles too become more politically part of the realm.[2] Both James III and James IV present themselves as emperors in their kingdom, an important change in political perception.[3] While James V (1512–1542) was famously concerned with pacifying the lawlessness on the Scottish border with England, the assumption of the English throne by his grandson changed the nature of that border and its government.[4] On the other hand, the ruling dynasty – in contrast to both England and France – remained constant; the Stuarts would even regain the crown after Charles I's (1600–1649) execution, and it was the more mundane difficulties of raising children that brought the dynasty to a close.[5]

An established ruling dynasty, however, did not guarantee stable government. From the beginning of the period until 1625, every Stewart monarch ascended the throne as a minor.[6] The chronicler Walter Bower (1385–1449) was not alone in lamenting the effects of minority government and regency, although more recent historians have not seen these periods as entirely disastrous.[7] The literary ramifications of such interludes are equally mixed. Where overt royal patronage was absent, magnates and other figures stepped in: this is most obviously and consistently true of Gaelic literature, but also pertains to writing in Older Scots and Latin.[8] The Campbells, the Douglases and the Sinclairs are perhaps the most obvious noble patrons, but writers like Andrew Wyntoun (c. 1350–c. 1422) and Hary (c. 1440–c. 1492) identify lesser lairds as commissioners of their work, whereas the title of the Book of the Dean of Lismore locates it in a church context.[9] The transmission and preservation of much Older Scots material rests in the circles around George Bannatyne (1545–1607/8) and Richard Maitland (1496–1586), and the preferences of an earlier lawyer, John Asloan (fl. 1513–1530).[10] The devolution of literary production outwith an only intermittently regal court provokes additional questions about audience and circulation, as well as about the relationship of the regions of Scotland to the centre. A metropolitan model of production and reception, still evident in discussions of early modern English literature, seems far less probable in a realm where there was not always a political centre, and where power was frequently devolved to regional magnates and burghs.[11]

To the peculiarities of Scottish government might also be attributed the recurrent concern – even an obsession – in Older Scots and Latin writing with advising their princes.[12] Political comment can also be found in Gaelic writing, particularly in relation to feud and regional concerns, but, because of the status of Gaelic, royal (in contrast to magnatial) government would be far less likely to encounter literature in that language, let alone pay it due attention.[13] Writers in Older Scots and Latin, in contrast, are willing to address both regional and national government, in both specific and general terms. One of the best-known examples is David Lyndsay (c. 1486–1555)'s *Ane Satyre of the Thrie Estaitis*:[14] first performed in its entirety in the minority of Mary, Queen of Scots (1542–1587), it begins and ends with considerations of government generally relevant to individual and nation, while presenting some quite particular solutions in the middle. The diversity of kinds of performance in Lyndsay's play, from literary modes such as morality play, farce, and sermon, to public acts like execution and the passing of laws, demonstrates the sophistication of the audience, not least in recognising the Pure [poor] Man as both their representative and also a part of the drama, when he invades the playing area.[15] The same sophistication applies in addressing the broad aspects of self-control required in a good king and a good person (Rex Humanitas), as well as the specific abuses that can be addressed by law and practice. The question of whether Folly's entrance at the end of the play undermines entirely the previous reforming decisions and renders them pointless, or whether it should be seen as a positive challenge to the audience to participate in both personal and political reform while acknowledging the imperfectibility of human society is open to debate. Folly was missing in Guthrie's adaptation of the play (1948);[16] Alan Spence's updating in 2000 for performance on the Castlehill in Cupar chose to foreground a particular strand of Protestantism.[17] Yet the repetition of key acts at the beginning of many medieval Scottish parliaments suggests that the frailty of government was well-known and fully acknowledged by generations preceding and following Lyndsay, as well as Lyndsay himself.[18] Such acknowledgement did not, however, preclude the hope of improvement. So, from the beginning of the period, where the *Kingis Quair* also addresses the relationship between self and royal governments to the end, where, through all kinds of text, literary work considers the effects of government under Charles and the Commonwealth, a primary concern remains: how readers should govern themselves, with a view to their divine salvation as well as their earthly one.

Although important, the influence of individual kings and dynasties is overshadowed by two broader, international, cultural phenomena: the Renaissance and the Reformation. While 'Renaissance' is a contested concept, particularly in a Scottish context where it is applied as much to the early twentieth century as it is to the sixteenth, there is plenty of evidence for the presence of humanism, one of the defining movements associated with the Renaissance, in Scotland from the late fifteenth century.[19] Through the rediscovery of lost Latin works such as Tacitus's *Annales,* and the engagement with classical Greek texts in the original language, humanism fostered direct engagement with language, literature and new interpretations of all kinds of ancient texts, including the Bible and Plato's philosophy.[20] From such academic beginnings came, amongst other things, renewed discussions of civic behaviour and the nature of the commonweal;[21] the study of classical rhetoric as a key aspect of advanced education; and a desire to emulate classical literary practice, either in writing Latin (as did Hector Boece (c. 1465–1536), George Buchanan (1506–1582) and Arthur Johnston (c. 1579–1641)), or in translating classical texts, such as the *Aeneid* or Livy's *Histories,* into the vernacular.[22] Although the changes attributed to humanism are profound, nevertheless their enactment was gradual and erratic: as the Tay is salt as far as Perth, so we can see that the literature of sixteenth- and seventeenth-century Scotland reaches back into the medieval tradition, both in Gaelic and in Scots.

However, in Northern Europe generally, humanist study did contribute to a more abrupt change in the cultural fabric. The rediscovery of classical languages, particularly Greek and Hebrew, and a concern for accurate representation of early texts also shed new light on the Bible, and produced texts independent of the Vulgate translation.[23] Reformers of all persuasions responded to these endeavours, reviewing church practice as well as theology.[24] Not all humanists were Protestant, and certainly not all humanists approved of enabling by translation lay access to holy texts, but many of the significant Reforming figures in Scotland had interests in humanist study, from Bishop William Elphinstone (1431–1514) to Andrew Melville (1545–1622).[25] The particularly Protestant focus on the Word also seems to have contributed to a promotion of literacy. The advent of print made texts more accessible, so that there was also possibly more to read. Moreover, religious principles also contributed to different kinds of writing and self-presentation, including psalm translations and hymns, polemic in many guises, and self-examination in the forms of diaries and letters.[26] Aside then from the practical matters of church and national government, the Reformation had a profound effect on cultural life: of Lowland Scotland in the eighteenth century, it has been said that every household that could afford it had a Bible and the collected works of Sir David Lyndsay, a writer equivocal about Protestantism but certain about the need for reform.[27]

If the Reformation is significant in our understanding of the literatures in Scotland, then the great political events of the seventeenth century, the Union of the Crowns in 1603 and the Wars of the Three Kingdoms (1639–1652), should also be visible in the cultural tradition.[28] It can be argued that the Union of the Crowns is less significant than has been imagined: although James VI's (1566–1625) departure took court patronage from Older Scots literature and probably encouraged writing in English orthography rather than Scots, he nevertheless left behind some notable writers and a sophisticated literary audience.[29] Furthermore, he was never a great patron of Gaelic writing, and thus, overall, 1603 may not have had as direct an impact as is sometimes imagined on the literatures he left behind. The Wars of the Three Kingdoms, however, like all civil wars, provoked all kinds of responses: while its presence in Gaelic material has been considered, seventeenth-century material in Older Scots is generally less explored, apart from Thomas Urquhart's (1611–1660) *The Jewel*.[30]

It will be obvious even from this brief survey that there were a variety of languages used in Scotland during this period. The native vernaculars were Scottish Gaelic and Older Scots; the primary language of education was Latin.[31] In the burghs trading with the Continent, and among those families associated with the court and government, as well as those who had received education abroad, there would have been other languages understood at least: particularly French, but also Flemish and Dutch, some German, some Danish, some Norwegian and Norse-inflected varieties in the Northern Isles, and even some Italian. There is not space to discuss in detail the full variety of languages used in Scotland at the period in this *Companion*; however, where possible the three main languages of Scottish literary production – Older Scots/English, Scottish Gaelic and Latin – are considered in conjunction. Previous collections have tended to focus on material in Older Scots, and to consider Latin and Gaelic texts in separate chapters:[32] while that arrangement reflects the usual divisions of academic expertise, where Older Scots tends to be studied in departments of English, and Gaelic in departments of Celtic, it does not really represent the experience of the writers and their audiences. The arrangement here is intended to represent the linguistic communities as porous and interactive and to consider what it might have been like to compose and to read where one form of bilingualism was an inevitable part of education, and others arose from daily experience. Considering the different languages together also reveals the different experiences that came with the use of each tongue, both at the time of composition, but also in their subsequent receptions, something which still has political and cultural ramifications today. The aim is also in part to challenge assumptions about which language is central and which marginal, and to interrogate common teleologies about literary influence and development: comparing the changes in Gaelic and Older Scots literature indicates that particular developments – such as changes in orthography and literary form – may arise as much from political and cultural happenstance as from any inherent pattern of (often English) literary history.[33] Bringing together Gaelic and Scots writing has demonstrated the features held in common: some uses of elegy, for instance, or the kinds of expression used in hymns. It has also made clear significant differences, notably the use of translation into Gaelic, and the perceptions of the purposes of literature. For this *Companion*, the result is that some chapters consider their material separately – such as those on language and translation – whereas others synthesise the discussion, such as those on historiography and elegy.

The other feature of this volume that distinguishes it from earlier essay collections and companions is its focus on topic and genre rather than author. Although there are clear advantages to focusing on individual authors, not the least of which is that it removes the need to define period boundaries, any attempt to list essential authors between 1400 and 1650 can easily produce fifteen to twenty names without any pretensions to being complete or representative. This is deeply frustrating. In addition, it is possible to get good author guides to poets such as Robert Henryson (d. c. 1490), Gavin Douglas (c. 1475–1522) and Lyndsay in other volumes and places.[34] However, there are fewer guides to individual Gaelic poets, less productive poets in Scots and Latin, and those who remain anonymous, although their works can be just as significant in our larger understanding of literary traditions.[35] Moreover, all poets and writers, great or less, function within political and cultural constraints and expectations, and are generally deeply knowledgeable about their literary traditions. This *Companion* aims to embed the literature in its context, not simply one of other great names, but a rich fabric of writers and readers. Finally, a great deal of recent work has focused on previously understudied material and areas, such as Neo-Latin polemic, satirical broadsides, and means of transmission, and this volume seems an appropriate place to integrate it into introductory essays, just as previous collections have reflected similar milestones in the discipline.[36] As a result, this *Companion* approaches the familiar writers through a variety of contexts, which inflects and informs understanding of the work as well as the writers.

To those ends, this *Companion* has three sections. The first deals with the basic requirements of literary culture: language and transmission. The second section addresses three broad cultural assumptions – the place of religious faith, the purposes of literature, and the uses of history – and the ways in which each of these underpin ideas of identity. The third section addresses questions of genre and approach, to consider the expectations created by generic choice and method of transmission, and the way in which each generation of writers responds to their predecessors. In so doing, contributors range widely through writers and writings, locating them in a Scottish context. The *Companion* is designed to be inclusive, offering approaches and information to illuminate both the material discussed and other material readers may encounter themselves. It does not replace other volumes, but complements them: the richness of Scottish literatures in this period can only be understood through diverse and broad engagement, and by regular reconsideration of previous readings and understandings. That is the ultimate task of this volume, to reconsider Scottish literature between 1400 and 1650 at this point in its critical history.

The *Companion* begins, therefore, with the essentials of literature. In the first chapter, Sara Pons-Sanz and Aonghas MacCoinnich outline the histories of the native languages, Gaelic and Scots, in these centuries. Pons-Sanz demonstrates the elaborated nature of Older Scots as a full language, and explores its different literary registers, while MacCoinnich discusses the status of Gaelic and the concomitant effects on its written usage. Although their relative statuses differed in these centuries, both languages are often positioned in relation to others, Classical Gaelic used in Ireland, and the Middle English of Scotland's southern neighbour, and both Pons-Sanz and MacCoinnich reflect on the effects of those centripetal forces. MacCoinnich also goes on to consider the effect of Older Scots as a dominant language of government and law on Gaelic speakers and writers, suggesting that for many Gaelic speakers, Scots orthography was the natural alternative to Classical Gaelic, hence the idiosyncrasies of the BDL, a vital piece of evidence for vernacular Scottish Gaelic writing.[37] Both critics discuss manifestations of literary register, and the ways in which language is used to reflect genre and expectation.

Without manuscripts and print, we would not know anything of the literature of this time in any language. Combining detailed examples with new work on the circulation of manuscripts and print, in chapter two Sally Mapstone explores questions of transmission and reception of literary material. She focuses on the transmission of William Dunbar (1460?–1513x1530), Douglas and Henryson to demonstrate its unpredictable nature: the ways in which early print determined later manuscript copies, and where English witnesses preserve Scottish texts before they are re-presented in Scottish material. Crucial is the fluidity between manuscript and print, but also the permeability of political and linguistic boundaries. Both Douglas and Henryson drew quite clearly on Continental as well as English productions as source material, some in print and some in manuscript, while Dunbar's reading is broad but impossible to specify. The obverse of this, the reception of Scottish writing in Continental Europe, particularly writing in Latin, is often overlooked, but in some very new work on the grammar of John Vaus, Mapstone explores the printing of Scottish works in Latin in Paris.[38] Mapstone's chapter introduces the material evidence and the way in which it mediates our understanding and experience of the writing it contains.

The presence of religion was common to all Scots in this period.[39] In chapter three, Sìm Innes and Steven Reid explore the expression of faith in Scots, Gaelic and Latin, noting that the conventions particularly of pre-Reformation Europe are also evident in Scotland, and that Continental influence remains significant throughout the sixteenth and seventeenth centuries. Innes and Reid note, for instance, that late medieval poetry of all kinds assumes shared understanding of, among other things, the place of the Virgin Mary and the patterns of the church's year. Although the literary conventions differ between the languages, nevertheless prior to the Reformation there was evidently a commonality of belief. Although the Reformation shattered much of that commonality, Innes and Reid point out the continuities between pre-Reformation and post-Reformation expressions of faith: while Biblical narratives may come to displace saintly exempla, the patterns of verse, such as dream-vision, remain the same across confessional boundaries. Such shared understanding of devotion is significant in appreciating the ways in which faith was experienced and expressed by individuals, in the face of hyperbolic polemic between Protestant and Catholic apologists.[40]

While the Reformation sharpened the attacks, Innes and Reid point out that there was already a satirical tradition in religious writing: all the languages of Scotland (and many others across Europe) have examples of late medieval anti-fraternal and anti-clerical attacks.[41] Indeed some of the aspects of Protestant polemic in particular can be seen to have roots in this kind of attack, especially around sexual continence and financial greed. The complex interweaving of religious and secular politics in the sixteenth and seventeenth centuries made it a particularly fertile period of satirical composition, in poetry as well as prose, but, as Innes and Reid argue, religious and theological polemic seemed to generate far more prose in Scots than had previously been written. Whether that is directly attributable to Reformation politics is questionable, but there is no doubt that the rise of literacy, the existence of Scottish printers, and acute political and ideological circumstances contributed writers, readers and means of distribution.[42] In these texts too, the complexity of linguistic politics is evident, for Catholic writers frequently accused Protestant ones of using English; the accusation was first made by Ninian Winzet of Knox. It is certainly possible to argue that where such anglicisation occurs (and it is by no means consistent), its writers might genuinely have sought an English audience:[43] such usage would mirror Bishop John Carswell's decision to use Classical Gaelic for his translations of the Book of Common Order to make his work more readily accessible in Ireland.[44]

Complementing this discussion of faith, William Gillies and Kate McClune consider the broader purposes of literature, indicating from the start some distinctions between the vernaculars. Gillies explores the nature of Gaelic composition, with its particular forms of poetic education and employment, as well as its deference to Classical Gaelic forms, and considers its role in reasserting family and social structures. McClune explores a feature that seems peculiarly heightened in Older Scots, namely the suggestion that there is a moral duty in reading correctly. She begins with *The Kingis Quair*, and its examination of the management of Fortune, and continues through Henryson to John Stewart of Baldynneis (c. 1545–c. 1605) to consider the significance of understanding and reading carefully. Such an anxiety about reading accurately can be found in texts in other traditions, but McClune's suggestion is that it is a consistent presence in literature from the fifteenth to the seventeenth centuries. The imperative on the individual reader to read carefully for their own improvement runs in parallel to the tendency of Older Scots writers to proffer advice to their lords and masters, but McClune argues that without the role of the individual reader, the advice to government has little weight.

Gillies also perceives a strain of advice regarding good rule in Gaelic verse. In that context, poetic authority is gained through traditional practice and inheritance of such poetic authority: for example, a eulogy to a noble patron composed in Classical Gaelic will quite often both celebrate the patron's achievements but also advise through what it foregrounds and what it omits. Thus, Gillies suggests, even the most apparently traditional material allows for political mediation. Such works reinforce the relationship between poet and patron whereby, in keeping the poet, the patron ensures his reputation in his own and subsequent generations. In the earlier part of the period, the post of poet to a particular patron could be inherited, as was common in several learned professions: the most famous bardic family was that of the MacMhuirichs. Such cultural practice was supported by bardic schools in Ireland, which trained poets in the use of Classical metres and style. Crucially, Gillies argues that because of these structures and expectations, and because of a largely stable culture in this period, Gaelic literature appears self-sufficient, running parallel to Older Scots writing but not dependent on it. Such self-sufficiency, and self-confidence in classical forms, does not mean that it was indifferent to European cultural patterns – Gillies draws particular attention to the conventions of courtly love – but rather that these were absorbed into traditional forms.

When Tudor policy in Ireland did its best to eradicate Gaelic culture there, Gaelic-speaking Scots lost their Irish models and began to develop their own;[45] the differences in style and language are described by Pons-Sanz and MacCoinnich. Notwithstanding the reliable patronage of Gaelic aristocrats, Scottish Gaelic poetry was further marginalised by royal indifference, and indeed hostility under James VI. It is tempting to attribute James's hostility to his tutor, George Buchanan, either because of Buchanan's own disparagement of his native tongue, or simply because Buchanan, a stern tutor, was a Gaelic-speaker; however, it is probable that there were other less personal reasons.[46] Whatever the cause, such hostility, as is discussed in several chapters, had significant impact on Scottish Gaelic writing, its written survival, and its circulation; by the end of the seventeenth century, the previous cultural stability had been lost. At all points, however, Gaelic literature articulated the 'shared inheritance and identity' of its speakers, and when the culture came under pressure, it continued to serve that purpose.

The narration of the past also contributes to the articulation of a culture and encodes key values of a community. In the last discussion of broad cultural assumptions, Ulrike Hogg and Martin McGregor focus on historiography, the way the communities of Scotland imagined themselves and their identities. They discuss the beginnings of historiography in John Fordun's *Chronica* (c. 1385) and the ways in which that narrative is reused and reshaped in subsequent elaborations. Hogg and MacGregor outline the development of Latin historiography and its presentation to an international as well as to an indigenous audience; Hogg points out the changes brought by print. They also consider the interaction between Latin material and vernacular writing, and the greater prevalence of Older Scots historiography in the sixteenth century, as well as the development of confessional historiography into the seventeenth century, as different religious groupings remembered the past in different ways. As the chapter begins with the Gaelic narratives that lie behind Fordun, towards the end it draws attention to the inconsistency in the presentation of Gaelic culture in Lowland historical writing, whether in Latin or in Older Scots. The Scottish origin myths, including Gathelos and Scota, derive from Gaelic tradition; such myths, because of their antiquity and flat contradiction of the English equivalents articulated in Geoffrey of Monmouth's *History of the Kings of Britain*, were adopted wholesale by most Lowland writers. At the same time, contemporary Gaelic society was presented as more threatening and problematic. Hogg and MacGregor consider the response to this ambivalence in Gaelic writing, and the ways in which the margins understood central political discourse around national identity and government.[47]

The last section of the *Companion* addresses genre. Genre is interpreted widely and here includes performance and translation. Where possible, these chapters bring together Gaelic and Scots practice, to illustrate the cultural overlap of shared European experience. In some cases, however, the nature of the witnesses, as with lyric, or the practice, as with translation, mean that a fully integrated chapter has proved impossible. Nevertheless, side by side, such chapters highlight the difference in linguistic experience and also challenge some standard cultural assumptions about literary movements and contacts. For instance, while the apparent absence of Gaelic translations of classical works might be imagined to be an effect of Gaelic's status, at the same time, it might also question whether humanism, at least as expressed by translation, is as integral to vernacular poetics in Scotland as common narratives of the Renaissance would suggest.[48] Only by asking such questions is it possible to refine understandings of cultural context and literary interpretation.

In discussing the use of various key genres in all languages, this section considers constraints, expectations and audience, as well as recurrent features. These chapters present one striking consistent point: the literary material exaggerates and subverts expectations, and gains affective literary power by engagement with those expectations. This is as true of the use of a female voice in Gaelic elegy, evoking the traditional female role in caring for the dead body, as it is of the political performances orchestrated by kings, as it is of Alexander Montgomerie's (c. 1550–1598) use of a sonnet sequence to address James VI. In directly comparing the practice in different languages, it is possible to see in action Gillies's assertion regarding parallel traditions in Gaelic and Scots, particularly in satire, elegy, and, in a different way, translation. Yet at other points, such as the performance of music, or the subjects for lyric, or indeed in the use of flyting, there seems some evidence of interaction, even if that is through a third common language.

The final section begins with lyric, considered in two parallel sections in chapter six by Mícheál Ó Mainnín and Nicola Royan. While lyric is the most familiar poetic genre for a modern audience, together with apparently universal experiences of love and loss, there are nevertheless poems that reveal striking differences in our own expectations and those of our ancestors. The lyrics in the BDL are, as Ó Mainnín argues, particularly notable in this respect: the BDL preserves bawdy poems addressed to a priest which are attributed to a noblewoman, the Countess of Argyll. Such poems reveal the various levels of coterie and audience, which, because of the compressed and elliptical nature of poems, are sometimes crucial to interpretation. Dunbar's lyrics for the court of James IV, for instance, assume in a few cases knowledge of court personnel: although now lost, such identities may well have been known to Richard Maitland, who served at court for most of his life and whose Folio Manuscript preserves a large quantity of Dunbar's lyric poetry. However, the relationships between the speaker and the other figures in these poems are easier to work out than those in the BDL. Broader audiences are suggested by some occasional verse: poems praising or addressing the sovereign demand public performance and reception, as do the liminal verses at the beginning of printed books. Often the most effective expressions of erotic passion do not depend on the direct identification of the lover and beloved, and again find a broad audience, whether attributed or anonymous.

Perhaps it is the focus on the speaker's experience that allows the lyric to be voiced and written by women. As Ó Mainnín records, in Gaelic certainly women are visible as poets in this genre and period, as they are in elegy, another genre driven by emotion. In Older Scots, too, towards the end of the period, there are women writers, of both devotional and secular material; the Casket Sonnets associated with Mary, Queen of Scots, however, demonstrate how contentious the female voice can be, particularly when negotiating power, erotic and political.[49] What is permitted in a coterie context for a Gaelic-speaking noblewoman is not permitted in a public context for the French-speaking queen.[50]

Although medieval and early modern love lyric often draws on the courtly element of chivalric literature, Rhiannon Purdie and Katie Stevenson point out that chivalry was more than just a literary code, even beyond the introduction of artillery. In chapter seven, Purdie and Stevenson consider where written representations of chivalry are to be found, from romances to more practical guides, through comic representations of those for whom chivalric practice was out of reach. They point out that the Scots version of chivalry in all these texts focuses on its primary function: that of warfare and knightly prowess. Because all kings, certainly in medieval practice, were also knights, chivalric conduct is also used as a means of commenting on government, that constant theme in Scottish literature: this occurs both in serious romance, such as *Golagros and Gawane*, and in subversive comic romance, such as *Rauf Coilyear* and *Squyer Meldrum*. Such examples have been less celebrated in the centuries after their composition: while medieval romance offers a kind of Pre-Raphaelite nostalgia, early modern romance has not been as appealing to modern tastes, perhaps because of an unease with a genre that celebrates chivalry in a world of artillery. Recent critical engagement has begun to re-examine these romances, some of which, like George

Mackenzie's (1636/1638–1691) *Aretina*, reshape inherited chivalric patterns to fit early modern political discussion.[51]

Some chivalric tropes, however, break out of romance and heraldic collections. Purdie and Stevenson demonstrate this with a discussion of the Nine Worthies, European epitomes of chivalry. As Purdie and Stevenson point out, they appear on a ceiling at Crathes Castle; they also appear in Lyndsay's *Armorial*, an important guide to all matters chivalric, particularly heraldry. Because they also have historical authority, the Nine Worthies are used as comparisons for the Scots' most distinguished chivalric figures in their eponymous narratives, the *Bruce* and the *Wallace*. Purdie and Stevenson argue that these poems have a complex relationship with chivalry, and display quite different interpretations: while the *Wallace* denies knightliness to anyone opposed to the Scottish cause, Barbour (c. 1330–1395) is more open to the idea of an honourable enemy. Chivalry's peculiar longevity, particularly its significance in organising government, lies partly in the European commonality of its assumptions as well as in the idiosyncrasies of its Scottish incarnations.

While laments for fallen soldiers and commanders are a significant feature of Scots elegy, in chapter eight Joanna Martin and Kate Mathis argue that it is far more capacious, mourning bureaucrats like Richard Maitland as well as chivalric figures.[52] They go on to argue that it becomes a genre for wider loss, loss that encompasses death most obviously, but also the rejection of love, political failure, and a change in family fortunes. As a genre, elegy is particularly recognisable in Gaelic writing, as a traditional form in bardic culture, with consistent rules and practice. Martin and Mathis examine the features of traditional Gaelic practice, such as the physical expression of grief, and the particular situations depicted in elegy, such as the loss of a patron. The experience of feud is also apparent in Gaelic elegy, where the form is used to give voice to women caught between fathers, brothers and husbands. Although it is not absolutely certain that all the poems in female voice were composed by women, nevertheless, they give space to feminine experience, which is not as evident in Older Scots and in Latin.

While Gaelic poetic practice is formalised, the experiences and the sentiments of elegy are also evident in other languages. Martin and Mathis pick out some recurrent themes: poems as gestures of solidarity as well as grief; expressions of public mourning as well as personal loss; and, more particularly in Scots and Latin, examinations of personal identity as affected by the loss of love. Elegiac expression is open to all these uses, and poets are able to deploy and manipulate typical features to various effects, whether serious, satiric or comic. In all its forms and in all its languages, elegy is deployed to construct and confirm networks of circulation and alliance. Such networks also locate the speaker in particular poetic patterns and fashions. Such location stresses the place of the writer as much as the subject, whether with reference to the immediate circumstances of composition or towards desired future generations of readers. A desire for poetic immortality, more evident as more elegies survive in the sixteenth and seventeenth centuries, in some pieces alters the balance of McClune's argument about poetic authority, from moral to aesthetic. Whether that balance is sustained over the seventeenth and into the eighteenth centuries is a question beyond the scope of this volume: answering that question offers an alternative prospect for examining the Scottish tradition after the Union of the Crowns.[53]

Although satire might seem diametrically opposed to elegy in its intent, the most successful can be just as immortalising of failure as elegy is of success. In chapter nine, Tricia McElroy and Nicole Meier examine both Gaelic and Scots practice. They present satire as fundamentally traditional in its targets and its accusations: poor leadership, hypocrisy, assaults on sexuality and gender. Although the word 'satire' is a sixteenth-century innovation, the use of words to attack is a perpetual phenomenon. Associated with magic and cursing in Gaelic writing, satire is described as having physical effects, such as causing blisters; as a genre, it inverts panegyric, deliberately presenting the opposites of all the qualities praised. Like panegyric too, satire is often directed at the individual; however, as Meier and McElroy argue, it can also be used to attack classes and types of people. Meier and McElroy explore in detail the various manifestations of satire. In particular, they compare the satiric practices of Dunbar and Henryson. They argue that Dunbar is prepared to mock named individuals, most notably Walter Kennedy (1455?–1518?), but also classes of people, both those in competition for royal favour, and familiar targets, such as the women in *The Tua Mariit Wemen and the Wedo*. In contrast, Henryson has more universal satire, aimed at corrupt members of the lawyerly and burgess classes. Drawing on both these writers, Lyndsay adapts Henryson's social satire in several of his works, including *The Testament of the Papyngo*, but, as Dunbar satirises individual rivals, Lyndsay has no compunction at satirising Cardinal Beaton (1494?–1546).[54]

As the sixteenth century progresses, satire circulates widely. Innes and Reid identify the contribution of religious divide to this development; McElroy and Meier point out the complex political situation, where the satire of female rulers derives much of its strength from misogynist arguments entirely familiar to Dunbar. McElroy and Meier also demonstrate the flexibility of satire as a literary genre, for on the one hand, it is the mainstay of broadsides, finding a popular and wide audience with blunt attacks, and on the other it includes George Buchanan's devastating caricature of William Maitland of Lethington (1525x1530–1573) in *The Chameleon*, which derives its force from combining specific detail with material drawn from bestiaries, and an acid tone. It is almost possible to believe that *The Chameleon* did indeed draw blisters from its target.[55]

To be effective, satire often has a public dimension, and many surviving satires have an element of performance. Drama, too, of course is a corporate enterprise, and also art with the potential to change in every iteration. While Scotland is notorious for its limited supply of play texts in the sixteenth and seventeenth centuries, in chapter ten John McGavin and Dòmhnall Uilleam Stiùbhart argue that performance requires a much broader definition, encompassing both performance (of plays and entertainments) and performative (where public concerns and decisions are played out before an audience of witnesses), and include music and dance as well as scripted text. They point out the importance of ritual, both religious and civic, and the ways in which audience can encompass people from all social classes and ranks and require them to respond to the material in front of them. Such events were used to reconfirm understandings of precedence or of justice, or – less positively – to describe and define Gaelic culture to a less-than-friendly Lowland community, as the opening examples of the chapter reveal.

In illustrating this, McGavin and Stiùbhart examine all kinds of poetic, chronicle and archival record of performance. This demonstrates the breadth and sophistication of audience understanding: in particular, they draw a line from Douglas's depiction of royal entertainment in *The Palice of Honour*, through Lyndsay's *Ane Satyre* to a ritualised performance of accord arranged by James VI. In each case, they draw attention to the importance of the role of the spectators, that who is watching is as significant as what is watched, and stress that these audiences are sophisticated in their understanding. Such sophistication regarding performance is evident across linguistic boundaries, for although there is even less evidence of play text in Gaelic, the understanding of ritual and location remains strong.

At the end of the chapter, McGavin and Stiùbhart take the example of the third and fourth Lords Elphinstone, father and son, whose lives cover over a century (1530–1638), and whose family accounts reveal all kinds of musical patronage. Their patronage, which included musicians from all over Scotland, and beyond, of a variety of levels and styles, demonstrates the fluidity of music in particular, but forms of performance more widely. The chapter encapsulates two recurrent themes of this *Companion*: firstly, that the experiences of Gaelic speakers and Lowland dwellers were different, sometimes parallel and sometimes overlapping; and, secondly, that some cultural aspects crossed the Highland line without issue, even if – as mentioned several times before – there is so little evidence of cross-fertilisation.

Translation, the subject of the last chapter in the *Companion*, is necessarily a genre of cross-fertilisation, although as Thomas Rutledge argues, there is a difference between translation that brings familiar ideas into a new language (such would be Gilbert Hay's (c. 1397–after 1465) prose treatises on chivalry) and translation that mediates a different culture into a new language (such as the *Eneados*). Of all the chapters in this *Companion*, this is the one where the practice of the different language groups contrasts most starkly. While Rutledge outlines the continuous presence of translated texts in Scots from the fifteenth century onwards, Kaarina Hollo describes the comparative lack of evidence for such practice in Gaelic at this period. Formal translation appears dependent on the ideological demands of the Reformation, to provide the Book of Common Order and the Bible in Gaelic. Through translations, Older Scots literature illustrates its engagement with literature in French, Latin, German and even Italian and Ancient Greek; Gaelic translations of classical material were made slightly earlier and largely in Ireland, but there is less evidence of direct Scottish Gaelic engagement with more recent material, such as romances. The lack of such evidence does not imply either ignorance or indifference. On the one hand, reading Latin was as common to the learned in the west of Scotland and Ireland as it was in the east, so some material would have been read in its original language. On the other, as MacCoinnich suggests, the use of Scots orthography to represent Gaelic in the BDL may well suggest that Gaelic speakers were more comfortable reading Scots than we might imagine. Consequently, if not read in the original languages, texts like Livy's *Histories* or Petrarch's *Trionfi* might have been read in Scots translation.[56] Even so, there remain many questions about survival and circulation, about Scots material, and writing in other languages, in Gaelic-speaking areas, and about the circulation of Gaelic material itself.

In contrast, Scots writers overtly embraced translation and adaptation. All kinds of works in the fifteenth century have Latin or French sources, often reshaped to fit local tastes, such as the romances *Golagros and Gawane* and *Lancelot of the Laik*.[57] As Rutledge argues, the growth of humanism in the sixteenth century led to another strand of translation, where respect for the base text is asserted by claims of accurate representation (notably, the *Eneados*). The latter form also had a significant part to play in Reformation writing, where translations of the psalms particularly, but also the rest of the Bible, carried additional ideological weight. Neither form of translation expels the other, however: the poets at the court of James VI were as likely to borrow and revise poetry in French and other languages, as they were to undertake an overtly signalled translation. These works, Rutledge points out, share the literary axes of external literatures and home-grown traditions, so that translations as diverse as Stewart's *Roland Furious* and William Fowler's (1560/1–1612) *Prince* refigure these works to fit expectations of princely advice and questions of good rule.[58] Counter-intuitively, therefore, translation seems to demonstrate all that is particular about Scottish writing under the Stewart sovereigns.

Altogether, these chapters reiterate certain essential points about literary cultures in Scotland between 1400 and 1650. Firstly, linguistic, literary and cultural experiences were plural, depending not simply on chronology, but also on geography, wealth and social status, education, and political and religious affiliations. These experiences seem often to have been discrete, for some audiences must have been partly monolingual, and even where they were not so, some poets looked towards their own vernacular models rather than seek those in other languages. Gaelic composers looked primarily west towards Ireland, Scots speakers looked south and east: the ways in which writers of Scots referred to Gaelic poetry, as in Dunbar's *Flyting* or Holland's (d. c. 1483) *Buke of the Howlat*, were rarely flattering.[59] Nevertheless these cultures co-existed, and also engaged – separately – with pan-European Latinate culture. To understand medieval Scottish culture, it is necessary to acknowledge the existence of all three, because both on the occasions where direct borrowing is evident, such as in the historiography of national identity, and where there appear to be common concerns about government of the self as well as the people, appreciating the particular nature of the interaction enables precise analysis rather than generalisation.

The benefits of such precision are also evident in those chapters that explore the interaction of international and national politics and culture on literary work. Some events and attitudes have obvious effects: writing in Gaelic came under particular pressure from royal policy in the late sixteenth and early seventeenth centuries, having already begun to change in part because of Tudor impositions on Irish culture. Comparing the effects of such overt linguistic condemnation to the evident changes in Scots orthography around the Reformation and the Union of the Crowns challenges easy narratives of cultural decline with more complex matrices of multiple causes. Still larger cultural changes, most obviously the Reformation, also brought new styles, concerns and genres; what is more striking often is the continuity in writing practice across such revolutions and how much continues to be passed on.

Finally, however, the breadth of the *Companion* gives a hint of the wealth of literary culture of Stewart Scotland: that the final text discussed is Thomas Urquhart's *Gargantua and Pantagruel*, a translation of Rabelais only serves to emphasise the richness of the linguistic and literary resources. The greatness of Henryson, Dunbar and Lyndsay is not diminished by their context, but rather enriched. Moreover, such a depth of material challenges facile notions of cultural crisis in the seventeenth century: while the absence of a royal patron affected certain kinds of material, just as James VI's hostility to Gaelic culture had identifiable impact on writing in that language, it did not remove either cultural production or wide reception from the realm. The cultural and political sophistication asserted by McGavin and Stiùbhart and the confident engagement with new ideas and inherited tradition continued beyond 1650, necessarily so since otherwise the Enlightenment could not have happened. But no literary period is important only because of what it precedes: writing in Scotland, in whatever language, between 1400 and 1650, is in and of itself surprising, demanding, enthralling, emotive and intellectual: if nothing else, this *Companion* displays that to best advantage.

PART 1: LANGUAGE AND TRANSMISSION

CHAPTER ONE

The Languages of Scotland

Sara Pons-Sanz and Aonghas MacCoinnich

Introduction

There were several languages in use in Scotland in the period this *Companion* covers. Of these the Scots tongue, closely related to but distinct from its southern neighbour, was the most widespread and influential spoken and written language throughout Scotland for most of the period. Scots had replaced Scottish Gaelic as the vernacular language in much of the south and east or the Lowlands of Scotland by 1400. By the fifteenth century Scots was the language of burgh, court and parliament; yet, during the course of the seventeenth century, it slowly gave ground to English.

Gaelic, however, was widely spoken, perhaps by half the population of Scotland by the beginning of the period, c. 1400, and possibly spoken as a first language by up to a third of all Scots by 1700. It remained as the predominant vernacular in the Hebrides and the Highlands as far south as Dumbartonshire, Stirlingshire and Perthshire and as far east as Aberdeenshire. South of 'the Highland line', Gaelic was also spoken in Galloway and Carrick probably until the end of the seventeenth century.

Latin had been the language commonly used in church, for formal and legal documents, conveyancing, in parliament and in business prior to 1400. Latin, however, was retreating before Scots, an assertive and confident newcomer during the fifteenth century.[1] The Reformation of 1560 and the move from the Latin Mass to vernacular worship diminished the status of Latin to an extent. Nevertheless, Latin remained as one of the predominant languages of education in schools and universities, was widely known and used throughout the period and it retained its importance in legal usage. It was often the medium through which Scots scholars demonstrated their learning and it remained a means of intellectual discourse before and after the Reformation.[2]

The dominance of Scots, Gaelic and Latin had supplanted the wider linguistic plurality of earlier centuries. Pictish and Cumbric ('P-Celtic' languages related to Old Welsh) had become extinct as spoken languages well before 1400 as, probably, had Norse, formerly used in the far north and the Hebrides. Norse or Norn lingered longer, however, in Orkney and Shetland, which did not become part of the Scottish kingdom until 1469, although there too it was under great pressure from Scots during the course of the sixteenth century. These languages, though, left a rich crop of place names and other linguistic features inherited by their successor languages to a greater or lesser degree.[3]

Some use of aristocratic French prevalent in earlier centuries, as represented for instance in the Anglo-French *The Romance of Fergus* (c. 1200), had also dwindled by this period.[4] Certainly, George Dunbar, the Earl of March, claimed in 1400 in a letter to Henry IV of England that, although he knew French, he was much more comfortable with 'Englishe'.[5] Ability to read French may have remained among noble and mercantile communities, reinforced perhaps by royal marriages and alliances up to 1560. Southern English, however, became increasingly important after the Reformation, with a significant amount of southern English print materials in circulation alongside native products during the latter half of the sixteenth century.[6] The Union of the Crowns of 1603 reinforced this drift towards southern English at the expense of Scots (see below).

The different approaches taken to Gaelic and Scots in this chapter mirror the position they found themselves in and the concerns they faced during the period. Gaelic was still widely spoken in Scotland, but increasingly marginalised socially and politically and with an archaic, obsolescent literary culture divorced from the vernacular. One of the many challenges that faced Gaelic in this period was the struggle to achieve orthographic stability against a background of official indifference, if not hostility. Scots on the other hand, the language of government and commerce in the kingdom at the start of the period, had a rich and well-established literary tradition. It faced a very different set of challenges. Scots, perhaps, both benefitted from and had its distinctiveness eroded due to its similarity to the English language. While the closeness of the languages allowed, for example, English books to be circulated in Scotland where they could be understood, this had, in the longer term, a deleterious effect on the status of Scots, accelerated by the departure of the court in 1603 and James VI's British agenda. Much of the discussion on Scots thus focuses on issues of syntax, register and on the differentiation of Scots from southern English before and after the Union of the Crowns in 1603.

The Sociolinguistic Situation

Although Gaelic had been the language of court and kirk during the formation of the kingdom, between 900 and 1100, and was used as far south as Galloway and Berwickshire, it fell out of fashion in the south and east of the country during the twelfth and thirteenth centuries. It lost ground at an elite level to Anglo-Norman, the language brought in or adopted by the ascendant aristocracy. Scots, known originally as 'Inglis', had been well established in the south and east of what became Scotland for centuries. During the period 1100–1400 'Inglis' expanded, slowly displacing Gaelic as an everyday speech in the south and east 'Lowlands' of Scotland by 1400.[7] Gaelic, while retreating in the south before Inglis, may, however, have been expanding northwards into Ross, Sutherland and Caithness and, perhaps, the Hebrides during the thirteenth century, largely at the expense of Norse.[8] By around 1400, however, Gaelic had retreated from the Lowlands north and west up to the 'Highland line' and to Galloway and Carrick, where it remained the everyday speech of much of the population. Gaelic, formerly known as 'the Scottish tongue', was at some time (possibly during the fifteenth century) rebranded as 'Irish' or 'Erse' by the speakers of what was now called 'Scots'. This may have happened around the same time as speakers of 'Inglis' appropriated the label 'Scots' for their own language. Not only was Gaelic becoming marginalised in the southern and eastern parts of the kingdom, but its speakers, by the fifteenth century, if not earlier, came to be labelled as 'barbarous' or 'hieland' by lowlanders, who in turn came to be called '*goill*', singular '*gall*' (which can be translated as 'strangers', if not 'foreigners') by speakers of Gaelic.[9]

While much of the detail of the process of language shift from Gaelic to Scots is unclear, it seems to have been tied to the domination of the new structures and institutions introduced in the early twelfth century by Anglo-Norman and Inglis speakers, such as ecclesiastical foundations and burghs. Gaelic also seems to have lost favour at court level at much the same time. An increasingly confident and assertive Scots language dominated commerce, church and government orally and, increasingly during the fifteenth century, came to be the written language of business and everyday correspondence (to a greater degree than Latin) throughout the kingdom.[10] The link between the establishment of burghs, the advancement of Scots, and the decline of Gaelic in and around these establishments, particularly in lowland Scotland, seems firm.[11] Yet, while burghs were undeniably engines of linguistic change from Gaelic to Scots in the south and east, there are exceptions to such a broad generalisation, particularly in the Highland area. Inverness, a burgh established in the twelfth century, had by the start of the eighteenth century about 3000 parishioners who could not understand English, and another 800 who were bilingual. Only forty people resident in Inverness in 1704, according to Synod papers, could not understand Gaelic.[12] Gaelic, having retreated to the Highland 'line' and to the Hebrides by 1400, remained unchallenged as the vernacular until the later eighteenth century. However, the position of Scots (and Latin) as the dominant languages of court, government, church and commerce during the period 1400–1650 meant that Gaels had to – and did – widely engage with Scots writings.

While one of the tenets of the Reformation was access to the Scriptures through the vernacular, Scottish Gaelic Protestants had to wait until 1767 for a translation of the New Testament published in their own tongue.[13] It followed on from the reluctant adoption of Gaelic instruction for children by the SSPCK (Scottish Society for the Propagation for Christian Knowledge) in the early eighteenth century. The clause in the Statutes of Iona (1609) stating that the children of wealthy Gaels should be educated in the Lowlands, and a proclamation by the Privy Council (1616) that Gaelic should be 'abolesheit' are often taken as the start of an official assault on Gaelic. In reality, however, a laissez faire attitude was taken to the language by the Privy Council and the wealthier elements in the Highlands, other than to ensure that all lairds' children could read and write Scots/English.[14] Almost all the families of Highland chiefs, inasmuch as the evidence survives, seem, in any case, to have had an education in Scots (and Latin) prior to the end of the sixteenth century.

Educated speakers of Gaelic were thus, typically, from at least the mid-sixteenth century onwards (if not much earlier), habitual writers of Scots and latterly English. The extant correspondence of the Campbell clan with their neighbours during the mid-sixteenth century – all in Scots – underlines this point.[15] According to one writer, Sir Robert Gordon (1580–1656), the Tutor (here meaning guardian or administrator) of Sutherland in 1620, the ability of a laird to be able to speak the 'vulgar language' of his tenants, Gaelic, was vital. However, despite this necessity, Gordon also wanted to 'ruit out' Gaelic on the Sutherland estates through education. Education and Scots/English-speaking were equated with progress, and Scottish Gaelic, labelled by Gordon as the language of the 'poor ones', was to be eradicated over time through the establishment of schools.[16]

The study of Latin and Greek texts dominated the syllabus of Edinburgh grammar school in 1614. The first-year students started with the study of Dunbar's 'Rudiments,' progressing in the second year to Erasmus and Cicero, with scholars in the third year tackling works such as Ovid's Epistles, Virgil and Suetonius.[17] Such an approach was probably mirrored in a network of schools from Stranraer to Shetland and to Stornoway in the west by the mid-seventeenth century, where, according to the traveller Martin Martin (1695), Latin and English were taught. The same observer also cautioned against the needless education of girls which, he observed, could lead to 'love intrigues'.[18]

Yet Margaret Sanderson's study of handwriting in the Lowlands of Scotland shows wide rates of literacy in women from the early sixteenth century. The evidence of signatures in Sanderson's study would suggest that a substantial proportion of women drawn from the noble, laird and burgess class were literate.[19] Despite Martin's comment, women of the wealthier families in the Gàidhealtachd did, like their Lowland counterparts, probably have an education, albeit probably in Scots/English. A substantial corpus of the work of at least three major female poets survives from seventeenth-century Gaelic Scotland: Sìleas na Ceapaich (c. 1660–c. 1729), Màiri nighean Alasdair Ruaidh (c. 1615–c. 1707) and Mairghread nighean Lachlainn (c. 1660–1750).[20] If they had an education, as presumably they did, it would almost certainly not have included formal Gaelic instruction. Indeed, their songs circulated in oral tradition and the earliest manuscript witnesses of their work dates from two to three generations after their lifetimes (1740–1800).

Gaelic as a Literary Language

Although Scottish Gaelic was widely spoken, it was not widely used in writing, as its speakers almost always employed Scots and Latin for written purposes. Thus, vernacular Scottish Gaelic made its debut as a published language as late as 1751, with a work by Alexander MacDonald (1698–1770) *alias* Alasdair mac Mhaighstir Alasdair. His *Ais-Eiridh na Sean-Chánoin Albannaich* (Resurrection of the Ancient Scottish Tongue) is a collection of seditious and bawdy Jacobite poetry that broke out of the traditional straitjackets of panegyric and convention embracing themes such as love and nature.[21] When speakers of Gaelic wished to write their own language prior to this, they often used an orthography with which they were familiar: that of Scots and latterly English. This can be seen in the two most voluminous and important collections of Gaelic made in this period, the Book of the Dean of Lismore (BDL) c. 1512–1542,[22] and the Fernaig Manuscript, 1689 (see further below).[23] Notably, of the sixty extant clan histories, the single biggest surviving cultural product bequeathed to us by the Gaelophone clans of Scotland in terms of written texts, fifty-eight were written in Scottish-flavoured English during the seventeenth and early eighteenth centuries.[24] Even when these English-language histories occasionally sought to illustrate an anecdote with Gaelic verse, they used English orthography to do so.[25]

Prior to the Norman influx of the twelfth century, there are indications that a form of Middle Gaelic (c. 900–1200) was used in the southern and eastern Lowlands, but little evidence survives other than the twelfth-century Gaelic notes in the Book of Deer, from Aberdeenshire.[26] After this the language used for written Gaelic was a form of the language based on a dialect of Irish, known variously as 'Classical Gaelic' or 'Early Modern Irish', devised in Ireland around c. 1200 (as distinct from Scottish Gaelic as Barbour's Scots is from modern English).[27]

Classical Gaelic (or Classical Irish) was used throughout Ireland and also in the written forms of Gaelic widely practised in the inner and southern Hebrides, Kintyre and Argyll c. 1200–1650. These were the areas most closely in touch with Ireland politically and culturally, under the auspices of the MacDonald Lordship of the Isles, a powerful dynasty that flourished on the western seaboard of Scotland from the mid-fourteenth century to the end of the fifteenth century. Classical Gaelic also seems to have been sponsored by and appreciated by the Campbells, who rose to prominence as Clan Donald power faded, expanding eastwards into Perthshire from their Argyll base from the late fifteenth century. The language used in the BDL, written in the Campbell worlds of Argyll and Perthshire, contains material composed in several varieties of Gaelic together with material in Scots and Latin.[28] However, there is little evidence that classical Gaelic was ever adopted elsewhere in Gaelic Scotland, such as Moray, Ross, Sutherland, Caithness, Angus, Aberdeenshire and Inverness-shire. The languages used in all areas of Gaelic Scotland for business were overwhelmingly Latin and, increasingly, Scots – even in the most undoubtedly 'Gaelic' of areas, the Lordship of the Isles.[29]

Classical Gaelic has, despite its seemingly limited range within Scotland, bequeathed us not only the *Books of Clanranald*, c. 1700, written at the very end of the tradition, but also a number of literary and non-literary texts mainly from the coast of Argyll and the Isles.[30] Several families were associated with the production of classical Gaelic manuscripts over several generations such as the MacMhuirich dynasty of poets and genealogists associated with MacDonalds of Clanranald, and other families such as the Beaton family, associated with medicine.[31] Most of these families using classical Gaelic had ties with Ireland (often as mercenaries during the sixteenth century) prior to the defeat of the Irish Gaels by English forces at Kinsale in 1601. One such clan chief, Ruairidh Mòr MacLeòid of Dunvegan (d. 1626), had particularly strong ties with Ireland, having spent long periods of time there in the 1590s, and was a sponsor of classical Gaelic.[32] Ruairidh's successor as chief, however, Iain Mòr, does not seem to have continued to support classical Gaelic writings, perhaps due to the collapse of the Gaelic order in Ulster, although the Dunvegan household did continue to support a harpist and a vernacular Scottish Gaelic poet until the end of the century. John MacInnes has cautioned, however, against seeing the difference between the vernacular and classical traditions as a stark one and has suggested that there was interaction between both traditions in terms of imagery and rhetoric.[33]

The year 1567 witnessed the publication of the first printed book in Gaelic, Classical Gaelic rather than the vernacular. This was the translation by Bishop John Carswell (c. 1522–1572) of the Genevan prayer book, *Foirm na n-Urrnuidheadh*.[34] Its publication was sponsored by Archibald Campbell (1538–1573), the devoutly Protestant fifth Earl of Argyll, and Carswell and Campbell opted for classical Gaelic rather than the Scots orthographic models found elsewhere on the Argyll estates. Classical Gaelic was probably chosen because of its prestige among the influential Gaelic 'learned classes' in the Hebrides, but it may also have been done with one eye on Ireland, where the Earl was heavily involved politically and where the prayer book might also have an audience. While this work had a very limited reception outside Argyll and the Isles, it did establish a precedent for printing classical Gaelic on which the Argyll family built a little during the seventeenth century by sponsoring the translation and publication of catechisms and psalms. The Episcopalian minister Robert Kirk (1644–1692) translated and published a psalter in 1684 and transliterated Bishop Bedell's classical Irish Bible (printed in a font mimicking Gaelic script) into the more familiar Roman font in 1690, but this Bible was not widely adopted. This was probably mainly due to the difficult nature of the 'classicisms' or 'Irishisms' in the language, although the tensions between the Episcopalian and Presbyterian factions within Protestantism may also have been a factor.[35]

Despite its presence in the written medium, classical Gaelic was probably little understood in the wider Scottish Gaelophone world (outwith an influential but numerically small caste of classical Gaelic 'literati' on the south western fringe of the Gàidhealtachd) and did not long survive the severing of ties with Gaelic Ireland at the start of the seventeenth century. By 1695, while noticing classical Gaelic manuscripts in the possession of a few families such as the MacNeils of Barra and MacDonald of Clanranald in the southern Hebrides, Martin Martin commented that the panegyric verse produced by the remaining classical Gaelic poets was 'understood by very few'.[36] Edward Lhuyd (c. 1699) was the only person to record someone in either Scotland or Ireland, John Beaton in the Isle of Mull, reading classical Gaelic (a passage from Kirk's Bible) before this orthographic tradition fell into disuse. Lhuyd observed that, although Beaton was 'from the Highlands, he was pronouncing as the Gaels of Ireland do'.[37]

The following versions of *The Lord's Prayer*, from 1567, 1659 and 1796, illustrate some of the differences between classical Gaelic and the vernacular over what is basically the same text.[38] The first version shows Carswell's classical Gaelic of 1567; the second shows prose printed by the Synod of Argyll in 1659; and the third shows vernacular Scottish Gaelic from 1767 in the first Gaelic *New Testament*. Speakers of modern Gaelic (apart perhaps from linguists) may find Carswell's text difficult to follow, but might find the language used by the Synod of Argyll in the mid-seventeenth century, which Thomson described as representing 'the vernacular language with a half-hearted attempt at keeping up the fiction of a standard literary language', a little more familiar.[39]

Foirm na N-Urrnuidheadh, (1567)[40]
AR N-ATHAIR-NE atá ar neamh
go mo beandaighthe th' ainm
go dtí do ríghe
go ma dēnta do thoil adtalmhuin mar atá ar neamh
tabhair dhúinn aniu ar narān laitheamhail;
agas maith dhúinn ar bfiacha, amhail mhaitmaoid-ne dār
  bfēicheamhnuibh;
Agas nā lēig a mbuaidhreadh sind, acht saor sind ó olc
Óir is leat-sa an ríghe, an neart agas an ghlōir, tré bhioth sīor.
  Biodh amhluidh.

Foirceadul Aithghearr Cheasnuighe (1659)[41]

AR Nathairne ata ar Neamh

Go ma beannuigte hainmsa

Ga dtig do Rioghachdsa

Dentar do thoilsi air dtalmhuin mar ata air Neamh

Tabhair dhuinn a nuigh ar naran laitheamhuil

Agas maith dhuinn ar bfiacha, amhuil mhathmuid dar bhfeicheamhnuibh

Agas na leig ambuaidhreadh sinn, achd saor sinn ó olc:

Oir is leatsa an rioghachd, an cumhachd, agus an gloir gu siorruidh, Amen.

An Tiomnadh Nuadh (1796)[42]

Ar n-Athair ata air neamh,

Gu naomhaichear t' ainm

Thigeadh do rioghachd

Deanar do thoil air an talamh mar a nithear air nèamh

Tabhair dhuinn an diugh ar n-aran laitheil.

Agus maith dhuinn ar fiacha, amhuil mar a mhaitheas sinne d'ar luchd-fiach.

Agus na leig am buaireadh sinn, ach saor sinn o olc:

Oir is leata an rioghachd, agus an cumhachd, agus a' ghlòir, gu siorruidh. Amen.

Another feature which would militate against the easy adoption of these early religious texts may also have been that most Gaelic speakers were simply not used to reading the language, their education, as noted above, typically having consisted of Latin and Scots. Nevertheless, there are clear similarities between the language in all three texts shown above, and the printing of Classical Gaelic did provide an influential template which could be modified to accommodate the vernacular during the course of the eighteenth century. Classical Gaelic, moreover, was perceived as having a higher status than the vernacular, not only due to the precedent of religious printing but through the association of Classical Gaelic with learned families who had tended to monopolise literate professions in the Gàidhealtachd. This meant that classical Gaelic forms were borrowed into the Scottish Gaelic translation of the Bible (1767–1801). The classical form of the language was drawn in the direction of the vernacular to make it what Donald Meek called an 'acceptable middle road' between the classical and the vernacular forms. One result of this was an enriching of the vernacular with higher register forms of classical origin.[43] This could give a similar effect in the Gaelic Bible to that achieved in the English King James Bible of 1611, which had consciously drawn on antique forms of language, resulting in an archaic higher register.[44]

Had it not been for the efforts of the Argyll family, Scottish Gaelic orthography, for better or for worse, may have followed the road taken by Manx and signposted by the BDL and the Fernaig Manuscript, which use the twenty-six-letter alphabet and orthographic style of Scots and English rather than the eighteen-letter classical Gaelic orthographic system. A transcription of two quatrains from a poem in the BDL, when compared with Watson's reconstruction of the same lines using classical Gaelic, illustrates the difference between the Scots and Gaelic orthographic conventional systems.[45]

Original Scots orthography
Ac so geil di clinn ʒalt*ir*
ag rair fille farda a ʒna
ga ta misse er dail o wron'w
is kist dawe is ollamh ai.

One stewart a c*r*ith ra'nyt
a lave geil if far boe
gawe a leith is solt in gaga
leith volt 7 bagre voyṁ

Watson's interpretation
Ag so Gaoidheal do chloinn Ghaltair
ag réir fileadh, feirrde a ghné
gé tá mise ar dál ó a bhronnadh
's ciste dámh is ollamh é

A Eoin Stiúbhart a crích Raithneach
a lámh Gaoidheal as fearr buaidh
gabh, a laoich as sola i gcagadh
laoidh mholta agus bagar uaim[46]

There are no yoghs in Gaelic orthographic systems nor are the letters <v>, <w>, <k> used above (or <j>, <q>, <x>, <y>, <z>) used in Gaelic, either classical or modern. A large number of the poems in the manuscript seem to have been composed in the medium of Classical Gaelic, some of the poems being of Irish (geographical) origin and others produced in Classical Gaelic within the Campbell sphere of influence in the southern Scottish Gàidhealtachd. However, other poems in the collection seem to have been in vernacular Scottish Gaelic. Readers familiar with Gaelic will struggle to read the original Scots orthographic version, not least because the unfamiliar sixteenth-century Scots orthographic norms present another layer of difficulty. If this were not enough, the difficulties presented by the unfamiliar Scots orthography obscures the language of the scribes' texts: some of these probably originating from classical Gaelic and some from the vernacular.[47]

These two important and substantial *duanaire* (song or poetry collections), the Fernaig Manuscript and the BDL, were not isolated instances of such orthographic treatments of Gaelic, although they are exceptional in scale. A range of fragmentary attempts at writing Gaelic survive in the hand of Gaelic speakers who were fluent and comfortable in Scots and English but who clearly had little or no knowledge of traditional Gaelic orthography or letters. Despite its restricted geographical range in Scotland, Classical Gaelic, having been designed for a distinctively different dialect of Gaelic in Ireland, was, nevertheless, much more fitted for serving the purposes of Scottish Gaelic orthography, than the English or Scots systems. Despite this it took some time, as noted above, before the classical Gaelic system was adapted to Scottish Gaelic in the mid-eighteenth century. Paradoxically, it may have been the sheer prevalence of Scots language writings among Gaels and their comfort and widespread usage of written Scots and English but oral Gaelic (together with growing antipathy to Gaelic in the Lowlands) – in other words written Scots but with extempore translation into Gaelic of religious materials – that delayed the development of Scottish Gaelic as a written language.[48]

Scottish Gaelic, though, had a prolific oral literary culture, represented by poetry, song and prose tales. Yet the oral nature of this vernacular culture militated against the survival of much Gaelic 'literature'. Many of the songs from the seventeenth and eighteenth centuries, and the Fenian tales and folktales in Gaelic oral tradition were not collected and written down until much later than their dates of composition. Similarly, while much poetry still popular in oral tradition during the later eighteenth century and onwards has tended to be preserved, much of the poetry of earlier centuries has been irrevocably lost.

Despite this, when collectors of Gaelic song started work from the mid-eighteenth century onwards, following the perceived threat to Gaelic culture in the wake of the failure of the last Jacobite rising (1745–1746) and the Hanoverian regime's measures in the Highlands, a great corpus of earlier material was preserved. Over five hundred songs in vernacular Scottish Gaelic have been recovered pre-dating 1730.[49] These include 'clan' poetry and elegiac works by poets such as Eachann Bacach (fl. 1649–1651) and An Clarsair Dall (c. 1656–c. 1714), and the blistering response to the political events and conflict of the seventeenth century by poets such as Iain Lom (c. 1624–c. 1710), whose works circulated widely in oral form. They provide a vigorous and dynamic vernacular Gaelic commentary on the upheavals of war and political unrest in the mid-seventeenth century: the equivalent, in oral Gaelic culture, of the English language propaganda 'broadsides' of the civil war period.[50]

Scots as a Literary Language

Older Scots, which had become the vernacular tongue in most of southern and eastern Lowland Scotland by the thirteenth or fourteenth century, can be further subdivided into three periods: Early Scots (1375–1450), Early Middle Scots (1450–1550) and Late Middle Scots (1550–1700).[51] The beginning of the period is, of course, marked by John Barbour's *Brus*, c. 1375, the first significant extant literary text written in Scots. If we examine the linguistic features of the first few lines of this text, we can see that at this point there are already very clear differences between Scots and the southern dialects of Middle English:[52]

Storys to rede ar *delitabill	*delightful*
*Suppos that thai be *nocht bot fabill,	*even if* *nothing*
Than suld storys that *suthfast wer	*true*
And thai war said on gud maner	
Hawe doubill *plesance in heryng.	*pleasure*
The first plesance is the *carpyng,	*telling*
And the tother the *suthfastnes	*truthfulness*
That schawys the thing rycht as it wes,	
And suth thyngis that ar *likand	*attractive*
Tyll mannys heryng ar *plesand.	*pleasant*
(I. 1–10)[53]	

In terms of spelling, we notice that the sound /x/ (which Scots speakers pronounce at the end of *loch*) was spelt <ch>, while southern English texts preferred <gh> (e.g. <rycht> vs Chaucer's <right>), and that initial

/ʃ/ was spelt <sch> instead of <sh> (e.g. <schawys> vs Chaucer's <sheweth>). Another important difference to bear in mind, particularly as far as later (mainly, post-1450) texts are concerned, is the use of <i> or <y> to mark a long vowel (e.g. <guid> 'good'), while in English length was normally marked by a following <a>, <e> or by the doubling of the vowel. Whereas these are just visual differences, others actually go back to differences in pronunciation: e.g. <suld> suggests that the word should be pronounced with /s/ not with /ʃ/ (cp. Chaucer's <should>); similarly, <gud> and <suth> suggest that /o:/ has been fronted to /ø:/ and then to /y:/ (cp. Chaucer's <go(o)d(e)>, <so(o)th>), while <schawys> indicates that /a:/ has not become /ɔ:/ as in southern English. Albeit not represented in this fragment, the use of <qu(h)-> instead of <wh->, which points to the fact that the initial cluster still retained some aspiration (i.e. it was pronounced as /ʍ/ instead of /w/), is also very characteristic of Older Scots.[54]

From a morphological perspective, the presence of <-is/-ys> to mark the plural (e.g. 'thyngis') and genitive of nouns (e.g. 'mannys'), as well as the third person singular present indicative forms of verbs (e.g. 'schawys'),[55] and the use of the Norse-derived <-and> to mark the present participle of verbs (e.g. 'likand') are very characteristic of early Scots texts (cp. <-es> and <-ing/-yng> in the Chaucerian corpus). The use of <-and> for the present participle maintains the Old English morphological difference between this verbal form and deverbal nouns (e.g. 'carpyng', 'heryng').[56]

As we have seen, these phonological and morphological features clearly differentiate Early Scots from other varieties of English, particularly its southern varieties. Given that *The Brus* is aimed mainly at those who were in a position of power (i.e. the 'Lordings! who chooses now to hear', I.445) rather than at the commoners, and that it voices a strong desire for freedom, it may seem tempting to interpret Barbour's decision to compose the poem in his native variety in a patriotic light.[57] However, we need to remember that, at this stage, English had no standard and all its dialectal varieties were considered to hold a similar sociolinguistic status (think, for instance, that in Chaucer's contemporary *The Reeve's Tale* no one makes fun of the students' northern accent and, in fact, they end up getting the better of their southern hosts). It is then not surprising that a Scottish man should write a poem aimed at the court in Scots (although it is, of course, noteworthy because he was the first we know who did so). Thus, it is not his choice of dialect, but rather his choice of language, that should attract our attention, because similar chivalric or (pseudo-) historical near-contemporary texts, such as Peter Langtoft's (d. c. 1307) chronicle,

Vita Edwardi Secundi (c. 1326), Sir Thomas Gray's *Scalacronica* (1355) and John of Fordun's *Chronica Gentis Scotorum* (c. 1360), were commonly written in French or Latin. From a linguistic perspective, Barbour's text should be interpreted as an example of the increasing status of Scots in the face of French and Latin (as well as Gaelic).[58]

The vocabulary of the *Brus* shares many terms, as we would expect, with other English dialects, with a large proportion of words (e.g. 'suthfast', 'heryng', 'thing', 'mann', etc.) of Old English origin (52%) and French origin (37%), although there are also many other terms which are characteristically Scots.[59] It is striking that, given the prevalence of Gaelic in the kingdom, the *Brus* contains only eight words of Gaelic origin.[60] When looking at the use of loans in Older Scots literature, we can see that, while Germanic terms (mainly Norse, Dutch, Flemish and Low German) tend to be everyday words and, therefore, not particularly associated with high style or formal registers (e.g. the Norse-derived 'yai', 'carpyng', 'tyll'), French terms are, generally speaking, somewhat more formal, commonly associated with particular lexical fields, such as government, law, literature (e.g. 'story', 'fabill'), the arts and knowledge in general, and leisure (e.g. 'delitabill', 'pleasance', 'plesand').[61] Thus, it is very important to pay attention to an author's lexical choices, both in terms of meaning and etymology, because this is one of the key elements that help establish the tone and style of a text.

Compare, for instance, the vocabulary of two of William Dunbar's (c. 1460–1513x1530) poems:

O reverend Chaucere, rose of *rhetoris all	*rhetoricians*
(As in oure tong ane flour imperiall)	
That *raise in Britaine ewir, quho redis ryght,	*rose*
Thou beris of makaris the tryumph riall;	
Thy fresch *anamalit termes *celicall	*enamelled celestial*
This mater coud *illumynit have full brycht:	*illuminated*
Was thou *nocht of oure Inglisch all the lycht,	*not*
*Surmounting ewiry tong terrestriall	*surpassing*
Alls fer as Mayes *morow dois mydnycht?	*morning*
(ll. 253–261 of 'Ryght as the stern of day', B 59)[62]	

Thow *speiris, *dastard, gif I dare with the fecht.	*ask coward*
3e, *Dagone dowbart, thairof haif thow no douwt.	*worthless villain*
*Quhair evir we meit, thairto my hand I *hecht	*wherever raise*
To red thy *rebald rymyng with a *rowt.	*perverted blow*

Throw all Bretane it salbe *blawin owt	*well-known*
How that thow, *poysonit pelour, gat thy *paikis;	*poisonous thief beating*
With ane *doig leich I *schepe to gar the schowt,	*dog-leash going to make*
And *nowther to the tak knyfe, swerd nor *aix.	*not axe*

(ll. 65-72 of 'Schir Jhon the Ros' B 65)[63]

The first poem honours Chaucer as an eminent figure in the English literary tradition, of which Dunbar sees himself part; it emphasises the relationship between language and power (e.g. 'flour imperiall', 'tryumph riall'), and places Chaucer, who has managed to take the language, through rhetoric and elaboration (e.g. 'rose of rhetoris', 'anamalit', 'illumynit') to a position that it had never achieved before, right in the centre of that relationship. The poet is presented as a craftsman, a maker, who, through his choices, can enhance the status of his language. Thus, the selection of heavily Latinate and French vocabulary, with its association with knowledge, power and sophistication, is fully appropriate; in fact, this poem can be considered to be one of the best examples of the aureate diction which characterises some of the works of Dunbar and his contemporaries.[64] In the second poem, which represents a flyting (or verbal fight) between Dunbar and his near-contemporary Walter Kennedy, although we encounter some Romance terms (e.g. 'rebald' and 'poysonit', perhaps seen as appropriate because, after all, Kennedy was also a makar), we are faced with a predominance of Germanic terms (e.g. 'tak knyfe, swerd nor aix'). Their association with unsophisticated, everyday speech makes them perfect choices for the topic of the poem. Similarly, the few Gaelic forms that Dunbar employs in his poems are of disparagement, reflecting the low status of Gaelic in the south and east by the mid-sixteenth century.[65]

Albeit very important, vocabulary is by no means the only linguistic feature that determines the tone of the poems. The first poem is characterised by fairly complicated syntax, partially due to the use of the rhetorical device known as hyperbaton, or departure from ordinary word-order: for instance, the expected word order has been altered in the first few lines; sandwiched between the two appellatives in apposition (viz. 'O reverend Chaucere, rose of rhetoris all') and the rest of the sentence, we find the second element of the comparison, within which we have two embedded subordinate clauses, namely, 'That raise in Britaine' and 'evir quho redis rygnt'. This sentence contrasts with the short, simple and colloquial sentences that open the second fragment: 'Thow speiris, dastard, gif I dare with the fecht: / 3e, Dagone dowbart, thairof haif thow no douwt'. The need of lexis and syntax to work together so as to maintain decorum is specifically acknowledged by James VI in Chapter III of *Ane Schort Treatise Conteining Some Reulis and Cautelis to be Observit and Eschewit in Scottis Poesie* (1584), a work with literary and patriotic interests very much in line with Du Bellay's *The Defence and Illustration of the French Language* (1549) and Puttenham's *The Arte of English Poesie*: 'Ye man also take heid to frame your wordis and sentencis according to the mater'.[66]

The 'frame' of the two poems also differs in terms of their stanzaic forms. The formality and high style of the 'Rycht as the stern of day', a love allegory, are emphasised by the demanding rhyming scheme of the nine-line stanza (*aabaabbab*), which Dunbar may have borrowed from Chaucer's *Complaint of Anelida*, the first text where it occurs, or from Gavin Douglas's *Palice of Honour*. Thus, topic, form and tradition are all fully in line in this poem. On the contrary, 'Schir Jhon the Ros' uses the *ballade* form, an eight-line stanza rhyming *ababbcbc* (in this case, though, without refrain). Dunbar commonly used this stanza for serious or celebratory poems, but, as far as this poem is concerned, the effect that he was aiming for is significantly different. Notably, while both poems include some level of alliteration, the latter is particularly heavy in 'Schir Jhon the Ros', where it works together with the other elements of the poem to create a low-style composition. In Older Scots, as in Middle English, there were, broadly speaking, two different types of poetic structure: the native alliterative poetry, which was based on unrhymed lines structured through sound similarity at the beginning of specific stressed syllables and which reappeared in the fourteenth century; and the poetry based on foreign models structured through metrical feet and rhyming schemes. This syllabic verse could still be combined with alliteration in Late Middle Scots to deal with serious topics,[67] but purely alliterative verse was, from the sixteenth century onwards, relegated to comic or insulting texts, as suggested by the fact that in his *Revlis and Cautelis* James VI calls it 'tumbling verse', and suggests that it is particularly appropriate for 'flytings'.[68]

Interestingly, we also find that in his more formal poem Dunbar has chosen a form which imitates English spelling and perhaps pronunciation, viz. 'quho' instead of 'quha'. A sprinkling of such forms is relatively common in Early Middle Scots literature, particularly in high style texts, even those which emphasise their Scottishness. They are a linguistic sign of significant cross-cultural relations, and, possibly, a hint of the status of English in some Scottish circles.[69]

After all, we need to remember that, although Dunbar's actual role in James IV's court was somewhat problematic, his main audience, at least as far as 'Rycht as the stern of day' is concerned, were the educated courtiers surrounding the king. Indeed, the association of anglicised forms with more formal and elevated texts can be seen in both literary and non-literary texts. For instance, Meurman-Solin points out that Gilbert Skeyne's (c. 1522–1599) *Ane Breve Descriptioun of the Pest*, a learned text composed in a Latinate style, has a higher degree of anglicisation (and a lower degree of clearly Scottish forms) than his rather less formal *Ane Breif Descriptioun of the Qualiteis and Effectis of the Well of the Woman Hill besyde Abirdene*.[70] Yet, while audience and style had a significant impact on the adoption or rejection of anglicised forms during the sixteenth and the seventeenth centuries,[71] the picture that texts paint is a very complicated one, with many other issues such as the author's dialectal origin, age, gender, education and socio-economic status, and the text's genre, source and circulation (i.e. printed or manuscript) having a bearing as well on anglicising and de-anglicising trends. Furthermore, the pace of anglicisation and the pattern of change also differed as far as each feature was concerned: for instance, the use of <wh-> instead of the Scottish <q(u)h-> appears to have spread later than the anglicisation of the third person plural subject pronoun (i.e. the adoption of <they> instead of <tha, thai, thay>).[72]

The complexity involved in the study of anglicising trends in Scots increases even more when we consider that, on the one hand, the anglicised forms could be attributable to a scribe or a printer rather than to the author himself.[73] On the other hand, while the term looks anglicised, an Older Scots pronunciation may actually have been intended. The fifteenth-century romance *Lancelot of the Laik* (c. 1460–1479) exemplifies these problems. It is only recorded in a slightly later manuscript, Cambridge, University Library MS KK.1.5 (late 1480s);[74] thus, we cannot collate various versions of the text to try to disentangle authorial from scribal forms. While some anglicised forms may indeed be attributable to the scribe, it may also be the case that the anonymous author followed English models such as Chaucer and Gower not only in style and ideas but also in the actual language he used.[75] Alternatively, he might have been trying to imitate other highly anglicised Scottish texts (e.g. *The Kingis Quair*).[76] What is clear is that in some cases a Scottish rather than English pronunciation of an English-looking form is needed for the poem to rhyme successfully. For instance, ll. 1571–72 have 'withstand' and 'lond' in rhyming position, while ll. 2857–58 rhyme 'hond' with 'Scotlande' and ll. 3083–84 rhyme 'Desyrand' with 'honde'; thus, <o> in these terms should be pronounced /a/ rather than /ɔ/, as in southern English. Similarly, ll. 2439–40 rhyme 'multitud' with 'wod', which indicates that the latter term should not be pronounced with English /oː/, but with the fronted Older Scots phoneme, commonly spelled with <u> (cp. <gud> and <suth> in the *Brus*).[77]

Anglicised forms can then be informative about possible cultural and literary connections, but can also be very problematic. In any case, we see that these forms become increasingly common in the Late Middle Scots period, following the Reformation and especially after the movement of the court of King James VI to London in 1603.[78] The second edition of the king's *Basilicon Doron* (or 'The King's Gift'), a book about how to govern addressed to his son, shows the immediate linguistic effects of such political change. While the 1599 text is indisputably Scots, the 1603 text, printed in London, exhibits instead the linguistic traits of the developing Standard English.[79] The new British sphere of James's power affected not only this text, but also the compositions of courtly poets, who, like the king, began to use English; the growing use of English Bibles in Scotland during the sixteenth century meant that most Scots had already become acquainted with southern English forms by 1603.

Very quickly after the Union of the Crowns, English became the most influential language in Scotland, at least as far as the written medium is concerned. This can be seen not only in James's attitude to his own texts, discussed above, but also in official papers such as the Privy Council Register and the estate papers of families such as the Hamiltons and the Mackenzies. Yet this written 'English' often retained Scotticisms to varying degrees.[80] The Scottish burghs were quick to embrace this linguistic switch. Edinburgh, anticipating the royal succession, gave a licence in 1601 to an 'Erasmus Drurye, Englishman, to keip and hald a wryting skoill'.[81] Aberdeen had, by October 1607, hired an Edward Diggens, Englishman, to teach English to the youth of Aberdeen over the age of ten years old. Diggens had previously been employed at Dumfries and Glasgow, 'Instructinge the youth to wreit fair and Perfyitlie'.[82] Written Scots usage did not disappear overnight in 1603, however, and continued to be used widely both in Scotland and on the continent in diplomatic and mercantile correspondence.[83] Yet the increasing drift towards anglicisation on the page during the seventeenth century almost certainly masks the continued use of Scots speech, with 'north Britons' of later generations requiring elocution lessons to bring their speech in line with the southern English standard.

Libraries and Circulation of Printed Materials in Scotland

The accounts of David Wedderburn (c. 1562–1634), merchant-burgess of Dundee, give us an insight into the range of reading materials possessed by a wealthy individual.[84] Wedderburn not only shared and lent from his collection but also carefully noted who borrowed his books. Wedderburn had copies of the Fables of Aesop, his edition of Hector Boece, 'lately weill bund', was lent to a number of people and an English book of Arithmetic (in 1607) which some unnamed rogue borrowed but did not return. An entry in his *compt buik* notes that 'The gudwyfe of Pitlathy' borrowed his copy of Chaucer and the 'Gude man of Ardowny boruit' his Chronicles, and 'Young Creich' borrowed his Ortelius.' He ordered a copy of 'Eneme to Athesme' and lent the 'Cronicles of Ingland, Scotland and Irland' to a Thomas Abercromby for 'xx dayes to reid on'. He lent the 'Frenshe Academy and ane uthir buik' to an Alexander Peirson. Other works he named as having lent included a paraphrase on the New Testament, his 'Blundeville book', Plutarch, a Latin Bible, Ovid, Homer's Iliad, John Mairis Chronicle, Drake's Voyages, an Hebrew Bible, Smyth's 'Sermons', a 'law buik', and works by or relating to Ortelius, Socrates, Erasmus (in English), Morcelphis and Doctor Faustus.

The list made by Wedderburn (in the Lowlands) of such works lent shows an eclectic taste and a culture of borrowing and reading of expensive books (none of which was in Gaelic). This suggests that, even if the actual number of volumes in circulation may not have been high, such works could have a wider impact due to these patterns of lending.[85] A list (c. 1660) of the items in the library of a Gaelic speaking Highlander, Mr James Fraser, shows a similarly eclectic selection of works, albeit reflecting his religious calling. The fact that most of these were in English and only two out of the fifty-three items in Fraser's collection were in or related to Gaelic is indicative of the status of the language in Scotland.[86] Patterns of book ownership expanded greatly in the mid-seventeenth century as presses proliferated and printed materials were used as a propaganda tool in the civil war period.[87] The possession of a manuscript copy (the Selden MS) of James I's *The Kingis Quair* (1423), in Scots, by Dòmhnall Gorm, one of the chiefs of the MacDonalds of Sleat (c. 1592), bearing not only Dòmhnall's signature in Gaelic script, but also a quatrain of classical Gaelic verse, is a further reminder that these cultures did not exist in isolation from each other even if the relationship between the languages was an unequal one.[88]

CHAPTER TWO

The Transmission of Older Scots Literature

Sally Mapstone

The publication histories of the three greatest Older Scots makars, Robert Henryson (d. c. 1490), William Dunbar (1460?–1513x1530), and Gavin Douglas (c. 1476–1522), convey the range of pathways through which an author's works could be transmitted as Scottish culture made its slow and often interrupted transition from manuscript to print.

Each of these poets shows a strong consciousness of the medium of manuscript. Henryson's poet-figure Mercury in *The Testament of Cresseid* is 'With pen and ink to report all reddie' (242), and his Aesop in the *Fables* has 'Ane roll off paper in his hand', and 'Ane swannis pen stikand vnder his eir' (1356–57).[1] The narrator of Dunbar's *Tretis of the Tua Mariit Wemen and the Wedo* records how at the end of the night he has spent listening to the three women talk 'I all prevely past to a plesand arber, / And with my pen did report ther pastance most mery' (B 3, 525–26).[2] Entering the last stage of translating Virgil's *Aeneid*, Douglas describes how he 'hynt a scriptour [the case containing his pen] and my pen furth tuke, / Syne thus begouth of Virgill the twelt buke' (XII, 305–06).[3]

The printed book is less immediately obvious in these writers' poetry. Yet all of them experienced forms of print culture during their lifetimes. Each had the opportunity to read printed works, but only Dunbar saw his own work in print, as far as we are aware. In some crucial instances it is now unclear whether they are thinking of manuscript, print, or allowing for both. The term 'quair' which Henryson uses in the *Testament* both for Chaucer's *Troilus and Criseyde* and the 'vther quair' on which the *Testament* is said to be based (40, 61) was employed in Older Scots to refer both to manuscript and printed books. When Henryson was writing (1470s–1490s) it was more commonly used in the context of manuscript, frequently to indicate unbound quires, and that is probably what he has in mind, not least because his references to *Troilus* are confined to its fifth book.[4] Dunbar's only use of the word is within the modesty topos at the end of his *Goldyn Targe*, one of the poems that was printed in his lifetime, c. 20 April 1508. Dunbar's concern that his 'lytill quair [...] wele aucht [...] be aferit of the licht' (B 59, 271-79) is deliberately recalling Chaucer's invocation to his 'litel bok' at the end of *Troilus* (V, 1786). But it could nonetheless suggest that Dunbar intended *The Goldyn Targe* to go to Walter Chepman (1471?-1528) and Andrew Myllar (fl. 1503-1508) for printing.

Chaucer's *Troilus* could have been available to both Henryson and Dunbar in either manuscript or print. They could have seen a manuscript like Oxford, Bodleian Library, Arch. Selden. B. 24, now the only surviving Chaucerian manuscript anthology from Scotland.[5] *Troilus* was the first item copied into this manuscript (fols 1-118^v), in the late 1480s, for Henry third Lord Sinclair. But they could also have read *Troilus* in the printed edition produced by William Caxton in Westminster in 1483 (*STC* 5094). Some works printed by Caxton made their way to Scotland quickly, though demand could lead to their transmission back into the older medium: a manuscript copy of Caxton's 1479 edition of Lord Rivers' *Cordial* (*STC* 5758), and extracts from his 1480 edition of the *Chronicles of England* (*STC* 9991), for example, had been made in Scotland by 1485 (NRS, GD 112/71/1/1 and 2).[6] That said, for Scottish poets to know Chaucer's *Legend of Good Women*, as Gavin Douglas clearly did (*Eneados*, I, 410-14, 445-48), they could only have done so in manuscript, since the poem was not printed until 1532. It was included in Arch. Selden. B. 24 (fols 152^v-91^v).[7]

Print and script come memorably together when Douglas, in the prologue to the seventh book of his *Eneados*, writes that 'And seand Virgill on a lettron stand, / To write onone I hynt a pen in hand' (VII, 143-44). For we know that the Virgil from which he was working was the edition printed by Josse Badius Ascensius (1462-1535) in Paris in 1501, as one of his early publications there in association with the bookseller Jean Petit (fl. 1493-1530).[8] Douglas undoubtedly worked from a library containing both manuscript and print, but he seems to have had more extensive access to printed texts than did Dunbar or Henryson: his aristocratic background, his university education at St Andrews, and his subsequent career in the church all affording him good opportunities for book purchase and library access. He is scathing about Caxton's *Eneados*, which had been printed in 1499 (I, 137-262); he probably knew other Continental printed editions of Virgil as well as Ascensius', including illustrated ones;[9] his knowledge of the early humanist commentators Valla and Landino seems to be derived from printed editions.[10] In this respect Dunbar is, as Priscilla Bawcutt points out, the antithesis of Douglas: widely read as he manifestly was, nonetheless, 'Dunbar rarely worked with *any* book at his elbow', and it would be difficult to plot what Dunbar read in manuscript and what in print.[11] However, that question is less of an issue for Dunbar than it is for Henryson and Douglas, for both of whom the identity of their source texts is such a significant matter.

The greater part of Henryson's own reading experience would have been in manuscript. He lived for much of his adult life in Dunfermline, whose Benedictine abbey had some tradition of a scriptorium and a recent abbot, Richard Bothwell (abbot 1444–1468) with a marked engagement in book culture.[12] The legal and historical nature of the manuscripts copied in Dunfermline would have been of interest to Henryson who was trained as a notary as well as working as a schoolmaster, but he would also have encountered other works influential on his poetry, such as Latin or French Aesopic and Reynardian collections and commentaries, and Nicholas Trevet's commentary on Boethius's *De Consolatione Philosophiae*, in manuscripts originating outwith Scotland, on the continent, or in England.[13] There is also evidence that in later years Henryson had some exposure to print. His possible acquaintance with Chaucer's *Troilus* in printed form has been mentioned. As Roderick Lyall has shown, his *Fables* were influenced by at least one printed collection – some version (whether in Latin or German, or French, English, or Dutch translation is unclear) of the collection of fables put together by Heinrich Steinhöwel and first printed in Ulm in 1476–1477 as a bilingual German and Latin edition of the *Vita et Fabulae*.[14]

Manuscript was a key form of transmission for the works of each of these makars, both initially and, significantly, after the establishment of printing in Scotland. With the exception of one manuscript of Douglas's *Eneados* copied by his amanuensis and containing some possible annotations by the poet (Cambridge, Trinity College o.3.12),[15] their holographs or the very earliest copies of their works no longer survive, and we must accept that we are thus always at some remove from their poetry as originally composed. Nonetheless, individual manuscripts preserve vital pieces of evidence.

The earliest witness of any of Henryson's works is a manuscript in which four of his poems appear as tangential to its main focus. The Makculloch manuscript (EUL MS 205, formerly La. III. 149) is a folio volume in Latin of notes from sets of lectures on Aristotelian logic made during 1477 at the University of Louvain by Magnus Makculloch (fl. 1477–1484).[16] He went on to become a notary public and professional scribe of some significance, particularly as a copyist of two surviving MSS of Walter Bower's *Scotichronicon* (NRS GD 45/26/48, c. 1481, and BL, Harley 712, 1483–84), and as secretary to the Scottish churchman, politician and book-collector William Scheves (c. 1440–1497), archbishop of St Andrews.[17] (Strikingly, a contemporary hand, closely resembling Makculloch's and possibly indeed his, has copied at the end of the Makculloch MS (fol. 202^v) a previously unidentified extract from the opening of Robert Baston's Latin poem on Bannockburn included in Book XII of the *Scotichronicon*.[18]) Makculloch's lecture notes appear to be written up after the fact as a reference copy; they are relatively carefully laid out, and there are some flamboyant attempts at illustration and rubrication. The notes are not always complete copies of the courses, as the scribe acknowledges in his *explicits*, and some gaps are left in the MS as a result. This provided an opportunity for other owners of the MS to use it as a repository for recording a very different body of material.

On flyleaves, empty leaves, and leaves with areas of blank space, a substantial quantity of dominantly vernacular verse and prose material has been added by a hand of the later fifteenth or early sixteenth century: devotional, Marian, and moral lyrics, a Latin/Scots glossary (including 'hic ysopus, ysop'), and Lydgate's *Dietary* (though not identified as Lydgate's as was common in Scotland with this work).[19] Henryson's poems are distributed across the manuscript. On the opening flyleaves are copied the Prologue to the *Fables* and the first fable in his collection, 'The Cock and the Jasp'. On fol. 87^r, within a group of devotional poems located in a gap in the text of a set of lectures by Petrus de Mera, is included Henryson's 'Praise of Age'. On folio 181^v, in between items by Andreas de Alchmaria and Theodricus Meysach, ll. 1–40 of Henryson's 'Reasoning between Age and Youth' precede a popular anonymous Marian lyric, 'Royss mary, most of vertu virginall' (*NIMEV* 1374).[20] None of Henryson's poems has an attribution. Despite the importance of the Makulloch MS as an early Henryson witness, the ascription of these particular poems to him is thus dependent on other witnesses, principally the later Bannatyne manuscript copied in Edinburgh by George Bannatyne c. 1565–1568 (NLS Adv. 1.1.6), in which all of these poems also appear, and in all of which they are attributed to Henryson by name (fols 55^r–6^r, 57^r–^{v}, 326^v–8^v) – though there is little to suggest any direct textual transmission from the Makculloch MS to Bannatyne.[21]

Opinions differ as to whether the hand that copies this material into the Makculloch MS is that of an early owner whose inscriptions can be found in the MS, a John Purde, possibly a chaplain whose name appears in documentation associated with Edinburgh between 1500 and 1509.[22] A student of that name features in the St Andrews university rolls for 1491–1493 within a year of Gavin Douglas.[23] The association with John Purde is encouraged by the note at the conclusion Henryson's 'Cock and Jasp':

> Qui scripsit scriptum capud eius ben*edictum*
> Nome*n* scripto*ris* Iohannes plen*us* amo*ris*. (fol. iii^v)

However, this kind of 'plenus amoris' tag was a common scribal rhetorical feature across European and English manuscripts and does little further to identify the scribe.[24] I do not myself think that the hand that copied the poetry is Purde's. His ownership, signed in a big display script on fols iii^v and 203^v of the MS, for example, is strongly associated with the lecture material. The vernacular poetry and prose, by contrast, looks as if added to the manuscript by a slightly later owner much less interested in its original content.

Paradoxically, the Makculloch MS's text of the first 140 lines of Henryson's *Fables* is deemed by Denton Fox to be both 'written carelessly and [...] clearly the most accurate witness for this section of the *Fables*'.[25] The Makculloch MS owner could have been working from memory, but the fluent way in which the poetry is written out does not suggest that, and the relatively close relationship of his text of the *Fables* to later witnesses would indicate too that he was working from an existing copy. The Makculloch manuscript also gives the earliest indication of a feature of the textual history of Henryson's *Fables*, their partial, or excerpted, transmission. It contains the Prologue and the first fable. The two later manuscript copies in which the *Fables* were included, the Asloan Manuscript (NLS MS 16500) anthology of prose and verse copied by the Edinburgh notary public John Asloan c. 1513–1530, and the Bannatyne Manuscript, contain seven and ten of them respectively – or contained, in the case of the Asloan Manuscript, since we know of these fables' inclusion from its contemporary contents list; a large part of the manuscript, containing six of the seven Henryson fables, has not survived.[26] They are not attributed to Henryson in the contents list or with the text of the one fable ('The Two Mice') now extant. In the Bannatyne MS the Prologue and six of the *Fables* are attributed to Henryson, but four are not.[27] In both the Asloan and Bannatyne Manuscripts three of the 'Reynardian' fables that feature in the second half of the corpus in the Charteris and Bassandyne orders, are absent: 'The Fox, the Wolf, and the Cadger'; 'The Fox, the Wolf, and the Husbandman', and 'The Wolf and the Wether'. The last two of these were almost certainly influenced by Steinhöwel's printed collection of 1476–1477.[28] It is not in fact until the print made in Edinburgh by Robert Lekpreuick (fl. 1561–1581) for Henry Charteris (d. 1599) of 1569–1570 (STC 185) and Thomas Bassandyne (d. 1577)'s Edinburgh print of 1571 (STC 185.5) that the *Fables* survive as a collection of thirteen with overall Henrysonian attribution and in the order that we now know them. This is the order also followed in an anglicised print produced in London by the bookseller Richard Smith in 1577, most probably derived from Bassandyne's print (STC 186.5).[29] One suggestive way of interpreting this evidence is that the run of Reynardian fables in the second half of the corpus was added by Henryson at a late point in the composition history of the collection, to balance the Reynardian run in the first half: 'The Cock and the Fox', 'The Fox and the Wolf' and 'The Trial of the Fox'. The Asloan and Bannatyne manuscripts would thus reflect earlier textual stages in the composition and publication of the *Fables*, the final statement of which is transmitted in the carefully constructed and symmetrical balance of source material and content that is apparent in the Charteris and Bassandyne versions.[30]

Another of Henryson's minor poems, 'The Annunciation', is transmitted in a quite early manuscript in which the dominant language is again Latin. NLS Adv. MS 34.7.3 is known as the Gray MS, as it was substantially compiled by James Gray, a priest and notary public with connections both to Magnus Makculloch (he rubricated MS NRS GD 45/26/48 of the *Scotichronicon*, which Makculloch copied in 1481) and to archbishop William Scheves, to whom, like Makculloch, he acted as secretary. Gray died c. 1505 but there are datable items in his MS as late as the early 1530s indicating that it continued to be added to by later owners or scribes.[31] His manuscript is a very small volume of both vellum and paper, containing a mixture of prayers, invocations, historical and parliamentary material, legal formulae, and an interesting item on 'Quid sit Notarius' (fol. 32^r). 'The Annunciation', which is attributed to Henryson, is one of a small number of devotional and moral vernacular poems in the MS, and is copied on fols 71^r–2^v after some acts of the reign of James IV, in a hand that is not Gray's. It is the only surviving copy of this poem.

In the early manuscript glimpses of Henryson, he is far from centre stage and he is often anonymous. An element of this paradox is present in his earliest appearance in print. Henryson had died by the time printing came to Scotland in 1507–1508: one of the first poems to be printed by Andrew Myllar, Dunbar's 'I that in heill wes' (B 21, 81–82; STC 7350), refers to his death (p. 191).³² With Walter Chepman Myllar printed two of Henryson's poems in 1508, 'The Praise of Age' (*STC* 7348) and *Orpheus and Eurydice* (*STC* 13166), though neither poem is ascribed to Henryson. This is particularly notable in the case of *Orpheus*, which survives as a complete print with (as was customary) Chepman's device on its title-page and Myllar's device on its final page (pp. 149, 168). The title-page advertises the poem's content and the fact that it comes with an additional item ('The Want of Wise Men', a poem occasionally attributed by editors to Henryson but without strong reason),³³ but makes no reference to an author, though there was space to do so: 'Heire begynnis the traitie of Orpheus kyng and how he yeid to hewyn and to hel to seik his quene And ane othir ballad in the lattir end.'

This makes a contrast with the six Dunbar poems surviving in Myllar or Chepman and Myllar prints only one of which ('I maister Andro Kennedy') does not name Dunbar as author on its title-page, in its colophon, or in the poem itself. Dunbar was almost certainly known to Chepman and Myllar.³⁴ Henryson, before his death, may not have been, which may explain the exclusion of his name from the prints. Asloan's manuscript version of *Orpheus and Eurydice* appears to be textually derived either from the Chepman and Myllar print, or a close relation of it.³⁵ Probably for that reason Henryson is not named by Asloan as author, either in the *incipit* or *explicit* to the poem itself or in Asloan's contemporary contents list. That list shows that, in its full form, this manuscript contained all or parts of all of Henryson's major works: the *Testament of Cresseid*, seven of the *Fables*, and *Orpheus and Eurydice*. None of them is, however, attributed to Henryson. Ironically, the one poem attributed to him by name in the contents list is one that no longer survives: no copy is known of 'master Robert hendersonnis Dreme On fut by forth'.³⁶

Henryson continues to be transmitted in anonymous guise in the early textual history of the *Testament*. In notable contrast to the textual transmission of Henryson's two other major works, no full Scottish manuscript copy of the poem survives (it was in that part of the Asloan MS which is no longer extant). A single stanza, part of Cresseid's concluding address, in ll. 561–67, is copied into the multilingual (predominantly Gaelic, but also containing Latin, Scots, and English) manuscript known as the Book of the Dean of Lismore (NLS Adv. MS 72.1.37, p. 92b), which was compiled in Perthshire at a roughly contemporary period to the Asloan MS, c. 1512–1542.³⁷ It is not attributed to Henryson, but rather headed 'In bocas [i.e. Boccaccio] þat wes full gwd'.

The same stanza was copied (probably from the Dean's book or a manuscript closely related to it) into a now-lost Perthshire manuscript of the Chronicle of Fortingall in the 1570s, without the attribution to Boccaccio. We do not know what the source of these copies was, but this single stanza exhibits some textual independence from other fuller (and generally later) witnesses, all of which seem more closely related to a transmission through print.[38]

It may be indeed that the reason for the paucity of surviving manuscript copies of the *Testament* is the fact that it was in print from an early stage. 'Henryson's "Cresseid", we may presume, was printed by Chepman and Myllar, with other popular works which are not now preserved', wrote with confidence one of his great early editors, David Laing in 1865.[39] It is a reasonable surmise, but if the *Testament* was printed c. 1508 it may well have been anonymous like the other Henrysonian poems printed by Chepman and Myllar. The contents list of the Asloan MS cites it by title only, but it is a title that has remarkable staying power in the history of the poem, which itself may be evidence of its early but now lost existence in printed form.

The earliest surviving full witness of the *Testament* is in fact an English one. It was included by William Thynne (d. 1546) in his edition of Chaucer's *Workes*, which was printed by Thomas Godfray in London in 1532. Thynne was a determined collector of 'Chaucerian' materials, and the fact that he added the *Testament* late to his edition of Chaucer is shown by a cancelled leaf and a gap in foliation.[40] That he placed it deliberately after *Troilus* and before the *Legend of Good Women* conveys even now something of his excited sense of its significance. Thynne's text of 'the pyteful and dolorus testament of fayre Creseyde' is anglicised and its version of Cresseid's 'Complaint' is particularly corrupted. The narrator of the *Testament* of course memorably enquires (in Thynne's anglicisation) 'Who wot if al that Chaucer wrate was trewe?' (64),[41] but Thynne's edition still presents the work as a Chaucerian follow-on to *Troilus* and Henryson's authorship is entirely occluded. English editions of Chaucer's works deriving from Thynne's continued to print the poem as Chaucerian throughout the sixteenth and seventeenth centuries.[42]

The *Testament of Cresseid* is not included in either of the great sixteenth-century Scottish manuscript anthologies, the Bannatyne MS, or the Maitland Folio MS (Cambridge, Magdalene College, MS 2553) which was compiled in the household of Sir Richard Maitland of Lethington, c. 1570–1585.[43] The *Testament*'s absence from the Bannatyne MS is the more remarkable, given that Bannatyne is otherwise such a major repository of Henryson's poems: as noted, the MS contains ten of the *Fables*. It also has *Orpheus and Eurydice*, and eleven of the twelve short poems now regarded as Henryson's, for four of which ('The Bludy Serk', 'The Garmont of Gud Ladeis', 'Robene and Makene' and 'Sum Practysis of Medecyne') it is the only witness.[44] The majority of Henrysonian items in Bannatyne's MS have an attribution to him and Bannatyne indeed plays a significant role in establishing the Henrysonian canon – at least for modern readers. The Maitland Folio, by contrast, contains little Henryson, particularly in comparison to its copious anthologising of Dunbar. It has none of the major works, and just four of the short poems ('The Abbey Walk', 'Against Hasty Credence', 'The Ressoning betuix Aige and Yowth', 'The Thre Deid Polis'), none of them uniquely.

Henryson was clearly less of a priority for the Maitland compilers, probably because of the availability of some of his work in print. Bannatyne's exclusion of the *Testament* is less easy to understand, given his predilection for Henrysonian works, his propensity to copy from printed witnesses, and his focus in the fourth section of his manuscript on poems concerning both faithful and false women, including some that have been argued to make allusion to the *Testament*.[45] And the poem was available to him. However, his now demonstrable access to it was in an English copy. Seven of the nine items by Chaucer or attributed to Chaucer in the Bannatyne Manuscript derive either from Thynne's 1532 edition of Chaucer or editions descended from it.[46] If there was a lacuna in the Scottish printing of Henryson between c. 1530 and some point in the latter part of the century, it is likely that Bannatyne knew the *Testament* principally in its English Chaucerian guise. He may consequently have been less interested in it, because he did not know that it was Henryson's and he did not realise it was Scottish.

A full Scottish witness of the *Testament* does not now survive earlier than the edition printed by Henry Charteris in Edinburgh in 1593 (*STC* 13165). Charteris started printing in the late 1570s, and it is probable that his 1593 edition of the *Testament* was a reprint of an earlier blackletter one.[47] The 1586 testament and inventory of the Edinburgh bookbinder Robert Gourlay records three blackletter copies of 'Testament of Cresside'; those to whom he owed debts included Henry Charteris.[48] So the most plausible reading of the transmission of the *Testament* as a print is that there was a very early Scottish edition that influenced Thynne's edition and in due course Charteris's, but that there was also a period from the 1530s through the 1560s when the dominant printed version in circulation in Scotland was Thynne's English one.

When Charteris printed the poem, however, its association with Henryson was finally strongly asserted. The title-page of the 1593 edition attributes the poem to 'M. Robert Henrysone, Sculemaister in Dunfermeling', using a form of words earlier established (with 'of' for 'in') in the transmission of printed editions of the *Fables* for Charteris and by Bassandyne in 1569–1571. Charteris, a serious enthusiast for Scottish literature, follows Bannatyne in contributing to the establishment of the Henrysonian canon. Henryson was 'master' from as early as Dunbar's 'I that in heill wes' (B 21, 82), and the Asloan manuscript, that designation referring to his university master's degree. The insistence on his schoolmaster role in the later Scottish prints of the *Fables* (Smith's 1577 English edition has him as Master but not as schoolmaster) and the *Testament* may look back to an original authorial self-designation in manuscript that transmitted itself to print, in the way that, for example, John Bellenden (c. 1495–1545x1548)'s designation of himself as 'Channon of Ross' in manuscripts of his translation of Hector Boece's *Scotorum Historia* made its way into the printed edition of his translation produced in Edinburgh by Thomas Davidson c. 1537–1538.[49] But Henryson's long separation from his *Testament* during the sixteenth century conveys the fickleness of transmission culture during this period. His name attaches itself more abidingly to the *Fables* in both Scots and English mid-sixteenth-century transmission than it does to the *Testament*. Neither print nor manuscript gave any guarantee of securing authorship.

William Dunbar writes about this phenomenon in one of his brilliant short poems, 'Schir, I complane off iniuris' (B 64), in which he complains about a would-be writer at court, called Mure, who has plagiarised one or more of Dunbar's poems by endorsing them as his own and by adding defamatory material to them. In the process he has 'magellit my making' (l. 3, mutilated my composition). Dunbar asserts that Mure has 'dismemberit' his metre, indicating a concern with precision that shows that writers like Dunbar did not loosely let the texts of their works go forth. This poem survives in the Maitland Folio MS (pp. 10–11) and a later (1622–1623) copy of that manuscript, the Reidpeth MS (CUL MS Ll.5.10, fol. 11ʳ).[50] The scribe of the Maitland Folio MS went to some effort to correct his transcription through marginal annotation as if alert to the necessity for the clear transmission of this particular poem. Both copyists firmly attribute the poem: 'Quod Dumbar'.

The colophons in the Maitland Folio manuscript indeed have the potential to reveal aspects of the transmission of Dunbar's poetry in the sixteenth century; this evidence is complex but fascinating. The manuscript contains over sixty poems by or attributed to Dunbar. The manuscript is copied by a variety of scribes, though one hand is dominant. That hand, designated by Sir William Craigie as hand A, accounts for fifty of Dunbar's poems. Eighteen other Dunbar poems are found in two separate groups, one of thirteen poems, and one of five, copied by a different hand, designated by Craigie as scribe L.[51] In Craigie's view, both of these sets of poems formed fragments of what was originally a separate earlier MS of Dunbar's poems. Bawcutt accepts this argument for the first fragment of thirteen poems, but not necessarily for the second of five, commenting on some notable differences in hand and orthography between the two sections attributed by Craigie to scribe L, which lead her to question both the identification of these poems as in scribe L's hand and their status as a fragment of the same original compilation.[52] I share Bawcutt's reservations, particularly because of something that she notes in passing: 'Several of the poems in the second section, but not in the first [...] have unusually elaborate colophons'.[53] I thus refer to the hand responsible for the second set of Dunbar poems assigned by Craigie to Hand L as hand X.[54]

'Quod Dumbar', sometimes preceded by 'Finis' and/or followed by '&c', is the dominant colophon form. It occurs much in the first half of the manuscript, in the run of poems copied by hand L and in subsequent clusters of poems copied by hand A, but there are two other significant variations on it. The first is found only in two poems that follow each other in the manuscript, being amongst those first appearing in the hand of scribe A. *The Goldyn Targe* and *The Tretis of the Tua Mariit Wemen and the Wedo* are each said to be 'quod maister william/e Dunbar' (pp. 81, 96). This designation appears to derive from the printed tradition of Dunbar's work, which began during his lifetime. The full colophon to *The Goldyn Targe* in the Maitland Folio MS states that it was 'compylit be maister william Dunbar', phrasing that echoes that used to introduce the poem on the title-page of the Chepman and Myllar print (p. 89). The text of *The Goldyn Targe* in the Maitland Folio MS also suggests that it derives from the Chepman and Myllar print or one related to it. The same is true of the textual relationship of the Maitland Folio MS copy of *The Tretis* to the Chepman and Myllar print. The elaborate title to *The Tretis* in the Maitland Folio manuscript uses similar phrasing to that in the Chepman and Myllar title-page to *The Goldyn* Targe: 'Heir beginis the Tretis of the Tua Mariit Wemen and the Wedo Compylit be maister William Dunbar' (p. 81). The *Tretis* lacks its opening pages in the surviving print copy and concludes with 'quod dunbar' (p. 189), but this is one of the earliest of the prints, possibly printed by Myllar only c. 1507, and it is probable that Chepman and Myllar reprinted this poem with a colophon more like those in their joint works, and that the Maitland copy derives from that. In the other Chepman and Myllar print of a Dunbar poem that survives with a title-page, *The Ballad of [...] Lord Barnard Stewart*, Dunbar's name again appears, once more with the phrasing 'compilit', in the form 'Maistir Willyam Dumbar' (p. 169). It is possible that Dunbar requested this particular designation in his print appearances. But, unlike Henryson, Bellenden, or indeed Douglas, Dunbar's name is not followed by a further descriptor. He has no equivalent of schoolmaster of Dunfermline, Canon of Ross, or Bishop of Dunkeld. The very formation that gives him a title exposes one of Dunbar's most vaunted vulnerabilities, his lack of a stable ecclesiastical living, 'A sempill vicar I can not be' (B 68, 64).

The only other place in the Maitland Folio where there is a magisterial colophon for Dunbar is at the end of *The Tabill of Confessioun* (copied by scribe A, p. 203), and this form of colophon is also paralleled in the copy of this poem in MS British Library Arundel 285 of c. 1540.[55] One wonders if a now-lost printed copy also lies behind this wording. There is moreover only one other attribution of a Dunbar poem to him as 'maister' in any other witness. Bannatyne's copy of 'Off Februar the fyiftene nycht' (B 47) concludes that the poem was 'maid be the nobill poyet maister William Dumbar' (fol. 111^r). This little accumulation of designations for Dunbar is in itself unusual, and may well be ironic on Bannatyne's part, deliberately invoking the 'print' associations of Dunbar in a manuscript context, and suggesting that the rude bawdy of Dunbar's joking at the tailor and souter backfires on the poet himself. That is to say that this colophon reference to Dunbar as 'maister' I take to be scribal, and indeed Bannatyne's; the other 'maister' formulations I believe may have originated with the poet himself.

The second 'quod' colophon variation in the Maitland Folio MS is to couple it with an informative and retrospective title. These occur mainly in the second half of the manuscript. There are two main sub-sets. The first is used both by scribe A and scribe X. It is not used by scribe L. It links Quod Dunbar with a form of title, as in 'Quod Dunbar of Iames Dog kepair of the quenis wardrep' (scribe X, p. 339; B 72), or, straight-faced but with possible irony, 'Quod Dunbar in prays of women' (scribe A, p. 295; B 40). The other subset links Quod Dunbar to a description introduced by a conjunction, frequently 'quhen', as in 'Quod Dumbar quhone mony Benefices vakit' (scribe A, p. 316; B 62). There can again be an ironic tinge to these colophons. That to 'My hartis treasure and swete assured fo' (B 34) is 'Quod Dumbar quhone he list to feyne' (scribe A, p. 323). All the colophons in this sub-set are in the hand of scribe A, but there is arguable overlap with one of the first sub-set since 'quod dunbar of ye said Iames quhen he had plesett him' is similar in kind, and is written by scribe X.

Six of Dunbar's poems are duplicated in the Maitland Folio MS. Poems copied in the section of the MS produced by scribe L with which the manuscript now starts are copied into a later portion of the MS by scribe A. Strikingly, three of these poems have differing colophons. While L's copies intone the standard 'Quod Dunbar', A's produce three variations, 'Quod Dumbar quhone many Benefices vakit' (p. 316; B 62), 'Quod Dumbar aganis the solistaris in court' (p. 316; B 5), and 'Quod Dumbar at Oxinfurde' (p. 318; B 82). There is generally little textual variation between the copies of the duplicated poems, but the fact that scribe L's copies are part of what was probably an originally separate MS later brought together with the Folio proper makes it entirely possible that the two scribes were working from different witnesses.[56] Bawcutt as editor tends to prefer scribe A's copies of these duplicated poems, but not exclusively. She comments rarely on whether she believes the poems share exemplars, but in the case of 'To speik of science' (B 82) does state categorically that 'MF contains two copies, which represent slightly differing exemplars'.[57] Thus it would be unwise to conclude that the extended colophons in the Maitland Folio are introduced into this MS by scribe A. The way in which they are clustered, the fact that scribe A will elsewhere simply write 'Finis' or 'Quod Dunbar' and the fact that scribe X also copies colophons of this ilk in a cluster (as in the two James Dog poems, B 72, 73), suggests that they reflect practice in underlying exemplars and as such that their ultimate point of origin could be Dunbar as author.

Where do these colophons originate? In my view they go back to the early transmission of Dunbar's poetry, originating either with the poet himself and/or with the scribes in his circle. For there is precedent for this kind of colophon in another witness of Dunbar's oeuvre. It starts within his lifetime, in the earliest of the Chepman and Myllar prints, indeed within the print possibly produced by Myllar himself ahead of his work with Chepman. This print contains three poems by Dunbar, the *Tretis*, 'I that in heill wes' and 'I maister Andro kennedy'. 'I that in heill wes' has the colophon 'Quod [D]unbar quhen he was sek &c' (p. 192). It is not obvious whether this colophon falls into the informative category or the ironic one; it may be a bit of both. It is unlikely to have originated with the compositors of this text, who may well have been French, and who often struggled with their text of Dunbar as it was, so its origins look to be either authorial or scribal.[58]

We may pick up another vestige of these styles of 'quod' colophons in the Bannatyne MS. The Bannatyne MS has far fewer of this kind of colophon in the forty odd Dunbar poems in its capacious bounds, but it has a notable instance in that to 'I maister Andro Kennedy' (B 19), where the explicit reads 'Heir endis the tesment of maister Andro Kennedy/ Maide be Dumbar Quhen he wes lyk to dy' (fol. 155ᵛ). Bannatyne's text of this poem is closely related to that of the very early Myllar print of it, where the colophon is simply 'Explicit' and the poem is not attributed to Dunbar. In my view Bannatyne's colophon is most likely to derive from a subsequent print of this poem made by Chepman and Myllar c. 1508 where this poem was linked more overtly to Dunbar, and this again raises some possibility of its being authorial in origin.

This style of colophon has moreover some contemporary parallel outside Dunbar's oeuvre. The first scribe of MS Arch. Selden. B. 24 writes ironically at the end of his copy of the anti-feminist lyric 'Deuice prowess and eke humilitee', commonly attributed to Chaucer in Scottish witnesses, 'Quod Chaucer quhen he was ry*ch*t auisit' (fol. 120ʳ). The colophon as commentary may have been a feature in Scottish courtly and bookish circles, seems to have particularly attached itself to the tradition of Dunbar, and is especially picked up in the exemplars underlying parts of the Maitland Folio MS. Some of these instances could originate with Dunbar himself; some could originate with contemporary scribes; and a few could also – as Bawcutt suggests of the colophon to 'To speik of science' (B 82) – be the imitative practice of later scribes.[59]

Well known enough in his lifetime to get into print and in some circles for half a century after it to be included in the major anthologies of Scottish poetry, Dunbar had, however, less sustained and widespread transmission than his contemporary and rival Gavin Douglas. Dunbar is lost to us in print after his initial foray during his lifetime until his poetry reappears, dominantly from the Bannatyne manuscript, in Allan Ramsay's *The Ever Green: Being a Collection of Scots Poems Wrote by the Ingenious before 1600* printed in two volumes by Thomas Ruddiman in Edinburgh in 1724.[60] His poetry was not entirely unknown in England, as the inclusion of 'In secreit place' (B 25) in the mid–late sixteenth century Osborn Manuscript (Music MS 13), now in the Beinecke Rare Book and Manuscript Library at Yale University, shows;[61] but the poem has no attribution. When Dunbar crossed the border, he did so anonymously.

Gavin Douglas, by contrast, crossed the border in his lifetime and stayed as an exile in England, dying in London in 1522, and his poetry travelled after him, taking his name with it. Both of Douglas's major poems were published during the reign of Mary Tudor. The *Eneados* was printed in London by William Copland in 1553 at the start of Mary's reign (*STC* 368.05), the first of three translations or partial translations of Virgil's poem to be published during her years: 'Because the *Aeneid* is the story of the founding of Rome and because Rome and the Catholic church were, on the Continent, virtually inseparable concepts, the appearance of [this edition] during Mary's reign speaks first of all to her Catholic identity and European connections'.[62] Douglas's bishopric doubtless also spoke to Mary's Catholicism. The title-page to the Copland print acknowledges that the poem is translated 'into Scottish metir bi the Reuerend Father in God, Mayster Gawin Douglas/Bischop of Dunkel'. The reference to the poem's original Scottishness was there in part to explain its potential difficulty, though the poem was also anglicised in this edition.

Copland probably published Douglas's *Palice of Honour* shortly afterwards (the title-page bears no date), trading on an interest in Douglas aroused by the publication of his *Eneados*. Its title-page makes reference to compilation in a formulation that looks back to those employed in the printed tradition of Dunbar 'THE PALIS OF Honoure Compyled by Gawyne dowglas Bysshope of Dunkyll' (*STC* 7073), and it is most likely that Copland was working from a Scottish print witness. Fragments survive of an edition probably produced in Edinburgh c. 1530–1540 (*STC* 7072.8) by Thomas Davidson (fl. 1532–1542), the printer who began the resurrection of the printing of Scottish poetry after the twenty-year gap that apparently followed the conclusion of Chepman and Myllar's enterprise and the aftermath of the Scottish defeat at Flodden in 1513. There is a close relationship between that edition and Copland's.[63] A recently discovered manuscript fragment of *The Palice* in the protocol book of the Dysart notary and cleric Mr David Bousie (also known as David Alexander; Edinburgh, NRS, MS B 21/1/1, fol. 1ʳ) dating from the early 1540s, may derive from that print or pre-date it; not enough material survives of this MS fragment or the 'Davidson' fragments to confirm this one way or the other. This fragment is the only surviving manuscript witness for the poem. The earliest full surviving Scottish witness is the print made in Edinburgh in 1579 by John Ross for the indefatigable Henry Charteris (*STC* 7074). The route of transmission from the 'Davidson' and London editions to this one is not straightforward. Charteris was aware of the edition 'quhilk hes bene Imprentit at London' but saw it as 'faultie and corrupt'.[64] The divergences between the 1553 and 1579 editions are such that Bawcutt has posited that Douglas revised the text and that differing versions of it were in circulation[65] (we have seen a somewhat comparable situation with Henryson's *Fables*). In his preface to the 1579 edition, Charteris implies that he may have had access to a manuscript of the poem in addition to the prints he claims to have consulted. This should not be ruled out. Charteris's access to manuscripts is demonstrable, for example, in his preface to his 1594 edition of the *Wallace*, where, as not previously recognised, he quotes from what is identifiable as the Coupar Angus MS (NLS Adv. 35.1.7) account of Wallace's sojourn in France with King Philip IV from Bower's *Scotichronicon*.[66] But the lack of surviving full manuscripts of the *Palice* suggests that, like Henryson's *Testament*, it was a poem whose early and repeated appearance in print led to a lessened transmission through manuscript and through anthologies.

Something comparable may have pertained in relation to Douglas's *Eneados*, despite the apparent absence of a contemporary Scottish printed edition. On the evidence now available, the *Eneados* was not printed by a Scottish publisher until Thomas Ruddiman's edition in 1710 shortly after the Union of the Parliaments. But it was clearly popular in Scotland during the sixteenth century. Five full manuscripts survive along with some fragments from what was once a complete manuscript (now EUL, MS Laing II 655).[67] These manuscripts date from the first half of the century. Parts of three of Douglas's Prologues to books of his translation were copied in the Bannatyne MS, apparently from the 1553 London print and/or one related to it.[68] Was this a Scottish edition? It is not obvious who would have been prepared to undertake this in Scotland in the 1550s or early 1560s. The two principal printers at work during at period, John Scot and Robert Lekpreuick, were producing mostly relatively short quarto or octavo publications.[69] It is slightly more likely that this was a variant English edition. Cumulatively this evidence suggests that after the poem was printed in London demand for it in Scotland was met from copies of that edition or others derived from it. The 1579 inventory of the goods of Thomas Bassandyne, who sold far more books than he printed, contained 'fyue Virgilis in Inglis', another possible reference to an edition of Douglas.[70]

Gavin Douglas did not see his works in print during his lifetime, but he saw himself in print. He featured in a dialogue with his Scottish contemporary philosopher and theologian David Cranston (c. 1480–1512) prefixed to John Mair's commentary on book one of Peter Lombard's

Sentences which was printed in Paris in 1510.[71] Mair (c. 1467–1550), like some other Scots scholars before him (James Liddell (fl. 1483–1500) was the first Scots writer to have a book printed in his lifetime, in Paris, in 1495[72]), had begun getting his books printed in Paris before the advent of printing in Scotland, his first publication appearing in 1499. That writers like Mair and his peers continued printing in Paris after the advent of Chepman and Myllar's printing press in Edinburgh c. 1507 is explicable for a number of reasons. Firstly, they were based there – in Mair's case, he arrived c. 1494 and left in 1518. Secondly, they intended their works to have a continental circulation ahead of, or as well as, a Scottish one – this was a feature of Scottish book culture that continued well into the seventeenth century.[73] Thirdly, there is little evidence that Myllar and Chepman were strongly interested in Latin scholarly printing. Their existing publications were in the vernacular, with the large exception of the Aberdeen breviary, a devotional rather than a scholarly publication, after the appearance of which their (or by that time Chepman's) printing enterprise seems to have ceased. Writers like Mair continued to print in France during the next twenty years because there was no Scottish press readily available to them.

The printer of the 1510 volume in which Douglas featured was Henri Estienne (the elder, also known as Henricus Stephanus), the founder of a celebrated printing dynasty. But the printing was carried out 'impensis [...] Jodoci badii ascensii [...]'.[74] A Fleming, based for much of his adult life in Paris, Josse Badius Ascensius played a seminal role in the printing of Latin texts by Scottish authors over the best part of three decades. A scholar of considerable distinction himself, he worked closely with a range of Scottish authors, either based in Paris or visiting there. In the first decade of the century Mair and others in his circle, such as Cranston and George Lockert (c. 1485–1547), often published with the Parisian printer and bookseller Denis Roce (or Ross as he sometimes styled himself; his origins would repay a separate study[75]). But after Roce's death in 1517 Ascensius came to dominate as the printer of choice of Scottish authors, amidst his very many other publications. In the 1520s his publications included the two major Latin histories of Scotland, Mair's *Historia Majoris Britanniae tam Angliae quam Scotiae* (1521) and Hector Boece's *Scotorum Historiae a prima gentis origine cum aliarum et rerum et gentium illustratione non vulgari* (1527).[76]

Ascensius was also the publisher of the celebrated Aberdonian grammarian, John Vaus (c. 1484–c. 1539).[77] Some of Vaus's publications were aimed more at a Scottish than a European market, but Vaus published with Ascensius because he had met him during his own sojourn in Paris at the beginning of the century, and because he was indebted to Ascensius as a scholar as well as a printer – as is particularly shown in the construction of Vaus's commentary on the first part of the *Doctrinale* of Alexander de Villedieu, which Ascensius published in 1522.[78] The transmission histories of this book and of Vaus's own grammar, his *Rudimenta puerorum in artem grammaticam*, afford a fascinating case-history of how a Scottish author worked closely with a printer and with a combination of print and manuscript in the revision of his materials.

Vaus travelled to Paris in 1522 to oversee the production of these volumes. He stayed there six months, working on his *Doctrinale* commentary with Ascensius himself, whose existing revision of the first part formed the basis for Vaus's edition, and with another Scot, Robert Gray, a professor at the college of Boncourt.

Three printed copies of Vaus' commentary on the first part of the *Doctrinale* survive, two complete, one partial. They appear to represent three slightly different impressions of the same edition. The partial copy constitutes over fifty fragments found in the binding of a mid-sixteenth-century manuscript of the *Regiam Maiestatem* of Inverness provenance and now in the NLS (Acc.11218/6, no.2). In terms of printing, this is very slightly the earliest of the three copies. It has a number of tiny press variants that distinguish it from the other two where they have been corrected. Its relationship to the two other copies illustrates Anthony Grafton's assessment that 'When errors came to light, the presses might be stopped and the forme corrected. But then the uncorrected sheets would be sold, alongside the corrected ones'.[79] The relationship of the other two copies to each other is less straightforward. The copy that until about fifteen years ago was thought to be the only surviving copy of this edition is that in Aberdeen University Library (Λ³ Vau r1). This edition is heavily marked up with manuscript corrections and revisions, many of which are in Vaus's own hand. He was a serial reviser of his work. Other comments are by subsequent owners of the book, often also manifesting a highly focused relationship to it, in which correction and supplementation feature prominently.

A few years ago another nearly complete copy of this edition surfaced in Glasgow University Library (Sp Coll RG 3053).[80] This copy contains at its end an extensive printed list of four pages of 'Emendanda' (sig. hh 1ʳ–hh2ᵛ), which are not found in the Aberdeen copy. They pertain to both the *Doctrinale* and to a version of Vaus's bilingual Latin and Scots *Rudimenta* that was here published as the first item ahead of the

Doctrinale. These two items have separate pagination but the errata list refers to them both. Thus, the Aberdeen and Glasgow texts of the *Doctrinale* are identical, and both are dated February 1522, but the Glasgow copy reveals that Badius produced two separate runs of this edition of the *Doctrinale*, in one of which it appeared on its own (the AUL copy) and in one of which (GUL) it was grouped with Vaus's *Rudimenta*. It is possible that the latter run was specifically intended for a Scottish market.

The fact that the errata list refers to both of Vaus's works indicates that he took the lead in identifying the errata, though Badius was an experienced corrector, having, like so many printers (including Andrew Myllar), begun his engagement with the printing business in that capacity.[81] Vaus describes these emendations as the product of his 'lucubrations', generated in part in relation to his text of Alexander, in part because of errors committed by the printers (*partim chalcographorum errore comissa*) and partly as the revisions to his commentary stemming from his further reflections on it. These kinds of comments become in due course the topoi of sixteenth-century errata lists, but this is a strikingly early example of them.

It has been suggested that Erasmus in his *Adagiorum opus* of 1528 was 'perhaps the first to refer to line numbers by counting from the top or bottom of the page, depending on which direction was shorter'.[82] Vaus can be shown counting from the top of the page in 1522. He indeed explains precisely how the system works, 'Signabuntur autem per signaturas foliorum, & numerum signaturarum, paginarum, & linearum: vt pa. sit pagina.li. linea. Et ponitur dictio bona ante emendandam'. (Moreover, they (the corrections) are indicated by the signatures of the folios, and the number of the signatures, pages, and lines: so pa. = page, li. = line. And the correct rendition is placed before the emendation.) That is the standard format, so the first correction for the *Doctrinale* reads 'a.iiii.pa.ii.lin.xxiiii.etiam est tertiae' (sig. hh 1^r; the original text reads 'etiam est seconde'). There is also a system for counting from the foot of the page as signalled by the occasional reference to the penultimate (li. penul.) or ultimate line. Additions and deletions are signalled by 'Adde' and 'Dele', sometimes with an explicatory comment.

A great many, though not all, of these emendations in the GUL copy errata list can be shown to have been marked up by hand by Vaus on the AUL copy. Thus, the first correction cited above for sig a iv^v has been made by hand in Vaus's copy with *seconde* crossed through and *tertie* added in the right-hand margin. Other emendations, especially additions, are more extensive and ambitious. Again, a great many of them are picked up in manuscript in the AUL copy. So the errata list in the GUL copy signals (sig. hh2ᵛ) that at sig k. iiii [ʳ] after line 29 'duos versiculos' which had been omitted due to a wandering mind (*hallucinatione*) should be added and in the AUL copy they are duly written in at the bottom margin. The majority of these particular manuscript changes are, in my view, Vaus's, and the intense scribbling over much of the AUL copy shows that he indeed went on refining his commentary, hence his exclusion of some of the changes suggested in the GUL errata.

This kind of attention to detail was obviously strongly connected to the fact that the *Doctrinale* was, and remained, a teaching text. Its revision at the hands of Ascensius and Vaus was designed to redeem it from some of the criticisms it had received from other humanist grammarians[83] and for Vaus it continued a work in progress. The AUL copy of the *Doctrinale* was clearly Vaus's working copy. In that sense it may be both earlier and later than the GUL one. It contains marking up that got into the errata list in the GUL, but its extensive MS notes show that Vaus went on marking up this text afterwards as he reflected on it. He exhibited something of a similar rigour in relation to the text of his own *Rudimenta*, a work itself derived from the Scots vernacular 'Donatus' printed probably by Andrew Myllar c. 1507, of which Vaus is the most likely author (AUL, Λ³ Vau r 1).[84] Here we are able to see changes working through from the errata list in the 1522 edition to a later printed edition of the work, because the 1531 edition, also printed by Ascensius, survives in a single copy in the AUL (Λ³ Vau r 2). This text is not identical to the 1522 edition. 1522 is shorter altogether and has less Scots. Both texts move from extended sections in Latin to sections in Scots (frequently using black letter for the vernacular), but the 1531 edition, having apparently been set up from the 1522 in its first half, moves far more independently into Scots in its second. Nonetheless, it takes on board a considerable number of the errata signalled in the 1522 edition, both making additions and deletions (e.g. a repeated line ('quia bis ponitur') sig. hh[1ʳ]; cf. 1522 sig. bb. vʳ, l. 11 with 1531, sg. bb iiiiʳ, l. 10). The 1531 edition has its own printed errata list (sig. hh.5ᵛ), with corrections both to the Latin and the Scots, and a further set of corrections in a slightly later manuscript hand on a piece of vellum inserted at the back of the volume.[85] Vaus's own habit of marking up his work continued with this grammar, and influenced its transmission long after his death in 1539. Once more, some but not all of the changes signalled in manuscript annotation in the 1531 edition can be seen to have been taken up and implemented in the text of the 1566 edition by Robert Lekpreuick that is a reprint of the edition produced by another

Parisian printer Robert Masselin in 1553.[86] Print and manuscript went hand in hand as closely related forms of transmission for Scottish works throughout the sixteenth century.

Personal ownership, family ownership, and institutional ownership have much to do with the history of the transmission of Older Scots literature to the present day. The involvement of individuals or institutions as patrons and owners can play a crucial role in whether we now have a copy of a work or know of its existence. A certain category of owner has been seen to recur significantly throughout this chapter, notaries public.[87] They both collected and transcribed texts, as we have seen in the cases of James Gray and John Asloan. And sometimes they collected them not only with other literary works but amidst copying that spoke to their activities as recorders of legal materials. David Bousie's MS is an instance of this. So too apparently was an MS known in the nineteenth century but currently unidentified. The Reverend W. Muir wrote of it, 'I have seen a protocol book of a notary public containing a song on the return of James the First from his captivity'.[88] How wonderful it would be if that resurfaced!

Some notaries were also authors, Richard Holland, Robert Henryson, and Andrew Cadiou (translator of *The Porteous of Noblenes* in the Chepman and Myllar prints) amongst them. Another notary public, Walter Chepman, played a key role in the transition from manuscript to print. But the survival of the Chepman and Myllar prints today owes as much to other early owners of these earliest examples of Scottish printing. One of these, Florentine Martin, whose name appears in manuscript on the title-page of Dunbar's *Golden Targe* (p. 89), was a laird in the Dysart region of Fife, placing him in the suggestive context of a literary nexus which included the Sinclairs of Ravenscraig (owners of the Selden MS) and the notary and copyist David Bousie.[89] Another name written after the 8 April 1508 colophon at the end of the print of *Golagros and Gawane* (p. 51) is hard to decipher but has recently been transcribed by Ian Cunningham, as M[aister/Magister] Robert Forrester.[90] I think this is highly likely to be correct. Forrester was abbot of the Cistercian abbey at Balmerino in Fife from 1511 to c. 1559.[91] But, as significantly, before that from 1509 he was provost of the collegiate church of Corstorphine (the rules were somewhat bent by the papacy to enable him to make his profession to the order in a compressed period in order to take on the abbacy).[92] The Forresters had been landholders in Corstorphine for a century or so and dominated the patronage of Corstorphine church. Robert must have been some form of relative of Sir Archibald Forrester of Corstorphine, in whose house Bernard Stuart, Lord D'Aubigny, died in June 1508.[93] Dunbar's *Ballade of* [...] *Barnard Stewart* (B 56) of course celebrated Stuart's arrival in Edinburgh from France on a diplomatic mission a month earlier and was printed by Chepman and Myllar around that time. The Forrester family may well have acquired a copy of the eulogy on Stuart around the time that they got the copy of *Golagros*, and they may thus have been amongst the various earliest owners of some or all of the Chepman and Myllar prints. For a notable Edinburgh family to own a series of the Chepman and Myllar prints would make sense. Whether Robert Forrester's move to Fife lies behind Florentine Martin's ownership of some of the prints is presently unclear, but more work on the attribution of the various inscriptions and *sententiae* scattered through the Chepman and Myllar prints should do much to elucidate this.

The early history of the transmission of Older Scots literature is one of transition: from manuscript to print, and sometimes back to manuscript. Authors, manuscript, and printed books travel from Scotland to Europe and from Scotland to England and back again. Texts transition through different forms, being revised, extended, or sometimes, as in the case of the *Scotichronicon*, abbreviated.[94] In Vaus's grammars or Dunbar's macaronic poetry texts transition fluidly between Latin and Scots. The fifteenth and sixteenth centuries were a period of formidable creativity in Scottish culture, and those who copied, printed, kept, and read these texts played a crucial cultural part in making that so.

PART 2: CULTURE AND IDENTITY

CHAPTER THREE

Expressions of Faith: Religious Writing

Sìm Innes and Steven Reid

Religious faith was the most prominent theme in literary discourse in the sixteenth and early seventeenth century, the bulk of which consists of theological tracts, biblical commentaries, and polemic. Concerned primarily with the nuanced exposition of scripture and the issues of liturgy and polity afflicting Scotland's fledgling Kirk, it mostly lacks the discussion of universal and timeless themes or the stylistic excellence that makes great literature. Moreover, the constant stream of vitriol poured forth against all those who were not part of the godly community, particularly the 'antichristian' forces of Catholicism, can be wearying and repugnant to read. However, as John Knox (c. 1514–1572) points out in Book I of his *History of the Reformation in Scotland*, works like his serve a higher purpose than the purely literary:

> This we wryte to lett the posteriteis to come understand, how potentlye God wrought in preserving and delivering of these that had butt a small knowledge of his trewth, and for the luif [love] of the same hasarded all; that yf that eyther we now in our dayis, having grettar lycht, or our posteriteis that shall follow us, shall see ane fearfull dispersioun of such as oppone [oppose] thame selfis to impietie [...] nor yitt dispare, butt that the same God that dejectes, (for causes unknawin to us,) will raise up agane the personis dejected, to his glorye and thare conforte.[1]

The Reformation century created several generations of writers, on both sides of the confessional divide, who like Knox were keen to document and disseminate their vision of Christianity as the one true path to salvation. The Reformation inadvertently contributed to significant shifts in the literary forms used by all three of early modern Scotland's major languages, albeit with differing levels of impact. While late-medieval Gaelic verse predominantly inhabited a pan-Gaelic context (incorporating both Scotland and Ireland), links can be made between religious poetry in both of Scotland's vernacular languages, although there are often considerable differences in form, reception and function. The advent of the Reformation saw certain topics fall out of favour in Protestant verse, but it is noteworthy that religious verse from seemingly opposed confessional traditions continued to be shared and enjoyed in some contexts.

For Scots prose, by contrast, the Reformation arguably resulted in its arrival as a genre, as Catholics and Protestants alike wrote historical narratives to justify their faith and polemical works denouncing their opponents. In doing so, they moved away from the traditional use of Latin for religious writing in the hopes of attracting – and keeping – the interest of the common parishioner. The use of the vernacular and indeed an appropriate register of the vernacular were major concerns for Scottish writers of religious literature, in both Scots and Gaelic, after the Reformation.[2] Collectively, the works produced during this period of religious turmoil help explain why so many were willing to die, or suffer persecution and exile, for their own 'true' version of the church; individually, some transcend their immediate context and have a merited place in the Scottish canon.

Religious Verse in the Vernaculars

Religious practice and specific devotion are evident in a whole range of primarily non-religious verse in both Gaelic and Scots. In the elegy for Niall MacNèill of Gigha (d. c. 1470), Aithbhreac inghean Coirceadail (fl. 1460–70) tells us that her grief is inspired by his Rosary.[3] The focus on the Rosary in this poem is somewhat reminiscent of another bardic elegy 'A Chros thall ar an dtulaigh' ('O Cross yonder on the hill') by the Irish poet Gofraidh Fionn Ó Dálaigh (d. 1387) which begins with a similar address to the wooden cross at his son's grave as cause of grief.[4] The works of Sir David Lyndsay of the Mount (c. 1486–1555) are full of descriptions of, and comment on, religious practice and Church governance, such as his verses on 'Imageis maid with mennis hand' in *The Monarche*.[5] Richard Holland (d. c. 1483), priest and notary public, includes bird-minstrels singing thirty seven lines of praise to the Virgin at the banquet in *The Buke of the Howlat*. The entertainment at the banquet also includes the Ruke (Rook), as 'a bard owt of Ireland', reciting in Gaelic before being attacked by the Tuchet (Lapwing) and Golk (Cuckoo) in the guise of fools, much to the amusement of the assembly.[6] Eachann Bacach's (c.? 1600–post-1651) 'A' Chnò Shamhna' ('The Halloween Nut'), a lament for Lachlan MacLean of Duart (d. 1648), perhaps provides a glimpse of religious practice:

> Bha gràdh is eagal Mhic Dè ort
> An àm sgriobtair a leughadh
> Ann ad chaisteal mun èireadh do bhòrd.

You had the love and fear of the Son of God / when the Scripture was read / in your castle before your table arose.[7]

The importance of the noble court is highlighted in both of these last examples. Much of the surviving late-medieval Scots religious verse that has received scholarly attention was written by poets with some attachment to the royal court of the Stewart kings. This is not true of Gaelic religious verse. In 1616, the Scottish Privy Council of King James VI and I, decreed that the 'vulgar Inglishe toung be universallie plantit and the Irische language, whilk is one of the chief and principall causis of the continewance of barbaritie and incivilitie amongis the inhabitantis of the Ilis and Heylandis, may be abolisheit and removit'.[8] This was to be done in order to advance the cause of the 'trew religion'. It is estimated that somewhere between a third and a half of the population of Scotland would have been Gaelic-speaking during the period 1400–1650[9] and the king had already made his feelings on his Gaelic subjects crystal clear in his *Basilicon Doron* (1599) stating that in his view the Gaels on the mainland were mostly barbarous and that the 'wolves or wild boars' of the Islands were beyond contempt.[10] With this in mind it is perhaps remarkable that any religious works were printed in Gaelic at all. The king was of course choosing to ignore the fact that the 'incivilitie' of the Gaelic nobility included the support of all sorts of Gaelic scholarship during our period. He cannot have been unaware of this since there is some evidence that he himself might have provided patronage for the Irish poet Fearghal Óg Mac an Bhaird (d. 1618x1630) around 1581. For his part, Mac an Bhaird in the poem 'Dursan mh'Eachtra go hAlbuin' ('A Hardship my Journey to Scotland') appears to have been rather traumatised by the Reformed faith he witnessed in Scotland.[11]

The literary high register of Gaelic, which had been designed for the composition of dán díreach (bardic poetry in syllabic metres), was in use in Scotland and Ireland from the thirteenth century until the end of our period. This register is referred to as Early Modern Irish, or more commonly in Scotland as Classical Gaelic. This literary standard had to be taught and guides that demonstrated correct usage were produced. A late Scottish guide from c. 1640 is thought to have been produced for a young Archibald Campbell (Gilleasbaig Fionn), the future 9th Earl of Argyll (1629–1685).[12] The use of this register allowed the learned orders to operate in both Scotland and Ireland. This pan-Gaelic context is important for an understanding of Scottish religious literature in Gaelic, although clearly not the only context. A number of Gaelic manuscripts containing religious material provide evidence for further contexts and literacy in Scots and Latin. The Murthly Hours (NLS, MS 21000) gives us an early glimpse of this multilingual setting since it includes instruction in Gaelic for the use of prayers, in Latin and Anglo-Norman French, as charms for healing. The Gaelic notes were added to the Murthly Hours around the beginning of the fifteenth century.[13] The Classical Gaelic manuscripts in the National Library of Scotland contain much religious material. These manuscripts range in date from the fifteenth century onwards, and the vast majority appear to have originated in Ireland and then been added to in Scotland.[14] They contain a whole range of different religious literary forms in Classical Gaelic: prayers and charms; religious verse; saints' lives; sermons; apocrypha; translations of *mirabilia*, such as the letter of Prester John; texts that seek to promote affective devotion, such as the *Dialogue of the Blessed Virgin and Anselm on the Passion*; and instructional tracts, such as one on the four reasons for prostration before the Cross. These kinds of religious writings, whether in Latin, Gaelic or Scots, often reflect the pan-European transmission of pre-Reformation devotional material, and it can be difficult to ascertain how much of this we can claim as Scottish. Once again the multilingual setting is apparent, as well as the pan-Gaelic reality, of many of the Gaelic manuscripts. For instance, NLS, MS 72.1.2 is a medical compendium compiled by the Beatons in Mull, containing much material that has come from Ireland.[15] It also includes a short tract on the periods of indulgence secured by the recitation of the *Saltair Mhuire* (Mary's Psalter) in Gaelic and a quatrain in Scots in the hand of Niall Beaton (fl. 1656):

> In my defend God me defend
> And bring my sauld to ane guid end.
> For I am sik and leik to die
> The Lord God sauld heve mercie of me.[16]

Our main source for late-medieval Classical Gaelic religious verse attributed to identifiably Scottish poets is the BDL (NLS, MS 72.1.37), compiled

1512–1542 by Seumas MacGregor, dean and notary public. It contains a large number of Classical Gaelic poems in bardic metres, as well as some items in Scots and Latin.[17] This manuscript miscellany was compiled in Perthshire and contains around twenty bardic poems of a religious nature as well as five poems that satirise lascivious clergy. These twenty are a mix of Irish and Scottish items with some as old as the thirteenth century and others perhaps as recent as the lifetimes of the compilers. The post-1400 Scottish poets of religious material are: Giolla-Críost Táilléar, thought to be poet to the fifteenth-century Stewarts of Rannoch; Maol-Domhnaigh mac Mhághnais Mhuileadhaigh, thought to be an Ó Muirgheasáin; and similarly unidentified poets such as Donnchadh Óg, and Roibéard Mac Laghmainn.[18] These poets provide us with Classical Gaelic poetry based on narratives drawn from Latin exempla collections such as the *Gesta Romanorum*, two of which are presented as Marian miracles[19] and another as a dream-vision.

Given these subject matters and source materials we can easily demonstrate some similarities between Gaelic and Scots religious verse, despite differences of convention. For instance, the use of exempla collections can also be demonstrated for Scots verse since 'The Bludy Serk' by Robert Henryson (d. c. 1490) is also based on a narrative from the *Gesta Romanorum*.[20] A significant amount of poetry survives in Scots on the Virgin and the dream-vision was also very popular. William Dunbar's (1460?–1513x1530) poem on the Passion, 'Amang thir freiris, within ane cloister', and his poem on the seven deadly sins, 'Off Februar the fyiftene nycht', are both presented as dream-visions.[21] The latter envisages Hell as full of Gaelic-speakers; even Mahoun (the Devil) who summons a Highland pageant is so deafened by their speech, which is again associated with the 'ruke', that he suffocates them with smoke![22] The religious dream-vision was to survive the Reformation since John Stewart of Baldynneis (c. 1545–c. 1605) uses it for 'Ane Schersing out of Trew Felicitie'.[23] 'Ane Schersing' was written for King James VI and is particularly sophisticated; while the importance of Biblical evidence is highlighted it does not concentrate on confessional identity.[24] Elizabeth Melville (fl. 1599–1631) in *Ane Godlie Dreame* (1603), another dream-vision, describes the journey of a Calvinist elect soul.[25] Christ assures the pilgrim that the 'Papists purging place, quhair [...] sillie saulles do dwell' is a figment of man's imagination and that 'My blude alone did saif thy saull from sin'.[26] Alexander Montgomerie (c. 1550–1598) in his sonnet 'Iniquitie on earth is so increst' had previously subtly recast Catholics as the elect.[27] We can look for subtle Catholic discourse in the works of Montgomerie, including in his masterpiece 'The Cherrie and the Slae'. However, it has been suggested that we do well to remember that the sixteenth-century Catholic Council of Trent may have resulted in something of a shared Catholic and Protestant devotional poetic language – to the point where a translation of Psalm 23 and a lyric 'Supreme essence' have early attributions both to Montgomerie and to the Protestant divine James Melville of Kilrenny (1556–1614).[28]

Religious verse in Scots also had recourse to more than one register. For instance, Scots with *aureate* or a large amount of Latinate vocabulary was used by a number of late-medieval poets for religious poetry: 'Hale, Sterne Superne' to the Virgin by Dunbar is perhaps the most well-known example. Dunbar became a priest in 1504. His poem 'Rorate celi desuper!' calls upon all of creation to proclaim the Nativity; even the flowers are to 'lay out your levis lustely'.[29] This is illustrative of the ways in which pre-Reformation poets could not only use scripture as inspiration but also expand upon it in order to induce feelings of wonder, pity and love in the audience. The long poem in Scots with the title 'The Passioun of Crist' by Walter Kennedy (1455?–1518?), apparently also a Gaelic-speaker, is a good example of the extended description of the events of the Passion.[30] Inviting the audience to 'se' the events of the Passion and Resurrection was a common device in Scotland and beyond. For instance, the anonymous poem 'Off the Resurrectoun' from BL, MS Arundel 285 which begins 'Thow that in prayeris hes bene lent' instructs the audience to

> Behald yi meik sueit Salviour
> The to embrace how yat he bowis.
> Se how he martirit wes with Iowis.[31]

Late-medieval verse in Scots provides more evidence than Gaelic for poetry that was intended to act as a devotional exercise. 'The Contemplacioun of Synnaris' by the Franciscan William of Touris (d. c. 1508), the original version of which may have been intended for King James IV, is split into separate sections meant for each day of the week.[32] However, certain sections of Classical Gaelic bardic poems use the first-person, and it may be that they were also used as prayer. Translations of Latin religious lyrics into Scots, and versions in Scots of English lyrics are also relatively common.[33] Translation of whole lyrics like this appears to have been much less common in Gaelic.

Scotland had a rich tradition of verse satire which could include satire of priests. George Buchanan (1506–1582), again thought to have also been a Gaelic-speaker, was forced to flee to England as a result of his Latin satires of the Franciscans: *Somnium, Palinodiae,* and *Franciscanus* written in the 1530s.[34] Satire on religious themes becomes even more vitriolic with the advent of the Reformation. *The Gude and Godlie Ballatis* (1565) includes some anti-Catholic verse polemic among the psalms and other songs.[35] The *Ballatis* contains many translations of Lutheran German originals. Robert Sempill (d. 1595?), in plain-style Scots, also used satire for the Reformist cause.[36] However, not all Protestant poetry is combative; William Drummond of Hawthornden (1585–1649), who wrote in English, published a collection of 'spirituall poems', *Flowres of Sion* (1623). His religious poetry borders on the mystical and allows for some use of common medieval allegory. For instance, his poem 'If that the world doth in a maze remaine' invites the reader to 'powre foorth teares to him pour'd Blood for thee', through meditation on the pelican feeding her young with the blood of her breast.[37]

Scotland saw some Protestant censorship of late-medieval verse. For instance, the Bannatyne Manuscript (NLS, Adv. MS 1.1.6), compiled in 1568 by George Bannatyne (1545–1607/8), includes a censored version of 'The Contemplacioun of Synnaris' but does however contain much pre-Reformation poetry that was apparently acceptable.[38] Such care is still evident a century later in the Fernaig Manuscript (Glasgow, University Library, MS Gen. 85/1 & 85/2) which provides another fascinating example of a collection that contains Protestant verse in Gaelic but also some carefully selected pre-Reformation material, as well as one poem from a distinctly Counter-Reformation context. It was compiled by Duncan MacRae of Inverinate (Donnchadh nam Pìos) (d. c. 1700).[39] MacRae was Episcopalian; he includes a Gaelic translation of a poem that prays to be protected 'bho bhreugan Phresbiterian is Shagart' ('*from the lies of Presbyterians and Priests*').[40] There are fifty-nine poems in the collection and over two thirds of these are religious. These include poetry by northern Gaelic nobility such as MacCulloch of Park, Strathpeffer (Fear na Pàirce) (fl. late sixteenth / early seventeenth century); Alasdair, the 4th MacKenzie of Achilty (Alasdair mac Mhurchaidh, Fear Àicheallaidh) (d. 1642); and Alexander Munro, minister of Durness (d. c. 1653). It has been said that over half of the poems in the collection are in bardic metres.[41] The majority of the verse from this collection is not concerned with confessional identity. Rather some continuity with pre-Reformation religious themes is evident, such as the struggle between body and soul and the futility of earthly pleasures. Biblical episodes provide the detail in a number of poems in the collection whereas apocryphal and exempla material was preferred in Gaelic pre-Reformation poetry. The poem from a Counter-Reformation context is 'Truagh cor chloinne Adhaimh' ('*Sad the state of the children of Adam*'); it is an adaptation of the popular medieval Latin lyric 'Cur Mundus Militat Sub Vana Gloria', adding the Gaelic hero Cù Chulainn to the list of classical heroes who have now perished.[42] The poem was composed by Giolla Brighde (Bonabhentura) Ó hEodhasa (d. 1614), an Irish friar at Louvain. Once again we might see MacRae's inclusion of this poem as reflecting something of the shared devotional language and themes of some post-Reformation poetry.

The Franciscan College of St Anthony of Padua founded in 1607 at Louvain in Flanders became a refuge for Irish friars. They wrote and printed a great deal of Counter-Reformation material in Irish in the early seventeenth century at the College and are often explicit about their decision to simplify Classical Gaelic for religious prose for use in Ireland. Many of these friars came from poetic lineages and were themselves poets. Giolla Brighde Ó hEodhasa explains that it is wrong to further ornament the teachings of God in his *An Teagasg Críosdaidhe* ('The Christian Doctrine'), first printed at Antwerp in 1611.[43] However, this was not the first mention of appropriate language register for Gaelic religious literature in print. The issue had been discussed by John Carswell (Carsualach Mòr Chàrn-Àsaraidh) (c. 1522–1572) in his translation and adaptation of the *Book of Common Order of the Church of Scotland* (1564), printed in 1567 as *Foirm na n-Urrnuidheadh* ('The Form of the Prayers'). One of his adaptations was the addition of a blessing for a ship. Carswell stated in the epistle to his patron, Archibald Campbell (Gilleasbaig Donn) the 5th Earl of Argyll (1538–1573), that while there are those who know Classical Gaelic better than he, he is aware

> nach a milis-bhriathruibh na bfeallsamh do cuireadh an sgriobhtúir diadha, agas nach bfuil feidhm aige ar dhath breadhdha brégach na bfileadh do chur air. Oir is lór don fhírinde í féin mar fhiadhnuise, gan brat oile do chur impe.

> *that the words of the holy scripture are not framed in the sweet words of the philosophers, and that it does not need the fine false colour of the poets. For truth is a sufficient witness to itself, requiring no other covering.*[44]

Yet despite these words, Carswell translated into Classical Gaelic, rather than something closer to the Scottish vernacular.[45] Classical Gaelic was perhaps the natural choice for a work that the translator envisaged being used by both the Gaels of Scotland and Ireland. Also, since the language of much Gaelic scholarship continued to be Classical Gaelic, and since bardic poetry was still highly prized, a move to the vernacular may have been out of the question. Carswell includes his own dedicatory poem and the Lord's Prayer, both in bardic metre, as well as two short carefully chosen excerpts from two pre-Reformation Irish religious bardic poems. Carswell's choice of register was to some extent successful. The Anglican reformers in Ireland printed Seán Ó Cearnaigh's (c. 1545–after 1572) *Aibidil Gaoidheilge & Caiticiosma* ('A B C of Gaelic & Catechism') in 1571; a primer that includes a translation of the catechism of the Anglican *Book of Common Prayer*.[46] It is noteworthy that four of the ten prayers in the *Aibidil* are based on Carswell's prayers in *Foirm na n-Urrnuidheadh*.[47]

The high regard in which bardic poetry was held in Gaelic Scotland and Ireland is underlined by the activities of the Counter-Reformation missionaries from Louvain in Gaelic Scotland. Aodh Mac Cathmhaoil 'Mac Aingil' (Hugh MacCaghwell) (c. 1571–1626), the Irish Guardian of St Anthony's College, is presumably referring to Gaelic Scotland, and indulging in wishful thinking, when he refers to 'Éiri amháin & a hinghean ionmhuin Alba' ('*Ireland alone and her beloved daughter Scotland*') as having the privilege of being uniquely free of heresy, in his *Scáthán Shacramuinte na hAithridhe* ('Mirror of the Sacrament of Penance', 1618).[48] There were a number of Scots at St Anthony's and the College sent groups of missionaries to the Highlands and Islands. In the reports the missionaries sent to the *Sacra Congregatio de Propaganda Fide* in Rome, they detail their great success and various miraculous happenings. The Irish missionary Conchobhair Mac an Bhaird (Cornelius Ward, d. 1641) gives us a fascinating insight into the regard the Highland nobility had for bardic poetry into the seventeenth century. In 1624 he writes of the way in which he was able to gain access to, and work towards the conversion of, John Campbell of Cawdor at Muckairn by:

> Simulandi me esse poetam Hybernum (hos inibi in maximo honore haberi solere novi) cumque unum poema encomiasticum in domini illius laudem composuerim, mox cum uno cytharoeda, et cantore (ut moris erat) ingredior, et honorificentissime excipior.

> *Pretending that I was an Irish poet (I knew it was the custom there to hold these in the greatest esteem) and when I composed a praise poem in that laird's praise, I straightaway went in, with a harper and, as was customary, a singer, and was most honourably received.*[49]

Here we see that the nobility's regard for Gaelic literature could be used as a conversion tool, and as Counter-Reformation missionaries did elsewhere in Europe their reports suggest that they also promoted the miraculous, as well as the veneration of holy objects and local native saints that were all a part of the late-medieval geography of the sacred.[50] It has been postulated that the large amount of Gaelic religious oral literature collected in the Highlands in the nineteenth century by Alexander Carmichael may to some extent bear their imprint.[51]

In Scotland the use of something resembling Scottish Gaelic for printed Reformed literature was not to take place until the 1640s and 1650s. Classical Gaelic was still used for a translation of the Latin version of Calvin's *Catechismus Ecclesiae Genevensis* (1545), printed by Wreittoun in Edinburgh around the year 1631. This is known as *Adtimchiol an Chreidimh* ('Concerning the Faith') and it is thought that Niall MacEoghain of the Clann MhicEoghain (MacEwen) poets to the Campbells may have carried out the translation. Once again *Adtimchiol an Chreidimh* included a number of poems in bardic metres. These include the *faoisid* ('confession') of Eòin Stiùbhart of Appin and two poems that may both be by Niall's father Athairne. The two poems by Athairne were known at Louvain as they appear in the Book of the O'Conor Don, a huge manuscript collection of bardic poetry compiled at Ostend in 1631 for Captain Somhairle Mac Domhnaill from the Glens of Antrim.[52] Therefore, the pan-Gaelic transmission (to and from Flanders) of some Classical Gaelic religious verse survives into the seventeenth century. However, vernacular Scottish Gaelic for religious printed literature was just on the horizon. Ministers of the Synod of Argyll, which covered a huge area, were extremely busy translating during the first half of the seventeenth century. Their *Foirceadul Aithghearr Cheasnuighe* ('A Brief Catechetical Lesson') of 1651, a translation of the Westminster Assembly Shorter Catechism, survives in its second edition print from 1659.[53] The language used in this is much closer to vernacular Scottish Gaelic.[54] Also in 1659 their *An Ceud Chaogad do Shalmaibh Dhaibhidh*, the first fifty metrical Psalms, was printed in Glasgow. The Synod had also parceled out translation of the Old Testament to various ministers in the 1650s but it did not make it into print.[55]

Classical Gaelic and Scots were thus used for religious verse throughout the late-medieval and early modern period, and poetry in both languages shared a number of key elements, including a common stock of tropes and themes and a flexibility of register. While the censorship and the need to address different audiences and polemical purposes caused by the arrival of the Reformation (processes that, indeed, were also seen at work within Protestantism as it split into a range of sects) fractured this shared heritage and its usage, it still remained as the basis for verse across all denominations. It was not until the seventeenth century that a more demotic register of Scottish Gaelic began to be used for printed religious works. This can be contrasted with the earlier and more extensive use of Scots in printed prose works, to which we now turn.

Religious Prose and Polemic

The *Breviarum Aberdonense* ('Aberdeen Breviary'), a liturgical calendar containing numerous prose *lectiones* (readings) for the feasts of many of Scotland's native saints, was finally printed in 1510 after some two decades of research by clerics working under Bishop William Elphinstone (1431–1514). It is testament to the existence of an earlier (and now largely lost) culture of Latin religious prose writing, also reflected in Walter Bower's religious digressions in the *Scotichronicon* (1440s) on topics as diverse as traditions relating to the Virgin Mary and the meaning of the word 'ave'.[56] However, vernacular prose expressing 'popular' piety and focused on matters theological only emerged in the very late fifteenth century, and rapidly grew in popularity.[57] John Ireland (c. 1440–1495), a theologian whose career included stints as a professor at the Sorbonne, as ambassador to the French court, and as confessor to James III, also produced the first vernacular treatise on religion, the *Meroure of Wyssdome*, an 'A B C of Christianitie' and advice manual for the young James IV.[58] Although its seventh 'book' has attracted most scholarly attention for its discussion of kingship and good governance and of the mutual obligations of responsibility that exist between God, the sovereign and his people,[59] the first six books are just as important for their portrayal of the major tenets of the Catholic faith so omnipresent in late-medieval Scottish life. Books one to three and six provide a straightforward exegesis of the Lord's Prayer, the Hail Mary, the Apostles' Creed and the Sacraments, while books four and five discuss the issues of faith and predestination in terms that, as we would expect, allow for man's free will and the place of good works and penance in his own salvation. The constant emphasis on the Virgin Mary and the life of Christ, notably the Passion, reflects similar preoccupations seen in material and cultural expressions of late-medieval Scottish piety such as the Confraternities of the Holy Blood and the Fetternear Banner.[60] The work shows the merest hint of a shift towards humanist modes of thought – sources cited include Seneca, Plato and Virgil alongside Aristotle, Augustine, Boethius, and Ockham, and there is a sense in Ireland's discussion of the preeminence of man above all created things that presupposes the renaissance view of the dignity of reason. However, although there are exhortations to James IV in the dedication to protect the church as 'meroure and exampil to all the pepil' and to 'put nocht jgnorant ore licht persounis and of euill lif jn benefice ore digniteis', there is little else to suggest Ireland desired a humanist reform of the church.[61]

By the second quarter of the sixteenth century, when Lutheran ideas were starting to make their way into Scotland's religious and intellectual communities, vernacular prose pamphlets and manuals began to appear articulating the basic doctrines of evangelical Protestantism. These were all produced by Scots exposed to reforming ideas in Switzerland or Germany, and, as these were functional texts aiming to ground the reader in basic Protestant theology, they lack stylistic or literary flair. John Gau's (d. c. 1553) *Richt Vay to the Kingdom of Hevine* (1533) was a translation of a Danish tract of the same name written by Christiern Pedersen in 1531 which offered a Lutheran interpretation of the Ten Commandments, the Creed, the Lord's Prayer and the Angelic Salutation to the Virgin.[62] John Johnsone's (fl. 1533) *An Confortable Exhortation of our mooste Holy Christen faith and her Frutes written unto the Christen brethren in Scotland after the pure word of God* (1533) was a work of spiritual advice exhorting the reader to piety via a collection of scriptural quotations, mainly derived from Coverdale's English version of the New Testament.[63] During his Continental exile between 1539 and 1542, George Wishart (c. 1513–1546) produced a translation of the Helvetic Confession drawn up by Swiss reformers in 1536, which was posthumously published after his execution for heresy at St Andrews in 1546 as *The Confescion of the Fayth of the Sweserlandes* (London, 1548?). Each author emphasises the importance of the doctrine of justification by faith and the primacy of scripture in the vernacular as the chief instrument of salvation for the common man. Gau describes the gospels as 'richt profetabil to reid and ramember apone', and Wishart describes scripture in the opening of the *Confession* as 'the moost perfyte and auncient science' which 'alone contayneth all godlynes and all sorte and maner of facyon of lyfe', and which is the judge of itself.[64] While all three texts exhibit intense evangelical piety, there is no evidence yet of the polemical aggression prevalent in religious writing of the latter half of the sixteenth century. Instead, each writer focuses on the acceptance of suffering for the true invisible church of all believers, on advocating passive resistance to the ungodly magistrate rather than direct action, and on articulating these ideas in a direct and clear Scots.[65]

Critics are sharply divided over the extent of John Knox's leadership of the early Kirk and the exact nature of his theological and intellectual outlook, but there is general agreement that his collection of writings represents the crucial cultural turn in the appropriation of prose for the purposes of religious polemic. Recent studies investigating Knox as a purely literary agent have been uniformly impressed with his command of a variety of genres, his ability to switch authorial voice, and his talent for producing arresting imagery and anecdotes that rhetorically enrich an otherwise plain and direct written style.[66] Turning his hand with equal ease to admonitory epistles to his parishioners and the Scottish ruling elite (*A Godly Letter of warning* and *Comfortable Epistles* (all 1554); *An Admonition to the Nobility* (1557)) and to theological and political tracts (most famously in the notorious *First Blast of the Trumpet against the Monstrous Regiment of Women* (1558)), his greatest work is the *History of the Reformation in Scotland*, written between 1559 and 1567. Comprising four books written by Knox and a fifth written by an unknown 'continuator' (possibly his 'secretary', Richard Bannatyne), the *History* creates a narrative that legitimises the actions of the Lords of the Congregation during the Reformation Rebellion, and sharply delineates the sufferings of the 'constant' Protestant elect against the 'bloody beasts' of the Catholic hierarchy and the 'dontybours' ('*full-bellies*') and 'munzeons' (a play on *minion* and *monsieurs*) of the court. Books II and III, which give an account of the rebellion against Mary of Guise between 1558 and 1560 down to the return of Mary Stewart from France in the following year, were probably in train by late October 1559, and thus written almost contemporaneously with the events described. Interspersed with vast swathes of documentary and epistolary evidence, these two books are less a compelling personal account of the Reformation than an urgent attempt to fashion a 'master narrative' that depicts the sweeping victory of Protestantism, complete with a self-contained collection of reference texts to prove it. Book I, which acts as a martyrology for Scottish Protestants down to 1558, and book IV, which narrates Knox's clashes with Mary Queen of Scots and her government between 1561 and 1564, were written during Knox's extended stay in Ayrshire in 1566. Relying more on Knox's immediate recollections, these flow far better in narrative terms than the other books and show his talent for lurid soundbites at its sharpest. His graphic account of the six hours it took Patrick Hamilton to die when being burned for heresy in 1528, and of the Perth matron Helen Stirk, drowned on the order of Cardinal David Beaton in 1544 despite 'having ane suckin babe upon hir breast', contrast sharply with the sexual and moral depravities of Beaton himself, who in the account of his murder is found sleeping in after a night 'busy at his comptis [accounts]' with his mistress Marion Ogilvy as his assassins enter the castle.[67] However, Knox reserves his greatest opprobrium throughout for his most feared opponent, Mary of Guise. In a particularly arresting line he describes the placing of a crown on her head when she is appointed to the regency in 1554 as 'als seimlye a sight, (yf men had eis,) as to putt a saddil upoun the back of ane unrewly kow'.[68]

Knox has been described by Robert Crawford as 'the first Scot to achieve literary mastery over English prose',[69] and there has been considerable debate over his frequent (but inconsistent) use of anglicised word-forms and whether he, or the relative dearth of printed books in Scots compared to the ubiquity of anglicised religious texts, played a greater role in the increasingly 'de-scotticised' tendencies of Scottish literature in the seventeenth and eighteenth centuries.[70] This issue was one that the earliest Catholic respondents to his polemic gleefully exploited, and several engaged Knox and his supporters in public disputations (recorded in Knox's *History*) and in a series of printed pamphlets where the defence of a 'purer' form of Scots vernacular, free from anglicised Protestant tendencies, became a key issue. Archbishop John Hamilton tried to appeal, apparently with little success, to both Catholics and moderate evangelicals with the production of a *Catechism* in Scots at St Andrews in 1552, and a simplified exposition of doctrine in broadsheet format in 1558, known as the *Twopenny Faith* due to its purchase price.[71] However, the Abbot of Crossraguel, Quintin Kennedy (c. 1520–1564), and the Linlithgow priest and schoolmaster Ninian Winzet (1518/19–1592) rose to the challenge of defending the Catholic faith publicly at the height of the Reformation. Kennedy's writings include the *Compendius Tractive conforme to the Scripturis of almychtie God* (1558), which argues that only the church fathers and a duly appointed council of church representatives have the right to judge scripture, and several tracts defending the Catholic doctrine of transubstantiation.[72] His works are so centred on adducing scriptural and learned proof for Catholic theology that they largely ignore criticisms of the church posited by Scottish evangelicals, although *Ane litil brief tractait [...] prevand cleirlye the real body of Iesu Crist to be present in the sacrament of the altare* (1561) does take to task the opinions on the Eucharist of the German Johannes Oecolampadius.[73] However, Winzet's *Certane Tractatis for Reformatioun of Doctryne and maneris* (1562), *The Last Blast of the Trompet of Godis worde aganis the vsurpit auctoritie of Iohne Knox* (1562) and *The Buke of Four Scoir Thre Questions*

(1563) combine impassioned rhetoric and acknowledgement of the failings of the pre-Reformation Catholic church with a series of questions aimed at systematically undermining the theological and political claims of Knox and his supporters.[74] In *The Buke of Four Scoir Thre Questions*, when justifying the liberal use of a broader Scots style, Winzet argues that religious truth requires 'familiar, and na curius nor affectat speche' and characterises the anglicising tendencies of Scottish Protestants as 'a cloke of finzeit eloquence' used to entice the gullible.[75] In a postscript added to the work in October 1563, Winzet directly lays this assertion at Knox's door, when he asks him:

> Gif ze, throw curiositie of nouationis, hes forzet our auld plane Scottis quhilk zour mother lerit zou in tymes cuming, I sall wryte to zou my mynd in Latin, for I am nocht acquyntit with zour Southeroun.[76]

Knox's *History* set several patterns for the wave of historical and biographical writings that emerged in the late sixteenth and seventeenth century, and which form a core strand of prose in post-Reformation Scotland. These include James Melville's (1556–1614) *Autobiography and Diary*, John Row's (1568/9–1646) *History of the Kirk of Scotland from the Year 1558 to August 1637*, and David Calderwood's (c. 1575–1650) multi-volume masterwork, *The History of the Church of Scotland*.[77] There is a gap of more than thirty years between the completion of Knox's text and the first of these later narratives (Melville's *Autobiography*, completed in 1601/1602), but they are linked to his work through their shared aim of narrating the struggle of God's 'elect' people against the forces of tyranny. In Knox's case, the object of opprobrium is the forces of French-backed Catholicism; in the later narratives, it is the Episcopal and absolutist leanings of James VI and I in his (increasingly successful) attempts to control the church after assuming full political control in the mid-1580s. To a far greater extent than Knox, these later works engross a vast amount of documentary material – the entire proceedings of the general assembly, full parliamentary acts, the books of discipline, and religious tracts and letters – so they can seem like little more than disjointed collections of edited sources. However, in the same way that they expand Knox's 'master narrative' of the trials and tribulations of the suffering Kirk, they also develop several of the literary devices and strengths that make his work so effective, including the use of pithy anecdotes to attack the failings of James' 'courtly' bishops (described in such unflattering terms as 'dumb dogges' and 'bellie gods').

Melville's *Autobiography and Diary* is by far the most 'literary' of these histories. His narrative is interspersed with accounts of his own life – his education at St Andrews, meeting his wife, the births (and deaths) of his children, and his ministry at Anstruther – that make it eminently readable and appealing. It is also thanks to Melville that his uncle Andrew has come down to posterity with a mythic status similar to that of Knox as a leader of the chosen people. Melville's frequent clashes with royal authority, including his forced exile to England for inflammatory sermons between 1584 and 1586, his warding benorth Tay in 1587, and his imprisonment in the Tower of London between 1607 and 1611, are all portrayed as the actions of an 'intrepid' mouthpiece for the one true faith in Scotland. So too is his most infamous sound-bite from a confrontation with James VI at Falkland Palace in 1596 where he grabbed James by the sleeve and harangued him as 'God's sillie vassall'.[78] However, when James introduces Andrew to his readers at the very beginning of his narrative he waxes at length on his uncle's great patience: 'whowbeit he was verie hat in all questions, yit when it tuiched his particular [his own private interest], no man could crab [enrage] him'.[79] There are also direct invocations of Melville as a prophet, including his almost supernatural ability to divine meaning from dreams – he foretells from the Glasgow regent Peter Blackburn's dream of two red toads climbing out of a 'cap full of barmie drink' that the college's legal action against its former accountants John Graham and Archibald Beaton will be successful – and his 'wounderfull sagacity and smelling out of men's naturals and dispositiones' so that he knew friends who were truly enemies and vice versa.[80]

Although only a handful of tracts and histories were produced by Scottish Catholic spokesmen to combat the rising tide of Protestant literature in the later sixteenth century, it is notable that nearly all their authors wrote in Scots, despite their common complaint that the Protestants had overturned the sacredness of the bible by translating it into the vulgar tongue.[81] While clearly essential for putting the Catholic message across to the non-Latinate Scottish reader, this linguistic choice seems also to have been a conscious attempt to continue the image established by Ninian Winzet of the Catholic Church as a defender of Scotland's traditional culture. John Knox attacked the letter sent to him by the Jesuit James Tyrie (1543–1597) in his *An Answer to the Jesuit Tyrie* (1572) as seeming 'rather scabrushly to haue translatit that which he wrytis furth of Latin', to which Tyrie responded in his *Refutation* (1573) that although his 'language and orthographie' are slightly rusty, he speaks so that he 'salbe easalie vnderstand'.[82] The ex-St Andrews regent John

Hamilton (c. 1547–1610/11), who fled from St Mary's College after revealing his Catholicism and who went on to enjoy great success as an academic at the University of Paris, published *Ane Catholik and Facile Treatise* at Paris in 1581 which ends with a similarly aggressive point about the increasing presence of English word-forms in Scotland's religious life.[83] Directed at the *Negative Confession* drawn up by Robert Bruce and signed by King James and the royal household in the same year, Hamilton pointedly asks:

> Giff king James the fyft var alive, quha hering ane of his subiectis knap suddrone, declarit him ane trateur: quhidder vald he declaire you triple traitoris, quha not onlie knappis suddrone in your negative confession, bot also hes causit it to be imprentit at London in contempt of our natiue language?[84]

Like Knox, Hamilton also displays a penchant for humour that adds to the polemic heat of his text, but which is recounted in earthy Scots. When discussing the nature of the Eucharist, he reels off a chain of scurrilous anecdotes about the misuse of communion wine in reformed parishes where they treat the sacrament as profanely 'as scheraris ressauing thair denner on the harvest field'. Hamilton rehearses an anecdote by James Martine (the provost of St Salvator's College St Andrews) about a minister who became so drunk on taking communion wine on an empty stomach that he fell asleep in the pulpit and woke up at the end of his allotted sermon time to a slightly bemused audience. He then recounts the tale of Katharene Lyon of Aberdeen, who had 'maid guid cheir at hame' before a service and refused the communion loaf, 'saying scho had eitin sufficientlie at hame, and come to ressaue of thair drink'.[85]

The extensive *De Origine, Moribus et Rebus Gestis Scotorum, libri decem* ('Ten Books on the Origin, Customs and Deeds of the Scots', Rome, 1578) produced by the Bishop of Ross, John Lesley (1527–1596), is the only narrative of the events of the Reformation from a Catholic viewpoint.[86] Developed from an earlier and much shorter manuscript in Scots presented to Queen Mary in 1570, but written in Latin for the benefit of the international Catholic community, Lesley's *De Origine* was a full-scale epic covering the span of Scottish history along the lines of those written by Hector Boece and George Buchanan. The work had several deficiencies that greatly limited its value as a piece of polemic. It studiously ignored the events of the Reformation until the final book on the reign of Mary Stewart (book X). Nor did it give the reformers due credit as a well-organised and widespread opposition, but rather treated them as a radical minority who seized power largely with luck and the aid of a cynical and opportunistic nobility.

Despite their plain style, Catholic tracts can be just as heavy to read as Protestant polemic, consisting as they so often do of impassioned but repetitive expositions of Catholic doctrine or the unpicking of the Protestant viewpoint in a series of questions, or both. However, several of these texts have features worthy of comment, and it is interesting to note that the devices they use often mirror those found in the polemic of their counterparts, not least in their affirmations of persecution at the hands of a cruel and corrupt Kirk. Adam King (c. 1560–c. 1625), a professor of philosophy and mathematics at Paris who returned to Scotland in later life to become an advocate (though it is unclear when or if he ever fully abandoned his Catholicism), used his astronomical learning to directly counter Protestant views of the liturgical calendar of worship. In Paris, he produced a translation of the lengthy *Cathechisme* (1581) by the Nimeguen Jesuit Peter Canisius (1521–1597), to which he appended a vernacular calendar of saint's feasts and a tide-table 'of Fvll Sey at all ye costes of Scotland', to counter a similar set of materials added to the Arbuthnot-Bassandyne Bible of 1579 by Robert Pont (1524–1606).[87] Nicol Burne (fl. 1574–1598) was another ex-regent from St Andrews (this time from St Leonard's College) who revealed his conversion to Catholicism to the Paisley minister Thomas Smeaton, and naively offered to defend his faith before the General Assembly due to meet in October 1580. Smeaton instead arranged for his arrest, and Burne was held for over three months in the Tolbooth in Edinburgh. His *Disputation* of 1581 recounts two separate interrogations – one led in Edinburgh by Andrew Melville, and the other in Paisley by Thomas Smeaton – where he was threatened because of his theological convictions.[88] The text ranges over many points of doctrine and shows Burne's considerable learning in patristic and philosophical writings. However, the *Disputation* is most effective as a persecution narrative, with Burne cast as a bold and unbroken spirit whose sinister captors attempt to have him executed, and then try to starve him to death by removing all access to alms (even resorting to cutting down a begging purse he hangs outside his cell window).[89] Burne is only saved by the dramatic intervention of James VI, and while this account may seem slightly over-wrought, the Jesuit missionary John Hay (1547–1607) also alleged similar levels of persecution during a visit to Scotland in 1579 (albeit without the starvation and imprisonment) in his *Certain Demandes concerning the Christian religion and discipline* (1580) when recounting an interrogation by ministers before the Privy Council at Stirling.[90] It is fascinating to see how both these Catholic writers invert the images of suffering and persecution so successfully used by Knox less than thirty years earlier.

Conclusion

The wealth of religious literature produced in early modern Scotland, ranging from devotional lyric to heated polemic, clearly reflects the multilingual and highly fractured state of the nation throughout this period. The changes to (and in some cases advent of) a host of different genres within Scots and Gaelic are often contradictory and complex, and lack any particular rhyme or reason. Themes such as the dream-vision and devotion to Christ provided a slim thread of continuity across verse productions before and after the Reformation, as did the fact that religious verse existed across a wide range of registers. By contrast, almost as soon as prose arrived as a genre it became the domain of history and polemic dictated by Scots Protestants of a particularly hard-line stripe. Although a small range of works by Catholic authors before and after the Reformation stand against this trend, it was only with the arrival of Scottish Gaelic religious prose in the mid-seventeenth century that this monopoly was challenged. At the same time, the increasingly fractured nature of discourse between and within confessions that emerged in the era of the Covenant and its aftermath meant that religious literature only became more fissiparous and venomous in tone as the century progressed.

CHAPTER FOUR

The Purposes of Literature

William Gillies and Kate McClune

Gaelic

The period 1400–1650, although politically turbulent, was relatively stable in cultural terms in the Highlands, sandwiched as it was between the major upheavals of the Wars of Independence and those of the War of the Three Kingdoms. It opened in the heyday of the Lordship of the Isles, when an older, more easterly dynamic centered on a Gaelic-speaking Scottish court had melted away, and the Norse presence in the North and in the Isles had likewise disappeared, allowing a new centre of gravity to develop on the Western seaboard. There were strong cultural ties with Ireland, reinforced by military service and settlement, at a time when the so-called 'Gaelic revival' was under way there, reversing the tide of Normanisation that had begun in the later twelfth century. To Celtic scholars this is the Early Modern period of Gaelic language and literature, in which we find a 'mandarin' class of professional lawyers, doctors and literati (principally the poets and the historians) supporting and supported by the leading families throughout the Gaelic world. The presence of these professionals, and their near-monopoly of literary activity, had powerful effects on the constituency and function of literature in Gaelic. Their position in Gaelic society was an honoured one, and they were jealous in guarding their privileges.[1]

As time went on, the Scottish Gaelic world came increasingly into conflict with the Scottish Crown, and the forfeiture of the Lordship of the Isles in 1493 was of enormous long-term significance. But the highly devolved system of chiefly patrons and native literati only felt the impact of this pressure when James VI and I intervened more drastically in the polity of the Highlands and Northern Ireland after the Union of the Crowns in 1603. Until the last half-century of our period, then, the social basis of Gaelic literature was relatively undisturbed. The evidence for this comes most clearly from the western area dominated or overshadowed by the Lordship, but the Book of the Dean of Lismore (BDL: compiled 1512–1542) shows that Gaelic literary activity, including amateur as well as professional poets, could also flourish much nearer to the eastern fringe of the Gàidhealtachd.

Formal discussion of the purposes of literature in Gaelic sources is rare in our period – and shows nothing like the theoretical treatment of artistic inspiration that we find in the early medieval *Cauldron of Poesy*.[2] Nevertheless, the Gaelic literati did express some views on the topic, and we can derive additional information from their practices and their relationship with their audiences. Additionally, despite radically changed circumstances, there were some strands of continuity from Early Medieval to Early Modern literature, e.g. in the use of the tale-cycles as a literary frame of reference, in the ideology of kingship, and in the so-called Milesian myth as an origin legend for the Gaelic aristocracy. Their use of these gives us insights into how they regarded themselves as practitioners and their place in the tradition within which they worked. Thus, Tadhg mac Dáire Mac Bruaideadha's (1570–1652) inauguration ode for Donnchadh Ua Briain, 4th Earl of Thomond, invoked the legendary judges and lawgivers to whom Old Gaelic wisdom texts were ascribed as his charter to advise his own patron on the attributes of a good ruler. Thus, too, the prose prologue attached to 'Maith an chairt ceannas na nGaoidheal' ('*The headship of the Gaels is a good charter*'), a poem to Gilleasbuig, the 4th or 5th Earl of Argyll (1530–1558 or 1558–1575), sets out much the same tokens of a good ruler, as the heads under which he is about to praise his patron.[3]

Categorising Gaelic literature in terms of its purposes is not easy. A literary trope with a long pedigree in Gaelic literature gave the three principal sorts of musical entertainment as *gentraige* ('smile-music'), *goltraige* ('wail-music') and *súantraige* ('sleep-music'), with the suggestion that its function was to induce a state of mind, whether cheerful, doleful or sleepy.[4] But things are not usually so clear-cut. Didaxis could be embedded in entertainment and vice versa; wisdom literature could be dressed up as a story and romances could carry a 'message'. Despite such complications in the disposition of the material, however, it is possible to draw broad distinctions between three different 'takes' on literature: the perspectives of (1) bardic eulogy (mainly poetry), (2) history (mainly prose) and (3) imaginative fiction (verse and prose).

Bardic eulogy was celebratory; it dealt with the deeds, ancestry, mental and physical attributes and personal qualities of its subject, the chief. It proceeded by setting him against a pre-formed picture of an ideal ruler, and meted out praise according as he measured up to the ideal picture. The bardic panegyric was a sort of hymn, and it is interesting to recall that these poets also composed religious verse, using the same ecstatic or adulatory tone in addressing Christ, the Virgin or the Saints.[5] Of course, the usual subjects of bardic eulogy were mere mortals, short of perfection in one or more respects, or undecided between different real-life courses of action. The bardic eulogy said to them, in effect, 'Pick up the accolades of fame by acting in a certain way'. In that light, bardic eulogy can be seen as admonitory and hortatory rather than toadying – seeking to shape a microcosm of the world by encouraging a certain sort of behaviour in its leaders. It can also be seen as exercising a sort of social control, with the underlying aim of securing the stability and continuity of the social organism – the ruling family or the clan.[6]

Implicit in all this was the idea of a contract between patrons and poets. In a culture in which fame and good name (we should call it 'image' today) defined and determined success, the ruler needed the poet as much as vice versa. For in an aristocratic society, if praise were withheld, its absence would undermine the chief's authority. As Giolla-Brighde Mac Con-Midhe (c. 1210–?1272) put it,

> Dá mbáití an dán, a dhaoine,
> gan sheanchas, gan sheanlaoidhe,
> go bráth acht athair gach fhir
> rachadh cách gan a chluinsin.

If poetry were suppressed, people, so there was neither history nor ancient lays, every man forever would die unheard of except for (the name of) each man's father.[7]

Several features of bardic verse are to be understood in the light of this basic fact about the poet-patron relationship. Many eulogies contain specific advice (e.g. on a political move), with the unspoken assumption that the poet is the right person to give such advice; in some others we find an explicit assertion of the poets' rights in this respect. It is possible for the poet to criticise the patron, a common approach being the threat of satire if the patron does not toe the line.[8] In a case like this the suggestion is that if the chief has departed from the norms of ideal chiefly behaviour – including, for example, generosity to his poet – he forfeits the rewards that only the endorsement of praise-poetry can give him. Actual satires are understandably rare in the literature; amongst other things, they were not likely to find their way into the patron-oriented *duanaire* or 'family poem-book'. But we know they existed; they had a place in the 'mythology' of the poets, inasmuch as the poet, once hired, was required to be ready to make a satire on another poet's patron or repel another poet's satire on his own patron. We are lucky that the eclectic interests and poetic contacts of the compilers of the BDL led them to include several specimens of satire. Noteworthy amongst these is 'Theasta aoindiabhal na nGaoidheal', ('*The prime devil of the Gaels is dead*'), which puts the images and tropes of eulogy into reverse; we may suspect that this poem was composed against another poet or poem as much as against its 'victim'.[9] And some such poetic skirmishing or badinage may likewise underlie 'Dá urradh i n-iath Éireann' ('*(There are) two chiefs in Ireland's land*') in the same source, where the two chiefs MacDiarmada and Maguire are contrasted in a symmetrical exercise of positive and negative reportage.[10] There is no room for such an explanation in regard to the satire 'Tá triúr cailín as searbh glóir' ('*There are three girls of sour repute*'), which directs a torrent of abuse at the allegedly squalid lives – immoral, incontinent and insanitary – of the three women in question. Significantly, the poet proclaims his purpose: ós éigean a gcur ar folbh '*to put them away*' or drive them out.[11] On a different tack, the idea of gift and counter-gift passing between poet and patron, symbolising the link between liberality and fame, becomes concrete in a number of poems of petition and (somewhat less frequently) of thanks. Fionnlagh Ruadh's poem 'Fada atáim gan bhogha' ('*Long am I without a bow*'), also in the Dean's Book, is an example of a poet making a request which his patron cannot, with honour, refuse.[12]

Some other features of bardic verse are linked, in various ways, to the primary poet-patron formula 'no poet, no prince'. These include the prickly tone that certain poets adopt when dealing with other poets whom they regard as being lower in the literary pecking order than themselves. By contrast, they lay claim to intimacy with their patron, whom they term their bosom friend or even their bed-fellow.[13] As for their craft, they make it clear that it is not their business to find something new to say about their patron; that work has been done for them. On the contrary, their job is to polish, gild and decorate, working with the elaborate linguistic and metrical skills that their long training has given them and operating within the thematic and rhetorical conventions they have been taught. These parameters are always there, but there is room for originality of presentation within the conventions. For instance, Giolla-Coluim Mac an Ollaimh (fl. 1490s)'s 'Mór an feidhm freagairt na bhfhoighdhe' ('*It is very important to respond to the thiggers [beggars]')*[14] appears to be an elegantly exasperated, mildly self-mocking reflection on how vulnerable a chief-poet is to the demands of the thiggers, up to the point where he declares that, since the thiggers have cleaned him out, he will go thigging himself to John MacDonald's court, where he will get back all he lost and more, and we see that the whole poem is an elaborate way of eulogising MacDonald. Finally, the political dimension in the professional poet's 'job description', which we see coming to the fore in the hortatory poem 'Ar sliocht Ghaoidheal ó ghort Ghréag' ('*Upon the race of the Gaels from the Grecian plain*')[15] eventually proved to be their undoing. This came about because the Irish bardic schools, whose prestige made them the destination of Scottish poets seeking the highest qualifications in poetry, were targeted for destruction during the Tudor re-conquest of Ireland and thereafter. Their demise brought the so-called 'Classical Early Modern' period of Gaelic literature effectively to an end.

While bardic poetry is fundamentally about chiefs and ruling, the bardic rhetoric and poetic techniques could be applied, *mutatis mutandis*, to churchmen, to women, to other poets and artists, even to inanimate objects. Its union with the conventions of courtly love was particularly fruitful.[16] While it has been criticised for being impersonal and starchy, mastery of its technicalities enabled it to be used to striking effect at moments of intense personal emotion, as in Muireadhach Albanach's (fl. late twelfth/early thirteenth century) elegy for his dead wife.[17] Although the over-riding impression one gets from bardic poetry is of supreme self-confidence, even arrogance, an element of doubt sometimes creeps in. There are poems in which the poet questions the validity of the bardic enterprise; and when the bardic schools were being destroyed the focus shifts to the sheer possibility of continuing with it.[18] And in some others again, composed about the time of the Plantation of Ulster, the subject of the elegy becomes the Gaelic world as such.[19] The bards were conscious of their public, social role till the very end.

In the Scottish Gàidhealtachd the families of official poets who were hereditarily attached to the principal families were often poets *cum historians*. Niall Mac Mhuirich (c. 1636–1726), of the descendants of Muireadhach Albanach who served the Clanranald MacDonalds, composed the elegy for Clanranald as poet (*file*, Mod ScG *filidh*) and the Clanranald Histories as historian (*seanchaidh*). In Ireland some learned families were specialists in genealogy and history, and the Lords of the Isles maintained historians as well as poets. But in general there was less of this specialisation in Scotland. There are three main sorts of text that contain history: (1) chronicles or annals, which had been kept in early medieval times in monasteries of the Gaelic Church (including Iona), and continued to be kept in some centres in post-Norman times (again including Iona under the patronage of the Lords of the Isles); (2) genealogies and supporting materials (e.g. origin legends, regnal lists) forming a compendium of knowledge about the inter-relationships and origins (back in some cases to fabulous, prehistoric times) of the leading families of the Gaelic world; and (3) the legendary prehistory of the Gaels – a massive compilation which had reached maturity in pre-Norman times under the heading 'Lebor Gabála Érenn' or '*Book of Conquests*' (literally, '*Book of the Taking of Ireland*') and purported to tell of the successive waves of settlers who had won and held Ireland since before the Deluge, together with the wandering of the Gaels from far-off Scythia until they themselves became masters of the Island. This immense fabrication was designed to fill a knowledge vacuum spanning the centuries when plenty was known about the 'Eastern World' through the testimony of Biblical and Classical sources, but the 'Western World' was a blank – and also, like Virgil's *Aeneid*, to glorify a contemporary ruling dynasty by making the sweep of earlier history culminate in its success through the achievements of its remote ancestors. In other words, 'Lebor Gabála Érenn' provided an elaborate national origin legend for the Gaels themselves, and also a sort of matrix into which could be plugged the genealogies of the leading families. It also provided a background for the happenings recounted in the literary and historical tale-cycles – the Mythological Cycle, the 'Cycles of the Kings', the Ulster Cycle, and the Fenian Cycle – all the way down to the Norman invasion of Ireland. So influential was this myth that the annals themselves contain 'legendary' sections that, in the eyes of their compilers, gave way pretty seamlessly to the historical period – broadly speaking, at the time of the coming of Christianity.[20]

The importance of the Gaelic origin legend in Scots chronicles and historiography outwith the Gàidhealtachd has been well studied.[21] To the Gaelic men of learning and their patrons in the late Middle Ages the thought of Gaelic culture flourishing at the national level was a receding but not yet wholly remote matter. They may well have found the idea of Scotland as a Gaelic nation to be a precious and empowering asset. Be that as it may, it came as part of a 'package' of organised knowledge about the past – one which complemented the picture derived from the Bible for early centuries, while at the same time it related to people's desire to know about their own family origins and derivation. The whole panorama of prehistoric, ancient and medieval lore was there to be used, as a unified field of literary reference, by the court poets. They referred to it constantly in their eulogies and elegies, whether in brief similes and fleeting allusions or in extended apologues. Certain aspects of it percolated throughout Gaelic society, as may be inferred from its appearance, in a more limited way, in vernacular Gaelic poetry from the seventeenth century on, and in its association with Gaelic place-names.

In the sixteenth and seventeenth centuries increased exposure to English and Scots antiquarian and historical writing, itself struggling to digest Classical Latin and Greek references to early circumstances and events in the British Isles, brought a sense of challenge and a need for positive reinforcement of the native accounts – as when Niall Mac Mhuirich explains his reasons for writing the section containing the Montrose campaigns in his Clanranald History:

> Do gheibhinn móran re na sgríobhadh do sgéluibh ar gnóidhibh na haimsir dá ccuirfinn romham é, acht as e tug oram an uradsa féin do sgríobhadh, mur do connairc mé gan iomrágh air bioth ar Ghaoidhealaibh ag na sgríobhnóiribh atá ag teacht ar ghnóidhibh na haimsire – an mhuinntear do-rinne an tseirbhis uile.
>
> *I could have found plenty to write about the deeds of the time if I had set myself that task; but what spurred me to write even the amount that I have done was the way I saw that the [non-Gaelic] writers who deal with the period make no mention of the Gaels, who did all the grafting.*[22]

Niall's older Irish contemporary Dubhaltach Mac Fir-Bhisigh provides us with an insight into his thinking about the material which provided his family of hereditary historians and genealogists with their livelihood. At the beginning of his great Book of Genealogies (1650) he states that his *causa scribendi* is 'do mhórughadh glóire Dé agus do geunamh iuil do chách i gcoitchinne', '*to magnify the glory of God and to provide guidance for everyone in general*'. He expands on this as follows: 'do thaispeanadh na fírinne iar sen-sgríbhnibh suidhighthe suadh sen-naomh agus sruith-sheanchadh Érenn, ní nach cuirthe i gcuntabhairt', '[*Our purpose is] to demonstrate the truth (fírinne) according to the settled ancient writings of sages, ancient saints and senior historians of Ireland besides, from the first beginning of ages till today – something on which doubt is not to be cast* [...]'. He acknowledges that there are doubters, but he is not concerned to take them on. That task was left to the Continentally trained priest Geoffrey Keating, whose own account of Irish history, though compiled slightly earlier than Mac Fir-Bhisigh's, belongs to a different era – that of the Renaissance and Counter-Reformation.[23]

From glimpses such as these we can derive a notion of what this version of the past meant to people; it was the articulation of a shared inheritance, a coherent universe filled with information and example, massive detail and human interest, and all linked to the present by the genealogical ties; it was the saga of 'us, the Gaels'. It remains to add two important riders. First, belief in this mythic past was not always absolute. We may occasionally detect a note of uneasiness about the status of this past, whether for reasons of Christian scruple or, by the end of our period, on account of rationalist doubts. But such qualifications only gradually and partially altered its status, and hardly diminished its importance as a cultural mainstay. Second, certain aspects of this past were malleable in the hands of the cognoscenti – for it was part of the job of the historians and genealogists to ensure that it reflected the ebb and flow of contemporary aspirations and political dynamics.[24]

Turning to literature as such, whether entertaining, moving or relaxing, the extraordinary flowering of Early Gaelic literature composed between the seventh and eleventh century AD, had already seen the birth and development of creative, experimental, fictive literature of many sorts. This existed beside, and sometimes overlapped with, other sorts of writing, which included scholastic writing – classificatory, exegetical, compendious, analytic, and so on. In the Early Modern period some of that early literature was forgotten; some survived but remained within the purview of the learned; and some was re-cycled, renewed and transformed for late medieval audiences, where this *matière d'Irlande* took pride of place beside the translated Classical and Medieval European literature that was also taking root more vigorously.

A pivotal text was 'Agallamh na Seanóireach' ('*The Colloquy of [or 'with'] the Ancients*'), which was based on the idea of a meeting between St Patrick, as the bringer of Christianity to Ireland, and the last surviving Fenian warriors, who are able to take him around the unknown country and tell him the stories of the famous deeds and adventures associated with each locality they pass through. This delightful frame gave rise to ballads and other texts built on the idea of the dialogue between cleric and warrior and sharing several important interwoven motifs: the old pagan world versus the new Christian world; the authority of ancient eyewitnesses to get us beyond the silence of the pre-literate era; nostalgia for a vanished age of simpler, purer, nobler values; and a sense of deep devotion to the land itself. It is not surprising that tales and ballads manifesting these characteristics were popular in the post-Norman period in Ireland and after the forfeiture of the Lordship of the Isles in Scotland. In fact, they became subtly woven into the fabric of Gaelic experience beyond the learned and literate few, as we can see from the mid-sixteenth-century 'Òran na Comhachaig' ('*The Song of the Owl*'), which combines all these themes in the poignant reflections of the aged hunter in conversation with the ancient bird.[25] The ripples spread further, indeed, to help create an image for 'the Highlands' both before and after James 'Ossian' MacPherson drank at this particular well.

If we must on that basis acknowledge a conservative, backward-looking thread in Gaelic imaginative literature, we should also note some more positive, outward-looking developments. The presence of these should not surprise us at a time when members of the Highland gentry (and their Irish counterparts) attended universities and had external and overseas contacts through military service, ecclesiastical business, court attendance, commercial engagement, pilgrimage, and so on. This was, after all, a period in which the Lords of the Isles could engage in European diplomacy in England and France, and the Earls of Argyll could attain the highest rank in the Scottish court. The translation literature just mentioned shows aristocratic tastes not greatly different from the rest of Europe: tales of Arthur and Charlemagne, for example, and the foreign travels of Mandeville and Marco Polo. There is evidence also for interest in *amour courtois*, where the convoluted agonisings of the courtly lover prompted our learned Gaelic poets to dally with *ogham*-encoded acrostics to conceal the name of the beloved one, and revel in the paradox of being 'alive but not alive, dead but not dead'. It is in the romances and in the *dánta grádha* ('love poems in syllabic metre') that we come on hints of private reading by 'amateurs' of literature, though it is clear that the romances were also read out aloud, i.e. as a public or communal experience like cinema or theatre, and the involvement of the literati in translating and adapting these texts for a Gaelic audience can be judged from many stylistic traits, including a weakness for explanatory 'footnotes'.[26]

Another innovative aspect is this: scholars have recently suggested that several sixteenth- and seventeenth-century adaptations of early prose texts owe their specific Early Modern form to their authors' deliberate intention to make them echo and comment on contemporary political circumstances that would have been well known to their audiences. Some of these interpretations are very persuasive, and they suggest that by the sixteenth century the courts of the Gaelic aristocracy had developed an appetite for sophisticated, 'edgy' commentary on current affairs.[27] A similar tone is struck by the prose elements in the verse-prose medleys known as crosántachta, in which the verse gives high-flown praise of the patron and the prose interjects sardonic or caustic comments on the doings and misdeeds of people who would, most likely, have been known to the audience – in equally high-flown language.[28] It is fair to say that the presence and special social standing of the professional literati in Gaelic society was the lubricant in all of this, though it also has to be added that the same presence is responsible for the often over-indulgent language that characterises these tales, invading even those that were translated from other languages into Gaelic.[29]

The aristocratic patronage on which this literature depended was undermined – spectacularly so in Ireland when the Flight of the Earls (1607) followed the English victory at the Battle of Kinsale (1601), and more gradually in Scotland where the impact of the Statutes of Iona (1609) prescribed anglophone Lowland education for the children of Highland chiefs. It fell to vernacular, non-literate bards, minstrels and singers, who had been part of the Gaelic 'entertainment industry' all along, but lacked the literacy-enhanced visibility of the learned poets, to chronicle the decline of the Early Modern Gaelic Heroic Age. The songs of Roderick Morrison ('The Blind Harper') (c. 1656–c. 1714) and Mary MacLeod (Màiri nighean Alastair Ruaidh) (c. 1615–c. 1707) are eloquent on this process in the case of the MacLeods of Dunvegan, as are those of Eachann Bacach (c. 1600–post 1650) and Mairghread Ní Lachlainn (c. 1660–post 1749) for the Macleans in Mull.[30] For despite their claims to exclusiveness, the learned poets and historians were only part of the Gaelic poetic order (*cliar*) – and the iceberg, as it were, survived the melting of its tip for centuries to come, in the halls of lesser chiefs and tacksmen who continued to encourage Gaelic arts. The celebrating and upholding of Gaelic society was likewise part of the function of the nameless women who composed celebratory songs for Domhnall mac Iain 'ic Sheumais, victor of the Battle of Carinish (1601), and Alasdair mac Colla Ciotaich, the victor (for so he was seen in the Highlands) of the Battles of Inverlochy and Auldearn (1645), which survived orally as Hebridean waulking songs until the age of the tape-recorder.[31]

At the end of the day, one's most lasting impression is of the self-sufficiency of the late medieval Gaelic tradition. Many genres, at both the most 'courtly' and the most 'popular' ends of the literary spectrum, appear as robustly native products. Even those genres that we know to have been imported have taken on a distinctly Gaelic *blas* – e.g. the romances, and the song-form known as amhran or òran, with its regular beat, four-line or eight-line stanzas and AABA musical structure. Looking at Gaelic literature from the Scots point of view, there are some points of contact or comparison, but by and large the presence of the 'men of art' (aos dána), whether it be the hereditary professional chief-poet (ollamh) or the 'strollers' (lorgánaigh) known to the Dean of Lismore and his associates, differentiates the place and function of literature in Gaelic society, and likewise the purposes of literature.

William Gillies

Older Scots

Among all the possible themes, the one that seems most marked in Older Scots writing is that of self-governance in the face of many challenges and threats, be those of love, war, power or pride. The importance of self-control is often demonstrated through an illustration of the contrast between reasoned self-governance, and excess that generally emanates from some kind of appetitive craving. This tension is presented in Older Scots texts spanning the period covered by this volume, from the behaviour of the greedy, morally blind animals in Henryson's *Moral Fables*, to the narrator's plight in Alexander Montgomerie's *The Cherrie and the Slae*, undone by his 'wilful' (l. 179) desire to fly like Cupid.[32] Similar preoccupation with dangerous passion is expressed in James I's *Kingis Quair* (c. 1424), in Gavin Douglas' *The Palice of Honoure* (c. 1500 or 1501) and his *Eneados* (1513). Sir David Lyndsay's *Ane Dialog* (1553) focuses on a courtier who questions the wisdom of earthly greed (lines 394–97), and John Stewart of Baldynneis' *Roland Furiovs* (c. 1576–1584) presents a vivid depiction of the madness caused by excessive love. But while these works have in common their recognition of dangerous desire, they differ in the extent to which they offer a workable solution to such conflict. Of course, concern about the hazardous impact of uncontrollable lust is not restricted to Scots texts; Gower's *Confessio Amantis* is clear about the threat to stability if one succumbs to bodily lust, while in Chaucer's *Troilus and Criseyde* the 'double wo' of Troilus is a direct result of his all-consuming desire for Criseyde. However, such is the sustained popularity of the theme with Scots writers that it suggests a particularised interest not reflected in English literature of the same period. This is partly explained by history. Although the Stewart dynasty governed Scotland in an unbroken line from 1370 to 1603, between 1406 and 1576 every Stewart monarch ascended the throne as a child, the eldest, James IV, only fifteen years old, while Mary, Queen of Scots, was seven days old when she inherited the throne. One of the distinctive features of Scots engagements is the way in which lack of self-governance is often examined in the particular context of kings or would-be rulers, whose intemperance has catastrophic effects for their nation.[33] Youth was a period in which one was thought to be particularly subject to external threats – self-aggrandising magnates, hostile border nations, ill counsel – but also, significantly, to more inward dangers: the temptations of excess,[34] a problem recognised by the narrator of the *Kingis Quair*, who comments that in his youth he was 'of wit wayke and unstable' (l. 95). The potential national and political dangers faced by a nation whose king is enslaved by his physical desires are obvious, and some of the Older Scots texts mentioned above have (implicit or explicit) regal connections. The *Kingis Quair* is a semi-autobiographical piece, attributed to a king; Douglas' *Palice* is addressed to James IV; Montgomerie was – periodically – an intimate of James VI; Lyndsay's *Dialog*, written during the minority of Mary, Queen of Scots, laments 'We have no kyng […] allace! / Quhilk to this countre bene ane cairfull cace' (ll. 10–11); and *Roland* is contained in the unique manuscript witness to Stewart's verse, which was dedicated to King James VI.

Examinations of self-governance (or its absence) were also used by Scots poets to indicate the more general hazardous implications of powerful carnal desires, which applied to all men, not just kings. The perils of emotional, physical or amatory excess – particularly in the case of the *Kingis Quair* and Henryson's longer poems – are often depicted through a modelling of the reading experience: characters grounded in the sensual or appetitive have limited interpretative abilities. Reading as a measure of moral value is also manifested in the way these authors interact with their literary predecessors: James I (1394–1437) and Henryson (d. c. 1490) poetically interrogate the writings of Chaucer, Gower, and others, enacting a distinctively Scots pattern of reading older texts. In doing so, they establish a new model for ethical and active reading from which valuable lessons can be learned, and which occasionally offers surprisingly optimistic readings of the possible reconciliation of reason and desire.[35]

The unique witness to the *Kingis Quair*, Bodleian Library, MS Arch. Selden B. 24,[36] attributes the poem to James I, who spent eighteen years as a prisoner of Henry IV in England. The biographical context for the poem is most notable because of what it suggests about the king's first-hand perception of the importance of self-governance and avoidance of passionate excess. In addition, the poem is profoundly literary, imbued with textual reference, most overtly to Boethius' *Consolation of Philosophy*, but also *Confessio Amantis*, *Troilus and Criseyde*, and 'The Knight's Tale'.[37] The narrator presents himself as reader whose literary creativity is inspired by active textual engagement, and he allows what he reads to inform his depiction of reason and desire.

The poem begins with a sleepless narrator reaching for a book, recalling Chaucer's *Book of the Duchess*. Chaucer's narrator demonstrates his unreliability through a selective reading of Ovid's 'Ceyx and Alcyone' that omits the metamorphosis and reunion to focus instead on the fact that Alcyone's vision of her dead husband comes during sleep, inspiring the narrator to promise the gift of an ostentatious bed to any god who will grant him similar repose. Such concentration on bodily relief (through sleep) and material reward (the bed) indicates his susceptibility to worldly appetite. The narrator of the *Kingis Quair*, who has chosen Boethius' *Consolation of Philosophy*, finds himself in a very different situation: the text acts not as a soporific, but as a stimulant. Sleep becomes even more unlikely; the questions raised by Boethius about Fortune's mutability ensure that the narrator retires to bed 'this mater new in my mynd rolling' (l. 54), and – another marker of a 'good' reader – applies aspects of the text to a recollected youthful dream.

This retrospective element is unusual. It allows James to identify youthful failings, and to propose a remedy, based on advice gleaned from his reading of Boethius. He remembers his capture, ascribed to Fortune, who 'it schupe non othir wayis to be' (l. 168) and how he would compare his unfavourable plight with that of 'the bird, the beste, the fische eke in the see' who 'lyve in fredome' (ll. 183–84). This envy of the animal world suggests an irrational misery: bestial metaphors are often deployed to demonstrate the extent to which an individual has succumbed to wilful excess, losing his reason, which was what distinguished humans from beasts.[38] Although the youthful prisoner is distracted from his misery by birdsong, this does not indicate a return to stability: the birdsong praises love (ll. 232–38), which causes him to ponder Love's nature, and ask what it is he has done to offend such a great personage. Earlier, his adult self acknowledged that in youth 'the ripeness of resoune lakkit I / To governe with my will' (ll. 108–9), and this prepares us for the fact that his youthful solution to his plight is a resolve to join Love's 'service digne, / And evermore for to be one of tho / Him trewly for to serve in wele and wo' (ll. 271–73, see also l. 1015). His unconscious comparison of himself to Troilus, who passes from 'wo to wele' (*Troilus* I, l. 4), reminds the literate reader of a text in which no lasting happiness comes from earthly love, suggesting that his initial response to his dilemma should not be emulated. The decision implies capitulation to dangerous desire, and this is reiterated when the narrator's intellectual capacities are overwhelmed by the sight of a beautiful maiden: 'my wittis all / Were so overcom' (ll. 282–83), culminating in his voluntary enslavement: 'my hert become hir thrall / For ever, of free wyll' (ll. 285–86). Even if this does not provoke a questioning response from the reader, the obvious overtones in this scene of Chaucer's 'The Knight's Tale' should. The narrator's apparently unconscious echoing of a tale in which desire has violent repercussions is significant, indicating the potential dangers of his uncontrolled passion. The tendency in the *Kingis Quair* to refract experience through other texts, to retreat into a self-consciously literary world (which mentally mirrors his physical imprisonment) is an index of the difficulty of reconciling the ethical and the amatory in a theoretically and practically satisfying way. Yet the dream experienced by the youthful *Quair* narrator, 'half sleping and half swoun' (l. 510), seems to depict the possibility of just such resolution. Venus, for many medieval writers the embodiment of sinful lust,[39] is an 'anker' (l. 698) for the lover tossed on wild seas of 'lufis rage' (l. 697), and her guidance further implies rehabilitation: she advises 'lat Gude Hope the gye' (l. 740) and significantly sends the dreamer to Minerva, Roman goddess of wisdom, whose advice is similarly measured. Desire is not innately detrimental:

> 'Desire,' quod sche, 'I nyl it nought deny,
> So thou it ground and set in Cristin wise.' (ll. 988–89)

She reveals that self-governance, good sense, is one means by which man can defend himself against the vagaries of Fortune, whose power is inversely proportional to the moral strength of the individual:

> [...] of wit or lore
> Sen thou art wayke and feble, lo, therefore
> The more thou art in danger and commune
> With hir that clerkis clepen so 'Fortune'. (ll. 1040–44)

However, given the intensely cerebral nature of the poem, an inevitable problem with this attempted compromise is that it is based in theory. The 'love-affair' is never dealt with practically: there is no climactic engagement either with the lady, or the forces of passion. Indeed, the most memorable physical encounter in this text comes when the dreamer voluntarily steps upon Fortune's Wheel, and has his ear pinched by Lady Fortune, 'so ernestly that therwithall I woke' (l. 1204).

The dream is analysed through the lens of other authors. In the case of Boethius, this has an apparently positive effect. The narrator's adult recognition that 'Now sufficiante is my felicitee' (l. 1281) – that is, he is satisfied with what he has, rather than desiring more – seems optimistic (although it does seem partially dependent on the restitution of his fortunes, see ll. 1274–75). However, the embedded references to Chaucer and Gower destabilise this hopeful conclusion. 'Go, litill tretisse' (l. 1352) echoes *Troilus* V.1786, invoking a work in which no happy balance between desire and reason exists, while the address to 'Gowere and Chaucere' (l. 1374) suggests Gower's *Confessio Amantis*, another work in which compromise between lust and rationality is impossible, and in which we see a far more hostile Venus. Surprisingly then, a text whose major preoccupation seems to be the quest for balance, one which contains a wealth of intertextual reference, consistently cites works that undermine the encouraging conclusion reached. The paradoxical relationship between what is implied and what is actually said seems designed to ensure that we read the *Kingis Quair* as its narrator reads Boethius: alertly. Such a reader has undeniable similarities with Henryson's ideal of the morally active reader. Notions of reading ethically, and the corresponding potential for self-knowledge are certainly of prime import to James and Henryson.

The idea of the ethically engaged reader is explicated in Henryson's famous image of the nut's shell in the prologue to his *Fables* (ll. 15–18): one must search actively for a moral meaning (the sweet kernell) beneath the 'hard and teuch' (l. 15) exterior. The analogy of the hard-working labourer (l. 9) emphasises that effort is necessary if we are to attain moral equilibrium. But an ethical dimension is essential. Many of Henryson's characters are accurate readers, but lack awareness of, or are simply not interested in, the importance of self-governance. The cock addressing the 'gentill Iasp, of all stanis the flour' (l. 110) adeptly manipulates rhetorical tropes, but his moralising is inadequate. He is unable to 'read' the jasp properly, and abandons the 'perfite prudence' (l. 128) that it betokens in order to 'seik his meit' (l. 114), symbolising the conflict between reason and bodily desire that characterises the fables. Likewise, the fox in 'The Fox and the Wolf' is a partially self-aware reader, who analyses the message of the stars 'My auenture is cleirlie to me kend / […] / Deid is reward off sin and schamefull end' (ll. 650, 652). He recognises his immorality, but is unable, or unwilling, to repent genuinely, and like the cock, is enslaved by his appetitive urges. His self-awareness is reiterated towards the end of the fable when, sated with 'new-maid salmond' (l. 753; the salmon is, in fact, a kid which he has 'baptised' 'schir Salmond', l. 751, so he can consume meat without technically breaking his penance to 'forbeir flesche', l. 723) and basking in the sunlight, he strokes his belly, musing that it would make a fine target for an arrow. He is not alone in his supposition: almost immediately, the angry human owner of the dead goat comes upon him and the fox's prediction is borne out. Both the cock and the fox mistakenly concentrate upon physical fulfilment at the expense of rational thought processes. Focus on food distracts from true wisdom. In the fox's case, emphasis on further bodily comfort – sunbathing – ensures that he is a prime target for his enemy. In contrast to the relatively optimistic conclusion offered by the *Kingis Quair*, Henryson's depiction of the possibility of 'man's higher part to control his lower part' is pessimistic.[40] In the central tale, 'The Lion and the Mouse', the only fable that contains a discrete prologue, the narrator dreams that he meets Aesop, whose tales he claims to be translating. But the father of fabular wisdom is doubtful about the educative value of literary texts 'Quhen haly preiching may na thing auaill' (l. 1390), and while his fable has a fairly optimistic denouement – the lion's life is saved by the same mouse to whom he showed mercy earlier – it contains significant warnings.[41] The lion, like the sun-worshipping fox, makes himself vulnerable at the outset, 'Beikand his breist and belly at the sun' (l. 1407); the mice dance upon him because he 'lay so law' (l. 1432), a position ill-befitting a king. The lion's subsequent capture is also associated with physical excess, in hunting he 'slew baith tayme and wyld' (l. 1512). The fable is pivotal: it reiterates Henryson's concern with the outcome of ill-judged behaviour, and, though it ends happily for the lion and the mouse, it is the last fable in which there is any semblance of hope about the fates of weaker characters. Subsequent fables demonstrate the bleak fortunes of individuals whose concentration on the fulfilment of physical desire (however justifiable) leads to their downfall. The birds ignore the swallow's preaching because they are 'for hunger famischit neir' (l. 1867), and are brutally killed, while the lamb who attempts to reason with the wolf is given short shrift ('The Wolf and the Lamb'). The final fable 'The Paddock and the Mouse' contains another greedy individual: a mouse who rejects the 'hard nuttis' (l. 2796; echoes of the prologue here) that are available because she craves tastier food on the opposite riverbank. She 'reads' the features of the toad who offers to help her cross, and recognises therein 'falset and inuy' (l. 2825), but her hunger is such that she disregards this physiognomical warning, and the fable concludes with the watery struggle of the toad (representative of 'mannis bodie', l. 2937) and the mouse ('the saull of man', l. 2949), which attracts the attention of the kite (death), who kills them both.

While the fables' extrinsic *moralitates* help alert the reader to the inadequacies of interpretation, in *The Testament of Cresseid*, a different pattern emerges. This is the only longer poem by Henryson that lacks a discrete *moralitas*, and the onus is squarely upon the reader to compensate for the absence of an authoritative ethical statement (however inadequate) by analysing the readings of Cresseid presented by other characters. This is complicated by Henryson's preference for flawed protagonists. Even his narrator is enslaved by bodily desires. He prays Venus will make his 'faidit hart [...] grene' (l. 24), suggestive both of a refusal to accept the natural process of ageing (one might identify similarities in Cresseid's assertion that the seed of love sown in her face 'ay grew grene' (l. 138), but was slain by frost) and an ominous vulnerability to worldly passions. Alongside his immersion in earthly desires is a corresponding inadequacy in moral judgement, exemplified in his subjective reading: 'I sall excuse [Cresseid] als far furth as I may' (l. 87). His incomplete analysis, which reduces her fate to a symbolic warning for 'worthie wemen' (l. 610) is mirrored in Troilus' inability to control his bodily desires. Seeing, but not recognising, Cresseid 'kendlit all his bodie in ane fyre' (l. 513); his similarity to the narrator is reinforced in their final rhymes 'moir; befoir',[42] and their reductive readings of Cresseid: Troilus' engraving on her tomb defines her on a bodily level of attractive femininity. Neither judges wisely, fundamentally because their verdicts are couched in the corporeal realm of physical desire.

The only character who rejects earthly desire is Cresseid. Although her judgement is originally as flawed as Troilus' and the narrator's, and she blames the gods (ll. 134–40) and fortune (ll. 412, 469) for her plight, Henryson allows her to read and analyse herself, returning her voice to her.[43] Notably, it is her vocality that damns her; her thoughtless criticism of the gods means that she is punished for verbal sins of 'sclander and defame iniurious' (l. 284). But inchoate awareness of culpability – '[...] "Lo, quhat it is [...] / With fraward langage for to mufe and steir / Our craibit goddis,"' (ll. 351–52) suggests a potential for self-awareness not equalled by the narrator or Troilus. Her epiphanic moment does not occur until her meeting with Troilus, after which she is imbued with the power of self-judgement, '"Nane but my self as now I will accuse"' (l. 574). This revelation is intimately connected to rejection of physical desire. She bequeaths her soul 'to Diane' (l. 587), goddess of chastity (but also the moon and mutability), and sloughs off her corrupt earthly actions and body, reaching a new purity, which contrasts with Troilus' physical reaction to her. Cresseid's bodily decay, her accelerated ageing, is directly proportional to her ability to read herself. She is liberated from the sexual incontinence of her youth and is free to approach an understanding of the need for temperance and self-governance:

> 'My mynd in fleschelie foull affectioun
> Was inclynit to lustis lecherous' (ll. 558–59)

Her self-analysis is underscored by the trite judgements of Troilus and the narrator in a structural device that implicitly holds their *moralitates* up for comparison. The absence of a formal *moralitas* is compensated for by this tacit invitation for our own moral reading. However, Cresseid's recognition of earthly transience is inevitably incomplete – as a pagan, she cannot have access to the hope offered by divine aid. Only if God will 'vndirput his haly hand' can we have 'grace to stand' (*Orpheus and Eurydice* ll. 630–31). The apparent solution offered by Henryson, that earthly desire can be mitigated as one ages, but controlled only when couched in a Christian ethical scheme, echoes James's in the *Kingis Quair*, but, while his method tends towards the theoretical, Henryson takes pains to depict the very physical struggle between reason and passion.

A similar tussle is apparent in Douglas's *Palice of Honour*.[44] The narrator witnesses in a dream the courts of excess and measure presided over by Venus and Minerva respectively. Though 'peirles of schap and portrature' (l. 454), Venus is a dangerous ally. The hazards of the extreme passions she provokes are depicted both via the portrayal of Mars, the war-god, as lover, and in her court song, so seductive that 'Baith wit and resoun half is loist of all' (l. 414). The risks of the opposite extreme – complete rejection of earthly love – are demonstrated too, in the aftermath of the narrator's blasphemous ditty. Terrified of punishment, all rational judgement is lost; he is unable even to 'say my creid' (l. 733) and fears the removal of his humanity: '[Venus] In till sum bysnyng beist [might] transfigurat me' (l. 740). He is rescued by Calliope's court of the muses; described with a vocabulary indicating measure: 'plesand steidfastnes [...] constant merynes [...] Ioyus discipline' (ll. 844–46). On his subsequent journey, the nymph gives him temporary access to a world of literature that implies that the instilling into poetry of moral purpose, the reconciliation of the ethical/amatory spheres leads to greater, more meaningful creation. Perhaps significantly though, this is what he *sees* when he looks in Venus' mirror; he is an observer of stories and narratives, but not an active participant, recalling the bookish narrator of Chaucer's *Parliament of Fowls*.

The *Palice*'s narrator is afraid that he will be dehumanised by love (Venus), transformed into an irrational, voiceless beast, and in John Stewart's (c. 1545–c. 1605) adaptation of Ariosto's *Orlando Furioso*, *Roland Furiovs* this outcome is enacted.[45] In canto 1, the eponymous protagonist is compared to a 'volf' (l. 41), his foes are 'terrefait haeir' (l. 49); by canto 11, he has degenerated into total insanity, and Stewart depicts the serious ramifications of inadequate reading in Roland's misinterpretation of Angelica and Medor's 'text'. Obsessive love clouds his moral faculties: intentional misreading results. He tries to convince himself that '[…] Scho, of hir guid grace / In his remembrance haid thois vordis vrocht' (canto 11, ll. 186–87). However, the text's true meaning cannot be misread; indeed, the reality it propounds grows 'Moir plaine and ampill' (canto 11, l. 256) in direct proportion to Roland's conscious misinterpretation. The final insult is Medor's poem, written in a 'langage Roland rycht expertlie knew' (canto 11, l. 252). Linguistic competence causes Roland such grief that he is 'almaist void of his vittis all' (canto 11, l. 260). In his subsequent monologue, he recognises his lack of control, but paradoxically this apparent self-awareness results in total self-negation:

> Bot quhom am I in quhom sic raidge dois grow?
> am I that Roland quho hes vonders vrocht?
> No. Roland treulie in his grafe is brocht (canto 11, ll. 465–68).

He realises grief is 'Quhat euerie ane may hoip for till attaine, / Quho thrallit in the links of luife dois go […]' (canto 11, ll. 473–74), and this brief clarity precedes the depiction of 'Raging Roland' (canto 11, l. 566), leaving us with an unfulfilled potential for self-knowledge. This is intensified by Stewart's decision not to '[…] expone in ilk degrie / The histoir veill As it at lenth is pend' (canto 11, ll. 629–30). The absence of explicit redemption demonstrates an apparent reluctance to reconcile passion and reason, and ensures that Stewart's main preoccupation appears to be with demonstrating the dangerous state of internal conflict that can result from amatory excess.

The relationship between literary authority and perceptiveness and excessive vulnerability to bodily excess is of lasting fascination for Scots authors, and it retains its prominence during the rise of humanism. The nature of the humanist endeavour emphasises individual engagement with the text, but in a work like Douglas' *Eneados*, for example, it is still possible still to identify attempts to reconcile ethical and amatory,[46] shown in the contrast between Dido's 'inordinate desyre' (IV Prol. 250), and the potential of 'lufe [...] rewlyt by mesure' (IV Prol. 125). Douglas' prologue to Mapheus' extraneous thirteenth book, which he includes despite his assertions of fidelity to Virgil, indicates the tense relationship between author and translator, but the book itself offers an apparently optimistic conclusion. By marrying Aeneas to Lavinia, Mapheus neutralises his vulnerability to the amatory pressures and dangers outlined by Douglas in Prologue IV. Book XIII becomes Douglas's closest approach to the reconciliation of reason and passion – within marriage. Turnus has 'gone aganyst reson', failing to temper desire with rationality, thus causing chaos. The subsequent narrative concerns the establishment of peace and reason, and the subordination of the amatory to the ethical is emphasised: Aeneas unites Trojans and Italians, ruling 'In ferm concord and gret tranquylite' (XIII.x.130).

Engagement with the theme is longstanding, and not just literary: Scots historical writings were also concerned with dangerous passions. In John Bellenden's (c. 1495–1545x1548) translation of Hector Boece's (c. 1465–1536) *Scotorum Historia*, the death of King Alexander III is described thus: 'rynnand ane fers hors at Kingorn with maist insolence and gawmondis [arrogance], he was dongin oute of þe sadill, and brak his crag, þe xxxvij ʒere of his regne.'[47]. Alexander defied stormy weather to ride back to his wife Yolande, presenting us with a rather complicated example of a king whose amorousness perhaps compromises his better judgement but is nevertheless framed by marriage.

I highlighted the connection at the beginning of this chapter between emphasis on self-governance and the tendency of Scots monarchs to ascend the throne at young ages. Yet the preoccupation was not confined to authors attempting (directly or indirectly) to advise kings. James VI's *Reulis and Cautelis* notes that love can render even the most skilled poet inarticulate, depriving them of reason, although he suggests exploiting this apparent weakness and turning it into a strength: if the poet is praising his love, say 'that ʒour wittis are sa smal, and ʒour vtterance so barren, that ʒe can not discryue any part of hir worthelie.'[48]

Clearly, identification and interrogation of the hazardous tension between reason and passion continued to preoccupy Scots writers. Their tendency to couch their analysis in images of reading, writing, and poetic creativity, and (often) to provide some kind of regal framework for their writings is a feature that differentiates the Scots engagement with that of contemporary English poets. For the authors of the Older Scots works discussed here, self-governance is inextricably linked to ethical reading, and wise interpretation. Whether such a link continues to be demonstrated after James departs for England, and Scotland no longer suffers the problems associated with minority rule, is a question outside the scope of this chapter, though the degree to which love inspires inadequate and inarticulate literary creation is alluded to by Alexander in his *Aurora* (1604) sequence: '[…] euery youth to entertaine his loue, / Did straine his wits as farre as they might reach […]' (59, ll. 1–2).

Kate McClune

CHAPTER FIVE

Historiography in Highlands and Lowlands

Ulrike Hogg and Martin MacGregor

In Scotland between 1100 and 1400, Gaelic speech retreated significantly on the ground as English – that in time came to be called Scots – advanced in the south and east, eventually resulting in the creation of linguistic zones that corresponded roughly to the physical realities of Highlands and Lowlands.[1] This hugely important but poorly understood phenomenon carried consequences for the historiography of the Scots, as for much else. Down to the later thirteenth century, Scottish historiography continued to operate within a milieu that was significantly Gaelic. The key prose texts that defined the kingdom's history – royal genealogy, king lists and origin legend – largely derived from Gaelic originals, even if their written expression was increasingly orientated towards Latin. The texts themselves pointed unequivocally to a Gaelic template for Scottish origins. The preservation and promulgation of these texts was primarily the responsibility of a Gaelic scholarly caste at whose apex was the king's poet.[2] After 1300, and particularly once we reach John of Fordun in the later fourteenth century, mainstream presentations of the history of the Scots passed to overwhelmingly non-Gaelic historians based in non-Gaelic speaking Scotland, and working in another genre, the continuous narrative chronicle, usually in prose.

The most momentous of these changes was in personnel. An argument for continuity in this respect can hardly be sustained on the basis of the unknown historian active in the later thirteenth century who seems to have known Gaelic, and to have been responsible for an intermediate stage in the evolution of the chronicle to which John of Fordun gave final form;[3] or of George Buchanan, whose *Rerum Scoticarum Historia* was published in 1582, and who knew Gaelic, but who would surely have baulked at any attempt to claim him as a Gaelic historian, given his own highly negative comments on the Gaelic approach to history.[4] In other respects, the continuities were significant. These prose chronicles were

Latin works, although sometimes accompanied, come the sixteenth century, by parallel versions in Scots, while Scots was also the language of composition of a number of shorter independent chronicles. They incorporated the substance of the texts of the middle ages, sometimes verbatim. As this implies, and even if much of the detail was rejected by Buchanan and his predecessor John Mair, the late medieval national chronicle tradition remained wedded to the Gaelic version of Scottish origins, and to belief in the Gaels as the *prisci Scoti* or aboriginal Scots. In Mair's words, 'we trace our descent from the Irish [...] at the present day almost the half of Scotland speaks the Irish [i.e. Gaelic] tongue, and not so long ago it was spoken by the majority of us'.[5] The same mindset explains why Bishop William Elphinstone and his protégé Hector Boece saw the likeliest repository of sources upon which to base their patriotic explorations of the Scottish past as the Gaelic west, and specifically Iona, 'where also are preserved the sepulchres of our ancient kings and the ancient monuments of our race'.[6]

However, this did not preclude – indeed, it may have encouraged – a diametrically opposed attitude towards the more recent Scottish past. The Gaelic contribution was to have provided deep roots and antiquity to the Scots as a people, and to their monarchy in particular – and, thus, to the kingdom as a whole. In subsequent history, insofar as they featured at all, the role of Gaelic-speaking Scots became that of inveterate troublemakers or enemies of a realm whose political centre of gravity had come to be located in non-Gaelic or Lowland Scotland. The Gaels had become a stereotype inhabiting the margins of the history of the kingdom to which, so that history still asserted, they had given birth and autonomous existence – the very history that they themselves had once authored and nurtured.[7]

From the late fourteenth and early fifteenth centuries onwards, written accounts of the past became increasingly accessible in Scotland, leading to a gradual increase in historical awareness among the people. Building on the king-lists that were first composed in the ninth century, and the annalistic entries kept in religious houses by anonymous scribes, the later Middle Ages in the Lowlands saw the development of Scottish historical writing into coherent and creative narrative. Historiography in Latin, although predominant in this period, was complemented by histories written in the Scots vernacular. Histories in both languages, just as is the case in other literary genres, were influenced in their style and presentation of facts by current politics and literary fashions on the one hand,

and the author's own purpose and agenda, imagination and love of story and description on the other. In what might be called an established canon of historiographical works, however, some areas are still awaiting detailed study, and most histories have seen no recent scholarly edition.

The *Chronica gentis Scotorum* ('The Chronicle of the Scottish People') of John of Fordun (d. in or after 1363) is the earliest surviving single-author narrative of the history of Scotland from the beginning.[8] According to Walter Bower, his successor in the field of Latin historiography, Fordun travelled widely throughout Britain and Ireland in order to collect information which, following the Wars of Independence, was scarce within Scotland itself.[9] Not all of what we find in his work is the result of his own research, however; Dauvit Broun's work has shown him to have incorporated into his work an unidentified, now lost, historical account written in Scotland in the second half of the thirteenth century.[10] While this earlier chronicle is the text that must be seen as the first step towards a presentation of Scottish history in continuous narrative, the account that we know as Fordun's history remains the work from which we have here to start. Written in a competent mediaeval Latin style, it presents the history of the Scots in five books and a half, beginning with the origins of the Scots in Greece and Egypt and ending with the reign of David I (1124–1153).

The starting point of Fordun's account, with its exotic locations, is based on one of several versions of what is known as the Scottish origin legend, a tale that aims to trace the origin of the Scottish people back to antiquity. Strongly political in its purpose, this myth existed in different versions. That found in Fordun is based on an Irish narrative and presents Ireland as the homeland of the Scots. It follows the idea that it was the marriage of the exiled Greek prince Gathelos with the Egyptian Pharaoh's daughter, Scota, and their subsequent journey first to Ireland and then to Scotland where they finally settled, that started off the new Scottish nation and the dynasty of Scottish kings. They brought with them the stone of Scone, which would from then on play a part in the initiation of Scottish kings. Their arrival in Scotland coincides with that of the Picts, whose true status as inhabitants of much longer standing is thus turned into that of competing newcomers; relations predictably worsen and culminate in the conquest and destruction of the Picts by Kenneth Mac Alpin in 839. The history of Scotland is then continued until the reign of David I.

While much of Fordun's account cannot be said to be based on fact, it offers a version of the past that could be set confidently against those of other countries, especially that of England. In 1286, when the death of the Scottish king Alexander III resulted in a succession crisis, Edward I of England embarked on a campaign to establish English overlordship over Scotland, drawing on a British origin myth that was best known in its presentation in Geoffrey of Monmouth's (c. 1100–c. 1155) *Historia regum Britanniae*.[11] According to this, Brutus, great-grandson of Aeneas of Troy, took possession of an island named Albion, named it 'Britannia' after himself, and at his death arranged for it to be divided among his sons Locrinus, Albanactus and Camber, who thereby inherited England, Scotland and Wales respectively. The legend chosen by Fordun, which began with the victorious Greeks rather than the defeated Trojans, conveyed an image of a nation whose origins were built on success.

Fordun's work owes its fame, and indeed its survival, to the fact that in the 1440s it was copied, expanded and continued by Walter Bower, born in Haddington in 1385, and abbot of Inchcolm from 1418 until his death in 1449. Under the title of *Scotichronicon*, Bower produced a historical account in which both Fordun's chronicle and his own additions are clearly marked as such, allowing for the reconstruction of Fordun's original text.[12] Due to his high ecclesiastical rank it is likely that, from James I's return from captivity in 1424 onwards, he attended parliament and meetings of the king's council. Bower's greater political awareness, his decidedly anti-English point of view and support of the king's decisive rule, his more vivid Latin style, and firm moral guidance meant that his expansion and rewriting greatly added to the impact of Fordun's original work. The *Scotichronicon* survives in a comparatively large number of manuscripts, as does an anonymous rewriting probably undertaken shortly after Bower's death, which is known as *Liber Pluscardensis*.[13] Other abbreviated versions, too, were popular until the sixteenth century, when Hector Boece's *Scotorum historia* (1527) took its place as the most widely read historical account in Latin.

While historiography in the Latin language was developing into a more creative form of literature, the subject was also embraced in the Scots vernacular. A number of shorter Scots prose chronicles – brought together in a recent edition[14] – were made to make history more widely accessible; a full translation of the *Scotichronicon* or even of an abbreviated version into Scots prose was never made. The other, quite different, type of vernacular history composed in the fourteenth and fifteenth centuries was written in verse. Out of these, only one account is comparable in its coverage to the *Scotichronicon*. This is the *Original Chronicle*, written between 1408 and 1424 by Andrew of Wyntoun (c. 1350–c. 1424), an Augustinian canon and from 1390 prior on St. Serf's Inch, Loch Leven. Written at the request of his patron, Sir John of Wemyss, Wyntoun's work gives an account of the history of the world from the creation and Scotland's place within it up to c. 1420. The first five books make no mention of Scotland, showing here, and elsewhere in his chronicle, a mind that was interested in many other global issues besides Scotland, and to a lesser degree concerned with national politics and ideology. Besides making use of orally transmitted Gaelic tales and motifs, Wyntoun had access to written sources now lost, such as a Stewart genealogy by John Barbour and the great register of St Andrew's priory. For the history of Scotland from 1325 to 1390 he used an anonymous source, supplied by an un-named contributor. Wyntoun's work was highly popular, as is obvious from its nine surviving manuscripts. Although its literary merit is not considered to be high, some of his imagery is evocative and memorable. The often-quoted eight lines of verse on the death of Alexander III in 1286, beginning 'Quhen Alexander our kynge wes dede', are also found in his chronicle, although they were possibly not his own composition.[15]

Contemporary with such global coverage of time and subject, which can be traced back to the fourteenth-century English writer Ranulph Higden's influential large-scale *Polychronicon,* there were other historical works written in the Scots vernacular that were focused more narrowly on certain episodes and persons. John Barbour's *The Bruce* and Hary's *The Wallace* are verse epics centred on the Wars of Independence. While they are formally works of literature and include fictional material, their focus on a historical rather than fictional protagonist means that they straddle the boundary between history and romance in a way that has almost no parallel in other verse romances.[16] Their influence on Scottish perceptions of nationhood and kingship was at least as strong as that of the *Scotichronicon,* and possibly more enduring.

John Barbour (c. 1330–1395) was archdeacon of Aberdeen from 1356 onwards, but was also pursuing studies in England and France after this date. He wrote *The Bruce,* an epic of almost 14,000 lines, between c. 1372 and 1375, covering Robert Bruce's fight for independence, the Scottish victory at Bannockburn, and Bruce's subsequent reign in Scotland.[17] Barbour had a strong attachment to King Robert II, and his epic on Robert I is not his only work written in honour of his patron's family; he is also believed to have written the the genealogy of the Stewarts that was used as a source by Andrew of Wyntoun.[18] Its style and idealistic portrayal of its protagonists shows the influence of French romances, although women, as has been pointed out, have no role in it at all. Barbour's focus on a single ruler and his leadership in Scotland's fight for independence creates in Bruce a personification of Scotland and Scottish identity. He, too, gave to the world a memorable, often-quoted passage on freedom, beginning 'A, fredome is a noble thing!'[19] His epic also raises the subjects of good kingship on the one hand – showing in Bruce a hero whose heroic potential is checked by his responsibilities as a leader – and of loyalty to the king on the other. To the Scots, it serves as a reminder that their country's independent status was largely the achievement of a member of the current dynasty, and to the troublesome contemporary Douglases, that their ancestor Sir James Douglas was – in his presentation here – Bruce's most loyal supporter.

Roughly a century later, Hary's *The Wallace,* written in the 1470s, likewise concentrates on the achievements of a single man in the fight for Scottish independence.[20] It highlights in more dramatic narrative than the *Bruce* the extremes of warfare and of dedication to a cause. Its use of longer Scots pentameter lines provides more scope for individual expression than the shorter lines of Barbour and Wyntoun. It is based on the works of Bower and Wyntoun and on 'gestes' of Wallace, but a good deal is also supplied by Hary's own imagination. William Wallace is here charged with the task of liberating Scotland by Saint Andrew and the Virgin Mary – a direct divine inspiration that stands in contrast to Bruce's more implied divine support as the rightful king of the Scots – and pursues this aim with single-minded idealism. His own and his followers' nobility of character and purpose, and his martyr-like end, appear here in sharp contrast to the unjust ambitions of the villainous enemy. In contrast to Barbour's depiction of a hero whose adversaries are found both outside Scotland and within, some of the *Wallace*'s popularity rests on the fact that Wallace's fight is very clearly against the English, revealing on Hary's part a greater concern for the fortunes of the Scottish people than for those of the Scottish king. While Barbour's epic celebrated King Robert I and through him his royal dynasty, Hary (c. 1440–1492 or thereafter) is thought to have belonged to a section of society that disagreed with the pro-English politics of James III, so that his *Wallace* is both a reminder of the immense struggles it cost the Scottish people to achieve its independence, and a call to defend it in the present times. The work's great and lasting popularity, which surpassed that of Barbour's, can also be attributed to its more vivid style, and to the greater proximity of its language to that spoken at the point at which printing began in Scotland. It was one of the first works to be published by Scotland's first printers,

Walter Chepman and Andro Myllar, in c. 1508, was printed again in 1594 and 1601, and in the wake of the Union of the Crowns of 1603, saw thirteen further editions during the seventeenth century. It also served as the basis of a controversial play, *The Valiant Scot,* printed in London in 1637, by an author whose initials 'J.W.' have not been identified.[21] Barbour's work, in contrast, was printed only six times until the end of the seventeenth century, although it, too, inspired another literary piece in the shape of a long verse epic by Patrick Gordon of Ruthven, *The famous historie of the renouned and valiant Prince Robert surnamed the Bruce King of Scotland,* which was published in Dordrecht in 1615.[22]

The early sixteenth century saw the beginnings of a different approach to Scottish historiography as it was now in the hands of authors who were increasingly influenced by humanist ideas. The first of these was John Mair (c. 1467–1550), born near North Berwick in East Lothian. He studied in Cambridge and Paris, remained in Paris until 1518 where he acquired fame as a teacher, and then returned to Scotland to teach in Glasgow. Here, he wrote the *Historia Maioris Britanniae* (printed in Paris, 1521). Although often described as a logician with a scholastic background, he was also touched by elements of early humanism. He was an industrious author who by the time of his return to Scotland had a sizeable list of philosophical publications to his name.[23] History was only one of many interests of his, and he made no attempt to present a new factual account based on his own research; rather, he treated the existing record as an object for analysis and criticism. The modest format and length of his history, a volume of 146 leaves printed in the same quarto format in which other works of his were published, signals from the start a sober, matter-of-fact approach. His stay in England as a student, and his more objective interest in Scotland brought on by long absence, may also have been factors that contributed to his rather novel point of view. Rather than continuing the presentation of Scotland as a country forever under threat from an overbearing neighbour and thus forced to keep intact its physical and ideological defences, Mair argued for the two countries to form a union of equals: he thought that there was little to distinguish them, and dismissed both the English and the Scottish origin myths as fabrications. Watching with some suspicion the development of new humanist fashions of history writing – which were enthusiastically followed by the next historian, his contemporary Hector Boece – John Mair advocated a truthful and unemotional account of history, where a simple style ensured that the account was not falsified through colourful language.

To be clearly and universally understood was an important aim; in fact, it has been commented that Mair 'narrowly [...] missed writing in the vernacular'.[24] The work is dedicated to the nine-year-old King James V, not so much as a manual of good kingship, but in the hope that an understanding of history will help him to avoid many mistakes; in the book, events and their causes are at times helpfully analysed. Concerned, like his predecessors, with the relationship between king and people, Mair was the first historian to question the concept of the divine right of kingship, that is, the idea that kingship was conferred on a ruler and his dynasty by God so that only a strict adherence to the law of primogeniture could be seen as being compliant with God's will. Instead, there are signs that he favoured a conciliarist approach, where legitimacy was reduced in importance and the king could forfeit his kingship if his rule was incompetent or damaging. His rule was seen as resting on the consent of the people, and he could be deposed by them if he showed himself to be unsatisfactory. Although in his narrative Mair finds little opportunity to demonstrate the workings of such a principle in practice, one historical figure who he thinks entirely lost all claim to kingship is John Balliol, for surrendering the throne to Edward I, which raises, once again, the Wars of Independence to a highly significant period in Scottish history.

Mair's history, at odds with popular feeling, may yet have fared better if the young king and the world at large had not so soon afterwards been presented with a far more appealing history of Scotland. Mair's successor in the field – and a man who fits rather well the description of the type of author at whom he aimed his stylistic advice – was Hector Boece (c. 1465–1536). He was born in Dundee, one of several sons of a wealthy burgess, and studied in Paris where he enjoyed the friendship of Erasmus and other humanists from Scotland and elsewhere. After he had achieved his MA he initially, like Mair, remained in Paris to work as a teacher and to study for a degree in theology; in 1497, however, he was invited by Bishop William Elphinstone to teach at the newly founded King's College in Aberdeen, and in 1505 he became the College's first principal. Boece's *Scotorum historia a prima gentis origine* – not his only, but his most important work – was printed in Paris in 1527.[25] It was thus published only six years after Mair's history, very probably begun and planned before Mair's work appeared, and followed none of Mair's recommendations for a more pared-down and less imaginative narrative. Divided into seventeen books, and coming down to the murder of James I in 1437, it is written in a classical Latin style and models itself on Roman historiography. Not only does it display the dramatic diction that Mair believed to be out of place in a history, but it also adds digressions, ethnographical matter and speeches in battle and council, and includes a lengthy re-telling of the Scottish origin myth. Divided into long books but with no further subdivision, it is nevertheless an accessible historical reference work due to the helpful name index at the front. While this gave Boece's work an impeccably humanist face, it is in many ways far more traditional than Mair's. It was printed in folio format with a highly decorated title page and is monumental in length – over four hundred leaves – as well as size. It was dedicated to the young King James V, and that good kingship is one of his concerns becomes evident in the sequence of exemplary narratives that illustrate the reigns of the early kings of Scotland. In the absence of a more detailed historical record, Boece uses the opportunity to develop these rulers out of single-line entries in king-lists into either model kings or tyrannical, weak or immoral rulers, drawing on the traditional *speculum principis* literature of instruction for young rulers. While the subjects of Boece's kings have a duty of loyalty, they also have the right to criticise or depose bad kings for the good of the country, and frequently make use of it. Like Mair, Boece shows an awareness of conciliarist ideas, but does not argue for this practice to be applied in modern times. Ridding the country of evil rulers was in keeping with the virtuous ideals of the ancient Scots, who were, besides, not yet following the law of primogeniture: this he presents as a much later development. The portrayal of the ancient Scots in his work as 'noble savages' shows the influence of classical sources such as Tacitus's *Agricola* and *Germania*, the latter newly discovered in his time and creating a certain fashion for northerly ethnography that was also taken up, for example, by the Swedish author Olaus Magnus in his *Historia de gentibus Septentrionalibus* ('History of the northern peoples'), first printed in Rome in 1555.

Further, Boece does not share John Mair's view that Scotland and England would benefit from forming a union. Instead, his account serves as a reminder that it is within Scotland itself that some effort at bringing different groups closer together might be made: in the Gaelic-speaking Scots Boece found a large demographic group that had long existed only at the fringes of the country's historical narrative. Later medieval Lowland Scottish historiography had until now been composed by writers whose origins lay east of the Highland line in counties such as East Lothian and Fife. These saw Scotland, correctly, as divided into Lowlands and Gàidhealtachd, but their attitude towards the Gaels was one of prejudice and suspicion: their barbarous neighbours, they felt, were nothing but trouble, and there is no acknowledgement that it was to the Gaels that Scotland owed the existence of any early historical record at all. John

Mair, whose knowledge of them is more detailed than might be expected, had expressed himself in a more differentiated way; he had seen different degrees of integration into the kingdom within the Highland population, and moreover much admired their playing on the harp.[26] Ownership of the Scottish past, however, was claimed for the Lowlands, while the original preservers of its records were sidelined and rarely brought into the narrative unless as troublemakers. Boece, on the other hand, according to his own account in his preface to James V, was in contact with Highlanders. Possibly on the grounds of the information accessed with the help of these contacts, he presented the Gaelic Scots as those that still preserved the original virtue and austerity of the ancient Scots; this fitted in well with the ideals expressed in Tacitus's *Germania*, and similarly results in a juxtaposition in his work of archaic Highland virtue and Lowland greed and unmanliness.[27] But although his humanist heart seems to be with the virtuous Highlanders, their lifestyle is unfit for modern times: both writer and reader have to accept that, regrettably, it is sophisticated Lowland decadence that will cause less embarrassment to the nation. Moreover, the difficulties for a Lowlander of access to Highland history, which for a great part remained preserved only in Gaelic oral tradition, meant that Boece did not change the established narrative record into a history that showed a more positive interaction between Highlands and Lowlands.

Boece's history proved highly influential on future historians. Later reprints published in 1574 and 1575 by Giovanni Ferrerio added two further books left incomplete at Boece's death. By then, three different translations into Scots had been written. The best known among these was ordered by King James V to be made by the poet John Bellenden (c. 1495–1545x1548); it may be noted that the king apparently did not commission a translation of Mair's history.[28] Bellenden's translation was first presented to the king in manuscript in 1533, and a revised version was printed in Edinburgh in the later 1530s. Two other translations into Scots – a verse translation by William Stewart, and an anonymous prose translation known as the Mar Lodge version – were written within the same timeframe but not published.[29] Bellenden's translation, which makes some substantial changes to the original narrative and also adds material from other sources, turned Boece's work into the first universally popular prose history in Scotland, after Barbour's and especially Hary's verse epics. For much of the sixteenth century, subsequent historians tended to add to, rather than question, what was considered the accepted account of the Scottish past both in Scotland and abroad. Raphael

Holinshed's historical work, the *Chronicles of England, Scotlande and Irelande*, first printed in London in 1577, shows its absorption into historical accounts in England: its version of the story of Macbeth was based on that of Boece/Bellenden, and then itself provided the basis for Shakespeare's *Macbeth*.

So far, historians had been able to take for granted a religiously and – on the whole – politically united Scottish readership. Although the authors' regional loyalties had always had a bearing on their presentation of certain events,[30] the impact of the Wars of Independence, and for the later authors also the battle of Flodden, meant that there was never any doubt that the main enemy was to be found outside Scotland. This did not mean, of course, that they had been unanimous in their treatment of fundamental constitutional and political themes. Views on the rights of kingship, the sacredness of the dynasty, the duties of a king and the role of the people varied greatly throughout the histories. While the older authors celebrated the shift from the Gaelic succession practice to the law of primogeniture, which had eventually resulted in a successful outcome of the Wars of Independence under the current dynasty, their sixteenth-century successors tended to regard national success as an achievement of the people and – following the *Institutio Principis Christiani* of Erasmus and similar literature for the education of princes[31] – emphasised the duties, rather than rights, of the king. They had been able to express such views in relative security, and there had been no expectation of their political theories ever being seriously acted upon.

However, the *Scotorum historia*, along with its translation, was the last work in the genre to be written before the Scottish Reformation, and before the forced abdication and later execution of Mary, Queen of Scots. The historians of the later sixteenth century and beyond, whose accounts extended that of Boece into their own times, were of necessity taking sides both religiously and politically, and neither was without danger. It had not been uncommon for the earlier historians to end their accounts a safe number of decades before their own times in order to avoid a variety of criticisms; now, however, some authors did not publish their works at all for fear of reprisals. An example is Robert Lindsay of Pitscottie (c. 1532–c. 1586), whose history is a continuation of Bellenden's Scots translation of Boece's work, from the death of James I in 1437 to 1575. It was not printed in his own lifetime, possibly because of the author's anti-Douglas sentiments; the first edition was published by Robert Freebairn in 1728 under the title *The history of Scotland; from 21 February, 1436, to March, 1565*. However, the fact that sixteen manuscripts survive suggests that the work must have been well known through private circulation, although only one of these goes beyond 1565. Three further printed editions followed: Aeneas J. G. Mackay's scholarly edition, published by the Scottish Text Society in three volumes, 1899–1911, used the title under which it is now better known, *The historie and chronicles of Scotland*.[32] Pitscottie used Bellenden and other sources until he reached the times when his own political awareness began, around the year 1555. Some source material was probably supplied by the poet and Lyon herald David Lyndsay of the Mount, his relative, whose poetry Pitscottie also quotes. However, much of his contemporary narrative is based on hearsay and oral accounts, giving his history its feeling of immediacy and closeness to the spoken word. Although there is a pronounced pro-Protestant bias in his work, which contributes to the general untrustworthiness of his history, Pitscottie is less polemical than his contemporaries Knox and Buchanan. He continued to support the Stewart dynasty, and about Mary, Queen of Scots, out of the country since 1568, he finds little to say, perhaps out of consideration for her son James VI.[33] With all its faults, Pitscottie's history is generally considered to be a likeable book and a vivid, enjoyable read.

John Lesley, bishop of Ross (1527–1596), remained a Catholic and through much of his career acted as supporter and negotiator on behalf of Mary, Queen of Scots. After her defeat and abdication he left Scotland for the Continent in 1573, and never returned. He wrote a *Defence of the honour of the right highe, mightye and noble Princesse Marie Quene of Scotlande* (1569), and a continuation of Hector Boece's work, entitled *De origine, moribus et rebus gestis Scotorum libri decem* (Rome, 1578). Lesley follows Hector Boece's account of the early Scottish kings, but in his narrative of better documented times his presentation is informed – sometimes in direct contradiction to what he repeats from Boece – by his own interest in the cause of Mary, Queen of Scots. He advocates firmly the law of primogeniture, the divine right of kingship, and the justness of the Catholic cause. Also, although he adopts Boece's view that the Highland Scots are those that preserve ancient Scottish virtue in Scotland, his account of more recent times contains frequent references to them as savages, an interesting fact in view of the Highland location of his episcopal see.

George Buchanan (1506–1582), a Protestant and one of Scotland's greatest humanists, wrote his *Rerum Scoticarum Historia* in the years leading up to 1582, but died while the work was in the press. Three years previously, he had already presented his views on kingship in his *De jure regni apud Scotos dialogus* (Edinburgh, 1579), but in his history the subject is taken up again. Relying on Boece's presentation of kings ruling by popular consent among the ancient Scots, Buchanan was strongly opposed to the rule of Mary Queen of Scots, and in favour of the deposition of unsuitable monarchs or even of tyrannicide. As for the presentation of the Highlanders, Buchanan, who was himself a Highlander from the Lennox with a knowledge of Gaelic, gives a similar account of the Gaels to that found in Boece. It is, however, enriched by more detail, and, while he retains Boece's image of the Highland Scots as the preservers of the austere virtue of the ancients, his ethnographical account lacks Boece's corresponding presentation of the Lowlanders as decadent and anglified. The reader is thus left with an impression of Scotland's cultural distinctness, for which the Highlanders are living proof, rather than its similarities with England that had led Mair and others to argue for a union with England.

In subsequent decades, Lowland historical writing showed a tendency to become more specialised and narrowed in its scope by subject or period. Genealogies, family memoirs and sometimes also heraldic works outlined the history of families and individuals against the background of more generally known historical fact. Protestant church histories, such as John Knox's *History of the Reformation in Scotland* (published 1587), and David Calderwood's *The True History of the Kirk of Scotland* (published posthumously in 1678), were limited chronologically as well as in their choice of subject. Thomas Dempster's (1579–1625) flawed but nevertheless valuable *Historia Ecclesiastica Gentis Scotorum* (Bologna, 1627) is a Catholic expatriate's attempt to chart the cultural rather than political achievements of the Scottish nation.[34] Rather than presenting a historical narrative, Dempster compiled an encyclopedia of – mostly – Catholic Scottish authors and their works, and although many persons on his list are wrongly identified as Scots, much of his information is still of great interest and was much copied until the early eighteenth century. Local history and topography, too, began to gain ground until, in the second half of the century, early Enlightenment scholars like Robert Sibbald (1641–1722) began to assemble on a larger scale the country's topographical picture.

What can be said of the expression, function and social significance of history between 1300 and 1650 in Gaelic-speaking Scotland? Did the process of Gaelic linguistic contraction and then retrenchment in the centuries after 1100 have any discernible impact upon Gaelic views of

Scottish origins, or of more recent history? Was the predominant vision pan-Gaelic, extending to Ireland as the homeland of the Gaels, or 'national' in a Scottish sense, or more narrowly focused upon the regional and local? Did agency and authorship continue to be vested purely in learned professionals – the intellectual, if not the biological, heirs of the king's poet – and employing the same genres?

If answers to these questions are to be sought in prose texts committed to the written or printed word within this timeframe, then in terms of texts in Gaelic, virtually nothing has survived, and the contrast with contemporary Gaelic Ireland – replete with annalistic and genealogical compilations, and much else besides – could not be starker.[35] Even taking into account the two other written languages in use in Gaelic-speaking Scotland in the era, Latin and Scots (which in time increasingly conformed to English), the improvement is marginal, and the contrast with Lowland Scotland no less stark. To a very few genealogical texts, mainly in Gaelic, can be added a very few chronicles orientated towards Latin and then Scots, essentially annalistic in form, highly localised in perspective, and associated with particular churches. One such chronicle survives in the famous early sixteenth century miscellany, mainly of Gaelic poetry, known as the Book of the Dean of Lismore, whose centre of compilation was the parish church of Fortingall in eastern Highland Perthshire. The BDL also includes various Latin and Scots texts relating to the kingship of the Scots, and insofar as their origins have been identified, they derive from the Lowland chroniclers.[36]

It is only after 1650 that the situation changes as a productive and enduring genre of genealogical or clan history comes into full visibility, composed in manuscript and overwhelmingly in English.[37] Even then, the authors of these works make liberal use of Fordun and his successors while occasionally lamenting the dearth of indigenous written antecedents available to them.[38] On that basis we might assume that they, and perhaps therefore the compilers of the BDL before them, turned to the Lowland historians to fill the vacuum left by the absence of a homegrown alternative. However, this was not the case. The clan histories offer a means of reconstructing a model, however tentative, of the shape and nature of historical enquiry within Gaelic Scotland in the later middle ages, and when this is complemented by other evidence, the unequivocal conclusion is that this was a society steeped in the knowledge of its own past. In the words of the author of one clan history, writing in the early eighteenth century, 'no people have their History so exactly kept by Tradition as the Highlanders'.[39]

Why then had a profoundly historicist society left such a paltry written legacy to bear witness to the fact? Explanations proffered in the early modern clan histories ranged from the unlikely – ingratitude towards their patrons, or simple ignorance, on the part of the historians concerned – to the more plausible assertion of destruction of manuscripts. Evidence for specimens now lost – Beauly and Bunchrew from Easter Ross, possibly Iona – may hint that the maintenance of local annalistic texts in ecclesiastical environments was fairly widespread in the late medieval Highlands.[40] Some of the clan histories were able to draw upon earlier texts apparently in the same mould as themselves, and which have failed to survive independently. Three Macintosh manuscripts had testified to 'the antiquity of the family and their pedigree', the earliest of them bringing the story down to c. 1500, and reputedly authored around that date by the chief of the clan, Fearchar Macintosh, then a prisoner in southern Scotland.[41] Loss has also undoubtedly diminished the written legacy left by those professional learned lineages in late medieval Gaelic Scotland that included history in their repertoire. The names that stand out are MacMhuirich, Ó Muirgheasáin, MacEwen and Beaton, all based in the west Highlands and Islands. They were ultimately of Irish origin (this is less clear-cut in the case of the MacEwens); in regular contact with the professional classes of Ireland, including their own kinsfolk; and espoused the so-called 'classical tradition' of Gaelic scholarship on lines that were consistent with Irish practice, including the use of the high-status literary dialect of Gaelic, and of Gaelic script, for manuscript composition. A MacEwen poem alludes to 'sein-leabhruibh suadh', '*the ancient books of the learned*',[42] but we have no surviving archive to speak of for them or for the Uí Muirgheasáin, while that of the MacMhuirichs has apparently suffered grievously from attrition.[43]

Yet this is very far from the whole story. According to the clan histories, the professional cultivation of history was not the preserve of these four lineages, but well-nigh universal: the MacLeans 'had their shenachies and bards as every family of distinction in the Highlands had'.[44] Within the 'classical tradition', 'shenachie' or seanchaidh was the appropriate technical term for a professional historian. Another history adds the gloss that 'the senachie was the prose writer, and the bard the poet, but very oft the bard supplied the place of both'. It goes on to define the primary function of these poet-historians as:

> to hand down to posterity the valorous actions, conquests, battles, skirmishes, marriages and relations of the predicessors by repeating and

singing the same at births, baptisms, marriages, feasts and funerals, so that no people since the curse of the Almighty dissipated the Jews took such care to keep their tribes, cadets and branches, so well and so distinctly separate.[45]

On this basis, two complementary explanations for the lack of written prose history in late medieval Gaelic Scotland can be offered. History was primarily conceived of as genealogy, and with material of this order, the preferred modus operandi was oral and aural. All this is present in the praise accorded Gilleasbuig Campbell, fifth earl of Argyll in 1567 by Eoin or John Carswell (c. 1522–1572), first Protestant bishop of the Isles, for his devotion to scripture rather than ancestral history:

> [...] oir is mo do chuir tu a suim an ni do dhearbh an soisgel diadha dhuit ina meid oirrdhearchais th'aoisi, agas fad an ghnathuighe do-chualais do bheith ag na sindsearaibh onoracha do-chuaidh romhad [...]

> *[...] for you have considered that which the divine gospel has proved to you of more account than the glory of your age and the old-established customs which you have heard were followed by your honourable ancestors who preceded you [...].*[46]

Secondly, Gaelic poetry and song was a fitting medium for rehearsing and memorialising history. An early sixteenth-century poem addresses the chief of the MacGregors thus:

> Mithigh a rádh réd rorg glas,
> éistidh, a Eoin, réd sheanchas,
> ríomh do fhréimhe – cá meisde? –
> ríoghdha séimhe saoirtheisde.

> *Fit time it is to state to thee, thou of the blue eyes – listen, Eoin, to thy history – the enumeration of thy line – what harm therein? – a line royal, gentle, of noble repute.*[47]

As this makes clear, Gaelic verse was also geared towards the spoken rather than the written word. Nevertheless, insofar as a corpus of late medieval historical writing in Gaelic has come down to us, it is provided by verse rather than prose. This might be explicable by the lottery of survival, above all else the poetry-centred BDL, but it could equally be argued that it is no accident that within that source, the verse is overwhelmingly Gaelic, the prose monopolised by Latin and Scots.

This is an appropriate juncture to return to the clan histories, for whenever their authors enlarge upon their sources, mention is made of oral informants of high social status, typically characterised as 'sensible old men of the last generation', 'the most intelligent and best informed men yet alive', or 'the oldest and wisest, not only of my own but of all our neighbours' families'.[48] Thus, inherited Gaelic oral narrative underpins these English prose texts. The clan histories further imply that these aristocratic amateurs were one element in a threefold engagement with history in Gaelic Scotland in the later middle ages, the others being the professional poet-historians, and all society viewed as a single consciousness sharing a 'collective memory'.[49] Noble laymen such as the Macintosh, Campbell and MacGregor chiefs already mentioned could hardly avoid imbibing what the specialists taught them, or being immersed in the history of their own lineages and clans. Such laymen were pivotal to cultural interchange and recycling across social strata, ideally placed to combine all three spheres of indigenous historical activity, and to initiate the process by which the results were committed to writing, in anticipation of what happened on a general and more deliberate scale after 1650. It was to men of this class that the term *seanchaidh* came to be applied in the later seventeenth century, as the professionals previously so designated died out.[50]

To summarise thus far, the practice of history in Gaelic Scotland in the later middle ages turned upon orality, and the noble lineages that exercised lordship over society. Professionals preserved and pronounced the history of these lineages, and instructed them in it, resulting in a lay aristocracy that was very historically minded. Individual members of this class may have developed reputations as amateur historians in their own right, and enjoyed greater latitude for experimentation and synthesis of sources which potentially included the 'vulgar traditions' of the people below. The two putative poles of this putative historical world were the chief's court, and its demotic mirror-image, the forerunner of the taigh-chèilidh or ceilidh house familiar from the fuller record of the modern era. In the seventeenth century, the changing self-perception and self-expression of the social elite generated an imperative for new history. In the van were the Campbells, initially offering patronage to non-Gaelic specialists in disciplines such as medicine and visual art as well as literature. William Bowie commenced *The Black Book of Taymouth* in 1598, a history of the Campbells of Glenorchy embellished with full colour portraits of the chiefs of the lineage.[51] Also of Lowland authorship was *Information anent the Pedigree of the Noble and Antient House of Lochow*, written in 1634, and treating of the main Campbell line.[52] However, as the genealogical history genre came to full flower after 1650, so indigenous authorship reasserted itself, but with a difference. With the professional historical class in advanced and terminal decline, the amateur seanchaidh now came into his own as the de facto 'new historian', putting history into writing in English and within a broader comparative framework, thereby acknowledging that outside audience that itself signified part of the rationale for change.[53]

The surviving evidence, with the poetry looming large, suggests that late medieval Gaelic Scotland depended upon history for its sense of self, order and ethos. The past was accessed via the rungs of genealogy, represented in the first instance by the mini-pedigree (sloinneadh) of two, three or even four generations that constituted part of the everyday naming system by which those of social standing were known. These pedigrees linked or associated the individual with the main chiefly line of a particular clan, whose genealogy and deeds were maintained by the professional historians. These clans in their turn were the limbs of the great craobhsgaoileadh or 'branching-tree' of the Gaels as a people: 'the race of the Gaels from the land of Greece'. This conceptualisation of the past as a domain inhabited first and foremost by those to whom one was related, and whose personal name one might well share, must have fostered social inclusion and collectivism, and made for a highly permeable frontier between the living and the dead. Blood was a finite and sacred commodity entrusted to the latest generation: 'fuil Ghrantach mád ghruaidh mar fhuil' (*'the blood of Grants is the blood that is in thy cheek'*), as one chief was reminded.[54] The kin-based past must necessarily be held in reverence, and in constant employ as a benchmark of morality and compass for action: 'ionnan moltar igcathaibh / Torcul is a athair áirmheach (*'praise equal to his renowned sire's doth Torquil win in battles'*); 'a mheic Aileín, ná toill féin / taibhéim nachar thoill Ailéin' (*'thou son of Ailean, do thou thyself no reproach that Ailean earned not'*); 'cuimhnigh nach tugsad na fir / umhla ar uamhan do Ghallaibh / cia mó fá dtugadh tusa / umhla uait an dula-sa?' (*'remember that these men made no submission for dread to Saxons; why shouldst thou, more than they, make submission now?'*).[55] For Gaelic Scotland, the past was not only present in the personal naming system *per se*, but in one type of epithet attached to ancestral names appearing in the pedigree of the clan's ruling line. Forms such as 'Gill-easbuig Arann', *'Gilleasbuig of Arran'* or 'Cailéin na gceann,' *Cailean of the Heads*', were shorthand for known historical events, and precisely analogous to place-names of the order of *Linn na Lùirich* ('the Pool of the Mailcoat'), *Loch MhicMhàrtainn* ('MacMartin's Loch') or *Coille na Baintighearna* ('the Lady's Wood').[56] While the origins and points of reference of these kinds of nomenclature may have been aristocratic, they became universals, part of the landscape and soundscape inhabited by all.

Ireland was the historic homeland of all Gaels, and the Scottish poet-historians existed to bear witness to 'the tribes who came from Ireland to Scotland and became heads of families and chiefs of clans'.[57] Texts relating to kindreds whose origins were understood to be impeccably Irish, such as the MacDonalds and MacDougalls, are dense in allusion to Irish history and pre-history; of one later fifteenth-century MacDougall chief it is said that 'gaisgeadh is eineach Éireann / 'gá nasgadh 'na luaithbhéimean', (*'the valour and honour of Ireland are knit in his swift blows'*').[58] Such was the inescapabilty of the relationship that even in cases where an Irish connection was non-existent or called into question, such would need to be found or reasserted, to render or maintain that lineage as a fully functioning limb of the Gaelic tree. Coinneach Cam, chief of the MacKenzies in the early seventeenth century, for whose kindred an ultimately Norman ancestry had come to be claimed (via the spurious Colin (Fitz) Gerald, who had supposedly prevented a stag from killing King Alexander III while hunting), was informed by MacLean's genealogist that he was 'not descended of the Geralds but of the Kings of Ireland, as the most of the clans of the west and south west parts of Scotland were'.[59] The Stewarts' roots in Brittany are nowhere visible in the characterisation of the fifteenth-century 'Eoin Stiúbhairt a crích Raithneach / a lámh Gaoidheal as fear buaidh [...] A Chú Chulainn cloinne Ghaltair [...] a shíl shlat ó chathach Chonn' (*'John Stewart from the bounds of Rannoch, thou whose hand has more virtue than all the Gael [...] thou Cú Chulainn of Walter's clan [...] thou scion of the princes of warrior Conn's race'*').[60] The MacLeods of Lewis were of indubitably Norse descent, and around 1500 a poet could acknowledge that the MacLeod chief Torcul might bestow upon him 'ó Charraig Bhoirbhe / séad as soirbhe fhuair file' (*'from the Rock of Bergen, a jewel the most precious that poet ever won'*').[61] But this was only one item in a wish-list comprising Fionn mac Cumhaill's shield and the horses of Cú Chulainn and Conall Cernach, for Torcul was endowed with a generosity equal to that of the revered Guaire son of Colmán, king of Connacht, as well as the endurance of Cú Chulainn.[62]

There were established tropes and pathways by which the connection to Ireland could be made, and the resultant descent groupings gave primary structure to Gaelic society in Scotland. At the level of individual clan pedigrees, the segment from the present chief back as far as the eponymous ancestor, from whom the clan derived its name, remained largely stable. The segment beyond the eponym, including the link to Ireland, became less strictly historical in its farthest reaches, and susceptible to alteration. Different origins might be claimed for the one clan, in response to variables such as the affiliation and intent of the genealogist involved, or the clan's changing fortunes and allegiances across time. Pedigree manipulation reinforces rather than diminishes the status of genealogy as the determinant of history, and confirms the intimacy of the relationship between past and present. Current political realities carried genealogical consequences and needed genealogical justification. Such manipulation had to be intellectually credible, necessitating the skills of the poet-historians who maintained the pedigrees both of their own employers and of others, and their knowledge of the Gaelic branching-tree in its entirety.[63]

As long as this caste remained in life, it asserted a vision of Scotland or Alba as the homeland of the Gaels beyond Ireland, and of Alba as an undifferentiated Gaelic entity. Whereas the Gaelic vernacular literature that becomes properly visible in the seventeenth century acknowledges a physical and cultural divide in Scotland between Gael and non-Gael, there seems to have been no comparable updating of the world-view of the Scottish Gaelic professional literati. To be a Gael in Scotland was to own Ireland as motherland and Scotland as fatherland. If Gaelic hero figures such as Fionn mac Cumhaill were charged with the protection of Ireland, the present-day chiefs of Scottish clans bore exactly the same responsibility towards Scotland. An abiding sense of the Gaels as one people, of ultimate Gaelic unity and solidarity, was not irreconcilable with the acknowledgement and maintenance of two homelands of equal weighting. In Scottish sources, whoever held ceannas nan Gàidheal, the 'headship of the Gaels' had the right and bounden duty to marshal the whole people to protect either Ireland, or Scotland, or both. The concept is absent from Irish sources, which see Scotland as an aberration, and the sovereignty of the Gaels as inseparable from Ireland and the high-kingship of Ireland.[64] The kingship of the Scots may have been a crucial legitimator of Scottish growth from Irish roots, a genealogical counterpart to the sense of place provided by Alba. Gaelic society in Scotland was in natural harmony with a royal dynasty claiming Irish origin, and a number of Scottish clans subscribed to the particular pathway in question, via the ruling stocks of Dalriada, the embryonic kingdom of the Gaels in Scotland. The BDL is a witness to the degree of interest in the ramifications of the royal house, and thus a marker of the desirability of being able to associate one's pedigree with that of the kings of Scots.

For late medieval Gaelic Scotland, history was no less than the morality of the present, providing explanations, warnings, encouragement and lessons. It was a repository of virtues, as embodied by archetypes, heroic and real, to whom one must aspire. The ultimate reward for the exhibition of virtue was a place in the past, and the collective Gaelic consciousness: to shine immortal as 'éinrinn ghaisgidh Gaoidheal nGréag', a *'unique star of valour among the Grecian Gael'*.[65] As one poet reminded his patron in an argument of perfect circularity, what deed was more lasting than the hospitality bestowed by Guaire, the seventh-century king of Connacht, upon Senchán Torpéist and his train?[66] The past began and ended with one's own kin, for 'eineach is eangnamh is iocht / do cheangladh ar a sliocht riamh' (*'generosity and prowess and mercy have been bound on their lineage ever'*).[67] But role models could be drawn from anywhere in Gaelic history, prehistory and mythology, as well as the Biblical or classical worlds. Another poet, clearly an aristocratic amateur, demonstrates his immersion in Gaelic heroic literature by seeing solutions for his condition in the wealth represented by the most conspicuous cattle-droves and horse herds from the sagas, the weaponry of Fionn and Cú Chulainn, the gold of Éibhear and of Éireamhón, the harp of Cuircheól and the ship of Laoimean.[68] In its moral aspect the past was shorn of the depth and distance created by time and space, and became akin to a flat screen or mirror in which the honoured dead of every past generation vied equally for the attention of the living.

Holding up the mirror were the arbiters of worth, the poet-historians. Their texts shuttle ceaselessly between present and past, the relationship formalised into the úrsgeul or comparative apologue, the point of transition effected by a statement such as 'do-chuala mé go roibh sin / uair éigin Inis Incin / fá smacht ag fine Fomhra' (*'I have heard that on a time Ireland was under the rule of a Fomorian race'*; or 'do chuala mé fada ó shoin / sgéal as cosmhail rér gcumhaidh' (*'I heard long ago a tale like unto our lament'*).[69] This last is from an elegy for Aonghas Òg, son of Eoin MacDonald, lord of the Isles, who was assassinated in 1490. The apologue, concerning the inadvertent death of Conlaoch at the hands of his father Cú Chulainn, provides an historic scale for present grief, and points a learned finger of suspicion.⁷⁰ The successive stages involved in the forging of the sort of reputation required to enter the pantheon of the past are staked out in the vocabulary of the poetic mission: approach and find; experience and know; estimate and pronounce. One to pass the test was Torcul MacLeod: 'adéara mé dhá h-aithle / d'éis a aithne is a éolais / nach dtánaig fear a aoise / as fearr ná an rí-se Leódhuis' (*I shall assert thereafter, after acquaintance and knowledge, that there hath come no man of his age who is better than this king of Lewis*').⁷¹ The same agency that recognised and validated virtue could then spread reputation wherever Gaelic was spoken and heard. The words of an Irish poet are equally applicable to the Scottish poet-historians as keepers of the gateway to the past, for 'muna leasaighdís laoidhe / a ndearnsad, gér dheaghdhaoine / le i bhfad a-nonn do bhiadh brat / ar Niall, ar Chonn, ar Chormac' (*'if poems did not preserve all that they had done, even though they were noble heroes, there would long since have been a cloak of silence upon Niall, Conn and Cormac'*).⁷²

In Lowland Scotland, historical writing in this period, with its increased availability through publication or distribution in manuscript, ensured that knowledge of history became more widespread. It resulted in an awareness of the nation's past and of past achievements, cultural discreteness and identity, and worked its way towards becoming part of the nation's general knowledge. However, outside the more explicitly political works its influence on Scottish literature is not always easy to define, and may sometimes merely result in an author's discernible feeling of pride in his nation's antiquity and success. In other cases, events from the past may be used in order to advise on the present, and sometimes this happens within the historical works themselves. Political prose and poetry made more direct reference to the historical framework of current events. A few examples for this are Richard Holland's *Buke of the Howlat*, Walter Kennedy's parts in *The Flyting of Dunbar and Kennedie*, and several of the works of Sir David Lyndsay, especially *The Testament of the Papyngo* and *Ane dialoge betuix experience and ane courteour*.⁷³

Some of the histories mentioned here were influential as works of literature in their own right. Some of them, such as the accounts of Hector Boece (through Bellenden's translation) and Lindsay of Pitscottie, contain masterpieces of storytelling that inspired those that followed them; as we have Boece to thank for Shaekespeare's *Macbeth*, so Pitscottie's history provided inspiration for Walter Scott's *Tales of a Grandfather*. Others, such as John Barbour and Hary, wrote epics that not only were most influential in the development of Scottish national feeling, but also have their firm place in the canon of Older Scots verse literature.

Between 1400 and 1650, Gaelic Scotland's approach to history was distinguished from its Lowland counterpart by the greater weight accorded to orality in transmission, dissemination and performance, the greater degree of overlap with literature in terms of personnel, form, content and intent, and the greater role of professionalisation and patronage. Writing in the later sixteenth century, Eoin Carswell and George Buchanan launched reformed and humanist critiques of a genre susceptible to the fallibility of memory, coloured by heroic literary narrative, and obsessed with singing the praises of great men and their ancestors. Gaelic historians replied in their turn after 1650, castigating Buchanan, Boece and their ilk as 'partial pickers of Scottish chronology and history', who portrayed Gaelic Scots either negatively or not at all.[74] Yet underlying difference and dissonance was a shared concern with legitimacy and constitutionalism. Just as Lowland historiography was preoccupied with Scottish sovereignty, and the rights and duties of kings and subjects, so too can the corpus of Gaelic poetry bear analysis as a sustained commentary on Scottish Gaelic identity, and the contractual relationship between chief, land and people, with the past as the touchstone.

Another point of contact was the impact of religious reformation and political rapprochement with England, which shook the entire edifice of Scottish historiography in the sixteenth century. Whether the same applied to the deposition of Mary, Queen of Scots cannot be gauged for lack of evidence on the Gaelic side, although George Buchanan was quick to justify the act by reference to Gaelic conciliarism and succession practice past and present. In the early 1540s, John Elder (fl. 1533–1565), a Gaelic Scot and (at this stage) committed Protestant who had the ear of Henry VIII, rejected the Scottish for the British origin legend in order to locate Scotland within an English Protestant imperium that should be cemented forthwith by dynastic union. Writing in the shadow of Boece as well as Mair, Elder extolled the atavistic Spartanism of his fellow Gaels in order to emphasise their fitness to fight for Henry and the true faith. Rather than importing the Scots from Ireland, Elder gaelicised the Picts, and naturalised Columba as a proto-Protestant, Gaelic-speaking Pictish bishop.[75] In 1567 Bishop Carswell advanced the Bible and the printing press as the twin bases of authority for a Scottish Gaelic Protestant nobility and its intelligentsia, including 'gach seancha gan seanchas saobh' ('*every historian without false history*').[76] A Catholic riposte came in 1626 in the form of a letter in Latin from the chief of the MacDonalds of Clanranald, Eoin Muideartach, to Pope Urban VIII.[77] This text recalls the Declaration of Arbroath in its depiction of the Scots as a conquering and unconquered people who even now had still not completely submitted to the English. Unlike Arbroath, however, it adheres to the older orthodoxies that the Scots were of Irish stock and arrived from Ireland, and that it was from Ireland – rather than through the agency of St Andrew and Bishop Palladius, which became the standard narrative in later medieval Scottish historiography – that they first received the faith. Hence it is in conjunction with their Catholic Irish brethren that the Gaelic Scots will exercise their historically attested military capability to bring counter-Reformation to all Scotland.

Both historiographies were now exhibiting signs of diversification and specialisation, while still adhering to the templates operative across the later middle ages. A case in point, which also exemplifies many of the themes discussed in this chapter, is Sir Robert Gordon's (1580–1656) *Genealogical History of the Earldom of Sutherland* (1630). Gordon surely made use of Gaelic traditions and informants to write with such authority about a Gaelic world whose language he nonetheless condemned elsewhere in the most virulent terms. Education and travel gave him access to the Lowland chroniclers, the classics and sources drawn from across the continent, all contributing to a truly European historical vision governed by neo-stoicism and Tacitean realpolitik.[78] Gordon's masterpiece hinted at an increasingly liberated and creative Scottish historiography, on the cusp of modernity. Nevertheless, this was a manuscript history steeped in the culture of kinship and the feud, written to legitimise the contested Gordon claim to lordship in the northern mainland, and to educate the next earl in the glory of the house and name whose honour and heritage he must at all costs uphold.

PART 3: GENRE AND APPROACH

CHAPTER SIX

Lyric

Mícheál B. Ó Mainnín and Nicola Royan

Love-Lyric in the Gaelic Tradition

Gaelic 'love-lyric' for the present purposes is a broad term for poetry that is concerned with love, sexuality and sexual relations. It ranges in tone from the courtly to what has been described as the 'uncourtly', verse that is bawdy and, on occasion, overtly misogynistic. This essay seeks to examine aspects of the Gaelic tradition of love-lyric based for the most part on the collection of poems preserved in Scotland's most famous Gaelic manuscript, the Book of the Dean of Lismore (BDL), which appears to have been compiled between 1512 and 1542 but which contains earlier material. Consideration will be given to two substantial and overlapping themes in these lyrics: the *querelle des femmes* ('argument about women'), and sexual decadence and the promiscuity of the clergy. These find expression in all of the three languages employed in the manuscript (Gaelic, Scots and Latin), although there are very few poems in BDL in which the medium is a language other than Gaelic. Questions relating to authorship, attribution and poetic voice are of particular interest; the collection has a playful and intimate quality which manifests itself in the coterie verse to which poets of various backgrounds (both professional and amateur) have contributed. The amateurs include churchmen and aristocrats, the latter seeming to embrace both men and women. If so, we have evidence of a mixed gender coterie composing love-lyric in Gaelic Scotland at least half a century before we find similar evidence in Lowland Scots tradition (in the case of the Maitland Folio and Quarto). A further question is whether we are dealing with a single coterie centred on the court at Inveraray of the Earl of Argyll (probably Cailéan/Colin, the first earl (d. 1492)), or with two interconnected coteries, the second revolving around his cousin, Donnchadh (Sir Duncan Campbell of Glenorchy (d. 1513)).[1] Either way, the Campbells are dominant figures; this is particularly interesting from a broader Scottish perspective because of this family's connections with the king and involvement at the highest levels in the Scottish court.

We are currently dependant to a large degree for our corpus of love-lyric on BDL, although there is material in other manuscripts that has yet to be subjected to proper scrutiny.[2] Edinburgh, NLS Advocates MS 72.1.36 has been described as 'an intriguing and under-worked collection' ranging from the 'mildly misogynistic to the outright unpalatable'[3] and contains a copy of our most famous love-lyric, 'Soraidh slán don oidhche aréir' (*'Farewell ever to last night'*). Few of its poems have received detailed treatment or yet appeared in print.[4] Further examples are to be found elsewhere; NLS Advocates MS 72.1.34 contains the poem 'Cá h-ainm atá ar Fearghal Óg' (*'What reputation has Fearghal Óg'*), in which the Irish poet Fearghal Óg Mac an Bhaird is warned off by an un-named and clearly Scottish love-rival,[5] while the Red Book of Clanranald is significant not only in containing another copy of 'Soraidh slán don oidhche aréir' but in assigning it to Niall Mór Mac Muireadhaigh (or Mac Mhuirich), a member of Gaelic Scotland's premier learned family, who is thought to have flourished c. 1580.

Niall Mór is also credited with the authorship of a well-known satire on the bagpipes, 'Èatroman muice ò hò' (*'The bladder of a pig, o ho'*).[6] However, while this poem is written in what is unquestionably vernacular *Scottish* Gaelic, his love poem is written in a form of Classical Early Modern Gaelic: the literary language that was the preserve of the professional poet classes of the highest order, in both Scotland and Ireland, and that was also practised by the aristocracy in both countries.[7] There are love-lyrics in vernacular Scottish Gaelic that may be dateable to our period and which are also distinguishable in prosodic terms from the poetry preserved in BDL; for example, ''S e MacAoidh an duine treubhach' (*'MacAoidh it is who's the man of valour'*), or 'Craobh an Iubhair' as it is also known, is composed in accentual metre and is thought to date from the late sixteenth century.[8] This composition is a world away from the courtly poems in syllabic metre witnessed in BDL and elsewhere; here the lover is elevated by raw emotion, rather than by the conventions of *amour courtois*, and the lyric has been described as 'an early example of the powerful and emotionally complex women's song tradition'.[9] There are also compositions that fall in between, poems that may be described as semi-classical or semi-bardic in that they are written in the vernacular but composed in loose syllabic metres. These include three poems that on the basis of their ascriptions (all of which are open to doubt) may date to the sixteenth century. One particularly notable example is ''S luaineach mo chadal a-nochd' (*'Restless my sleep tonight'*) – said to have been composed by Eachann Mòr MacGill'Eathain, eleventh chief of Duart, to his wife Mòr – which bears striking similarities to courtly love-lyric in the classical language, both in terms of its tropes and depictions of female beauty.[10]

Our present discussion will necessarily be limited to lyric preserved in BDL, which we can reasonably assume was composed in Scotland in the fifteenth and early sixteenth centuries by poets both professional and amateur. This lyric is related to formal praise poetry not only in terms of language and metrical form but also in terms of style and imagery. Gaelic love-lyric has been described as a merger of two traditions, the themes deriving from the broader European tradition of *amour courtois* (but differing in some respects such as the absence of the connection between love and nature) and the aesthetics being supplied by the native men of learning, the professional poets.[11]

There are two particular contexts for our courtly and uncourtly lyric, therefore, that concern us at this point. First, the pan-Gaelic context inevitably connects with Ireland and the schools, the courts of the elite poets, which for the most part appear to have been located there. Second, the pan-Scottish context, with the king of Scots at the apex of aristocratic society, is particularly important in the case of BDL, a manuscript described as having two central preoccupations: women and the kingship of the Scots, the latter clearly drawing upon the late medieval Lowland chronicle tradition.[12] The manuscript departs from traditional Gaelic orthography in employing a spelling system based on Older Scots, and it also contains some specimens of verse of Scots and English provenance. Furthermore, BDL emanates from within the orbit of Campbell lordship and, in numbering the Earl of Argyll and the Campbell laird of Glenorchy among its contributors, can be connected (as was noted earlier) with individuals who formed part of the king's retinue and played an important role in the government of the kingdom at the highest level.

These contexts cannot be reduced to a simple binary opposition that places Ireland in the role of metropolitan centre in literary terms while political and other considerations place the book in the pan-Scottish context. William Gillies, Martin MacGregor and, latterly, Thomas Clancy have pondered the significance or otherwise of the fact that, in terms of Gaeldom, the Scottish courtly material largely predates the Irish; Clancy suggests that 'the dead hand of the Irish [literary] paradigm' and the 'slow rapprochement between scholars of Gaelic and Scots in the period 1450–1650' have prevented us from seeing lyrics such as those preserved in BDL 'as part of a wider Scottish phenomenon'. In the particular case of 'Soraidh slán don oidhche aréir', it seems to him to be 'part of the same world as the poems of Alexander Scott and Alexander Montgomerie, to partake of some of the same instincts (and be surrounded in its MSS by some of the same kind of companion pieces) as a poem like [...] Scott's 'Only to zow in erd that I luve best [...]'.[13] If this is true of a poem from the heart of the Gaelic west in the late sixteenth or early seventeenth century, one might expect it to be equally true of poems preserved in BDL with its geographical hub in Breadalbane and Fortingall in Perthshire.

While much of the Scottish material in BDL has been edited – the panegyric material by Watson and the Ossianic verse by Ross and Meek – the love-lyric has received much less scrutiny by editors, with the notable exception of Edmund Quiggin and, especially, Gillies.[14] However, as the orthography employed in the manuscript departs from traditional Gaelic orthography and, as Quiggin had only begun the work of transliteration (none of which is published) at the time of his death in 1920, the love-lyrics in BDL remain opaque to most students of late medieval Gaelic literature. They had also been ignored by scholars (Watson and, presumably, others) on account of their 'indecency'[15] until Gillies turned his attention to this material in his seminal article in 1977, and he has returned to survey this material again very recently (2016).[16]

We have noted that the love-lyrics preserved in BDL are among the earliest datable examples in the Gaelic tradition as a whole. These include two poems by the earliest professional poet known to have composed courtly verse about whom we have any broader contextual knowledge, Eóin Mac Muireadhaigh; he must have belonged to the same learned family as Niall Mór. One of these poems, 'Námha dhomh an dán' ('*Fate or the poem/poetry is hostile to me*'), bears some comparison with that by his later kinsman. In both poems, the subject is the passing of night and the departure of love at daybreak. In this case, however, the implication of the fourth quatrain appears to be that the nocturnal liaison was the subject of fantasy:

> Far bhean an dán díom
> is mór m'fhíoch is m'fhearg:
> cneas mar chubhar tonn,
> glac chorr is [gruaidh dhearg];
> béal ar dath na subh
> tug mo chruth ar searg.

> Ór chodlas-sa a-réir
> truagh, a Dhé, mo chor:
> do bhí sí fa-riom,
> ar liom, gion go robh;
> gan í ann ó ló
> do-chuaidh ar bhrón domh. (vv. 3–4)

Great is my fury and anger at what Fate or the poem/poetry took from me: skin like foam on the waves, dainty hand and red cheek; a mouth the colour of raspberries has withered my form.
Since I went to sleep last night my condition, o God, is sad: she was beside me, [or] so I thought, although she was not; her absence since day[break] has ended with sorrow for me.[17]

This poem exhibits some universal features of *amour courtois*, in particular the depiction of love as an illness that impairs the lover's physical condition. The anonymous author of another poem in BDL, 'Fada atú i n-easbhaidh aoibhnis' (*'Long am I lacking happiness'*) puts it succinctly: he is neither dead nor alive ('ní béo is níor cailleadh mise', *'I'm not alive, and I haven't died'*, q. 3d) and he has lost interest in everyone and everything:

> Saoilim nách bhfuil ar thalmhain
> aon mhac-samhla mo ghalair;
> gé tá mo chorp ar marthain
> táim ar scarthain re m'anaim.
>
> Éinneach dá bhfuil ar domhan,
> do chomthach nó do charaid,
> cha chluinim, is chan fhaicim
> éinní as ait liom nó as an-ait. (qq. 4–5)

I reckon that there is not on earth any likeness for my sickness; although my body has survived I have parted from my soul.
Of all the people of the world, (even) companions and friends, I hear none, and I see nothing that I consider pleasing or unpleasing.[18]

These poems and a few others like them, e.g. 'Tugas ró-ghrádh do mhnaoi fhir' (*'I have given great love to a certain one's/another's wife'*),[19] correspond closely to the bulk of the poems that are preserved in Irish manuscripts.

Eoin Mac Muireadhaigh's poem presents the same images of idealised beauty (skin white as sea foam, scarlet cheeks, lips red like raspberries and slender hands) that we encounter not only in Irish love-lyric but also in standard eulogy in the supplementary verse dedicated to the wives of chieftains and even, in the case of some elements of that imagery, in the depiction of men.

It is not courtly love-lyric but its antithesis – poetry which stands in opposition to the courtly ideal and which is concerned principally with what has been termed the 'argument about women' – that is most prominent in BDL and gives the manuscript its distinctiveness. Here the lady of courtly verse is thrown off her pedestal, mercilessly and unceremoniously; women rather than men are deemed to be rendered helpless but, taking the misogynistic view, not by love but by nature: their dependence on men for sexual gratification. A poem ascribed to the Earl of Argyll, 'A bhean dá dtugas-sa grádh' ('*Woman to whom I have given love*'), is particularly blunt in this regard; when forced to voice her preference, the poet has the woman opting for sex over love.[20] It also has a lash at the feeble courtly lover who pledges himself to his lady but who cannot compete with the virile fly-by-night stud who alone can satisfy her:

> Cia as annsa leat – fear gan bhod,
> is é a ngeall ort do\<n\> ghnáth,
> nó giolla an bhuid bhríoghmhoir chruaidh,
> bhíos ag imtheacht uait gach lá?[21] (q. 2)

Which do you prefer – a prickless man pledged to you forever [i.e. the courtly lover], or the lad with the potent, hard penis who departs your chamber every morning?[22]

A second and related theme is the voracious sexual appetite of the clergy pithily encapsulated in the single unattributed quatrain beginning 'Do-chuaidh mise, Roibeart féin':

> Do-chuaidh mise, Roibeart féin,
> don mhainistir a-né a-nonn;
> agus níor léigeadh mé a-steach,
> ó nach raibh mo bhean far riom.

I myself, Robert, went across yesterday to the monastery – and was not allowed inside, since my wife was not with me![23]

The two themes, the sexual gratification of women and the sexual appetite of the clergy, are linked in a poem attributed to the Earl of Argyll's wife, Iseabal (Countess Isabella, d. 1510), which celebrates the masculinity of her chaplain, 'Éistibh, a lucht an tighe-se' ('*Listen, people of this house*').[24] If so, it would appear to owe less to anti-clericalism than to what has been termed the 'subversive, satiric dimension' of BDL that is widespread across the range of Gaelic, Latin and Scots material.[25] Gillies has also referred to the considerable corpus of 'merry' verse in the Book and poems such as this seem tongue-in-cheek, particularly when one considers the clerical dimension to the compilation of the manuscript, most notably in the person of the Dean himself.[26] Also noteworthy is the poem 'Créad fá seachnainn-sa suirghe' ('*Why should I avoid courtship*'), attributed to 'The Parson', in which he suggests that philandering is the appropriate response to the faithlessness of women.[27] The positions taken on the nature of women and of the clergy's treatment of them may appear on occasion to have their apologists. A poem ascribed to Gearóid Iarla (Gerald, Earl of Desmond), 'Mairg adeir olc ris na mnáibh' ('*Woe to him who speaks ill of women*'), seems to take the part of women, arguing that it is wrong to criticise them. The concluding verse, however, which appears to be preserved only in BDL, strikes a misogynistic tone: with its apparent assertion that women would choose the redoubtable 'bod' ('*penis*') over all the wealth and riches of the world, we are brought back again to the argument that women are only interested in sexual gratification.[28] The intriguing thing, however, is that this additional verse in BDL may not have been composed by the Irish poet, but by a member of the broader coterie or immediate scribal circle of the Dean, as there is evidence elsewhere in the manuscript for accretion of this kind (as we shall see below).

The identity of the authors of love-lyric and the nature of the literary circles that lie behind the compilation is one of the most intriguing aspects of BDL. The manuscript as a whole is extremely diverse in terms of its authors; alongside professional poets (who appear to vary in status), there are clerics (sometimes belonging to the same professional families, sometimes not), and amateurs who belong to the various levels of the aristocracy up to the level of the Earl of Argyll. MacGregor has noted that 'much of the generic sweep, innovation and élan' of the Book's poetry is attributable to these amateurs and that they betray no lack of confidence in what they do.[29] By far the greater number of identifiable poets are male; however, the presence of noble women among the named authors is notable in terms of the pan-Gaelic tradition where ascriptions to women are rare. This is in contrast to the later vernacular tradition in Gaelic Scotland which can boast of some very prominent female poets.

Three poems are attributed in BDL to female members of the Earl of Argyll's immediate family: 'Éistibh, a lucht an tighe-se', ascribed to Iseabal, 'Countess of Argyll' and wife of the first earl, has already been discussed. The other two poems – 'Atá fleasgach ar mo thí' (*'There's a young man in pursuit of me'*) and 'Is mairg dá ngalar an grádh' (*'Woe to the one whose sickness is love'*) – are attributed to Iseabal Ní Mheic Cailéin who some believe may be the first earl's daughter (rather than his wife).[30] Both of these poems are short pieces of three quatrains each and (if the compositions of Isabel the younger) may concern the same man: Aonghus Óg Mac Domhnaill (MacDonald; d. c. 1490), son of the Lord of the Isles, with whom Iseabal had a relationship and by whom she had a son, Domhnall Dubh (d. 1545). It has been suggested that this was not 'a canonically orthodox marriage' but it does seem to have been sanctioned by Argyll at some point.[31] 'Atá fleasgach ar mo thí' would fit better the initial stages of their relationship, perhaps: Iseabal is being pursued by a young man who is currently at sea; their desire is mutual but there are difficulties that lie in the way:

> Atá fleasgach ar mo thí
> a Rí na ríogh go rí leis!
> a bheith sínte ré mo bhroinn
> agus a choim ré mo chneis!
>
> Dá mbeith gach ní mar mo mhian,
> ní bhiadh cian eadrainn go bráth,
> gé beag sin dá chur i gcéill,
> 's nach tuigeann sé féin mar tá.
>
> Acht ní éadtrom gan a luing,
> sgéal as truaighe linn 'nar ndís:
> esan soir is mise siar,
> mar nach dtig ar riar a rís.[32]

> *There's a young man in pursuit of me, O King of Kings, may he have success! Would he were stretched out by my side with his body pressing against my breast!*

> If everything were as I would wish, no distance would ever cause us separation, though that is all too little to say with him not yet knowing the situation.
> But it isn't easy if his ship doesn't come, for the two of us it's a wretched matter: he is East and I am West, so what we desire can never again happen.[33]

The second poem, 'Is mairg dá ngalar an grádh', also suggests that the course of love is not yet running smoothly:

> Is mairg dá ngalar an grádh,
> gé bé fáth fá n-abrainn é;
> deacair sgarachtainn ré pháirt;
> truagh an cás i bhfeilim féin.
>
> An grádh-soin tugas gan fhios,
> ó's é mo leas gan a luadh,
> mara bhfaigh mé furtacht tráth,
> biaidh mo bhláth go tana truagh.
>
> An fear-soin dá dtugas grádh,
> 's nach féadtar a rádh ós n-aird,
> dá gcuireadh sé mise i bpéin,
> gomadh dó féin bhus céad mairg.[34]

> Woe to the one whose sickness is love, no matter the grounds I might present, hard it is to get free of its hold, sorry the state I'm in.
> That love I have given in secret, it being better not to declare it, unless I find relief before long, my bloom will grow wan and wretched.
> That man to whom I have given love, (this should not be said out loud), if he should ever cause me hurt, may he suffer a hundred times the woe.[35]

On one level this second poem is typical of *amour courtois* in that love is portrayed as a sickness that the lover cannot escape and which leaves her in a sorry state (q. 1); if she cannot find relief, she will fade away (q. 2cd). Furthermore, there is a furtive element which is also a commonplace of *amour courtois*: her love is given in secret as it is safer for her not to declare it (qq. 2ab, 3b). In this particular context, however, the use of this trope may reflect the reality of the situation if the man concerned is indeed Aonghus Óg MacDonald; after all, relations between the families of the Earl of Argyll and the Lord of the Isles were often very delicate. For me at least, there is a personal note to the poem: Iseabal has invested in a relationship that is fraught with difficulty. Consequently, should her lover happen to let her down, her wish would be that he should 'suffer a hundred times the woe'. The 'self-possession' of the poet in delivering the 'veiled threat of the final verse' has been noted by others.[36]

A particular criticism that has been levelled at love-lyric more generally, including Gaelic lyric, is the absence of the female voice: usually, the only real person in these poems is male and women are 'lacking in autonomy, character and even name'.[37] Interestingly, we have evidence from Ireland of love poetry being composed on behalf of patrons by professional poets, notably in the case of Cú Chonnacht Óg Mág Uidhir (Maguire, lord of Fermanagh) who employed his poet, Eochaidh Ó hEoghusa, to compose a poem to Brighid, daughter of the Earl of Kildare, in his name: 'Ní mé bhur n-aithne, a aos gráidh' ('*Friends, I am not your acquaintance*').[38] Brighid replied with 'A mhacaoimh dhealbas an dán' ('*O young man who composes the poem*'), a poem that may or may not have been composed by Brighid herself.[39] The relevance of this Irish evidence to us is that it prompts the question as to whether any of the poems ascribed to Campbell and other women in BDL (such as Máire inghean Stiúbhairt and Aithbhreac inghean Corcadail (d. c. 1470)) may not have been composed by them. Indeed, BDL more broadly is of great interest in terms of poetic voice and the attribution of texts to legendary or fictitious 'authors' and so forth.[40] These include a series of poems attributed to another woman, the tenth-century Irish queen Gormfhlaith, which could not have been composed by her,[41] and poems attributed to Earl Gerald of Desmond which may include poems not written by him.[42] Is it possible, therefore, for a poem such as 'Éistibh, a lucht an tighe-se' to have been attributed to the Countess of Argyll in mischief?[43] If so, it is also the case that the Countess may have acquiesced in this when one considers that there is much posturing and game-playing in BDL, particularly as far as the amateur poets are concerned.[44]

Despite evidence for the practice of writing on behalf of individual women, and the general absence of female ascription in Irish love-lyric, the poems ascribed to Scottish women in BDL may well have been composed by them. There is no compelling reason to dismiss the possibility that the voice encountered in the poems 'Atá fleasgach ar mo thí' and 'Is mairg dá ngalar an grádh' is anybody's other than the person to whom they are ascribed: Iseabal Ní Mheic Cailéin. BDL contains five poems in total that are attributed to members of the senior house of Clan Campbell: the three poems by Iseabal (be that one woman or two) that we have just discussed and two poems that are probably both the work of Colin, first Earl of Argyll (d. 1493). The broader context, then, is that of a literary circle or coterie centred upon the court of Argyll and involving members of his family, both male and female. The poem by the Countess, 'Éistibh, a lucht an tighe-se', evokes this court setting in which verse is composed and recited to an audience for recreational purposes. We should also include circulation and reading: Argyll himself may be depicted as a reader of the verse being compiled in BDL in what has been interpreted as the dedicatory poem, 'Duanaire na Sracaire' (*The Songbook of the Pillagers*'). In the context of verse such as ours, there is reason to believe that women may also have had an active role as readers and critics of texts and that, in the process of transmission, they may have served as important conduits of material from external sources.[45]

'Éistibh, a lucht an tighe-se' is directly followed in BDL by 'A shagairt na hamhsóige' ('*Priest with the kept woman(?)*'), a poem by Sir Duncan Campbell of Glenorchy (c. 1443–1513) on a similar theme: the sexual depravity of a priest. Gillies's view of the poem by the Countess is that the 'overriding attitude expressed is one of acclaim rather than censure', and that the two poems together may form 'a sort of *jeu parti* on the same subject'.[46] Nonetheless, Duncan's poem seems to have an edge to it, in my view.[47]

> Dá mbeith leabhair dhiadhachta
> san tigh as gearr dod dhoras,
> d'fhiarfaighidh a n-iasachta
> ní rachthá – <fá> cuid ded dhonas.
>
> An Bíoball bláith, bionnghlórdha,
> dá mbeith agat 's ad chomas,
> is pit fhairsing iomnochta –
> is í do glacfaidhe ar tosach.
>
> Pit óg nō pit airsighthe
> ó nach bhfuil tú 'ga cagailt,
> gach ainspiorad aimsighthe
> go dtí thugat, a shagairt!

If there were theology books in the house next door to you, you would not go to borrow them – part of your evil, this.

> *Suppose you had in your grasp and at your disposal the warm sweet-tongued Bible, and a yawning naked crutch – that is the one that would be seized first.*
> *Young crutch or aged crutch, since you spare none, may every tormenting demon visit you, priest!*[48]

The use of metonymy throughout – there is no mention of 'women', who are consistently referenced by 'pit', the female genitals, in five of six quatrains – is effective in depicting the priest's wantonness as being particularly base. That the poem may not constitute mock-satire may be inferred from the juxtaposing of the priest's lack of commitment to the Bible (and interest in reading religious texts) with his voracious sexual appetite and, also, the fact that the last word on the matter is the poet's cursing of the priest in the final verse.[49]

Six of Duncan Campbell's poems, including 'A shagairt na hamhsóige', may be classified as contributions to love-lyric.[50] In the case of the others, 'Bod bríoghmhor atá ag Donncha' ('*A potent prick has Duncan*'), extends the panegyric mode to praise the prowess of an associate's penis; in 'Teachtaire chuireas i gcéin' ('*I sent a messenger afar*'), the poet reproaches himself for choosing an untrustworthy love messenger; and the other three focus on the denigration of women. 'Atá amhghar fá na mnáibh' ('*Women are fraught with affliction*') is a particularly explicit contribution to the 'argument about women' as it is in the form of a dialogue between two men. The first verse is put in the mouth of the person who offers advice in the matters of courtship and marriage; women are trouble and one must be slow and cautious in dealing with them. The next three quatrains express the concerns of the other party to act appropriately, and the final two constitute the counsellor's response in which he reiterates his original advice: there are few good women in the world ('ní h-iomdha dhíobh atá maith') and they should not be committed to in terms of love until material matters, 'gold and cattle', are settled. Other dialogues in BDL have been noted as 'vehicles' for anti-feminist verse:[51] Argyll's 'A bhean dá dtugas-sa grádh' above; Eóin Mac Muireadhaigh's 'Maith do chuid, a charbaid mhaoil' ('*You are well off, (Mister) Bare Cheek*');[52] and a poem by Ailéin mac Dhubhghaill Bháin, 'Sgéal beag agam ar na mnáibh' ('*I have a little tale about women*'). In the latter, the male party to the debate accuses women of innate infidelity:

> An aoinbhean lérbh annsa a fear
> dá bhfacaidh tú thear nó thiar,

> dh'fhéadte go bhfacaidh 'san lá
> fear nó dhá i mbíodh a mian. (q. 3)

The woman who loved her husband most, of all women you've seen, east or west, it might be that she has seen one man – or two, perhaps – per day that she'd fancy.

The woman counters with professions of eternal devotion: he will find 'no living man to whom I have secretly given my kiss' ('chan fhaighfir éanduine beó/ dá dtug mé mo phóg gan fhios', q. 8cd); and, even in the event of his death, she would remain loyal to him (q. 6). Of all men under the sun, he is the one for her and, were the whole world at her disposal, she would give him half of it (qq. 4–5). Most importantly, she could indeed get better offers although she would of course turn them down:

> Ghéabhainn airgead, ghéabhainn spréidh,
> dá dtugainn mé féin dá chionn;
> ó n-as duit-se bhá mo ghaol
> cha b'fheirrde duine a thaobh riom (q. 9)

I could get money, I could get cattle if I were to give myself for them; (but) since my love was for you, no man would be any the better off for approaching me.

To which the husband replies sarcastically that she would need to have an offer from one or two men infinitely better off than him to be tempted!

> Fiosrach mé ar sin, a bhean,
> go bhfeadhmadh tú fear nó dhó
> ab fhearr ná mise fá chéad,
> dá mbadh áil leat féin dol dóibh. (q. 10)

I'm well aware of this, woman, that you'd need a man – or two – a hundred times better than me – if you yourself would want to go to them![53]

Ailéin mac Dhubhghaill Bháin was quite possibly an associate of Duncan Campbell's, and we should note at this point Campbell's poem 'Mairg ó ndeachaidh a léim lúidh' ('*Woe to him whose vitality has left him*') which regrets his loss of virility. As a consequence of his diminished sexual vigour, he is unable to satisfy his wife and, taking a position that runs counter to that taken by Ailéin mac Dhubhghaill Bháin, one is left with no doubt that, for Duncan Campbell, material wealth is not enough to sustain a woman's interest. The poem concludes with a reference to Gearóid Iarla who had also been ill-used by his wife and appears among the stock example of men who have been ruined by evil women.[54] Further evidence of the influence of Gearóid Iarla upon Duncan Campbell may possibly be deduced from the position of Duncan's poem 'Fada ó mhalluigh Dia na mná' ('*Long ago God cursed women*') in BDL where it forms part of a sequence of poems including one ascribed to the Irish poet.[55]

Duncan Campbell also mentions individuals in his poems from much closer to home, people who undoubtedly formed part of the broader literary and/or social circle in which he was the key figure in Breadalbane. His poem 'Teachtaire chuireas i gcéin' deals in characteristically subversive fashion with the convention of the love messenger,[56] a figure who features more broadly in the courtly love tradition as evidenced in poems by Gearóid Iarla himself.[57] What is interesting here, however, is that this messenger is named as Domhnall Mac an Aba, mostly likely a member of the ruling family of the MacNabs of Glen Dochart, who appears in documents of the period between 1487 and 1513 alongside individuals who played a key role in BDL: Fionnlagh Mac an Aba, head of the kindred, the Dean and his father, and particularly Duncan Campbell himself.[58] Campbell's playful subversion of classical panegyric, 'Bod bríoghmhor atá ag Donncha',[59] a poem that may be considered as an extension of uncourtly or anti-courtly verse, is also noteworthy in this respect:

> Bod bríoghmhor atá ag Donncha,
> fada, féitheach, fíordhorcha,
> reamhar, druimleathan, díreach
> sleamhan, cuirneach, ceirtlíneach.
>
> Cluaisleathan, ceannreamhar, crom,
> go díoghainn, data, dubhghorm;
> atá breall ag an fhleascach,
> is ē ceannsa (?) go conachtach (?).

> Maolshrónach, mallghormtha, glas,
> fuachdha, forránach, fíorchas;
> go cronánach, ceannghorm, cruaidh,
> móirbhéimneach i measc banshluaigh.

A potent prick has Duncan, long, sinewy, truly swarthy, fat, broad-backed, erect, smooth, hornlike, well-swaddled(?).
Wide-eared, fat-headed, crooked, substantial, shapely, blue-black; the stalwart has a gland which is now placid (?) now fretful (?).
Snub-nosed, stately-purple, lissom (?), fearsome, violent, densely matted (?); humming, purple-headed, hard, dealing mighty blows amongst womenfolk.[60]

Elsewhere the poem refers to its subject as Donnchadh Riabhach and a *duncanus reoch* appears alongside our poet as witness to a document that dates to 1503. The evidence points to him being a very close political associate of Duncan Campbell: the *duncanus reouch makgill quhamyll* who was a member of Glenorchy's retinue and that of Colin, first Earl of Argyll, when they took part in the seizure of King James III at Lauder in 1482. The death of one Donnchadh Riabhach MacGille-Chonaill is recorded in 1526 and this may possibly be the individual in question here.[61]

There is an intimate and familiar dimension to the love-lyric in BDL, therefore, not least in the poetry of Duncan Campbell, which is attributable to a considerable degree to the substantial element of coterie verse. Not only do we get an insight into the literary coterie at work in the connections that can be made between individual compositions but we also, on occasion, witness poets passing comment or making reference to fellow poets within the circle. There is a striking example in a poem by Duncan Campbell, 'Cé don Phléid as ceann uidhe' ('*To whom can Disputation turn*'), which satirises another poet Lachlann Mac an Bhreatnaigh, who, if the poem is to be believed, had recently died. A second satire by Duncan on a certain Domhnall Donn, 'Créad dá ndearnadh Domhnall Donn' ('*What is Brown Donald made of*'), follows directly in the manuscript in the same hand, pen and ink. 'Cé don Phléid as ceann uidhe' invites others to add additional verses and Duncan's request did not go unanswered: a quatrain has been added to the bottom of folio 110 in a different hand bemoaning this poem (while expressing delight at the following composition on Domhnall Donn):

> Ionmhain liom dán Domhnaill Duinn,
> ní mholaim marbhnaidh Lochlainn;

mór do mhill a déanamh dhomh:
ní féaghthar linn an laoidh-se.

Brown Donald's poem delights me, (but) I do not praise the elegy for Lachlann; its being composed has destroyed a lot for me; this poem is not expected by us.[62]

This, then, may be the comment of one of the compilers in view of the distinct hand that distinguishes it from the surrounding verse. There is further comment on the poetic output of Duncan Campbell elsewhere. Of the four items in BDL which are ascribed to An Bard Mac an tSaoir,[63] two – 'Créad í an long-sa ar Loch Inse' (*'What ship is this on Loch Inch?'*) and Tánaig long ar Loch Raithneach (*'A ship has come on Loch Rannoch'*) – are intriguing poems in which the poet has a vision of a 'ship of evil women' manned by 'specimens of female wantonness, pride, inconstancy, quarrelsomeness and so on'.[64] Crucially, the second of Mac an tSaoir's poems, 'Tánaig long ar Loch Raithneach', refers to this 'ship of evil women' as the 'ship of Donnchadh mac Cailéin (Duncan son of Colin)':

Tá lán Luicifeir i luing
mheic Cailéin, Donnchaidh dhearccuirr,
ar ghalraighe ar ghnáth ar dhath,
do mhnáibh na ndeárna ndathta.

In the ship of mac Cailéin, round-eyed Duncan, there is a devil's load, for sickliness, for habits, for hue, of women with dyed palms.[65]

In view of the subject matter of these poems and his particular interest in women, this is very likely to be a reference to our Duncan of Glenorchy,[66] who succeeded his father Colin, first Lord of Glenorchy, in 1475, according to the Chronicle contained in BDL.[67] The dates fit: we know that An Bard Mac an tSaoir became attached to the Clan Macintosh not long after 1493,[68] which confirms that he was contemporary with Duncan of Glenorchy. This verse, then, suggests that An Bard Mac an tSaoir was familiar with Duncan Campbell's misogynist verse on the theme of women, and that he may have been a member of the coterie that was led by Campbell. We should add that there is an intriguing record of payment by King James IV to Duncan Campbell's 'bard' while visiting this part of the Highlands in 1506.[69] The bard is unnamed but it has been suggested that he may have been one of the Clann Mhic Eoghain, the

MacEwans who served as professional poets to the Campbells.[70] However, it may be that Duncan Campbell, as Lord of Glenorchy, employed a member of a different family of professional poets and that he entertained the king on this occasion. It is also possible that the 'bard' who entertained the king may not have served Duncan Campbell in a traditional capacity but may have been simply one of a number of poets which constituted his coterie. Either way, it is possible to imagine that Mac an tSaoir himself may even have been the unnamed bard in question.

Duncan Campbell is the pivotal figure in the literary circles that lie behind the production of BDL. As author of nine poems himself, he is the most prolific Scottish poet in the manuscript; Gillies notes his linguistic and technical competence, and his 'confident and recognisable "voice".[71] Significantly, he appears to link all of the major parties – poets, clergy and aristocracy – that have contributed lyrics to the collection. A close ally and first cousin of Colin, Earl of Argyll, Duncan is also believed to have been a nephew of Colin's wife, the Countess (as his mother is most likely to have been Janet Stewart, Isabel's sister).[72] We have seen that the Countess's poem 'Éistibh, a lucht an tighe-se' is immediately followed in BDL by Duncan's 'A shagairt na hamhsóige', and that the two poems are linked thematically. Isabel's poem, in extolling the sexual prowess of her personal chaplain, is also important as evidence for the inclusion of clergy in the coterie, whether as poets or the subjects of poetry. It has been suggested that household chaplains may have been key figures within the coterie; we might note, at this point, 'Tuig [gura?] feargach an t-éad' ('*Know that jealousy is ferocious*') by Sir Donnchadh Mac Diarmaid, a man described elsewhere as a chaplain, possibly with reference to the household of Glenorchy rather than that of the Earl.[73]

The intimacy and extent of the coterie is further illustrated by a composition such as 'Mairg bean nach bí ag éansagart' ('*Woe to the woman whom no priest possesses*') by the Dean of Lismore's brother, the poet and scribe Donnchadh Mac Griogóir, which alludes to the sexual excesses of the clergy, including deans![74] Not only does the theme and tone connect this poem to others by the Countess of Argyll and Duncan of Glenorchy; we should recall that it was through the patronage either of the Earl of Argyll or the Campbells of Glenorchy that Séamas Mac Griogóir was appointed to the deanery of Lismore, and it was as chaplains that both he and his son, Dubhghall, witnessed the will of Eóin Campbell of Glenorchy in 1550.[75] It is undoubtedly the case, therefore, that the MacGregors were included in the coterie in which their lord, Duncan

Campbell, played a central role. The coterie's particular interest in women constitutes a 'running debate' among members of the Dean of Lismore's and broader Campbell circles, some of whom have been identified as associates of the MacGregors and Campbells in other contexts.[76] BDL includes not only formal and more sustained compositions on the theme but also short epigrams in the form of isolated couplets and quatrains to women or on women which have been described as 'mostly scurrilous sallies at the expense of local worthies of the Dean of Lismore's day, their wives and daughters'.[77]

The two poems by An Bard Mac an tSaoir prompt us to consider the issue of the origins of love-lyric in BDL and of external influence upon the genre. Although they are formally (and, in some respects, thematically) very different, it has been suggested that Sebastian Brant's *Das Narrenschiff*, 'The Ship of Fools', first printed in German at Basle in 1494, may have served as the inspiration for the poems by Mac an tSaoir. A Latin version appeared in print in 1497 while two English versions were published in 1509. Brant's former pupil, Jodocus Badius Ascensius, responded to his master's work with his own *Navicula stultarum mulierum* ('Little Ship of Foolish Women') c. 1500 which, despite the title, does not bear close comparison with our poems. However, as Gillies has argued, 'even a fleeting exposure to the idea of a Ship of Foolish Women could have been the germ that inspired a response' from our bard.[78] In any case, we know that the Campbells were collectors of both English and European literary texts at this time and that literary contact with the continent could have facilitated the transmission of texts to at least parts of the Scottish Highlands reasonably quickly.[79]

Gillies points out elsewhere in this volume that Highland gentry attended universities in the Lowlands and had external and overseas contact through military service, and ecclesiastical, legal and commercial business; this, obviously, would have brought them into contact with other literatures.[80] We have noted the presence of material not just in Latin but also in Scots and English in BDL. The manuscript contains two stanzas taken from the English poet John Lydgate's treatment of Samson and Delilah in *The Fall of Princes*. It also contains two stanzas from the poem generally known as the *Ballate aganis Evill Women*, which it attributes to Chaucer (but which is actually in Scots and is sometimes attributed to Dunbar). This raises interesting questions about the networks in which the compilers of BDL participated, not least because of the fact that it contains what may be the earliest extant witness of two Scots texts: the

Ballate aganis Evill Women, and a single stanza from Robert Henryson's *Testament of Cresseid*, which begins 'Luffaris, be war and tak gwd heid about'. The manuscript also contains an anonymous and unidentified quatrain beginning 'Gyf that zor wyf be deid' and an anonymous version of part of Juvenal's sixth satire beginning 'Quhat alyt ye man to ved a vyff'.[81] This material is clearly not significant in terms of volume; its real significance lies in the fact that it contributes to one of BDL's prominent themes. MacGregor has remarked that it is 'blatantly obvious' that the compilers were 'single-mindedly targeting texts' on the 'argument about women' whether for personal gratification or for the benefit of the literary circles that lie behind the compilation.[82]

The other great theme in BDL, the kingship of the Scots, also provides evidence for networks that extend to and include the Lowlands. Material copied from John Bellenden's translation of Hector Boece's *Scotorum Historia* (or perhaps taken directly from Boece's original) and the presence of other unidentified sources has also been noted in the manuscript and some of these sources may have become available to the compilers through their connections with Perth and Dunkeld or, indeed, by virtue of contact with Boece himself as he was closely connected to the Campbells. As to more general similarities with contemporary manuscript anthologies in the Lowlands, and the possibility of influence in that respect, consideration has been given to the Asloan Manuscript. John Asloan was a notary public, like Séamas MacGregor and his father, and MacGregor has noted that the manuscript's subject matter is reminiscent of BDL in some respects, 'in its melding of literature and history [...], in a shared fondness for instructional and devotional exempla, and in the occurrence of specimens of misogynist literature'. However, BDL differs greatly from this compilation too, particularly in terms of its presentation of texts, and MacGregor has described it as 'anarchic and chaotic' by comparison.[83] Furthermore, the Asloan Manuscript does not have a great amount of lyric among its contents and he also seems to copy a substantial part of his material from print.

On the other hand, BDL is also distinctive in the pan-Gaelic context in that it extends the parameters of classical verse (within and beyond the genre of love-lyric) to include compositions on topics which appear not to be witnessed in the Irish corpus (despite that corpus being much larger). As well as poems which resemble in every respect the bulk of the Irish collection assembled in O'Rahilly's *Dánta Grádha*,[84] there are aspects of the corpus in BDL that find no or few parallels in Irish tradition.

There is the possibility that compositions on the more bawdy end of the spectrum (such 'Bod bríoghmhor atá ag Donncha' and 'A shagairt na hamhsóige') were to be had in Ireland also but that they have yet to be unearthed in our surviving manuscripts. Alternatively, it could be argued that poems of this kind were lost at some stage of transmission from the late medieval period to the nineteenth century when the manuscript tradition in Ireland came to an end. Equally, differences between the Irish and the Scottish literary traditions as evidenced in BDL might occasionally point to influences from the Lowlands and beyond; the potential evidence of Mac an tSaoir's poems is certainly instructive in that regard. However, we always have to reckon with the intimate nature of the compilation process which has produced BDL – the 'insider's view of the literary tradition that *The Book* provides for us', as Gillies puts it – as the uniqueness of the manuscript may owe much more to this than to any external influence.[85]

We have a fascinating collection of Gaelic love-lyric in BDL (of Scottish and Irish provenance) – with further snippets from the Scots and English traditions, and some examples in Latin – which indicates that its compilers were open to, and in touch with, the world well beyond Perthshire. Nonetheless, it is primarily a Gaelic collection which may be linked in particular with literary circles centred upon the courts of the Earl of Argyll and the Campbells of Glenorchy. These circles were comprised of aristocrats, clergy and professional poets, and included the Dean and other members of his family. Their members were mostly men, but the contribution of verse by women belonging to the senior branch of Clan Campbell (possibly both the wife and daughter of Colin, first Earl of Argyll) is also a distinguishing feature of the manuscript. Although the Earl of Argyll is also a contributor, it is his cousin, Sir Duncan Campbell of Glenorchy, who is the driving force; while our love-lyrics may have been the product of two interconnected coteries, it was the hub in Breadalbane rather than Inveraray that took the lead and made the greater contribution in terms of BDL as we now find it. This should not surprise us; as the Earl of Argyll had many calls on his time, both on the local and national stages, it may have been easier to leave the task of taking the initiative in terms of literary activity in the capable hands of his cousin and his associates.

The male members of these circles do not focus exclusively, or even primarily, on poems of courtly love or love of any kind: rather, they had a particular interest in conversing about the 'nature' of women, a conversation which was misogynist and characterised by sexual explicitness. They composed for their own amusement and at the expense of people who appear to be well-known to them, including members of the clergy who are charged with sexual licentiousness; this is particularly interesting when considered in the context of the compilers, the Dean and other members of his family, who were part of the ecclesiastical establishment. The catholicity of the compilers in terms of taste has been often commented upon; their sense of humour (and that of the literary circles on which they drew) reflects an attitude towards those who are satirised within BDL which is not so much one of reprehension but, as MacGregor observes, of 'indulgence and affection, aimed at those within the circle or known to it'.[86]

Although most datable examples of Irish love-lyric seem to be rather later than those in BDL,[87] Gillies had doubted the possibility (when he first directed our attention to this subject) that the emergence of Gaelic love-lyrics in Scotland and Ireland could have been the result of entirely independent developments. Noting that 'our poems show eccentricities – judged from a continental standpoint – otherwise confined to the *dánta grádha* alone', he concluded that the most likely hypothesis is that 'these *dánta grádha* came to Scotland through the agency of the poetic order – through Scottish poets training in Irish seminaries and Irish poets visiting Scottish patrons and colleagues on their circuits'.[88] More recently, he has stressed that 'the features that make Gaelic manifestations of *amour courtois* distinctive [...] relate in one way or another to the Gaelic learned orders, especially the learned poets' and the evidence for this is extremely strong.[89] One might add that as these learned orders operated on a pan-Gaelic level, we may need to be open to the possibility that elements of the tradition of love lyric as we find it in our *dánta grádha* may owe something to Scottish initiative and that some of these could have been introduced to Ireland from Scotland 'through the agency of the poetic order' (to paraphrase Gillies). This would not be incompatible with the dating horizon for Gaelic love-lyric, i.e. that a large number of the earliest examples (including the earliest examples by professional poets) are preserved in Scottish rather than Irish sources.[90]

The circumstances in which a genre may emerge may not be the same as those in which it subsequently develops. While I find myself cleaving to the view that Gaelic love-lyrics in Scotland and Ireland have shared origins, this is not to say that poems composed in either country could not have been influenced by contact with other literatures.[91] In the case of BDL, we have seen that the excerpts of poetry derived from and recorded in other languages resonate with the Gaelic corpus of love-lyric in that the misogynist voice is dominant. The prospect that these non-Gaelic texts may have provided inspiration for some of BDL's Gaelic poetry cannot be discounted. Influence need not always involve an external source acting as an actual model for a particular poem; it could be the case, rather, that external influence served as a catalyst that inspired experimentation with aspects of the native tradition or indeed, transformation of native sensibilities in terms of what was 'acceptable' love-lyric.[92] I am thinking here, in particular, of the explicit and subversive element of those lyrics preserved in BDL that are encountered very rarely or not at all in Irish tradition. Furthermore, we should recall that those members of Clan Campbell who played a leading role in the coteries which can be discerned in the background to the compilation of BDL were people who partook of an aristocratic worldview that they shared with their counterparts elsewhere (irrespective of ethnic differences and linguistic boundaries); this must have had an impact on literary taste.

Having acknowledged all of that, the amount of non-Gaelic verse contained in BDL is very small relative to the total amount of poetry that is preserved in the Book and, in most cases, involves no more than snippets; these could have been recalled from memory and derived from reading or recitation by members of the literary circles who lie behind the compilation of BDL. Furthermore, the possibility of Scots verse, for example, influencing (in some ways) the corpus of Gaelic lyric does not necessitate deep familiarity with the Scots lyric tradition on the part of all the compilers or members of the literary circles involved in the production of BDL. It is important to recall that when the single most important author of love-lyric in BDL, Sir Duncan Campbell, provides evidence of the influence of other poets, it is to Ireland (and not Lowland Scotland) that our attention is directed. We have seen that the only discernible influence on him was the poetry attributed (whether correctly or not) to the Earl of Desmond, Gearóid Iarla; there is a real possibility that some of this verse was deliberately targeted and sourced from Ireland,[93] and that it circulated more widely in Breadalbane (as witnessed in the case of poetry composed by another member of the local gentry, Fearchar Grant).[94] One is left with an impression of Gaelic love-lyric that is largely self-referential in terms of how it presents and positions itself, despite the possibility of other currents under the surface.[95]

Mícheál B. Ó Mainnín

Older Scots Lyric

Lyric is the most ephemeral of medieval literary genres: its frequent anonymity, its shorter form and its close association with music did not appear to encourage its formal record.[96] This is possibly truer of lyrics in Older Scots than it is in Middle English, for while in addition to the ones scribbled on manuscript flyleaves or inserted in blank pages, there are also a few significant English collections, such as the Harley manuscript where a body of anonymous work has been brought together.[97] In Older Scots, no such early collections survive, and indeed there is very little material evidence of the circulation of lyric in Scotland prior to the sixteenth century. Yet lyrics of all kinds must have been well known. For instance, in discussing the Wars of Independence, both Barbour and Wyntoun allude to a much older piece of lyric writing, 'Quhen Alexander the king was deid', in such a way to suggest a familiarity among their audience.[98] Similarly, embedded in *The Buke of the Howlat* is a vernacular hymn to the Virgin Mary, clearly evoking other lyrics that Holland and his audience already knew.[99] Moreover, even allowing for the absurd improbability that there was no lyric composed in Older Scots between the death of Alexander III and the enthronement of James IV, poets like Holland, Dunbar and Henryson would have encountered lyric in English as well as in French and especially Latin. While the nature of lyric, namely its comparative brevity, its connection to music, song and dance, and its presentation of a viewpoint with which the reader might easily identify, make it ephemeral, those features also allow it to travel freely and circulate widely.

By the beginning of the sixteenth century, however, substantial witnesses to Older Scots lyric begin to appear. For instance, the manuscript containing the *Kingis Quair* contains a few (late fifteenth and early sixteenth century), as do the Makculloch (c. 1477) and Asloan (c. 1515–25) manuscripts, among others.[100] The larger collections, however, are from later in the century: the Bannatyne Manuscript (c. 1568) and the Maitland Folio (c. 1570–c. 1585) and Quarto (c. 1586).[101] These are not the manuscripts of aristocrats, but of burgesses and royal servants: to quote Alasdair MacDonald, 'it is somewhat alarming to realise how much the modern notion of the Middle Scots literary corpus has been conditioned by the preferences of just three families of Edinburgh lawyers'.[102] These are the manuscripts that contain most of Dunbar's lyrics, as well as those by Richard Maitland himself, and other poets of the court, both minor, such as George Clappertoun, and major, such as Alexander Scott, as well as the extensive oeuvre of Anonymous. The range of lyric contained in these witnesses, as well as the religious lyrics and *contrafacta* associated with the Reformation demonstrate the wealth of material written and read by Older Scots poets.

Because of the lack of early evidence, however, a description of Older Scots lyric almost inevitably begins with William Dunbar (1460?–1513x1530).[103] Dunbar's virtuosity and variety is another indication that the forms and techniques of lyric were well known in late fifteenth-century Scotland: although his predecessor, Robert Henryson, also demonstrates mastery over the shorter form, Dunbar takes lyric to new heights. He plays elaborately with form to deal with themes religious and secular, and topics eternal and occasional. 'Haile sterne superne', for instance, is a pinnacle of aureation.[104] This quatrain demonstrates the sheer abundance of rhetorical features:

> Haile, bricht be sicht in hevyn on hicht,
>   Haile, day sterne orientale,
> Our licht most richt in clud of nycht,
>   Our dirknes for to scale.[105]

The internal rhyme on <-icht> stresses the power of light both by association (*bricht, sicht, licht*) and by contrast (*bricht* and *nicht*). A similar contrast is also indicated by the repeated beginning of 'our' in 27–28, followed by 'licht' and 'dirknes'. The complex grammar of the single sentence marks out the high register of the poem, as does the use of 'orientale' (26). Such features are replicated across the eighty-four lines of the poem, appropriate as a hymn to the Virgin. Yet for all his gifts with ornateness, sometimes Dunbar makes the greatest mark with simple form. For instance, his lyric 'My heid did ȝak ȝester nicht' reserves its punch for the metafictional conceit of apologising for not writing a poem by writing a poem.[106] The excuse given is a headache, whose impact is measured by alliteration ('scant I luik may on the licht'(5), 'Dullit in dulnes and distress' (10)). Similarly, although 'I that in heill wes and gladnes' gets much of its power from the repetition of the refrain *Timor mortis conturbat me* at the end of every four-line ballad stanza, that power may be as much ironically concerned with the speaker's living literary reputation as it is with his fear of corporeal death.[107]

Moreover, for the first time in Older Scots, we have in Dunbar a poet whose lyrics can be unambiguously located within the royal court:[108] in some poems, he addresses specifically a court audience, and locates himself in that milieu by means of direct reference. The poems concerned with Sir James Doig, the queen's wardrober, for instance, locate Dunbar in the queen's circle. This can be a matter of occasional humour: in 'Sir Jhon Sinclair begowthe to dance', we must assume that the audience would recognise 'dame Dounteboir' (36) as much as they would enjoy Dunbar's self-presentation as a 'pillie wanton' (25), and that licence was given to the poet to tease Sir James Doig, either by the queen or by Doig himself, in 'The wardraipper of Wenus boure' and 'O gracious princes guid and fair'.[109] As in the case of the poems in the Book of the Dean of Lismore outlined in the other half of this chapter, here too we are conscious that we cannot always recreate the precise context of a given lyric and need to make a best guess.

The next great Scottish poet of the court, Sir David Lyndsay (c. 1486–1555), is less known for his lyric than for his longer pieces. However, works such as 'The Answer to the Kingis Flyting' and 'The Deploratioun of the Deith of Quene Magdalene' fit the definition, at least in their stanzaic form and their presentation as emotional response.[110] In its two hundred lines, 'The Deploratioun' not only presents a formal lament for the death of the new queen, through the expected classical references and accusations against Fortune and Nature, but also outlines the loss to the body politic through a description of the Edinburgh entry planned for Magdalene before she died. 'The Answer to the Kingis Flyting' presents Lyndsay as having a much more personal (albeit carefully negotiated) relationship with his sovereign than any of Dunbar's poetry. Ostensibly a response to a composition by the king mocking Lyndsay for impotence, the poem challenges the king's licentiousness in direct language and obscene images.[111] At the same time, Lyndsay denies his own poetic attainment ('Wer I ane poeit'(15)), instead identifying James as 'of flowand rhethorik the flour' (70); indeed, Lyndsay insists that he only writes in response to James's order (22–24). The lyric thus explores the complicated nature of royal counsel, and the relationship between moral and political authority, while embodying the comedy of an extremely low register.

Although Lyndsay dominates the poetry of the court of James V, other, less familiar, poets there include John Bellenden (c. 1495–1545x8), George Clappertoun (d. 1574) and William Stewart (fl. 1499–1541).[112] As writers of lyric, they are competent: generally, they deal with traditional tropes, without Dunbar's distinctiveness or Wyatt's wit. For instance, the poem attributed to Clappertoun in the Maitland Folio, 'In bowdoun on blak monunday', can be described as a *chanson de mal mariée*, comparable in subject to Dunbar's *Tretise of the Tua Mariit Wemen and the Wedo*.[113] The narrator overhears a young woman lamenting her marriage to 'ane schrew/ quhilk dow nothing of chalmer glew' (26–27), and wishing either for death or, more extensively, for a widowhood in which she could be 'ane wantoun' (37). The refrain is 'way worth maryage for evirmair'. There is nothing to differentiate this female voice from any others: she is interested in sex, clothes and sovereignty in her choice of lovers ('I suld luif þame þat wald luif me' (47)), but there is little depth. As it happens, it is followed in the Maitland Folio by an anonymous poem presenting 'ane heynd cheild' lamenting his marriage, 'God gif I wer wedo now'. His complaint is that 'Off sturtsumnes scho has no peir', namely that she is quarrelsome.[114] In neither of these poems do the women come off particularly well, nor are they presented with individualised complaints; the lyrics themselves are perfectly competent but not striking.

As well as owning the Folio, Richard Maitland (1496–1586) himself was a prolific lyric poet and his writing life extended into Mary's reign. The majority of his works are preserved in the Maitland Folio and the Maitland Quarto; the Folio particularly is also an important witness for Dunbar, as well as lyrics from the court of James V. Maitland's concerns focus on living the good life, government and surviving at court, rather than love. Such poems as 'My sone in court gif thow pleisis remane' and 'Ground þe ay on gudnes' are clearly poems of moral advice, generic enough in content, even though the first is ostensibly addressed to one of Maitland's sons.[115] The situation of court life is of course also considered by Maitland's English contemporaries, Thomas Wyatt and Henry Howard, Earl of Surrey.[116] The concerns are similar, dealing with flattery, gambling, true friendship as well as serving God and the prince, in a profoundly uncertain and unpredictable environment. Wider political laments can be found in 'At moirning in ane garding grene' and 'ȝe nobilliz all þat sould þis cuntrie gyd'.[117] The former takes the trope of the pleasant garden and the isolated speaker, more familiar from love poetry and deploys it in a consideration of the state of Scotland: the poem invokes God rather than Cupid or Venus, saves its 'petie' for the 'pure commounis' (19–20), and identifies 'the grittest caus of þis discord/ [as] for our synnis pvneisment' (46–47). The lyric ultimately argues that political resolution lies in compromise between factions, and where the nobles will put the realm (or the commonweal, as Maitland might have described it) before individual interests. A similar argument can be found in 'ȝe nobilliz all þat sould þis cuntrie gyd'. Such a view is idealistic, traditional and long-lasting: when George Buchanan describes his opponents as 'Machiavel mokkers', he does not mean it as a compliment.[118]

Good government and a peaceful realm are not simply bureaucratic concerns, however, for we can compare Maitland's address to the new queen Mary, with that of Alexander Scott (c. 1520–1582/3), a musician of the Chapel Royal, and a better poet than Maitland.[119] In Maitland's poem, 'Off the Quenis Arryvale in Scotland', there is evident the same kind of negotiation regarding counsel that is evident in Lyndsay:[120] Maitland is the mature royal servant attempting both to advise the new queen but also to retain his own position. The poem begins with general statements of hope for the new rule:

> Now sen thow art arryvit in this land
> Our native princes and Illustir queen
> I traist to God this regioun sall stand
> Ane auld fre realme as it lang tyme hes bein
> Quairin richt sone thair sall be hard and sein
> Grit joy, justice, gude peax and policie,
> All cair and cummar banist quyt and clein
> And ilk man leif in gude tranquillitie. (9-16)

Explicit is the hope for an independent realm, in this case as much from France as from England, and the twin duties of monarch, peace and justice. At the heart of the stanza, Maitland plays with time, contrasting 'auld' and 'lang tyme' of history with the 'richt sone' of new government. Maitland goes on to assert the value of reliable counsel (25–32), and then concludes with his own qualifications ('I wes trew servand to thy mother' (49)). The last stanza contrasts his actual physical blindness with his prayer that he 'heir thy peple with hie voce/ […] cry continewlie/ 'Viva Marie trenobill royne de escois' (62–5). This contrast is notable in comparison to the pairing of 'hard and sein' above (13), emphasising the totality of Maitland's 'national' hope compared to his personal experience.

Scott's poem, 'Ane New Yeir's Gift to the Quene Marie, quhen scho come first home 1562', covers similar ground.[121] Scott also identifies a longing for 'peax tranquillitie and rest' (10), and raises the issue of royal marriage, for instance (185–192). In the line 'Still on þe common weill haif E and eir' (38), Scott evokes the same totality of experience found in Maitland's poem, but he attributes it proactively to the sovereign, rather than reactively to the realm and counsellor. This is in line with Scott's general presentation of Mary as an active agent in her own right, for the poem opens with the unequivocal attribution of Scottish royal symbols to Mary ('oure Lyoune', 'oure thrissill' (2-3)) alongside the gendered 'quene', 'genetryce' and 'princes' (1, 5, 7). Maitland, in contrast, uses only 'princes' and 'quene' (1, 3, 9). In addition, Scott's is also more formally ornate, evoking perhaps Dunbar's 'Quhen Merche wes with variand windis past' (*The Thrissil and the Rois*). There is consistent alliteration, used, for instance, to link the different estates into a whole: 'barron clerk and burges' (164), 'majestratis [...] merchandis [...] mechanikis' (172-74). There is one striking image, comparing true Christians to bees and 'reprobatis' to wasps (105-109), whereas Maitland's poem is devoid of conscious metaphor. Overall, through its techniques, Scott's piece manages to convey its concerns without the delicate negotiation of the relationship between speaker and recipient that underlies Maitland's presentation.

Scott's other lyrics deal with love, anticipatory, fulfilled and disappointment; his work also includes some psalm translations.[122] All of his poems are preserved in the Bannatyne Manuscript, and the evidence indicates that Scott was known to the family.[123] As a result, some of Bannatyne's colophons for the lyrics, such as 'Quod Scott quhen his wyfe left him' offer tantalising biographical clues.[124] Whether or not that is the case, for the poem is by no means as specific to people or to situations as the colophon suggests, 'To luve unluvit it is ane pane' demonstrates Scott's skill both in the formal elements of metre and rhyme as well as a conciseness in expression. Each of the five stanzas has five lines, and ends with a variant of the refrain '[...] brekis my hert and nocht the bettir'; consistently, 'bettir' is rhymed with 'hir', both stressing the speaker's happier state with her, and also her place his love object. Only once, in the opening stanza, is 'scho', the subject pronoun used, and even there, she is rapidly translated into 'hir', manipulated by 'some wantoun man' (2-3): she may escape blame in her vulnerability, but also lacks agency. Like many lyrics, therefore, the interest lies entirely with the experience of the voice of the speaker: the other party is silent. Scott moves from general observations about love to the specific experience of the speaker ('and now I leif in pain and woe'(14)) and concludes with more cynical general views ('gude luve cumis as gais'(22)). Embedded in the simple expression is bitter emotion, including self-condemnation ('Quhattane a glaikit fule am I' (16)); despite the bravado of the last stanzas, the conclusion ('God give him dolour and diseiss/ that brekis thair heart and nocht the bettir' (24-25)) allows both a curse on the seducer and on the betrayed.

Scott and Maitland continued writing into Mary's personal reign and possibly beyond.[125] However, in contrast to her father and her son,

Mary does not have close associations with Older Scots poetry.[126] Instead, on the one hand, George Buchanan (1506–1582), famous across Europe for his Latin poetry, was a notable court presence until the murder of Darnley in 1567; on the other hand, the most explosive lyric collection associated with her court devoted is the Casket Sonnets, which was originally written in French, although translated into Scots to serve a directly political purpose.[127] The question of authorship of the Casket Sonnets is highly vexed, and not soluble in this essay. This is in part because of their impressive deployment of Petrarchan tropes, both to claim and to undermine female sovereignty of the body, the moral will and the realm.[128] They are highly sophisticated pieces of work for a highly sophisticated audience, familiar with poetic ventriloquism as well as the formation of the lyric subject.

Mary was not the only Scottish woman to whom poems might be ascribed:[129] the Maitland Quarto appears to preserve sophisticated lyrics that allude to Marie Maitland (d. 1596), Richard's daughter, as a poet.[130] Since Marie Maitland is quite possibly the main scribe of the manuscript and since the collection is largely concerned with poems composed in or associated with the Maitland family circle, it is entirely possible that she included some of her own work, even though none are attributed to her. Poem 85 is particularly concerned with female poetic confidence.[131] Entitled 'To Your Self', it associates Maitland with Sappho and Olimpia, 'O lamp of Latin land', probably Olimpia Morata, a contemporary Protestant convert and poet.[132] Its theme is to encourage Maitland in her own poetry and 'the laurell win/ Adorn'd with cumlie croun of poesie' (15–16). The choice of comparators demonstrates confident familiarity with classical (albeit as much by reputation as by reading in Greek) and contemporary poetry, and a sense of self-worth. Although there survive a few other poems known to be by women from the late sixteenth century (there are most probably more amongst the collections of anonymous works), more significant work appeared in the seventeenth. In particular, Anna Hume's (fl. 1644) *Triumphs*, a translation of Petrarch's *Trionfi*, stands out: not only was it the first printed secular book by a Scottish woman, its precision and particular inflections of Petrarchan tropes bear closer inspection.[133] Her consciousness of translation and her self-presentation as a poet are shown in her verse to the reader at the beginning of the work:

> Reader, I have oft been told,
> Verse that speake not Love, are cold.

> I would gladly please thine eare,
> But am loth to buy 't too deare.
> And 'tis easier farre to borrow
> Lovers tears, then feel their sorrow.
> Therefore he hath furnish't me,
> Who had enough to serve all three.[134]

This stanza emphasises the vicariousness of the experience described in the poetry that follows: given her innovation in print, such attribution of experience to Petrarch and her understanding of the importance of love to poetry to unnamed authorities allows her to maintain a degree of feminine modesty. The writer is merely a conduit.

The printing of Hume's work illustrates the growing importance of print to the transmission of lyric. Although there is no Scottish equivalent of *Tottel's Miscellany* (although it has been argued that the Bannatyne Manuscript was intended as a copy-text for a printed collection)[135] more lyric, particularly satirical and religious works, can be found in printed collections. For instance, the collection known as the *Gude and Godlie Ballatis*, first printed in 1565, not only contained Older Scots versions of Lutheran hymns, but also psalm translations and numerous *contrafacta*, where popular secular lyrics were rewritten as religious pieces to enable wide transmission.[136] Factional, or satirical, lyric, printed on broadsides, also circulated. Many of these poems are attributed to Robert Sempill (d. 1595?), and deal directly with contemporary political circumstances.[137] That they served a useful propaganda purpose, like the religious *contrafacta*, suggests a sophisticated audience for lyric, able to marry form and content.

James VI's assumption of power in the 1580s has been associated with an increase in court poetry and lyric in particular.[138] James himself wrote a guide to the writing of poetry, *Ane Schort Treatise Conteining Some Reulis and Cautelis to be Observit and Eschewit in Scottis Poesie*, and illustrated it with his own work as well as the work of Alexander Montgomerie, his 'maister poet' (early 1550s–1598).[139] Like Dunbar, Montgomerie wrote occasional verse, and poems in praise of his sovereign, such as *In praise of his Majestie*, which uses classical references to the muses, Caesar and Minerva to praise James' acumen and martial courage.[140] More telling of Montgomerie's view of James, however, may be a line from *In praise of Maister John Maitland chanceller*, 'A Cunning King a Cunning Chancellor chuisis' (8).[141] In his poems regarding the failure of his pension, however, Montgomerie constructs a relationship with James more akin to Lyndsay's with James V, than Dunbar's with James IV.[142] The short sequences such as *To his Majestie for his Pensioun* and *To Robert Hudsone*, refer to shared experience and former affection.[143] The sequence to Hudsone is particularly evocative of shared poetic practice, as Montgomerie associates himself with 'old Scot and Robert Semple' and recalls 'Hou I chaist Polwart from the chimney nook'.[144] While these sonnets present a projection of Montgomerie's own voice and experience, his other poems are not necessarily so personal. Some of his work is ventriloquism:[145] this might well apply to the poem attributed to Christian Lyndsay, but also to such pieces as 'James Lauder I wald se mare' and 'Issobell yong by loving so', occasional sonnets for a bride and groom, and *The Ladyis Lamentatioune*, a short sequence reflecting a female repentance for an unspecified sexual offence.[146] Love, both human and divine, is the subject of many of Montgomerie's poems: one in particular, 'Come my children deir drau neir me', with its central conceit of marriage with Christ, seems strikingly to presage the tone of George Herbert's devotional verse.[147]

Montgomerie is one of several notable poets of the Scottish Jacobean court. While there may be some doubt as to whether James engineered a Castalian Band, nevertheless lyric poetry, including that by the king himself, is a significant feature of his Scottish rule.[148] It was certainly outward-facing, for as well as James himself, poets such as John Stewart of Baldynneis (c. 1545–c. 1605) and William Fowler (1560/61–1612), as well as Montgomerie, translated and reworked French and (in Fowler's case) Italian lyrics into Older Scots.[149] While Fowler took on the challenge of an Italianate sonnet sequence, Stewart experimented with formal innovations, including 'Ane Literall Sonnet', where each line alliterates (e.g. 'Dull dolour dalie dois delyt destroy').[150] Such experimentation is typical of the Scots poets of these decades, in part inspired by their engagement with contemporary European as much if not more than English literature, and in part domesticating that engagement in response to traditions in Older Scots.

Like Robert Aytoun (1570–1638) and William Alexander (1577–1640), William Fowler went south with James, and thereafter appears to write in English as much as in Scots.[151] Appearances can be deceptive, however: Aytoun's poem 'On the Tweed', contains one rhyme that only works in Scots, appropriate to a sonnet concerned with the annihilation of Scottish identity.[152] Other lesser-known poets also considered the Union of the Crowns but also address other topics:[153] one striking collection by Alexander Craig of Rosecraig (1567?–1627) directs sonnets to ten female figures, exploring different forms of love.[154] Even under James, however, the court did not preserve a stranglehold on lyric writing. Religious lyric continued in the work of James Melville (1556–1614) and, a little earlier, Alexander Arbuthnot (1538–1583);[155] Alexander Hume (c. 1557–1609), a younger brother of Montgomerie's alleged rival, Patrick Hume of Polwarth, attempted Protestant aesthetics in 'Of the Day Estivall'. What these might be can be illustrated by the opening stanzas:

> O perfite light, quhilk schaid away
> The darkenes from the light,
> And set a ruler ou'r the day,
> Ane uther ou'r the night;
>
> Thy glorie when the day foorth flies
> Mair vively dois appeare
> Nor at midday unto our eyes
> The shining sun is cleare.[156]

As throughout the poem, nature is here seen as a witness for God, His rule and His benignity; that dawn is more glorious than noon implies the difficulties of facing God directly, as well as the relief at the end of night. Both the form – cross-rhymed quatrains – and the lexis is straightforward, a middle style, and the metaphors are consistent and arise from the experience of a summer day.

Hume's poetry speaks to an audience of the pious and the literate, including those of middling rank as well as those with connections to court and government. Other work suggests other audiences. The great Latin collection, *Delitiae Poetarum Scotorum*, compiled in Aberdeen by Arthur Johnston (c. 1579–1641) and others, addresses a more educated audience, both in Scotland and beyond;[157] William Drummond (1585–1649) also found an audience beyond Scotland's border, as well as a more local one presumably overlapping Alexander Hume's or Arthur Johnston's. Like his predecessors at the Scottish Jacobean court, Drummond was also engaged with European writing, including Petrarch's.[158] His most famous work, the sonnet sequence, *Poems*, including songs and madrigals as well as sonnets, is closely modelled on Petrarch and wrestles with the purposes of writing as well as love.[159] In addition, he wrote a devotional sequence *Flowres of Sion*, memorial verse and other madrigals, as well as verse not formally lyric such as *Tears of the Death of Moeliades* and *Forth Feasting*.[160]

Modern anthologies of Scottish verse tend not to include a large number of seventeenth-century lyrics after Drummond. As is the case with the fifteenth century, it is unlikely that this absence reflects an absence of composition and circulation, but rather that poems have either not been found, or else are harder to identify as Scots, since the practice of Drummond and Hume in particular suggests a tendency to use English rather than Scots.[161] This is certainly true of one frequently anthologised writer: James Graham, Marquis of Montrose (1612–1650), whose poetry presents the refined feelings of the cavalier.[162] In contrast, Robert Sempill of Beltrees (1595–1669), in his poem *The Life and Death of the Piper of Kilbarchan* uses Scots to lament the passing of a particular Scottish culture and offers a stanza form that becomes known as 'standard Habbie'.[163] The early eighteenth-century acts of recovery, James Watson's (c. 1664–1722) *Choice Collection* and Allan Ramsay's (1684–1758) *The Evergreen*, are as keen to revive material from the fifteenth, sixteenth and early seventeenth centuries (especially the latter) as they are to record their immediate predecessors;[164] ballad rather than lyric comes to dominate views of Scots inheritance.[165] Nevertheless, Scots lyric of the sixteenth and seventeenth centuries demonstrates the breadth and the depth of Lowland Scotland's literary traditions.[166]

Nicola Royan

CHAPTER SEVEN

Chivalric Literature

Rhiannon Purdie and Katie Stevenson

What is chivalric literature? This seemingly straightforward label is complicated by the fact that both terms, 'chivalric' and 'literature', carry different meanings for different groups of readers, both medieval and modern. Chivalry is a fluid concept. Stripped of the sentimental romanticism encouraged by the Gothic revival of late eighteenth and nineteenth centuries, it can be defined as the cultural ethos of the medieval military elites. The term 'chivalry' comes from Old French *chevalerie*, itself a derivative of Latin *caballerius* or 'horseman', and implies a focus on the deeds and mores of the military elites as represented by the figure of the mounted knight. 'Courtliness' – the courteous behaviour that knights were expected to display but which could be equally displayed by others (such as women) – did not define knighthood in the same way as *prowes, worschip, manheid* or *price*, to use some of the favourite terms of praise of the fourteenth-century Scots poet John Barbour. Thus the term chivalry has a more specific application than the broader notion of 'courtliness', or Barbour's *curtasy*. If the chivalric ethos originated on the battlefield, its relevance to wider medieval society must nevertheless be recognised: the knightly class was that from which all medieval secular leaders were drawn, so everyone had a stake in the ethos governing the 'order of knighthood' to which they all (at least in theory) subscribed. 'Knycthede is the hyest temporale order þat is jn the warld [...] ffor quhy þat all Emperouris and kingis aw to bere that ordre or ellis thair dignitee is nocht perfyte' wrote Sir Gilbert Hay, the fifteenth-century translator and embellisher of several important continental works of chivalric literature.[1] The centrality of the ideals of chivalry to medieval social order meant that it remained a subject of keen interest and debate throughout the period. It was regularly re-shaped or customised by individual writers and commentators, in Scotland as much as elsewhere, and inevitably developed multiple shades of meaning for different groups.

Bearing in mind the shifting definition of chivalry, 'chivalric literature' may be defined as a body of works that either engages directly with chivalric themes, or is informed by chivalry in its composition or potential audience. The genre of romance may be the most obvious representative this, but the term 'chivalric literature' also includes works that offer incidental comment on the values and practices of chivalry, such as the comic mock-tournament poems by William Dunbar and Sir David Lyndsay, amongst others. More importantly, it includes a large body of descriptive or instructional material on chivalry – commentaries on chivalry and knighthood, and instruction manuals for various aspects of knightly conduct – upon which the student of late medieval and early modern chivalry might fruitfully draw. This material provides a crucial context for understanding both the imaginative works of chivalric literature, and the late medieval and early-modern audience(s) for whom such works were designed.

Medieval Romance

The medieval genre of romance is often seen as the most characteristic representative of chivalric literature, and much has been written on its symbiotic relationship with actual chivalric practice.[2] Setting aside the two great historical epic poems, Barbour's *Bruce* and Hary's *Wallace*,[3] and Lyndsay's 'chivalric biography' of William 'Squyer' Meldrum (which are discussed separately below), there are twelve Scottish 'medieval' romances that survive in whole or part from the fifteenth and sixteenth centuries and a small handful of later sixteenth- and early seventeenth-century romances written more clearly in the renaissance mode.[4] The medieval romances are: two fifteenth-century romances of Alexander[5] and about five hundred surviving lines of a romance about Alexander's fictional grandfather *Florimond of Albany*;[6] the Arthurian romances *Golagros and Gawane* and *Lancelot of the Laik*;[7] a Scottish *Troy Book* (ca. 3,700 lines of which survive incongruously in two separate sixteenth-century manuscript copies of Lydgate's *Troy Book*);[8] *Rauf Coilȝear*;[9] *Eger and Grime* (first cited in 1497 but surviving only in two related but very different versions from the seventeenth century);[10] *King Orphius* (fragments of a rather different Scottish version of the Middle English *Sir Orfeo*); *Sir Colling the Knycht* (a fantastical tale associated with the powerful Campbells of Argyll);[11] *Clariodus* (the first romance in this list that was demonstrably composed after 1500, though before 1550);[12] and finally *Roswall and Lillian*, a medieval romance in style and form but whose internal citations of *Clariodus* help to date it to the sixteenth century at the earliest.[13]

Viewed together, the small collection of Scottish medieval romances indicates an overwhelming preference for the more strictly 'chivalric' features of the genre: displays of knightly courage and fighting prowess complemented by the equally masculine pursuits of royal governance and diplomatic negotiation. There are no Scottish contributions to the 'calumniated queen' category of romance (focusing on the virtuous endurance of a female protagonist)[14] and relatively few significant female characters within Scottish romances generally until we reach the sixteenth century. The Scottish author of *Golagros and Gawane* expunges the distracting 'amie' of the Old French source the better to concentrate on Golagros's loyalty to his (male) followers and Gawain's masterful mediation of the conflict between Golagros and Arthur.[15] The author of the admittedly incomplete *Lancelot of the Laik*, whose tale of Lancelot's devotion to Guinevere is framed as a means for the poet to woo his own lady, ignores the most obviously relevant episodes such as Lancelot's introduction to court by the Lady of the Lake, when Lancelot first meets Guinevere and 'was tak / By love and was iwondit to the stak' (lines 225–6). Instead he narrates Arthur's wars with Galiot and greatly expands a disquisition on good governance.[16] Sir Colling in *Sir Colling the Knycht* and Sir Eger in *Eger and Grime* both fight to impress their ladies, but Sir Colling wins the unnamed lady in his very first battle and the story moves swiftly on to his thrilling defence of the 'kingdom' of Argyll against a gigantic invader, followed by his near-mauling by a lion which had been set upon him by the jealous steward: the temptation to read political allegory into Colling's final triumph is strong but ultimately fruitless in the face of the tale's otherworldly vagueness. *Eger and Grime*, meanwhile, has at its centre the bond of brotherhood between the title characters: Grime defeats the mysterious Graysteel (after whom this story is also sometimes named)[17] in Eger's name to salvage the latter's honour and allow him to win the haughty Winglaine. Grime himself marries the much nicer lady Loosepaine who had healed both knights' wounds, but the focus of the text – in each of its rather different extant versions – is firmly on knightly prowess, brotherly loyalty and the importance of knightly reputation. In the longer Huntington-Laing version (in which Winglaine is called 'Winliane', Loosepaine is 'Lillias' and Grime is 'Grahame', though still rhymed as 'Grime'), Grime/Grahame's death some years later causes a guilt-racked Eger to admit to the deceit: his affronted wife takes the veil while he goes on a repentant pilgrimage to Rome followed by two years' valiant fighting in Rhodes, restoring his reputation at last before returning to find he is a widower, at which point he pragmatically marries Grime/Grahame's widow.

Taken together, the medieval Scottish romances accord very well with other evidence for Scotland's full participation in the pan-European enthusiasm for literature that helped to define, illustrate or evaluate the ideals of chivalry. *Golagros* and *Rauf* weigh up the relative merits of raw martial prowess and shrewd diplomacy; *Golagros*, *Lancelot* and the two *Alexander* romances consider the limits and dangers of imperial power through their studies of Alexander's and Arthur's aggression (an admired chivalric value in isolation but one acknowledged as problematic in practice). *Eger and Grime* tests the moral limits of renown and loyalty. The role of women in the maintenance of chivalric values is also explored in this latter romance. The doublet of Eger and Grime is mirrored by that of Winglaine and Loosepaine, with Winglaine taking the traditional romance heroine's role as the haughty inspiration for chivalric derring-do, while Loosepaine, whose apparent fairy-status may suggest its own comment on ordinary mortal women, takes the healing and advisory role.

Early Modern Romance

Two romances survive that are clearly post-medieval in both date and style but which pre-date the 1603 Union of the Crowns. The first is an abortive attempt in 1571 by Charles Stewart, later earl of Lennox, to translate (from a French rendition) the first book of the wildly popular sixteenth-century Spanish romance *Amadis de Gaule* for his mother.[18] The second is the unjustly neglected *Roland Furious* of John Stewart of Baldynneis, a verse translation of part of Ariosto's *Orlando furioso* which he completed in the later 1580s and dedicated to James VI ('One suspects that those who praise only Montgomerie among Scots poets of this period have simply not read Stewart's poem', enthuses McDiarmid).[19] After 1603, the increasing integration of Scottish and English literary culture is evident in the palpable influence of Spenser's *Faerie Queene* on Patrick Gordon's *Penardo and Laissa* of 1615,[20] and Patrick Hannay's *Sheretine and Mariana* of 1622 (dedicated to the countess of Bedford),[21] or the allusions to Sidney's *Arcadia* in John Kennedie's *Calanthrop and Lucilla* of 1626, which was swiftly reprinted in London as *The ladies delight, or:*

The English gentlewomans history of Calanthrop and Lucilla (the mere fact of circulation in London distinguishes these seventeenth-century romances from their earlier Scottish predecessors).[22] Although Patrick Gordon's *Penardo* has languished in obscurity ever since – as have all of these late Scottish romances in comparison to some of their medieval forerunners – Gordon's other major work, also published in 1615, gained a brief foothold in literary history. He explains that he wrote his *Famous Historie of the Renouned and Valiant Prince Robert surnamed the Bruce* in order that he might 'with more mildness modifie that which our writers most sharplie have written: thereby to extinguish, if possibill, the evil opinion that hath bin so long engraftid in the hearts of manie by reading of these old historeis'.[23] This attempt to provide a history of Robert Bruce more acceptable to Unionist sensibilities was reprinted twice in the eighteenth century before it, too, disappeared from the literary radar.[24]

The elaborate rhetoric of the later renaissance romances may distinguish them immediately from their late-medieval precedents, but the one group should not be seen as replacing the other: medieval romances – both Scottish and English – continued to be read, copied and printed in Scotland throughout this later period. Of the twelve 'medieval' romances cited above, only three – *Golagros, Lancelot* and *Clariodus* – survive in copies pre-dating the accession of James VI to the throne in 1567. Meanwhile, although the sixteenth- and seventeenth-century romances show a far greater interest in portraying love stories, they retain their determination to illustrate what makes an ideal knight. Ideas of, and interest in, chivalry changed over the centuries covered by this volume, but as a concept it nevertheless proved to be as buoyant as 'the unkillable genre' of romance itself.[25]

The Nine Worthies

The medieval European drive to define and exemplify chivalry had crystallised by the early fourteenth century in the popular identification of a group of nine figures who epitomised the ideals of chivalry and thereby provided it with what Maurice Keen has called a 'historical mythology'.[26] This group – the Nine Worthies – was tripartite in structure, with three pagan heroes (Hector, Alexander, Julius Caesar), three Jewish Old Testament heroes (Joshua, David, Judas Maccabeus), and three heroes of Christian chivalric culture (Arthur, Charlemagne and Godfrey de Bouillon). The grouping of the nine took its earliest and most influential literary form in Jacques de Longuyon's *Voeux du Paon*. This originally independent romance of Alexander, composed for Thibaud, Bishop of Liège before the latter's death in 1312, proved tremendously popular – over thirty manuscripts survive – and was swiftly assimilated into the vast *Roman d'Alexandre*, whether appended to it or interpolated into the third branch of this cycle.[27] *Les Voeux* was first translated into Scots as part of the *Buik of Alexander* of c. 1438, where it is preceded by a part of the second branch known as the *Fuerre de Gadres*, which provides the background to the eponymous vows on the peacock ('paon') made before the battle with Gadifer. Both parts would be translated again in the mid-fifteenth-century *Buik of King Alexander the Conquerour* generally attributed to Sir Gilbert Hay, although Scottish knowledge of the Nine Worthies predates both of these.

The Nine Worthies' reputations were soon cemented in the language of chivalric culture. Collectively they represented all facets of the ideal chivalric warrior, including some of its inherent dangers: in literature or art, only one needed to be named or represented to evoke the memories of all. The cult of the worthies underpinned the description of Robert Bruce in the 1320 'Declaration of Arbroath' as 'another Maccabeus or Joshua' who had delivered his people from their enemies.[28] Later in the century, Barbour would describe Bruce's beleaguered party as being 'lik to the Machabeys' in their determination to fight those that 'throw iniquite / Held thaim and thairis in thrillage', while the exploits of Edward Bruce in Ireland are likened to those of Judas Maccabeus himself in the way that he led his men into battle against tremendous odds.[29] Interest in these figures drove the demand for romances of Arthur, Alexander and Troy.

The desire to measure more recent figures against these epitomes of chivalric virtue sometimes led to the designation of a tenth worthy. In Scotland, this was Robert Bruce. The best known example is in a brief poem that its first modern editor, David Laing, christened 'Ane Ballet of the Nine Nobles',[30] although the most recent edition calls it more accurately 'The Ballettis of the Nine Nobles', since its final lines refer to the preceding stanzas as '*thir* balletis' (i.e. 'these stanzas').[31] The poem appears among the endpapers of four separate manuscripts of Walter Bower's *Scotichronicon*, including the working copy apparently made at Inchcolm Abbey in the 1440s under Bower's own supervision, Cambridge, Corpus Christi College MS 171. Although it is untitled in the Corpus manuscript (the ultimate source of the other three manuscript copies), its subject – the Nine Worthies – would have been immediately obvious to its medieval readers since it consists of a single stanza on each figure, presented in the order given by Longuyon. Following these is a tenth stanza on Bruce:

> Robert the Brois throu hard feichtyng
> With few venkust the mychthy Kyng
> Off Ingland, Edward, twyse in fycht,
> At occupit his realme but rycht
> At sum tyme wes set so hard,
> At hat nocht sax ['six'] till hym toward.
> (lines 55–60)

A concluding couplet asks:

> ȝe gude men that thir balletis redis,
> Deme quha dochtyast was in dedis.

The implication that Robert Bruce should be regarded as a tenth member of the group is clear.[32]

From the mid-fifteenth century onwards there was an exponential increase in references to the Nine Worthies in late medieval and early modern Scottish literature and art. Their (imaginary) coats of arms appeared prominently in Sir David Lyndsay of the Mount's 1542 *Armorial* which he compiled in his capacity as Lyon King of Arms. They also appear in the late sixteenth-century room dedicated to them at Crathes Castle, decorated with images and short verses describing their achievements.[33] It is notable that both the Crathes inscriptions and *The Balletis* finish by inviting the audience to consider which is the most worthy, although there is no direct textual relationship between the two. The worthies are not indistinguishable exemplars of chivalry but individuals representing slightly different aspects of it, inviting comparison, judgment and critical evaluation even as they are held up as ideals.

Scottish Historical Epics

It has been argued that a native Scottish 'matter' emerged in the late Middle Ages, echoing the pattern of the traditional three romance 'matters' of France (Charlemagne), Britain (Arthur) and Rome or Antiquity (for example, Alexander).[34] The 'matter of Scotland' is represented by two major historical narratives – Barbour's *Bruce* and Hary's *Wallace*. These two epics are significant for several reasons: they constructed a historical narrative of the recent Scottish past and created a focal point around which nascent Scottish national identities could be articulated – and they did so by reflecting the preoccupation of the kingdom's elite with chivalry.

These are not texts directly concerned with chivalry, or even court life, but they certainly reveal a great deal about Scottish chivalric ideals and culture in the fifteenth century.

The Bruce was completed around 1375 by John Barbour, archdeacon of Aberdeen.[35] Shortly after Robert II (1371–1390) was crowned, Barbour was in the employ of the king's household as clerk of the audit and later as auditor of the exchequer. Around the time of the completion of *The Bruce*, arrangements were made by the crown for Barbour to receive an annual pension. Although the original commission is unproven, it is widely held that Barbour wrote this work under the patronage of the Stewart family and most probably at the behest of Robert II. As part of a careful programme of consolidation of Stewart royal power, the historical narrative presented in *The Bruce* was crafted to bolster the image of the Stewarts as the rightful heirs of Robert Bruce. Its principal focus is a narrative history of the lives of Robert Bruce and Sir James Douglas, but one that showcases Douglas to such an extent that the natural assumption has been that Barbour was working, in part, from a substantial work on the life of Douglas that has now been lost.[36] The poem also features the acts of the Stewart family, especially in relation to the Battle of Bannockburn (the poem's centrepiece) and its aftermath. The poem is written using chivalry as its ideological currency, but it is a chivalry nuanced by a genuine appreciation of the realities of warfare and violence, and one based upon the concerns of a community facing tremendous pressures on 'fredome' and loyalty. It may be no coincidence that the two earliest surviving manuscripts of Barbour's poem date to 1487 and 1489, near to the close of James III's reign (1460–1488) and the commencement of James IV's (1488–1513).[37] The themes Barbour explored were of acute concern at this time, when loyalty to the crown was an issue at the heart of Scottish politics.

During James III's reign, 'Blind' Hary contributed a second historical narrative to the emerging 'matter'. The *Wallace* was written between 1474 and 1479.[38] It should be recalled that Barbour was writing much nearer in time to the events and drew from a range of sources including oral testimonies: Hary was writing over century and a half after the events of his history and thus flavoured his narrative with a far more liberal sprinkling of emotive embellishment. Nevertheless, its impact on the political community was considerable and a connection was immediately drawn between the *Bruce* and the *Wallace*, including their binding together in manuscript form in 1487.[39] Although the *Wallace*'s central character belonged to the knightly community, the poem was not a traditional chivalric tale of glorious knighthood but instead a story of warfare and violence between the Scots and the English. It was a clear articulation of 'nationalist' sentiment in which the English were consistently portrayed as the enemy (unlike *The Bruce*, in which Barbour sees chivalric virtue irrespective of national origin). Hary's poem is a political commentary on his own time and a denunciation of James III's policy of peace with England. This, in effect, renders the poem devoid of extensive commentary on chivalry. Hary did not judge knights by their adherence to the codes of chivalric practice, nor by their violations of it; instead, he conceived of good knights as those who were loyal to Wallace, simply on the grounds that they were engaging in war and violence for the right cause. In Hary's view, Wallace's enemies (especially the English) were not knights who should or could be considered admirable for their chivalry.

Chivalric and Heraldic Manuals

At the same time as these historical epics were developing and a violent and nationalistic 'Scottish' chivalry was being woven into the memory of the recent past, more practical guides to chivalric practice and culture were also proving popular in Scotland. These ranged in scope from instructions on how to arrange a duel to the production of armorials, from descriptions of weaponry used in battle to observations on chivalric court rituals. These represent some of the most underused resources for the study of chivalry in late medieval and early modern Scotland, principally due to their lack of transcription from manuscript form (although in recent years the Scottish Text Society has made considerable inroads on this front with the publication of the *Prose Works of Sir Gilbert Hay* and *The Deidis of Armorie*). Other Scottish texts survive in forms that cast doubts on their authority, such as the *Order of Combats for Life in Scotland*.[40] This treatise claims to originate in James I's reign (1424–1437), but the manuscript actually dates from the late seventeenth or early eighteenth century and was discovered in the family papers of the House of Erroll in the early nineteenth century. It details the role of officials during duelling and it is most likely that it belonged to the family of the Hays of Erroll, who were the hereditary constables of Scotland. As constables, the Hays of Erroll had a well-established role in the tournaments and judicial duels held in the kingdom. Nothing is known of the author: if the treatise does date from James I's reign, it has certainly been edited and modernised from its original fifteenth-century form. This, of course, causes serious problems with authenticity and it is plausible that a later author attributed it to James I's reign to bestow antique authority and precedence upon it: as a consequence scholars have shied away from its potential as a source. Whilst its provenance makes it difficult to come to reliable conclusions about fifteenth-century duelling, the *Order of Combats* can still be used to illuminate the function of the early-modern duel in Scotland.

From the mid-fifteenth century, we are on a firmer footing and there was a flourishing of practical guides to chivalry produced in Scots. These types of text were increasingly popular elsewhere in Europe from the fourteenth century, with Geoffroi de Charny's *Livre de chevalerie* influencing contemporary debates on the nature of chivalry.[41] Manuals of this sort had also appeared much earlier with the anonymous thirteenth-century *Ordene de Chevalerie* and the exponentially popular thirteenth-century Catalan work, the *Llibre de l'orde de cavalleria* of Ramon Llull.[42] Llull's work was translated into French in the fourteenth century as the *Livre de l'ordre de chevalerie* and was widely distributed, with the consequence that it was to be translated into other vernaculars in the fifteenth century, including into Scots by Sir Gilbert Hay as *The Buke of the Ordre of Knychthede* in 1456 (with substantial additions – Hay's text runs to approximately 34,000 words against about 17,000 in his French source),[43] and into English as the *Book of the Ordre of Chiualry or Knyghthode* printed by William Caxton in 1484.[44]

Sir Gilbert Hay's contribution to the knowledge of continental and domestic chivalric culture and practices was considerable. He had himself seen military service in France and was a member of Charles VII's household, where he had received his knighthood.[45] His additions to the texts are in part to explain differences between French and Scottish practices, and in part a reflection of his own experiences in war. Under the commission of Sir William Sinclair, Earl of Orkney, in addition to the substantially enhanced version of Llull, Hay also worked on and expanded two further texts in 1456. These were the *Buke of the Law of Armys* and the *Buke of the Gouernance of Princis*.[46] All three were bound in the same manuscript, although the juxtaposition of the *Law of Armys* and the *Ordre of Knychthede* was not Hay's innovation as these two works had appeared side-by-side for the first time in a late fourteenth-century French manuscript, which may have been the source Hay used.[47] The *Law of Armys*, a version of Honoré Bouvet's French work of 1382, was a practical guide to warfare, concerned primarily with the laws of war and the position of the soldier in society, suggesting ideas for making knights more efficient on the battlefield. The *Buke of the Ordre of Knychthede* promoted knighthood, especially in times of peace, firmly within its social and civic setting. Both placed emphasis on the commitment of the chivalric elite to be loyal to their king and on the obligations they had to their wider communities. Whilst not strictly speaking a chivalric text, the *Buke of the Gouernance of Princis*, a version of the *Secreta Secretorum*, seems to have had considerable influence on Hay's later translations: the *Buik of King Alexander the Conquerour* attributed to him borrowed directly and extensively from the *Secreta Secretorum*. Hay's translations were well known in Scotland and reached a more extensive audience in the fifteenth and sixteenth centuries than just those with access to Sinclair's library at Roslin. The surviving copy of his prose chivalric works was made in the late 1480s,[48] while the contents page of the Asloan manuscript of c. 1513–30 indicates that it once contained some of Hay's work.[49] Dunbar and Lyndsay both included Hay in their lists of eminent Scottish poets.[50] The inclusion of Hay's work in the aforementioned manuscript compilation of Edinburgh notary John Asloan shows that the appeal of such works extended far beyond those who might have to put the chivalry there described into practice themselves.

By the end of the fifteenth century, an emerging body of custodians of chivalric culture saw the value of producing companions or handbooks that might assist them in their interests. These handbooks were much more diverse and broad-ranging than the manuals of the sort produced by Hay, and they contain a wealth of information that has barely been used by scholars to date: treatises, poems, protocols, drawings and letters can all be found in their bindings. The compilers of the handbooks were the kingdom's heralds, by this time usually drawn from the knighthood themselves, who were principally concerned with monitoring, organising and recording all components of chivalric culture.[51] To do this, they were avid collectors of books and manuscripts relating to their areas of interest and expertise. The glimpse we have of even a small part of their libraries attests to the resources available to them. The first surviving handbook of this type is a manuscript of 173 folios dating to 1494, compiled by Adam Loutfut, Kintyre Pursuivant, for Sir William Cumming of Inverallochy, Marchmont Herald (and later Lyon King of Arms).[52] The Loutfut manuscript contains twenty-seven items, twenty in Scots and the remainder in Latin. These include a mid-fifteenth-century Breton description of the rights of kings of arms and heralds and where they should walk when accompanying the king on official occasions; *The Gaige of Battaill* dealing with judicial duels; Loutfut's translation from French into Scots of the *Deidis of Armorie*, a heraldic history and bestiary; a short piece for heralds on how to cry largess; a treatise on the organisation of tournaments; three short texts describing the various ceremonial duties of heralds at tournament, in war, at feasts and at funerals; a treatise on the rules of battles; a short treatise on the origin of officers of arms; a Scots version of the late Middle English *Liber Armorum*; an extract from Nicholas Upton's *De Officio Militari*; a copy of a letter from Pope Pius II dealing with the place in society of officers of arms; a Scots version of William Caxton's *Book of the Ordre of Chiualry or Knyghthode*; a treatise on the law of arms at judicial duels; a treatise on coronation rituals; a treatise on the relationship between war and crowns; two short notes on war; a translation of Vegetius's *De Re Militari*; a tract on preparations for battle; two different treatises on officers of arms; practical examples of the art of blazoning; a poem on heraldry; and a copy of Bartolus of Saxoferrato's *Tractatus de insigniis et armis*.[53] Subsequent Scottish officers of arms copied and adjusted versions of this manuscript for their own usage.[54] Many of these treatises were essential for assistance in the heralds' role as organisers and participants in public, royal and chivalric ceremonies.

Rolls of arms were also held in heraldic libraries, from which heralds derived their knowledge of the genealogies and histories of the Scottish and wider European nobilities. Heraldry was the universal labelling of chivalry – a language through which elites communicated ideas about themselves and their relationship to others. Whilst initially heraldic devices were used on shields and armour to proclaim identity, later they were also employed as an ornamental device on personal property to demonstrate ownership. While no late medieval domestic armorials have survived, there is ample evidence to indicate that these were circulating throughout Europe and the inclusion of Scots arms in English and continental armorials of the period is considerable. The mid-fifteenth-century *Scots Roll* forms part of an English heraldic handbook by Sir Thomas Holmes,[55] and the *Armorial de Gelre*, the *Armorial de Bellenville* and the *Armorial de Berry*, for example, all contain Scottish coats of arms.[56] It was not until 1542 that the first attempt was made at a complete record of all arms used in the kingdom. This was undertaken by Sir David Lyndsay of the Mount in his role as Lyon King of Arms, and in addition to contemporary Scottish arms, we find depictions of historic Scottish arms, European royal arms and the heroes of chivalric culture.[57]

Heraldry could be depicted visually through a drawing, but the heraldic language known as blazon could draw upon this tradition in written works. A superb example of this occurs in Richard Holland's *Buke of the Howlat*, a demonstration of how heraldry, chivalry and propaganda could intersect in literary form.[58] *The Buke of the Howlat* celebrates and promotes the Douglas family's standing in mid-fifteenth-century Scotland just prior, as it turned out, to their spectacular downfall in 1455. Holland conveys the greatness of the family through a lengthy description and explication of the main Douglas arms as borne by the current earl and master of Douglas (lines 408–585, stressing amongst other things the importance of their ancestor Sir James Douglas to Robert Bruce), but he also describes the specific arms of his patron, Archibald Douglas, Earl of Moray, (lines 586–97) and notes those of his brothers Hugh and John (lines 599–601), earl of Ormond and lord Balvenie respectively. His audience is also expected to recognise the continental arms of the anti-pope Felix V (lines 339–47) and the emperor-elect Frederick III (lines 352–9). Holland wrote the *Howlat* for Archibald's wife, Elizabeth Dunbar, Countess of Moray, but, as with chivalric literature more generally, it should not be supposed that an interest in heraldry was restricted to heralds or armigerous families themselves. The *Howlat* was printed by Chepman and Myllar in 1508 – presumably in expectation of decent sales – and it was copied by both the Edinburgh notary John Asloan and the young Edinburgh merchant George Bannatyne.[59]

Chivalry and Social Rank

Occasionally, chivalric literature turns its attention to the question of exactly who should be expected or allowed to participate in chivalric culture. This was especially noticeable towards the end of the fifteenth century and during the first half of the sixteenth century when increasing social mobility brought these issues to the fore.[60] In, for example, Sir David Lyndsay's mid-sixteenth-century chivalric biography *Squyer Meldrum*, chivalry and social standing are key themes. William Meldrum is a documented person of Lyndsay's acquaintance, and there is historical evidence for some of the events described.[61] In the poem Meldrum supposedly performs feats of arms that should have seen him knighted many times over, although he dies a squire.[62] Modern commentators have tended to see the poem as a critique of the outdated ideals of romance rather than of Meldrum himself.[63] The portrayal of Meldrum offered by its lesser-known companion-piece, the *Testament of Squyer Meldrum*, however, is less uniformly positive, suggesting that Lyndsay's views on both the chivalric ideal and Meldrum himself were rather more complex. Nevertheless, *Squyer Meldrum* can be read as a shrewd observation of contemporary knighthood, incorporating a new understanding of social and civic responsibility within chivalric ideology's fundamental concepts.

In *The Justing Betwix James Watsoun and Jhone Barbour*, Lyndsay's contribution to the popular slapstick 'mock-tournament' sub-genre, the relationship between chivalry and social rank is highlighted.[64] It is interesting to compare this poem to Dunbar's earlier mock-tournament between a tailor and a soutar (the second half of 'Off Februar the fyiftene nycht') and Alexander Scott's later sixteenth-century 'Justing and Debait up at the Drum', which includes more specific parody of romance conventions.[65] Although Lyndsay's men make a better show of fighting than either Dunbar's or Scott's (the former crash into each other once; the latter never manage to fight at all), the physical weakness and terror of all combatants are comically stressed. Scott's man runs away; Dunbar's and Lyndsay's men both defecate in fear and the latter then ignore protocol by agreeing they are too exhausted to continue. This highlights by implicit comparison the great hardiness and courage of real tourneying knights. In Dunbar's and Scott's poems, the 'jousters' are explicitly lower class – distant not only from the knightly world they imitate, but even from the well-to-do mercantile or gentry circles from which many members of the poems' audiences would be drawn.[66] Lyndsay's failed jousters, by contrast, are respected yeomen of the king's household, one of whom had been awarded lands near Perth.[67] Lyndsay's poem can thus be read as a light-hearted demonstration that knightly qualities could not be gained merely by moving in knightly circles, an observation that delimits social boundaries much more subtly than the comically low origins of Dunbar's and Scott's jousters can do.

The Taill of Rauf Coilȝear is an unusual variant of the popular comic king-in-disguise tales in which a monarch enjoys the over-rough hospitality of an unsuspecting non-gentle subject before summoning his victim to court and magnanimously rewarding his hospitality rather than punishing his disrespect. A typical example of this type is the fifteenth-century English tale *John the Reeve* (told of Edward I), which is known to have circulated in Scotland thanks to citations of both tales together by Dunbar and Douglas: it probably influenced the composition of *Rauf*.[68] Although still a comic poem, *Rauf Coilȝear* shows the same sort of interest as *Golagros and Gawane* in exemplifying the ideal chivalric pairing of martial prowess with well-considered diplomacy. The king in *Rauf* is Charlemagne, whose rank amongst the Nine Worthies and reputation as an exemplar of chivalry is unchallengeable. The newly knighted Rauf, uniquely among the heroes of king-in-disguise tales, goes on to prove his fitness for knighthood by fighting and ultimately converting a Saracen champion who conveniently happens past on a camel. Rauf's non-noble origins are stressed: this is no 'Fair Unknown' tale of a knight's son discovering his birthright, but a genuine movement from low to elite social status.

There were inevitable differences of opinion on the nature of the relationship between chivalry and social status, but it is clear that this was a live issue throughout our period. Moreover, questions were specifically raised as to whether the qualities esteemed by knightly society could be achieved by those of non-gentle birth. The pressure of this challenge to the traditional association between knightly ideals and heredity can be sensed in some of the literature commissioned by the nobility.[69] This was even more acutely felt from the second half of the fifteenth century with its increased possibilities for social and financial mobility. Concerns were exacerbated by the favouring of 'low-born' men at the Scottish royal court.[70]

Conclusion

Chivalry in 1400 looked very different to chivalry in 1650, both in its literary forms and practical execution. At the beginning of this period, it was still closely allied to military and knightly practices. By the sixteenth century, however, it was evident that the concept of chivalry had become more remote from its militaristic origins, bringing a broader range of qualities to prominence. Several factors contributed to this, including the rapid rise of gunpowder technology, which eclipsed the use of more 'knightly' weapons and permitted those who had less experience or skill in hand-to-hand combat to be successful in war and duelling. Indeed, duelling with lances and swords was replaced in this period by pistols.[71] Chivalric literature, meanwhile, had taken on something of an antiquarian sheen. As a set of ideals, chivalry had always looked back to a supposed golden age – this was what lay behind the development of concepts such as the Nine Worthies – but at the beginning of our period the ideals and practices illustrated in chivalric literature (both imaginative and practical) still maintained direct links with contemporary military practice. Over the course of our period, however, these had weakened. The genuine martial element of chivalry and its relevance as training for battle declined, while the performance element became more prominent: for example, the tournaments held at the courts of James IV and V were theatrical showcases of the kingdom's chivalric skill, whereas a hundred years earlier jousts were still used to settle a protracted siege. Nevertheless, the description 'antiquarian' for later sixteenth- and seventeenth-century chivalric literature should not be taken to mean that its audience had somehow grown narrower or more specialised. The audience for both imaginative and instructive chivalric literature had always included people who were largely excluded from chivalric practice, from the sixteenth-century Edinburgh notaries and merchants who copied the works of Holland and Hay to the early seventeenth-century antiquarian James Balfour of Denmilne. Nor did the commitment to knighthood as an ideal lessen during our period: indeed, this is the constant that underlies the many and various types of chivalric literature produced over these fertile two and half centuries of Scottish letters.

CHAPTER EIGHT

Elegy and Commemorative Writing

Joanna Martin and Kate L. Mathis

Elegiac and commemorative writing was important to Scotland's literary culture in all three of the nation's medieval languages. It is to Scottish Gaelic culture, however, that elegy and lament verse is central. The second part of this chapter will explore the importance of the genre and the variety of uses to which it was put between c. 1400 and 1650. The practice of composing Gaelic-language panegyric and elegiac verse is attested from the earliest written record,[1] its composition governed by a set of long-established literary conventions. The continued relevance of these conventions and the remarkable stability of the genre enabled it to flourish well into the seventeenth century. As we will see, the contexts that fostered the composition of Gaelic elegy may explain the longevity of many of its characteristic features: poets were often trained in bardic schools (c. 1200–1600) and much of their literary culture was clan- and household-based, located within close-knit networks of hereditary poets and patrons. Many of the elegies that will be discussed here were preserved in family collections known as 'duanairean'. Moreover, as this chapter demonstrates, the stability of the literary tradition gave Gaelic poets the freedom to work with ingenuity and originality.

In Scots and Latin literature, elegy and commemorative writing took more varied forms, including succinct epitaph and expansive prose family history. Elegiac writing in Scots and Latin also overlapped with other kinds of moral and religious writing on death. It was thus less coherent in development than its Gaelic counterpart. The conditions of its composition also varied markedly. Only a few extant elegies survive from close family or household settings, the elegies and epitaphs in the Maitland Quarto Manuscript being important examples, although some texts, such as George Buchanan's poignant Latin epitaph for Anne Walsingham, wife of Thomas Randolph, and her baby,[2] were composed for friends and close contacts. Many of the Scots and Latin elegies discussed below were composed in formal settings for distinguished individuals to whom the poet may not have had a particularly close connection (in direct contrast to the often intimate connection between Gaelic poets and the subjects of their laments). Furthermore, not all Scots and neo-Latin elegies were the result of a direct commission from a patron with whom the poet had a close and lasting relationship. Several elegies related to important events at the Stewart court may have been commissioned works, but this is hard to determine; they may also have been unsolicited bids for preferment. Examples of Scots and Latin elegy survive from the early fifteenth century onwards, and although some themes and forms of expression remain consistent, a shift in the attitudes to death and the expression of grief becomes apparent towards the end of the period.

Gaelic elegiac writing from Scotland has also an intimate connection with Irish Gaelic literary culture, and, while its elegy makes use of classical and Biblical sources, it also draws upon a distinctive set of allusions and references from wider Gaelic tradition, well known to its intended audience, but not found in Scots and Latin writing (several poets' careers and networks of patronage also spanned both sides of the Irish Sea). It is difficult to believe that the rich tradition of Gaelic elegy exerted no influence upon Latin and Scots commemorative writing. Conclusive evidence for influence in either direction, however, has yet to be presented, and scholarly opinion is divided concerning the attitudes towards Gaelic culture amongst the writers of Lowland Scotland. The hostile mockery of Dunbar's *Flyting* is often taken as representative of the views of Scots poets on their counterparts in the Gàidhealtachd, but Martin MacGregor has recently questioned the extent to which this apparent antipathy was shared.[3]

Several themes, nevertheless, are common to all the Scottish traditions of late-medieval elegiac writing. Most obviously, Gaelic, Scots, and Latin writing uses elegy in the commemoration of major celebrated figures, often claiming to articulate public grief. In each tradition elegy is also used to offer protest or to comment upon the wider political situation. In Gaelic elegy, however, regional and clan-based politics, rather than national events, are given most attention. In Scots, elegy for public figures is used by poets to make observations on the political situation and to give advice to those in power; amongst neo-Latin writing from Scotland, some elegies, such as those of George Buchanan, also offer satirical comment on international affairs.

In each tradition, the overlap between amatory loss and bereavement is also exploited. In Scots and Latin writing, elegy, on the basis of classical literature and contemporary continental revivals of the form, was employed to mark the loss of love, either through death or abandonment, as well as the loss of an esteemed individual, while other forms such as epitaph were used to commemorate the deceased. Gaelic elegiac verse also focuses regularly upon the motif of love lost through death, but the poet's method of expressing such loss varies from the description of an intimate personal relationship with his subject to sometimes overt, politicised commentary upon events leading to their demise. Gaelic lament poetry, however, focuses to a greater extent than Scots and Latin examples upon the expression of personal grief, especially within amatory and marital contexts, and only rarely includes some of the more explicit moralising – often aimed at discouraging the act of grieving – found in Scots and Latin examples. Although women (usually of high rank) are the subject of some of the Scots elegies discussed here, none can be proven to have been composed by female writers in this period. In contrast, a significant number of women are known to have composed elegies in Gaelic, often addressing the same subjects, and using the same registers as male contemporaries. Furthermore, Gaelic elegy sometimes presents the reader with ambiguities of interpretation surrounding the poem's speaking voice or persona, as male poets adopted female personae for a variety of reasons, sometimes political and satirical, suggesting a need for anonymity or discretion, or to incite and shame a specific audience. Indeed, the variation in attitudes to gender in Scots/Latin and Gaelic elegy is one of the most fascinating and striking differences between the traditions examined in this chapter.

Latin and Scots

This part of the chapter focuses on the development of commemorative verse, the funerary elegy, and the related but shorter epitaph, in Latin and Scots. Elegies and epitaphs in the two languages survive from the period as stand-alone lyrics preserved in manuscript anthologies, or as set-pieces inserted into longer works such as romances and chronicles; some also survive as printed texts.[4] Their subjects include real figures, historical or contemporary, usually royalty or aristocracy, as well as legendary and imagined ones. This section will consider examples of 'public' elegiac verse, perhaps commissioned by a patron or employed by a poet in an attempt to gain preferment, and designed to elide the destructiveness of death by forging a sense of the community amongst its readers through the articulation of shared grief.[5] Some elegies and epitaphs, however, emerged from more private contexts, such as the family, and a few include the poet's reflection on his own mortality. Both the public and more private forms of commemorative writing, however, share a concern with how loss should be understood, and the nature of the relationship of the dead to those who remain living. Moral or religious didacticism is seldom completely absent from pre-Reformation commemorative poems, and is often also shared by elegies and epitaphs from after 1560, although these later poems also begin to develop the concern for the exemplary status of the dead and seek to make their subjects' (and, more boldly, sometimes even their author's) fame immortal.[6]

Elegy and epitaph were just two of several genres employed in this period for writing about death. As we will see, many of these other forms, including *memento mori* poems – such as debates between the body and soul – and *ars moriendi* – treatises on making a good end, such as the Scottish *The Crafte of Deyng*, c. 1480s[7] – also influenced the literature of mourning and commemoration. The term 'epitaph' is attested in English from the late fourteenth century, and 'elegy' from the early sixteenth century, but it should be noted that to an early-modern reader, elegy was not just a lament on death, but also a term for a complaint on love lost, perhaps through death, but also through unrequited desire. This understanding of elegy was modelled on French usage, such as similar works by Marot and Ronsard.[8] Alexander Montgomerie's translation of Marot's *Elégie III*, a poem on the parting of lovers, demonstrates this transmission. Also in this tradition is a poem in the Maitland Quarto Manuscript (c. 1586), entitled 'Ane Elagie translatit out of Frenche in English meter', which laments, from a female perspective, an unhappy marriage and thus the loss of both hope and love.[9] The emphasis upon sadness and loss is shared by love elegy and elegiac writing on death, both kinds of text dealing with unfathomable and unsettling human experiences. Frequently, too, the funerary lament deals with both lost love and death. It is with the latter that we must be primarily concerned in this chapter.

The earliest Older Scots funeral elegy concerns a high-ranking historical figure, Princess Margaret of Scotland (d. 1445), wife of Louis XI of France. Margaret's death was marked in several French elegies, but only one Scottish poem on the subject survives. It is based, though with considerable freedom, on a French original ('*Complainte pour la mort de Madame Marguerite d'Escosse, daulphine de Viennoys*'), and survives in some copies of a late fifteenth-century Scottish chronicle, the *Liber Pluscardensis*.[10] The poem is introduced by the rubric, 'Incipit Lamentacio domini Dalphini Franciae pro morte uxoris suae, dictae Margareta', and an introductory Latin note explains that the Scottish translation was commissioned by James II: thus the poem emerges from family grief and voices the sorrow of two princes (i.e. the husband to and brother of the deceased princess). As Priscilla Bawcutt has shown, one of the most significant adaptations made by the Scottish poet-translator is the abridgement of the French original, in particular the removal of much of its extensive apostrophe to death. In the Scots poem, only five stanzas are spent on mourning the 'princes but peire' (l. 9). These describe the 'woful waymentyng' (l. 8) of the bereaved husband and his desire that the whole of nature and all of human society are permitted to join him in his sorrow: 'Quhill we haue murnyt the dule of our mastres, / Lat nature thole, na kyng leife heire gladly' (ll. 58–59). Very little space is given in these hyperbolic stanzas to celebrating Margaret's life, though some of her qualities are described conventionally – her cultivation of the 'floure of nobilite' (l. 18) and her status as 'The mirroure of vertu and warldis glore' (l. 28), for example. Rather, the emphasis of the poem is on consolation and recovery from grief. A prose note cuts the lamentation short and counsels that although there is 'mare of this lamentacioun', it is more efficacious that the 'Ansuere of Resoune' to the complainer is given instead, 'for the complant is bot feynit thing' – something not to be trusted or indulged. The ensuing consolation of Reason extends to eighteen stanzas, advising that as a 'man resonabile' (l. 72), the prince should face grief in accordance with philosophical and Christian teachings and put away his inconsolable despair. Everything, the voice of Reason reminds the reader, takes place according to the 'wisdome and resoun' (l. 109) of God, who 'maid this warld nocht to be ay lestande' (l. 100). By the end of the poem, elegy begins to intersect with ideas familiar from the *ars moriendi* tradition, which offered instruction on making a good end. Thus, Reason encourages the mourner to 'Think on thi selfe and all this mys amend' (l. 237) in anticipation of his own death.

The elegy for Margaret uses a stanza form – ten decasyllabic lines – that continued to be employed in Scottish complaints on death, lost love, or misfortune. For example, this form is used for Orpheus's elegiac 'sangis lamentable' (l. 184) for his lost queen in Henryson's *Orpheus and Eurydice*, with their mournful *ubi sunt?* complaints.[11] Furthermore, the approach to grieving taken in the elegy for Margaret, with its exhortations to reason and pious self-governance, is one that dominates later Scottish and neo-Latin elegy. This is not to say that the act of mourning is always one which is rejected in these texts, but poets sought to encourage a beneficial expression of grief. Thus, in *The Buik of King Alexander the*

Conquerour (c. 1499) it is suggested that formalised mourning may offer moral encouragement and promote self-reform. Accordingly, Aristotle assembles the lords around Alexander the Great's sepulchre, 'For to rehears [...] / The wirschip quhilk he worthie was to haife' (ll. 18694–95):

> And guide maner is in evirie sted
> To love all guide [men] eftir þat þai be dead;
> And namelie worthie empriour and king
> Eftir guide lyife sould euir haue guide loving –
> For sic thingis giffis men curage guid to be. (ll. 18696–18700)[12]

In contrast, unrestrained mourning is dangerous because it focuses upon the mourner and not on the subject mourned. In a passage that prefaces the formal 'lamentatiounis' (l. 18704) around Alexander's tomb, the narrator describes how some of the king's men 'become wod and witles' (l. 18681) in grief and 'mony deit for sorrow of thair lord' (l. 18685). The inset elegies given by his followers at the tomb instead create a sombre and dignified poetic equivalent of the cadaver tomb,[13] contrasting Alexander's past splendour and present corruption in death, thus constituting a *memento mori*. Aristotle concludes the mourning by remarking on the comfort of 'perpetuall memoir' (l. 18810), the inevitability of worldly transience, and the importance of faith. Similarly, in Henryson's *Orpheus and Eurydice*, Orpheus's first formal laments (in ten-line stanzas) on the loss of his queen facilitate his quest to recover her, but his less formalised 'weping and [...] wo' when Eurydice is lost to the underworld for a second time, is futile.[14] Such sentiments seem to be heightened by the Calvinistic theology of the Reformation period, despite the differences between Catholic and Protestant attitudes to salvation. Buchanan's elegy for John Calvin (d. 1564) is confident that 'empty pomp and pathetic laments' have no place in mourning those who are guaranteed eternal life through faith.[15]

It is not until the later sixteenth century that the poetic expression of personal grief becomes a way of memorialising without moralising. Thus, in its opening 'Elegie', the distraught speaker of William Fowler's lyric sequence *Of Death* (late 1580s?)[16] can bid farewell without censure to 'counsell, ressoun, hope', admitting, 'To greif I lose the vains [ability to write]!';[17] and by the closing 'Fantasie' of the sequence reveal that commemorative poetry can immortalise both its subject – the narrator is told by his dead lover that 'thy verse dois mak me liue' (l. 13) – and its author. Thus death, and writing in response to it, may advance the poet's fame rather than offer a path to moral improvement.[18] This position is very different to that taken in Dunbar's earlier 'I that in heill wes and gladnes' (B 21 'The Lament for the Makars'), with its liturgical refrain, 'Timor mortis conturbat me', and conventional *ars moriendi* ending. The speaker's list of vernacular poets who have been claimed by death forms a literary memorial: mentioned here are English poets and Scottish makars, some of whom (including 'Clerk of Tranent', 'Sandy Traill', 'Merseir', 'Roull', 'Schir Iohne the Ros') can no longer be identified or linked securely to surviving texts,[19] thus adding a poignancy to the commemoration perhaps not envisaged by Dunbar. But there is much less confidence here in the poet's fame triumphing over the anonymity of death than there is in the poems of Fowler just mentioned, or in Sir Robert Ayton's Latin elegies (composed in the early seventeenth century) for fellow poets such as Thomas Reid.[20] Rather, for Dunbar, the act of recalling the transience of these creative lives turns the poet-narrator's fearful mind to his own inevitable demise, rather than to poetic immortality: 'Sen he has all my brether tane / He will naught lat me alane' (ll. 93–94). The tone is one of acceptance and humility – the purpose of the poem didactic as well as commemorative and ultimately also sanguine about personal loss.

Many Scots and Latin elegies for notable individuals combine explorations and censorship of grieving with reflections on the nature of political power. Two Latin epitaphs for James I of Scotland (Margaret's father), preserved uniquely in the Perth Manuscript of Walter Bower's *Scotichronicon*,[21] put lamentation to political ends.[22] Both mourn James's murder in 1437 and the simultaneous destruction of political virtues in Scotland: 'Laus, honor omnis, lex perit et mos murmure multo' ('*Glory, honour, the law and morality all perish with much murmured lamentation*').[23] By extension, the laments are designed to encourage the urgent revivification of these virtues in the reader. Indeed, the loss of James I is characterised in the Perth epitaphs as the death of Scotland's stability: 'Nunc jacet exuta gens Scotica lumine mentis/luctibus induta' ('*Now the Scottish people lies prostrate [...] clad in sorrows*'),[24] and the poems anticipate the numerous complaints for Scotland, made in times of political crisis, which recur in Older Scots literature.[25]

In this tradition too is Sir David Lyndsay's *The Deploratioun of the Deith of Quene Magdalene* (1537). James V's union with Madeleine was solemnised in Paris on 1 January 1537. On the journey back to Scotland Madeleine fell ill, and she died soon after arriving in Edinburgh, aged only seventeen.[26] Lyndsay had been involved in the arrangements for

Madeleine's official welcome and was present as Lyon Herald at her funeral, thus the poem may have been composed in connection with his official duties.[27] It considers the nature and significance of this loss to different mourners, including the realm and people of Scotland. For all concerned, Madeleine's death is a reminder of the fragility of worldly power in the face of the 'cruell tyrane' death (l. 4). In particular, both Madeleine's father, François I, 'the most hie cristinit king' (l. 62), and James himself have to confront their lack of 'micht' (l. 66) against death.[28] And, while James is cast in the poem in the role of Madeleine's 'lustie lufe and knicht' (l. 64), as he voyages 'throw bulryng stremis wode' (l. 45) to 'seik his lufe' (l. 49), he does so leaving 'his realme in greit disperance' (l. 48), only to be overcome by a power greater than his own, bringing his country to further 'disperance'. There is at least a little criticism of James's marital policy implied in Lyndsay's observations, although the focus soon shifts to the safer subject of the nation's shared grief. Scotland is deprived of its 'hail plesance' (l. 199) and future in the form of the 'fruct [...] of hir bodie' (l. 28): Madeleine's ability to provide an heir. The loss suffered by the 'Thre Estaitis of Scotland' is the subject of thirteen out of the poem's twenty-nine stanzas. While the marriage celebrations for James and Madeleine – which took place in Paris – are referred to in the poem, it is dominated by the fact that Edinburgh's 'greit preparativis' (l. 99) can never come to fruition and her ladies, knights, townsfolk, and clergy can never fulfil the roles they wish to embrace in welcoming their queen.[29] The poem attempts to offer some consolation: Scotland is left not just with the 'perpetuall memorie' of the young queen, but also with the sweet 'smell' of the 'peice and amite' forever renewed between Scotland and France as a result of this brief union, a political legacy of sorts.[30] Ultimately, however, the disappointing absence of Madeleine is mirrored by the lack of space she actually takes up in the poem.

Lyndsay's elegy for a lost princess, a lost public occasion, and a loss of hope for Scotland's future, is highly allusive and hyperbolic, and in this it anticipates the elaborate pastoral elegy, *Teares on the Death of Meoliades*, written by William Drummond of Hawthornden on the death of James VI and I's son, Henry, Prince of Wales, in 1612, and subsequently printed in London and Edinburgh.[31] Like Lyndsay's poem, this is an expression of the 'fading hopes' (l. 9) of 'this woefull ile' (l. 2). The loss to Scotland, as well as the rest of Britain, is marked in a passage in which Moeliades's nurse, the Forth, grieves along with the Clyde and Tweed: Henry had of course been raised in Scotland. The pastoral nature of the elegy keeps explicit Christian moralising at a distance, but it is nonetheless subtly introduced in the acknowledgement that grief belongs to those 'weake' (l. 144), loving minds left behind:

> Our losse, not thine (when we complaine) wee weepe,
> For thee the glistring walles of Heaven doe keepe (ll. 145–46).

In contrast to these elegies for deceased young royals, William Dunbar's 'Illuster Lodouick, of France most cristin king' (c. 1508; B 23), is a concise and restrained statement of public mourning. Like the poems by Lyndsay and Drummond, however, it may well have been written in view of the poet's role at court, or his desire for advancement there. The subject is Bernard Stewart (c. 1452–1508), third seigneur d'Aubigny, ambassador and military commander to Louis XII, to whom the poem is addressed as chief mourner. Stewart had died in 1508 not long after he had returned to Scotland on diplomatic business, a happier occasion that had been marked in a poem by Dunbar which was printed at the time by Chepman and Myllar. The poem belongs to an environment (the city of Edinburgh) similar to that of Lyndsay's poem, but the mourning it purports to record is confined to masculine and military contexts: it is 'euerie noble valiant knycht' who will join the French king in lamenting this loss of a distinguished military life. Although all those who 'loueit' (l. 25) Stewart are mentioned, Dunbar is not concerned with private grief. The poem ends piously, but, unlike the other elegies examined so far, is notable for its lack of an impulse towards explicit didacticism. Indeed, its allusions to public contexts along with its form (the stanza *ababbcbC* was often used for panegyric and religious verse)[32] seem to negate the need for warnings against the disruptions of melancholy. Although the poem's third stanza contains an apostrophe to 'duilfull death', a 'dragoun dolorous' (l. 17), against whom even the most valiant earthly warriors are powerless, this point is not overworked. No attempt is made at consolation and no particular morals are drawn: the narrator merely exhorts all 'of Scottis natioun' (l. 29) to remember Stewart in their prayers, an appropriate pious injunction for a pre-Reformation poem. The succinctness of the poem simply and powerfully serves to foreground Stewart's exemplary status as knight – 'the flour of chavelrie' (l. 8) as he is described in the refrain to each stanza – and this is how he is to be remembered.[33]

Dunbar's poem has much in common with the emphasis upon social order and collective memory of the epitaph, and with the brevity of that form, to which this chapter now turns. The epitaph, usually a composition on a deceased person intended to be inscribed on a tomb or at least to be imagined thus, grew in popularity in this period, and many Latin and Scots examples survive. Some early epitaphic verses are akin to elegy and do not necessarily exploit their connection with the physical monument, which necessitates condensed expression: the epitaphs for James I, already mentioned, fall into this category. They draw attention to the grave: one remarks on the irony of the king, murdered by his magnates in Perth in 1437, who has been 'pacis petra suis, sub petra clausa manescit' ('*a rock of peace for his people*', being now '*shut in under a stone*');[34] while the other more simply alludes to his resting place 'sub humo jacet imus' ('*deep down in the earth*').[35] Yet they are too long to have been inscribed on a tomb.[36] The epitaphs for James, however, anticipate later features of the form, especially the stress on the exemplariness of the dead, for they focus on James's valour, wisdom and nobility, and even his poetic skill: 'Cultor Amoris obit; heu qui nunc metrica psallent?' ('*The devotee of Love is dead; alas, who will now sing his songs?*').[37] Epitaphs also tend to assume the collective nature of the grief they document:[38] in those for James, earth and rivers spontaneously decry his murder, where in the elegy for Margaret, the narrator had to appeal to others to join his mourning.

A more obvious imitation of what might plausibly be inscribed on a tomb became favoured by later writers of epitaphs, with Thomas Maitland's and James VI's succinct Latin epitaphs for Philip Sidney being cases in point.[39] James VI's epitaph for his chancellor, John Maitland, appears *in situ* in St Mary's Church, Haddington.[40] This epitaph is a sonnet, the most popular vehicle for such poetry by the late sixteenth century. Of course, as a form of succinct occasional verse, the epitaph could be rather conventional, especially if its composition related to the author's desire for patronage or his public role. R. J. Lyall describes Alexander Montgomerie's epitaphs for Robert Lord Boyd and Robert Scott as 'undistinguished pieces' composed out of duty.[41] Nevertheless, writers of epitaphs also exploited brevity of expression to produce stylistic ingenuity. Montgomerie's sonnet epitaph for the brothers Patrick and John Shaw, who were killed defending James VI at Holyrood in 1591, juxtaposes classical and Christian allusion, and uses Latinate diction, oxymoron and complex syntax to build up to the praise of the brothers as 'praisuorthie Pelicans [...] / Quhais saikles bluid wes for ȝour souerane shed'.[42] The poem ends with the arresting and pious paradox that confirms the eternal life and fame of the dead men: 'Deid shawis ȝe live, suppose ȝour lyfis be lost' (l. 14). Fowler brings together not one but two Spenserian sonnets in his epitaph for the English ambassador M. Robert Bowes (d. 1597). These are linked by elaborate word play on the subject's name to create metaphors for his contribution to public life: thus, the martial ('Whose bodie was the BOWE, and Soule the Shaft'), architectural ('Statuaes, Arches Bowes / And Tombes [...] to his liuing fame') and metaphysical ('Raine-Bowes of peace') resonances of 'Bowes' provide Fowler with ample material for a fitting valediction.

It was common to group epitaphs (and elegies) at the end of manuscript miscellanies in the sixteenth and seventeenth centuries.[43] Often such pieces commemorated famous individuals not necessarily known to the compiler (or even the author), but in the case of the epitaphs at the end of Maitland Quarto Manuscript – a collection of verse apparently formed within the Maitland household with commemorative intentions (it is dated 1586, the year of Richard Maitland of Lethington's death, and contains the earliest complete collection of his poems) – family members are remembered.[44] In this the anthology may have something in common with the Gaelic 'duanaire', which, as the next part of the chapter describes, frequently contained family elegies that would have had real significance to their audience. The extent to which such Gaelic collections were known and influential in the Lowlands of Scotland is a fascinating subject that requires further research. In the Maitland Quarto, there are three epitaphs for Richard Maitland, all sonnets, and one joint epitaph for him and his wife Mary/Mariota Cranstoun (who died, according to a note in the manuscript, on the day of her husband's funeral), as well as two longer elegiac verses, one of which is also a double commemoration of Maitland and his wife. These epitaphs perhaps lack the sophistication of those by Montgomerie and Fowler, and in some ways look back to medieval traditions of epitaph writing. For example, the double epitaph is followed by a *memento mori* quatrain entitled 'A luid to the passer by':

> Loke to thy self by vs
> Suche wer we ons as thow
> And thow by tyme sall be consemud
> To dust, as we ar now.

The Maitland epitaphs, however, also exemplify important trends in commemorative writing in late sixteenth-century Scotland with their interest in family history as a means of memorialisation and didacticism.[45] The two epitaphs attributed to the court musicians, Thomas and Robert Hudson, emphasise Maitland as exemplar of virtue for those left behind, peerless in his execution of his public duties, and celebrate his role in ensuring family continuity.[46] According to the poem attributed to Robert

Hudson, Maitland exemplified the qualities of his 'antient race' and ensured its longevity: 'his childrens children flourishit day by day' (l. 7). It is therefore fitting that Richard Maitland made his own contribution to family history writing: a prose account of his mother's family, the *History of the House of Seyton* (c. 1560).[47] The commemorative writing associated with the Maitlands seems to stand out in Lowland Scottish literature of this period for its concentration on remembering family, though claims for its distinctiveness must be modified by an acknowledgement of the great amount of non-aristocratic household-based compositions of this sort which have surely now been lost. Gaelic elegiac literature, to which this chapter now turns, appears to focus more than Scots and Latin on the family and the local, and the differences between the traditions may reflect different poetic priorities or just the unpredictable survival rates of literary ephemera. Its lack of epitaphs for our period, as observed by the historian John Ramsay of Ochtertyre (1724–1824),[48] reflects the central role of the oral tradition, not the written, in commemorating the dead.

Gaelic

A detailed exploration of the full range of Gaelic-language elegy and lament poetry composed within our period falls outside the scope of this chapter. The 'caoineadh' (graveside lament, or '*keen*'), for example, will not be discussed, due primarily to a lack of evidence concerning its practice in Scotland,[49] nor laments occurring within a prose context, such as compendia of heroic death-tales also containing commemorative verses for fallen warriors.[50] Several important laments are preserved within the Book of the Dean of Lismore [BDL] – compiled 1512–1542 but containing material composed at least a century beforehand – arguably the most important of the collections of poetry to have survived from later-medieval Scotland. Several elegies composed by members of the MacMhuirich family during the first half of the seventeenth century will also be considered, chiefly those made by Cathal MacMhuirich (fl. 1620s–1630s) for successive chieftains of Clanranald;[51] others, by non-professional poets, were made for private individuals involved in the early conflicts of the Wars of the Three Kingdoms. Very few elegies extant from the period in question pre-date the 1490s. Some are the work of male, some of female authors, both known and anonymous; some represent the private sphere of personal grief, others the public commemoration of celebrated individuals.

The central place of elegiac poetry within Gaelic literary tradition has long been recognised, especially during the Classical period (i.e. c. 1200–c. 1600). This era, the heyday of poets trained in traditional bardic schools and of a language, the high-register 'dán díreach', common to the literati of both Ireland and Scotland,[52] was characterised less by the testimony of independent commentators such as David Lyndsay or William Fowler than by the mutually dependent relationship between a poet and his patron (see below). Whereas, moreover, deeds of persons and events of far-reaching national significance for the Scottish people were documented amply by Scots writers, especially those based at court, the attention of the Gaelic poets focused primarily, during this period at least, upon the clans and clan-chieftains of the regional Gàidhealtachd.[53] A notable exception, the only extant Gaelic poem concerning the battle of Flodden (1513), is addressed to Archibald, Earl of Argyll, who died in the field. Rather than an elegy for his passing, however, the poem is a rousing 'brosnachadh catha' ('*incitement to battle*'), probably sung before his household set out upon their expedition.[54] The majority of elegies pre-dating 1600, i.e. prior to the eventual dissolution of the bardic system, were produced within the context of a poet's relationship with his patron.[55] At odds with the range of families patronised in contemporary Ireland, many examples of which have survived, the extant Scottish bardic corpus is addressed to only a handful of kin-groups, chiefly the Campbells, MacDonalds and MacLeods.[56] Many of these verses are preserved within 'duanairean' ('*family anthologies*'),[57] of which BDL is the most important example (as well as a notable exception to the rule, since it contains verses addressed to several other families too, notably the MacGregors).[58] Martin MacGregor has argued recently that the range of kin-groups and territories represented within BDL reflects less upon the extent of power wielded by the Lordship of the Isles,[59] than upon the 'sphere of influence achieved by the Campbells within Gaelic Scotland by the first half of the sixteenth century'.[60] The verses' contents, overall, reflect the extent of the poet/patron relationship throughout the patron's lifetime, whether celebrating or condoling with momentous occasions during his career, such as victory or defeat in battle, marriage, or strategic political alliance. The cessation of this career gave rise to the poet's final obligation: lamenting his patron's death and the loss represented by his demise to the patron's family and clan. Rarer, elegiac-style verses may also attest to a poet's transition between patrons, often following his former sponsor's decline in fortune,[61] or meditate upon loss caused by leave-taking other than death, such as emigration.[62]

Conventional grief for a patron's loss is epitomised by the elegy made by Giolla Coluim Mac an Ollaimh (fl. 1480s–1490s) for Aonghas Óg, son of John IV, last hereditary Lord of the Isles.[63] Aonghas Óg's death occurred in 1490 and was described by the poet as arousing such grief that the wounds it caused should be visible to all who saw him (ll. 787–88). Aonghas's death is interpreted as an omen of the poet's own (ll. 803–04), as his body is weakened by grief and his strength diminished (ll. 795–96). The poet extols Aonghas's many virtues, of which his relatives, his clan, and the poet himself are now deprived. We hear of his former hospitality, his distribution of 'cairdreabh is comhól is támh' (l. 859, '*society, feasting and rest*'), and of his excellent comradeship, now withdrawn (l. 854). The excellence of his genealogy, another theme common within elegiac verse, is not referred to by Giolla Coluim, for reasons discussed below. References by Cathal MacMhuirich to 'síol Leóid' (v. 8a, '*the race of Leòd*'), 'deaghmhac ríoghamhuil Ruaidhrí' (v. 10b, '*Ruaidhrí's noble kingly son*'), and 'ua Tormóid' (v. 16b, '*Tormód's grandson*'), i.e. to the heritage of Iain MacLeod of Dunvegan, are more typical examples of their kind, from MacMhuirich's lament for Iain composed c. 1649.[64] Finally, Giolla Coluim compares the excellence of Aonghas to the excellence of other poets' patrons, even to the son of Mary Himself and the care He once bestowed upon His people. Without Aonghas, his poet claims, his people are left 'gan duine taisgidh againn' (l. 848, '*without a man to cherish us*').

The comparison of a poem's subject to well-known paragons of bravery, honour or other fame is commonplace within bardic elegies. By drawing upon its audience's prior knowledge of literary tradition, Gaelic and otherwise, the poet enhances the effectiveness of his or her chosen imagery significantly. Popular objects of comparison include characters from the Old Testament, as in Donnchadh MacRaoiridh's (fl. 1590s–1620s) address on the death of Alasdair, only son of Cailean Ruadh, Earl of Seaforth, in 1629.[65] The bereaved father is reminded by the poet of Abraham's willingness to sacrifice his only son: 'fuair e gràsan bho mo Rìgh, / An geall a-rìst aige fèin' (v. 3c–d, '*favours he was granted from my King in return for this as a pledge to himself*'). Donnchadh suggests further that 'aig ro-mheud diadhachd do chuirp/ bheir Se dhuit a dhò no trì' (v. 2c–d, '*for your body's godliness in return He will give you two or three [more sons]*'). Cathal MacMhuirich's elegy for MacLeod of Dunvegan also utilises Old Testament imagery, comparing Iain's remaining kindred after his death to Noah's family in the wake of the Flood.[66] Characters from classical history and mythology, such as Alexander the Great, Caesar, and Hector, may also be invoked, often in a genealogical context.[67] Most commonly, however, the subject of the elegy will be compared to figures renowned elsewhere within Gaelic literature, notably to the exemplary warrior, Cú Chulainn.[68] Verses composed on the deaths of two Clanranald chieftains, Ailean and Raghnaill, circa 1514, include the comparison of Ailean's former protection of his lands to Cú Chulainn's defence of Ulster against invasion.[69] Other popular comparators include the warriors of Fionn Mac Cumhaill, as in Iain Lom's address to Dòmhnall Gorm Òg, MacDonald of Sleat, and his men, circa 1643,[70] and Noísiu, son of Uisneach and his brothers, as in another of Cathal MacMhuirich's elegies composed on the death of four chieftains of Clanranald in 1636 (see below).[71]

Giolla Coluim Mac an Ollaimh's elegy for the death of Aonghas Òg also entwines his subject's biographical experience with Cú Chulainn's. The elegy, comprised of twenty-three stanzas in Watson's edition, begins on page 240 of BDL.[72] The following lines in the manuscript begin, 'do chuala mé fada ó shoin/ sgéal as cosmhail rér gcumhaidh' (ll. 873–74, '*I heard long ago a tale like unto our lament*'). This is almost certainly a reference to the poem, also the work of Giolla Coluim, beginning on page 236 of BDL, in which the poet presents a version of 'Oidheadh Conlaoch' ('*The Death of Conlaoch*'), an Ulster Cycle tale in which Cú Chulainn's only son is slain. William J. Watson was the first to suggest that these texts should be interpreted alongside each other as a co-ordinated elegy for Aonghas Òg.[73] Ostensibly, the connection made by Giolla Coluim is to the intensity of grief felt by Cú Chulainn for Conlaoch, shared by those who mourn Aonghas.[74] There is, however, a deeper level of connection between the two subjects. Within 'Oidheadh Conlaoch', Cú Chulainn himself is responsible for his son's death, following a series of challenges made by Conlaoch to his father's authority in Ulster. Aonghas's relationship with his father, John, was similarly contentious, leading upon several occasions to open conflict between their rival factions. Aonghas met his death at the hand of his own harper, Diarmaid Ó Cairbre, which deed was almost certainly carried out at the behest of a third party.[75] As Thomas Clancy has observed, 'it is hard not to suspect that political factors were behind Aonghas's assassination, [or] indeed, that his own still politically active and dangerous father may have been behind his death'.[76] The juxtaposition of Giolla Coluim's conventional – and uncontroversial – lament for Aonghas with a description of Conlaoch's death at his own father's hand invites the audience to consider

John's culpability in a similar light to Cú Chulainn's – without, crucially, an overt accusation of his involvement being made. The sentiments aroused, however, and the suggestion of the poet's anger at the manner of Aonghas's death, remain clear, and were probably apparent even several decades later at the time of their insertion into BDL, resulting in the otherwise curious separation of the elegy from its apologue.[77]

Giolla Coluim's response to his patron's murder demonstrates that elegiac verse of this period was not intended solely to express conventional grief. It provided also a powerful vehicle for the communication of anger, protest, and criticism of a particular series of events (usually, though not always, those resulting in the death of the poem's subject).[78] Occasionally, as in a poem by the Dean of Knoydart, Eoin MacMhuirich (d. 1510),[79] also concerning the murder of Aonghas Óg, these sentiments are addressed to the deceased directly. Here, the poet berates Diarmaid Ó Cairbre, Aonghas's killer, for his role in the death, addressing his anger towards, specifically, Diarmaid's head, now severed from his body in punishment for his crime (e.g. 'mairg do chréacht a chneas niamhgheal,/ a chinn Diarmaid Uí Chairbre' (*'woe to him who wounded [Aonghas's] bright white skin, thou head of Diarmaid Ó Cairbre'*).[80] The poet claims to feel no pity for Diarmaid, despite the fact that he was hanged for his crime (l. 944), since his betrayal of Aonghas has wrought such devastation. The circumstances of his treachery unfold alongside more traditional descriptions of Aonghas's virtues: he was 'Rí Íle na gcorn gcomhóil' (l. 957, *'Islay's king of festive goblets'*), 'nár dhoichleach óir ná airgid' (l. 962, *'ungrudging of gold or silver'*). Diarmaid, claims the poet, was involved in a conspiracy – others should fear, who 'nach badh námha do chairdis' (l. 950, *'would not be a foe to [his] alliance'*) – and he gained, at least initially, 'th'airgne agus t'uaille' (l. 942, *'spoils and thy pride'*) from his involvement. His fellow perpetrators are unnamed, due possibly to the poet's desire to reserve explicit judgement upon their behaviour.

Both Eoin MacMhuirich's address to Diarmaid Ó Cairbre and Giolla Coluim's elegy for Aonghas Óg provide fairly transparent indications of the poet's relationship to his subject. Both poets associate themselves openly with the aftermath of Aonghas's murder, and Giolla Coluim twice identifies his role as someone responsible for publicising what has taken place.[81] Other elegies in which similar judgement is passed upon their subject's death – and the manner in which it was procured – present more complex issues of interpretation. Many of these concern the speaking-voice, or persona, of the verses, at times singularly misleading with regard to their actual authorship and origins. Such examples are more common within the so-called sub-literary tradition, post-1600 (see below),[82] but may be found also within the bardic corpus, though less frequently in Gaelic Scotland.[83] Chief amongst these are the laments, discussed at length by Proinsias Mac Cana[84] and Katharine Simms,[85] in which a chieftain's death is mourned in language reminiscent of someone with whom he was once upon intimate terms. These elegies were interpreted initially as the work of women, their subjects' anonymous wives or lovers, and the frequency of their occurrence was used to support arguments for the commonplace existence of professional female poets.[86] This assumption was challenged first by James Carney,[87] who proposed that the verses' female voice was actually a male poet's adopted persona, underlining the strength of his grief for his departed patron by assuming the posture of a bereaved spouse. Genuine female poets did, of course, exist,[88] but similar masking techniques are prevalent elsewhere within Celtic-language literature,[89] in which use of the poet's own, first-person voice is rare, and is often disguised by gender-switching or, alternatively, by adopting the assumed voice of a traditional character.[90] The reference may be overt, as in his widow's lament for a MacDonald of Glengarry, Dòmhnall Gorm, slain at Killiecrankie (1689), in which she compares her grief at her husband's loss to Deirdre's sorrow "n deis a gràidh thoirt do Naoise' (*after she gave her love to Noísiu*').[91] It may also be implied, indirectly, by the cumulative description of events experienced, actually or otherwise, by the speaker, common also to the recognisable biography of a traditional character.[92] Within Cathal MacMhuirich's elegy for the deaths of four chieftains of Clanranald (1636) we see another example of this technique, where he mourns the loss of four men but names only three comparators: Noísiu, Ainnle, and Ardán, the sons of Uisneach.[93] Prior knowledge of the brothers' biography, described initially by another Ulster Cycle tale, 'Longes mac n-Uislenn', (*'The Exile of the Sons of Uisliu'*), would suggest a further comparison being drawn between the chieftains' loss and the fourth character central to that tale, i.e. Deirdre. It may be Deirdre's own death to which the loss of the fourth chieftain is compared, but it is more likely that Cathal himself has assumed Deirdre's voice, reminding his audience that she remained alive, albeit temporarily, to compose her own laments for the brothers' demise.[94]

The general effect of such masking, as we have seen already in the case of Giolla Coluim's elegy for Aonghas Óg, is to associate the poem's subject, and a significant experience that he or she has undergone, with the circumstances of a similar event in the renowned life of the chosen character.[95] As well as providing convenient descriptive shorthand for the sentiments he hopes to arouse in the minds of his audience, the poet's desire to criticise the events from which his elegy arose could also be managed effectively, depending upon the context of its composition.

Passing judgement upon the behaviour of a patron – or, more often in the case of elegiac verse, upon the behaviour of those responsible for his death – placed the poet in a delicate position vis-à-vis potential consequences of his words. Various techniques of composition appear to have been designed to distance the poet from those persons he sought to criticise, or the series of events at which he hoped to protest (especially in cases where the parties concerned were those to whom he was closely connected, or the events those in which he had been personally involved).[96] Use of a borrowed persona is the most important of these techniques, apparently gaining significant freedom for the poet to express sentiments for which, ordinarily, he may have been condemned. In the wake of the Keppoch murders in 1663, Iain Lom (c. 1624–c. 1695)[97] composed a lament for the deceased, Alasdair the thirteenth chieftain and his brother Raghnall, in which he claimed to have rushed to the scene of their deaths upon hearing the news, staunching the blood flowing from their wounds with his own hands, and placing the corpses in their graves.[98] These duties would normally have been performed by women.[99] Whether or not his claims are sincere, by asserting that he behaved in this way the poem assumes an essentially feminine voice of grief.[100] His purpose may have been to insinuate that no other mourners had gathered to lament the murdered men, with no women present to bury them appropriately – an accusation of indifference amongst the men's kindred concerning their deaths, when the poet himself took an active part in pursuing those suspected.[101] The effectiveness of the poem's imagery depends upon the inversion of a commonplace occurrence, in this case the expectation that women rather than men would have assumed post-mortem care of the victim's bodies. A similar use of inverted motif occurs in the song known as 'Grioghal Cridhe' ('*O Gregor, my heart*'), Mòr Chaimbeul's (fl. 1560s) lament for her murdered husband Griogair Ruadh MacGregor of Glen Strae.[102] Composed c. 1570, its verses describe, retrospectively, Mòr's relationship with her husband, from the time of their first meeting to his execution at the behest of her own kindred, part of the on-going feud between the Campbells and MacGregors in the 1550s and 1560s.[103] Concerning his death, by beheading, Mòr states that:

> chuir iad a cheann air ploc daraich,
> 's dhòirt iad 'fhuil mu làr;
> nam biodh agamsa an-sin cupan,
> dh'òlainn dhith mo shàth

they placed his head on a block of oak, and spilt his blood on the ground; had I but had a cup there I'd have drunk of it my fill. (v. 5)

Whereas the wish to consume blood from a loved one's corpse is relatively common in Gaelic elegy,[104] Mòr intends to make use of a cup to collect it, rather than her own hands. The foreign object introduces an element of distance from the scene described; Mòr, in fact, is unlikely to have been present at her husband's execution, due to her own captivity at the time as well as the advanced nature of her contemporary pregnancy.[105] 'Grioghal Cridhe' is couched ostensibly as a lullaby addressed to her new-born son, a style of composition often employed in order to distance the poet even further from his or her subject-matter.[106] Its apparent insignificance as a genre amongst professional poets may also have been deliberate: Màiri nighean Alasdair Ruaidh (c. 1625–c. 1707),[107] poet to the MacLeod chieftains of Harris and Dunvegan, is said to have countered objections to the content of one of her songs by claiming that it was 'only a *crònan*', i.e. a croon or lullaby.[108]

Not all critical elegies, however, were coded. A poem composed c. 1645, following the battle of Inverlochy, has been attributed to the authorship of Fionnghal Campbell (fl. 1640s), wife to Iain Garbh, eighth Maclean of Coll.[109] Their marriage appears to have been intensely unhappy, with the poem's speaker claiming that she has been physically abused, and her possessions taken from her and bestowed upon 'Seònaid', either her daughter or her husband's mistress.[110] Worse still in the speaker's eyes, her husband's family took the field at Inverlochy on the opposite side to her own kindred; her brother, Mac Dhonnchaidh Ghlinne Faochainn, Donnchadh Campbell of Auchinbreck, was slain, perhaps by the hand of the Marquis of Montrose's second-in-command, Alasdair mac Colla MacDonald.[111] The speaker's grief at his loss is so vivid that she wishes for her own son, Eachann Ruadh, to be destroyed in return: 'a chur air ròsta / air diol na muice duibhe dòite / no diol na circe thig an chòcair!' ('*to be set roasting, given the scorched black pig's treatment or the handling the cook gives the chicken!*').[112] In the wake of her brother's death, she claims, there is no one left to defend her. If the poem is not

Fionnghal's own work it was composed by someone with the deepest sympathy for her predicament, with few qualms concerning a negative response to their accusations – the situation, perhaps, could get no worse. The lament is one of very few to mourn the Campbells slain at Inverlochy, despite the significant number of their dead; another, attributed to Campbell of Auchinbreck's widow,[113] claims that 'thall 'sa bhos mu Inbhir-Aora, / Mnathan 'sa bhasraich 's am falt sgaoilte' (*'round and about Inveraray, women are wringing their hands and tearing their hair'*). Iain Lom's poem 'Là Inbhir Lochaidh' (*'The battle of Inverlochy'*) exulted specifically at the quantity of laments being made by the losers' widows;[114] akin to the barely concealed violence of Eoin MacMhuirich's elegy for Aonghas Óg (discussed above), his own lament for Montrose, executed at Edinburgh's Mercat Cross in May 1650, expresses the fervent hope that he will live to see the latter's betrayers hanged themselves.[115]

In several other directly accusatory elegies, either the circumstances to which the poet objects have been exposed already to others' critique, or else he or she draws deliberate attention to his subject's flaws. BDL contains a vicious satire[116] by Donnchadh Campbell of Glenorchy (1443–1513)[117] upon the allegedly degenerate conduct of one Lachlann Mac an Bhreatnaigh, who may have been a member of a noted family of harpers from Gigha.[118] Whereas the traditional elegy commemorates the life of its subject, Donnchadh's address to Lachlann chastises the dead man upon every possible level, concluding that 'is subhach bhíos gach dúnadh; / dá éag is buidhe gach bioth, / is ní cuibhdhe giodh éinchioth' (v. 23b-d, *'every court can [now] be happy; every being is thankful for his death, and not a single tear is in order'*). Accusations are made against Lachlann's bad practice in his profession, accepting gifts belonging rightfully to his apprentice (v. 13), and his constant requests for money, food, shoes, and clothes, even to 'léinte ban n-óg' (v. 12, *'the undergarments of young girls'*). Donnchadh's poem also parodies another common aspect of traditional laments, referring, here insincerely, to persons who might carry on his subject's legacy to the next generation: 'deacra liom ná éag an fhir / gan a oighre dhá éis-sin' (v. 21, *'I think it more vexing than the man's death that he should be without an heir to follow him'*).

Another example of the satirical lament, also from BDL, was described by William J. Watson as 'the most ferocious one known to me'.[119] Attributed to Fionnlagh am Bard Ruadh (*'the Red Bard Finlay'*, fl. 1510s), it is addressed to the same Ailean of Clanranald lamented more conventionally by the MacMhuirich bard (as above).[120] Its extreme rancour against Clanranald may connote the anti-Isles stance of BDL's predominantly MacGregor compilers, with Ailean and his family representing territories into which their own kinsmen had failed to expand.[121] Ailean is labelled 'aon diabhal na nGaoidheal' (*'the prime devil of the Gael'*),[122] a son of the hell-fires to which death has returned him (ll. 1237–44). He is accused of the most obscene crimes, including the desecration of burial grounds and sacred gospels (ll. 1265–8), and of conducting incestuous liaisons with his mother and sister (ll. 1295–96). The poet also suggests that Ailean had long been 'ó b'ionchrochtha' (l. 1294, *'gallows-ripe'*), an insult which may have given rise to the – almost certainly false – tradition that he was executed.[123] Although, akin to the 'elegy' to Lachlann Mac an Bhreatnaigh, the poem is styled as a post-mortem address, Watson speculated that Ailean may yet have been living when it was composed, suggesting that some aspect of his recent relations with Fionnlagh's patrons must have given rise to such extremity of verbal assault.[124]

The existence of two elegiac poems addressed to the same person, so different in style, content, and context, testifies also to the effects upon the genre of the decline of the Classically-trained bards and their high-register metres. In Scotland, this decline was more gradual than the dramatic de-gaelicisation across the Irish Sea, but its origins still comprised a complex mixture of foreign immigration, and the abandonment of Gaelic traditional culture.[125] Lower-register, vernacular poetry had begun to develop following the dissolution of the Lordship of the Isles at the end of the fifteenth century,[126] accounting for an increasing proportion of elegiac verse towards the end of our period. Lower-register metres, such as óglachas, did not displace dán díreach automatically but, at least at first, co-existed, with various types of poets producing various kinds of poetry, sometimes for the same patrons.[127] The contents of BDL, for example, are the work of 'professional poets of varying status, of ecclesiastics, and of lay amateurs, including women, representing a range of social strata within the aristocracy and perhaps beyond'.[128] One of its most poignant poems is the elegy composed by Aithbhreac inghean Coirceadail (fl. 1450s–1460s) upon the premature death of her husband, Niall Óg Mac Néill.[129] Certain sentiments expressed by the poet are not unlike Giolla Coluim Mac an Ollaimh's lament for Aonghas Óg. Aithbhreac praises her husband's eloquence, and extols his many physical virtues with heroic terminology: he is the 'leómhan Muile na múr ngeal' (*'lion of white-walled Mull'*),[130] the 'seabhag seangglan Sléibhe Gaoil' (l. 581, *'slim bright hawk of Sliabh Gaoil'*), and the 'dreagan Leódhuis'

(l. 583, '*dragon of Lewis*'). She finds also a more unusual focus for her grief: a rosary, formerly her husband's, upon which her eye has come to rest:

> a phaidrín do dhúisg mo dhéar,
> ionmhain méar do bhitheadh ort;
> ionmhain cridhe fáilteach fial
> 'gá raibhe riamh gus a nocht

> *thou rosary that has waked my tear, dear the finger that was wont to be on thee; dear the heart, hospitable and generous, which owned thee ever until tonight.* (ll. 557–60)

Aithbhreac's poem refers also to a deterioration in her own condition, stating that she is 'gan chluiche, gan chomhrádh caoin, / gan ábhacht, gan aoibh i gcéill' (ll. 587–8, '*without sport, without kindly talk, without mirth, without cheer to show*', and that her strength is failing (l. 610). The latter claim recalls Giolla Coluim Mac an Ollaimh's description of his physical decline since Aonghas Óg's death (discussed above), a comparison between the mourner's former and current status are also characteristic of descriptions of the grieving process as a whole; similar debility may be linked to psychological distress at being witness to their subject's burial, or preparing the corpse to be interred. Màiri nighean Aonghais (fl. 1590s–1610s),[131] widow of Dòmhnall, 3rd MacDonald chieftain of Clanranald (d. 1618), observed: ''s e chuir mo shùilean o léirsinn / Bhi càradh na léine mu d' thuairms' ('*it has wrenched the sight from my eyes, to be folding the shroud around you*'),[132] claiming more than once that her grief has torn her apart (e.g. vv. 8c, 13a), and that 'tha mo chridh' air a mhùchadh' (v. 16a, '*my heart has been extinguished*') since '[...] m' ulaidh is m' àbhachd, / Ann an ciste nan clàr 'ga chur sìos' (v. 17c–d, '*my treasure and my joy is being laid down in a chest of boards*'). The widow of Iain Stiùbhard of Strone (fl. 1640s) grieves that putting his body in the earth has left him ''s gun aon socair fo d' cheann ach bòrd' (v. 3c, '*no comfort but a board beneath your head*').[133] Conversely, however, distress could also arise when the mourner was unable to attend their subject's burial in person, such as the anonymous widow (fl. 1640s)[134] of a man of Clan Callum who was buried in Kingussie, apparently far from his home:

> Gur e siud mo sgeul deacair,
> Gu'n do thaisg iad 's Taobh Tuath thu [...]

'S truagh nach robh fir do dhùthcha'
Ga do ghiùlan air ghualainn [...]
'S nach robh i bean d'fhàrdaich
'S a' ghàirich m' an cuairt duit

That is my grievous tale, that they buried you in the north [...] it's a shame that your country-men did not carry you shoulder-high [...] and that it was not a woman of your [own] house that wept around you. (vv. 16, 17–18)

The poet begins her lament by describing a night-time vision (v. 1), from which she awoke to the newly-alarming revelation of her loss: "S a bhi cur mo làmh tharad, / 'S ann a dh'fhairich mi bhuam thu [...] / Gu'n d'thug siud orm briosgadh; / 'S mor is misde mo shnuadh e!' (vv. 2–3, '*stretching my hand across [towards] you, I felt that you were gone from me [...] that startled me: great and worse my complexion for it!*').[135] Other mourners exhibited more frantic physical symptoms of their grief, like the Campbell women of Inveraray noted above, common especially to cases of women informed only recently of a loved one's death. Their elegies may claim that they, like Iain Lom, rushed to the scene whilst the corpse was still warm, wringing their hands, tearing their clothes, and dishevelling their hair.[136] Màiri nighean Aonghais paces the length of her room, recollecting others for whom she has grieved as well as her husband: ''S mi a' cuimhneachadh uaislean, / 'Chuir sgaoilidh 's a ghruaig bh' air mo cheann ('*I am remembering [those] noblemen for whom I have torn out the hair of my head*').[137] She claims that the process, perhaps all-too familiar, is liable to ruin her health: 'Gur mis' th' air mo sguabadh' (v. 14, '*I have been swept clean away*');[138] Iain Lom makes a similar observation, worn out by the effort of grieving for several deceased MacDonald chieftains within a few years.[139] In 'Grioghal Cridhe', Mòr Chaimbeul claims that since her husband's death she has been unable to sleep, and sits 'aig bruaich mo leapa / a' bualadh mo dhà làimh ('*at the edge of my bed beating my two hands*'),[140] an aspect of grieving taken sometimes to extremes, forming blisters upon the mourner's hands.[141]

Reference to the waning or delicate health of the mourner is not, as we have seen, limited to poems composed by women. There are actually few notable differences in tone or subject-matter between male- and female-authored elegies from our period, with the exception that women poets seem to have composed fewer verses in high-register metres.[142] Women even composed poetry, including elegies, for male patrons, a possibility more apparent during the late-seventeenth and eighteenth centuries in the work of Màiri nighean Alasdair Ruaidh and Mairghread nighean Lachlainn (fl. 1690s–c. 1750).[143] Most often, however, as we have seen, it is a husband or sweetheart whom female-authored elegies mourn, and more examples of female lament poetry belong to the so-called sub-literary tradition, post-1600 (e.g. the elegy for Iain Stiùbhard, discussed above).[144] It is also more common for a female-authored poem to lack context, with little more than the fact of their subject's decease itself revealed by its verses, accompanied sometimes by the cause of death and, if we are very fortunate, by their name. Plenty of laments, such as the anonymous tribute to the man buried in Kingussie, withhold this, even when the subject appears to have belonged to an important family (the Killiecrankie elegy, noted above, names its probable subject in only one version, and his identity as well as the poet's remain open to dispute).[145] Some are almost impossible to date, or contextualise: we are left only with the poignancy of an unknown mourner's grief for an unknown subject, like the waulking song known as 'Cumha peathair' ('*A sister's lament*'),[146] in which we learn only her brothers' first names, and that both appear to have drowned:

> Ach a' cumha mo bhràithrean
> A' cnàmh anns a' chuain.
> Cumha Eachann 'is Lachlainn
> 'Dh' fhàg tàna mo ghruag
> 'S oil leam dìol ar cùil chlannaich
> 'S an fheamainn 'ga luaidh'

But I'm grieving for my brothers, who were swallowed up by the sea. A lament for Eachann and Lachlan, on whose account my hair has thinned; I grieve that your luxuriant hair is being fulled by the seaweed. (vv. 3–5)

The lament attributed to the otherwise unknown Mòr Nic Phàidein (fl. c. 1620s)[147] also focuses primarily upon the effects of her subject's death upon herself; we learn only his name, Niall Óg (v. 4), that he looked good in a kilt (v. 8), and that he died in equally noble company (vv. 6–7). Clearer is Mòr's inconsolable grief, worsened by others' laughter (v. 2), and the fact that she cannot entertain the possibility of other suitors (v. 11). It would seem, however, that Niall Óg's death has not been detrimental to Mòr financially, unlike the widow of a hunter identified only as Gilleaspuig,[148] whose premature loss has left her destitute in every sense:

Dh' fhuirich mise gun tacar
O' n mhadainn sin fhèin
Anns an deachaidh do thasgaidh
Ann an clachan nan geug

I have been without provisions since that very morning when you were stored up in the churchyard of the boughs. (ll. 1677-80)

In more affluent times, she recalls, though she had neither bread nor milk, 'thigeadh tu dhachaigh / ['S] bu leam tacar nam beann' (ll. 1675-76, '*you'd return home [and] the spoils of the hill would be mine*'); today, unable to replicate her husband's skills, she and her child go hungry (ll. 1681-84).[149]

Even such intensely personalised expressions of the effects of loss, intended primarily, we must assume, as either catharsis or a private record of the mourner's grief, are not limited to women's compositions. A lament on the death of Fearchar Ó Maoilchiaráin, composed perhaps c. 1500, was made by his father, whose own first name is unknown; he becomes, however, another archetype of tremendous sorrow for later poets.[150] Aside from the fact that Fearchar's death, apparently the result of murder, occurred whilst he was making a poetic circuit of Ireland (and, thus, that his profession was the same as his father's), we learn little from the poem itself besides the intensity of the speaker's grief and his desire for retribution.[151] Cathal MacMhuirich also composed a series of poems following the death of Catrìona, daughter of Domhnall Gorm Óg, eighth MacDonald of Sleat (d. 1643), to whom he had probably once been tutor.[152] One poem, 'Leasg linn gabháil go Gearrloch' ('*I am loth to go to Gairloch*') recounts how everything connected to the girl has become hateful to him, accentuating the strength of his loss.[153] Another, 'A Sheónóid, méaduigh meanma' ('*O Seonaid, cheer up*') counsels Catrìona's mother against permitting her grief to become excessive,[154] a rare Gaelic-language example of the 'moralising' verse so prevalent in the Scots tradition (see above).

Towards the end of our period, elegiac-style verses composed in honour of troubling occasions other than their subject's death also become more common. Poets lament the declining fortunes of entire kindreds, often in the wake of a conflict in which their objectives were not achieved. Such is the poem, attributed to Ailean Mac Gilleasbaig, whose context appears to have been the aftermath of the battle of Glen Fruin (1603), as it refers to Alasdair and Iain MacGregor (the sons of Mòr Chaimbeul and Griogair Ruadh), both of whom died as the result of their involvement.[155] Similar is the poem known as 'MacGriogair á Ruadhshruth' ('*MacGregor from Roro*'), another of those made within the atmosphere of the 'fearful sufferings' inflicted upon the MacGregors from the mid-sixteenth century onward.[156] Such is the significance of their persecution, especially to the political and cultural landscape in which BDL was compiled, that arguments have been made for the volume itself to be read as a testament to 'past glories', expressed in the 'predominantly elegiac tone of its heroic ballads, with their preoccupation with warrior death, the *ars moriendi*, and commemoration of the passing of an heroic age'.[157] For many in Gaelic Scotland, this age drew finally to a close during the Wars of the Three Kingdoms in the late 1640s and 1650s, as a result of which the attention of their poets focused ever more closely upon events of national significance as well as local. An untitled poem by a Maclachlan of Kilbride (probably John, who died c. 1681), composed on the death of Oliver Cromwell in 1658, reflects upon the 'inevitability of death even for the most powerful among us'.[158] In 'Òran cumhaidh air cor na Rioghachd' ('*A lament for the state of the country*'), one of many poems addressing its worsening plight,[159] Iain Lom entwines his grief for the death of Alasdair mac Colla MacDonald (d. 1647)[160] with his anger at the exile of the future Charles II (v. 6), expressing the conviction that Scotland is now 'mar luing air uachdar sàile, / gun stiùir gun ràimh gun phort' (v. 7, '*like a ship on the top of the ocean, without rudder or oar or port*'), whose future is bleak if God has truly abandoned them:

> Tha Sasannaich gar fairgneadh,
> Gar creach, gar murt 's gar marbhadh;
> Gun ghabh ar n-Athair fearg ruinn –
> Gur dearmad dhuinn 's gur bochd

> We are plundered by the English, despoiled, slain, and murdered; we must have caused our Father anger – for we are neglected and poor. (v. 4)

His eloquent frustration foreshadows the era of Jacobite detractors and sympathisers alike, also amongst the greatest poets of both personal grief and national devastation: such is Sìleas na Ceapaich's lament for the death of James MacDonald of Oronsay and Sleat (d. 1720), ostensibly a politicised elegy for the loss of her chieftain, but also informed by the sudden deaths of her own husband and daughter within a week of each other shortly before.[161] Her elegy for Alasdair Dubh, eleventh MacDonald of

Glengarry (d. 1724), shares the complaint made by Iain Lom (discussed above), that too much grief over too short a time is also damaging to the poet who must observe it:

> 'S beag ionghnadh mi bhith fo chreuchdaibh
> 'S gur tric 'gan reubadh as ùr iad;
> 'S beag ionghnadh mi bhith trom-osnach,
> 'S meud an dosgaidh th' air mo chàirdibh;
> Gur tric an t-eug uainn a' gearradh
> Rogha nan darag as àirde

Small wonder that I am covered with wounds and that they are repeatedly being burst open; small wonder that I am filled with deep sighing, considering all the misfortune that has befallen my friends. Death is constantly cutting us off from the best of the tallest oaks. (ll. 801–06)

From high-register panegyric verses to fallen chieftains, through vernacular paeans to beloved husbands and sweethearts, and startlingly abrupt political critiques, Scottish Gaelic elegiac poetry of the later medieval period provides unusual insight into both public and private spheres of grief, attesting to the range, expertise and eloquent power of its bards.

CHAPTER NINE

Satire

Tricia A. McElroy and Nicole Meier

Idealistic and discontented, the satirist produces art that sets up for exposure and ridicule the foibles and sins of society. The strategies of satire are various: irony, sarcasm, mockery, hyperbole, understatement, parody, distortion, word play, humour, wit, and sometimes invective and direct attack. The tone can range from gentle mocking to bitter scorn, and the result can be immensely entertaining but can also cut in unexpected directions, always at risk of being misinterpreted and causing offence. While the satirist's impulse to criticise may arise from personal indignation, it usually stems also from an earnest desire to reform human behaviour, whether the target is an individual, a group of people, or a social institution. Speaking of satire's strategy and purpose, Horace claimed that satire aims to laugh men out of their follies. Yet critics have always been divided about the extent to which satire is efficacious: can it really bring about change, or does it operate more as a safety valve for the satirist to let off steam?

Moreover, satire is notoriously difficult to define. As one critic puts it, 'no omnibus definition can ever pigeonhole all types of satire'.[1] It is not a genre itself, so much as a parasitic mode of writing, bursting to life through a variety of literary forms. In the Middle Ages, for example, satire appears 'episodically' in 'works such as romances, fables, sermons, visions, songs, or other medieval genres';[2] it attacks the familiar evils of human society – vanity, hypocrisy, corruption, greed, perversity, exploitation of the poor – and often specifically targets women, the clergy, the church or state. At the heart of any satire – certainly the Scottish examples surveyed below – lies both a commitment to art and a belief in the power of words. The former manifests itself in the often-complex rhetorical structures and fictions through which the satirist presents his critique[3] – beast fable, for instance, flyting competition, or dream-vision. So essential is this aspect of the satirist's craft, in fact, that Ruben Quintero argues,

'Though some form of attack or ridicule is necessary for something to be satiric, without intentional art there is no satire'.[4] And the power of words – to bless, to curse, to change – seems rooted in something more deeply mystical, whether biblical prophecy or the eulogistic or shaming power of the Gaelic poets.

Gaelic satire, especially in early texts, had strong associations with magic,[5] and was a means of wielding or exerting power. The term '*áer*' could refer to incantational satire (spell and enchantment), as well as to satire without the aid of magic (lampoon, personal attack, or curse).[6] Satirists were feared and respected in Celtic society: 'the words of a satire were believed to be capable of inflicting both physical and social damage'[7] – hence, the metaphors of satire as a weapon, with its effects of lacerating, cutting, blemishing, and dishonouring.[8] The sagas of Early Gaelic literature contain numerous references to satire's unpleasant effects, which could cause facial blemishes and blisters, and in extreme cases, even death. In 'Talland Etair'('*The Siege of Howth*'), for example, the poet Aithirne, refused by Luaine, makes a satire on the latter, which causes three blisters to appear on Luaine's face.[9] The same is reported of Néde, who makes a satire on his uncle Caiér. In 'Cath Maige Tuired' ('*The [Second] Battle of Moytura*'), the satire of poet Cairbre mac Étaíne causes Bres mac Elathan, king of the Tuatha Dé Danann, to lose his health and position as king.[10] In a society where reputation and honour were paramount, facing desocialisation by means of satire constituted a powerful threat.

The tradition of earlier Gaelic satire strongly influenced the Gaelic literature of the Middle Ages. The Gaelic satirical literature composed during the Stewart Kingdom falls within the Classical Early Modern period, when it is not linguistically possible to distinguish between Irish and Scottish Gaelic texts.[11] This body of poetry was written by poets trained in the bardic schools as they existed in Ireland and parts of Scotland.[12] The 'file' was a professional poet, attached to noble families and patrons, and a highly esteemed member of Gaelic society whose 'principal function was to uphold and protect his chief's good name and fame'.[13] The bardic poets were renowned for two kinds of poetry: eulogies for their chieftain and satires on their enemies. However, the corpus of satires which has come down to us is not large, 'because such compositions would not commend themselves for inclusion in the *duanaire* class of manuscripts'.[14] Since the duanaire was a family poem book and anthology of bardic poetry, censorious verse – caustic and unappealing – is less likely to have been preserved. The learned compendium known as the Book of Ballymote (Royal Irish Academy MS 23 P 12), compiled c. 1400, contains a treatise on types of satire ('Cis lir fodla aíre?' '*How many types of satire are there?*'),[15] but the most interesting anthology made in Scotland during the Stewart Kingdom is certainly the Book of the Dean of Lismore (NLS Adv. 72.1.37). In several satires from this collection, the complementary relationship between satire and eulogy becomes evident. Satire is dispraise and inversion of the positive values enumerated in panegyrics such as hospitality, generosity, valour, prowess, nobility of birth. The satirised person is hence credited with the opposites: meanness, low birth, inhospitality, cowardice and physical defects. While eulogy creates and enforces renown and social standing, satire destroys good name. One example of eulogy and satire as counterparts is Giolla Críost Brúilingeach's (fl. 1440s) 'Dá urradh i n-iath Éireann' ('*Two chiefs are there in Ireland*'), which compares the good chief Tomaltach MacDermot and Tómas Maguire, the bad chief. Tómas is 'lom lochtach' ('*mean and faulty*', l. 469) whereas Tomaltach is 'cródha' ('*valiant*', l. 470). Their horses, mailcoats and weapons are compared; the contrast is epitomised when McDermot is called 'láidir aithnid eólach' ('*strong, renowned and skilful*') and Maguire is feeble and helpless ('anbhfann aintreórach'). Likewise, 'Theast aon diabhal na nGaoidheal' ('*The prime devil of the Gael is dead*') is a satiric elegy on Ailean mac Ruairi MacDonald (Allan, son of Roderick MacDonald of Clanranald) by Fionnlagh, am Bard Ruadh (Finlay, the Red Bard, fl. 1510s). It is a kind of black praise, in which the author enumerates every hellish deed said to have been performed by Ailean, as a means of shame, hurt and humiliation, something also discussed in the previous chapter.[16]

Some of the satires in the BDL can be classified as 'arguments about women' and are 'concerned principally with women in general rather than with particular women'.[17] A poem ascribed to Earl Gerald (1335–1398), 'Mairg do léimeas thar a each' ('*Woe to him who dismounts from his horse*') satirises treacherous and scheming women whereas Duncan Campbell's (d. 1513) 'Mairg ó ndeachaidh a léim lúith?' ('*Woe to him whose vigour has now departed*') is an old man's lament about the loss of virility and the consequential lack of female interest this causes.[18] But there is also satire directed against specific women – a black inversion of the courtly love poems which are also present in the BDL (and are discussed in the chapter on Lyric, above).

Hence, Gaelic satire is very much invective, threatening and insulting individuals or groups, and thus functions as a sanction or threat and instrument of social control, enforcing norms and social values while at the same time punishing offences. Techniques at work are very often black praise, inversion of the panegyric code, and use of 'obscenities', such as vulgar words, usually referring to sex and excretion, blasphemy and profanity, as well as animal imagery.[19]

Types of satire recalling these Gaelic modes can be found in the poetry of Dunbar, Kennedy, Henryson and other Middle Scots poets of the fifteenth and sixteenth centuries. In the poetry of William Dunbar (c. 1460–c. 1513), which is notoriously difficult to categorise, satire crops up as 'manner' in poems of various sorts and different genres.[20] The most intriguing poem in this context is *The Flyting of Dunbar and Kennedy*, a collaborative work of Dunbar and his fellow poet Walter Kennedy (c. 1455–c. 1518), which, on the one hand, appears to be a verbal slanging match with tirades of insults and, on the other, exhibits a clear structure and displays the verbal skills of both poets who assume different personae in order to vilify each other. They caricature each other's way of life (Kennedy as thieving Highlander, beggar, layabout and bad poet; Dunbar as descendent of a family of devils and traitors and inept poet) and tell anecdotes and accounts of disreputable incidents in order to discredit their opponent and denigrate their ancestry and life-style. Like Gaelic satire, the *Flyting* is personal attack, lampoon and invective, very much *ad hominem*, and relies on the power of words. The portraits of the antagonists are illustrated by vivid animal imagery, thus underlining unattractive character traits and shortcomings. Both poets use the techniques of Gaelic satire, as the *Flyting* contains a wide range of references to illnesses (and venereal diseases), to lineage, and makes use of scatology.

Several of Dunbar's shorter poems in satirical manner also attack specific individuals. In a petition for advancement ('Schir, I complane of injuris,'[21]), Dunbar complains about the poet Mure whom he accuses of plagiarism and of corrupting his poetry. Interestingly, the charges Dunbar makes against Mure are similar to those uttered in the *Flyting*: the other poet is a fool who 'has tynt baith wit and ressoun' (l. 20) and would best be hanged as 'crewall sclander servis ded' (l. 12). Dunbar also threatens the poet to make 'him knawin' (l. 6) and anticipates a mobbing scene staged as a bull-baiting. The poem 'In vice most vicius he excellis' (B 27) attacks Donald Owyr, who is generally identified with Donald Dubh, a grandson of the last Lord of the Isles and prominent in the failed attempt to restore the Lordship in James IV's reign (1503–1506). In his poem, Dunbar vilifies Donald and describes him as being as ugly as an owl and resembling a 'fals fox' (l. 31). As in the *Flyting*, outward appearance and the comparison to animals serve a more general aim: to portray vices.

The owl is not only ugly, but also an animal of the night and often associated with treachery.[22] And traditionally the fox, as in Henryson's *Fabillis*, is cunning and crafty, nothing but a villain and a thief. It becomes apparent that here Dunbar is not merely vilifying an individual but also attacking general vices, above all treachery: Donald Owyr is a 'reffar, theiff, and tratour'[23] (l. 32). 'In vice most vicius he excellis' thus comprises personal attack and a more general castigation of treachery, and the poem probably contains an indirect complaint to the king who granted traitors like Donald Owyr pardons – although according to Dunbar 'the murtherer ay murthour mais' (l. 43).

Dunbar's capacity to strike different tones in one poem can also be traced in 'As ʒung Awrora with cristall haile', which takes the form of a dream-vision.[24] The dreamer describes the career of John Damian, who became abbot of Tungland (Kirkcudbrightshire) in 1504, his diabolic origin and his success, which is characterised by greed and deception. After fleeing from Europe, Damian became James IV's protégé and was renowned for his alchemical experiments. The Asloan Manuscript entitles the poem 'a ballat of the abbot of tungland', and, though Damian is never explicitly mentioned, Dunbar's readers would immediately have identified the figure of the poem with someone as prominent as Damian. According to Dunbar, Damian attempts to fly from Stirling castle with wings made from birds' feathers, but is attacked by birds, defecates all over himself, and ends up in a mire. The first part of the poem seems concerned solely with expressing Dunbar's spite at Damian, but the poem is more than merely a personal invective. Dunbar not only attacks Damian but also alchemy, false science, greed, and incompetence. Personal abuse is thus coupled with a broader satirical thrust, and the dream-vision serves as a vehicle for a poem narrative in mode and satirical in manner.[25]

Figures at James IV's court frequently become the targets of Dunbar's satire, very often also bordering on the comic. As in 'Schir, I complane of injuris', Dunbar combines the language of complaint and invective when he complains about James Doig to the queen ('The wardraipper of Wenus boure')[26]. Doig is accused of having behaved disobligingly to Dunbar who therefore mockingly plays on Doig's name, using canine imagery. Doig is a 'tyk' (l. 14), a 'mastive' (l. 17), of ugly appearance and hence unfit to keep the queen's wardrobe. In 'Schir, ye have mony servitouris'[27] Dunbar first gives a list of people serving the king: craftsmen who deserve the king's thanks and reward. In the second stanza Dunbar asserts that his making is also a craft, although he describes himself as unworthy. He then enumerates people at James's court, concentrating this time on parasites. They are endowed with unpleasant traits like the contestants of the *Flyting*; they are 'fantastik fulis' (l. 57), and yet, they are rewarded. Dunbar complains about this injustice: if they be rewarded, why not he? Dunbar declares that his 'mind so fer is set to flyte' (l. 79) and threatens the king that he will avenge himself by flyting. If he does not communicate his displeasure – that is, to 'lat the vennim ische all out' (l. 85) – he will die of melancholy. The last stanza expresses the destructive potential of flyting and is directly in line with the Gaelic concept of satire which results in loss of honour and good name. Satire is poisonous to its victims, but also detrimental to the satirist himself. The fact that he cannot communicate his satire makes him sick. This idea can be found in Gaelic satirical writings,[28] but Dunbar picks up a metaphor prominent in Early Renaissance satire. Dunbar's anger at the idlers and parasites at court is a disease, a kind of melancholy that needs a remedy. In the Early Renaissance of the fifteenth and sixteenth centuries, descriptions of satire abound in medical imagery and the main aim of Early Renaissance satire was catharsis.[29] Dunbar seems to combine an older destructive notion of satire with this cathartic function.

Several of Dunbar's poems address corruption at court and in the church. In his petition to James, 'Complane I wald, wist I quhome till',[30] Dunbar complains about upstart courtiers who climb at the expense of others. The catalogue of these persons recalls the tone of the *Flyting* when the upstarts are '[m]isgydit membris of the devellis / Mismad mandragis of masits strynd / Crawdones, couhirttis and theifis of kind' (ll. 21–23). These 'monsteris' (l. 27) are associated with ugly appearance, treachery, filth and theft, and Dunbar employs a whole range of fanciful abusive epithets. Dunbar especially abuses a low-born churchman who is a 'pykthank in a prelottis clais' (l. 53) and 'fenyeing the feirs of ane lord' (l. 61). Ecclesiastical abuses and familiar shortcomings of the clergy are also the object of Dunbar's satire: in 'Off benefice, sir, at everie feist' he criticises greedy churchmen who neglect the poor people of the parish, and in 'This hinder nycht, half sleeping as I lay' he attacks pluralism.[31] Duplicity of friars and of Franciscans in particular are the target of Dunbar's dream-vision 'This nycht befoir the dawing cleir', in which a figure who first seems to be St Francis but then turns out to be the Devil, appears to the dreamer and urges him to become a friar.[32] The central symbol in the poem is the friar's habit, and various pretensions of the friars are revealed, such as 'wrink and wyle' (l. 42), falsehood, venality and deceit. Dunbar combines religious and legal satire in 'Ane murelandis man of uplandis mak' in which he has a naïve countryman recounting shocking 'tythinges', such as the corruption of lawyers and the worldliness and unchastity of various religious orders.[33]

In his longest poem, 'Apon the Midsummer Ewin, merriest of nichtis' (B 3), Dunbar combines various literary conventions to satirise women and marriage.[34] The poem opens like a *chanson d'aventure* with a narrator hiding in a shrubbery and secretly watching and listening to three beautiful women. The idealised scene is shattered when the three women, a widow and two married women, begin to speak and start to gossip and complain about their husbands and the miseries of their marriages. The women talk about their old and/or impotent husbands in repulsive and scathing terms, and the men are likened to animals (dogs, horses, insects). Contrasts heighten the effect of Dunbar's satire: the angelic appearance of the three women is contrasted with their experiences and their derisive talk and the realities of marriage with the artifices of courtly love. The poem certainly does not paint a sympathetic picture of the women, with the widow advising the women how to deceive and use men, yet 'Ane aigit man, twyß fourty ʒeiris'[35] by Dunbar's contemporary Walter Kennedy is a far more misogynist poem. In Kennedy's poem an old man complains about the miseries of old age: he used to devote his time, money, and riches to 'mouth thankles' (ll. 8, 16, 24), (the word is a noun plus a postposed adjective, literally meaning 'ungrateful mouth', but 'mouth' certainly signifies 'female pudendum' here) and now, since he is old, the women whom he used to please and gratify will not look on him any more. The poem vilifies women as greedy and faithless, reducing them to their genitals. In Dunbar's 'Apon the Midsummer Ewin', however, the husbands are also repellent, and 'the overall vision seems less misogynistic than misanthropic'.[36]

Whereas Dunbar often depicts human beings as animals in order to denigrate them and to satirise follies and vices, in the *Morall Fabillis* of Robert Henryson (1425?–1506) animals are portrayed as human beings mainly in order to teach moral lessons. Henryson's *Fabillis* have two main models: Aesopian fables lie behind seven of Henryson's poems, and beast epic, such as the *Roman de Renart,* underpin the other six. Although Henryson's overall cast is a moral one (man has to control the appetites of his senses that belong to his animal nature and let himself be governed by reason), with attacks on general vices such as greed, injustice, vanity, hypocrisy or duplicity, the fables also serve as a vehicle for specific social criticism and satire. In 'The Two Mice',[37] a town mouse visits her sister in the country and is offered a simple meal by her relative at which she scoffs and invites the country mouse back to the city. There they share a sumptuous meal, but are interrupted first by the arrival of the spenser (the household steward) and then by the cat. The country mouse escapes the cat's attack, but decides to return home, preferring security to plenty. Since Henryson's town mouse belongs to a guild, she is a burgess mouse and Henryson not only satirises and criticises people who get above themselves – as the burgess mouse has obviously forgotten the reality of her childhood – but also the pretensions of the rising bourgeoisie, the third estate, in Scotland and their impious materialism (the town mouse eats large amounts of food, takes wine instead of water and skips the grace). The gluttony, covetousness and snobbishness of the burgess mouse are underlined by contrasting her with her country sister. The fable and the moralitas recommend and praise simple living, contentment with small possessions. The 'Wolf and the Wedder' strikes similar tones when a wether, after his shepherd has lost his dog, insists on replacing the dog by putting on a dogskin.[38] The wether overreaches himself when he believes he is able to guard the rest of the flock and is killed by the wolf. The fable thus advises sticking to one's station in life and satirises those who proudly rise above their station.

Henryson also contrives to attack general misdemeanours such as violence and injustice and abuse of power, while at the same time employing social satire to comment on the state of contemporary Scotland. In 'The Sheep and the Dog', a dog sues a sheep for a loaf of bread, but the court is packed with predators and enemies of the sheep: the raven is the summoner/apparitor, the fox the notary, kite and vulture are advocates, and the wolf functions as the judge.[39] Here, Henryson turns the Aesopian pagan law court into an ecclesiastical court in order to warn against the corruption of justice: false bearing of witness, altering of names in return for bribes. The 'The Wolf and the Lamb' also focuses on abuse of power.[40] The lamb and the wolf drink from the same stream and although the lamb is drinking downstream, the wolf accuses the lamb of sullying the water. Although the lamb argues with logic from natural, divine and human law, the wolf pitilessly kills his victim. In his moralitas, Henryson makes clear that the lamb symbolises the Scottish peasantry and that the wolf stands for three kinds of oppressors: manipulators of the legal system, greedy landlords, and land-owners exploiting their tenants.

Even with its customary targets – women, corrupt clerics, negligent rulers – medieval satire usually tilted toward complaint, concerned with the underlying moral causes of social misbehavior and resigned to the belief that change comes only from God.[41] The Renaissance and Reformation period brought about both a transformation in tone and in attitude. The familiar plagues of immorality, injustice, and corruption continued to preoccupy Scottish authors, but, with real reform movements under way on the continent and in England, literary satire began to venture into more strident and specific commentary. Religious change, increased factionalism, and, importantly, the power of the printing press freed the satirist to demand and to expect more – including more involvement from the populace in addressing and solving the problems of public life. Sir David Lyndsay of the Mount (c. 1486–1555) is the key Scottish author bridging these periods – and, incidentally, the first to use 'satyre' to describe one of his works. Committed to the idea of reform from within the Church, steeped in but willing to experiment with medieval literary conventions, and pushing the boundaries between the purely literary and the controversially political, Lyndsay would later be embraced by the Reformers as their prescient forerunner, someone to whom they looked for models and inspiration.[42] He may have been attached to the Scottish court as early as 1508, and he went on to have a long career as a companion and 'maister uschar' to King James V, a traveling diplomat, and the Lyon King of Arms.[43] Writing into the reign of Mary, Queen of Scots, he produced a number of important works, in which he took up the familiar matters of good governance, church corruption, and social justice, using a variety of modes (advice, complaint, satire) and conventions (dream poem, testament, beast fable). The difference, according to J. H. Burns, was that, unlike his predecessors, Lyndsay handled the relevant public issues of his day from 'a perspective of broader experience, and with correspondingly greater depth and elaboration'.[44]

Lyndsay's works reveal his deeply felt investment in advising the king well, reforming the church, and addressing the needs of the Scottish community. His contribution to the genre of flyting is the 'Answer to the Kingis Flyting' (c. 1536), in which he vividly snaps the satirist's tightrope:[45] how does one respond to a superior, one's king, admonishing him for moral shortcomings while paying him compliment, through the potentially explosive game of flyting? Lyndsay begins his reply to the king's 'ragment' by wavering between bravado and intimidation. He wishes for a 'tygerris toung' (4), swears to 'cry ane loud vengeance' (14), and, at the same time, admits that 'with my prince pertenit me nocht to pley. / Bot sen your grace hes gevin me sic command, / To mak answer, it must neidis me obey' (22–24). His is an unenviable position. Describing himself as a failure in matters of love, Lyndsay can then tease the king about his amorous encounter with a kitchen maid, scold him gently for being a 'furious fornicatour' (49), warn him about the dangers of such behaviour, and encourage him to get a wife. The poet thanks God 'tymes ten score' for preventing James from contracting venereal disease (62), hinting at the familiar political relationship between the king's moral health and the health of the body politic.[46] Lyndsay then bows out of the flyting gracefully, by complimenting the king as 'of flowand rethorik the flour' (70). The balance between abuse and humour, seriousness and game, is delicate in any flyting, but, by responding to James's challenge as he does, Lyndsay carefully draws attention to the inherent anxieties of the genre and to the political perils and possibilities when the contestants are so unevenly matched.

In the *The Testament and Complaynt of our Souerane Lordis Papyngo* (1530), Lyndsay again advises his king, but moves into broader political territory, deftly combining several genres to humorous and satiric effect: bird fable, *de casibus* tragedy, *chanson d'aventure*, as well as the more obvious complaint and testament.[47] Lyndsay's advice comes from the mouth of a dying parrot, who falls from a tree after climbing too high. Horrified and grief-stricken, the poet records the parrot's dying words. Her 'complaynt' opens with the admonitory proverb, 'Quho clymmit to hycht, perforce his feit mon faill' (73), conventional political wisdom that both sets up the parrot's tragi-comic fall and frames her ensuing testament: calling out to 'fals Fortune' (192), she now testifies to the dangers of the court, where a life of indulgence has caused her to ignore 'prudent counsell' and succumb to vanity and pride (199). Two epistles follow, first, one to her king, James V, in which the bird presents a concise 'mirror for princes'. James is praised, but reminded that he is 'vassall to that kyng incomparabyll' (256), God; he is advised to practice good king-craft, to be prudent, to dispense justice, to heed good counsel, to study history and governance, and to guide himself first: 'For quhou suld prencis govern gret regiounis, / That can nocht dewlie gyde thare awin personis?' (295–96) – echoing the *Flyting*'s interest in the monarch's personal morality. In her second epistle, to 'hir Brether of Courte', the bird characterises the court as a place of fickle fortune and corruption, launching into an extended 'fall of princes'. But in the final section of the poem Lyndsay turns fully to anti-clerical satire, in which the parrot gives an account of the degradation of the church from its early purity into sensuality, worldliness, and lack of learning. Swooping in to prey on the dying bird, a magpie (canon regular), raven (monk), and kite (friar) listen grudgingly to her recriminations, as they prepare to divvy up her worldly goods. In a grotesque and symbolic final gesture, they tear apart her body 'full gormondlyke' (1149).

Lyndsay remains best known for *Ane Satyre of the Thrie Estaitis*, a play built on the foundations of the medieval morality, but groundbreaking in its use of drama to intervene in the social and political concerns of contemporary Scotland – principally, clerical corruption and oppression of the poor.[48] The history of *Ane Satyre*'s recorded performances – first, in an early, non-extant version for James V at Linlithgow in 1540 and, later, the surviving longer version at Cupar in 1552 and in Edinburgh in 1554[49] – mirrors the ethical movement of the play's structure, from the arguably private drama of the king's struggle toward moral reform to the more public drama of cleansing the Scottish commonweal through a very specific legislative agenda. Using the familiar allegorical conventions of a morality play, *Ane Satyre*'s first section presents Rex Humanitas – the hero 'everyman' politically transformed into a Scottish king – succumbing to the temptation of Lady Sensualitie and the bad counsel of Placebo, Solace, and Wantonness. Despite the comic disguises and exploits of the Vices Dissait, Falset, and Flatterie, Rex ultimately prevails over his fleshly weakness with the arrival of Divine Correctioun, who orchestrates the king's receiving of Gude Counsell, Veritie, and Chastitie.

In the second section of the play, however, with Rex morally transformed and his attention re-directed toward the needs of his country, Lyndsay achieves 'something new and quite distinct – a continuation of the action in which the issues raised and seemingly resolved in the allegorical space of the first section are explored afresh in a verisimilitudinous play-world with a much greater geographic and cultural scope'.[50] The movement might also be characterised as a collapse, of the universal abstractions of medieval allegory into historical reality, in which a member of the audience, Pauper, can enter the play-world, begging for alms and demanding reparation for the taxation, exploitation, and poverty he has suffered. In this world, at the command of Rex, Diligence convenes a parliament of the estates – Spiritualitie, Temporalitie, and Merchand – which hears and attempts to redress the complaints of John the Commonweal and Pauper. The entrance of the estates is emblematic of the current state of affairs: they enter 'gangand backwart led be their vyces' (2315), with Gude Counsell instructing Rex to 'them reforme as ye think best / Sua that the realme may live in rest, / According to Gods lawis' (2356–8). And although the temporal estates, the lords and merchants, eventually clothe John the Commonweal 'gorgeouslie' and place him rightfully in the parliament (3802), the clergy clings more stubbornly to their customary privileges, claiming peevishly that they will 'want nathing that wee haue in use' (2828). Lyndsay strongly criticises the Church as the most recalcitrant and troublesome branch of the commonweal – corrupt, unlearned, and predatory. In the end, however, the clergy is disciplined, the vices are punished, and, importantly, legislation is enacted to address the wrongs perpetrated – primarily by the church – against John and Pauper. Although Lyndsay does not leave his audience securely with the sense that all has been solved – Flatterie escapes and Foly bursts in to deliver a concluding sermon[51] – he persuasively models the monarchical leadership and the cooperation and shared sacrifices required from the Scottish community in order to realise a more just polity. His significant literary achievement is to 'to reconfigure a dramatic form based upon abstraction and idealism to represent concrete and pragmatic ends'.[52] Lyndsay's play, particularly *Ane Satyre* with its movement from allegory to real-world solution, modelled for later satirists the political interventions possible – if not always entirely efficacious – with the transformation of literary forms and traditions.

When the Protestant Reformation did arrive in Scotland, after Lyndsay's death, it intensified debate about the sources of authority, stiffening religious and political division. The controversial reign of Mary, Queen of Scots spawned the most significant outbreak of satirical literature in the period. The crises of the late 1560s and early 1570s – the murder of Henry, Lord Darnley; the rebellion against Mary; the ensuing civil war between her and her son James's supporters – provided the satirist with seemingly endless material and prompted him to use late-medieval literary conventions for direct political comment. That satirist, principally, was Robert Sempill, a poet who left behind scant biographical details but who, along with printer Robert Lekpreuik, produced an astonishing series of broadside poems. Written from a strongly Protestant perspective, these broadsides began appearing in Edinburgh in 1567 after the sensational murder of the Queen of Scots' second husband, Darnley, and her rumoured affair with the prime suspect, the Earl of Bothwell. The queen was depicted as an adulterous, murderous Jezebel who should be removed from the throne. Posted surreptitiously, unsigned and unambiguous, these satires caused real alarm, and Mary and her advisors immediately addressed the threat by outlawing the 'placards and billis and ticquettis of defamatioun sett up under silence of nycht'.[53] But the damage was real, the effect swift. After Mary's overthrow in summer 1567, what had begun as a campaign to traduce the queen shifted focus to address the developing political fallout: a succession of regents during James VI's minority, the murder of the Earl of Moray; military skirmishes; religious conflict; and the general suffering that accompanies a protracted civil war.

About forty poems survive to comment on this period – a few in manuscript but most on printed broadsides – as well as a handful of prose pieces.[54] Like political satire of any era, these relentlessly severe and topical poems have often been regarded as aesthetically unappealing and have not always received their critical due.[55] Yet this satire is compelling precisely because of its polemical character and political engagement, because it suggests the possibility of a mutually productive relationship between literature and politics, especially during the momentous period of Reformation. In contrast to previous Scottish satire, Sempill's language, his barbed use of well-worn literary conventions, could have real political effect – as the parliamentary act of 1567 implies. The sharpness of his art emerges most obviously in the tone of the poems, many of which rely on exhortation and invective. A poem like 'Ane Answer maid to the Sklanderaris' reveals its debt to flyting, for example, although, unlike Dunbar and Kennedy's colourful abuse and performative one-upmanship, here the insults are notable for their humourless sincerity. Surviving in one manuscript copy, the 'Answer' suggests the possibility of a verbal battle played out on the market cross between Maddie, Sempill's kale wife and *nom de plume*, and the alleged 'papistis of this toun' (VIII.62).[56] Attacking her adversary as a 'papist loun' and 'blasphemus baird' (6, 11), Maddie warns him that, unless he rightly supports Moray as Regent, 'Thow sould haif waige, durst thow avow It, / The gallowis, for thi gratitude' (39–40). And, in a later poem 'The Spur to the Lordis', Sempill responds to the assassination of Moray by associating the murderous Hamiltons with Cain, hissing, 'Thay Renigats, thay Rubiatouris / Hes stollin our Regentis lyfe, / Thay treuthles Tygars, thay trinfauld Tratours / Hes steirit up this stryfe' (XXI.17–20). Thus, in the satirical poems, political and historical reality intensifies the aesthetic effect of an already vigorous poetic form.

Their most remarkable feature is the strategic use of literary tradition. Whereas invective and complaint are 'rhetorically straightforward', as Roderick Lyall argues, satire 'involves a more complex rhetorical structure, a fictional device, or other persuasive weapon'.[57] Sempill attempts to shape his readers' understanding of contemporary events in just these ways. Despite being offered up on the market cross in the popular broadside form, the poems are notable for their variety of metrical forms and for their learned range of allusion, to the Scottish poetic tradition, medieval conventions, homely proverbs, biblical narrative, even classical models. The transformation of real 'events and people into "fictive" creations'[58] converts familiar literary *topoi* into tools of political persuasion: a minstrel embarks on a *chanson d'aventure* to learn of murder and adultery in Edinburgh; Darnley's ghost delivers his *de casibus* testament; two men debate the sources of political authority in a *locus amoenus*; 'Honour' and 'Gude Fame' appear in a dream-vision after the murder of Moray; an allegorical Lady Scotland mourns the disappearance of her husband, John the Commonweal; and Maddie the market's kale wife, like a medieval ploughman figure, offers brutally honest social criticism.[59] Strategically and innovatively deployed, these devices of medieval poets both transform and are transformed by a specific political and religious context.[60]

Individual targets included Mary herself, but also her associates and supporters. The shifting allegiances of William Maitland of Lethington, once Mary's secretary, earned him a prominent place in the satires of Sempill and his fellow satirists. Poems like 'The Cruikit liedis the blinde' and 'The Bird in the Cage' deride Lethington for having 'miscuikit' the commonweal (XVI.8), for holding the nobles 'at variance' (XVI.13), and for being a 'Scurvie Schollar of Machiavellus lair' (XXII.8). The most notorious attack on Lethington was penned by none other than George Buchanan, humanist of European renown, architect of the case against Mary, Queen of Scots, and tutor of the young King James VI. His prose pamphlet *The Chamæleon* employs a sustained caricature of Lethington as the creature of changing hues, gifted at dissimulation and deception, a student of Machiavelli concerned only with self-interest: 'he changeit dailie colouris sumtyme flattering ye ane, sumtyme ye other, and making euery ane of yame belief that he laubourit onelie for yame'.[61] Having got wind of Buchanan's satire, Lethington, clearly alarmed, orchestrated a raid on Lekpreuik's house in April 1571 in order to prevent the 'Chamæleon' from being printed. Lethington's concern was well founded. As the nineteenth-century editor of Buchanan's vernacular writings observes, Lethington would have known Buchanan as 'one of the most formidable satirists of the age', notable (and notorious) for his *Franciscanus*, 'one of the most brilliant pasquinades ever written against the ancient Church'. Whereas Robert Sempill posed as the 'simple' poet, mostly anonymous if ardent and sharp, Buchanan enjoyed a reputation far beyond Scotland's borders: his work would not 'be the mere birth of a day'.[62]

Two other important examples of prose satires survive from this period of conflict: 'An Account of a Pretended Conference held by the Regent, Earl of Murray' and 'The Dialogue of the Twa Wyfeis'.[63] Both provide a sense of the one-upmanship among those responsible for contributing to this body of satire (Sempill, Buchanan, the Maitland brothers), as well as a fuller picture of the range of tools at the satirist's disposal.[64] The

'Pretended Conference' provides a welcome relief from the anti-Marian point of view by ridiculing the Earl of Moray and his cronies. Generally attributed to Thomas Maitland, Lethington's brother, the 'Pretended Conference' uses the common fictional device, like many of Sempill's satires, of a hidden listener who reports an overheard conversation or dialogue. In this case, the listener eavesdrops on Moray and a group of supporters, including John Knox, as they scheme to strip the infant King James of the crown and replace him with Regent Moray. Circulated only after the Regent's death, the 'Pretended Conference' aims to tarnish Moray's reputation, and those loyal to his memory considered this satire to be the work of 'impudent liaris, or sones of the dewill'.[65] Knox even fulminated against it from the pulpit and prophesied that its author would die alone in a strange land.[66] Knox seems to perform similarly in the 'Pretended Conference', looking to the heavens before he speaks, 'as gif he had bene begynand a prayer befoir the sermon, [...] and efter he had keipit silence a guid space he begynis with a stuir and brocken voice, and sayis, "I praise my God grittumlie that hes hard my prayer"' (40). Liar or not, the author of the 'Pretended Conference' succeeds in giving the reader vivid and amusing caricatures of these well-known men.

The anonymous 'Dialogue of the Twa Wyfeis' derives from the anti-Marian party and, if Sempill did not write it, then his methods certainly influenced an anonymous satirist. This piece shares a series of images with broadsides like 'The Cruikit Leads the Blind' and 'The Bird in the Cage': sailing and weathercock metaphors, allusions to children's games ('nevy nevy nak', 'blind Hary', 'pluk at the craw'), the presence of Maddie (wife of the Caill Mercat), and cutting descriptions of the Scottish Machiavel, Maitland of Lethington. The single manuscript copy of the 'Twa Wyfeis' can be dated confidently, thanks to an endorsement by William Cecil, Lord Burghley, in London: '30 April 1570. a Scottish dyalog betwixt 2 Scottish women of the state of Scotland'. The 'Dialogue' opens with a narrator resting in an Edinburgh tavern, where he overhears a conversation between two wives who have just 'sat doun to the drink'. He cannot identify them because there is no 'hoill in the dur', so he dubs them A and B. Addressing one another genially as 'cummer' (used to indicate a female friend), the wives lament the state of affairs in Scotland – rising prices, bad weather – and then direct their attention to the members of the queen's party (289). With canny wit, the wives ridicule Lethington and attack Mary's supporters, one by one, for their deceitful motives and ability to hedge their bets. The 'Dialogue' adapts several literary and rhetorical traditions – obviously, the dialogue form itself[67] – but perhaps most interestingly the *chanson d'aventure* and the gossips' meeting. These two forms are natural partners: here, the eavesdropper may not wander outdoors, but, like his fellow medieval poets, he encounters the women in a tavern unexpectedly and unnoticed – and when gossips gather in taverns to carouse, they almost always exchange stories and advice about men.[68] One detects the influence of Dunbar's 'Apon the Midsummer Ewin', and, like Dunbar, the author of the 'Dialogue' plays on our generic expectations, leading us to expect gossip about men and surprising us with the wives' chinwag about politics. In the end, the satirical effect is sophisticated and multi-directional: the 'Dialogue' effeminises members of the queen's party, ridicules their figurehead Mary, Queen of Scots, and makes the wives themselves look capricious and cunning – another likely swipe at Mary. The wives finally resign themselves to 'drink away sorow' and let men deal with civil conflict 'as thai think best'. Anyway, confides wife A, if 'my man wer slane this nycht I haif ane uthir in his steid'. 'Marie cummer', wife B approves, 'that is the forsycht and wisdome that wyfeis suld steik be' (297).

The sharpest Scottish satire from the Reformation and into the next century retains characteristics paralleled in the earlier Gaelic material, particularly its interest in either shaming or praising. Rarely does it generalise about the follies of the time but rather focuses keenly on specific individuals and political events – lampooning, excoriating, and occasionally eulogising. The anonymous satirical poem 'Rob Stene's Dream' (c. 1591), for example, targets John Maitland, Chancellor for James VI, in the midst of the political crisis that eventually saw him retire from public life. A convincing case for Sempill's authorship has been made, but, in any case, the *Dream* recalls in style, forcefulness, and malice the satirical broadsides of the early 1570s, and reveals the literary influence of Dunbar and Henryson.[69] The tradition of flyting also enjoys tremendous continuity into the sixteenth century, from Dunbar and Kennedy to Sempill's broadside skirmishes on the market cross to the *Flyting* between Alexander Montgomerie and Patrick Hume of Polwarth (c. 1580). Popular well into the seventeenth century, Montgomerie and Polwarth's *Flyting* was probably presented as a court entertainment for James VI, in which the contestants use invective, scatological humour, and eldritch fantasy to attack one another, with Montgomerie later claiming to have 'chaist Polwarth from the chimney nook' – the coveted place of favour nearest the king. James, in fact, demonstrated his aesthetic approval of Montgomerie's verse by quoting lines from the *Flyting* in his own *Reulis and Cautelis* (1584).[70] Finally, it is worth reiterating the impact of the mostly anonymous Robert Sempill, who draws heavily on the makars who precede him and brings a new intensity and ferocity to Scottish satire. In the *Flyting*, Polwarth accuses Montgomerie of stealing from Sempill,[71] and James Melville, in his *Autobiography and Diary*, claims to have learned from Sempill's ballads 'sum thing bathe of the esteat of the country, and of the missours [measures] and cullors of Scottes ryme'.[72] Sempill's satirical verse provided not only a kind of political news – albeit fiercely partisan – but also a repository for the essentials of a Scottish literary tradition past and present.

CHAPTER TEN

Performance

John J. McGavin and Dòmhnall Uilleam Stiùbhart

No drama texts exist in medieval Scottish Gaelic sources, and medieval and early-modern Scotland has left few plays in Scots (although those survivors are high quality). It was nonetheless a country immensely rich in that wide field of performance before spectators which can incorporate music, narrative, debate and poetry, and even military displays like tournaments, or theatrical sporting events such as horse racing, as well as text-based theatre.[1] But performance is not a term that can be restricted to actions that entertain. Communities, groups and individuals might also employ the public language of performance for other ends, and in other contexts. Thus, one finds performance in ritual, in ceremony, and in staged political events – in the processions of kings entering their major towns; in the staged charity of the rich man to the poor at his gate or his overt patronage of retained fools; in aristocratic funerals; in public demonstrations of judicial punishment; and in those displays of clothing and accoutrements by which men and women who had the financial capacity chose to affirm their identities to their neighbours. Performance is thus central not only to the realm of pleasure but to the public world of assertion; there is often an overlap between these realms and one event can have many different functions.[2] This chapter selects examples to reveal the broad range of early Scottish performance; to explore points of connection between apparently differing traditions, modes and genres; and to demonstrate that performance must be understood in relation to the nuances of context.

The Edge of Performance

The potential of classical Gaelic *dán díreach* ('strict metre') poetry to be performed has recently been the subject of detailed study and speculation. This body of complex, syllabic verse, dating between the twelfth and seventeenth century, primarily panegyric affirming aristocratic and heroic values, conferring honour and fame, represents a key element of the shared inheritance of the Gaelic culture-region stretching from Munster to Sutherland. Frustratingly, although much is understood concerning the complex metrical and linguistic rules governing its composition, relatively little evidence survives concerning the actual performance of this high status, long-lasting and once ubiquitous genre. Relatively late ethnographic descriptions suggest that typically two individuals were involved: the reacaire or bàrd (not necessarily the poet who composed the piece) responsible for the recitation before the chief or patron, and the clàrsair or harper who offered some manner of musical accompaniment. Given the primary focus upon the meaning of the texts themselves (in which classical linguistic forms were increasingly divorced from everyday speech),[3] the construction of the verse according to syllabic count rather than regular metrical rhythm, and the lack of allusion to instrumental accompaniment within the poetry itself, it seems probable that the harper's contribution was limited to flourishes performed at the beginning and end of verses.[4]

Later evidence also suggests that certain genres of vernacular poetry and song, extant at least since the end of the medieval period, could be performed for an audience under particular circumstances: these include Fenian or Ossianic lays – most notably in the case of dialogues purportedly between the aged Ossian and St Patrick – and flyting competitions such as those described by Angus Fraser in the early nineteenth century as 'Rainn co'chaineadh': a poem consisting of alternate verses of mutual satire between two bards. Satirical contests of this kind were frequent in ancient times as tests of skill and ability in the profession, but it was deemed a disgrace to exhibit any bad feeling towards an opponent – they generally concluded with an embrace, and mutual professions of regard.[5] This genre of patently staged antipathy also offered a 'jocound and mirrie' opportunity in Scots for William Dunbar and Walter Kennedy, respectively, to exploit prejudicial Highland and Lowland stereotypes in their *Flyting* at the turn of the sixteenth century.[6] The earthiness that they showed in their invective had a counterpart in the enduring popularity of 'crosántacht', a medley of semi-classical verse and prose well larded with buffoonery and obscenity.[7] The evidence of these genres, and in particular the self-consciously regional slant given to flyting by Kennedy and Dunbar, indicates awareness that tastes could be shared between the Highland and Lowland Scots in the area where poetry shades into para-dramatic performance. However, flyting is not a simple case of parallel traditions, but rather of a genre that allowed for self-reflexive performed engagement between cultures.

Place of Performance

Scotland was only beginning to establish purpose-built commercial theatres at the very end of the period under review, though these may well have been sited in locations that had become traditional from earlier use, such as the Blackfriars Wynd, Edinburgh, which had been employed by English comedians in November 1599, with the support of James VI against the kirk.[8] However, the general lack of a theatrical infrastructure along commercial English lines through the bulk of this period should not blind us to the subtle connections of publicly theatrical events to the spaces chosen to perform them.

Medieval and early-modern Scots towns, like their English counterparts, enjoyed religious plays put on by craft and religious guilds or, latterly, by committed individuals claiming civic institutional support against reforming opponents. It is not always possible to determine in specific cases whether such performances were tableaux or texted drama, and whether they were processional through the town, sacralising its space in the way that the York biblical plays did by moving from the city wall to its heart, or were pragmatically located in play fields, where other forms of public event such as execution might easily take place. Both forms and locations, however, seem to have been used. It is evident that powerfully different effects and meanings could be generated by performing in spaces that were already ideologically weighted. A good example is offered by early Scotland's most famous play, Sir David Lyndsay's *Ane Satyre of the Thrie Estaitis*, also discussed in the chapter on Satire, above.[9] The full version of this was first performed in the open air in Cupar (1552), probably positioned between the castle and the burgh for practical purposes, though no doubt with symbolic effect, since it would have offered its audience an overtly signified axis of burghal and noble power, enhancing the play's own notion of a common cause between these two estates against the corrupt clergy. It was then performed before the Queen Regent at the Edinburgh Greenside (1554), a location that had been established for outdoor events such as jousts in 1456 by James II, but which, as a venue for such a play as the *Satyre*, combined pragmatism with wider significance. Visible to the north was the port of Leith, the main sea-road in and out of Scotland, and beyond that the noble and ecclesiastical houses and royal palaces of Fife. To the south within an easy walking distance lay Edinburgh Castle, an expanding capital city, and the royal seat of Holyrood Palace. Above it, Calton Hill would have been a landmark readily reached by the 'landwart' inhabitants of the broad East Lothian plain from which at least one of the play's characters (Pauper) was presented as coming. Spectators would have felt very much at the heart of the nation whose health was the principal concern of the play.

The *Satyre's* adumbration in interlude form (1540) had been in a location that could lay even greater claim to being the ideological heart of the nation: the Great Hall of Linlithgow Palace under the gaze of its Renaissance monarch, James V. Unlike the full-text plays, this early version draws us closer to the tradition of performance in halls that we know from English court, burgh and university sources, while the Scottish Exchequer records similarly point to courtly interlude performances under James IV. But widespread evidence for indoor performance of masques, interludes, and music to limited (though often still mixed) audiences potentially misrepresents the diversity, even opportunism, shown in Scottish performance venues, and the prevailing iconic conception of performance as something which could, and often should, accommodate the different estates of this small, divided, multilingual, and frequently embattled country in a single experience, thus requiring a larger open space. One finds this notion represented in poetry and drama as the following strangely congruent examples show.

In *The Palice of Honour* (c. 1501), Gavin Douglas brings his dreamer to a meadow, where he sees the Muses at a banquet.[10] The location is a tent or pavilion (1167) pitched in a field, but Douglas evidently had no problem about envisaging this kind of structure as a possible location of drama, for the Muses watch interludes: 'At ease thay eit with interludyis betweene' (1181). The dreamer is described as entering it, and the tent/pavilion does not seem to offer much privacy from the outside world, for the Porter certainly does not keep people away. Douglas envisages, as so many performance records do at this time, that the noble audience itself fell under the gaze of others: 'Grete wes the preis the feist ryall to sene' (1180), so what went on in this probably temporary structure is not presented by him as reserved for a coterie. The location thus combines the outdoors of the meadow with a covered, though not enclosed, environment. As the focus of the immediate audience in the tent, the 'interludyis' feel like indoor performances, but they and their audience together constitute a spectacle for the press of onlookers, as in the many forms of public event, such as processions and open-air civic entries, where the royal party would have been presented with shows, themselves providing an additional show for the citizens. Without apparently being driven by the poem's allegorical needs, this episode assumes both hybridity in performance venue and inclusiveness in the audience. It additionally implies that public spectatorship can be multiple and complex, involving performance within performance, as here there is interlude within spectacle.

Lyndsay was to create just such an effect in the *Satyre* when he showed to his large open-air audiences a scene of Rex Humanitas slothfully listening to music performed by ladies in the sanctuary of his court, and then brought in Lady Verity to comment on the responsibilities of governors: here there was a scene within a scene, courtly entertainment turned into an emblematic image by the perspective provided by the drama around it, and the reserved pleasures of the king laid open to public view. It is not inconceivable that Lyndsay thought of this scene as a travesty of the Feast of the Muses in Douglas's *Palice*, but, even if Lyndsay himself was unconscious of any link, Douglas's poetic text recognises, and Lyndsay's play directly employs, use of multiple perspective in performance and a similar notion that spectatorship links the highest and lowest in the land, performance thus opening up reserved space to scrutiny by the people. In the context of the *Satyre*'s demands for change in Scotland, one could reasonably claim that this was not incidental to the dramatic action of the morality but was a self-conscious deployment of a traditional understanding of performance and spectatorship in the service of a new forensic examination of the state. Performance, along with the spectatorship it implied, was thus not only the medium but part of the message also. The self-reflexivity of this performance also recalls the intercultural negotiations staged in the *Flyting of Dunbar and Kennedy* – whether expressed through poetry, a quasi-dramatic genre, or full theatre, performance offered that multiple, contested space in which Scots could reflect on the complex nature of their realm.

Public Theatricality

Although formal dramatic texts are absent from the medieval literature of the Scottish Gàidhealtachd, evidence suggests, as one might expect, a culture-region where social interaction, social structure, and the expression of social identities were imbued with theatricality, shaped and informed by diverse and flexible performance practices and rituals. The paucity of contemporary sources, however, and the inevitable unreliability of later material purporting to refer back to the period, mean that even recorded episodes of overt theatricality in the Gàidhealtachd tend to defy easy interpretation.

Two 'Highland performances' in the Lowlands from the centuries before the period under discussion, precisely datable and from the same area, afford relatively well-known examples of Lowland 'othering' of the figure of the Scottish Highlander. Firstly, the mid-fourteenth-century chronicler John of Fordun records how, at Scone on 13 July 1249, an unidentified *Scotus montanus* hailed the newly inaugurated Alexander III by reciting in Gaelic the young king's pedigree back to its source. Secondly, on 28 September 1396, before Robert III and his court on the North Inch at Perth, a staged battle was fought between thirty representatives of the Clan Chattan and thirty from the still mysterious 'Clahynne Quhewyl', resulting in the near annihilation of the latter kindred. Traditional or popular historical readings of these events would represent the Highlander as contemporary ancestor, performing a specific role before monarch and court, to employ Martin MacGregor's words, 'for legitimisation of origins and validation of progress'.[11] Thus the former event might suggest the Gael as mysterious visitant, symbolising continuity with remote origins. The latter, on the other hand, relegates the Gael to cruel and barbarous relic.

Scholarship, recent and not so recent, has reassessed the meanings ascribed to these events by later medieval chroniclers and historians, suggesting fundamental misinterpretations of the performances involved. Rather than being a venerable, enigmatic interloper, the *Scotus montanus* – recorded as having read (*legebat*) the king's pedigree – was more likely to have played a formal, integral rôle in the inauguration ceremony. The 'Battle of North Inch', on the other hand, can be read as an admittedly late example of *duellum* or trial by combat, 'a gigantic appeal in the Scottish Court of Chivalry' over landholding rights, drawing upon contemporary western European legal practice. Despite more recent re-framings of these events, however, it remains the case that a recitation in Gaelic was considered somewhat odd and worthy of recording by the original observer, while the sheer numbers involved in the gruesome North Inch contest bear little comparison with other contemporary examples of trial by combat through jousts and tournaments under courts of chivalry from the period.[12]

These two instances of public theatricality which, in their original manifestation, both showed points of contact between the cultural worlds of the Gaelic- and Scots-speaking prove also to have been enduring modes of performance. Ambiguous though they may be in respect of the representation of the Highlander, as *performances* they had close parallels elsewhere in Scotland and abroad: tournaments provided spectacular public theatre, and could involve symbolism, exotic disguise, cross-dressing, an underlying narrative, stage scenery, international audiences and the semiotic eclecticism that tends to accompany grandiose acts of public self-definition.[13] As a genre of public performance they have proved extraordinarily long-lived, with the most obvious contemporary instances being the Royal Tournament in England and the Royal Edinburgh Military Tattoo. The mid-thirteenth-century reading of royal ancestry by the *Scotus Montanus* was also to have its distant, fully theatrical, descendant in the form of over one hundred portraits of past Scottish kings, painted on a triumphal arch, who greeted Charles I in Edinburgh in 1633. Led by Mercury, the first of these kings, Fergus, stepped forward to advise the latest member of the royal line.[14]

Decorum, Protocol, and the Spectator

Performance is a kind of language: its use depends on the performer's sense of how the spectator or auditor can best be spoken to in context, of what they want to hear, what they need to hear, what they will be receptive to, and what social decorum or the genre of communication dictates as appropriate language. It is thus deeply embedded in the protocols of public life, with which it is in dialogue.

The instances of the *Scotus montanus* and the Battle on the North Inch suggest how hard it is to surmount prejudices and presuppositions concerning Highland exceptionality, traditionality, and otherness when interpreting historical examples of theatricality involving Gaels, and attempting to achieve a satisfactory construal of even some of the meanings felt to underlie performance practices. As in any society in which honour-claims were paramount, achieving or transgressing the agreed norms of social performance could be a matter of life and death. Hugh MacDonald, composer of the late seventeenth-century manuscript History of the MacDonalds, recounts how 'one John Macdonald, tutor to Roderick his nephew, Laird of Mudort [Clan Ranald]', offered to 'MacLean' to take on himself the duty of seating the principal men at dinner at the Lord of the Isles in return for a black hound. This being agreed,

> [a]t dinner time next day, John stood at the end of Macdonald's table, and desired the Laird of Ardnamurchan to sit down. This family, indeed, might claim to be lords since King David Bruce's time; but the old Scots

were careless of their prerogatives. Then he desired MacFinnon and MacQuire to sit, for MacQuire was an ancient Thane. Then desired Beatton, the principal physician, then MacMurrich, the poet, to take their seats. Now, saith he, I am the oldest and best of your surnames here present, and will sit down; as for these fellows who have raised up their heads of late, and are upstarts, whose pedigree we know not, nor even they themselves, let them sit as they please.[15]

According to MacDonald, in return for this affront, MacLeod of Harris ravaged and plundered Clan Ranald lands, seized John Macdonald and confined him in a windowless dungeon in Dunvegan where he went blind.[16]

More routine matters of precedence are touched upon in admittedly late and synthetic oral historical traditions concerning a battle in Balquhidder in the mid-fifteenth century between Clann Labhrainn, the native MacLarens, on the one side, and the expansionist kindred of the Buchanans of Ardprior on the other. The narrative commences:

> Bha Clann Laubhrain anns an am o shean ro lion-mhor laidir ann am Bogh-chuidir, agus bha iad cho uaibhreach dhiubh fein, is nach leigeadh iad le dream air bhith eile dol a stigh do n eaglais dì-domhnaich gus gu'm bitheadh Clann Laubhrainn gu léir riaraichte le aiteichean suidhe, b iad dream de Chlann an t-shaoir a b' fhaigse do Chlann Laubhrain ann an lion-mhoraid, gidheadh b eiginn doibh geilleadh do neart Chlann Laubhrain.

> *A long time ago Clann Labhrainn were very numerous and strong in Balquhidder, and they were so proud that they wouldn't allow any other group to enter the church on Sunday until all of Clann Labhrainn were satisfied with their seats. It was a group of Macintyres who were the closest to Clann Labhrainn in numbers, but they still had to bow to the power of Clann Labhrainn.*[17]

As a result of the assistance lent by the smaller kindred, following their unexpected victory 'Clann Labhrainn did not hinder people from going into the church and taking a seat when it would be suitable for them'.

In such examples one finds that the scrutiny of spectators could turn ordinary action into performance, imbuing acts with meaning and revealing the social investment which individuals and groups made in their public identity. This is the quasi-dramatic sphere of public ceremony, where performance and what is now known as the 'performative' blend, and again one finds that the Gaelic- and Scots-speaking parts of the kingdom offer comparable instances.

In 1587, James VI set out to reconcile his feuding nobles or, perhaps more accurately, to make the inevitable feuding more difficult for them. The event staged for this purpose had two parts, the second of which was at least partially a public version of the first. David Calderwood records it thus:

> At this conventioun, the king reconciled the noblemen who were at variance, and upon the Lord's day, the 14th of May, made a bankett unto them. The Lords satt at a long table by themselves. The king dranke to them thrise, willed them to mainteane concord and peace, and vowed to be a mortall enemie to him who first brake. Upon Moonday, the 15th May, after supper, the king came from the Palace of Halyrudhous to the Castell of Edinburgh; from that to the Tolbuith, [and] releeved the prisoners warded for debt; from thence came to the Mercat Croce, where a long table was sett, furnished with bread, wyne, and sweete meates. The Croce was covered with tapestrie, and upon it the trumpeters blowing, and the musicians singing. The king, in presence of the multitude, dranke to the nobilitie, and everie lorde dranke to another. The gibbets at the Croce were brokin doun with fire-balls and fire-speares; the glasses, with wyne, sweet meates, were cast abrod in the streets, and from the fore stairs. They went backe to the palace, in the same order as they came up. The king, with my Lord Hammilton on the right hand, and the secretar on the left; the duke and Lord Claud in other's hands before the king; Angus and Montrose in hands; Huntlie and Marshall; Crawfurd and the Master of Glames likewise. In the mean tyme, the cannons of the castell thundered.[18]

The performance at the Cross was not exactly dramatic in the literary sense. It was probably not scripted, though it must have been planned and stage-managed, and there may have been words planned for the toast. These words were probably not in verse as would have been expected for drama. There was no point in the performance being repeated, as plays could be, since it had been designed for a single occasion and specific context. It was more ceremony or ritual than 'mimesis' in the Aristotelian sense of a representation of an action. But such distinctions need qualification when one compares the event's constituent parts with Lyndsay's *Satyre*.

Like the *Satyre*, this was colourful, theatrical spectacle, with a large cast, theatrical props, a constructed scene for the central action, and a clear structure of actions that were both powerfully immediate and symbolic of important political aspirations for the realm. Like the *Satyre*, it also exploited a breach of the notional boundary between spectators and performers. In James's event this took the optimistic and wholly traditional form of distributing wine and sweetmeats to the crowd. Lyndsay had used an equally traditional, but more ominous, insurgency from the audience, in the shape of the characters Pauper and John the Commonweill, but crossing the gap between the action and the audience was common to both. The principal difference was, of course, the fact that a real king and real nobility were involved, not Rex Humanitas and Nobilitie, and in this sense the event was a performative act by people acting *in propria persona* as well as a performance. But for the participants, the ceremony of establishing harmony at the Cross would have had a quasi-mimetic element nevertheless: it represented the action they had been involved in on the previous day, and they would certainly have known they were 'putting on a show', no less than those who performed in the *Satyre*. Like the *Satyre*, this show was a foreshadowing of the future as much as an immediate experience.

Furthermore, just as the *Satyre* evidently drew upon traditional forms of medieval drama that are now, alas, unavailable to us except through English and continental examples or Scottish records of performance, so James's event at the Cross carefully mixed tradition with innovation for an audience that would recognise both. Having the nobles process hand in hand alluded to a tradition of signalling concord at less noble levels: when in 1532 the Haddington guilds fell out over precedence in their Corpus Christi processions, the town sent to get advice on relative status from Edinburgh, eventually concluding that the masons and wrights would henceforth walk arm in arm with the smiths and hammermen as 'brethern and companions'.[19] The form in which the amity of the nobles was displayed thus implicitly performed the unifying power of a higher authority. This was what Balfour meant when he wrote that James made the nobles walk in pairs 'to that end, that the haill realme might take the better notice that this was his maiesties auen proper worke'.[20] But the event also strikingly varied tradition by employing actions, such as the relief of prisoners, which would have been internationally recognised as a feature of royal entries at the beginning of a new reign. The occasion was thus signalled as a figurative fresh start.

Finally, and most significantly for this study, the performance at the Cross acknowledged the people as witnesses to concord by staging their admittance to the private world of power – no less than Lyndsay had done when laying bare the court of Rex Humanitas: now, the banqueting and pledging of nobles that had been done first in the reserved conditions of the convention were replayed in the open air. No doubt, as in Gavin Douglas's account of the Muses' banquet, 'Grete wes the preis the feist ryall to sene'. It is unlikely that the nobles actually ate from the long table set up at the Cross under the gaze of the spectators. Instead, the table was probably set up only with such comestibles as could be easily distributed to the onlookers, a traditional feature of celebratory progresses by monarchs. However, the effect was to create a simulacrum of the banqueting that the nobles had enjoyed at a long table by themselves on the previous day, almost as if the windows of the banqueting hall had been opened to allow the gaze of ordinary folk into the exclusive court world of tapestries and musicians, now displayed to all at the Cross. Through this doubling James not only employed the people as spectators to witness the nobles' public harmony, but, as a political act, he staged the people's spectatorship to the nobles, letting them feel the gaze of the ordinary man and woman fall on a scene the court would expect to enjoy in private, and had indeed enjoyed the previous day. Of course, it also allowed the people under the figuration of public theatre to eat from the same table as the nobility, with the implicit benefit that from aristocratic harmony would flow plenty to the realm as a whole, but James's dramaturgical skill was shown most powerfully by his staging the people as spectators to put pressure on the nobility. Gavin Douglas's Muses evidently welcomed such scrutiny. The Queen Regent and those in Lyndsay's audiences who represented the three estates must have felt the pressure of the public eye upon them as they watched the *Satyre* in the company of those over whom they had power. James ensured that the nobility enacted their ritual of friendship under the public's enforcing gaze. It is likely that at least some of the audience would have been conscious of the role that they were performing as witnesses to such an action. Performance in Scotland, whether in poetic description, drama or political action, in the Gàidhealtachd or not, consistently shows awareness that it is not only what is performed but who is seen to be watching it that matters.

This display at the Cross, as with other acts of public theatricality, far from being secondary to the written word or the spoken promise, was employed to convey meaning in difficult circumstances where only an action seen and remembered would suffice. Distinguishing on the basis of quality, style or effect between such theatrically performative acts and the scripted theatre of imagined actions would have seemed otiose to many spectators, even if they demanded that pretence should be absent from the former. If one adds to these overlapping characteristics the fact that a play such as the *Satyre* was itself as much a political intervention as a theatrical performance, and conversely that publicly performative ceremonies such as royal entries and progresses were scripted by poets of quality like David Lyndsay and William Drummond of Hawthornden (for Charles I's entry in 1633), the gap between the performative and performance seems even narrower.

Rituals and Calendar Customs

Given that the principal Scottish burghs, where funded regular processions or popular drama performances served as a focus for civic identity, were situated in the Lowlands (whether central or coastal), the most prominent theatrical occasions in popular culture in the Gàidhealtachd would have been supplied primarily through religious ceremonial and ritual. The late seventeenth-century description of the Hebrides compiled by Martin Martin bears witness to plentiful examples of horse racing, clergy-led 'cavalcades', and celebrations held throughout the islands on Michaelmas (29 September), even after the dissolution of the Catholic church across much of the archipelago. Despite later folkloristic accounts portraying these rites as timeless Celtic enactments of harmonious community devotion, it is likely that these and similar practices were geographically diverse, subject to change, given to multiple interpretations by participants, and, crucially, best understood as outlying examples of religious harvest festivals widespread throughout western Europe. In fact, Hebridean Michaelmas rites as recorded later may well date no further back than the late medieval era, a rural reflection, perhaps, of the contemporary vogue for Corpus Christi processional pageantry in European urban localities. By the beginning of the nineteenth century most of these festivals had ceased: not just as a result of evangelical repression, but because of a need for increased work discipline as well as the withdrawal of upper classes and middling sorts from wider community life.[21]

Calendar customs at a more domestic level would have offered a faint echo of the theatricality of the grand religious pageants. The many modern recordings of the customs connected with Oidhche Challainn, or Hogmanay, may offer insights into earlier practices: groups of boys processed round each house three times sunwise reciting a rhyme while hitting with sticks one of their companions wrapped in a cow hide. On gaining entrance, the caisean uchd – the skin from a sheep's breastbone – which they carried was singed in the fire and passed around the occupants to ensure a prosperous new year.[22]

Finally, the ritual calendar was certainly marked in the early modern period, and doubtless before, by the performance of folk dance-dramas. A number of accounts of such dances were recorded before the genre had become effectively moribund at the beginning of the twentieth century, under pressure from fashionable European-influenced hybrid dances disseminated by itinerant dance masters. Although it should be stressed that the genre undoubtedly admitted of wide diversity across time and place, later dance-dramas such as 'Cailleach an Dùdain' (*the Hag of the Quern-Dust*), 'Marbhadh na Bèiste Duibhe' (*the Killing of the Otter*), and the 'Fir Chlis' or '*Merry Dancers*' probably had parallels in the earlier period.[23]

Outside the Gàidhealtachd, but, one assumes, frequently open to Gaelic-speaking spectators, as also to international guests, early Scotland had a rich tradition of seasonal festivity based in the educational, clerical, court and civic institutions. This often involved the nuanced and controlled subversion by which ideology keeps itself in place: Boy Bishops during Advent, and Kings and Queens of the Bean, Corpus Christi drama, May plays, guisings, and those authorised revelries that promised disorder by their association with Robin Hood, Little John, the Abbots of Unreason, Bonaccord or Narent, but which may in the earlier years just as easily have delivered opportunities for local career development, and a chance to show off oneself in costume or one's horse in procession. Later, things were to become more difficult.

There is no doubt that the religious craft or guild plays (possibly on occasion tableaux) that are so richly represented in the early records of Aberdeen and other towns in Scotland, and are clearly comparable to the late-medieval English efflorescence of Catholic lay piety, were gone by the end of our period, along with their playfully subversive counterparts. Abbots of Unreason were formally banned under Mary, Queen of Scots, and 'clerk' plays on the scriptures in 1575, though the records around this time reveal a degree of incomprehension at local level about whether this really meant that one could not take part in or watch them. There can be no doubt that Reformation helped to prevent any revival of playing on religious subjects, but long before the establishment of the Reformation Kirk, the writing had been on the wall for such events as expressions of civic identity because of financial pressures, war, and tension between urban craft and merchant groups. Changes in the perceived status of the civic office of master of revels had preceded the ban – what had been once an indicator of good present or future local standing had become a trivial distraction.

It is only later in the sixteenth century that an impetus in the records seems to build up against playing, and then specifically if it infringed limits set by the kirk, or when supporting and opposing it had become, or might become, a useful tool in local and national power politics. Undoubtedly a reformation of moral outlook meant that certain kinds of performance or their seasonal occasions or their venues gradually became unacceptable to groups of potential spectators. The benefits to be gained from participation would have been eventually outweighed by the potential social damage it could cause or by the incongruence between that activity and how the potential spectator imagined his or her own identity. In this way reformed practice became more diffused and society began to look more homogenous, but throughout this period there were other groups either powerful enough to withstand notice or too insignificant to attract it. James VI and I reportedly said to a recalcitrant Protestant bookseller, 'Farts on you and the session of your kirk baith. Quhen I was in Scotland, I keeped Yule and Pasch in spite of all your harts'.[24] This was true also of the performance activities associated with such celebrations. At this end of the social scale, cross-dressing and exotic masking might bring criticism but escape control. Calderwood reports, for example, that at the baptism festivities for James VI's son, Prince Henry Frederick, in 1594, 'The Abbot of Halyrudhous, in woman's apparell, tooke up the ring sindrie tymes. The Lord Hume, in Turkish rayment, the king himself, in his masking geir, with a white overthwart croce, the badge of the Knights of the Holie Spirit, which was much mislyked by good men'.[25] Such cross-dressing play, used also by Mary, Queen of Scots and her ladies, could have still greater longevity at the other end of the social scale, below the level of institutional organisation with its corresponding susceptibility to pressure from other power groups. There must have been many young people whose low-cost, rural, cross-dressed 'guising' escaped kirk notice (that many did not gives us the evidence for the practice) since the tradition was still strong in the twentieth century. It is demonstrable from the records that long after the disorderly play associated with Abbots of Unreason had been banned, activities were still judged sufficiently comparable with them to allow the authorities to use the appellation, though with what justice one cannot tell, and the celebration of superstitious occasions such as Yule or Pasche or Mayday were an enduring problem throughout the period.

Changing Rituals

One might argue that the reason the Scottish Reformation took as close a hold as it did is that Scotland was already well used to thinking about the health of the realm through the medium of public performance. The three examples discussed above from the *Palice of Honour*, the *Satyre*, and James's banquet at the Cross display a strikingly cohesive tradition in stressing performance before a witnessing public, and the developing ceremonial practices of the Kirk were consistent with this.[26] When the Roman Catholic priest Ninian Winzet complained about the Reformed Kirk's inconsistently opposing ceremonies except those 'expresly commandit in scripture' while creating unscriptural ceremonies of its own, such as refusing to baptise children unless 'the fader theirof hald It in his Armis' in front of the pulpit, his focus on theological contradiction missed the point that the fundamental battle was over the power to communicate through public performance.[27] For example, the ceremony used for the Induction of a minister was essentially a performative theatrical event in which members of the congregation were audience for a variety of staged and stagey actions and, to a limited degree recognisable from James's staged banquet, were active participants in them as well as being profoundly important for their role as witnesses.[28] The induction could include a sermon, a formal reading of the presbytery ordinance, an explanation of its meaning, a question and answer session about desires and goals between the presiding minister and the applicant, a direct address to a congregation drawn from the different estates of society about its own past actions and desires, a repeated invitation at the church door to those who might have any charges to lay against the proposed minister to come and do so (the performative equivalent of intrusion into the theatrical space), a unanimous spoken call from the congregation, symbolic handshaking, procedural objections, and hands raised to God in promise by the congregation.[29]

The Induction from which the preceding details were drawn took place in Stirling in October 1587 only a few months after James's staged banquet of harmony in Edinburgh. It is quite possible that some of the 'barrones, gentill men [and] commones'[30] present in the congregation had also been at the political event. If they were, the salient features of Scotland's public demonstrations would have felt remarkably homogenous despite national tensions, and strangely traditional despite the powerful forces of change. This is symptomatic of a major difficulty for the scholar, for the central truth about Scottish performance in this period is its resistance to interpretative grand narratives. Homogeneity at one social level is balanced by diversity if one includes others; major cultural shifts prove to have been less secure and less diffused through society than either the energy of contemporary recorders or the evidence of posterity would suggest; major publicly performative acts may look alike and have a recognisably traditional character, but performance in the sense of 'playing' seems at once traditional and more opportunistic, occasional, and improvised. The chronological span of the period, the geographical extent and cultural diversity of the country, its multi-lingual, ethnically diverse and multi-cultural character all point to diversity, yet they intersect, and could be crossed and linked in the experiences of individuals, as the following test case will suggest. A recent major project, on the tensions between homogeneity and diversity in Scotland's nationhood before the Wars of Independence, was entitled 'The Paradox of Medieval Scotland'.[31] Late-medieval and early-modern performance history may suggest the cultural continuation of this paradox.

Perspectives on Performance: Chronology and Geography

In fashioning a history of early performance in Scotland, one has to recover the notion of performance as social action undefined by later certainties. Allowing major political or cultural events to provide the grid references for performance history seems inappropriate because they do not capture the experience of the individual as a culturally responsive being through time. Major events retrospectively define phases, which the performers and spectators actually lived through with no certain knowledge or understanding of the present drawn from future end-points. While performance unfolds it is managed by reference to existing categories not future facts. Our historical interpretations are thus inevitably different from that experience since they can use moments of apparent closure or climax retrospectively to analyse what was actually inchoate, experienced within the flux of events, and constantly referenced to the past rather than a known future. The span of the individual spectator's life may often make a mockery of periodisation, demanding that things that now appear extraordinarily diverse be understood more as inflections in lived experience. Early modern Scotland offers such a case, and helps us to consider the diversity of performance in a different temporal perspective from what is customary.

In May of 1602, Robert, Lord Elphinstone, died aged seventy-two, and was succeeded by his son Alexander the fourth Lord Elphinstone, who was to be High Treasurer of Scotland. Alexander still had another thirty-six years to live, but was no spring chicken when he succeeded to the title. He was already fifty, having been born in 1552, the year of the *Satyre's* performance at Cupar, and he was eight years old when the Reformed Kirk of Scotland was founded in 1560. His father, who had just died on the threshold of a new united monarchy of Great Britain, was born in 1532, eight years before Lindsay's interlude version of the play at Linlithgow Palace. Perhaps he even saw it, since there were Elphinstone lands in adjacent Stirlingshire and aristocratic allies in West Lothian. He could certainly have seen it as an adult. So only two men's lifetimes, albeit men long-lived by the standards of the day, take us from the first third of the sixteenth century, with its early signs of fragility in medieval play traditions; through the first Scottish court-sponsored drama of reform, the performances of the last medieval morality play, now in Renaissance guise; the many court and provincial performances of Mary's and James's reigns together with growing reformist sentiment against any playing that implied the maintenance of superstition, or threatened financial ruin, social disorder or loss of Kirk influence; a short-lived attempt to re-establish civic theatre in Haddington in the mid-1570s; the reign of a king who invited English actors to visit Scotland, and then, when in England, sponsored Shakespeare and the King's Men; the celebration of his son Charles's visit with lavish pageants; and finally the National Covenant, which sought among other things, to re-assert the control of a revived Kirk over those habits of play which had evidently continued quite happily and traditionally throughout the entire period. These two men's lives covered the royal entries, celebrations, and progresses of half a dozen regents, monarchs, consorts, and children – at root, medieval events, whose forms and stage machinery tended to re-use what was still serviceable from the older traditions while gradually adopting new fashionable models and styles, and inflecting foreign genres with national characteristics.[32]

These two generations also cover George Buchanan's compassionate, humanist Latin plays, *Jephthes* and *Baptistes*, written probably c. 1542 when he was teaching in Bordeaux, and later his poetic celebration of the very season that was to be the occasion of local persecutions by his successors: May Day dedicated to playing and fun (*ludisque dicatae iocisque*).³³ Erotic, learned, and strongly influenced by continental sources, *Philotus*, Scotland's other early extant vernacular play comes from the second half of the sixteenth century, though Jamie Reid Baxter has shown it might be as convincingly located in either the 1560s court of Mary, Queen of Scots, or that of James VI, and with high-level Protestant acquiescence, if not actual authorship.³⁴ But either Elphinstone might have seen the play at either time. Through this period also continued educational theatre, though the specifics of performance, timing, venue, content, language, and, more likely, the religious sensibilities of the schoolmaster drew Kirk attention. Drama as an intellectual exercise on the page can also be found in Sir William Alexander's Senecan *Monarchick Tragedies* (1604). Fifteenth-century editions of Terence, Plautus, Aristophanes and Seneca appear in the early holdings of the sixteenth-century reformed university of Edinburgh, the Faculty of Advocates Library and that of the Writers to the Signet, and, while the dates of accession may not be precisely known, this material does correspond to the holdings of contemporary printers, where many copies of Terence appear. The potential exposure of the student to drama on stage or page reached its apogee in the extensive English and continental play-reading and spectating of William Drummond of Hawthornden in the first fifteen years of the seventeenth century; similarly well-financed young men were seeking out and noting performances of various kinds in the early years of what would later become the Grand Tour.

The rich seam of Elphinstone family accounts which began with Alexander's accession also permits us to see how geographical distance may be crossed and cultural diversity be accommodated within an individual experience.³⁵ For this, however, one must acknowledge that the realm of 'performance' may include music. One might argue sophistically that this is reasonable since, until the gramophone, music was experienced visually in public, but a more convincing justification for its inclusion is that it constituted Scotland's most ubiquitous form of public performance for pleasure, enjoyed in itself, as accompaniment, and in relation to other forms of performance. Gavin Douglas's Muses may have watched interludes, but these would almost certainly have involved music, as would the *Satyre*, and as James's banquet at the Cross also did. It would have made little sense to Scots of this period to separate literary and musical performance. Both gave pleasure and were ideally to be combined.

The form and auspices of the music experienced by the fourth Lord Elphinstone were extremely diverse. What the records show is a blend of music-making that might be arranged or opportunistic, performed by élite or non-élite, sponsored or unattached performers, by men with local or national identity, by visitors from England or from the north-western Gaelic-speaking parts of Scotland, using instruments which bore an ancient resonance, like the clàrsach, or implied the grandeur of power, such as the trumpet, or civic auspices, like the pipe and drum (or 'swasche'). In 1617, the year of James VI and I's return to Scotland, Lord Elphinstone paid twenty-four shillings to Thomas Ferguson, a violer, as part of a major banquet in Holyroodhouse for the visit of the Earl of Mar in March. We might regard this as the archetypal aristocratic activity, but in fact it was the diversity, ubiquity, and social range of musical engagement that was the real benchmark of the aristocrat. Aristocratic itinerancy between locations of different types of power, royal, civic, and narrowly, or widely, familial, ensured cultural contacts that cut across the kinds of genre we might use to distinguish types of entertainment. In that same year, at the highest social level, Elphinstone was responsible for paying the tuners of the organ that King James had sent to Holyroodhouse in preparation for his visit. But he also gave money to a drummer at his gate, three English pipers who seem to have been an established consort regularly visiting or possibly even resident in Scotland, two other named and unnamed violers, an English piper met (possibly fortuitously) as he was passing over a bridge, the official piper and drummer of Stirling who would usually announce his formal entry to the town, four trumpeters who appeared at his gate three days after the English pipers, and a band of Yule-tide guisers from a village close to his seat – this in addition to money given to maintained fools and unmaintained 'daft' people.

In the years when he made a summer trip to his lands of Kildrummy in the north, this extreme diversity of entertainment would be widened probably linguistically, and certainly stylistically, by various western Highland (or Irish) clàrsach players. Elphinstone seems to have been as happy to listen to the harper Mams Gario or clàrsair William MacGeigan, at least one of whose names suggests the Gàidhealtachd, as to violers in the House of Seton near Edinburgh or to English pipers. Performances could be predictable or impromptu (while Elphinstone was out hawking a man was given a tip for collecting a rebeck from elsewhere, presumably because it was discovered that someone could play but did not have an instrument available). In the far north, a duet was formed between a member of the Innes family he was visiting and one of his own men. The social range of his entertainment also seems broadened by a payment recorded to an unnamed 'auld man that Sang to your Lordship at Super' in Perth while Elphinstone was en route from Stirling to Kildrummy.[36] One can add to this range of performance, the formal entertainment of greeting provided by his noble friends' official pipers, who always appear in the list of gratuities that he gave on leaving the northern castles he had stayed at. One man's experience as an auditor and spectator of music serves to qualify those distinctions of geography, culture, genre and social level, which one might be tempted to employ to manage intellectually the business of how people enjoyed performance in the period.

Conclusion

A history of early performance in Scotland will therefore seem truer to the original experience of spectators if it acknowledges overlaps between genres and styles, and between full performance and the many types of display and enactment which approximated to it. Points of contact, between regions and cultures have to be identified together with the generic parallels, translations and knowing adaptations that resulted from them. Cultural change needs understood anew – less in terms of traditional historic 'turns', and more as a measure of the conflicted responses of spectators, as they tried to adapt to the 'new guise' with eyes guided by the memory of previous forms and meanings. It is also necessary to understand the political dimension of performance in terms of a series of pressure points, in which the subtlest nuances of context determined the outcome, and the record maker, one should not forget, tried to limit the possible interpretations of the event. Performance tradition in Scotland emerges as diverse, yet complexly integrated; entertaining, but also self-reflexive and politically dialogic; and expressive of major upheavals, but also subtly resistant to change.

CHAPTER ELEVEN

Translation

Kaarina Hollo and Thomas Rutledge

Into Scottish Gaelic

If we wish to consider translation and Gaelic during this period, we must keep in mind the linguistic situation as discussed in Chapter 1. There were multiple 'Gaelics' in use in Scotland – Classical Gaelic (the *lingua franca* of the pan-Gaelic learned classes), vernacular Gaelic as spoken (of which we have no exact record), and compromises between the two.[1] There is the additional complication of the employment of two different orthographies within Scotland, one inherited and also used in Ireland, and the other based on that of Scots; when the latter is employed it can be difficult at times to determine which form of the language (classical or vernacular) is being represented. Two different scripts are used to write Gaelic during this period as well – the traditional manuscript hand and typefaces based upon it ('corra-litir'), also used in Ireland, and the Roman script (as used for the writing of Latin, Scots, and English). The linguistic and cultural complexity of Scotland during the fifteenth, sixteenth and seventeenth centuries presents us with particular challenges in the consideration of translation activity. Among the types of translation to be considered are those from other languages into the target language of Gaelic, from the source language Gaelic into other languages, and from one form of Gaelic to another (arguably intralingual translation). Also important in the Scottish context are the translations that occur when a written text in a source language is translated/interpreted in either written or non-written form, and delivered orally to audiences in the target language (in this chapter section, Gaelic). Although not translation in the strictest sense, the use of more than one orthography for Gaelic and the employment of different manuscript hands and print types, as mentioned above, are important considerations.[2]

The discussion here is structured in a broadly chronological fashion, starting with earlier translations of secular texts and then moving on to Reformation scriptural and catechetical material. But first we must address some general considerations relating to the nature of the Gaelic manuscript tradition shared between Scotland and Ireland. How do we distinguish between a Scottish text in a Scottish manuscript, an Irish text in a Scottish manuscript, a Scottish text in an Irish manuscript, and an Irish text in an Irish manuscript? Does a Scottish scribe make a manuscript Scottish, even if he is working in Ireland? How relevant are the terms 'Scottish' and 'Irish' in this context?

The definition of 'a Scottish manuscript' is in itself rather slippery. Ronald Black, who has devoted a lifetime of research to Scottish Gaelic manuscript studies, puts it like this:

> It will be clear [...] that what I call 'the classical Gaelic manuscripts of Scotland' simply represent the Scottish end of a tradition held in common by the Gaels of Scotland and Ireland [...]. It should be borne in mind however, that with few exceptions the 'Gaelic manuscripts of Scotland' either originated in Scotland or at least passed through the hands of Scottish poets or physicians who were as much part of the Gaelic tradition as those who originally wrote them [...]. It would be impossible to separate the classical Gaelic manuscripts of Scotland from the classical Gaelic manuscripts of Ireland.[3]

This commonality of tradition must be kept in mind in considering any aspect of Scottish manuscript culture, including the transmission of translations of literary texts. Well before the period under consideration here, a considerable number of classical literary texts had been translated into Gaelic. By the end of the twelfth century there were Gaelic prose or prosimetrum versions of the Alexander saga, the *De excidio Troiae* attributed to Dares (*Togail Troí*), Lucan's *Pharsalia* (*In Cath Catharda*) and Statius' *Thebaid* (*Togail na Tebe*) as well as a looser reworking of the Odyssey.[4] In the course of the twelfth century a Gaelic prose translation of Vergil's *Aeneid* was also produced, *Imtheachta Aeniasa*; this is the earliest known translation of Vergil into a vernacular.[5] Although *Imtheachta Aeniasa* has survived in only three fourteenth- or fifteenth-century manuscripts, none of them of an obviously Scottish provenance, others of the classical translations are found in Scottish manuscripts from our period, including *Togail Troí*, *In Cath Catharda*, and *Togail na Tebe*. Although these were translated several hundred years earlier, they continued to be copied into fifteenth- to seventeenth-century manuscripts and form an integral part of the prose literature of our period. However, there is no Scottish equivalent of the fifteenth-century Irish author and translator Uilleam Mac an Leagha who created Gaelic versions of English texts including Caxton's *Recuyell of the Histories of Troy*, *Guy of Warwick*, *Beves of Hamtoun* and a life of St Mary of Egypt, nor do we have any known Scottish copies of Mac an Leagha's work. Uilleam worked for patrons including members of the gaelicised Anglo-Norman Butlers.[6] Scottish patrons of equivalent status may well have been able to access such texts in English or Scots, therefore obviating any need for translation into Gaelic.[7]

There is not the space here for a full discussion of the topic of the transmission of Latin medical texts and commentaries in Gaelic translation in Scotland and Ireland during this period. There are over a hundred Gaelic medical manuscripts extant from the period 1400–1700,[8] and twenty-nine of them are Scottish.[9] Almost thirty per cent is a substantial proportion, and Scotland can certainly be said to play an important role in the transmission of the texts represented, even if it is difficult to establish the provenance of the translators in most cases. These twenty-nine manuscripts also represent a healthy share of the 138 manuscripts identified by Ronald Black as 'classical Gaelic manuscripts of Scotland'.[10]

Among the earliest of the dateable medical translations is that by Aonghus Ó Callanáin and Niocól Ó hIceadha (both of Munster provenance) in 1403 of a commentary on the Aphorisms of Hippocrates. Although we do not have the original, there are more than a dozen copies, and 'the earliest dated copy [...] was written on an island in Loch Gara, Co. Sligo, in 1413 by a scribe who signs himself simply "Giolla Pádraig Albanach", "Giolla Pádraig the Scot"'.[11] As Aoibheann Nic Dhonnchadha points out, 'his cognomen is ambiguous, being equally descriptive of a Scottish scribe working in Ireland or of an Irish scribe who had close associations with Scotland'.[12] Although we cannot be certain that Giolla Pádraig was a Scot, the very fact that his epithet is ambiguous underlines the unified nature of the Gaelic medical fraternity.

One of the more unusual of the Gaelic medical tracts is the unique copy of the compendium in NLS MS 72.1.4, a bilingual Latin and Gaelic encyclopaedia of definitions, primarily relating to 'Medicine, Natural Science (Physics) and Philosophy'.[13] The manuscript is written primarily by Beaton (Mac Beatha) scribes, members of one of the foremost Scottish medical families. The scribe of the tract itself, Maol-Sheachlainn mac Iollainn Mhic an Leagha Ruaidh, is 'also the chief scribe of King's Inns

Library ms 15, a medical manuscript written in counties Sligo and Kildare in 1512', and probably a Beaton as well.[14] This encyclopaedia is most probably drawn from contemporary Gaelic medical and philosophical sources and may yet prove of importance in estimating the extent of the translated corpus, as works not extant elsewhere may well be cited here.[15]

NLS MS 73.1.22 exemplifies the close connections between Scottish and Irish medical families. It was written by a young Scottish scribe, Donnchadh Albanach Ó Conchubhair (1571–1647), between 1596 and 1600 at a school of medicine in Aghmacart in Ossory (modern Co. Laois), under the supervision of Donnchadh Óg Ó Conchubhair, official physician to Finghean Mac Giolla Pádraig, third Lord Baron of Upper Ossory.[16] The manuscript was in Scotland from 1600, presumably travelling there with Donnchadh Albanach, who 'appears to have divided his time between Lorne and Ossory'.[17] There was a least one other Scottish student at Aghmacart in 1596, Niall MacIomhair, who is mentioned in this manuscript.[18]

The response to the Reformation in Scotland, as in the rest of Europe, is integrally bound up with both print and translation; indeed, the first book printed in Gaelic in Scotland is a translation of a central Reformation text. Bishop John Carswell's (1522–1572) *Foirm na n-Urrnuidheadh*, a translation of the Book of Common Order appeared in 1567, five years after its publication in English in 1562.[19] In 1564 the General Assembly had urged that every minister, exhorter, and reader should have a copy of this book.[20] Carswell saw his work, in translating and publishing, as making good a deficit:

> Acht atá ní cheana, is mór an leathtrom agas an uireasbhuidh atá riamh orainde, Gaoidhil Alban agas Eireand, tar an gcuid eile don domhan, gan ar gcanamhna[21] Gaoidheilge do chur a gcló riamh mar atáid a gcanamhna agas a dteangtha féin a gcló ag gach uile chinél dhaoine oile sa domhan; agas atá uireasbhuidh is mó iná gach uireasbhuidh oraind, gan an Bíobla naomhtha do bheith a gcló Gaoidheilge againd, mar tá sé a gcló Laidne agus Bhérla, agas in gach teangaidh oile o sin amach, agus fós gan seanchus ar sean nó ar sindsear do bheith mar an gcédna a gcló againd riamh, acht gé tá cuid éigin do tseanchus Ghaoidheal Alban agas Eireand sgríobhtha a leabhruibh lámh, agas a dtámhlorgaibh fileadh agus ollamhan, agas a sleachtaibh suadh. Is mór-tsaothair sin ré sgríobhadh do láimh, agas féchain an neithe buailtear sa chló ar aibrisge agas ar aithghiorra bhíos gach én-ní dhá mhéd dá chríochnughadh leis.[22]

> *Great indeed is the disadvantage and want from which we, the Gaels of Scotland and Ireland, have ever suffered, beyond the rest of the world, in that our Gaelic language has never been printed as all other races of men in the world have their own languages and tongues in print; and we suffer from a greater want than any other in that we have not the Holy Bible printed in Gaelic as it has been printed in Latin and English, and in all other tongues besides, and likewise in that the history of our ancestors has never been printed, although a certain amount of the history of the Gaels of Scotland and Ireland is written in manuscripts, and in the tabular staves of poets and chief bards, and in the transcripts of the learned. It is great labour to write that by hand, when one considers what is printed in the press, how smartly and how quickly each work, however great, is completed thereby.*

With the publication of *Foirm*, the Gaelic language had made it into print. Nonetheless, Carswell saw that there was still much to be done, and the above passage from his introduction to *Foirm* shows that he eagerly awaited both the translation of the Bible into Gaelic and also the appearance in print form of the seanchas (or traditional lore) of the Gael. Carswell's coupling of these two desiderata within the confines of one sentence is worthy of note. With print Bibles and print histories in circulation, Calvinist Gaels would be able to see themselves represented as a modern nation defined by language, history, and religious belief. This could only come about through linguistic translation (of the Bible into Gaelic) and translation of medium (of traditional Gaelic seanchas from manuscript to print).

Carswell was presented with an interesting linguistic challenge. He wanted his work to be intelligible to as wide an audience as possible, without alienating the traditional literati. The language of his translation reflects this balancing act. Although Classical Gaelic in its essence, there is an attempt made to move towards the vernacular to enhance comprehensibility; scholarly opinion is divided on the success of this strategy.[23] Despite Carswell's somewhat formulaic protestations of his linguistic and stylistic shortcomings, he had a good grasp of Classical Gaelic.[24] Keeping close to the Classical Gaelic standard was not only necessary if he wished to retain the respect of the Gaelic learned classes in Scotland; it also made it possible for his work to potentially function in an Irish as well as a Scottish context. It is clear that Carswell directed his work towards an Irish audience as well as towards a Scottish one. Thus, he refers, in the letter to the reader quoted from above, specifically to 'the Gaels of Scotland

and Ireland', and in a short poem that addresses the book itself, he tells it to travel not just through Scotland but around Ireland as well. Carswell's patron, the fifth Earl of Argyll, had a great interest in Ulster, and Carswell's work could well have had a role to play there. It is difficult to assess the distribution and use of the book within Scotland itself, let alone Ireland. It is worth noting that in 1574, seven years after its publication, the sixth Earl of Argyll thought it worthwhile to urge adoption of the book by 'ministreis and rederis at ilk paroche Kirk'.[25]

Some of the choices made by Carswell in his translation reflect an overt acculturation of the work to its anticipated context. He adds a blessing for a boat, 'no doubt especially relevant to the maritime topography of his diocese'.[26] Although the catechism in *Foirm* is based upon Calvin's Little Catechism as found in his source, it is 'a free adaptation designed to suit his needs'.[27] Carswell omits the metrical psalms, but does include his own metrical version of the Lord's Prayer.[28] The reason for the omission of the psalms may well have been simply that Carswell wished to publish his work sooner rather than later: translating the psalms was not only a large job, but a tricky one. The first Scottish Psalter was only published in English with the approval of the General Assembly in 1564. It used 87 of the psalms in the Book of Common Order, with other drawn from the English Psalter of 1562 and elsewhere. It may well be that Carswell saw it as redundant and outside his brief to translate the psalter in the Book of Common Order when it had already been superseded by a new English version. In addition, the skills required to translate the psalms to conform to pre-existing melodies and metres, most of which were foreign to Gaelic prosody, may well not have been at Carswell's disposal.

Certain emphases, additions, and omissions in Carswell's translations reflect a somewhat conservative religious and political stance. Although he does not dispute the principle of election, Carswell emphasises the importance of good works. A positive reference to saints and archangels is inserted, and the Book of Common Order's negative references to purgatory, *limbus patrum* and free-will are omitted. Carswell tends to downplay the role of the congregation and elders, and to emphasise the importance of the secular ruler's role in promoting true faith and the suppression of idolatrous worship.[29]

It was over sixty years before Scotland's second Gaelic printed book, and second printed translation into Gaelic, *Adthimchiol an Chreidimh* (1630) appeared. This work, a translation of Calvin's Larger Catechism, was commissioned by the Synod of Argyll. In 1653 the

Synod also commissioned the translation of the psalms into Gaelic, and the first fifty appeared in print as *Ceud chaogad do Shalmaibh Dhaibhidh* in 1659 (a translation of all the psalms was not to appear until 1694).

The primary concern of translators into Gaelic in Scotland during the sixteenth and seventeenth centuries was to make available material for the instruction of individuals in the reformed religion. To limit the discussion to books printed in Scotland, however, might be a mistake. *Foirm na n-Urrnuidheadh* was closely followed in 1571 by the publication in Dublin of *Aibidil Gaoidheilge agus Caiticiosma*. This volume, compiled by Seaán Ó Cearnaigh, the Oxford-educated treasurer of St Patrick's Cathedral, contains an epistle, a short tract on the Irish alphabet, an Anglican catechism, ten prayers (four of which are based on the translations in *Foirm na n-Urrnuidheadh*)[30] and a translation of Sir Henry Sidney's 1566 proclamation on the principles of religion.[31] Though the project may have been in hand before the publication of Carswell's work, it could well be that 'the spectre of the dissemination of Calvinist doctrine in Ireland [...] may have prompted the authorities in Dublin to expedite the publication of Anglican material in Irish',[32] and 'it would seem reasonable to conclude that Ó Cearnaigh did have before him both Carswell's work and a copy of BCO [The Book of Common Order]'.[33] Like Carswell, Ó Cearnaigh 'articulates a paradigm in which Protestantism, print, and Gaelic literary scholarship are complementary',[34] albeit a different variety of Protestantism and in a different type.

The use of Roman type for Gaelic texts in Scotland was not necessarily a foregone conclusion. A different choice was made for Ireland. Before 1567 (the year of *Foirm*'s publication) Queen Elizabeth and her privy council had committed £66 13s 4d to the project of creating a 'character' (type) for the printing of the New Testament in Irish.[35] The origins of the type eventually used in the *Aibidil* of 1571 and subsequent Irish printed books are disputed;[36] however, the fact that the manuscript Irish language primer prepared for Queen Elizabeth in the 1560s by Christopher Nugent was in Irish script may well have been a significant factor in her decision to facilitate such a type's creation. The very title of Ó Cearnaigh's book – 'a Gaelic alphabet and Catechism' – forges a union between religion, language, and script. Matthew Staunton argues that this is a result of a deliberate policy:

> [Ó Cearnaigh's] book was not only written in the language of the place, but it was also printed using letterforms based on the Irish minuscule

manuscript. As such, it was doubly vernacular. Elizabeth's strategy was to turn this into a tripartite relationship with the addition of a religious message. It was hoped that the Irish would accept these homely looking books and that Protestantism would be allowed to slip in like the Greeks inside the Trojan horse.[37]

In Ó Cearnaigh's introduction, it is the cló (*type*) itself that will open up the road to knowledge for the reader. Staunton proposes that '[a]t the same time, the road to Edinburgh was symbolically blocked. The Gaels of Ireland had an exclusive typeface and a religion to go with it. The Gaels of Scotland were literally written out of the plot',[38] as was, the argument goes, the Earl of Argyll and his designs upon Ulster. The relative lack of success of this trinity of language, religion, and type in terms of successful proselytisation of the Irish should, of course, be noted.

If we take a look at the question of type from the Scottish point of view, we might ask if any disadvantage or advantage accrued to the furtherance of the reformed religion in Scotland through the use of Roman script.[39] There was a long tradition in Scotland of writing Gaelic in the same hands used for Latin and Scots. Although traditional script was favoured in manuscripts with a Highland provenance, even there Scots literacy was widespread, so familiarity with Roman type was assured. The expense of establishing a Gaelic script would not have been repaid in any great measure. The texts of the new religion in Scotland would not have looked sufficiently more 'Gaelic' or native in a more traditional type to justify the additional difficulty and cost of providing one. On balance, Roman type was the sensible option.

A complete Bible was not available in Gaelic until 1801, long after the end of the period under discussion here. However, an Irish New Testament was published in Dublin in 1603 (in Gaelic type), and there is evidence that it circulated within Scotland as well. The lack of a printed Bible in vernacular Gaelic could be seen as a serious handicap in the effort to educate Gaelic-speakers in the reformed religion. There were, however, a number of factors that ensured that, despite this lack, Protestantism was able to spread throughout the Gàidhealtachd. One was that, although there was no published vernacular Gaelic Bible, there were numerous translations made by ministers for their own use. Proof of this is provided by the search made by the Synod of Argyll in 1657 'for 'sundrie parcells translated alreadie' by the ministers of the Synod of Argyll to provide the basis for their proposed translation of the Scriptures'.[40] Another factor that ensured the successful spread of the reformed religion was the nature of the church services. Weekly worship

> started with the Reader's service. This was a hour-long reading of the Bible which the reader would translate directly from the English printed version in his hand. Further instruction would be given in the exegetical sermon which followed [...]. The advantage of these informal systems of translation was that the Biblical content could be conveyed in the vernacular and even in the particular local dialect so that it was completely comprehensible to the listeners.[41]

As Dawson notes, Gaelic ministers 'were far more effective in spreading Calvinism through a remote rural area than their struggling counterparts in comparable regions of Europe [...]. The traditional role of the learned orders in bridging the language gap was taken over by the Gaelic ministers'.[42] This success was in large part due to the manuscript and oral translations of the Biblical narrative created by these multilingual ministers.

The ministers' skill in extempore translation came to the fore as well in the treatment of two questions from the catechism that was customary in the lecture after the Sunday sermon. As Dawson observes, 'The careful explication of the Classical Common Gaelic phrases of the catechism by the minister helped this Calvinist text to become "the theological classical poetry" of the early modern period in the Highlands'.[43] This practice of explication and translation from Classical Gaelic to the vernacular helped to form a modern vernacular religious register which is later seen in print in the very popular Shorter Catechism of 1653, the Gaelic metrical psalms and eventually in the Gaelic Bible of 1801.

The translation of the Bible into Gaelic verse was another way of getting the Protestant message across. Although there are only two of his poems extant, Alexander Munro (c. 1605–c. 1653), minister of Durness from 1634, 'had a reputation as a versifier of Scripture',[44] with his compositions used to educate his Gaelic-speaking parishioners in the Biblical narrative. This type of poetry becomes more prominent in the eighteenth century, with Dúghall Bochanan (1716–1768) perhaps its most significant exponent.

The above discussion has concerned itself with translation of various types into Gaelic. There is, however, one type of text for which we have evidence of translation from Gaelic into Latin or English: official letters. Davies/Duncan Omey, a Scot, was acting in 1587 as secretary to Toirdhealdbeach Luineach Ó Néill.

> It is further recorded that a Gaelic letter from [...] Sir Toirdhealbhach Luineach ÓNeill [sic], intended to be the 'ground' for a letter in Latin to Queen Elizabeth of England, had been translated into English by Davies or Duncan Omey for the benefit of Sir John Perrot, the English lord deputy in Ireland.[45]

There seems to have been an implication that Omey was responsible for introducing material unfavourable to Sir John not present in the Gaelic original into his Latin version, and that this is the reason that Sir John sought him out (with some difficulty), questioned him, and required an English translation.[46] Omey exemplifies the multi-lingual nature of literacy in Gaelic Scotland, and the pan-Gaelic nature of the Scottish Gaelic-speaking learned classes.

We have Latin translations of two Gaelic letters dating from 1629, one from Donald MacDonald on Colonsay, and the other from Islay. These letters were translated as part of a dossier to attest to the success of the Franciscan mission in Scotland.[47] Two Scots translations of Gaelic letters with an Irish provenance are extant: one of a letter sent from the Lord of Tyrone, Seán Ó Néill to the Earl of Argyll in 1560, suggesting an 'alliance between them to be cemented by the marriage of ÓNéill himself to Archibald's sister', and another by the same Ó Néill to a fellow-countryman in Scotland in 1567.[48] Although these Scots translations would not fall under the heading of what we would now call literary, and were clearly produced in response to a political need, they are further evidence of the existence of bi-lingual literacy.

Fluency in Gaelic, Latin, Scots, and English among the literate learned classes enabled the translation activity here discussed.[49] It might also have in some ways inhibited it. Those literate in Gaelic in Scotland were largely literate in Scots and Latin as well. The multilingual Book of the Dean of Lismore embodies this multi-literate culture. If, as a scribe or scholar, one can read both Gaelic and Scots with ease, and those for whom one writes can do the same, one important motivation for translation – to make texts accessible – is greatly weakened. The use of Scots orthography for Gaelic in some of our most significant manuscripts and the use of the same script and type for texts in Scots, Gaelic, and Latin reduces the appearance of difference between them, creating a visual equivalence between the languages that echoes the ease of movement between them of those who wrote and read the manuscripts. The most significant contributions of Scottish translators in this period can be seen as functional rather than literary, in the translation of medical texts from Latin and the provision of material for religious instruction. The high-register vernacular language forged in the process of oral explication of Classical Gaelic religious translations, however, developed over time into a new medium of literary expression.

Kaarina Hollo

Into Older Scots

> For out of olde feldes, as men seyth,
> Cometh al this newe corn from yer to yere,
> And out of olde bokes, in good feyth,
> Cometh al this newe science that men lere.[50]

The array of translations produced in southern and eastern Scotland between 1400 and 1650 will always resist summary. The difficulties may be suggested, in part, through Chaucer's articulation of literary principle in *The Parliament of Fowls*. First, the range of material is almost intractably rich: because medieval and early modern writing so persistently returns to traditional material, proceeding by gleaning 'newe corn' from 'olde feldes', translation, of some form or another, is not a marginal or narrowly confined practice but a (even the) culturally central one. On the other hand, the complex and motile tension that Chaucer traces between 'olde bokes' and 'newe science' may suggest the difficulty of defining and delimiting the terms and procedures of 'translation' itself. For translation inevitably presupposes both the continuing pertinence of older work and the need to transform that work in some way to enable it to speak to new readers and new circumstances. It is this dialectic of retrieval and reimagining that gives translations their distinctive energy; it also makes distinguishing translation from other forms of medieval and early modern intertextual practice especially difficult. And to these difficulties we may add a third – the complex linguistic situation within Scotland in this period in which we see translations not only into Scots and English (itself, as we shall see, a problematic pairing), and Gaelic, but also into Latin, as, for instance, in George Buchanan's renderings of the Greek tragedies of Euripides, *Medea* and *Alcestis*. Our focus here will be on translations into the vernacular; the traditions of Biblical translation into Scots (and English) and of metrical psalm translation will also not be considered. These are approached in different ways elsewhere in the volume and to discuss them here would entail broaching questions of humanism, religious polemic, and prosody, to the complexities of which we should be unable to do justice.

The temptation is to start an account of Scots translation with Gavin Douglas's *Eneados*. Completed in 1513, just six weeks before the disaster of Flodden, the work is a landmark in Scottish cultural history. The quality of Douglas's achievement has often been celebrated. Ezra Pound, for instance, observed 'I am inclined to think that he gets more poetry out of Virgil than any other translator,'[51] and the great Virgilian scholar, R. G. Austin, proposed that Douglas

> makes one want to keep turning on and on to see how he has handled this or that passage [...]; each interpretation has seen something of the essential Virgil; and because of his more direct approach, Douglas often has things to tell the professional scholar that cannot be learnt from Dryden.[52]

Moreover, Douglas himself, in his discussion of his translation practice within the *Eneados*, emphatically distinguishes his work from earlier, freer handlings of the Virgilian material. He forcefully repudiates William Caxton's 'Virgill in Eneadoß' ('Quhilk that he says of Franch he dyd translait, / It haß na thing ado tharwith, God wait, / Ne na mair lyke than the devill and Sanct Austyne' (1.Pro.140-43)) and, in terms that may, perhaps, mirror our own instinctive assumptions about the nature of translation, marks the proximity of his rendering to Virgil's original:

> Quha is attachit ontill a staik, we se,
> May go na ferthir bot wreil about that tre:
> Rycht so am I to Virgillis text ybund,
> I may nocht fle leß than my falt be fund. (1.Pro.297-300)

Before Douglas, Louis Brewer Hall suggests, 'were the adaptations, and after him the translations'.[53]

Douglas displays a sophisticated sensitivity to the difficulties that confront the translator of Virgil's terse, allusive verse:

> Sum tyme the text mon haue ane expositioun,
> Sum tyme the collour will cauß a litill additioun,
> And sum tyme of a word I mon mak thre. (1.Pro.347-49)

He laments that the expressive possibilities of his own young Scots cannot match the richnesses of Virgil's mature Latin. That it is specifically *Scots*, though, into which Douglas translates, is especially important, for Douglas also forcefully distinguishes between 'Scottis', his own tongue, and 'sudron' or 'Inglys': he proposes to translate 'Kepand na sudron bot our awyn langage, / And spekis as I lernyt quhen I was page' (1.Pro.111–12). There is, no doubt, also a political charge to his rejection of Caxton's English Virgil. In this sense too, then, the *Eneados* may be seen to stand self-consciously at the beginning of a specifically Scottish tradition: 'the first major literary translation *into* Scots [emphasis added]', John Corbett suggests, 'is, for good reason, held to be' the *Eneados*.[54]

And yet Brewer Hall's formulation, richly suggestive as it is, will not quite do. For one thing, there certainly were Scots translations before Douglas. Probably the most notable of these were those of Gilbert Hay. In the *Buke of the Law of Armys*, his translation of Honoré Bouvet's late-fourteenth-century *L'Arbre des batailles*, Hay records that he translated the work 'at the request of ane hye and mychty Prince and wor/thy lord . williame erle of Orknay – and of Cathnes / lord synclere and chance/lare of Scotland . jn his castell of Rosselyn . The 3ere of oure lord . a thow/sand . four hundreth fyfty and sex',[55] and there is little reason to doubt that he also completed his other translations, the *Buke of the Ordre of Knychthede*, and the *Buke of the Gouernaunce of Princis*, for Sinclair about the same time.[56] All three works were almost certainly translated from French sources (although, ultimately, the *Ordre of Knychthede* derives from Ramon Llull's Catalan *Libre de Caballeria*) and collectively 'provide a comprehensive guide to chivalric principles, emphasising a knight's responsibilities to Church, lord and people'.[57] The final book of John Ireland's *Meroure of Wyssdome*, completed in 1490 and, like the *Buke of the Gouernaunce of Princis*, another work in the long tradition of Scottish 'Advice to Princes' literature, contains much material taken 'frequently verbatim' from the sermons of Jean Gerson, 'preached before Charles VI and the French court between 1391 and 1413'.[58] Hay is also accredited with a role in the 'translatioun' of the Scots *Buik of Alexander* (l. 19312) and the poet of *Lancelot of the Laik* imagines himself engaged in an act of translation from the French vulgate *Lancelot* (l. 211).

The intertextual freedoms of these two romances, moving at times more proximately to their sources and at times with greater independence, might encourage us to think of them more properly as adaptations. Yet the *Eneados*, too, for all its sustained attentiveness to Virgil's Latin (Douglas proposes that if he cannot reproduce Virgil's 'eloquens', he will at least work to retrieve his 'sentens' (1.Pro.307–10)), also contains elements that complicate Brewer Hall's classification. One might point to Douglas's poetic prologues that relate to the books they precede in varied and shifting ways or to his inclusion of a version of the extraneous 'Thirteenth Book' of Maphaeus Vegius, composed in 1429 to 'complete' Virgil's narrative. I am thinking more particularly, though, of elements such as the notes of euhemerism and allegoresis introduced within the 'Comment' with which Douglas accompanies the opening chapters of his translation:

> Neptun or Neptunus, brother to Ioue and Pluto and son to Saturn. For that the partis of his heritage lay in Creit by the sey cost, and for he vsit mekill salyng and rowyng, and fand the craft or art therof, therfor is he clepit god of the sey. He was alsswa an the first tawcht to dant and taym horsß (*ad* 1.3.54).

> Iohn Bocas, be Eolus set hie in his chare to rewle and dant the windis, ondirstandis raison set hie in the manis hed, quhilk suld dant, and includ the law in the cave or boddum of the stomak, the windis of peruersit appetyte, as lord and syre set be God almychty therto. (*ad* 1.2.12)

Douglas's euhemerism rationalises the figures of the Roman gods as outstanding heroes whose earthly exploits led to their credulous memorialisation as divinities. His allegoresis is either broadly 'moral' (Eolus as reason ordained to control the appetites), or 'physical' (Juno as 'the erth and the watir', Jupiter as 'the ayr and the fyr' (*ad* 1.1.82); the meddling of Venus in earthly affairs as an allegory of planetary influence (*ad* 1.6.1)). Euhemerism and allegoresis both work to disable potentially transgressive pagan elements within the classical poem by reconciling them with a Christian perspective. In this they may be compared with Douglas's efforts in his sixth prologue to find Christian orthodoxies within Virgil's classical underworld. They mediate the cultural difference of the classical poem by transforming the structures of its original conception.

This is, of course, to suggest that there is a very serious sense in which the *Eneados* is both translation and adaptation: Douglas carefully and closely reproduces Virgil's 'sentens' and offers ways of fundamentally reimagining the poem for a new, non-Roman, Christian audience. It is a work that especially powerfully embodies the dialectic of retrieval and transformation that is so central to all projects of translation. Whenever I return to the *Eneados* I am reminded of nothing so much as of Walt Whitman's retort in the 'Song of Myself': 'Do I contradict myself? / Very well then I contradict myself, / (I am large, I contain multitudes.)'.[59] In this way above all, perhaps, it serves to introduce the tradition of Scots translation.

The *Eneados* is certainly the first major classical translation into Scots. This is important, not only because it marks Scottish engagement with the wider developments of European humanism, which were characterised, in part, by a new interest in the classical legacy and a new valuation of it, but also because Douglas's classical material confronted him, as a translator, with a new sense of historical discontinuity. Douglas's mediating strategies were, of course, prompted by the cultural difference of Virgil's antique poem. By contrast, the translations of Hay and Ireland reveal an essential confidence in the continuities that bind together their world and that of their sources. Hay's chivalric translations seem straightforwardly to presume the pertinence of their continental models to his own aristocratic audience; in this they may be seen to partake of something of the quality of medieval chivalry itself. Ireland's use of Gerson's political lessons from almost a hundred years earlier, as though they could speak directly to the new circumstances of the courts of James III and James IV, is even more striking. In each case prevailing continuity is assumed in a manner that also illustrates the degree of Scotland's participation in the culture of medieval Europe. As a classical translation, by contrast, the *Eneados* brings much more sharply into focus the tensions at the heart of translation as an act of dialogic engagement between different cultures.

John Bellenden was Douglas's successor, not only in that he, too, as a translator turned to a classical source, for, having first completed a version of Hector Boece's *Scotorum Historia* (1527), *The Chronicles of Scotland* (a copy of this work was presented to James V in 1531, though Bellenden seems to have continued to work on it throughout the 1530s), he produced a translation of the first five books of Livy's *Ab Urbe Condita* in 1533, but also because his work seems programmatically to declare its indebtedness to Douglas's.[60] There may have been political as well as literary reasons for this, as Bellenden, particularly early in his life, seems to have been closely aligned with Douglas family interests. Even Bellenden's choice of classical text may have been partly prompted by Douglas: clearly Bellenden was interested in historiography, but Livy's work is also frequently cited within the 'Comment' and, in one note (*ad* 1.5.81), Douglas himself translates a short passage from the *Ab Urbe Condita*. On the other hand, it is interesting that Bellenden, although an accomplished poet, chose to translate prose sources into Scots prose.[61]

Livy's history presented Bellenden with problems comparable to those with which the *Aeneid* confronted Douglas; here, though, the difficulties are a function less of an alien pagan pantheon (Livy himself treats the Roman gods with convenient scepticism) than of the particularities of place and custom. Livy's work has a sharply local, Roman character – it is tied tightly to the landmarks and social practices of the city within and for which Livy wrote. It is interesting to track the variety of gestures by which Bellenden makes this local material imaginatively available to his Scottish readers; the central question must remain, though, to what effect did he produce this translation, in what ways might Livy's history have resonated within James V's Scotland.

Bellenden's strategies as a translator may be loosely grouped into two types: those that work to explain Livy's Roman material on its own Roman terms (an approach we might, with Christopher Baswell, call 'pedagogical') and those that work to reimagine that material in sixteenth-century Scottish terms (which we might call 'domesticating').[62] The former approach is most evident in the marginal notes that Bellenden, like Douglas, composed to accompany his translation. These are preserved most visibly in the manuscript partly in Bellenden's own hand, BL Add. MS. 36678, a copy of which Craigie has transcribed at the end of the second volume of his edition of the *Livy*. They are also, however, present throughout the Advocates' manuscript, now NLS MS 18.3.12, though often badly cropped. They clearly formed part of Bellenden's conception of his translation project. The notes explain many of the technical terms Livy uses in the course of his history or particular aspects of Roman political and religious practice:

> Interregnis war callit certane tymis bethuix þe election of new consulls & þe ald (vol. 2, p. 296).

> Feciales war certane preistis as afor is declarit quhilkis had allanerlie powar to denunce veire or mak confideration of peace (vol. 2, p. 261).

A similar approach may be seen within the translation when Bellenden expands Livy's 'in campo Martio' (1.44.1) with the explanatory 'in þe place of generall convencioun, namyt campus marcius' (vol. 1, p. 96).

It is also implicit in Bellenden's account of the lessons that may be gleaned from Livy's narrative in the prologue to his translation (vol. 1, p. 3, ll. 10–28). There Bellenden acknowledges the religious difference of the Romans without this being seen to compromise the continuing pertinence of their history. This is generally the manner in which the *Eneados* proceeds, most visibly in the sixth prologue. As Bawcutt suggests, the effect is to 'emphasize the gulf between the "they" of the *Aeneid* and the "we" of Douglas and his readers; between "then" and "now on dayis"; between "thair leid" and "our language" [and to] create, if fleetingly, a sense of the remoteness of the *Aeneid* from Douglas's world'.[63]

In fact, though, Bellenden's approach in his *Livy* is much more consistently of the domesticating type. John MacQueen has noted a number of the most conspicuous instances of this: Bellenden reimagines the Roman games and playing places as medieval processional theatre; his 'banerman' (for Livy's 'signifer', the standard-bearer), 'officiare' (for 'praeco', herald) and 'garde' (for 'Celeres', the royal bodyguard), for MacQueen, imply distinctively Scottish contexts; in the account of the dictatorship of Cincinnatus, 'Rome is seen as if it were Edinburgh with its merkat cross where proclamations were made, its Luckenbooths or covered stalls, and its law-courts'.[64] To MacQueen's examples we may add one more, from Book Two, in which the sacred games are disrupted (and polluted) before they have begun:

> ane houshaldare nocht onelie scurgit his servand arelie in þe morow throw þe placis quhare þe playis war ordanit to be, bot als gart him bere þe gibbet on his bak throw þe said place, afore þe pepill was convenit to þe contemplatioun of þir playis. (vol. 1, p. 191)

Livy's scourged servant is ironically termed 'praesultatorem' (2.36.2), the public dancer whose performance precedes the public show. Bellenden stylishly recasts the theatricality of Livy's language: the 'skurgeing of þe servand' is 'þe first padʒeane [...] of þare playis' (vol. 1, p. 191). The image of a servant scourged '*throw* þe *placis* quhare þe playis war ordanit to be' also seems to reconceive the nature of the playing space originally envisaged by Livy as the middle of the Circus Maximus (2.36.1).

MacQueen's term for this is 'equation' ('the method mainly adopted is the equation, wherever possible, of Livy's Rome with Bellenden's Scotland and Europe') and he suggests that Bellenden's 'modernisation and Scotticising of the text is sometimes carried out almost at an unconscious level'.[65] This may not, though, quite do justice to the consistency and cumulative force of Bellenden's domestication. Domestication is evident again, for instance, in the pervasive presentation of the Romans' martial exploits in chivalric terms. This colouring is anticipated in the 'proloug': Bellenden recommends his translation to James V as 'Richt proffittabill till undermynde ȝoure fais / And for to lere þe arte of chevelrie' (vol. 1, p. 5, ll. 4–5), for 'Sa knichtly dedis in bukis historiall / Sall neuer be fundin quhil þe warld Induris' (vol. 1, p. 3, ll. 11–12). It is striking how similarly battle and heroism are presented in *The Chronicles of Scotland* and the *Livy*; in each case, Bellenden turns to a characteristic and overlapping lexis of 'manhede', 'curage', 'ingyne', 'auenture', 'knichtis', 'cheualry'. His Romans strikingly echo his Scots.

It is frequently observed that James V's assumption of majority rule was accompanied by a renewed interest in chivalry at the Scottish court.[66] Carol Edington, for instance, suggests that 'James V was an enthusiastic devotee of the cult of chivalry' and places Bellenden's works at the centre of this chivalric revival: '[t]he popular literature of the period and indeed that specifically commissioned by James V (the translations of Bellenden) were decidedly chivalric in character.'[67] The interest in chivalry seems to have been tied both to the elaboration 'of a cult of Stewart kingship',[68] and to a celebration of Scottish martial culture rooted in the venerable tradition of armed resistance to the predatory English. Here, then, we may have both an explanation for Bellenden's domestication and an answer to the question of how his Livy might have resonated: the more compellingly his translation appropriates Livy's history, the more vividly available its ideals of chivalric valour.

Let me suggest two further ways in which Bellenden's classical translation speaks to his own distinctive Scottish circumstances. First, he presents Livy's history as a piece of Advice to Princes literature. In the 'proloug,' Bellenden directs his work to James V and the treasurer's accounts confirm that he received royal patronage for his translations. Bellenden consistently works to recast Livy's narrative within the conventional terms of good and bad kingship. The principles of justice, personal morality, and counsel, so familiar from so much more overtly advisory writing, also structure Bellenden's work. This is hardly surprising in the opening sections of Livy's history devoted to the Roman kings and culminating in the tyranny of the Tarquins. It is more striking in Bellenden's handling of Livy's republican material. One might compare, for instance, the parallel terms in which he presents the abuses of Sextus Tarquinius and of the decemuir, Appius Claudius (Sextus, 'birnand in desire of his lust' is overwhelmed by 'Inordinate desire' (vol. 1, pp. 123–24); Appius is 'enragit with blynd desire of luste,' acts 'aganis ressoun,' and is asked 'Is it als lefull to þe, appius, to rage in lust of body as dois þir brutall beistis?' (vol. 2, pp. 3, 4, 9). In each case, the treatment conspicuously recalls the imagery of Bellenden's own 'Proheme to the Cosmographe' and it is hardly surprising to find Appius, too, accused of 'manifest tyranny' (vol. 2, p. 10). Or, again, the terms in which the young nobles fondly recall the rule of the exiled Tarquins, at the beginning of Book Two, do not distort Livy's account, but quietly align it with the emphases of Scottish advisory literature: they affectionately recall the time when they were 'licent during þe empire of kingis to frequent þare lustis with mare opin renȝeis þan ony vtheris', under a king (or tyrant) who might be 'recounseld with his liegis, havand all tymes braid defference betuix freyndis & vnfreyndis' and lament the new 'equale administracion of Iustice' where genuine 'Innocence' is the only defence (vol. 1, pp. 133–34).

The final resonance requires a little introduction. The histories of John Mair (the *Historia Maioris Britanniae tam Angliae quam Scotiae* (1521)) and Hector Boece had given a new energy to considerations of the relations between the Scots and their kings.[69] Advisory writing characteristically avoids engaging explicitly with the possibilities available to a people afflicted with a bad king – redress is left to God. By contrast, Mair's history explores the terms on which deposition might be legitimate and Boece's, perhaps even more influentially, presents a succession of legendary Scottish kings who *were* deposed. How much more provocative, then, Livy's narrative, in which we are shown not only the celebrated banishment of Tarquin, but also a polity without any king at all. It is fascinating to ask to whom – or to what – Bellenden imagines his Sextus and Appius to have been guilty of 'tressoun' (vol. 1, p. 123; vol. 2, pp. 1–2).

Implicit in the preceding discussion is a tension between a royal and courtly audience and an aristocratic one, between the interests of the king and those of his nobles. It is a tension that structures much Older Scots writing. It may be seen, for instance, in Douglas's tentative dedication of *The Palis of Honoure* to James IV ('Til cum in plane, se that thow not pretend tha [...] Thow art bot stouth, thyft louys lycht but lyte' (ll. 2163–67)),[70] but of the *Eneados* to his kinsman Henry Sinclair (and the ninth prologue seems pointedly to mark a distinction between Virgil's 'wark imperiall, / Endyt onto the gret Octauyane, / The emperour excellent and maste souerane' (9.Pro.56–58) and Douglas's own 'wark addressyt and dycht, / I dar sa, baith to gentil barroun and knycht' (9.Pro.87–88)). It is evident, too, in Hay's completion of an advisory *Buke of the Gouernaunce of Princis* for William Sinclair. The tension would seem to resolve decisively in a centripetal, courtly direction with the cluster of Scottish translations produced in close proximity to James VI in the 1580s and 1590s: James himself translated Guillaume de Salluste Du Bartas's *L'Uranie* (1584); Thomas Hudson (d. before 1605) translated another of

Du Bartas's works, his *Judith* (1584); William Fowler (1560/1–1612) produced Scots versions of Petrarch's *Trionfi* (1587) and Machiavelli's *Il Principe*; John Stewart of Baldynneis's (c. 1545–c. 1605) *Roland Furious* (c. 1585) translated and reworked parts of Ariosto's expansive *Orlando Furioso*; and the sonnets of these men and of a number of their contemporaries – most notably, Alexander Montgomerie (c. 1550–1598) – revisited and 'translated' (old fields, new corn) passages from poems of Petrarch, Ronsard, Du Bellay, Saint Gelais, and Desportes.[71]

These works have generally been seen to constitute a collective project to enrich the Scottish literary tradition and Scots as a literary language through engagement with the developments of European vernacular culture.[72] This is translation as self-consciously nationalistic enterprise and the model here is *La Pléiade*, a group of French writers (prominent among whom were Ronsard and Du Bellay) who, in the middle of the sixteenth century, worked, through translation and more independent poetic composition, to perform this role for French and for France. It is an attractive model and positions these writers as the direct successors of Douglas, for whom enrichment of the 'fouth' of Scots certainly was one of the aims of the *Eneados*.[73] And James is central to it as poet, patron, and prescriber of literary principles in his *Ane Schort Treatise Conteining some Reulis and Cautelis to be Observit and Eschewit in Scottis Poesie* (1584).[74] More recently, however, the model has been seen to require considerable qualification and to exaggerate the unity of the disparate purposes and practices of these writers.[75] James himself, after all, expressly discourages translation in the *Reulis and Cautelis* in favour of poetic practices which more fully engage one's 'awin ingyne of *Inuentioun*' (an injunction, in turn, belied by the *Uranie* and by the 'Dedication' of Hudson's *Judith* in which Hudson records James's direct influence on his decision to translate Du Bartas's work).[76]

The model may perhaps be most fully exemplified by John Stewart of Baldynneis's *Roland Furious*.[77] Stewart not only dedicates the work to James but also emphatically invokes the king as ennobling stay and support in an effusion of introductory poems and continues to mark the relationship at important turns in the work that follows (9.25–36; 11.21–26).[78] Stewart also introduces his manuscript of poems with a profession of his particular commitment to the poetic principles of the *Reulis and Cautelis*: 'SIR, haifing red ʒour maiesteis maist prudent Precepts in the deuyn art of poesie, I haif assayit my Sempill spreit to becum ʒour hienes scholler'.[79] The profession seems largely to be confirmed by the practice.[80] This is most conspicuous in the *Roland Furious* in Stewart's use of alliteration. James urges 'Let all zour verse be *Literall* [...] By *Literall* I meane, that the maist pairt of zour lyne, sall rynne upon a letter' and such alliteration gives the verse of the *Roland Furious* much of its distinctive energy.[81] It is evident, too, in the very intertextual freedoms of Stewart's reworking of Ariosto. Stewart describes the work as 'Ane abbregement of roland furiovs translait ovt of Ariost', but there are additions as well as omissions, expansions as well as the rather sharper excisions.[82]

Stewart's 'Inuentioun' is principally exercised in sharply narrowing the focus of Ariosto's extravagantly (and wonderfully) rambling poem.[83] The *Roland Furious* concentrates on the stories of Roland (Orlando) and Angelique (Angelica), disentangling them from Ariosto's many and varied threads. Stewart characterises his practice at the beginning of the fifth cant:

> The historie all interlest I find
> With syndrie sayings of so great delyt,
> That singlie most I from the rest out spind
> As the unskilfull prentes imperfyt
> Quho fyns the gould frie from the laton quyt (5.9–13)

There is an intriguingly slippery humility here: Ariosto's 'flowing feild of sic profound indyt' (5.15) is seen also to contain much 'laton quyt' and, however unskilful a 'prentes' Stewart may be, his work promises to be spun gold.

In his more disciplined reorganisation of his material, Stewart has also been held to clarify and strengthen its ethical inflection. This argument was proposed by R. D. S. Jack in *The Italian Influence on Scottish Literature* and has been rehearsed again by the poem's most recent editor, Donna Heddle:[84] the story of Roland, who abandons his king and his religious duty to defend his kingdom against the heathen invaders in order to pursue an ever-elusive object of desire, exemplifies the dangers and errancies of illicit passion; Angelique's exaggerated pride in her chastity is illustratively humbled when she falls for the barely worthy Medor having rejected a string of the very noblest of suitors; and the two narratives together negotiate the familiar opposition of love and reason. This more firmly didactic shaping of the material emerges most clearly in the final cant. Here Roland's pursuit of Angelique is expressly condemned as a dereliction of his religious duty for which his madness is divine punishment, while his recovery illustrates the infinitely redemptive generosity of divine grace (12.21–34). It might also be seen at the beginning of the eleventh cant, where Roland's precipitous fall is presented as a model *de casibus* tragedy and placed alongside a series of conventional historical instances which it is seen to recall and exceed (11.1–152). It is probably there too in Stewart's presentation of Angelique's fall in cants 9 and 10: he emphasises Medor's unworthiness and excludes those passages in Ariosto which encourage sympathy for him, thereby sharpening the sense that Angelique truly *falls*; and the qualification at the opening of cant 9 – Love's 'fyrie force the fellest may offend / Thair dournes dompting with his amorus mist [...] / Yit I except all thois quho reson knaws / And may protect them be that puissant scheild' (9.3–10) – is particularly resonant.

These are inflections that are also present in Ariosto's *Orlando Furioso*, but they are much less prominent there, more forcibly challenged by competing elements.[85] Moreover, it is worth noting that moves to tighten Ariosto's focus and sharpen his didacticism would seem precisely to turn away from those very aspects of the *Orlando Furioso* that made it such an exciting and influential poem in the sixteenth century. For Ariosto's romance response to Virgilian epic (the generic terms merit more scrutiny than we can give them here) is principally characterised by a new digressiveness (an irrepressible proliferation of heroes and adventures) that quite overwhelms any sense of a single, central hero and a single, central, privileged narrative line, and by a new attitude to love that has become the fundamental driving force of poem and heroes alike.[86] The new emphasis is announced in the poem's opening line ('I sing of knights and ladies, of love and arms') and it is at once evident, too, in Charlemagne's use of the promise of Angelica to spur Rinaldo and Orlando to greater martial deeds.[87] The contrast with the *Aeneid*, in which Aeneas is forced to sacrifice personal love (Creusa, Dido), which is figured as seductive distraction, in order to assume his fated role in the teleological advance of history, is sharp. Stewart would seem to have effected a freshly Virgilian unpicking of Ariosto.

And yet it is not clear that the *Roland Furious* is quite so coherently sustained as this. The pattern is certainly articulated clearly in the final cant, but it is much less visible earlier in the poem. For one thing, Stewart so successfully captures so much of Ariosto's opening canto in cant 2 that he also reproduces its centrifugal, digressive momentum. The succession of figures introduced – Rennault, Ferragus, Sacripant, Bradamant – gesture towards further imaginative possibilities. This is most evident in the figure of Sacripant whose lament introduces the poem's focus on Angelique's chastity and contributes another of its models of love, but also contains an irreducible rhetorical energy that resists ready co-option within any other interpretative line. This is partly the result of Stewart's 'rhyming rhyme' which displays his poetic virtuosity, but also compellingly articulates the obsessively recursive and self-divided mind of the despairing lover. There is something similar in the broad comedy of Stewart's expanded handling of the Hermit's vain attempt to rape Angelique in cant 3 which surely exceeds and defers the emergence of any clear didactic line. Nor is the relationship between the amorous and the heroic simply or uniformly oppositional in the *Roland Furious*: it is as Roland pursues Angelique that he rescues Olimpe (4.149–72) and Isobell and Zerbin (8.106–25) and performs the other martial exploits celebrated in the eighth cant (8.18–105). There is, finally, too much in the raw material of the *Orlando Furioso* that resists neat reorganisation – and Stewart's poem is all the richer for it.

William Fowler's translation of *The Prince* may illustrate the dangers of exaggerating the centripetal, courtly quality of these works. It has been suggested that Fowler may have worked on this translation in close association with James and that the work is an expression of a shared interest in political theory which resulted also in the completion of the *Basilicon Doron* in the late 1590s.[88] The suggestion has been strongly rejected by the most recent editor of Fowler's work, Alessandra Petrina,[89] and it is worth observing that James in fact cautions against 'wryting any thing of materis of commoun weill [...] because [...] they are to grave materis, for a Poet to mell in' in the *Reulis and Cautelis*.[90] Moreover, it is hard to imagine two more dissonant political perspectives than Machiavelli's profoundly secular demystification of princely power and James's theocratic conception of sacred kingship. Machiavelli signally divorces principles of effective rule from conventional Christian morality (as suggested by a chapter addressing 'after and in what maner prences suld keip there faith' (Chapter 18)) and one suspects that the stark clarity of his presentation of the 'tua dyvers maner of wayes [...] all principaliteis and empires [...] ar governed' would have appealed rather more to Bellenden's constitutionally sensitive aristocratic readers than to Fowler's king:

> ather be the will of ane king and his subiects as servants quha be his licence grace and permissioun assisteth him [...]. or be a prence and his nobilitie that are vnto him coadjuteurs in the government of these dominions as for the antiquitie of there house and nobilitie of thair race and bloode that autorise them of themselfs in this handling.[91]

Thus, the king of France, Fowler's translation continues, 'is placed as it wer in the midst of ane [...] multitud of lords quha having there auen vassalls sa far and lovinglye affected vnto thame reteneth that autoritie quhilk ther king can not with draw fra thame nor diminish without perell and felony'.[92] James's absolutist inclinations led him to a rather different conception of the nature of his own kingship.

The most interesting aspect of this cluster of translations is the manner in which they engage both with the developments of European vernacular culture and with older Scottish traditions. To place Fowler's *The Prince* alongside Hay's *Buke of the Gouernaunce of Princis*, for instance, is to be afforded a wonderfully revealing – and economical – window onto the concerns and developments of fifteenth- and sixteenth-century Scottish political culture. Something similar might be said of Stewart's and his contemporaries' interest in love in its complex and varied forms. So many of these translations explore not only the opposition of love and reason and a Petrarchan or Ovidian self-dividedness of love, but a Platonic model of love and reason reconciled. This is the model articulated most fully by Diotima/Socrates in the *Symposium*, in which physical desire is sublimated into a transcendent and transformative force. It is there in the succession of Fowler's *Triumphs* and in the modulations of his *Tarantula of Love*, but it is there, too, in its own distinctive way, in *The Kingis Quair*, in the progression of the dreamer from the attentions of Venus to the counsels of Minerva.

The seventeenth century produced two of Scotland's most brilliantly virtuosic translators: William Drummond of Hawthornden (1585–1649) and Sir Thomas Urquhart of Cromarty (1611–1660). This final section concentrates on Urquhart, in part because Drummond has been better served by recent criticism and in part because Drummond's work – with its own distinctive urgencies – returns us to questions we have already had occasion to introduce: the dialectics of invention and translation, exploration of the ethical and philosophical implications of love in all its complex variety, and the difficulty of demarking and characterising a specifically Scottish tradition (these questions would also serve to introduce writers (translators) such as Alexander Craig (?1567–1627), Sir William Alexander (1577–1640), David Murray (1567–1629), and Sir Robert Ayton (1570–1638)).[93] Urquhart's translation of Rabelais allows us to consider a further philosophical inflection to the cultivation of linguistic 'fouth' and to give a final turn to the complexities of translatorly fidelity, for his work has been consistently praised for the success with which it recaptures the spirit and energy of its French source precisely through the very liberties of its handling.

Urquhart translated the first three books of Rabelais's *Gargantua and Pantagruel*; the first two were published in London in 1653 (a two-fold measure of how far we have moved from the translations of the 1580s and 1590s), while the third appeared only posthumously, in 1693 or 1694, edited (perhaps quite intrusively) by Pierre Motteux (or by a Mr Kimes for him) who then also added his own translations of Books 4 and 5.[94] It is a critical commonplace to celebrate the remarkable intellectual and imaginative sympathy of the translator and his material: Charles Whibley, in his influential introduction, proposed that Urquhart's is 'a translation, unique in its kind, which has no rival in profane letters. Indeed, it can scarcely be called a translation at all; rather it is the English Rabelais',[95] and J. Lewis May extended the trope with the beguiling images of metempsychosis and transubstantiation.[96]

Certainly Urquhart's other, more independent works also evince a distinctively Rabelaisian mix of irrepressibly ambitious learning, linguistic inventiveness, and hyperbolic mode, as their titles alone may perhaps sufficiently attest: *Trissotetras, or, A most exquisite Table, for resolving all manner of triangles* (1645), a wonderfully impenetrable mathematical treatise; *Pantochronochanon, or, A Peculiar Promptuary of Time* (1652), in which Urquhart, with improbable verve, traces his family lineage from Adam and Eve to the seventeenth century; *Ekskubalauron, or, The Discovery of a Most Exquisite Jewel* (1652), a vertiginous generic farrago of history, romance, learned treatise, and polemic;[97] and *Logopandecteison, or, An Introduction to the Universal Language* (1653), another generic medley in the first book of which Urquhart again (this is also one of the central elements of the *Ekskubalauron*) outlines the principles of his model universal language.[98] Within the works Urquhart deploys lexical coinages taken from Rabelais ('pentissim,' 'Septembral juyce,' 'honderspondered');[99] the *Pantochronochanon* recalls and outdoes the genealogy Rabelais gives Pantagruel in the first chapter of Book 2, while the account of the Admirable Crichton's disputations at the College of Navarre is surely modelled on an episode in chapter 10 of the same book; and the utopian community at Cromarty that Urquhart, in the *Logopandecteison*, imagines he should have fostered had he been unencumbered by other trials, rehearses ideals championed by Rabelais in the education of Gargantua (*Gargantua*, Chapters 23–24) and Pantagruel (*Pantagruel*, Chapter 8) and in the account of the Abbey of Theleme (*Gargantua*, Chapters 52–57). It is little wonder, then, that readers continue to sense that '[f]ew translators can have identified themselves so closely with their subject'.[100]

Rabelais does, though, present particularly sharp challenges to his translator. His work, for all the breadth of its influence and reception, is often acutely local in its topical and geographical allusion. The treelessness of Beauce, for instance, ascribed to the destructiveness of Gargantua's giant mare's tail (*Gargantua*, Chapter 16), is a local geographical joke, while the events of the war with Picrochole (*Gargantua*, Chapters 26–51) famously unfold over territory within a few miles of La Devinière, Rabelais's father's vineyard.[101] We may be reminded of the difficulties that details of Roman custom and topography presented Douglas and Bellenden. Similarly, much of Rabelais's satire (especially in the first two books), while its general contours may be recognisable, is rooted in particular events and controversies in Paris in the early 1530s.[102] Linguistically, Rabelais's writing also presents formidable challenges, as he borrows – eruditely and playfully – not only from Latin, Greek, and Hebrew, but also from the riches of French dialect and freely fashions his own coinages. And this linguistic range is matched by a corresponding breadth of register and material: there are few writers as learned or as coarse as Rabelais; surely there is none who is both.

Urquhart's response is to embrace and extend Rabelaisian abundance with his own virtuosic inventiveness.[103] As we should expect, he comfortably meets Rabelais's coinages with his own: 'Ha, for favour sake, (I beseech you) emberlucock or inpulregafize your spirits with these vaine thoughts and idle conceits' (vol. 1, p. 41); 'Liripipionated' (vol. 1, p. 72); 'I latrially venere the supernal Astripotent' (vol. 1, p. 219); 'ragamuffianisme' (vol. 1, p. 225). Often he extends the effect with a kind of 'double translation', formally reminiscent of Douglas's practice in the *Eneados*, in which he pairs a French or Greek word with his own equivalent: 'torcheculatif' is rendered 'torcheculatife, or wipe-bummatory' (vol. 1, p. 63); 'Et, pour l'appaiser, luy donnerent à boyre à tyre larigot' becomes 'in the meanwhile to quiete the childe, they gave him to drink a tirelaregot, that is, till his throat was like to crack with it' (vol. 1, p. 42); 'rataconniculer' is translated 'retaconniculation, and reiterated lechery' (vol. 1, p. 33); 'les spondyles du coul' is turned 'spondyles or knuckles of the neck' (vol. 1, p. 102).[104] Urquhart also retains the French where it is needed to explain a play on words. This is most sustained in *Gargantua*, Chapter 9, where the weak puns of courtly *imprese* are mocked:

In the like darknesse and mist of ignorance, are wrapped up these vain-glorious Courtiers, and name-transposers, who going about in their impresa's, to signifie *esperance*, (that is, hope) have portrayed a sphere and birds pennes for peines: *Ancholie* (which is the flower colombine) for melancholy [...] *un lit sans ciel*, that is, a bed without a testerne, for *un licencié*, a graduated person (vol. 1, pp. 48–49).[105]

In all of this Urquhart was aided greatly by Randle Cotgrave's *Dictionarie of the French and English Tongues* (1611). The dictionary is itself a landmark in the reception of Rabelais and its influence on Urquhart's translation is profound.[106] Cotgrave's glosses not only explained many of the lexical difficulties in Rabelais, they also provided Urquhart with a range of alternatives with which to enrich the copiousness of his work. Only the first of the double translations quoted above does not pair a word from Rabelais with its gloss in Cotgrave ('torche-culatif' is less colourfully explained as 'taile-wiping') and Huntington Brown has turned the fine phrase, 'an ascending scale of amplification', to characterise the process by which a word or phrase in Rabelais generates multiple glosses in Cotgrave which are then co-opted and further added to by Urquhart in his translation.[107] Let us provide a single, representative example: where Rabelais writes 'Que Diable (dist Panurge) veult pretendre ce maistre Alliboron', Urquhart offers 'What the Devil (quoth Panurge) means this busie restless Fellow? What is it that this Polypragmonetick Ardeloine to all the Fiends of Hell doth aim at?' (vol. 2, p. 111). Cotgrave has glossed Alliboron 'A polypragmon, medler [...] busiebody'.[108]

This tendency to amplify Rabelais is also evident in Urquhart's more general use of pairs of synonyms to translate a single word or phrase in his source: in the same paragraph in Book 3, for instance, we have, in each case for a single French equivalent, 'scrubbing and swindging', 'raise and elevate', 'at certain intervals and such spaces of time', 'vex and trouble', 'perplexed and disquieted', 'represented and signified', 'agree, and are consonant', 'utterly abjure and deny' (vol. 2, pp. 111–12). It is evident at a more substantive level too. Where the Cake-Bakers of Lerné in Rabelais hurl twenty-nine terms of abuse, in Urquhart's translation they unfurl forty-two. Urquhart adds four books seemingly entirely of his own invention to the end of the catalogue of the Library of Saint Victor (whether 'The ingrained rogue, by Dwarsencas Eldenu' (vol. 1, p. 227) quite strikes the authentically Rabelaisian note is presumably a matter for debate). The thirteen terms of affection Rabelais's governesses find for Gargantua's 'braguette' (*Gargantua*, Chapter 11) turn into almost three times as many in Urquhart. As Urquhart warms to his task two chapters later, 'torchecul' is expansively rendered as 'torcheculs, arsewisps, bumfodders, tail-napkins, bunghole cleansers and wipe-breeches' (vol. 1, p. 63). And the epithets proposed for 'cod' and 'fool' in Book 3 (Chapters 26, 28, and 38) are similarly extended and as often replace Rabelais's suggestions as conventionally translate them ('Crestfallen' and 'Weatherbeaten' (vol. 2, pp. 147, 149) are notably successful examples). It is the energy of these inventive additions that gives Urquhart's translation its distinctive character and it is the very freedom of the treatment that seems most faithful to the spirit of the Rabelaisian source. This is fidelity neither to 'sentens' nor to 'eloquens' but to literary mode.

We must ask again, finally, to what end might Urquhart have produced his translation and here Urquhart himself supplies us with a surprisingly simple answer. Urquhart fought on the side of the defeated Royalists at Worcester in 1651 and the *Pantachronochanon*, *Ekskubalauron*, *Logopandecteison*, and translation of Rabelais (or the first two books, at least) were all completed while in captivity.[109] This partly explains the ostentatious erudition of the works (as well as their aspects of personal polemic) and Urquhart's exaggerated championing of the utility of his various schemes: they are intended to advertise the exceptional service their writer could perform for the commonwealth if restored to liberty and his Cromarty estates (as well as the current injustice of his fate). Thus, in a preface to the second book of his translation, Urquhart marks the difficulty and singular success of his work ('so difficult neverthelesse to be turned into any other speech, that many prime spirits in most of the Nations of Europe, since the yeare 1573, (which was fourescore yeares ago) after having attempted it, were constrained with no small regret to give it over, as a thing impossible to be done'), laments his current plight ('his lands be sequestred, his house garrisoned, his other goods sold, and himself detained a Prisoner of warre at London, for his having been at Worcester fight'), and promises to complete the translation, if others wish it and so long as 'the continuation of the rigour whereby he is dispossest of all his both real and personal estate, by pressing too hard upon him, be not an impediment thereto' (vol. 1, pp. 192–93). On the face of it, Rabelais would seem an improbable choice for Urquhart in such a context (for all that he allows the translator to showcase his linguistic versatility): his bawdy humour seems quite alien to Puritan rigour and only likely to align Urquhart further with disgraced Cavalier wit.[110] Nicholas McDowell, though, has suggestively explored the kind of political work support for

Urquhart's *Rabelais* might have done for the new government (and for Urquhart).[111]

And yet I am not convinced that Urquhart's translation can really be explained politically rather than philosophically. Rabelais's 'great theme' is '[a]bundance.'[112] He celebrates human possibility, the richness of the material world and the human body, the infinite potential of the free human spirit. As Erich Auerbach expresses it,

> the thing which lies concealed in his work, yet which is conveyed in a thousand ways, is an intellectual attitude, which he himself calls Pantagruelism; a grasp of life which comprehends the spiritual and the sensual simultaneously, which allows none of life's possibilities to escape.[113]

We may, from Bakhtin, be most familiar with the philosophical implications of Rabelais's celebration of the materiality of the human body: it is notable how many of the substantive additions in Urquhart's translation allow him to luxuriate in passages of coarse physicality. Yet there is no less energy to his rendering of the education of Gargantua and Pantagruel, of the brilliantly Platonic prologue to *Gargantua*, of Panurge's wonderful encomium of debt, of the learned satire of the defence of Bridlegoose, or of the exploration of folly in all its different kinds. The studies of kingship we are given in Gargantua's Speech to the Vanquished (*Gargantua*, Chapter 50) or in Pantagruel's treatment of the conquered Dipsodie (*The Third Book*, Chapter 1) will stand comparison with anything from the *Buke of the Governaunce of Princis* or *The Prince* and the confident and learned humour of the consultation of the Virgilian Lottery (*The Third Book*, Chapter 12) deserves to be read alongside the more tentative beginnings of a tradition in Douglas's *Eneados*. Moreover, the very linguistic playfulness and amplification of Urquhart's translation itself entails a celebration of material abundance. Douglas's use of double translation to cultivate Scots 'fouth' has acquired here a quite new philosophical freighting. It is Urquhart's participation in abundance that marks him as Rabelais's heir and in translation as philosophy we have another instance of translation at its very richest.

Thomas Rutledge

Endnotes

Introduction: Literatures of the Stewart Kingdom

1. Many thanks are due to Joanna Martin, Rhiannon Purdie and Theo van Heijnsbergen, who read this introduction for intelligibility and accuracy. Such errors that remain are all my own.
2. See Jane E. A. Dawson, *Scotland Re-Formed 1488–1587*, (Edinburgh: EUP, 2007), pp. 41–42 and 71–74; and Norman Macdougall, *James III* (Edinburgh: John Donald, 1982), pp. 78, 90–91 and *James IV* (East Linton: Tuckwell, 1997), pp. 100–05.
3. See Roger A. Mason, '*Regnum and Imperium*: Humanism and the Political Culture of Early Renaissance Scotland', in Mason, *Kingship and Commonweal*, pp. 104–38.
4. For James V's campaigns in the Borders, see Dawson, *Scotland Re-formed*, pp. 122–23 and Jamie Cameron, *James V: The Personal Rule, 1528–1542* (East Linton: Tuckwell, 1998), pp. 70–97; for James VI's attitudes, see Julian Goodare and Michael Lynch, 'The Scottish State and its borderlands, 1567–1625' in Julian Goodare and Michael Lynch (eds), *The Reign of James VI* (East Linton: Tuckwell, 2000), pp. 186–207.
5. William Ferguson, *Scotland: 1689–present*, (Edinburgh: Mercat Press, 1965), pp. 36–69.
6. Although technically James IV ascended the throne as king after the battle of Sauchieburn in 1488, he went back in tutelage. See Michael Brown, *James I* (Edinburgh: SAP, 1994); pp. 9–44; Christine McGladdery, *James II* (Edinburgh: John Donald, 1990), pp. 5–31; Macdougall, *James III*, pp. 36–87; Macdougall, *James IV*, pp. 24–111; Dawson, *Scotland Re-formed*, pp. 89–114 and 264–301; and Jenny Wormald, *Mary, Queen of Scots: A Study in Failure* (London: Collins and Brown, 1991), pp. 43–101.

7   *Chron. Bower* 8, pp. 322–28; Jenny Wormald, *Court, Kirk and Community: Scotland 1470–1625* (Edinburgh: EUP, 1981), pp. 13–14.
8   Sally Mapstone, 'Was there a Court Literature in Fifteenth-Century Scotland?', *SSL* 26 (1991), 410–22 and also Sally Mapstone, 'Older Scots Literature and the Court', in *EHSL*, pp. 273–85.
9   See F. J. Amours (ed.), *The Original Chronicle of Andrew of Wyntoun* 6 vols., STS (1902–1914), vol. 2, p. 6–7 (Book 1, chapter 1, ll. 57–58 – Wemyss MS); M. P. McDiarmid (ed.), *Hary's Wallace* 2 vols. STS (1968–69), vol. 2, p. 122 (Book 12, ll. 1442–48); Martin MacGregor, 'Creation and Compilation: The Book of the Dean of Lismore and Literary Culture in Late Medieval Gaelic Scotland', in *EHSL*, pp. 209–18; and Gillies on Purpose, below.
10 See A. A. MacDonald, 'Lyrics in Middle Scots' in T. G. Duncan (eds), *A Companion to Middle English Lyric* (Cambridge: D. S. Brewer, 2005), pp. 242–61, esp. pp. 246–48; and also Sally Mapstone on Transmission, below.
11 James Simpson, in *Reform and Cultural Revolution* (Oxford: OUP, 2002) begins with a statement about centralisation (p. 1).
12 The most influential articulation of this is Sally Mapstone, 'The Advice to Princes Tradition in Scottish Literature, 1450–1500', (D. Phil thesis, Oxford University, 1986). Subsequent developments include Joanna Martin, *Kingship and Love in Scottish poetry, 1424–1540* (Aldershot: Ashgate, 2008) and Rhiannon Purdie, 'The Search for Scottishness in *Golagros and Gawane*' in R. Purdie and N. Royan (eds), *The Scots and Medieval Arthurian Legend* (Cambridge: D. S. Brewer, 2005), pp. 95–108.
13 Gillies, below.
14 See Sir David Lindsay of the Mount, *Ane Satyre of the Thrie Estaitis*, ed. Roderick Lyall (Edinburgh: Canongate, 1989).
15 A report on the AHRC-funded project, *Staging and Representing the Scottish Renaissance Court*, headed by Greg Walker, makes clear the sophistication of Lyndsay's play: www.stagingthescottishcourt.org/wp-content/uploads/2013/02/Staging-the-Renaissance-Court-v4.pdf (accessed 6 May 2015).
16 See Adrienne Scullion, 'Political Theatre or Heritage Culture? *Ane Satyre of the Thrie Estaitis in Production*', in D. G. Mullan and C. Gribben (eds), *Literature and the Scottish Reformation* (Aldershot: Ashgate, 2013), pp. 213–32, esp. pp. 216–17.
17 See Alan Spence and Angus Calder, *The Thrie Estaites: The Millennium Version* (Edinburgh: EUP, 2002).

18 Full records of Scottish parliamentary proceedings can be found at Records of the Parliament of Scotland until 1707 (www.rps.ac.uk). A typical account of royal intentions can be found under 17 October 1499 (1488/10/37–50).

19 See, for instance, 'The Twentieth-Century Scottish Literary Renaissance' in Douglas Gifford, Sarah Dunnigan and Alan MacGillivray (eds), *Scottish Literature* (Edinburgh: EUP, 2002), pp. 505–720. For a brief account of Renaissance, see Jerry Brotton, *The Renaissance: A Very Short Introduction* (Oxford: OUP, 2006), and for its Scottish reception see John MacQueen (ed.), *Humanism in Renaissance Scotland* (Edinburgh: EUP, 1990).

20 For an introduction to the varieties of humanism, see Jill Kraye (ed.), *Cambridge Companion to Renaissance Humanism* (Cambridge: CUP, 1996).

21 For a view of its political reception in Scotland see Roger Mason, 'Chivalry and citizenship: Aspects of National Identity in Renaissance Scotland', in Mason, *Kingship and Commonweal*, pp. 78–103 and J. H. Burns, *The True Law of Kingship* (Oxford: Clarendon Press, 1996), pp. 205–09.

22 See A. E. B. Coldiron, *Printers without Borders: Translation and Textuality in the Renaissance* (Oxford: OUP, 2014) for a discussion of translation into English (but only English).

23 For a full account of the European Reformation, see Diarmaid MacCulloch, *Reformation: Europe's House Divided 1490–1700* (London: Allen Lane, 2003); for a description of the scholarly engagement with the Bible, see Alister McGrath, *The Intellectual Origins of the European Reformation* (Oxford: Blackwell, 1995). The Scottish Reformation is outlined in Dawson, *Scotland Re-formed*, pp. 200–39.

24 See Alex Ryrie, *The Origins of the Scottish Reformation* (Manchester: MUP, 2006).

25 See L. J. Macfarlane, *William Elphinstone and the Kingdom of Scotland 1431–1514* (Aberdeen: AUP, 1985); Jane E. A. Dawson, *John Knox* (New Haven, CT: Yale University Press, 2015); and Roger A. Mason and Steven Reid (eds), *Andrew Melville 1545–1622: writings, reception and reputation* (Aldershot: Ashgate, 2014).

26 See Mullan and Gribben (eds), *Literature and the Scottish Reformation*.

27 See Carol Edington, *Court and Culture in Renaissance Scotland: Sir David Lindsay of the Mount (1486–1555)* (Amherst, MA: University of Massachusetts Press, 1994), p. 1.

28 For a short account of events of the seventeenth century, including the War of the Three Kingdoms, see Jenny Wormald, *The Seventeenth Century, 1603–1688* (Oxford: OUP, 2008) and Ian Gentles, *The English Revolution and the Wars in the Three Kingdoms 1638–1652* (London: Pearson, 2007).

29 See Michael Spiller, 'Poetry after the Union, 1603–1660', in *AHSL*, pp. 141–62 for the writers, and for potential readers, Marie-Claude Tucker, 'Scottish Students and Masters at the Faculty of Law of the University of Bourges in the Sixteenth and Seventeenth Centuries', in Van Heijnsbergen and Royan, *Literature, Letters and the Canonical* pp. 111–20.

30 See Gillies, 'Gaelic Literature in the Later Middle Ages'. Accounts of seventeenth-century writing are rarer: see Sally Mapstone, 'Older Scots and the Sixteenth and Seventeenth Centuries' in Mapstone, *Older Scots Literature*, pp. 413–23.

31 See Pons-Sanz and MacCoinnich on Language, below; also Jeremy J. Smith, *Introduction to Older Scots: A Linguistic Reader* STS (2012), pp. 1–10 and Christine Robinson and Roibeard ò Maolalaigh, 'The Several Tongues of a Single Kingdom: The Languages of Scotland 1314–1707' in *EHSL*, pp. 153–63.

32 See, for example, *AHSL* and *EHSL*.

33 See for example, S. Greenblatt (gen. ed.), *The Norton Anthology of English Literature* 9th edn, vols. A and B (New York: W. W. Norton, 2012), which includes Robert Henryson but not William Dunbar.

34 See Douglas Gray, *Robert Henryson* (Leiden: Brill, 1979); Priscilla Bawcutt, *Gavin Douglas: A Critical Study* (Edinburgh: EUP, 1976); Priscilla Bawcutt, *Dunbar the Makar* (Oxford: OUP, 1992); and Edington, *Lindsay*.

35 See, for example, R. J. Lyall, *Alexander Montgomerie* (Tempe, AZ: ACMRS, 2005); Sarah Dunnigan, *Eros and poetry at the courts of Mary Queen of Scots and James VI* (Basingstoke: Palgrave, 2002); and R. J. Goldstein, *The Matter of Scotland: Historical narrative in medieval Scotland* (Lincoln NE and London: Nebraska University Press, 1993).

36 In addition to general histories, there are recent seminal essay collections, mostly arising from the triennial International Conference on Medieval and Renaissance Scottish Literature and Language: Aitken et al, *Bards and Makars* (1976); Caie et al, *European Sun* (2001); van Heijnsbergen and Royan, *Literature, Letters and the Canonical* (2002); *Older Scots Literature* (2005); Royan, *Langage Cleir illumynate* (2007); Hadley Williams and McClure, *Fresche Fontanis* (2013), but

also Bawcutt and Hadley Williams, *Medieval Scottish Poetry* (2006); L. A. J. R. Houwen, A. A. MacDonald and S. L. Mapstone (eds), *A Palace in the Wild* (Leuven: Peeters, 2000); and S. M. Dunnigan, C. M. Harker and E. S. Newlyn, *Women and the Feminine in Medieval and Early Modern Scottish Writing* (London: Palgrave Macmillan, 2004).

37 The Book of the Dean of Lismore (BDL) (Edinburgh, NLS, MS Adv. MS.72.1.37) is mentioned in nearly every essay in this *Companion*, but particularly those by Pons-Sanz and MacCoinnich, Gillies, Mathis and Martin, and Hollo.

38 Earlier work in this field was undertaken by Alexander Broadie, in *The Circle of John Mair: Logic and Logicians in Pre-Reformation Scotland* (Oxford: OUP, 1985).

39 For Europe, see MacCulloch, *Reformation*, pp. 3–52, and for Scotland in particular, see Dawson, *Scotland Re-Formed*, pp. 16–20.

40 See Innes and Reid, on Faith, below.

41 For some Middle English anti-fraternal satire, see James M. Dean *Six Ecclesiastical Satires* (Kalamazoo, MI: MIP, 1991). Dunbar, Henryson and Lyndsay also deploy these positions.

42 See Dawson, *Scotland Re-Formed*, pp. 7–8, and for a fuller account of the book trade, see Alastair J. Mann, *The Scottish book trade 1500–1720* (East Linton: Tuckwell, 2000). For images of the first books printed in Scotland, see digital.nls.uk/firstscottishbooks/.

43 See Smith, *Older Scots*, pp. 15, 61–67, 200–05.

44 See Hollo on Translation, below.

45 For Tudor attitudes to Ireland, see Susan Brigden, *New Worlds, Lost Worlds: The Rule of the Tudors 1485–1603* (London: Penguin, 2000) pp. 149–62, 228–31, 342–55 and Steven G. Ellis, *Tudor Ireland: Crown, Community and Conflict of Cultures, 1470–1603* (Harlow: Longman, 1985).

46 See Michael Lynch, 'James VI and the "Highland Problem"', in Goodare and Lynch (eds), *The Reign of James VI*, pp. 208–27 for James's attitude to his Gaelic-speaking territory.

47 MacGregor and Hogg on History, below.

48 See, for instance, Clare Carroll, 'Humanism and English literature in the fifteenth and sixteenth centuries', in Kraye (ed.), *Renaissance Humanism*, pp. 246–68.

49 Dunnigan, *Eros and Poetry*, pp. 15–45.

50 The Casket sonnets were written in French and translated into Scots/English. See Dunnigan, *Eros and Poetry*, p. 10.

51 See Clare Jackson, 'Mackenzie, Sir George, of Rosehaugh (1636/1638–1691)', *Oxford Dictionary of National Biography*, Oxford University Press, 2004; online edn, Jan 2007 www.oxforddnb.com/view/article/17579, accessed 8 May 2015.

52 See Joanna M. Martin (ed.), *The Maitland Quarto* STS (2015).

53 Most general narratives move almost directly to the eighteenth century, although with the editing of writers such as Archibald Pitcairne (J. MacQueen (ed.), *Archibald Pitcairne: The Phanaticks*, STS (2012) [more commonly entitled *The Assembly*]), opportunities to refigure the seventeenth century are growing.

54 See Williams, *Lyndsay,* pp. 112–27.

55 See D. Webster (ed.), *The Works of George Buchanan, in the Scottish Language: Containing the Chameleon, a Satire Against the Laird of Lidingtone* (1823), reprinted (Whitefish MO: Kessinger Publishing, 2010). For a sample of the text, see Smith, *Older Scots: A Linguistic Reader*, pp. 206–07.

56 For *The Triumphs of Petrarke* , see H. W. Meikle (ed.), *The Works of William Fowler* 3 vols., STS (1914–1940), vol. 1, pp. 13–134, and for Gilbert Hay's work, see Jonathan A. Glenn (ed.), *Gilbert Hay's Prose Works* vols. 2 and 3, STS (1993 and 2005).

57 Ralph Hanna (ed.), *Golagros and Gawane* STS (2008) and M. M. Gray (ed.), *Lancelot of the Laik*, STS (1912).

58 For Fowler's translation of Machiavelli, see Alessandra Petrina (ed.), *Machiavelli in the British Isles* (Aldershot: Ashgate, 2009), and for *Roland Furious*, see T. Crockett (ed.), *Poems of John Stewart of Baldynneis,* vol 2, STS (1913), pp. 3–100.

59 See Ralph Hanna (ed.), *Richard Holland: The Buke of the Howlat*, STS (2014), pp. 79–80 (ll. 794–832) and *Dunbar* pp. 201–02 (ll. 49–56).

1. The Languages of Scotland

1 See David Sellar, 'Legal Writing, 1314–1707', in *EHSL* pp. 238–44.

2 See Keith Williamson, 'Lowland Scots in Education: An Historical Survey, Part 1', *SL* 1 (1982), pp. 54–77; Jack MacQueen, 'From Rome to Ruddiman: The Scotto-Latin Tradition,' in *EHSL* pp. 184–208, especially pp. 187–202; and Jane E. A. Dawson, *Scotland Re-formed, 1488–1587* (Edinburgh: EUP, 2007), pp. 224–29.

3 On the influence of Norse on Scots, see Jeremy J. Smith, 'Norse in Scotland', *SL* 13 (1994), pp. 18–33; and Susanne Kries, *Skandinavisch-schottische Sprachbeziehungen im Mittelalter: Der altnordische Lehneinfluss*, North-Western European Language Evolution

Supplement 20 (Odense: University Press of Southern Denmark, 2003). See also Christine Robinson and Roibeard Ó Maolalaigh, 'The Several Tongues: The Languages of Scotland, 1314–1707', in *EHSL* pp. 153–63.

4 See Guillaume le Clerc, *Romance of Fergus* ed. Wilson Frescoln (Philadephia, PA: W. H. Allen, 1983).

5 See Ranald Nicholson, *Scotland: The Later Middle Ages* (Edinburgh: Mercat Press, 1974), p. 274.

6 See Alastair J. Mann, *The Scottish Book Trade, 1500–1720* (East Linton: Tuckwell Press, 2000), pp. 112 and 236–52.

7 On the linguistic shift from Gaelic to Scots in this period, see Simon Taylor, 'Babbet and Bridin Pudding or Polyglot Fife in the Middle Ages', *Nomina* 17 (1994), pp. 99–118.

8 See Thomas Owen Clancy, 'Gaelic in Medieval Scotland: Advent and Expansion', *PBA* 167 (2011), 349–92, especially pp. 389–90.

9 The shift in attitudes to Scottish Gaelic in the Lowlands during this period is clearly shown in some contemporary works. While there was a recognition by some sixteenth-century Lowland historians of the Gaelic roots of the Scottish nation, others took a different view. For instance, William Dunbar (on whom see further below) presented Gaels in the last stanza of his poem *The Dance of the Sevin Deidly Synnis* as being condemned to the deepest part of hell, and hence the greatest sinners, and their language as something that could give a headache even to the Devil. See *Dunbar*, B 47 and B 65 and notes. For a review of the treatment of Gaelic and the Highlands by Lowland 'literati' such as Dunbar, Boece, Bower, Lyndsay and others in this period, see D. S. Thomson, 'Gaelic Literary Inter-actions with Scots and English Work: A Survey', *SL* 5 (1986), pp. 1–14, especially pp. 4–5; Dòmhnall Eachann Meek, 'Gàidhlig is Gaylick anns na Meadhan Aoisean', in Gillies, *Gaelic and Scotland*, pp. 131–45, especially pp. 137 and 144–45; and Martin MacGregor, 'Gaelic Barbarity and Scottish Identity in the Later Middle Ages,' in Dauvit Broun and Martin MacGregor (eds), *Mìorun Mòr nan Gall, 'The Great Ill-Will of the Lowlander'?* (Glasgow: University of Glasgow, 2007), pp. 7–48, available at eprints.gla.ac.uk/4960/. For Highland perspectives on the Lowlands, see John MacInnes, 'The Gaelic Perception of the Lowlands', in Gillies, *Gaelic and Scotland*, pp. 89–100.

10 See the wide ranging historical introduction and range of documents in Grant G. Simpson, *Scottish Handwriting, 1150–1650* (East Linton: Tuckwell Press, 1998).

11 See Simon Taylor, 'Babbet and Bridin Pudding or Polyglot Fife in the Middle Ages', *Nomina* 17 (1994), pp. 99–118.
12 See Victor Edward Durkacz, *The Decline of the Celtic Languages* (Edinburgh: John Donald, 1983), p. 13.
13 *Tiomnadh Nuadh ar Tighearna agus ar Slanuighir Iosa Criosd. Eadar-Theangaichte o'n Ghreugais chum Gaelic Albannaich* (Edinburgh, 1796). Accessed on 27 April 2011 via *Eighteenth Century Collections Online*. For an account of Gaelic religious publication from 1567 onwards, see Donald E. Meek, 'The Gaelic Bible', in David F. Wright (ed.), *The Bible in Scottish Life and Literature* (Edinburgh: Saint Andrews Press, 1988), pp. 9–23.
14 See Charles W. J. Withers, *Gaelic Scotland: The Transformation of a Culture Region* (London, Routledge, 1998), pp. 112–13. See, however, Allan I. Macinnes, *Clanship, Commerce and the House of Stuart, 1603–1788* (East Linton: Tuckwell Press, 1996), pp. 76–77.
15 See Jane E. A. Dawson (ed.), *Campbell Letters, 1559–1583*, SHS (1997), p. 7.
16 See Aonghas MacCoinnich, 'Where and How Was Gaelic Written in Late Medieval and Early Modern Scotland? Orthographic Practices and Cultural Identities', in Colm Ó Baoill and Nancy R. McGuire (eds), *Caindel Alban. Fèill-Sgrìobhainn do Dhòmhnall E. Meek. SGS* 24 (2008), 309–56 (available at eprints.gla.ac.uk/4940/), especially p. 335.
17 See Marguerite Wood (ed.), *Extracts from the Records of the Burgh of Edinburgh, 1604 to 1626* (Edinburgh: Oliver and Boyd, 1931), p. 121.
18 See Martin Martin, *A Description of the Western Islands of Scotland, circa 1695* (Edinburgh: Birlinn, 1999), p. 79; and D. Withrington, 'Education in the 17th Century Highlands', in Loraine Maclean (ed.), *The Seventeenth Century in the Highlands* (Inverness: Inverness Field Club, 1986), pp. 60–69.
19 Margaret H. B. Sanderson, *A Kindly Place? Living in Sixteenth Century Scotland* (East Linton: Tuckwell Press, 2002), pp. 125 and 137.
20 See J. Carmichael Watson, (ed.), *Orain agus Luinneagan le Mairi Nighean Alasdair Ruaidh: Gaelic Songs of Mary MacLeod* (Edinburgh: SGTS, 1934); Colm Ó Baoill, *Bàrdachd Shìlis na Ceapaich: Poems and Songs by Sìleas Macdonald, c. 1660–c. 1729* SGTS (1972); and *Mairghread Nighean Lachlainn: Song Maker of Mull* SGTS (2009).
21 Alastair Mac-Dhonuill, *Ais-eiridh na Sean Chánoin Albannaich; no an Nuadh Oranaiche Gaidhealach* (Edinburgh, 1751), available at www.archive.org/details/aiseiridhnaseancoomacd; accessed via the Internet

Archive, 11 May 2011. This volume was revolutionary not just in the sense of its choice of language and overt and covert Jacobitism. It pioneered, according to Ronald Black, 'metamorphosis from within the tradition, taking themes and ideas from the rhetorical codes of Gaelic panegyric and making them blossom in their own right'; see Ronald Black, 'Alexander Macdonald's *Ais-Eiridh*, 1751', *JEBS* 5 (2010), pp. 45–64, at p. 45.

22 See Watson *Scottish Verse,* and Neil Ross (ed.), *Heroic Poetry from the Book of the Dean of Lismore,* SGTS (1939); Donald E. Meek, 'The Scots-Gaelic Scribes of Late Medieval Perthshire: An Overview of the Orthography and Contents of the Book of the Dean of Lismore', in McClure and Spiler, *Bryght Lanternis*, pp. 387–404; and Martin MacGregor, 'Creation and Compilation: The Book of the Dean of Lismore and Literary Culture in Late Medieval Gaelic Scotland', *EHSL,* pp. 207–18.

23 See C. MacPhàrlain (ed.), *Làmh-Sgrìobhainn Mhic Rath. Dòrlach Laoidhean do Sgrìobhadh le Donnchadh MacRath, 1688: Fernaig Manuscript: Handful of Lays Written by Duncan Macrae, 1688* (Dùn Dè: Calum S. MacLeòid, 1923).

24 See Martin MacGregor, 'The Genealogical Histories of Gaelic Scotland', in Adam Fox and Daniel Woolf (eds), *The Spoken Word: Oral Culture in Britain, 1500–1800* (Manchester: MUP, 2002), pp. 196–239; and 'Writing the History of Gaelic Scotland: A Provisional Checklist of "Gaelic" Genealogical Histories', in Colm Ó Baoill and Nancy R. McGuire (eds), *Caindel Alban. Fèill-Sgrìobhainn do Dhòmhnall E. Meek, SGS* 24 (2008), pp. 357–79.

25 See MacCoinnich, 'Where and How Was Gaelic Written in Late Medieval and Early Modern Scotland?'; and '"Scribis le pen de henchis;" Criomagan de Ghàidhlig ann an Eachdraidhean Beurla Chloinn Choinnich, ca. 1550–1711', in Kenneth E. Nilsen (ed.), *Rannsachadh na Gàidhlig 5, Fifth Scottish Gaelic Research Conference* (Nova Scotia: Cape Breton University Press, 2010), pp. 149–94.

26 See Dauvit Broun, 'Gaelic Literacy in Eastern Scotland between 1124 and 1249', in Huw Pryce (ed.), *Literacy in Medieval Celtic Societies* (Cambridge: CUP, 1998), pp. 183–201; and Roibeard Ó Maolalaigh, 'The Scotticisation of Gaelic: A Reassessment of the Language and Orthography of the Gaelic Notes of the Book of Deer', in Katherine Forsyth (ed.), *Studies on the Book of Deer* (Dublin: Four Courts Press, 2008), pp. 201–96.

27 See Colm Ó Baoill, 'A History of Gaelic to 1800', in Moray Watson and Michelle Macleod (eds), *The Edinburgh Companion to the Gaelic Language* (Edinburgh: EUP, 2010), pp. 1–21, especially p. 11–12.

28 See William Gillies, 'Courtly and Satiric Poems in the Book of the Dean of Lismore', *ScotStud* 21 (1977), pp. 35–53, especially pp. 36–37, 41–42 and 48.

29 MacCoinnich, 'Where and How Was Gaelic Written in Late Medieval and Early Modern Scotland?', pp. 313–22 and 353–56. Cf. Ó Baoill, 'A History of Gaelic to 1800', p. 12.

30 See Black, 'The Gaelic Manuscripts of Scotland'; and MacCoinnich, 'Where and How Was Gaelic Written in Late Medieval and Early Modern Scotland?'.

31 See Derick S. Thomson, 'The MacMhuirich Bardic Family', *TGSI*, 43 (1963), pp. 276–304, and 'Gaelic Learned Orders and Literati in Medieval Scotland', *ScotStud* 12 (1968), pp. 57–78; also John Bannerman, *The Beatons: A Medical Kindred in the Classical Gaelic Tradition* (Edinburgh: John Donald, 1998).

32 For the MacLeods and their use of classical Gaelic, see John Bannerman, 'Gaelic Endorsements of Early Seventeenth Century Legal Documents', *Studia Celtica* 14–15 (1979–80), pp. 18–33. For Ruairidh Mòr MacLeòid's activities in Ireland, 1594–96, see Annie I. Cameron (ed.), *Calendar of State Papers Relating to Scotland and Mary, Queen of Scots, 1547–1603*, Vol. 11: *1593–1595* (Edinburgh: H. M. General Register House, 1936), pp. 477, 497–98, 676 and 683–84; and M. S. Giuseppi (ed.), *Calendar of State Papers Relating to Scotland and Mary, Queen of Scots, 1547–1603*, Vol. 12: *1595–1597* (Edinburgh: HMSO, 1952), pp. 156–57. For more on the nature of such classical Gaelic language and manuscripts, see William Gillies, 'Gaelic: The Classical Tradition', in *AHSL*, pp. 245–62; Colm Ó Baoill, 'Scotticisms in a Manuscript of 1467', *SGS* 15 (1988), pp. 122–39; and R. I. M. Black, 'The Gaelic Manuscripts of Scotland', in Gillies, *Gaelic and Scotland*, pp. 146–74. For recent attempts at understanding the performance context of classical Gaelic verse, see Virginia Blankenhorn, 'Observations on the Performance of Irish Syllabic Verse', *Studia Celtica* 44 (2010): 135–44; and William Gillies, 'Music and Gaelic Strict Metre Poetry', *Studia Celtica* 44 (2010), pp. 111–34.

33 John MacInnes, 'The Panegyric Code in Gaelic Poetry and its Historical Background', *TGSI* 50 (1978), pp. 435–98, especially pp. 444–45. This has been reproduced in M. Newton (ed.), *Dùthchas nan Gaidheal: The Selected Essays of John MacInnes* (Edinburgh: Birlinn, 2006),

pp. 265–319. For a list of classical Gaelic works related to Scotland, see Wilson McLeod, *Divided Gaels: Gaelic Cultural Identities in Scotland and Ireland, c. 1200–c. 1650* (Oxford: OUP, 2004), pp. 228–41.

34 R. L. Thomson (ed.), *Foirm Na N-Urrnuidheadh: John Carswell's Translation of the Book of Common Order* (Edinburgh: SGTS, 1970). See also Hollo, Chapter 11.

35 See Meek, 'The Gaelic Bible'. For a consideration of the differences in language, see Ronald Black, 'Gaelic Orthography: The Drunk Man's Broad Road', in Watson and MacLeod (eds), *Companion to Gaelic*, pp. 229–61, especially pp. 230–34.

36 Martin, *A Description of the Western Islands of Scotland*, p. 79. A few writers in Argyll were still using classical Gaelic by the end of the seventeenth century, however; see Colm Ó Baoill, 'Robert Campbell, Forsair Coire an t-Sìthe', *SGS* 23 (2007), 57–84, especially pp. 57 and 64. For the demise of the tradition in the Beaton family, hereditary practitioners of medicine, see Bannerman, *The Beatons*, pp. 120, 124, 127, 131 and 133.

37 See John Lorne Campbell and Derick S. Thomson, *Edward Lhuyd in the Scottish Highlands, 1699–1700* (Oxford: OUP, 1963), p. 78; Ó Maolalaigh, 'The Scotticisation of Gaelic', p. 265; and MacCoinnich, 'Where and How Was Gaelic Written in Late Medieval and Early Modern Scotland?', p. 340, n. 44.

38 Donald E. Meek, 'Language and Style in the Scottish Gaelic Bible', *SL* 9 (1990), pp. 1–16, especially pp. 8–9.

39 R. L. Thomson (ed.), *Adtimchiol an Chreidimh: The Gaelic Version of John Calvin's Catechismus Ecclesiae Genevensis* SGTS (1962), pp. xxxv–xxxix.

40 'Foirm na N-Urrnuidheadh' (1567) [Gaelic translation of the Book of Common Order]; see Thomson, *John Carswell's Translation of the Book of Common Order*, ll. 1132–49.

41 'Foirceadul Aithghearr Cheasnuighe' (1659). This is the second edition of the Shorter Catechism, published by the Synod of Argyll, 1659, from which this version of the prayer is taken. The first edition, of which no copies survive, was printed in 1651. See Thomson, *The Gaelic Version of John Calvin's Catechismus Ecclesiae Genevensis*, p. 249; and Ronald Black, 'Gaelic Religious Publishing, 1567–1800', *SGS* 24 (2008), pp. 73–86, especially p. 74; and idem, 'A Handlist of Gaelic Printed books, 1567–1800', *SGS* 25 (2009), pp. 35–94, especially pp. 43–44.

42 'An Tiomnadh Nuadh', Mata 6: 10–14. *Tiomnadh Nuadh ar Tighearna agus ar Slanuighir Iosa Criosd. Eadar-Theangaichte o'n Ghreugais*

chum Gaelic Albannaich (Edinburgh, 1796). Accessed on 27 April 2011 via *Eighteenth Century Collections Online*.

43 For 'learned' families in the Gàidhealtachd, see Thomson, 'Gaelic Learned Orders and Literati in Medieval Scotland'. For a discussion of the language, style and register of the Gaelic Bible and the transition between classical Gaelic and the vernacular, see Meek, 'Language and Style in the Scottish Gaelic Bible'; Ó Baoill, 'A History of Gaelic to 1800', pp. 14–17; and Black, 'Gaelic Orthography', pp. 230–34.

44 See Laurence Muir, 'The Influence of the Rolle and Wyclifite Psalters upon the Psalter of the Authorised Version', *The Modern Language Review* 30 (1935), pp. 302–10.

45 Watson, *Scottish Verse*, pp. 186–87.

46 Watson's translation into English is as follows. 'Here is a Gael of John Stewart's family who pleasures poets, whereby the better is his estate; though I am separated from his bounty, he is a treasury of poet-bands and learned men. / Thou John Stewart from the bounds of Rannoch, thou whose hand has more virtue than all the Gael, receive from me, thou warrior stout in warfare, a poem of praise and threat withal.'

47 While much of the Gaelic material in the Book of the Dean was in classical Gaelic, some of it was in vernacular Gaelic. Classical Gaelic, however, rather than vernacular Scottish Gaelic was used by Watson in his edition of the verse in the BDL, which may, on occasion, have obscured vernacular features in these poems; see Watson *Scottish Verse* p. xxi. For a linguistic description of Gaelic orthography, see William Gillies, 'Scottish Gaelic' in Martin J. Ball and James Fife (eds), *The Celtic Languages* (London: Routledge, 1993), pp. 145–227, especially pp. 147–56. For a recent appraisal of the cultural background to this manuscript, see Martin MacGregor, 'The View from Fortingall: The Worlds of the Book of the Dean of Lismore', *SGS*, 22 (2006), pp. 35–85.

48 MacCoinnich, "Where and How Was Gaelic Written in Late Medieval and Early Modern Scotland?', pp. 322–30. For the birth of modern Gaelic spelling systems in the late seventeenth and early eighteenth centuries see Black, 'Gaelic Orthography', pp. 230–39.

49 See Colm Ó Baoill and Donald MacAulay, *Scottish Gaelic Vernacular Verse to 1730: A Checklist*, 2nd edition (Aberdeen: University of Aberdeen, Department of Celtic, 2001). For anthologies of verse from this period see, Wilson McLeod and Meg Bateman (eds), *Duanaire nan Sracaire: The Songbook of the Pillagers: Anthology of Scotland's Gaelic Verse to 1600* (Edinburgh: Birlinn, 2007); and Colm

Ó Baoill (ed.) and Meg Bateman (trans.), *Gàir nan Clàrsach: The Harps' Cry: An Anthology of 17th-Century Gaelic Poetry* (Edinburgh: Birlinn, 1994).

50 See Annie M. Mackenzie (ed.), *Òrain Iain Luim: Songs of John Macdonald Bard of Keppoch* SGTS (1964); and A. I. Macinnes, 'Scottish Gaeldom, 1638-1651: The Vernacular Response to the Covenanting Dynamic', in John Dwyer et al. (eds), *New Perspectives on the Politics and Culture of Early Modern Scotland* (Edinburgh: John Donald, 1982), pp. 59-94.

51 J. Derrick McClure, 'English in Scotland', in Robert Burchfield (ed.), *The Cambridge History of the English Language*, Vol. 5 (Cambridge: CUP, 1994), pp. 23-93, at p. 46.

52 We should not forget, though, that the text is actually only preserved in two late-fifteenth-century manuscripts: Cambridge, St John's College MS G.23 (1487), and Edinburgh, National Library of Scotland MS 19.2.2 (1489), which exhibits more conservative linguistic features. See A. A. M. Duncan (ed.), *The Bruce* (Edinburgh: Canongate, 1997), pp. 2-4 and 32.

53 *John Barbour: The Bruce* (Edinburgh: Canongate, 1997), p. 47.

54 For a more detailed description of Older Scots phonology, see Adam J. Aitken, 'How to Pronounce Older Scots?', in Aitken et al, *Bards and Makars*, pp. 1-21, and *Older Scottish Vowels*, ed. by Caroline Macafee, STS (2002); Paul Johnston, 'Older Scots Phonology and its Regional Variation', in Charles Jones (ed.), *The Edinburgh History of the Scots Language* (Edinburgh: EUP), pp. 47-111; and Caroline Macafee, 'The Phonology of Older Scots', in John Corbett et al. (eds), *The Edinburgh Companion to Scots* (Edinburgh: EUP, 2003), pp. 138-69.

55 Cf. <-it.-yt> for the past and past participle of weak verbs (e.g. 'anamalit' and 'illumynit' in Dunbar's *The Goldyn Targe*; see below.

56 On the inflectional morphology of Older Scots, see further Anne King, 'The Inflectional Morphology of Older Scots', in Jones (ed.), *History of Scots* pp. 156-81; on its syntax, see Lilo Moessner, 'The Syntax of Older Scots', in Jones (ed.), *History of Scots*, pp. 112-55.

57 For examinations of the themes found in Barbour's *Bruce* and other early chronicles, see Nicola Royan, 'A Question of Truth: Barbour's *Bruce*, Hary's *Wallace* and *Richard Coeur de Lion*', *International Review of Scottish Studies* 34 (2009), pp. 75-105, www.irss.uoguelph.ca/issue/view/94.

58 See Duncan, *The Bruce*, pp. 4-8.

59 Ibid., pp. 2-8.

60 See J. Derrick McClure, 'What Scots Owes to Gaelic', *SL* 5 (1986), pp. 85–98, especially p. 85. For Scots and English borrowings into Gaelic poetry, see Thomson, 'Gaelic Literary Interactions with Scots and English Work'; and I. Quick, 'English and Scots Military Loanwords in Scottish Gaelic', *SL* 5 (1986), pp. 99–105. On the relationship between the two languages, see also Colm Ó Baoill, 'Scots-Gaelic Interface', in Jones (ed.), *History of Scots* pp. 551–68.

61 On the make-up of Older Scots vocabulary, see further Caroline Macafee, 'Older Scots Lexis', in Jones (ed.), *History of Scots*, pp. 182–212.

62 Bawcutt., *Dunbar,* B 59.

63 Ibid., B 65.

64 On aureation in Dunbar's poetry, see further Bengt Ellenberger, *The Latin Element in the Vocabulary of the Earlier Makars: Henryson and Dunbar* (Lund, CWK Gleerup, 1977); and John Corbett, 'Aureation Revisited: The Latinate Vocabulary of Dunbar's High and Plain Styles', in Sally Mapstone (ed.), *William Dunbar, 'The Nobill Poyet'* (East Linton: Tuckwell Press, 2001), pp. 183–97. Corbett reminds us that we cannot always consider Latinate and French terms as indicators of high style because on some occasions those terms had become the unmarked words to refer to a particular concept; therefore, it is their avoidance rather than their use that creates a particular stylistic effect. While in these cases we are talking about the use of Latin loans, it is important to bear in mind that Dunbar, like many of his contemporaries and predecessors, also engaged in code-switching in his works, alternating between Scots and Latin, which could be used in the refrain, at regular intervals or in random insertions; see Elizabeth Archibald, 'Tradition and Innovation in the Macaronic Poetry of Dunbar and Skelton', *Modern Language Quarterly* 53 (1992), pp. 126–49.

65 See S. Lucas, 'Foreign Influences in the Vocabulary of William Dunbar', *SL* 9 (1990), pp. 52–65, especially p. 55; and above, note 8.

66 See Neil Rhodes et al. (eds), *King James VI and I: Selected Writings* (Aldershot: Ashgate, 2003), p. 31.

67 See Felicity Riddy, 'The Alliterative Revival', in *AHSL* pp. 39–54.

68 Rhodes et al., *King James VI and I,* p. 36.

69 See Gregory Kratzmann, *Anglo-Scottish Literary Relations 1430–1550* (Cambridge: CUP, 1980).

70 Anneli Meurman-Solin, 'Differentiation and Standardisation in Early Scots', in Jones (ed.), *History of Scots,* pp. 3–23, at p. 14.

71 See Anneli Meurman-Solin, 'The Author-Addressee Relationship

and the Marking of Stance in the Characterization of Sixteenth- and Seventeenth-Century Genre Styles', *Revue Belge de Philologie et d'Histoire* 71 (1993), pp. 733–45.

72 See Amy J. Devitt, *Standardizing Written English: Diffusion in the Case of Scotland, 1520–1659* (Cambridge: CUP, 1989); Annelie Meurman-Solin, *Variation and Change in Early Scottish Prose: Studies Based on the Helsinki Corpus of Older Scots*, (Helsinki: Suomalainen Tiedeakatemia, 1993); 'Differentiation and Standardisation in Early Scots', 'Geographical, Socio-Spatial and Systemic Distance in the Spread of the Relative *who* in Scots', in Ricardo Bermúdez-Otero et al. (eds), *Generative Theory and Corpus Studies: A Dialogue from 10 ICEHL*, (Berlin: Mouton de Gruyter, 2000), pp. 417–38; 'On the Conditioning of Geographical and Social Distance in Language Variation and Change in Renaissance Scots', in Dieter Kastovsky and Arthur Mettinger (eds), *The History of English in a Social Context*, (Berlin: Mouton de Gruyter, 2000), pp. 227–55; 'Genre as a Variable in Sociohistorical Linguistics', *European Journal of English Studies* 5 (2001), pp. 241–56; and 'The Progressive in Early Scots', in Teresa Fanego, María José López-Couso and Javier Pérez-Guerra (eds), *English Historical Syntax and Morphology*, (Amsterdam: John Benjamins, 2002), pp. 203–29.

73 In the case of Dunbar's poem, this is however somewhat unlikely because the form is already recorded in the copy printed during Dunbar's lifetime by Walter Chepman and Andrew Myllar in Southgait.

74 See Joanna Martin, *Kingship and Love in Scottish Poetry, 1424–1540* (Aldershot: Ashgate, 2008), p. 41.

75 See Alan Lupack (ed.), *Lancelot of the Laik and Sir Tristrem* (Kalamazoo, MI: MIP, 1994), p. 2.

76 See Kratzmann, *Anglo-Scottish Literary Relations*, p. 231. On the linguistic features of this poem, see William A. Craigie, 'The Language of the *Kingis Quair*', *Essays and Studies* 25 (1939), pp. 22–38.

77 On the linguistic features of literary compositions in Older Scots, see further Alex Agutter, 'Middle Scots as a Literary Language', in *AHSL* pp. 13–25; Ronald D. S. Jack, 'The Language of Literary Materials: Origins to 1700', in Jones (ed.), *History of Scots* pp. 213–66; and Jeremy Smith, 'The Language of Older Scots Poetry', in Corbett et al. (eds), *Companion to Scots*, pp. 197–209.

78 See Mann, *Scottish Book Trade*, p. 225; and Joanna Bugaj, 'Middle Scots as an Emerging Standard, and Why it didn't Make it', *SL* 23 (2004), pp. 19–34.

79 For an edition of this text, see James Craigie (ed.), *Basilicon Doron of James VI*, 2 vols, STS (1944–50).
80 See H. Peters, 'The Duke's English: The Language of the Hamilton Papers', *SL* 16 (1997), pp. 63–73; Adam J. Aitken, 'The Pioneers of Anglicised Speech in Scotland: A Second Look', *SL* 16 (1997), pp. 1–36; and Veronika Kniezsa, 'Of the Orthographie and Congruitie of the Britan Tongue', *SL* 16 (1997), pp. 52–62.
81 Marguerite Wood and R. K. Hannay (eds), *Extracts from the Records of the Burgh of Edinburgh, AD 1589 to AD 1603* (Edinburgh: Oliver and Boyd, 1927), p. 282.
82 John S. Stuart (ed.), *Extracts from the Council Register of the Burgh of Aberdeen, Volume 2: 1570–1625* (Aberdeen: Spalding Club, 1848), pp. 293–94.
83 See Dauvit Horsbroch, 'Nostra Vulgari Lingua: Scots as a European Language, 1500–1700,' *SL* 18 (1999), pp. 1–16.
84 For the circulation of texts within Scotland, see Mann, *The Scottish Book Trade*, pp. 112 and 236–52. See also Sanderson's work on the printing of Bibles and Psalm books and on the libraries of clergymen in the late sixteenth century: M. H. B. Sanderson, 'The Printing and Distribution of the Bible and Psalm Books in Sixteenth Century Scotland: Some Additional Documentation', *Records of the Scottish Church History Society* 29 (1999), pp. 139–49; and 'Service and Survival: The Clergy in Late Sixteenth-Century Scotland', *Records of the Scottish Church History Society* 36 (2006), pp. 73–96, especially pp. 93–95. See also John Durkan, 'The Libraries of Sixteenth Century Scotland', in John Higgitt (ed.), *Scottish Libraries* (London: The British Academy, 2006), pp. lxv–lxxvi.
85 See A. H. Millar (ed.), *The Compt Buik of David Wedderburne, Merchant of Dundee, 1587–1630, together with the Shipping Lists of Dundee, 1580–1618* SHS (1898), pp. 45, 57, 73, 75, 87, 104–05, 114, 148, 168–70 and 173.
86 The Rev. James Fraser (1634–1709), a Gael from the outskirts of Inverness, wrote a chronicle, in English, of the Fraser clan. His library contained a list of fifty-three items. It appears from the titles of these works that ten of these may have been in Latin, two were related to Gaelic (a volume of verse and a dictionary, both lost) and the rest, forty, were in English; see William Mackay (ed.), *Chronicles of the Frasers: The Wardlaw Manuscript Entitled Polilcratica Temporum or the True Genealogy of the Frasers, 916–1674 by Master James Fraser* SHS, (1904), pp. xliv–xlv. For more on the distribution of written

materials in Gaelic Scotland, see Black, 'The Gaelic Manuscripts of Scotland'; and MacCoinnich, 'Where and How Was Gaelic Written in Late Medieval and Early Modern Scotland?'.

87 See Mann, *The Scottish Book Trade*, pp. 31–33; and R. Scott Spurlock, 'Cromwell's Edinburgh Press and the Development of a Print Culture in Scotland', *SHR* 90 (2011), pp. 179–203, especially pp. 180–82.

88 The sole surviving whole copy of the *Kingis Quair* (the Selden MS) commissioned by the Sinclair family around 1513 was owned, presumably, at some point by Dòmhnall Gorm, chief of the MacDonalds of Sleat, Skye. MacDonald managed to acquire it sometime in the 1590s. He scribbled a quatrain of classical Gaelic verse on folio 231. See Bannerman, 'Gaelic Endorsements of Early Seventeenth Century Legal Documents', p. 26, and 'Literacy in the Highlands', in I. B. Cowan and Duncan Shaw (eds), *The Renaissance and Reformation in Scotland* (Edinburgh: SAP, 1983), pp. 214–35, especially pp. 230–31; and Thomson, 'Gaelic Literary Interactions with Scots and English Work'.

2. The Transmission of Older Scots Literature

1 Quotation is from Fox, *Henryson* and numbers are line numbers from that edition.
2 Quotation is from Bawcutt, *Dunbar*.
3 Quotation is from *Virgil's Aeneid Translated into Scottish Verse by Gavin Douglas, Bishop of Dunkeld*, ed. David F. C. Coldwell, 4 vols. STS (1957–64).
4 *DSL*, quair, n; Fox, *Henryson*, p. 345.
5 Julia Boffey and A. S. G. Edwards (introd.), *The Works of Geoffrey Chaucer and The Kingis Quair: A Facsimile of Bodleian Library, Oxford, MS Arch. Selden. B. 24* (Woodbridge: D. S. Brewer, 1997).
6 R. J. Lyall, 'Books and Book Owners in Fifteenth-Century Scotland', in Jeremy Griffiths and Derek Pearsall (eds), *Book Production and Publishing in Britain 1375–1475* (Cambridge: CUP, 1989), pp. 239–56 (242); Emily Wingfield, '"Ex Libris duncani/Campbell de glenwrquhay/miles": *The Buik of King Alexander the Conquerour* in the household of Sir Duncan Campbell, seventh laird of Glenorchy', in Rhiannon Purdie and Michael Cichon (eds), *Medieval Romance, Medieval Contexts* (Cambridge: D. S. Brewer, 2011), pp. 161–74 (171–72); Priscilla Bawcutt, 'English Books and Scottish Readers in the Fifteenth and Sixteenth Centuries', *RoSC* 14 (2001–02), pp. 1–12 (3).
7 Walter Scheps, 'Chaucer and the Middle Scots Poets', *SSL* 22 (1987), pp. 44–59.

8   Priscilla J. Bawcutt, 'Gavin Douglas and the Text of Virgil', *Transactions of the Edinburgh Bibliographical Society* 4.6 (1973), pp. 213–31; P. H. Renouard, *Bibliographie des Impressions et des Oeuvres de Josse Badius Ascensius Imprimeur et Humaniste 1462–1535*, 3 vols (Paris: Paul and Guilleman, 1908), I, pp. 19–21, III, pp. 356–63.

9   Douglas Gray, '"As quha the mater beheld tofor thar e": Douglas's Treatment of Vergil's Imagery', in Houwen et al, *Palace in the Wild*, pp. 95–123.

10 Priscilla Bawcutt, 'The "Library" of Gavin Douglas', in Aitken et al, *Bards and Makars*, pp. 107–26.

11 Priscilla Bawcutt, *Dunbar the Makar* (Oxford: OUP, 1992), p. 25.

12 Sally Mapstone, 'Robert Henryson', in Larry Scanlon (ed.), *Cambridge Companion to Medieval English Literature 1100–1500* (Cambridge: CUP, 2009), pp. 243–55 (243–44); Lyall, pp. 246–48; John Higgitt, 'Dunfermline Abbey and its Books', in Richard Fawcett (ed.), *Royal Dunfermline* (Edinburgh: The Society of Antiquaries of Scotland, 2005), pp. 177–86 (187–81).

13 Edward Wheatley, *Mastering Aesop: Medieval Education, Chaucer, and his Followers* (Gainesville, FL: 2000), pp. 85–89, 149–89; Douglas Gray, *Robert Henryson* (Leiden: E. J. Brill, 1979), pp. 60–66; I. W. A. Jamieson, 'The Poetry of Robert Henryson: A Study of the Use of Source Material' (Ph.D. dissertation, Edinburgh, 1964); *Henryson*, pp. 384–91.

14 R. J. Lyall, 'Henryson's *Morall Fabillis* and the Steinhöwel Tradition', *FMLS* 38.4 (2002), pp. 362–81.

15 Coldwell, I, p. 97; Priscilla Bawcutt, *Gavin Douglas* (Edinburgh: EUP, 1976), p. 108.

16 Fox, *Henryson* pp. xxxix–xli; Catherine R. Borland, *A Descriptive Catalogue of the Western Medieval Manuscripts in Edinburgh University Library* (Edinburgh: T. and A. Constable, 1916), pp. 291–96.

17 *Chron. Bower*, vol. 9, pp. 188–91; Lyall, 'Books and Book Owners', pp. 245–46.

18 For the opening of the poem see *Chron. Bower*, vol. 6, pp. 366–67; Borland prints the first line and terms this 'various doggerel verses' (p. 295).

19 W. H. E. Sweet, 'Lydgate Manuscripts and Prints in Late Medieval Scotland', in Mark P. Bruce and Katherine H. Terrell (eds), *The Anglo-Scottish Border and the Shaping of Identity, 1300–1600* (New York: Palgrave Macmillan, 2012), pp. 141–59 (145–46).

20 Ian C. Cunningham, 'Two Poems on the Virgin (National Library of

Scotland, Adv. MS 18.5.14'), *Transactions of the Edinburgh Bibliographical Society*, 5.5 (1988), pp. 32–40.

21 Fox, *Henryson*, pp. lxix, 450, 459; for the MS, Denton Fox and William A. Ringler (introd.), *The Bannatyne Manuscript, National Library of Scotland Advocates' MS 1.1.6* (London: Scholar Press, 1980).

22 *Henryson*, pp. xl–xli; Keith Williamson, 'A Latin-Older Scots Glossary in EUL MS 205', *Selim: Spanish Society for Medieval English Language and Literature* 14 (2007), pp. 221–76 (222–23).

23 *Acta Facultatis Artium Universitatis Sanctiandree 1413–1588*, vol. 2, ed. Annie I. Dunlop SHS (1964), pp. 239–42.

24 Williamson, pp. 222–23; Lucien Reynhout, *Formule Latines de Colophons*, 2 vols (Turnhout: Brepols, 2006), I, pp. 186–94, 315; John B. Friedman, *Northern English Books, Owners, and Makers in the Late Middle Ages* (Syracuse, NY: Syracuse University Press: 1995), pp. 67–72.

25 *Henryson*, p. lxix.

26 *The Asloan Manuscript*, ed. W. A. Craigie, 2 vols STS (1923–25), I: pp. xiii–xv; I. C. Cunningham, 'The Asloan Manuscript', in MacDonald et al, *Renaissance in Scotland*, pp. 107–35.

27 Fox and Ringler, pp. xxxviii–xxxix.

28 Lyall, 'Steinhöwel Tradition'.

29 *Henryson* pp. lv–lvi, lxiv–lxviii; Priscilla Bawcutt, 'Crossing the Border: Scottish Poetry and English Readers in the Sixteenth Century', in Sally Mapstone and Juliette Wood (eds), *The Rose and the Thistle* (East Linton: Tuckwell, 1998), pp. 59–76 (70).

30 My comments here are influenced by discussion over the years with R. J. Lyall. A suggestion of this sort is included in his excellent unpublished commentary produced c. 1990 for unit 1c (Henryson and Dunbar) of the University of Glasgow's M.Phil. in Scottish Literature, p. 9.

31 Fox, *Henryson*, pp. 426–27; Lyall, 'Books and Book Owners', p. 245.

32 See the discussion in the Introduction in Sally Mapstone (gen. ed.), *The Chepman and Myllar Prints, Scotland's first printed texts, digitised facsimiles* (Edinburgh: STS and the National Library of Scotland, 2008; subsequent parenthetical reference is by page number to this edition) and William Beattie, 'Some Early Scottish Books', in G. W. S. Barrow (ed.), *The Scottish Tradition* (Edinburgh: SAP, 1974), pp. 112–13.

33 *Henryson*, p. cxvi; Mapstone, headnote to this poem in *Chepman and Myllar Prints*.

34 Sally Mapstone, 'William Dunbar and the Book Culture of Sixteenth-Century Scotland', in Sally Mapstone (ed.), *William Dunbar, 'The Nobill Poyet'* (East Linton: Tuckwell, 2001), pp. 1–23 (4–12).

35 Denton Fox, 'Manuscripts and Prints of Scots Poetry in the Sixteenth Century', in Aitken et al, *Bards and Makars*, pp. 156–71.

36 Craigie, *Asloan Manuscript*, I, pp. xiii–xv; R. J. Lyall, 'The Lost Literature of Medieval Scotland', in McClure and Spiller, *Bryght Lanternis*, pp. 33–47 (40–41).

37 Digital images are available via the Irish Script On Screen project. On the MS Martin MacGregor, 'The View from Fortingall: the worlds of the Book of the Dean of Lismore', *SGS* 22 (2006), pp. 35–85, and 'The Campbells: Lordship, Literature, and Liminality', *Textual Cultures* 7.1 (2012), pp. 121–57.

38 Sally Mapstone, '*The Testament of Cresseid*, lines 561–67: a new manuscript witness', *Notes and Queries* 230 (1985), pp. 307–10; Fox, *Henryson*, p. c.

39 *The Poems and Fables of Robert Henryson*, ed. David Laing (Edinburgh: William Paterson, 1865), p. 257.

40 *Henryson*, pp. xciv–xcv; Sally Mapstone, *Scots and their Books in the Middle Ages and the Renaissance* (Oxford: Bodleian Library, 1996), p. 8; Brian Donaghey, 'William Thynne's Collected Edition of Chaucer: Some Bibliographical Considerations', in John Scattergood and Julia Boffey (eds), *Texts and their Contexts* (Dublin: Four Courts Press, 1997), pp. 150–64.

41 For a transcript of Thynne's text, *The Poems of Robert Henryson*, vol. 3, ed. G. Gregory Smith, STS (1908), pp. 177–98.

42 Kathleen Forni, *The Chaucerian Apocrypha: a Counterfeit Canon* (Gainesville, FL: University of Florida Press, 2001), pp. 108–09.

43 Joanna M. Martin and Katherine A. McClune, 'The Maitland and Quarto Manuscripts in Context', *English Manuscript Studies 1485–1603* 6 (2009), pp. 237–63.

44 *Henryson*, pp. xxxiv–xxxviii.

45 David Parkinson, '"A Lamentable Storie": Mary Queen of Scots and the Inescapable *Querelle des Femmes*', in Houwen et al, *Palace in the Wild*, pp. 141–60 (155).

46 Fox and Ringler, pp. xix (D 25; also xxiii, 53); xxxiv (283), xxxvi (341, 343), xxxvii (361 362), xxxviii (371); see also Carolyn Ives and David Parkinson, 'Scottish Chaucer, Misogynist Chaucer', in Thomas A. Prendergast and Barbara Kline (eds), *Rewriting Chaucer* (Columbus: Ohio State University Press, 1999), pp. 186–202.

47 Fox, *Henryson*, p. xciv; Robert Dickson and John Philip Edmond, *Annals of Scottish Printing* (Cambridge: Macmillan and Bowes, 1890), pp. 348–76.
48 *The Bannatyne Miscellany*, vol. 2, ed. D. Laing (Edinburgh: Bannatyne Club, 1836), pp. 209–17.
49 *The Chronicles of Scotland Compiled by Hector Boece, translated into Scots by John Bellenden 1531*, vol. 1, ed. R. W. Chambers and Edith C. Batho STS (1938), p. 13 (from New York, Pierpont Morgan Library, MS M. 527); *The History and Chronicles of Scotland: Written in Latin by Hector Boece, Canon of Aberdeen; and Translated by John Bellenden, Archdean of Moray and Canon of Ross*, ed. T. Maitland, 2 vols (Edinburgh: W. and C. Tait, 1821), I: p. cxii (cf. *STC* 3203, c. 1537–38).
50 For the scribe, John Reidpeth, see Sally Mapstone, 'Older Scots and the Sixteenth Century', in Mapstone, *Older Scots Literature* pp. 175–88 (181–82).
51 *The Maitland Folio Manuscript*, ed. W. A. Craigie, 2 vols, STS (1919–27), II, pp. 2–3. Parenthetical references are to this edition.
52 Bawcutt, *Dunbar* I, p. 8; see also Julia Boffey, 'The Maitland Folio Manuscript as a Verse Anthology', in Mapstone, *William Dunbar*, pp. 40–50 (42); Mapstone, 'Dunbar and the Book Culture of Sixteenth-Century Scotland', p. 13.
53 Bawcutt, *Dunbar* I, p. 8.
54 For the record, only two other poems by Dunbar in the Maitland Folio MS are copied by a hand (C) other than A, L, or X.
55 *Devotional Pieces in Verse and Prose From MS. Arundel 285 and MS. Harleian 6919*, ed. J. A. W. Bennett, STS (1955), p. 6.
56 Craigie, *Maitland Folio*, I, p. v; II, p. 6; Boffey, 'The Maitland Folio Manuscript as a Verse Anthology', pp. 40–50.
57 *Dunbar*, II, p. 484.
58 Catherine van Buuren, 'The Chepman and Myllar Texts of Dunbar', in Mapstone, *William Dunbar*, pp. 24–39 (28).
59 *Dunbar*, II, p. 484.
60 A. S. G. Edwards, 'Editing Dunbar: The Tradition', in Mapstone, *William Dunbar*, pp. 51–68.
61 Bawcutt, *Dunbar* II, pp. 9–10; Priscilla Bawcutt, 'New Texts of William Dunbar, Alexander Scott and Other Scottish Poets', *SSR* 1 (2000), pp. 9–25.
62 Donna B. Hamilton, 'The Tempest and the Printed English *Aeneid*', in Peter Hulme and William H. Sherman (eds), *The Tempest and its Travels* (London: Reaktion Books, 2000), pp. 114–20 (115).

63 *The Shorter Poems of Gavin Douglas*, rev. edn, ed. Priscilla Bawcutt STS (2003), pp. xv–xvi.
64 Ibid, p. 7.
65 Ibid., p. xxxvi.
66 Cf. the Latin quotation on sig. ** iii^r of the preface as printed in *The Actis and Deidis of Schir William Wallace, 1570*, introd. Sir William A. Craigie STS (1940) with *Chron Bower* vol. 6: p. 243, n. to l. 67.
67 Coldwell, I, pp. 96–101.
68 Fox, 'Manuscripts and Prints', pp. 161–62.
69 Dickson and Edmond, pp. 150–272.
70 *Bannatyne Miscellany* II: p. 192.
71 J. Durkan, 'John Major: after 400 Years', and 'The School of John Major: Bibliography', *IR* 1.2 (1950), pp. 131–39, 140–57.
72 W. Beattie, 'Two Notes on Fifteenth-Century Printing: I. Jacobus Ledelh', *Transactions of the Edinburgh Bibliographical Society* 3 (1950), pp. 75–77.
73 Arthur Williamson, 'Scotland: International Politics, International Press', in Sabrina Alcorn Baron, Eric N. Lindquist, and Eleanor F. Shevlin (eds), *Agent of Change: Print Culture Studies after Elizabeth L. Eisenstein* (Amherst and Boston: University of Massachusetts Press, 2007), pp. 193–215.
74 Renouard, II, p. 58. Also Paul White, *Jodocus Badius Ascensius* (Oxford: OUP, 2013).
75 Beattie, 'Two Notes', observes that 'the devices of Denis Roce contain the arms of the Liddels, and Roce himself may have been a Scot', p. 75.
76 Mapstone, *Scots and their Books*, pp. 21–22.
77 Renouard I: pp. 119–25; III: pp. 351–52.
78 Sally Mapstone, 'A Newly Discovered Copy of a Work by John Vaus and its Manuscript Context', in Kevin J. McGinley and Nicola Royan (eds), *The Apparelling of Truth* (Newcastle upon Tyne: Cambridge Scholars Press, 2010), pp. 30–47.
79 Anthony Grafton, *The Culture of Correction in Renaissance Europe* (London: British Library, 2011), p. 108.
80 See the important blog entry by Julie Gardham at universityofglasgowlibrary.wordpress.com/2010/03/04/a-rare-book-lost-and-found/
81 Renouard, I, pp. 11–14; Dickson and Edmond, pp. 30–1.
82 Ann Blair, 'Errata Lists and the Reader as Corrector' in Baron, Lindquist and Shevlin, *Agent of Change*, pp. 21–41 (30).

83 Mapstone, 'Newly Discovered', pp. 43, 47.
84 Ibid., pp. 39–43; Kylie Murray, 'John Vaus, Aberdeen, and Early-Modern Scottish Book Culture', in Iain Beavan, Peter Davidson, and Jane Stevenson (eds), *The Library and Archive Collections of the University of Aberdeen: an Introduction and Description* (Manchester: MUP, 2011), pp. 120–23.
85 A description in James Fowler Kellas Johnstone and Alexander Webster Robertson, *Bibliographia Aberdonensis*, 2 vols (Aberdeen: 3rd Spalding Club, 1929), I, pp. 34–35.
86 One of the most significant revisions is at sig. O3^r of the 1566 *Rudimenta Artis Grammaticae* (*STC* 341:01), in the section on 'Quhair fra is the comparative gre formit', where a substantial section has been revised on the basis of changes signalled in the 1531 edition (sig dd i^v) by scoring through the paragraph and writing alternative text into the left-hand margin.
87 John Durkan, 'The Early Scottish Notary', in Ian B. Cowan and Duncan Shaw (eds), *The Renaissance and Reformation in Scotland* (Edinburgh: SAP, 1983), pp. 22–40.
88 The Rev. W. Muir, *Notices from the Local Records of Dysart* (Glasgow: James Hedderwick, 1853), p. 25.
89 Mapstone, Introduction, *Chepman and Myllar Prints*; Emily Wingfield, 'The Manuscript and Print Contexts of Barbour's *Bruce*' in Boardman and Foran, *Barbour's Bruce,* pp. 3350 (43).
90 Mapstone, *Chepman and Myllar Prints*.
91 James Campbell, *Balmerino and its Abbey* (Edinburgh and London: William Blackwood and Sons, 1899), pp. 223–61.
92 Julie Kerr, 'Balmerino Abbey: Cistercians on the East Coast of Fife', in *Life on the Edge: The Cistercian Abbey of Balmerino, Fife (Scotland), Cîteaux* 59.1–2 (2008), pp. 37–60 (41–42)
93 *The Scots Peerage*, vol. 4, ed. Sir James Balfour Paul (Edinburgh: David Douglas, 1909), p. 86; Charles Rogers, *Monuments and Monumental Inscriptions in Scotland*, vol. 1 (London: Charles Griffin, 1871), p. 158.
94 Sally Mapstone, 'The *Scotichronicon*'s First Readers', in Barbara E. Crawford (ed.), *Church, Chronicle and Learning in Medieval and Early Renaissance Scotland* (Edinburgh: Mercat Press, 1999), pp. 31–55.

3. Expressions of Faith: Religious Writing

1 *The Works of John Knox*, ed. David Laing 6 vols (Edinburgh: James Thin, 1895), vol. 1, pp. 234–35; a modern version can be found in John Knox, *The History of the Reformation of Religion within the Realm of*

Scotland, ed. W. C. Dickinson 2 vols. (London: Nelson, 1949), vol. 1, p. 112.
2 The wide range of Biblical commentaries, catechetical textbooks, and devotional paraphrases written in Latin by Scots in the early modern period cannot, for reasons of space, be discussed here. Useful starting points for discussions of Scottish Latin religious literature can be found in Alan Macquarrie, *Legends of Scottish saints* (Dublin: Four Courts Press, 2012), and Steven J. Reid, 'A Latin Renaissance in Reformation Scotland? Print Trends in Scottish Latin Literature, c. 1480–1700', *SHR* 95.1 (2016), pp. 1–29.
3 Watson, *Scottish Verse*, pp. 60–65.
4 L. McKenna, 'Historical Poems of Gofraidh Fionn Ó Dálaigh', *The Irish Monthly* 47 (1919), pp. 622–26.
5 John Higgitt, *'Imageis Maid with Mennis Hand': Saints, Images, Belief and Identity in Later Medieval Scotland* (Whithorn: Friends of the Whithorn Trust, 2003).
6 Richard Holland, *The Buke of the* Howlat, ed. R. Hanna, STS (2014), pp. 77–80; Nicola Royan, "Mark your Meroure be Me': Richard Holland's Buke of the Howlat', in Bawcutt and Hadley Williams, *Companion*, pp. 49–62. For discussion of the attitudes towards Gaelic, see Martin MacGregor, 'Gaelic Barbarity and Scottish Identity in the Later Middle Ages', in Dauvit Broun and Martin MacGregor (eds), *Mìorun Mòr nan Gall, 'The Great Ill-Will of the Lowlander'? Lowland Perceptions of the Highlands, Medieval and Modern* (Glasgow: Centre for Scottish and Celtic Studies, University of Glasgow, 2007), p. 20.
7 Colm Ó Baoill (ed.), *Eachann Bacach and other Maclean poets* (Edinburgh: SAP, 1979), pp. 22–23.
8 Gordon Donaldson, *Scottish Historical Documents* (Glasgow: Neil Wilson, 1970), p. 178.
9 Charles W. J. Withers, 'The Geographical History of Gaelic in Scotland', in Colin H. Williams (ed.), *Language in Geographic Context* (Clevedon: Multilingual Matters, 1988), p. 140.
10 J. Craigie (ed.) *The Basilikon Doron of James VI*, 2 vols, STS (1942–4), vol. 1, p. 70, l. 21 (Waldegrave 1599).
11 Wilson McLeod and Meg Bateman (eds), *Duanaire na Sracaire: Anthology of Medieval Gaelic Poetry* (Edinburgh: Birlinn, 2007), pp. 46–55.
12 Ronald Black, 'A Scottish Grammatical Tract, c. 1640', *Celtica* 21 (1990), pp. 3–16.
13 John Higgit, *The Murthly Hours* (London: The British Library, 2000).

14 Ronald I. M. Black, 'The Gaelic Manuscripts of Scotland', in Gillies, *Gaelic and Scotland,*, pp. 146–74.
15 The manuscript and a description by Ronald Black are online at *Irish Script On Screen* www.isos.dias.ie/.
16 John Bannerman, *The Beatons* (Edinburgh: John Donald, 1998), p. 110.
17 William Gillies, 'The Book of the Dean of Lismore: the literary perspective', in Hadley Williams and McClure, *Fresche Fontanis*, pp. 179–216.
18 Sìm Innes, 'Gaelic Religious Poetry in Scotland: the Book of the Dean of Lismore' in Tadhg Ó hAnnracháin and Robert Armstrong (eds), *Christianities in the early modern Celtic world* (Basingstoke: Palgrave Macmillan, 2014), pp. 111–23.
19 Sìm R. Innes, 'Is Eagal Liom Lá na hAgra: Devotion to the Virgin in the Later Medieval Gàidhealtachd', in Steve Boardman and Eila Williamson (eds), *The Cult of Saints and the Virgin Mary in Medieval Scotland* (Woodbridge: The Boydell Press, 2010), pp. 125–41.
20 Douglas Gray, *Robert Henryson* (Leiden: Brill, 1979), pp. 263–64.
21 Bawcutt, *Dunbar*, B 1 and B 47.
22 Bawcutt, *Dunbar*, vol. 1, pp. 155–56.
23 Thomas Crockett (ed.), *Poems of John Stewart of Baldynneis*, STS (1913), pp. 193–268.
24 R. D. S. Jack, 'Obscure Ways to God?: Ane Schersing Out of Trew Felicitie and The Cherrie and the Slae', in Kevin J. McGinley and Nicola Royan (eds), *The Apparelling of Truth* (Newcastle: Cambridge Scholars Publishing, 2010), pp. 119–33.
25 Sarah M. Dunnigan, 'Scottish Women Writers c. 1560–c. 1650', in Douglas Gifford and Dorothy McMillan (eds), *A History of Scottish Women's Writing* (Edinburgh: EUP, 1997), pp. 31–34.
26 David Laing, *Early Popular Poetry of Scotland and the Northern Border*, 2 vols (London: Reeves and Turner, 1895), II: pp. 293–94.
27 C. R. A. Gribben, 'The Literary Cultures of the Scottish Reformation', *RES* 57 (2006), p. 79.
28 Roderick J. Lyall, *Alexander Montgomerie* (Tempe, Arizona: ACMRS, 2005), p. 281. For the psalm and lyric see David J. Parkinson (ed.), *Alexander Montgomerie: Poems*, 2 vols, STS (2000), vol 2, p. 172.
29 John Burrow, 'William Dunbar', in Bawcutt and Hadley Williams, *Companion*, p. 139.
30 J. A. W. Bennett, *Devotional Pieces in Verse and Prose*, STS (1955), pp. 7–63.

31 Bennett, *Devotional Pieces*, p. 276.
32 Alasdair A. MacDonald, 'Catholic Devotion into Protestant Lyric: The Case of the *Contemplacioun of Synnaris*', *IR* 35.2 (1984), pp. 58–87.
33 A. A. MacDonald, 'The Latin Original of Robert Henryson's Annunciation Lyric', in MacDonald, *The Renaissance in Scotland* pp. 45–65.
34 George Robinson, *Court Politics, Culture and Literature in Scotland and England 1500–1540* (Aldershot: Ashgate, 2008), pp. 137–43.
35 A.A. MacDonald (ed.), *The Gude and Godlie Ballatis*, STS (2015).
36 James Cranston (ed.), *Satirical Poems of the Time of the Reformation*, bound as 2 vols, STS (1889–92).
37 William Drummond of Hawthorne-denne, *Flowres of Sion* ([Edinburgh]: [The Heirs of Andro Hart], 1623), p. 8; available on *Early English Books Online*.
38 W. Tod Ritchie (ed.), *The Bannatyne Manuscript*, 4 vols, STS (1928–34).
39 Calum Mac Phàrlain, *Làmh-Sgrìobhainn Mhic Rath: Dòrlach Laoidhean do Sgrìobhadh le Donnchadh Mac Rath, 1688* (Dun Dè: Calum S. Mac Leòid, 1923).
40 Ibid., p. 251.
41 Kenneth MacDonald, 'Fernaig Manuscript', in Derick S. Thomson (ed.), *The Companion to Gaelic Scotland* (Glasgow: Gairm, 1994 [1983]), pp. 71–72.
42 Ludwig Christian Stern, 'Crosanachd Illebhrighde', *Zeitschrift für Celtische Philologie* 2 (1899), pp. 566–88; Cuthbert Mhág Craith (ed.), *Dán na mBráthar Mionúr*, 2 vols (Dublin: Dublin Institute for Advanced Studies, 1980), poem 11; Terence P. McCaughey, 'Protestantism and Scottish Highland Culture', in James P. Mackey (ed.), *An Introduction to Celtic Christianity* (Edinburgh: T & T Clark, 1989), p. 184.
43 Mícheál Mac Craith, 'Literature in Irish, c. 1550–1690: from the Elizabethan settlement to the Battle of the Boyne', in Margaret Kelleher and Philip O' Leary (eds), *The Cambridge History of Irish Literature*, vol. 1: To 1890 (Cambridge: CUP, 2006), p. 203.
44 R. L. Thomson (ed.), *Foirm na n-Urrnuidheadh*, SGTS (1970), p. 8 and pp. 177–78.
45 Donald E. Meek, 'The Reformation and Gaelic Culture: Perspectives on Patronage, Language and Literature in John Carswell's translation of "The Book of Common Order"', in J. Kirk (ed.), *The Church in the Highlands* (Edinburgh: Scottish Church History Society, 1998), pp. 51–55.

46 For a modern edition see Brian Ó Cuív (ed.), *Aibidil Gaoidheilge and Caiticiosma: Seaán Ó Cearnaigh's Irish Primer of Religion published in 1571* (Dublin: Dublin Institute for Advanced Studies, 1994).
47 Marc Caball, 'Gaelic and Protestant: A Case Study in Early Modern Self-Fashioning, 1567–1608', *Proceedings of the Royal Irish Academy* 110C (2010), p. 205.
48 Cainneach Ó Maonaigh (ed.), *Scáthán Shacramuinte na hAithridhe* (Dublin: Dublin Institute for Advanced Studies), 1952), p. 190; Mac Craith, p. 202.
49 Cathaldus Giblin (ed.), *Irish Franciscan Mission to Scotland 1619–1646: Documents from Roman Archives* (Dublin: Assisi Press, 1964), p. 54; translation from Alan J. Fletcher, *Drama, Performance, and Polity in Pre-Cromwellian Ireland* (Toronto: University of Toronto Press, 2000), p. 50.
50 See for instance Giblin, *Irish Franciscan Mission*, p. 68 and pp. 84–89. For similar tactics in Wales see Alexandra Walsham, 'Holywell: Contesting Sacred Space in Post-Reformation Wales', in Will Coster and Andrew Spicer (eds), *Sacred Space in Early Modern Europe* (Cambridge: CUP, 2005), pp. 211–36.
51 Derick S. Thomson, 'Carmina Gadelica' in Thomson (ed.), *Companion to Gaelic Scotland*, p. 36; Diarmuid O' Laoghaire, 'Prayers and Hymns in the Vernacular' in J. Mackey (ed.), *An Introduction to Celtic Christianity* (Edinburgh: T & T Clark, 1989), pp. 276–77.
52 Mac Craith, 'Literature in Irish, p. 217.
53 Ronald Black, 'Gaelic Religious Publishing 1567–1800', *SGS* 24 (2008), p. 74.
54 John MacInnes, 'The Scottish Gaelic Language', in Glanville Price (ed.), *The Celtic Connection* (Gerrards Cross: Colin Smythe, 1992), p. 112. For the text see R. L. Thomson (ed.), *Adtimchiol an Chreidimh: The Gaelic Version of John Calvin's Catechismus Ecclesiae Genevensis* SGTS (1962), pp. 230–50; R. L. Thomson, 'The Language of the Shorter Catechism (1659)', *SGS* 12.1 (1971), pp. 34–51.
55 Donald MacKinnon, *The Gaelic Bible and Psalter* (Dingwall: Ross-shire Printing and Publishing, 1930), pp. 42–44.
56 We now are extremely fortunate to have a critical edition and translation of the Scottish parts of this formidable text. See MacQuarrie (ed.), *Readings, hymns and prayers*.
57 R. J. Lyall, 'Vernacular Prose before the Reformation', in *AHSL* pp. 163–82, at p. 163.

58 *The Meroure of Wyssdome*, Books I-II, ed. Charles MacPherson STS (1926), Books III-V, ed.. F. Quinn STS 4th Ser 2 (1965), and Books VI-VII, ed. Craig MacDonald STS (1990).
59 J. H. Burns, 'John Ireland and 'The Meroure of Wyssdome', *IR* 6.2 (1955), pp. 77–98; Roger A. Mason, 'Kingship, Tyranny and the Right to Resist in Fifteenth-Century Scotland', *SHR* 66 (1987), pp. 125–51, and *Kingship and the Commonweal:* (East Linton: Tuckwell, 1998), pp. 8–35.
60 Audrey-Beth Fitch, *The Search for Salvation: Lay Faith in Scotland 1480–1560* (Edinburgh: Birlinn, 2009).
61 *Meroure*, Books I-II, p. 13; Brother Bonaventure, 'The Popular Theology of John Ireland', *IR* 13.2 (1962), pp. 130–46.
62 J. Gau, *The Richt Vay to the Kingdom of Hevine*, ed. A. F. Mitchell, STS (1888).
63 J. K. Cameron, 'John Johnesone's *An Confortable Exhortatioun of our mooste Holy Christen Faith and her Frutes*: an early example of Scots Lutheran Piety', in D. Baker (ed.), *Reform and Reformation: England and the Continent, c. 1500–c. 1750* (Oxford: Blackwell for the Ecclesiastical History Society, 1979), pp. 133–47.
64 'The Confession of Faith of the Churches of Switzerland, translated from the Latin', by George Wishart, 1536, in David Laing (ed.), *The Miscellany of the Wodrow Society*, I (Edinburgh: Wodrow Society, 1844), pp. 1–23, at p. 11.
65 J. K. Cameron, 'Aspects of the Lutheran Contribution to the Scottish Reformation', *Records of the Scottish Church History Society* 22.1 (1984), pp. 1–12.
66 The standard biography of Knox is now Jane Dawson, *John Knox* (New Haven, CT: Yale University Press, 2014), but for detailed assessments of Knox as a writer see Ronald D.S. Jack, 'The Prose of John Knox: A reassessment', *Prose Studies*, 4 (1981), pp. 239–51; Kenneth D. Farrow, *John Knox: Reformation Rhetoric and the Traditions of Scots Prose 1490–1570* (Bern: Peter Lang, 2004); Rudolph P. Almasy, 'John Knox and *A Godly Letter*: fashioning and refashioning the exilic 'I'', in C. Gribben and G. Mullen (eds), *Literature and the Scottish Reformation* (Farnham: Ashgate, 2009), pp. 95–110.
67 Knox, ed. Laing, vol. 1, pp. 11–19, 118, 174–79; Knox, ed. Dickinson, vol. 1, pp. 11–14, 55, 76–8.
68 Knox, ed. Laing, vol. 1, p. 242; Knox, ed. Dickinson, vol. 1, p. 116.
69 Robert Crawford, *Scotland's Books* (London: Penguin, 2007), p. 122.
70 See note 63 and Maria Dossena, 'Language Attitudes and Choice in

the Scottish Reformation', in *Literature and the Scottish Reformation*, pp. 45–62, esp. pp. 48–55.
71 For a full discussion of these texts and their context, see Alec Ryrie, 'Reform without Frontiers in the Last Years of Catholic Scotland', *The English Historical Review* 119 (2004), pp. 27–56, and *The Origins of the Scottish Reformation* (Manchester: MUP, 2006), chapter 5.
72 Quentin Kennedy, 'Ane Compendius Tractive conform to the Scripturis of almychtie GOD, ressoun, and authoritie' (1558), in David Laing (ed.), *The Miscellany of the Wodrow Society*, I (Edinburgh: Wodrow Society, 1844), pp. 88–174 ('Ane Answer to the Compendius Tractive' (1563) by John Davidson, Principal of the University of Glasgow, follows at pp. 175–258); Cornelius Henry Kuipers, *Quentin Kennedy (1520–1564): Two Eucharistic Tracts* (n.p, 1964).
73 Kuipers, *Quentin Kennedy*, p. 64.
74 Ninian Winzet, *Certain Tractates together with the Book of Four Score Three Questions and a Translation of Vincentius Lirinensis*, ed. James King Hewison 2 vols, STS (1888–90).
75 Winzet, *Certain Tractates*, vol. 1, pp. 60–61.
76 Winzet, *Certain Tractates*, vol. 1, p. 138.
77 *The Autobiography and Diary of Mr James Melvill*, ed. R. Pitcairn (Edinburgh: Wodrow Society, 1842) [*JMAD*]; John Row, *The History of the Kirk of Scotland, from the year 1558 to August 1637*, ed. D. Laing (Edinburgh: Wodrow Society, 1842); David Calderwood, *The History of the Kirk of Scotland*, ed. T. Thomson and D. Laing, 8 vols (Edinburgh: Wodrow Society, 1842–49).
78 *JMAD*, pp. 369–71.
79 *JMAD*, p. 65.
80 *JMAD*, pp. 63–64.
81 Thomas Graves Law (ed.), *Catholic Tractates of the Sixteenth Century, 1573–1600* STS (1899).
82 Ibid., p. 9.
83 Ibid., pp. 93–105.
84 Ibid., p. 105.
85 Ibid., pp. 90–91.
86 John Leslie, *History of Scotland*, ed. E. G. Cody, 4 vols, bound as 2, STS (1888–95).
87 Law, *Catholic Tractates*, pp. 173–216; table at pp. 204–05.
88 Ibid., pp. 106–72.
89 Ibid., pp. 109–17.
90 Ibid., pp. 31–70, at pp. 33–34.

4. The Purposes of Literature

1. See, for example, the contributions of W. Gillies, M. MacGregor, R. Ó Maolalaigh and K. Simms to the '1314–1707' section of *EHSL*.
2. L. Breatnach, 'The caldron of poesy', *Ériu*, 32 (1981), pp. 45–94.
3. The text of Mac Bruaideadha's poem, *Mór atá ar theagasc flatha*, is printed with a Latin translation in *Gaelic Journal*, 1 (1882), pp. 352–58. For the preamble to *Maith an chairt ceannas na nGaoidheal* see W. Gillies, 'The Classical Irish tradition', in D. E. Evans, J. G. Griffith and E. M. Jope (eds), *Proceedings of the Seventh International Congress of Celtic Studies* (Oxford: OUP, 1986), pp. 108–20 (p. 111). For the poem itself, see W. McLeod and M. Bateman (eds), *Duanaire na Sracaire* (Edinburgh: Birlinn, 2007), no. 24.
4. K. Ralls-MacLeod, *Music and the Celtic Otherworld* (Edinburgh: EUP, 2000), pp. 80–86.
5. For bardic religious verse see the Introduction to L. McKenna, *Dán Dé* (Dublin [1922]); for examples see McLeod and Bateman, *Duanaire*, especially nos. 6 and 7.
6. See J. MacInnes, 'The Panegyric Code in Gaelic poetry and its historical background', in M. Newton (ed.), *Dùthchas nan Gàidheal: Selected essays of John MacInnes* (Edinburgh: Birlinn, 2006), pp. 265–319.
7. Cf. N. J. A. Williams, *The poems of Giolla Brighde Mac Con Midhe* (Dublin: Irish Texts Society 1980), 208–09 (stanza 21).
8. E.g. the anonymous *Cóir feitheamh ar uaislibh Alban*, addressed to John Stewart of Rannoch (Watson, *Scottish verse*, no. XXIV); cf. McLeod and Bateman, *Duanaire*, no. 20.
9. Watson, *Scottish verse*, no. XVI; cf. McLeod and Bateman, *Duanaire*, no. 38. As it happens, we have an elegy for the same man by one of the MacMhuirich poets (presumably Clanranald's own poet): see A. Cameron, *Reliquiae Celticae* (2 vols, Inverness: Northern Counties, 1892–94), 2, pp. 216–25.
10. Watson, *Scottish verse*, no. VII.
11. Unedited in the BDL (p. 199), where it is attributed to a certain Donald Liath, son of Dougall MacGregor, who may possibly have been a brother of the Dean himself.
12. Watson, *Scottish verse*, no. XVIII
13. See P. A. Breatnach, 'The chief's poet', *Proceedings of the Royal Irish Academy*, 83 C (1983), pp. 37–79.
14. Watson, *Scottish verse*, no. IX; McLeod and Bateman, *Duanaire*, no. 60.

15 Watson, *Scottish verse*, no. XX; McLeod and Bateman, *Duanaire*, no. 36.
16 See R. Flower's Introduction to T. F. O'Rahilly, *Dánta grádha* (2nd edn, Cork: Cork University Press, 1926), pp. xi–xxxiv. A more recent appraisal is provided by M. Mac Craith, *Lorg na hiasachta ar na dánta grádha* (Dublin: Clóchomhar, 1989).
17 Most of Muireadhach's elegy *M'anam do scar riom-sa a-réir* ['My soul parted from me last night'] is printed in O. Bergin, *Irish bardic poetry* (Dublin: Dublin Institute for Advanced Studies, 1970), no. 22, pp. 101–03 and 257–58. Cf. McLeod and Bateman, *Duanaire*, no. 27.
18 For cynicism about praise poetry compare Gofraidh Fionn Ó Dálaigh's *Déana mo dháil, a Ghearóid* ['See me right, Gerald'] (text in L. McKenna, *Dioghluim dána* (Dublin: Stationery Office 1938), no. 67, stanzas 44–47; discussion in E. Knott, *Irish Classical poetry* (Dublin: Cultural relations Committee of Ireland 1960), pp. 72–73. For doubts about the viability of poetry see Mathghamhain Ó hIfearnáin's *Ceist! cia do cheinneóchadh dán* ['A question: who would buy a poem?'], i.e. Bergin, *Irish bardic poetry*, no. 37 (pp. 145–46 and 279–80).
19 See Fearflatha Ó Gnímh's *Mo thruaighe mar táid Gaoidhil* ['Alas for the state of the Gaels'], printed by T. F. O'Rahilly, *Measgra dánta II* (Cork: Cork University Press, 1927), no. 45; and Lochlainn Ó Dálaigh's *Cáit ar ghabhadar Gaoidhil* ['Where have the Gaels gone to?'], ed. by W. Gillies, *Éigse*, 13 (1969–70), pp. 203–10.
20 A restrained example is contained in the Clanranald Histories of Niall Mac Mhuirich, which open with the coming of the Sons of Míl (i.e. the Gaels) to Ireland: see Cameron, *Reliquiae Celticae*, 2, pp. 148–55.
21 See D. Broun, *The Irish identity of the Kingdom of the Scots* (Woodbridge: Boydell & Brewer, 1999), ch. 6; W. Ferguson, *The identity of the Scottish nation* (Edinburgh: EUP, 1998), chh. 1–3.
22 Cf. Cameron, *Reliquiae Celticae*, 2, pp. 202–03; W. Gillies, 'After "The Backward Look": trials of a Gaelic historian', in van Heijnsbergen and Royan, *Literature, letters and the canonical*, pp. 121–37.
23 For Mac Fir-Bhisigh see T. Ó Raithbheartaigh, *Genealogical tracts I* (Dublin: Stationery Office, 1932), pp. 1–106 (2); N. Ó Muraíle, *The Celebrated Antiquary: Dubhaltach Mac Fhirbhisigh (c. 1600-71)* (Maynooth: An Sagart, 1996). For Keating see Breandán Ó Buachalla, Foreword to G. Keating, *Forus Feasa ar Éirinn* ['A basis of knowledge about Ireland'] (repr. ed., Dublin: Irish texts Society, 1987); B. Cunningham, *The world of Geoffrey Keating* (Dublin: Four Courts, 2000).

24 See, for example, D. Ó Corráin, 'Irish origin legends and genealogy: recurrent aetiologies', in T. Nyborg et al. (eds), *History and heroic tale: a symposium* (Odense: Odense University Press, 1985), pp. 51–96, and 'Historical need and literary narrative', in Evans, Griffith and Jope, *Seventh International Congress of Celtic Studies*, pp. 141–58.

25 R. A. Rankin, 'Òran na Comhachaig', *Transactions of the Gaelic Society of Glasgow*, 5 (1958), pp. 122–71; P. Menzies (ed.), *Òran na Comhachaig* ([Edinburgh]: SGTS, 2012).

26 A. Bruford, *Gaelic folk-tales and mediaeval romances* (Dublin: Folklore of Ireland Society, 1969); W. Gillies, 'Arthur in Gaelic tradition. Part II: Romances and learned lore', *Cambridge Medieval Celtic Studies*, 3 (1982), pp. 41–75.

27 See especially C. Breatnach, *Patronage, politics and prose* (Maynooth: An Sagart, 1996); cf. Bruford, *Gaelic-folk-tales*, p. 72, n. 2.

28 A. Harrison, *The Irish trickster* (Sheffield: Sheffield Academic Press/ The Folklore Society, 1989), ch. 4.

29 For further discussion on translation into Gaelic, see Hollo, ch. 11.

30 Roderick Morrison: W. Matheson (ed.), *The Blind Harper* SGTS (1970); Mary MacLeod: J. C. Watson (ed.), *Gaelic songs of Mary MacLeod* SGTS (Glasgow, 1934); Eachann Bacach: C. Ó Baoill (ed.), *Eachann Bacach and other Maclean poets* SGTS (1979); Maighread Ni Lachainn: C. Ó Baoill (ed.), *Mairghread nighean Lachlainn, song-maker of Mull* SGTS (2009).

31 J. L. Campbell and F. Collinson (eds), *Hebridean Folksongs* (3 vols, Oxford: OUP 1969–81), 2, no. LXXI (*Alasdair mhic Colla gasda*); 3, no. CIV (*A mhic Iain 'ic Sheumais*).

32 All quotations are taken from the Wreittoun print, in *Alexander Montgomerie: Poems*, ed. David J. Parkinson, 2 vols, STS (2000). For the composition history of the poem, see R. J. Lyall, *Alexander Montgomerie* (Tempe, AZ: ACMRS, 2005), p. 107. Pages 318–31 contain literary analyses of the various versions of the poem.

33 While concern with good kingship is not confined to fifteenth- and sixteenth-century Scotland, the marked preoccupation with appropriate kingly behaviour is linked by Wormald and Martin to the preponderance of minority rule. See Jenny Wormald, *Court, Kirk, and Community: Scotland 1470–1625* (Edinburgh: EUP, 2001), pp. 13–14; Joanna Martin, *Kingship and Love in Scottish Poetry, 1424–1540* (Aldershot: Ashgate Press, 2008), pp. 11–13; Sally Mapstone, 'Robert Henryson', in Larry Scanlon (ed.), *Cambridge Companion to Medieval English Literature 1100–1500* (Cambridge: CUP, 2009),

pp. 243–55, 244–45. For further discussion on the advisory tradition in Scotland, see Sally Mapstone, 'The Advice to Princes Tradition in Scottish Literature 1450–1500' (unpublished doctoral thesis, University of Oxford, 1986).

34 This scenario is played out in 'King Hart', for which see *The Shorter Poems of Gavin Douglas*, ed. Priscilla Bawcutt, rev. ed., STS (2003). Martin discusses the poem pp. 131–54.

35 Sarah Couper proposes that certain texts – including the *Kingis Quair* and Douglas' *Eneados* – display optimism 'about their [reason's and desire's] reconciliation'. See her 'Reason and Desire in Older Scots Poetry, c. 1424–1560' (unpublished doctoral thesis, University of Oxford, 2001), p. 2.

36 See *The works of Geoffrey Chaucer and the 'Kingis Quair': a facsimile of Bodleian Library Oxford, MS. Arch. Selden B. 24*, intro. Julia Boffey and A. S. G. Edwards (Cambridge: D.S. Brewer, 1997). For an edition of the poem, see Julia Boffey, ed., *Fifteenth-century dream-visions: an anthology* (Oxford: OUP, 2003), pp. 90–157.

37 Parallels are both thematic and verbal: *Kingis Quair* '"A, swete, ar ye a warldly creature, / Or hevinly thing in liknesse of nature?/ Or ar ye god Cupidis owin princesse [i.e. Venus]?"' (lines 293–5); *Knight's Tale* '"I noot wher she be womman or goddesse, / But Venus is it soothly, as I gesse"' (*CTs*. I. 1101–02). (All Chaucer quotations from *The Riverside Chaucer* ed. C. D. Benson (Oxford: OUP, 1988)).

38 See C.S. Lewis, *The Discarded Image* (Cambridge: CUP, 1994), p. 79.

39 See *Henryson, Testament*, ll. 218–38, and Chaucer, 'The Knight's Tale', ll. 1918–66, and *The Parliament of Fowls* ll. 211–301.

40 See *Henryson*, pp. xi–xii.

41 For more on the conversation between Aesop and the narrator, see Tim Machan, 'Robert Henryson and Father Aesop: Authority in the *Moral Fables*', *Studies in the Age of Chaucer* 12 (1990), 193–254; Edward Wheatley, *Mastering Aesop: Medieval Education, Chaucer, and His Followers* (Gainesville, FL: University of Florida Press, 2000), pp. 149–89.

42 The rhyme is also used by Henryson in 'The Preaching of the Swallow' lines 1886–87 and *Orpheus and Eurydice* lines 411–12 and seems to indicate a state of incomplete mental activity.

43 See Anne M. McKim., '"Makand hir mone"': Masculine Constructions of the Feminine Voice in Middle Scots Complaints', *Scotlands* 2 (1994), 32–46.

44 Bawcutt (ed.), *The Shorter Poems of Gavin Douglas*, pp. 1–133.

45 For the text of the poem, see *Poems of John Stewart of Baldynneis* vol. 1, ed. Thomas Crockett, STS (1913). See also *John Stewart of Baldynneis Roland Furiovs: A Scots Poem in its European Context*, ed. Donna Heddle (Leiden: Brill, 2008). A new edition of Stewart's poetry is in preparation by the present author for the STS.
46 G. Douglas, *Virgil's Aeneid*, ed. D. F. C. Coldwell, 4 vols, STS (1957–1964).
47 See *The Chronicles of Scotland Compiled by Hector Boece, translated into Scots by John Bellenden 1531*, (eds) R. W. Chambers, Edith C. Batho and H. Winifred Husbands, 2 vols, STS (1936, 1941), vol. 2, p. 243. This is an edition of the manuscript, dated 1531, presented by Bellenden to James V.
48 *The Poems of King James VI of Scotland*, ed. James Craigie, 2 vols, STS (1955–1958), vol. 1, p 78.

5. Historiography in Highlands and Lowlands

1 See Chapter 1, 'The Languages of Scotland', pp. 19–37.
2 John Bannerman, 'The king's poet and the Inauguration of Alexander III', *SHR* 68 (1989), pp. 120–49; John Bannerman, 'The residence of the king's poet', *SGS* 17 (1996), pp. 24–35; and Dauvit Broun, *The Irish Identity of the kingdom of the Scots in the Twelfth and Thirteenth Centuries* (Woodbridge: Boydell, 1999), pp. 3–5.
3 See Broun, *Irish Identity*, p. 262; Dauvit Broun, *Scottish Independence and the Idea of Britain from the Picts to Alexander III* (Edinburgh: EUP, 2007), p. 260; and also Dauvit Broun, 'Attitudes of *Gall* to *Gaedhel* in Scotland before John of Fordun' in D. Broun and M. MacGregor (eds), *Mìorun Mòr nan Gall, the Great ill-Will of the Lowlander? Lowland Perceptions of the Highlands, Medieval and Modern* (Centre for Scottish and Celtic Studies: University of Glasgow 2009), p. 77.
4 George Buchanan, *Rerum Scoticarum historia* (Edinburgh: Alexander Arbuthnot, 1582). The most recent translation, by Dana F. Sutton, can be found on the *Philological Museum* website www.philological.bham.ac.uk/scothist/contents.html, accessed 28 August 2013.
5 John Mair, *A History of Greater Britain, as well England as Scotland*, trans. by A. Constable, with a Life of the Author by Aeneas J.G. Mackay SHS (1892), p. 50.
6 *Hectoris Boetii Murthlacensium et Aberdonensium Episcoporum Vitae*, ed. J. Moir, New Spalding Club (Aberdeen, 1894), p. 99.
7 Martin MacGregor, 'Gaelic Barbarity and Scottish Identity in the Later Middle Ages', in Broun and MacGregor (eds), *Mìorun Mòr nan Gall*, pp. 7–48.

8   For an edition of Fordun, see W. F. Skene (ed.), *Johannis de Fordun Chronica Gentis Scotorum* Historians of Scotland (Edinburgh, 1871) and F. J. Skene (trans.), W. F. Skene (ed.) *John of Fordun's Chronicle of the Scottish Nation* (Edinburgh, 1872). For the problems with these editions, see Broun, *Irish Identity*, pp. 16–20.
9   *Chron Bower*, vol. 9, p. 13.
10 Broun, *Irish Identity*, esp. pp. 63–81.
11 This is accessible in Geoffrey of Monmouth, *History of the Kings of Britain*, ed. and trans. Lewis Thorpe (Harmondsworth: Penguin, 1966). A more recent edition is Geoffrey of Monmouth, *The History of the Kings of Britain* ed. M. D. Reeve, trans. N. Wright (Woodbridge: Boydell, 2007).
12 See *Chron Bower*, vol. 3, p. 343, vol. 9, pp. 3, 7, 13 and 15.
13 *Liber Pluscardensis*, ed. W. F Skene, trans. F. J. H. Skene (Edinburgh: Paterson, 1877–80).
14 D. Embree et al. (eds), *Short Scottish Prose Chronicles* (Woodbridge: Boydell, 2012).
15 *The Original Chronicle of Andrew of Wyntoun*, ed. F. J. Amours, 6 vols., STS (1903–1914), Book vii, ch. 10; but see also Chris Jones, '*Inclinit to diuersiteis*: Wyntoun's song on the death of Alexander III and the "origins" of Scots vernacular poetry', *RES* 64 (2012), 21–38.
16 See Nicola Royan, 'A question of truth: Barbour's *Bruce*, Hary's *Wallace* and *Richard Coer de Lion*', *International Review of Scottish Studies* 34 (2009), 75–105 for further discussion of the genre of these texts.
17 John Barbour, *Barbour's Bruce*, ed. M. P. McDiarmid and J. A. C. Stevenson, 3 vols, STS (1980–85).
18 The source for Barbour's authorship of a Stewart genealogy is found in Wyntoun Bk III, chap. III (vol. 2, p. 315 of the Amours edition; see also vol. 1, pp. lxxv–lxxvi of the same edition). See also Stephen Boardman, *The Early Stewart Kings: Robert II and Robert III 1371–1406* (East Linton: Tuckwell Press, 1996), pp. 59–60.
19 *Bruce*, Bk I, ll. 225ff.
20 *Hary's Wallace* ed. M. P. McDiarmid, 2 vols., STS (1968–9).
21 I. W. Gent, *The Valiant Scot* (London: Thomas Harper for Iohn Waterson, 1637).
22 Patrick Gordon, *The Famous Historie of the Renouned and Valiant Prince Robert surnamed the Bruce King of Scotland e&c, & of sundrie other valiant knights both Scots and English. [...] A historye both pleasant and profitable set for the and done in heroic verse* (Dordrecht: George Waters, 1615).

23 For more detailed discussion of Mair's philosophies, see A. Broadie, *The Circle of John Mair* (Oxford: OUP, 1985) and J. H. Burns, *The True Law of Kingship* (Oxford: OUP, 1996); Mason, *Kingship and the Commonweal*.
24 *A History of Greater Britain*, p. lxxviii; see also Mair's own preface, p. cxxxv.
25 Hector Boece, *Scotorum historiae a prima gentis origine XVII libri* (Paris: Iodocus Badius Ascensius, [1527]). A translation of the 1575 edition by Dana F. Sutton can be found on the website *The Philological Museum* www.philological.bham.ac.uk/boece/, accessed 26 August 2013.
26 *A History of Greater Britain*, Bk 1, ch. viii.
27 See in particular Boece's preliminary discourse or 'exhortation' concerning the ancient and modern Scots before Book 1 of the *Scotorum historia*, 'De Scotorum priscis recentibusque institutis ac moribus paraenesis Hectoris Boethii accommodatissima', ff. 17^v–20^v.
28 A modern edition of the manuscript version can be found in John Bellenden, *The Chronicles of Scotland compiled by Hector Boece*, eds. R.W. Chambers, E.C. Batho and H. W. Husbands, 2 vols. STS (1938 and 1941); the print version is edited in John Bellenden, *The History and Chronicles of Scotland* ed. T. Maitland, 2 vols. (Edinburgh: Tait, 1821).
29 *The Mar Lodge Translation of the History of Scotland by Hector Boece*, ed. G. Watson STS (1948): only one volume was produced. For the metrical version, see William Stewart, *The buik of the cronicles of Scotland*, ed. William Turnbull, Rolls Series (London: Longman, 1858).
30 For an example of this, see Stephen Boardman, 'Chronicle propaganda in fourteenth-century Scotland: Robert the Steward, John of Fordun and the "Anonymous Chronicle"', *SHR* 76 (1997), 23–43.
31 Erasmus's work can be read in translation in Erasmus, *The Education of a Christian Prince*, trans. Neil M. Cheshire and Michael J. Heath, with *The Panegyric for Archduke Philip of Austria*, trans. Lisa Jardine, ed. Lisa Jardine (Cambridge: CUP, 1997).
32 Robert Lindsay of Pitscottie, *The Historie and Cronicles of Scotland from the slaughter of King James the First to the ane thousand five hundreith thrie scoir fyftein zeir*, ed. Ae. J. G, Mackay, 3 vols, STS (1899–1911).
33 Grace Wilson, 'History and the common reader? Robert Lindsay of Pitscottie's *Cronicles*', *FMLS* 29 (1993), pp. 91–110.
34 The title of Dempster's work, modelled on the Venerable Bede's

Historia Ecclesiastica Gentis Anglorum and somewhat misleading in more than one way, was probably coined by his posthumous editor Matteo Pellegrini.

35 For a lost 'Gaelic chronicle of the kings of Scotland down to King Robert III' see M. Pía Coira, *By Poetic Authority: The Rhetoric of Panegyric in Gaelic Poetry of Scotland to c. 1700* (Edinburgh: Dunedin Academic Press, 2012), p. 71, n. 87.

36 Martin MacGregor, 'The View from Fortingall: the worlds of The Book of the Dean of Lismore', SGS 22 (2006), pp. 35–85.

37 Martin MacGregor, 'The genealogical histories of Gaelic Scotland', in A. Fox and D. Woolf (eds), *The Spoken Word: oral culture in the British Isles, 1500–1850* (Manchester: MUP, 2002), pp. 196–239.

38 *Genealogical Collections Concerning Families in Scotland Made by Walter MacFarlane*, ed. J. T. Clark, 2 vols SHS (1900), vol. 1, pp. 118–19; c.f. A. Campbell, *Records of Argyll* (Edinburgh, 1885), p. 4.

39 'The Genealogical and Historicall Account of the Family of Craignish', ed. H. Campbell, in *Miscellany of the Scottish History Society* SHS (1926), vol. 4, p. 193.

40 MacGregor, 'The genealogical histories of Gaelic Scotland', pp. 89–90, 211–12, 225 and nn. 89, 90, 110, 208.

41 Ibid., p. 209.

42 W. J. Watson, 'Unpublished Gaelic Poetry-IV., V', SGS 3 (1929–31), pp. 152–59, at pp. 156–57.

43 J. W. M. Bannerman, 'The MacLachlans of Kilbride and their Manuscripts', ScotStud 21 (1977), pp. 1–34, at p. 17; Henry Mackenzie (ed.), *Report of the Committee of the Highland Society of Scotland, appointed to enquire into the nature and authenticity of the poems of Ossian* (Edinburgh: Archibald Constable & Co., 1805), pp. 275–79; Derick S. Thomson, 'The MacMhuirich Bardic Family', TGSI 43 (1960–63), pp. 276–304, at pp. 297, 302.

44 MacFarlane, *Genealogical Collections*, vol. 1, pp. 118–19; c.f. C. A. Gordon, 'Letter to John Aubrey from Professor James Garden', SGS 8 (1955–58), pp. 18–26.

45 'The Genealogical and Historicall Account of the Family of Craignish', p. 190.

46 R. L. Thomson (ed.). *Foirm na n-Urrnuidheadh: John Carswell's Gaelic Translation of the Book of Common Order* SGTS (1970), p. 175.

47 Watson, *Scottish Verse*, pp. 212–13.

48 MacGregor, 'The genealogical histories of Gaelic Scotland' p. 209.

49 Ibid., pp. 204, 215, 224.

50 Ibid., pp. 210–12, 224; Martin MacGregor, 'Writing the history of Gaelic Scotland: a provisional checklist of "Gaelic" genealogical histories', *SGS* 24 (2008), pp. 357–79.
51 *The Black Book of Taymouth*, ed. C. Innes (Edinburgh: Bannatyne Club, 1855).
52 Archibald Campbell, *Records of Argyll* (Edinburgh: Blackwood, 1885), pp. 3–12.
53 MacGregor, 'The genealogical histories of Gaelic Scotland', pp. 224–25.
54 Watson, *Scottish Verse*, pp. 216–17.
55 Ibid., pp. 100–01, 180–81, 162–63.
56 Ibid., pp. 162–3; *Highland Papers*, ed. J. R. N. MacPhail, 4 vols. SHS (1914–34), vol. 2, p. 92; 'Account of the Family of Craignish', pp. 213, 218.
57 *Highland Papers*, vol. 1, pp. 198–99.
58 Watson, *Scottish Verse*, pp. 182–83.
59 A. MacDonald, 'Fragment of a MacKenzie MS.', *TGSI* 36 (1931–33), pp. 204–05.
60 Watson, *Scottish Verse*, pp. 186–9, 192–03.
61 Ibid., pp. 102–03.
62 Ibid., pp. 100–03.
63 W. D. H. Sellar 'Highland Family Origins: Pedigree Making and Pedigree Faking', in *The Middle Ages in the Highlands* (Inverness: Inverness Field Club, 1981), pp. 103–13.
64 Pia Dewar, 'Kingship Imagery in Classical Gaelic panegyric for Scottish chiefs' in W. McLeod, J.E. Fraser and A. Gunderloch (eds), *Cànan & Cultar / Language and Culture: Rannsachadh na Gàidhlig* 3 (Edinburgh: Dunedin Academic Press, 2006), pp. 39–55.
65 Watson, *Scottish Verse*, pp. 204–05.
66 Ibid., pp. 100–01.
67 Ibid., pp. 208–09.
68 Ibid., pp. 194–95, 297.
69 Ibid., pp. 158–59, 88–89.
70 Thomas Owen Clancy, 'Court, king and justice in the Ulster cycle', in Helen Fulton (ed.), *Medieval Celtic Literature and Society* (Dublin: Four Courts Press, 2005), pp. 163–82.
71 Watson, *Scottish Verse*, pp. 100–01.
72 N.J.A. Williams (ed.), *The poems of Giolla Brighde Mac Con Midhe* (Dublin: Irish Texts Society, 1980), pp. 210–11; Katharine Simms, 'Images of Warfare in Bardic Poetry', *Celtica* 21 (1990), pp. 608–19, at 610.

73 Richard Holland, *The Buke of the Howlat,* ed. R. Hanna, STS (2013); *The Poems of Walter Kennedy,* ed. Nicole Meier STS (2008), pp. 88–179 and *passim*. Lindsay's works can be found in *The Works of Sir David Lindsay of the Mount, 1490–1555,* ed. Douglas Hamer, 4 vols. STS (1931–1936), complemented by more recent editions of individual works that are easily accessible.

74 *Highland Papers,* vol. 1, p. 10; Ulrike Morét, 'Some Scottish humanists' views on the Highlanders', in Caie et al, *European Sun,* pp. 323–332; Ulrike Morét, 'Histories and languages: medieval and humanist views of Celtic Britain', in Terry Brotherstone and David Ditchburn (eds), *Freedom and Authority: Scotland c. 1050–c. 1650.* (East Linton: Tuckwell Press, 2000), pp. 60–72.

75 *Collectanea de Rebus Albanicis* (Edinburgh: The Iona Club, 1847), pp. 26–27; Roger A. Mason, 'The Scottish Reformation and the Origins of Anglo-British Imperialism', in Mason, *Kingship and the Commonweal,* pp. 242–69, esp. pp. 252–53.

76 Thomson, *Foirm na n-Urrnuidheadh,* pp. 13, 181.

77 J. L. Campbell, 'The Letter sent by Iain Muideartach, Twelfth Chief of Clanranald, to Pope Urban VIII, in 1626', *IR* 4 (1953), pp. 163–82.

78 David Allan, 'Ane Ornament to Yow and your Famelie: Sir Robert Gordon of Gordonstoun and the Genealogical History of the Earldom of Sutherland', *SHR* 80 (2001), pp. 124–44.

6. Lyric

I would like to thank the editors for their helpful comments on earlier drafts of this essay and to acknowledge my debt to the work of other scholars who have done so much to elucidate the BDL and its contents, in particular William Gillies (to whom we are especially indebted in terms of the provision of editions of love-lyric from the manuscript), Donald Meek and Martin MacGregor. My thanks also to Stephen Boardman for discussion of the Stewarts of Lorn and their marital relationships with the Campbells.

1 See Martin MacGregor, 'The View from Fortingall: The Worlds of the *Book of the Dean of Lismore*', SGS 22 (2006), pp. 35–86, esp. p. 57.

2 We should note at this point the unfortunate loss of Edinburgh, NLS Advocates MS 72.1.35 which contained poems of this kind; three of these (all of which are unattributed) are noted by MacKinnon and one at least (*Gluais, a leitir, ná léig sgís*) has a Scottish subject. See Donald MacKinnon, *A Descriptive Catalogue of Gaelic Manuscripts in the Advocates' Library, Edinburgh and Elsewhere in Scotland*

(Edinburgh: W. Brown, 1912), pp. 221–25; John MacKechnie, *Catalogue of Gaelic Manuscripts in Selected Libraries in Great Britain and Ireland*, 2 vols (Boston: G. K. Hall, 1973), vol. 1, pp. 175–76; Ronald I. M. Black, 'The Gaelic Manuscripts of Scotland', in Gillies (ed.), *Gaelic and Scotland*, pp. 146–74; at p. 158, §136. For the text of the poem 'Gluais, a leitir, ná léig sgís', see Thomas F. O'Rahilly (ed.), *Dánta Grádha. An Anthology of Irish Love Poetry (AD 1350–1750)*, second edition (Cork: Cork University Press, 1926), §27, pp. 35–36.

3 Thomas Owen Clancy, 'A Fond Farewell to Last Night's Literary Criticism: Reading Niall Mór Mac Mhuirich', *Rannsachadh na Gàidhlig* 4 (2010), pp. 109–26, esp. p. 113.

4 Cf. John MacKechnie and Patrick McGlynn (eds), *The Owl Remembers: Gaelic Poems Selected and Edited with Notes* (Stirling: E. Mackay, 1933).

5 Wilson McLeod and Meg Bateman (eds), *Duanaire na Sracaire: Songbook of the Pillagers.* (Edinburgh: Birlinn, 2007), 45, pp. 274–77.

6 McLeod and Bateman (eds), *Duanaire na Sracaire*, 46, pp. 278–81.

7 See also discussion of this issue in Chapters One and Four.

8 For the distinction between syllabic and accentual metres, see McLeod and Bateman (eds), *Duanaire na Sracaire*, pp. xxxviii–xl, xliii–iv.

9 McLeod and Bateman (eds), *Duanaire na Sracaire*, 80, pp. 460–65.

10 McLeod and Bateman (eds), *Duanaire na Sracaire*, 50, pp. 290–93. The other two poems are 'Tha bean an crìch Albainn fhuar' (*'There is a lady in the cold land of Scotland'*), ascribed to Alasdair MacMhathain (McLeod and Bateman (eds), *Duanaire na Sracaire*, 51, pp. 292–96) and 'Trèig t'uaisle 's na bi rinn' (*'Stop boasting of your noble birth'*), ascribed to Bishop Eòin Carsuel (McLeod and Bateman (eds), *Duanaire na Sracaire*, 52, pp. 296–99).

11 For the treatment of love and nature, see Seán Ó Tuama, *An Grá in Amhráin na nDaoine* (Dublin: An Clóchomhar, 1962), p. 173 and William Gillies, 'Courtly and Satiric Poems in the Book of the Dean of Lismore', *ScotStud* 21 (1977), pp. 35–53, esp. p. 38. For the professional poets, see Robin Flower, Introduction to O' Rahilly (ed.), *Dánta Grádha*, p. xii and Mícheál S. Mac Craith, *Lorg na hIasachta ar na Dánta Grá* (Dublin: An Clóchomhar, 1989), p. 18.

12 See MacGregor, 'The View from Fortingall', p. 68.

13 Clancy, 'A Fond Farewell', p. 114. See also Gillies, 'Courtly and Satiric Poems', p. 38; Martin MacGregor, 'Creation and Compilation: The Book of the Dean of Lismore and Literary Culture in Late Medieval Gaelic Scotland', in *EHSL*, pp. 209–18, esp. p. 214.

14 See Watson, *Scottish Verse*, Neil Ross (ed.), *Heroic Poetry from the Book of the Dean of Lismore*, SGTS (1939); Donald E. Meek, 'The Corpus of Heroic Verse in the Book of the Dean of Lismore', unpublished doctoral dissertation, University of Glasgow, 1982; and Edmund C. Quiggin, *Poems from the Book of the Dean of Lismore with a Catalogue of the Book and Indexes* (Cambridge: CUP, 1937).

15 Watson, *Scottish Verse*, p. xvii. O'Rahilly (*Dánta Grádha*, p. ix) notes that he had encountered only two or three poems of an 'unwomanly' or 'immodest' kind ('aon ní i bhfuirm mí-bhanúlachta') in Irish manuscripts containing love-lyric; however, he admits that this is in marked contrast to collections of later love songs of the eighteenth century. This may also be true of later manuscript anthologies more generally; see Diarmaid Ó Doibhlin, *The Ulster Irish Translation of the De Imitatione Christi* (Monaghan: Seanchas Ardmhacha 2000), p. 16, and fn. 48.

16 Gillies, 'Courtly and Satiric Poems', pp. 35–53. William Gillies, 'The *Dánta Grá* and the Book of the Dean of Lismore', in Matthieu Boyd (ed.), *Ollam. Studies in Gaelic and Related Traditions in Honor of Tomás Ó Cathasaigh* (Madison, N.J.: Fairleigh Dickinson University Press 2016), 257–69.

17 Uilleam MacGill'Ìosa, 'Dàn le Eòin Mac Mhuirich ann an Leabhar an Deadhain', in Eoin Mac Cárthaigh and Jürgen Uhlich (eds), *Féilscríbhinn do Chathal Ó Háinle* (Indreabhán: Cló Iar-Chonnacht 2012), 317–45, at pp. 327, 329. Cf. William Gillies, 'The Book of the Dean of Lismore: The Literary Perspective', in Hadley Williams and McClure (eds), *Fresche Fontanis*, pp. 179–216 (p. 197); Gillies, '*Dánta Grá* and the BDL', p. 259.

18 Gillies, '*Dánta Grá* and the BDL', pp. 261–62.

19 Ibid., p. 261.

20 Cf. Ibid., p. 260.

21 Gillies, 'Courtly and Satiric Poems', pp. 41–2; cf. Quiggin, *Poems from the BDL*, §LXX, p. 81.

22 I have departed from Gillies' translation at a couple of points here to emphasise the explicitness of the contrast. Gillies renders *fear gan bhod* as 'a stingless fellow' and *giolla an bhuid* 'the potent, virile lad'.

23 Gillies, 'Courtly and Satiric Poems', p. 42.

24 Quiggin, *Poems from the BDL*, §LXII, p. 78; Gillies, 'Courtly and Satiric Poems', p. 42.

25 William Gillies, 'Gaelic Literature in the Later Middle Ages: The *Book of the Dean* and beyond' in *EHSL*, pp. 219–25 (p. 224).

26 Ibid, p. 224. Cf. also 'Mairg bean nach bí ag éansagart' ('*Woe to the woman whom no priest possesses*') by the Dean's own brother which is discussed further below.
27 William Gillies, 'Créad fá Seachnainn-sa Suirghe?', in Colm Ó Baoill and Nancy R. McGuire (eds), *Caindel Alban. Fèill-sgrìobhainn do Dhòmhnall E. Meek. SGS* 24 (2008), pp. 215–43.
28 In BDL, this poem has eight quatrains (Quiggin, *Poems from the BDL*, pp. 75–6); part of one of these is missing as quatrains 6 and 7 are run together and contain six lines in total. There are three further Irish versions and a fragment, and O' Rahilly (*Dánta Grádha* §4, p. 4) provided an edition which has only six verses. See, for text and further discussion, Mac Craith, *Lorg na hIasachta*, pp. 43–47; Máirín Ní Dhonnchadha, 'Courts and Coteries I, c. 900–1600' in Angela Bourke et al. (eds), *The Field Day Anthology of Irish Writing. Volume IV. Irish Women's Writing and Traditions* (Cork: Cork University Press 2002), pp. 324–25; Gillies, '*Dánta Grá* and the BDL', p. 260.
29 MacGregor, 'Creation and Compilation', p. 213.
30 Opinion seems divided. Watson (*Scottish Verse*, p. 307) and Gillies ('BDL: Literary Perspective', p. 206) are inclined to the view that all three poems are the work of the Countess; both MacGregor ('The View from Fortingall', p. 57) and myself (Mícheál B. Ó Mainnín, 'Gnéithe de Chúlra Leabhar Dhéan Leasa Mhóir', in Máirtín Ó Briain and Pádraig Ó Héalaí (eds), *Téada Dúchais. Aistí in Ómós don Ollamh Breandán Ó Madagáin* (Indreabhán: Cló Iar-Chonnachta 2002), 395–422; at p. 402) have expressed the view that the poems may be assigned to mother and daughter.
31 See Stephen Boardman, *The Campbells 1250–1513* (Edinburgh: Birlinn, 2006), pp. 228–29 and 251–53.
32 Watson, *Scottish Verse*, pp. 307–08.
33 McLeod and Bateman (eds), *Duanaire na Sracaire*, p. 289. The last line of Watson's translation reads 'so that our mutual desire comes not to pass again' (*Scottish Verse*, p. 308).
34 Watson, *Scottish Verse*, p. 234.
35 McLeod and Bateman (eds), *Duanaire na Sracaire*, pp. 288–91. Cf. Watson, *Scottish Verse*, p. 235.
36 McLeod and Bateman, (eds) *Duanaire na Sracaire*, p. 289.
37 Grace Neville, 'Medieval Irish Courtly Love Poetry: An Exercise in Power-struggle', *Études Irlandaises* 8 (1983), pp. 19–30 (p. 27).

38 Osborn Bergin (ed.), *Irish Bardic Poetry* (Dublin: DIAS, 1970), §32, pp. 133–35; O'Rahilly (ed.), *Dánta Grádha* §47, pp. 66–69.
39 The text of both these poems, together with a translation, has been provided by Cathal G. Ó Háinle, 'Flattery Rejected: Two Seventeenth-century Irish Poems', *Hermathena* 137, (Summer 1985), pp. 5–26. The two poems have been dated to the period 1603–1607 and Brighid was a bilingual Irish-English speaker who was aged between thirteen and seventeen years of age at the time. The question is whether or not she would have been competent enough in Irish to have composed the poem herself, therefore. See Ó Háinle, 'Flattery Rejected, pp. 5–10; Mac Craith, *Lorg na hIasachta*, pp. 185–87.
40 Note, for example, the poems attributed to the legendary Fenian hero Oisín alongside poems ascribed to one Ailéin mac Ruaidhrí (possibly the author or narrator) in the corpus of heroic verse.
41 See Bergin, *Irish Bardic Poetry*, p. 202.
42 See Séamas Mac Mathúna, 'An Fhilíocht a Leagtar ar Ghearóid Iarla i Leabhar Fhear Maí: Iontaofa nó Bréagach' in Wilson McLeod, Abigail Burnyeat et al. (eds), *Bile ós Chrannaibh: A Festschrift for William Gillies* (Ceann Drochaid: Clann Tuirc, 2010), pp. 245–70.
43 This has also been pondered by Gillies ('Gaelic Literature in the Later Middle Ages', p. 224).
44 See the well-known poem in BDL, 'Mór tubaist na táiplisge' (*'Great was the upset of the tables'*), which, while ostensibly a description of a game of backgammon, is really about a sexual encounter (Quiggin, *Poems from the BDL*, XLII, pp. 62–63; David Greene, '*Un joc grossier* in Irish and Provençal', *Ériu* 17 (1955), pp. 7–15 (p. 8)).
45 The Irish corpus provides evidence of this in the person of Eilionóir, daughter of Sir Murchadh Caomhánach (d. 1643); the poem 'Do mhúscail mé d'éis luighe go sáimh' (*'I awoke after lying peacefully'*), which is ascribed to Cearbhall Óg Ó Dálaigh in at least one source, lauds her familiarity with English texts. Cf. Mac Craith, *Lorg na hIasachta*, p. 75.
46 William Gillies, 'The Gaelic Poems of Sir Duncan Campbell of Glenorchy (III)', *SGS* 14.1 (1983), pp. 59–82 (p. 72).
47 In this I would suggest a parallel with other poems in BDL such as that by Domhnall Liath Mac Griogóir, possibly the dean's brother, which illustrates that, despite the playfulness of BDL, contributors to the manuscript were not beyond expressing deep indignation and true censure. The poem in question, 'Tá triúr cailín as searbh glóir'

('*There are three girls of sour repute*'), directs 'a torrent of abuse at the allegedly squalid lives – immoral, incontinent and insanitary – of the three women in question' (See Gillies in Chapter 4, above).

48 Gillies, 'Gaelic Poems of Duncan Campbell (III)', pp. 73–74.
49 See Chapter 9, below.
50 This excludes three of his poems: 'Uch, is mise an giolla mór' ('*Uch, I am the big lad*'), 'Cé don Phléid as ceann uidhe?' ('*To whom can Disputation turn?*'), and 'Créad dá ndearnadh Domhnall Donn?' ('*What is Brown Donald made of?*').
51 William Gillies, 'The Gaelic Poems of Sir Duncan Campbell of Glenorchy (I)', *SGS* 13.1 (1978), pp. 18–45 (p. 35).
52 Gillies, 'BDL: Literary Perspective', p. 210.
53 Gillies, 'Courtly and Satiric Poems', pp. 40–41.
54 William Gillies, 'The Gaelic Poems of Sir Duncan Campbell of Glenorchy (II)', *SGS* 13.2 (1981), pp. 263–88 (pp. 280–82).
55 See Gillies, 'Gaelic Poems of Duncan Campbell (I)', p. 31. More recently, Gillies ('*Dánta Grá* and the BDL', p. 260) has amended this title as 'Mairg ó ndeachaidh a léim lúith'.
56 Gillies, 'Gaelic Poems of Duncan Campbell (I)', pp. 26–7.
57 See Gearóid Mac Niocaill (ed.), 'Duanaire Ghearóid Iarla', *Studia Hibernica* 3 (1963), pp. 7–59; §§XXV, XXIX.
58 MacGregor, 'The View from Fortingall', p. 59.
59 In the panegyric mode, all that relates to the lord may be taken to reflect his greatness. Praise is not restricted to his leadership and valour, therefore; his physical beauty, his house, his horse and all that pertains to him may constitute further manifestations of his capability and success (as evidenced in the corpus of poetry in BDL which is concerned with the praise of Eóin Dubh Mac Griogóir (d. 1519)). Duncan Campbell's poem subverts the element which is concerned with physical beauty in taking the penis as its particular and exclusive focus.
60 Gillies, 'Gaelic Poems of Duncan Campbell (III)', pp. 66–67.
61 MacGregor, 'The View from Fortingall', p. 44.
62 Gillies, 'Gaelic Poems of Duncan Campbell (II)', pp. 264–66 and 271.
63 Cf. William Gillies, 'From Milk-cow Blues to Hardheaded Women: Decoding the Bard Macintyre', in Georgia Henley and Paul Russell (eds), *Rhetoric and Reality in Medieval Celtic Literature* (Colgate University Press 2014), pp. 47–62 (p. 47); also William Gillies, 'The Gothic Poems of the Bard Macintyre', *SGS* 30 (2016), pp. 136–90.
64 Gillies, 'Courtly and Satiric Poems', pp. 46–47. The poems have been published in Watson, *Scottish Verse*, pp. 218–33, and discussed most

recently in Gillies, 'From Milk-cow Blues', pp. 56–57, 61–62. In the latter, Gillies now sees his earlier placement of these poems amongst the antifeminist pieces in BDL as being 'a slightly uncomfortable fit' and considers other readings which would position the ship, for example, rather than the women as the primary focus. However, he acknowledges that, whatever the reading, 'bad women' are clearly important and 'may have excited the antifeminist interests of the compilers of BDL and ensured the poems a place in their collection' (p. 56). One should also note the presence of vision poems in the contemporary Scots tradition, e.g. Dunbar's 'Ryght as the sterne of day', Bawcutt, *Dunbar* B 59, pp. 184–92.

65 Watson, *Scottish Verse*, pp. 232–33.
66 The text was read as Mac Cailéin (i.e. the Gaelic style of the chief of the Campbells) by Watson with specific reference, possibly, to Donnchadh (Duncan), first Lord Campbell (d. 1453). However, I remain convinced that the reference is to our Duncan (see Ó Mainnín, 'Gnéithe de Chúlra Leabhar Dhéan Leasa Mhóir', p. 405) and I have amended the text and translation accordingly.
67 This date is contradicted by the Black Book of Taymouth, however, which notes his death in 1480. See Watson, *Scottish Verse*, p. 260.
68 MacGregor, 'The View from Fortingall', pp. 55–56. Gillies, 'From Milk-cow Blues' (p. 48) dates this to 'in, or shortly after, 1496.'
69 James Balfour Paul, *Accounts of the Lord High Treasurer of Scotland*, vol. iii (AD 1506–07), (Edinburgh 1901), p. 339.
70 MacGregor, 'The View from Fortingall', p. 56.
71 Gillies, 'Gaelic Poems of Duncan Campbell (I)', p. 20.
72 Isabel and Janet Stewart were daughters of John Stewart, Lord of Lorn (cf. Boardman, *The Campbells*, pp. 186–87); a third sister (Marion?) was married to a Campbell of Otter (Boardman, personal correspondence). We have noted the presence of verses ascribed to Máire inghean Stiúbhairt 'Mary daughter of the Stewart' in BDL and one wonders might there be a connection to this family.
73 See Quiggin, *Poems from the BDL*, LIII, p. 72, Gillies, 'Courtly and Satiric Poems', p. 44, and MacGregor, 'The View from Fortingall', p. 58.
74 Gillies, 'Courtly and Satiric Poems', p. 42; Gillies, 'BDL: Literary Perspective', p. 207.
75 MacGregor, 'The View from Fortingall', p. 58.
76 Gillies, 'Gaelic Literature in the Later Middle Ages', pp. 224–25; MacGregor, 'The View from Fortingall', passim.

77 Gillies, 'Courtly and Satiric Poems', p. 47.
78 Gillies, 'From Milk-cow Blues', pp. 57–58.
79 Cf. MacGregor, 'The View from Fortingall', pp. 70–73.
80 See Gillies in Chapter Four above.
81 For the location of these texts in BDL, see Ronald Black's unpublished catalogue which is available online as part of the 'Irish Script on Screen' collection (www.isos.dias.ie/english/index.html). For discussion, see MacGregor, 'The View from Fortingall', pp. 71–72, and MacGregor, 'Creation and Compilation', p. 217.
82 MacGregor, 'The View from Fortingall', p. 72.
83 MacGregor, 'Creation and Compilation', pp. 215–17; MacGregor, 'The View from Fortingall', pp. 70–71; Gillies, 'BDL: Literary Perspective', p. 184.
84 See Gillies, '*Dánta Grá* and the BDL', pp. 259–60, 262.
85 Gillies, 'Gaelic Literature in the Later Middle Ages', p. 223.
86 MacGregor, 'The View from Fortingall', p. 57.
87 Although the poems ascribed to Gearóid Iarla in the Book of Fermoy would belong to the fourteenth century, if we could be sure that they were written by him, it is also the case that scholars see little of the *amour courtois* tradition in his poetry as a whole. See Mac Craith, *Lorg na hIasachta*, pp. 58–59; 201, n. 70a; Mac Mathúna, 'An Fhilíocht a Leagtar ar Ghearóid Iarla i Leabhar Fhear Maí', p. 245.
88 Gillies, 'Courtly and Satiric Poems', p. 38. We should remind ourselves, however, that distinct elements of the Gaelic tradition of love-lyric in Scotland (as opposed to Ireland) have also been highlighted in the intervening period, in particular by Gillies himself in the case of poems such as those by An Bard Mac an tSaoir (as we have seen).
89 He alludes, in particular, to the '"bardic" elements in the mix' such as imagery and phraseology, punning and wordplay, and the citing of literary precedent; cf. Gillies, '*Dánta Grá* and the BDL', p. 265.
90 One might add that a fuller exploration of the material which has yet to be edited from Irish manuscripts such as RIA 23 D 4 is a major desideratum in trying to advance our understanding of Gaelic love-lyric as a whole, not to mention the light which would be gained from a diplomatic edition of BDL. There is much benefit to be derived from 'a final (or at least a major) assault on BDL', as advocated by Gillies, 'BDL: Literary Perspective', p. 180.
91 This is precisely the case that has been made on the Irish side in that lyrics that were composed in Ireland in the latter half of the sixteenth

and first half of the seventeenth centuries have been shown to be indebted to English influence (Mac Craith, *Lorg na hIasachta*, passim).
92 See Mac Craith, *Lorg na hIasachta*, pp. 151, 160.
93 We should note that he may have had access to material from Ireland through his half-brother John who was Bishop of the Isles and may have served as a conduit for such materials. There are other routes, however, by which materials such as these could have reached Glenorchy, including more direct contact. Intriguingly, we find him standing surety for an Irish nobleman, Séan Ua Catháin, who had been kidnapped and held captive in Scotland in 1490–91 (cf. Boardman, *The Campbells*, pp. 252, 327–28).
94 Cf. 'A bhean 'gá bhfuil crodh', Angus Matheson (ed.), 'A Ughdar so Fearchar mac Phádraig Grannd', *Éigse* 5.3 (1946), pp 156–57.
95 Cf. Gillies, Chapter Four above, who refers to 'the self-sufficiency of the late medieval Gaelic tradition'.
96 See Rosemary Greentree, *The Middle English Lyric and Short Poem* (Cambridge: D. S. Brewer, 2001) and Thomas G. Duncan (ed.), *A Companion to Middle English Lyric* (Cambridge: D. S. Brewer, 2005) for broader considerations of the emergence of medieval lyric.
97 See Julia Boffey, 'Middle English lyrics and manuscripts' in Duncan (ed.) *Lyric*, pp. 1–18.
98 For a fuller discussion of this poem and its implications for Scottish literature, see C. Jones, 'Inclinit to diuersiteis: Wyntoun's song on the Death of Alexander III and the "origins" of Scots vernacular poetry', *RES* 64 (2013), pp. 21–38.
99 Richard Holland, *The Buke of the Howlat*, ed. Ralph Hanna, STS (2014), pp. 77–78, ll. 716–54.
100 *The Kingis Quair* is preserved in Oxford, Bodleian Library MS Arch. Selden B. 24 (see J. Boffey and A. S. G. Edwards (intro), *The Works of Geoffrey Chaucer and the 'The Kingis Quair': A Facsimile of Bodleian Library, Oxford MS Arch. Selden B. 24* (Cambridge: D. S. Brewer, 1997)). The Asloan Manuscript is now Edinburgh, National Library of Scotland MS 16500 and the Makculloch manuscript is Edinburgh, Edinburgh University Library MS 205. For full accounts of these as repositories for lyric, see A. A. MacDonald, 'Lyrics in Middle Scots' in Duncan (ed.) *Lyric*, pp. 242–61, esp. pp. 243, 246–68, and also Mapstone, above, pp. 38–59.
101 The Bannatyne Manuscript is now Edinburgh, National Library of Scotland, MS Advocates 1.1.6. The Maitland Folio is now Cambridge,

Magdalene College MS Pepys 2553, and the Maitland Quarto is Cambridge, Magdalene College MS Pepys 1408.

102 MacDonald, 'Lyrics in Middle Scots', p. 247.

103 For a full text of Dunbar's poetry, see *Dunbar*.

104 For further discussion, see Priscilla Bawcutt, *Dunbar the Makar* (Oxford: OUP, 1992), pp. 354–58 and Douglas Gray, '"Hale Sterne Superne" and its Literary Background' in Sally Mapstone (ed.) *William Dunbar: 'The Nobill Poyet'* (East Linton: Tuckwell Press, 2001), pp. 198–210.

105 *Dunbar* B 16, ll. 25–28.

106 *Dunbar* B 35. See Bawcutt, *Dunbar the Makar*, pp. 115–17.

107 *Dunbar* B 21. See Bawcutt, *Dunbar the Makar*, pp. 153–58, and also MacDonald, 'Lyrics in Middle Scots', p. 258.

108 Although *A Ballade of good Counsel* used to be associated with James I, this is no longer held to be the case: see A Lawson (ed.), *The Kingis Quair and the Quare of Jelusy* (London: A & C Black 1910), pp. 102–03.

109 *Dunbar* B 70, B 72, B 73. See also Bawcutt, *Dunbar the Makar*, pp. 244–49 and John Burrow, 'William Dunbar' in Bawcutt and Hadley Williams, *Companion* pp. 133–48.

110 Hadley Williams, *Lyndsay* , pp. 98–100 and pp. 101–08.

111 See, e.g. Hadley Williams, *Lyndsay*: 'The Answer', ll. 43–56.

112 For further details, see A. A. MacDonald, 'William Stewart and court poetry of the reign of James V', in J. Hadley Williams (ed.) *Stewart style, 1513–1542: essays on the court of James V,* (East Linton: Tuckwell Press, 1996), pp. 179–200; T. van Heijnsbergen, 'The interaction between literature and history in Queen Mary's Edinburgh: the Bannatyne manuscript and its prosopographical context', in A. A. MacDonald et al, *Renaissance in Scotland* , pp. 183–225.

113 See W. A. Craigie (ed.), *The Maitland Folio Manuscript,* 2 vols. STS (1919, 1927), vol. 1, p. 243.

114 Craigie (ed.) *Maitland Folio*, vol. 1, p. 244.

115 Craigie (ed.) *Maitland Folio* vol. 1, Poem XIV, pp. 21–24 and Poem CIII, pp. 323–24.

116 See A. Holton and T. McFaul (eds) *Tottel's miscellany: songs and sonnets of Henry Howard, Earl of Surrey, Sir Thomas Wyatt and others* (London: Penguin, 2011) for their early printed verse.

117 Craigie (ed.) *Maitland Folio* vol. 1, Poems XCVII and XCVIII, pp. 305–12.

118 "Machiavel, n." OED Online. OUP, December 2014. Accessed 17 February 2015.

119 For more detailed discussion of Alexander Scott, see Theo van Heijnsbergen, 'Studies in the Contextualisation of Mid-Sixteenth-Century Scottish Verse', unpublished PhD thesis, University of Glasgow, 2010.
120 Craigie (ed.) *Maitland Folio* vol. 1, Poem XIX, pp. 34–36.
121 W. Tod Ritchie (ed.) *The Bannatyne Manuscript*, 4 vols. STS (1928–34), vol. 2, Poem CLII, pp. 235–42.
122 Tod Ritchie (ed.) *Bannatyne Manuscript* vol. 2, Poems XVII and XVIII, pp. 38–42.
123 See van Heijnsbergen, 'Interaction between literature and history', pp. 186–88 and also Theo van Heijnsbergen, 'The Bannatyne Manuscript Lyrics: Literary Convention and Authorial Voice' in Caie et al, *European Sun:* pp. 423–44.
124 Tod Ritchie (ed.) *Bannatyne Manuscript* vol. 4, Poem CCCXXXIV, pp. 17–18.
125 See A. A. MacDonald, 'Scottish Poetry of the reign of Mary Stewart', in Caie et al, *European Sun*, pp. 44–61.
126 See Sarah Dunnigan, *Eros and poetry at the courts of Mary Queen of Scots and James VI* (Basingstoke: Palgrave Macmillan, 2002).
127 The sonnets can be found in *Detectioun of the duinges of Marie Quene of Scotts, touchand the murder of her Husband, and hir Conspiracie, Adulterie and pretensit Mariage with the Erle Bothwell. Translatit out of the Latine, quhilk was written be M. G. B.* ([London: John Day, 1571]), sigs. Qiiijv-Sir. For a brief account of their political significance, see Jenny Wormald, *Mary Queen of Scots: A Study in Failure* (London: Collins and Brown, 1991), pp. 171–78. See also Dunnigan. *Eros and Poetry*, pp. 15–21.
128 See Sarah Dunnigan, 'Scottish Women Writers, c. 1560–c. 1650' in Douglas Gifford and Dorothy McMillan (eds) *A History of Scottish Women's Writing* (Edinburgh: EUP 1997), pp. 15–43, esp. pp. 17–26 for further consideration.
129 See Dunnigan 'Scottish Women Writers' for discussion of other women poets of the period.
130 Joanna M. Martin (ed.), *The Maitland Quarto*, STS (2015).
131 Martin (ed.) *Maitland Quarto*, p. 262.
132 See Martin (ed.) *Maitland Quarto*, pp. 443–45 and Dunnigan 'Scottish Women Writers', pp. 29–31.
133 The first female religious poet in print was Elizabeth Melville. See above, 'Religious verse'. For more details on Anna Hume, see Dunnigan 'Scottish Women Writers' pp. 34–39.

134 Anna Hume, *The triumphs of love: chastitie: death: translated out of Petrarch* (Edinburgh: Evan Tyler, 1644), sig. A4r.
135 See A. A. MacDonald, 'The printed book that never was: George Bannatyne's poetic anthology (1968)' in J. M. M. Hermans and K. van der Hoek (eds) *Boekenin de late Middeleeuwen* (Groningen: 1994), pp. 101–10.
136 See A. A. MacDonald (ed.) *The Gude and Godlie Ballatis*, STS (2015) and A. A. MacDonald, 'Contrafacta and the *Gude and Godlie Ballatis*', in H. E. Wilcox, M. Todd and A. A. MacDonald (eds), *Sacred and Profane: Secular and Devotional Interplay in Early Modern British Literature* (Amsterdam: VU Press, 1996), pp. 33–44.
137 See below, Chapter on Satire.
138 For still influential discussion, see Helena M. Shire, *Song, Dance and Poetry at the Court of James VI* (Cambridge: CUP, 1969), and for recent perspectives, see David J. Parkinson (ed.) *James VI and I, Literature and Scotland: Tides of Change, 1567–1625* (Leuven: Peeters, 2013).
139 This was part of *The Essays of a Prentise in the Divine Art of Poesie*, published in Edinburgh by Thomas Vautroiller in 1584. For a modern edition, see R. D. S. Jack and P. A. T. Rozendaal (eds) *The Mercat Anthology of Scottish Literature 1375–1707* (Edinburgh: Mercat Press, 1997), pp. 460–73.
140 Alexander Montgomerie, *Poems* ed. D. Parkinson, 2 vols., STS (2000), vol. 1, Poem 65, p. 104.
141 Montgomerie *Poems*, vol. 1 Poem 66, p. 104. For fuller accounts of Montgomerie, see Roderick J. Lyall, *Alexander Montgomerie* (Tempe, AZ: ACMRS, 2005).
142 See Lyall, *Montgomerie*, pp. 63–117, 145–94.
143 Parkinson (ed.) *Montgomerie Poems*, vol. 1, Poems 68 (pp. 107–08) and 72 and 72a (pp. 112–15).
144 Parkinson (ed.) *Montgomerie: Poems*, vol 1, 72.I, line 12, and 72.III, line 14.
145 See Theo van Heijnsbergen, 'Masks of Revelation and "the 'female' tongues of men": Montgomerie, Christian Lyndsay, and the Writing Game at the Scottish Renaissance Court' in Van Heijnsbergen and Royan, *Literature, Letters and the Canonical*, pp. 67–89.
146 Parkinson (ed.), *Montgomerie: Poems* vol 1, Poems 72a (p. 115), 78–79 (p. 121) and 75 (pp. 116–17).
147 Parkinson (ed.), *Montgomerie: Poems*, vol 1, Poem 98, pp. 136–37 and also Lyall, *Montgomerie*, pp. 309–17.

148 The idea of a Castalian Band was first suggested by Helena M. Shire in *Song, Dance and Poetry*. More recently, Priscilla Bawcutt has questioned the accuracy of the idea in P. Bawcutt, 'The Castalian Band: A Modern Myth', *SHR* 80.2 (2001), 251–59.

149 See W. Calin, *The Lily and the Thistle: The French Tradition and the Older Literature of Scotland – Essays in Criticism* (Toronto: University of Toronto Press, 2014), pp. 236–51; R. D. S. Jack, *The Italian Influence on Scottish Literature* (Edinburgh: EUP, 1972); and R. D. S. Jack, 'Poetry under James VI', in *AHSL*, pp. 125–40.

150 T. Crockett (ed.), *The Poems of John Stewart of Baldynneis* vol. 1, STS (1913), Poem 59, p. 185, line 1. See also Kate McClune, 'Poetry and the In-Crowd: The Case of John Stewart of Baldynneis', in Parkinson (ed.) *James VI and I*, pp. 119–37.

151 For further discussion on seventeenth-century poetry, see Michael Spiller, 'Poetry after the Union 1603–1660', in *AHSL*, pp. 141–62. For editions, see Charles Gullans (ed.) *The English and Latin Poems of Robert Aytoun*, STS (1963); H. W. Meikle (ed.) *The Works of William Fowler* vol. 1: verse, STS (1914); and L. E. Kastner and H. B Charlton (eds) *The Poetical Works of William Alexander, Earl of Stirling*, 2 vols., STS (1921 and 1929).

152 Gullans (ed.) *Poems of Robert Aytoun*, Poem 24, p. 167, ll. 2, 4, 5 and 7.

153 See Morna R. Fleming, '"Kin[g]es be the glas, the verie scoole, the booke,/Where priuate men do learne, and read, and look" (Alexander Craig, 1604): The Translation of James VI to the Throne of England in 1603', in Heijnsbergen and Royan (eds), *Literature, Letters and the Canonical*, pp. 90–110.

154 Spiller, 'Poetry after the Union', pp. 147–48; for Craig's works, see David Laing (ed.), *The Poetical Works of Alexander Craig of Rosecraig*, Hunterian Club (Glasgow, 1875).

155 For discussion of James Melville, see Sally Mapstone, 'James Melville's Revisions to *A Spiritvall Propine* and *A Morning Vision*' in Parkinson (ed.), *James VI and I, Literature and Scotland*, pp. 173–94, and for Arbuthnot, see Joanna M Martin, 'Alexander Arbuthnot and the Lyric in Reformation Scotland', *SSL* 41.1 (2015), pp. 62–87. Available at scholarcommons.sc.edu/ssl/vol41/iss1/10

156 Alexander Hume, 'Of the Day Estivall', in Bawcutt and Riddy, *LSP*, pp. 291–302, ll. 1–8.

157 For the most recent work on the *Delitiae*, see the project, 'Bridging the Continental divide: neo-Latin and its cultural role in Jacobean

Scotland, as seen in the *Delitiae Poetarum Scotorum* (1637); www.dps.gla.ac.uk.
158 See Michael Spiller, '"Quintessencing in the Finest Substance": the *Sonnets* of William Drummond', in Royan, *Langage Cleir Illumynate*, pp. 193–205.
159 See Robert H. MacDonald (ed.), *William Drummond of Hawthornden: Poems and Prose* (Edinburgh: SAP, 1976), pp. 8–72.
160 MacDonald (ed.), *William Drummond, Flowres of Sion*, pp. 88–128. For a discussion, see David Atkinson, '*Flowres of Sion*: The Spiritual and Meditative Journey of William Drummond', in Royan, *Langage Cleir Illumynate*, pp. 181–91, and for discussion of *Tears on the Death of Moeliades*, see Chapter 8, below.
161 For further discussion of early seventeenth-century circulation, see Sebastiaan Verweij, *The Literary Culture of Early Modern Scotland* (Oxford: OUP, 2016).
162 See Spiller, 'Poetry after the Union', p. 159 and Edward J. Cowan, 'Mistress and Mother as Political Abstraction: The Apostrophic Poetry of James Graham, Marquis of Montrose, and William Lithgow' in Caie et al, *European Sun*, pp. 534–44.
163 Spiller, 'Poetry after the Union', p. 160.
164 H. Harvey-Wood (ed.), *James Watson's Choice Collection* 2 vols, STS (1977 and 1991) and Allan Ramsay (ed.) *The Ever Greene being a collection of Scots poems: wrote by the ingenious before 1600*. 2 vols. (Edinburgh, 1761). For a comparison of Ramsay and Watson, see Leith Davis, 'Imagining the Miscellaneous Nation: James Watson's Choice Collection of Comic and Serious Scots Poems', *Eighteenth Century Life* 35.3 (2011), pp. 60–80 (esp. pp. 79–80).
165 See, for instance, Douglas Gifford, Sarah Dunnigan and Alan MacGillivray (eds), *Scottish Literature* (Edinburgh: EUP, 2002), which places a chapter on ballads in between Renaissance Poetry and the Eighteenth Century (pp. 48–104).
166 I would like to thank Joanna Martin, Theo van Heijnsbergen and Sebastiaan Verweij for reading and commenting upon this chapter section in draft.

7. Chivalric Literature

1 *The Buke of the Ordre of Knychthede*, cap. iii, lines 113–34, 121–23, in *The Prose Works of Sir Gilbert Hay*, vol. III, ed. Jonathan A. Glenn, STS (1993), p. 16.

2   See for example, Louise Olga Fradenburg, *City, Marriage, Tournament: Arts of Rule in Late Medieval Scotland* (Madison: University of Wisconsin Press, 1991); Richard W. Kaeuper, *Chivalry and Violence in Medieval Europe* (Oxford: Clarendon Press, 1999), pp. 30–40, 111–20, 231–72; Andrew Taylor, 'From Heraldry to History: the Death of Giles D'Argentan', in Royan, *Langage Cleir Illumynate*, pp. 25–41.
3   The genre of Hary's *Wallace* and (even more so) Barbour's *Bruce* has been a matter of critical controversy: both poems present themselves as historiographical while also calling upon the genre of romance, two modes of writing which medieval and modern audiences alike sometimes have difficulty in reconciling. See for example Lois A. Ebin, 'John Barbour's *Bruce*: Poetry, History and Propaganda', *SSL* 9.4 (1972), 218–42; R. James Goldstein, *The Matter of Scotland: Historical Narrative in Medieval Scotland* (Lincoln & London: University of Nebraska Press, 1993), pp. 133–49 (*Bruce*) and 250–81 (*Wallace*); Nicola Royan, 'A question of truth: Barbour's *Bruce*, Hary's *Wallace* and *Richard Coer de Lion*', *International Review of Scottish Studies* 34 (2009), 75–105; Susan Foran, 'A Great Romance: Chivalry and War in Barbour's *Bruce*', in *Fourteenth Century England* VI, ed. Chris Given-Wilson (Woodbridge: Boydell Press, 2010), pp. 1–26; Rhiannon Purdie, 'Medieval romance and the generic frictions of Barbour's *Bruce*', in Boardman and Foran, *Barbour's* Bruce, pp. 51–74.
4   For surveys of medieval romance in Scotland see: A. S. G. Edwards, 'Contextualising Middle Scots Romance', in Houwen et al, *Palace in the Wild* (Leuven: Peeters, 2000), pp. 61–73: Rhiannon Purdie, 'Medieval Romance in Scotland', Bawcutt and Hadley Williams, *Medieval Scottish Poetry*, pp. 165–77; Sergi Mainer, *The Scottish Romance Tradition c. 1375–1500* (Amsterdam & New York: Rodopi, 2010).
5   *The Buik of Alexander*, ed. R. L. Graeme Ritchie, 4 vols., STS (1921–29): originally printed by A. Arbuthnet [Edinburgh, 1580]: STC (2nd ed.) 321.5. Ritchie's attribution of this text to Barbour is not generally accepted, although the colophon's date of 1438 is. The second *Alexander* is commonly, but not universally, accepted as the work of Sir Gilbert Hay: *The Buik of King Alexander the Conquerour*, ed. John Cartwright, STS (only vols. II and III published), (1986 and 1990). Joanna Martin sets out the arguments for rejecting Hay as the author of the extant work: '"Of Wisdome and of Guide Governance": Sir Gilbert Hay and the *Buik of King Alexander the Conquerour*', in Bawcutt and Hadley Williams, *Medieval Scottish Poetry*, pp. 75–88 (pp. 76–77).

6 Edited in Rhiannon Purdie, *Shorter Scottish Medieval Romances*, STS (2013), pp. 87–103.
7 *The Knightly Tale of Golagros and Gawane*, ed. Ralph Hanna, STS (2008); *Lancelot of the Laik and Sir Tristrem*, ed. Alan Lupack (Kalamazoo: MIP 1994), or *Lancelot of the Laik*, ed. M. M. Gray, STS (1912).
8 *Barbour's des Schottischen Nationaldichters Legendensammlung nebst den Fragmenten seines Trojanerkrieges*, ed. C. Horstmann, 2 vols. (Heilbronn, 1882), II, 215–307. On the question of how these fragments ended up in the Lydgate MSS, see Angus McIntosh, 'Some Notes on the Language and Textual Transmission of the *Scottish Troy Book*', *Archivum Linguisticum* n.s. 10 (1979), 1–19; Emily Wingfield, *The Trojan Legend in Medieval Scottish Literature* (Cambridge: D. S. Brewer, 2014), pp. 89–120; Sebastiaan Verweij, 'Reading and Mending the *Troy Book* in Renaissance Scotland', *JEBS*, 7 (2012), 11–30.
9 In Bawcutt and Riddy, *LSP*, pp. 94–133 or *The Tale of Ralph the Collier* in *Three Middle English Charlemagne Romances*, ed. Alan Lupack (Kalamazoo: MIP, 1990).
10 For a parallel-text edition of both Percy Folio and Huntington-Laing versions, see *Eger and Grime*, ed. J. R. Caldwell, Harvard Studies in Comparative Literature IX (Cambridge, Mass., 1933); on the date, see note 17 below.
11 See *Shorter Scottish Medieval Romances*, ed. Purdie, pp. 113–23 (*Orphius*) and 104–11 (*Colling*). Both texts were discovered in the 1970s by Marion Stewart: see her '*King Orphius*', *ScotStud* 17 (1973), 1–16 and 'A Recently-Discovered Manuscript: "ane taill of Sir colling ye kny^t"', *ScotStud* 16 (1972), 23–39. For *Sir Colling*'s connection to the Campbells, see Stephen Boardman, *The Campbells 1250–1513* (Edinburgh: John Donald, 2006), p. 42.
12 *Clariodus: A Metrical Romance*, ed. D. Irving (Edinburgh, 1830).
13 See *Shorter Scottish Medieval Romances*, ed. Purdie, pp. 125–99.
14 See Lillian Herlands Hornstein, 'Eustace-Constance-Florence-Griselda Legends', in *Manual of the Writings in Middle English 1050–1500*, gen. ed. J. Burke Severs (New Haven: The Connecticut Academy of Arts and Sciences, 1967), pp. 120–32.
15 See for example W. R. J. Barron, '*Golagros and Gawane*: A Creative Redaction', *BBIAS* 26 (1974), pp. 173–85, and Rhiannon Purdie, 'The Search for Scottishness in *Golagros and Gawane*', in Rhiannon Purdie and Nicola Royan (eds), *The Scots and Medieval Arthurian Legend*, (Cambridge: D. S. Brewer, 2005), pp. 95–107.

16 The importance of the advisory section is stressed by Sally Mapstone in 'The Scots, the French, and the English: an Arthurian Episode', in Caie et al, *European Sun,* pp. 128–44. Elizabeth Archibald questions the critical emphasis given to this advisory section ('*Lancelot of the Laik*: Sources, Genre, Reception', in *The Scots and Medieval Arthurian Legend,* eds. Purdie and Royan, pp. 76–79, as does Alan Lupack in the introduction to his edition.
17 See for example a reference to the performance of 'Graysteil' before James IV's court in 1497: *Compota Thesaurariorum Regum Scotorum,* ed. T. Dickson (Edinburgh, 1877), i, p. 330.
18 London, British Library, Lansdowne 766: see Ronald S. Crane, 'The Vogue of *Guy of Warwick* from the Close of the Middle Ages to the Romantic Revival', *PMLA,* 30.2 (1915), p. 146 note 32.
19 Matthew P. McDiarmid, 'Notes on the poems of John Stewart of Baldynneis', *RES* 24 (1948), p. 17.
20 *The first booke of the famous historye of Penardo and Laissa other ways callid the warres, of love and ambitione* (Dort: George Waters, 1615). STC (2nd ed.) 12067. For discussion of both of Gordon's works see Michael R. G. Spiller, 'Dungeons and Larders: the romances of Patrick Gordon', in McClure and Spiller, *Bryght Lanternis,* pp. 364–72.
21 *Sheretine and Mariana* (London : Printed by Iohn Haviland for Nathaniel Butter, 1622); STC (2nd ed.) 12748. See p. 90 for 'The Epistle Dedicatorie'. For a recent assessment of the Spenserian influence on *Penardo* and *Sheretine,* see Louise Hutcheson, '"Unpredictable symmetries": the discursive functions of early seventeenth-century Scottish romance', (unpublished MPhil thesis, University of Glasgow, 2010), pp. 33–7.
22 *The historie of Calanthrop and Lucilla* (Edinburgh: Iohn Wreittoun, 1626); STC (2nd ed.) 14929 and (London: Thomas Harper for Michael Sparke, 1631); STC (2nd ed.) 14930.
23 Preface, as quoted in Spiller, 'Dungeons and Larders', p. 366.
24 Spiller, 'Dungeons and Larders', p. 366.
25 The wry description is from James Simpson, *Reform and Cultural Revolution* (Oxford: OUP, 2002), p. 296.
26 Maurice Keen, *Chivalry* (New Haven & London: Yale University Press, 1995), pp. 102–24.
27 Edited in parallel with the Older Scots translation by Ritchie in Vols 3–4 of *The Buik of Alexander.*
28 Carol Edington, 'Paragons and Patriots: National Identity and the Chivalric Ideal in Late-Medieval Scotland', in Dauvit Broun, R. J.

Finlay and Michael Lynch (eds), *Image and Identity: The Making and Re-making of Scotland Through the Ages* (Edinburgh: John Donald, 1998), p. 75.

29 See John Barbour, *The Bruce*, ed. A. A. M. Duncan (Edinburgh: Canongate, 1977 rep. 2007): 1.465 and 470–71; 14.312–16.

30 *Select Remains of the Ancient Popular Poetry of Scotland*, ed. David Laing, rev. John Small (Edinburgh & London: Blackwood, 1885), pp. 185–91.

31 'The Ballettis of the Nine Nobles' in *Six Scottish Courtly and Chivalric Poems, Including Lyndsay's* Squyer Meldrum, eds. Rhiannon Purdie and Emily Wingfield (Kalamazoo, MI: MIP, 2018), pp. 11–32. Ritchie had attributed the poem to John Barbour, but the dates do not support this: see 'The Ballet of the Nine Worthies', in Ritchie (ed.), *The Buik of Alexander*, I, pp. cxxxiv–cl. W. A. Craigie argued it must have been written by the author of the *Buik of Alexander* in the later 1430s or early 1440s: 'The "Ballet of the Nine Nobles"', *Anglia: Zeitschrift für Englische Philologie* 21 (1898–99), 359–65 (p. 365, and see also Purdie and Wingfield, p. 19). Sally Mapstone suggests authorship by, or at least association, with Gilbert Hay: Sally Mapstone, 'The *Scotichronicon*'s First Readers', in Barbara E. Crawford (ed.), *Church, Chronicle and Learning in Medieval and Early Renaissance Scotland* (Edinburgh: Mercat Press, 1999), pp. 31–55 (p. 46).

32 Another attempt to add Bruce to the list of Worthies occurs in some Latin lines copied c. 1380 into a manuscript of the Vulgate from Sweetheart Abbey, Kirkcudbright: see R. S. Loomis, 'Verses on the Nine Worthies', *Modern Philology* 15.4 (1917), p. 211.

33 Henry Hargreaves, 'The Crathes Ceiling Inscriptions', in *Bryght Lanternis*, pp. 374–8; Michael Bath, *Renaissance Decorative Painting in Scotland* (Edinburgh: NMS, 2003), pp. 185–90.

34 Goldstein, *Matter of Scotland*; Steve Boardman, 'Late Medieval Scotland and the Matter of Britain', in E. J. Cowan and R. J. Finlay (eds), *Scottish History: The Power of the Past* (Edinburgh: EUP, 2002), pp. 47–72.

35 On the question of Robert II's patronage, see *The Bruce*, ed. Duncan, pp. 3, 10. For recent reassessments of the poem, see Boardman and Foran, *Barbour's* Bruce.

36 Duncan, ed. *The Bruce*, pp. 25–8.

37 St John's College, Cambridge, MS G23 (1487) and Edinburgh, NLS Adv. MS 19.2.2 (1489): see *The Bruce*, ed. Duncan, p. 32.

38 *Hary's Wallace*, ed. Matthew P. McDiarmid, STS (1968–9): on the poem's date, see pp. xiv–xxvi; on authorship, see pp. xxvi–xl.
39 Edinburgh, NLS MS Adv. 19.2.2.
40 'The Order of Combats for Life in Scotland as they are anciently recorded in ane old Manuscript of the Law Arms and Offices of Scotland pertaining to James I King of Scots', *The Miscellany of the Spalding Club*, ii, (Aberdeen, 1842). See also the mid-sixteenth century rules of the lists at NLS Fort Augustus MS (Acc 11218/5).
41 See *The Book of Chivalry of Geoffroi de Charny: Text, Context and Translation*, eds. Richard W. Kaeuper and Elspeth Kennedy (Philadelphia: University of Pennsylvania Press, 1996).
42 See *Raoul de Hodenc; Le Roman des Eles; the anonymous L'Ordene e Chevalerie*, ed. Keith Busby (Amsterdam: Benjamins, 1983) and Ramon Llull, *Llibre de l'orde de cavalleria*, ed. Albert Soler i Llopart, Els Nostres Clàssics A127 (Barcelona: Editorial Barcino, 1988).
43 Sally Mapstone, 'The Advice to Prince's Tradition in Scottish Literature, 1450–1500' (unpublished D.Phil, University of Oxford, 1986), p. 56.
44 STC (2nd ed.) 3356.7.
45 Sally Mapstone, 'The *Scotichronicon*'s First Readers', pp. 32–3; *Chron. Bower* Book xvi, 26, notes; Katie Stevenson, *Chivalry and Knighthood in Scotland, 1424–1513* (Woodbridge: Boydell & Brewer, 2006), p. 35 n. 115.
46 NLS, Acc. 9253; Glenn, ed., *The Buke of the Law of Armys*; Jonathan A. Glenn, ed., *The Prose Works of Sir Gilbert Hay Volume III: The Buke of the Ordre of Knychthede and The Buke of the Governaunce of Princis* STS (1993).
47 St John's College, Cambridge, MS 102; Mapstone, 'The Advice to Prince's Tradition', p. 56.
48 NLS MS TD 209; Mapstone, 'The Advice to Prince's Tradition', p. 47.
49 Edinburgh, NLS MS 16500: see Sally Mapstone, 'The Scots *Buke of Phisnomy* and Sir Gilbert Hay', in A. A. MacDonald, et al., *Renaissance in Scotland*, pp. 1–44.
50 See 'I that in heill wes and gladnes', B line 67, in *Dunbar* II, 94–97; 'The Testament and Complaynt of our Soverane Lordis Papyngo', line 19, in Hadley Williams, *Lyndsay*, pp. 58–97.
51 For more on this see Katie Stevenson, 'Jurisdiction, Authority and Professionalisation: The Officers of Arms of Late Medieval Scotland', in Katie Stevenson (ed.), *The Herald in Late Medieval Europe* (Woodbridge: Boydell & Brewer, 2009), pp. 41–66.

52 London, BL Harley MS 6149.
53 BL, Harley MS 6149; Houwen, ed. *Deidis of Armorie*, i, pp. xl–lv.
54 See Oxford, Queen's College, MS 161, c. 1500; NLS, Adv MS 31.5.3, of the first half of the sixteenth century, copied for John Scrymgeour of Mures, Master of the King's Works; NLS, Adv MS 31.3.20 from the later sixteenth century, for David Lindsay of Rathillet; and an incomplete version at NLS, Adv MS 31.7.22 belonging to Peter Thomson, Islay Herald, dating to the first half of the sixteenth century. John Meldrum, Marchmont Herald, also had a copy of Bartolus's *Tractatus* in the mid-sixteenth century: NLS, Adv. MS 31.6.5. For more see Houwen, ed., *Deidis of Armorie*, i, p. xxxi; Carol Edington, *Court and Culture in Renaissance Scotland: Sir David Lindsay of the Mount* (Amherst: University of Massachusetts Press, 1995), pp. 28–29; Stevenson, 'The Officers of Arms of Late Medieval Scotland', pp. 58 n. 97, 64–66.
55 BL Add 45133, ff. 46b–50b; *The Scots Roll: A Study of a Fifteenth Century Roll of Arms*, ed. Colin Campbell (Kinross, 1995); Rae Redfern Brown, 'The Scots Roll', (unpublished M.Litt dissertation, University of St Andrews, 2007).
56 Robert Riddle Stodart, *Scottish Arms, Being a Collection of Armorial Bearings, A.D. 1370–1678: Reproduced in Facsimile from Contemporary Manuscripts with Heraldic and Genealogical Notes* (Edinburgh, 1881). On the *Armorial de Berry* see J. Storer Clouston, 'The Armorial de Berry (Scottish Section)', *Proceedings of the Society of Antiquaries of Scotland* lxxii (1937–38), pp. 84–114. On the *Bellenville Roll* see Paris, Bibliothèque Nationale, MS Français 5230; Colin Campbell, 'Scottish Arms in the Bellenville Roll', *The Scottish Genealogist* 25:2 (1978), pp. 33–52.
57 NLS, Adv MS 31.4.3; John Horne Stevenson, *Heraldry in Scotland* (Glasgow, 1914), i, p. 62; Edington, *Court and Culture*, p. 37; Stevenson, 'The Officers of Arms in Late Medieval Scotland', p. 57.
58 Richard Holland, *The Buke of the Howlat*, ed. Ralph Hanna, STS (2013). For discussion see: Michael Brown, *The Black Douglases* (East Linton: Tuckwell, 1998), pp. 10–11, 122–31, 203, 277–8; Felicity Riddy, 'Dating the Buke of the Howlat', *RES* 37 (1986), 1–10; Matthew P. McDiarmid, 'Richard Holland's *Buke of the Howlat*: an interpretation', *Medium Aevum*, 38 (1969), 277–90; Flora Alexander, 'Richard Holland's "Buke of the Howlat"', in *Literature of the North*, ed. David Hewitt and Michael Spiller (Aberdeen, 1983), esp. pp. 22–3; Marion Stewart, 'Holland's "Howlat" and the Fall of the Livingstones', *IR* 23

(1972), esp. p. 74; Nicola Royan, '"Mark your Meroure be Me": Richard Holland's *Buke of the Howlat*', in Bawcutt and Hadley Williams, *Medieval Scottish Poetry*, pp. 49–62; Katie Stevenson, 'Contesting Chivalry: James II and the Control of Chivalric Culture in the 1450s', *Journal of Medieval History*, 20 (2007), p. 9. For a recent reassessment of the poem's date, see Alasdair A. MacDonald, 'Richard Holland and *The Buke of the Howlat*: Remembrance of Things Past', *Medium Aevum* 86 (2017), 108–22.

59 NLS MS 16500, c. 1515–25; NLS Adv. MS 1.1.6, copied 1568; Bawcutt and Riddy, *LSP*, p. 44.
60 Stevenson, *Chivalry and Knighthood*, pp. 148–50.
61 For edition and discussion, see *Six Scottish Courtly and Chivalric Poems*, eds Purdie and Wingfield, pp. 149–269.
62 We find this same idea in Froissart's *Chronicles* of the fourteenth century: when the Scots are defeated at Otterburn, it was remarked on the death of one Scottish squire that he had refused knighthood just before the battle because it would be better, should he meet his demise, to die a renowned squire than an unknown knight. Jean Froissart, *Chronicles*, ed. Geoffrey Brereton (London: Penguin, 1978), pp. 344–45. See also Stevenson, *Chivalry and Knighthood*, pp. 51–52.
63 Felicity Riddy, '*Squyer Meldrum* and the Romance of Chivalry', *Yearbook of English Studies* 4 (1974), pp. 26–36; Edington, *Court and Culture*, pp. 122–24; Hadley Williams, *Lyndsay*, p. 284; Purdie and Wingfield, *Six Scottish Courtly and Chivalric Poems*, pp. 159–63 and 172–75.
64 Hadley Williams, *Lyndsay*, pp. 109–11.
65 Bawcutt, *Dunbar* I, B 47, lines 121–228; Bawcutt and Riddy *LSP*, pp. 269–78.
66 On tailor and soutars ('cobblers') and the common names 'Will' and 'Sym' assigned to Scott's antagonists, see Bawcutt, *Dunbar* II, 383 and 391 (headnote to 'Betuix twell houris and ellevin'). See also Stevenson, *Chivalry and Knighthood*, pp. 86–89.
67 Hadley Williams, *Lyndsay*, pp. 267–68.
68 Dunbar, 'Schir, 3it remember as befoir', B line 33, in Bawcutt, *Dunbar* I pp. 225–28; Gavin Douglas, *The Palis of Honoure*, ed. David J. Parkinson (Kalamazoo: MIP, 1992), lines 1711–12.
69 Aldo Scaglione, *Knights at Court: Courtliness, Chivalry and Courtesy from Ottonian Germany to the Italian Renaissance* (Berkeley, Los Angeles & Oxford: University of California Press, 1991), p. 21; Robert L. Kindrick, 'Kings and Rustics: Henryson's Definition of Nobility in

The Moral Fabillis', in Roderick J. Lyall and Felicity Riddy (eds), *Proceedings of the Third International Conference on Scottish Language and Literature (Medieval and Renaissance), University of Stirling, 2–7 July 1981* (Stirling & Glasgow, 1981), p. 281; Stevenson, *Chivalry and Knighthood*, pp. 148–50.

70 Norman Macdougall, *James III* (Edinburgh: John Donald, 2009), pp. 145–55. This is also the point of Dunbar's snide remarks about 'Raf Coilȝearis kynd and Iohnne the Reif' in B 'Schir, ȝit remember as befoir' (see note 68 above).

71 For more on these issues see D. J. B. Trim (ed.), *The Chivalric Ethos and the Rise of Military Professionalism* (Leiden: Brill, 2003).

8. Elegy and Commemorative Writing

1 E.g. 'Amra Choluim Chille', an elegy for St Columba (d. 597), edited T. O. Clancy and Gilbert Markús (eds), *Iona: The earliest poetry of a Celtic monastery* (Edinburgh: EUP, 1995), pp. 96–128.

2 Philip J. Ford, *George Buchanan: Prince of Poets* (Aberdeen: AUP, 1982), p. 173.

3 Martin MacGregor, 'Gaelic Barbarity and Scottish Identity in the Later Middle Ages', in Dauvit Broun and M. MacGregor (eds), *Mìoran mór nan Gall, 'The great ill-will of the Lowlander'? Lowland perceptions of the Highlands, medieval and modern* (Glasgow: Centre for Scottish and Celtic Studies, University of Glasgow, 2009), pp. 7–49.

4 V. B. Richmond, *Laments for the Dead in Medieval Narrative*, (Pittsburgh, PA: Duquesne Studies, 1966), pp. 29–39; A. M. Kinghorn, 'Death and the Makars: *Timor Mortis* in Scottish Poetry to 1600', *English Studies* 60 (1979), pp. 2–13.

5 Andrea Brady, *English Funerary Elegy in the Seventeenth Century* (Basingstoke: Palgrave MacMillan, 2009), p. 10.

6 W. Pigman, *Grief and English Renaissance Elegy* (Cambridge: CUP, 1985), p. 3; Dennis Kay, *Melodious Tears: The English Funeral Elegy from Spenser to Milton* (Oxford: OUP 1990), p. 4; Robert M. Cummings, 'The Poet as Hero: Sir Robert Aytoun on Thomas Reid and Raphael Thory', in Kevin J. McGinley and N. Royan (eds), *The Apparelling of Truth* (Newcastle: Cambridge Scholars Press, 2010), pp. 207–23.

7 For an edition of this work see R. Girvan (ed.), *Ratis Raving and Other Early Scots Poems on Morals*, STS (1939), Appendix, Item 1, *The Craft of Deyng*, pp. 166–74.

8 Christine M. Scollen, *The Birth of the Elegy in France, 1500–1550* (Geneva: Librarie Droz, S.A., 1967), pp. 13–37.

9   J. Martin (ed.), *The Maitland Quarto*, STS (2015), pp. 224–27.
10 E. Wingfield (ed.), *Complaint for the Death of Margaret, Princess of Scotland*, in R. Purdie and E. Wingfield (eds), *Six Scottish Courtly and Chivalric Poems* (Kalamazoo, MI: MIP, 2018).
11 See Fox, *Henryson*, pp. 132–53.
12 John Cartwright (ed.), *The Buik of King Alexander the Conqueror*, STS (1986–90).
13 Kathleen Cohen, *Metamorphosis of a Death Symbol* (Berkeley CA: University of California Press, 1973); Peter Sherlock, *Monuments and Memory in Early Modern England* (Aldershot: Ashgate, 2008), pp. 46–52.
14 *Henryson*, pp. 136–38, ll. 134–81.
15 Ford, *Buchanan*, p. 169.
16 Sebastiaan Verweij, 'The Manuscripts of William Fowler: A Revaluation of *The Tarantula of Love, A Sonnet Sequence*, and *Of Death*', *SSR* 8 (2007), 9–23, esp. pp. 11, 18–20.
17 *DOST*, Van(e), n. sense 6.
18 H.W. Meikle (ed.) *The Works of William Fowler* vol. 1, STS (1914), p. 233.
19 Bawcutt, *Dunbar*, pp. 336–37.
20 Cummings, 'Poet as Hero', p. 209.
21 Edinburgh, NLS, Adv. Lib. MS 35, pp. 6–7.
22 *Chron. Bower* 9, Perth Epitaph 1, pp. 128–30, Perth Epitaph 2, pp. 130–33.
23 *Chron. Bower* 9, Perth Epitaph 1, l. 8.
24 *Chron. Bower* 9, Perth Epitaph 1, ll. 37–38.
25 See, for example, the inset elegy for Wallace in Hary's poem, 'Allace Scotland, to quhom sall thou compleyn?', M. P. McDiarmid (ed.), *Hary's Wallace*, 2 vols., STS (1968–69), vol. 2, p. 112, lines 1109–28.
26 Jamie Cameron, *James V: The Personal Rule, 1528–42* (East Linton: Tuckwell Press, 1998), pp. 132–33.
27 Carol Edington, *Court and Culture in Renaissance Scotland: Sir David Lindsay of the Mount* (Amherst: University of Massachusetts Press,1995), p. 27.
28 *The Deploratioun of the Deith of Quene Magdalene*, in Williams, *Lyndsay* , pp. 101–08.
29 Douglas Gray, 'The Royal Entry in Sixteenth-Century Scotland', in Sally Mapstone and Juliette Wood (eds), *The Rose and the Thistle:* (East Linton: Tuckwell Press, 1998), pp. 10–37, esp. pp. 23–24.
30 Janet Hadley Williams, 'Lyndsay and Europe: Politics, Patronage, Printing', in Caie et al. *European Sun*, pp. 333–46, p. 340.
31 Bawcutt and Riddy *LSP*, pp. 302–09.

32 Bawcutt, *Dunbar*, pp. 301–02.
33 Priscilla Bawcutt, *Dunbar the Makar* (Oxford: OUP, 1992), pp. 84–87.
34 *Chron. Bower* 9, Perth Epitaph 1, l. 5.
35 *Chron. Bower* 9, Perth Epitaph 2, l. 1.
36 *Chron. Bower* 8, book 16, chapter 28, pp. 303–05.
37 *Chron. Bower* 9, Perth Epitaph 1, l. 15.
38 Joshua Scodel, *The English Poetic Epitaph* (Ithaca NY and London: Cornell University Press, 1991), p. 2.
39 J. Bain (ed.), *The Poems of Sir Richard Maitland of Lethington, Knight* (Glasgow: Maitland Club, 1830) p. 135; James Craigie (ed.) *The Poems of James VI of Scotland*, STS (1958), p. 162.
40 Craigie (ed.), *James VI*, p. 166.
41 R. J. Lyall, *Alexander Montgomerie* (Tempe AZ: ACMRS, 2005), pp. 157–59.
42 David Parkinson (ed.), *Alexander Montgomerie: Poems*, STS (2000), vol. 1, p. 99.
43 Mary Hobbs, *Early Seventeenth Century Verse Miscellany Manuscripts* (Aldershot: Ashgate, 1992), pp. 35–36.
44 A. A. MacDonald, 'Sir Richard Maitland and William Dunbar: Textual Symbiosis and Poetic Individuality', in *William Dunbar, The Nobill Poyet*, ed. Sally Mapstone (East Linton: Tuckwell Press, 2001), p. 139.
45 Martin (ed.), *Maitland Quarto*, pp. 268–72; Keith M. Brown, *Noble Society in Scotland.* (Edinburgh: EUP, 2000), pp. 222–24.
46 Full attributions appear in the Maitland Folio Manuscript. The Quarto attributions are abbreviated to 'T.H.' and 'R.H.'.
47 See Chapter 5, above.
48 "An epitaph [upon a grave-slab] could have contributed little to fame, since the persons in whose esteem the dead man wished to live, could seldom read. [Sculpted images], in conjunction with the poetical tales of their bards and sennachies, were so many helps to remembrance [instead]"; NLS MS 1644, Ramsay's manuscript on 'Highlanders and the Highlands', at fol. 87^r, printed in Alexander Allardyce (ed.), *Scotland and Scotsmen in the eighteenth century; from the mss. of John Ramsay, esq. of Ochtertyre – Vol. ii* (Edinburgh: William Blackwood and Sons, 1888), p. 426. Ramsay's exception to his rule is men of the clergy, such as the abbots of Iona; for commemorative sculpture in the western Gàidhealtachd, see most recently David Caldwell et. al., 'The image of a Celtic society: medieval West Highland sculpture', in Pamela O'Neill (ed.), *Celts in Legend and Reality* (Sydney: University of Sydney Press, 2010), pp. 13–59.

49 Rachel Bromwich, 'The keen for Art O'Leary: its background and its place in the tradition of Gaelic keening', *Éigse* 5 (1947–48), pp. 236–52; cf. Patricia Lysaght, '"Caoineadh os Cionn Coirp": The lament for the dead in Ireland', *Folklore* 108 (1997), pp. 65–82, and Dòmhnall Uilleam Stiùbhart, 'Keening in the Scottish Gàidhealtachd', in Peter Jupp (ed.), *Death in Scotland* (forthcoming, 2019).

50 Such as National Library of Scotland Adv. Lib. MS. 72.1.40; for a detailed discussion of this manuscript see Thomas Clancy, 'Die like a man? The Ulster Cycle death-tale anthology', *Aiste* 2 (2008), pp. 70–94.

51 E.g. Ronald Black, 'The genius of Cathal MacMhuirich', *TGSI* 50 (1976–8), pp. 327–67.

52 William Gillies, 'Gaelic: the classical tradition', in *AHSL*, pp. 245–63, esp. pp. 251–52. See also Gillies, Chapter 4, above.

53 E.g. John MacInnes, 'The panegyric code in Scottish Gaelic poetry and its historical background', *TGSI* 50 (1976–78), pp. 435–98.

54 Pía M. Coira, 'The Earl of Argyll and the *Goill*: the 'Flodden Poem' revisited', *SGS* 24 (2008), pp. 137–68, esp. p. 158; the contents of BDL may have been purged of other laments for those killed at Flodden – including, most remarkably, Donnchadh Campbell of Glenorchy – in an attempt to 'omit any possible reminders that the Scots had actually been defeated'. Cf. Martin MacGregor, 'The view from Fortingall: the worlds of the Book of the Dean of Lismore', *SGS* 22 (2006), pp. 35–87, esp. p. 74. A different interpretation of the poem is given by MacGregor in 'Ar sliocht Gaodhal ó Ghort Gréag: An Dàn "Flodden" ann an Leabhar Deadhan Lios-mòir', in Gillian Munro and Richard V. A. Cox (eds), *Cànan & Cultar: Rannsachadh na Gàidhlig* 4 (Edinburgh: SAP, 2010), pp. 23–35.

55 E.g. P. Breatnach, 'The chief's poet', *Proceedings of the Royal Irish Academy* 83/C (1983), pp. 37–79.

56 Wilson McLeod, *Divided Gaels: Gaelic Cultural Identities in Scotland and Ireland c. 1200–1650* (Oxford: OUP, 2004), pp. 79–81.

57 E.g. Gillies, 'Classical tradition', p. 250.

58 McLeod, *Divided Gaels*, p. 79.

59 E.g. K. A. Steer and J. W. M. Bannerman, *Late Medieval Monumental Sculpture in the Western Highlands* (Edinburgh: RCAHMS, 1977), p. 206.

60 MacGregor, 'View from Fortingall', pp. 53–54.

61 McLeod, *Divided Gaels*, pp. 70–1; cf. MacGregor, 'View from Fortingall', pp. 54–55.

62 William Gillies, 'Gun ann ach an ceò/ "Nothing left but their mist": Farewell and elegy in Gaelic poetry', in Mapstone, *Older Scots Literature*, pp. 370–96.
63 Watson, *Scottish Verse*, pp. 82–89 (i.e. ll. 781–867).
64 J. Carmichael Watson, 'Cathal Mac Muireadhaigh Cecinit', in E. Ó Riain (ed.), *Féil-Sgríbhinn Eóin Mhic Néill/ Essays and Studies presented to Professor Eoin MacNeill* (Dublin: Three Candles, 1940), pp. 170–71, vv. 8, 10, and 16.
65 C. Ó Baoill and Meg Bateman, *Gàir nan Clàrsach/ The Harp's Cry: an Anthology of Seventeenth-century Gaelic poetry* (Edinburgh: Birlinn, 1994), p. 78.
66 Carmichael Watson 'Cathal Mac Muireadhaigh Cecinit', p. 173, vv. 33–38; cf. Black, 'Cathal MacMhuirich', p. 339. Noah was a popular Old Testament comparator within bardic verse, probably due to claims made for the descent of the Milesian line from his family by 'Lebor Gabála', the twelfth-century *Book of Invasions* [of Ireland]; McLeod, *Divided Gaels*, p. 117.
67 McLeod, *Divided Gaels*, pp. 117, 118–24.
68 McLeod, *Divided Gaels*, p. 117.
69 A. MacBain and J. Kennedy (eds), *Reliquiae Celticae vol ii: Poetry, History and Philology* (Inverness: The Northern Counties Newspaper and Printing and Publishing Company Ltd., 1894), p. 222; McLeod, *Divided Gaels*, p. 133.
70 'Òran do Dhòmhnall Gorm', in A. MacKenzie (ed.), *Òrain Iain Lom/ The Songs of John MacDonald* (Edinburgh: Oliver and Boyd, 1964), pp. 14–19, ll. 134–36.
71 MacBain and Kennedy, *Reliquiae Celticae ii*, p. 236.
72 Watson, *Scottish Verse*, pp. 277–78 (text at pp. 82–89, ll. 781–872).
73 Watson, *Scottish Verse*, pp. 277–78; cf. Thomas Owen Clancy, 'Court, king and justice in the Ulster Cycle', in Fulton, *Medieval Celtic Literature and Society*. pp. 163–83.
74 Clancy, 'Ulster Cycle', p. 164.
75 Cf. Norman MacDougall, 'Achilles heel? The earldom of Ross, the lordship of the Isles and the Stewart kings, 1449–1507', in E. J. Cowan and R. Andrew MacDonald (eds), *Alba* (East Linton: Tuckwell Press, 2000), pp. 248–75, esp. pp. 262–64.
76 Clancy, 'Ulster Cycle', p. 163.
77 Clancy, 'Ulster Cycle', p. 164; text of apologue in Neil Ross, *Heroic Poetry from the Book of the Dean of Lismore* (Edinburgh: Oliver and Boyd, 1939), pp. 168–75.

78 Cf. Angela Bourke, 'More in anger than in sorrow: Irish women's lament poetry', in J. Newton Radner and S Lanser (eds), *Feminist Messages: Coding Strategies in Women's Folklore* (Champaign-Urbana, IL: University of Illinois Press, 1993), pp. 160–82, esp. pp. 160–61.
79 Derick S. Thomson, 'The Mac Mhuirich bardic family', *TGSI* 43 (1960–63), pp. 276–304, at pp. 287–88.
80 Watson, *Scottish Verse*, ll. 959–60.
81 Watson, *Scottish Verse* ll. 789–90.
82 James Ross, 'The sub-literary tradition in Scottish Gaelic song-poetry', *Éigse* 7 (1954–5), pp. 217–31, and James Ross, 'The sub-literary tradition in Scottish Gaelic song-poetry', *Éigse* 8 (1955–6), pp. 1–17.
83 M. Pía Coira, *By Poetic Authority: the Rhetoric of Panegyric in Gaelic Poetry of Scotland to 1700* (Edinburgh: Dunedin Academic Press, 2012), p. 36.
84 P. Mac Cana, 'The poet as spouse of his patron' *Ériu* 39 (1988), pp. 79–85.
85 K. Simms, 'The poet as chieftain's widow: Bardic elegies', in Donnchadh Ó Corrain, Liam Breatnach, and Kim McCone (eds), *Saints, Sages and Storytellers* (Maynooth: An Sagart, 1989), pp. 400–12.
86 Cf. Máirín Ní Dhonnchadha, 'Travellers and settled folk: Women, honour and shame in Medieval Ireland', in Sarah Sheehan and Ann Dooley (eds), *Constructing Gender in Medieval Ireland* (New York: Palgrave Macmillan, 2013) pp. 17–38.
87 James Carney, *Studies in Irish Literature and History* (Dublin: Dublin Institute for Advanced Studies, 1955), pp. 243–76.
88 Thomas Owen Clancy, 'Women poets in early medieval Ireland: Stating the case', in Christine Meek and Katharine Simms (eds), *The Fragility of her Sex? Medieval Irishwomen in their European Context* (Dublin: Four Courts Press, 1996), pp. 43–72.
89 M. Tymoczko, 'A poetry of masks: the poet's persona in early Celtic poetry', in Kathryn A. Klar, E. E. Sweetser, and Claire Thomas (eds), *A Celtic Florilegium* (Lawrence, MA: Celtic Studies Publications, 1996), pp. 187–210.
90 Gillies, 'Classical tradition', pp. 252–53.
91 Glasgow University Library, Gen 1042, MS 152, printed in J. Kennedy, 'Poems from the MacLagan MSS', *TGSI* 22 (1897–98), pp. 168–92, at p. 172 (cf. William Gillies, 'Clan Donald bards and scholars', in *Cànan & Cultar*, pp. 108–09). I am grateful to Professor Gillies and Dr Dòmhnall Uilleam Stiùbhart for this reference. Deirdre's overwhelming grief for her loss of Noísiu and his brothers became a literary standard

by which others' extreme mourning could be quantified, akin to the strength of her love itself; cf. Kate L. Mathis, 'Mourning the *maic Uislenn*: Blood, death and grief in *Longes mac n-Uislenn* and "Oidheadh Chloinne hUisneach"', *SGS* 29 (2013), pp. 1–21, and '"Tha Mulad Air M'Inntinn" and Early Modern Gaelic dialogue poetry', *Aiste* 5 (forthcoming).

92 Kate L. Mathis, 'An Ulster Tale in Breadalbane? Personae and literary allusion in the poetry of Mòr Chaimbeul', *Aiste* 2 (2008), pp. 43–69, esp. pp. 45, 52–62.

93 MacBain and Kennedy, *Reliquiae Celticae ii*, pp. 232, 234, 236, vv. 6, 19, 21. I am grateful to Professor Gillies for permitting me to refer to his forthcoming edition of Cathal MacMhuirich's elegy to the four chieftains of Clanranald (from RMS MCR 39, 85–94).

94 Cf. Mathis, 'Mourning the *maic Uislenn*'.

95 Cf. Tymoczko, 'Poetry of masks', p. 189.

96 Cf. Anja Gunderloch, 'Donnchadh Bàn's Òran do Bhlàr na h-Eaglaise Brice – literary allusion and political comment', *SGS* 20 (2000), pp. 97–117, esp. pp. 99–103.

97 Colm Ó Baoill, 'Bàs Iain Luim', *SGS* 16 (1990), pp. 91–94.

98 'Murt na Ceapaich', in MacKenzie, *Òrain Iain Lom*, ll. 990–97.

99 Roxanne Reddington-Wilde, 'Violent death and damning words: Women's lament in Scottish Gaelic poetry', in Ronald Black, William Gillies, and Roibeard Ó Maolalaigh (eds), *Celtic Connections: Proceedings of the Tenth International Congress of Celtic Studies Vol. 1: Language, literature, history, culture* (East Linton: Tuckwell Press, 1999), pp. 265–87, esp. p. 282.

100 The blood-imagery, though not the element of burial, occurs also in a contemporary lament for the brothers said to have been composed by their sister, 'Ni Mhic Raonuill', i.e. another child of the twelfth chieftain of Keppoch, Dòmhnall Glas (d. c. 1651). Observing the aftermath of their deaths she exclaims: 'Dh' fhosgail mi dorus ur seòmair; / Thàinig ur fuil thar mo bhrògan! / 'S teann nach d' òl mi-fhìn mo leòr dh'i' (MacKenzie, *Òrain Iain Lom*, p. 281, 'Your chamber's door I opened; / Your blood spilled over my shoes! / I barely refrained from drinking my fill').

101 Seven men were indicted by the Privy Council for the crime, for which all were beheaded (MacKenzie, *Òrain Iain Lom*, pp. 272–3); Iain Lom's graphic description of their execution suggests that he was present: ''N deidh am plaosgach fhuair bhur ploicne, / Claigne 'gam faoisgneadh a copar, / Mar chinn laogh an déidh am plotadh' ('An

Ciaran Mabach', ll. 1635–36, 'Your skulls had the flesh / boiled off them in copper pots, / like calves' heads after they have been steeped in hot water').

102 Martin MacGregor, '"Surely one of the greatest poems ever made in Britain": The lament for Griogair Ruadh MacGregor of Glen Strae and its historical background', in E. J. Cowan and D. Gifford (eds), *The Polar Twins* (Edinburgh: John Donald, 1999), pp. 114–53.

103 MacGregor, 'Lament', pp. 118–25.

104 Mathis, 'Ulster Tale in Breadalbane', pp. 56–60; cf. Derick S. Thomson, 'The blood-drinking motif in Scottish Gaelic tradition', in Roland Bielmeier and Reinhard Stempel (eds), *Indogermanica et Caucasica: Festschrift für Karl Horst Schmidt zum 65 Geburtstag* (Berlin and New York: Walter de Gruyter, 1994), pp. 415–24; cf. Mathis, 'Mourning the maic Uislenn'.

105 Mathis, '"Tha Mulad Air M'Inntinn"', note 5.

106 Barbara Hillers, 'Dialogue or monologue? Lullabies in Scottish Gaelic tradition', in Michel Byrne, Thomas Owen Clancy, and Sheila Kidd (eds), *Litreachas & Eachdraidh: Rannsachadh na Gàidhlig 2/ Literature and History: Papers from the second conference of Scottish Gaelic studies* (Glasgow: Roinn na Cnanan Ceilteach, 2005), pp. 33–56.

107 C. Ó Baoill, *Màiri nighean Alasdair Ruaidh: Song-maker of Skye and Berneray* (Llandysul: Gwasg Gomer for the SGTS, 2014), pp. 1–2.

108 Ó Baoill, *Màiri nighean Alasdair Ruaidh*, pp. 8, 137; John MacInnes, 'Gaelic songs of Mary MacLeod', SGS 11 (1966), pp. 3–23, at pp. 9–10.

109 Ó Baoill and Bateman, *Gàir nan Clàrsach*, pp. 112–17. Meg Bateman points out (p. 112) that the song, whose loose structure is similar to a typical waulking song ('òrain luaidh'), has several widely divergent versions within the oral tradition. It is possible that, similar to the dissemination of 'Grioghal Cridhe' and its gradual detachment from the historical circumstances of its composition, the lament associated with Fionnghal Campbell's grief for her brother may represent a later response to the memory of her perceived ordeal as a whole (cf. MacGregor, 'Lament'). For the waulking tradition, see J. Campbell and F. Collinson (eds), *Hebridean Folksongs* vol. 1 (Oxford: OUP, 1969), pp. 3–16, and Morag Macleod, 'Gaelic Song', in Alexander Fenton and Margaret MacKay (eds), *An Introduction to Scottish Ethnology* (Edinburgh: John Donald, 2013), pp. 257–77, at pp. 266–69.

110 Ó Baoill and Bateman, *Gàir nan Clàrsach*, p. 112; cf. Sorley Maclean, 'Obscure and anonymous Gaelic poetry', in Loraine Maclean (ed.),

The Seventeenth Century in the Highlands (Inverness: Inverness Field Club, 1986), pp. 89–105, at p. 97.

111 Ó Baoill and Bateman, *Gàir nan Clàrsach*, p. 114. MacDonald's agency for Campbell of Auchinbreck's death is asserted by a contemporary waulking song, 'Òran Luathaidh do Alasdair Mac Colla', printed in A. MacDonald and A MacDonald (eds), *The MacDonald Collection of Gaelic Poetry* (Inverness: The Northern Counties Newspaper and Printing and Publishing Company Ltd, 1911), pp. 40–42; cf. MacKenzie, *Òrain Iain Lom*, p. 241.

112 Ó Baoill and Bateman, *Gàir nan Clàrsach*, p. 114.

113 Printed in Alexander Maclean Sinclair, *Mactalla nan Tùr* (Sydney, Cape Breton: Mactalla Publishing Co. Ltd., 1901), pp. 92–93, with the colophon ''S e Caimbeulach a bha am Fear Ghlinne-Faochain. A reir coltais 's i a bhean aige a rinn an t-oran' ('The lord of Glen Faochain was a Campbell. In all likelihood, it was his wife who made the song'); cf. J. L. Campbell, *Songs remembered in exile* (Edinburgh: Birlinn, 1999), pp. 205–06, and Coira, *By Poetic Authority*, pp. 147–48.

114 MacKenzie, *Òrain Iain Lom*, pp. 20–25, ll. 270–73.

115 'Cumha Mhontrois', in MacKenzie, *Òrain Iain Lom*, pp. 56–59, ll. 691–701 (cf. pp. 259–61).

116 William Gillies, 'The Gaelic poems of Sir Duncan Campbell of Glenorchy (II)', *SGS* 13/2 (1981), pp. 263–88, at pp. 263–76.

117 William Gillies, 'The Gaelic poems of Sir Duncan Campbell of Glenorchy (I)', *SGS* 13/1 (1978), pp. 18–45, p. 18.

118 Gillies, 'Campbell of Glenorchy (II)', p. 263.

119 Watson, *Scottish Verse*, p. 285.

120 McLeod, *Divided Gaels*, pp. 94–95, 156. For the poems attributed elsewhere in the manuscript to the authorship of 'Ailéin Mac Ruaidhrí', see Donald Meek, 'The death of Diarmait in Scottish and Irish Tradition', *Celtica* 21 (1990), pp. 335–61, at p. 358.

121 MacGregor, 'The View from Fortingall', p. 53.

122 Watson, *Scottish Verse*, l. 1233.

123 Watson, *Scottish Verse*, p. 285.

124 Watson, *Scottish Verse*, p. 285; cf. Gillies, 'Classical tradition', p. 257.

125 E.g. W. F. H. Nicolaisen, *Scottish Place-names* (London: B. T. Batsford, 1976), pp. 121–48; G. W. S. Barrow, 'The lost Gàidhealtachd of medieval Scotland', in William Gillies (ed.), *Alba agus a' Ghàidhlig/ Gaelic and Scotland*, (Edinburgh: EUP, 1989), pp. 67–89; cf. McLeod, *Divided Gaels*, pp. 20–29; Martin MacGregor, 'Writing the history of Gaelic

Scotland: a provisional checklist of "Gaelic" genealogical histories', *SGS* 24 (2008), pp. 357–81, at pp. 358–61.
126 E.g. MacGregor, 'The view from Fortingall', pp. 65–70.
127 McLeod, *Divided Gaels*, pp. 66–70.
128 MacGregor, 'The view from Fortingall', p. 38.
129 Watson, *Scottish Verse* p. 271 (text at pp. 60–64). The precise date of Niall's death is unclear. A charter affirming his possession of lands on Gigha was issued by John IV of the Isles in 1455 (Jean Munro and R. Munro, *Acts of the Lords of the Isles, 1336–1493* (Edinburgh: Printed for the Scottish History Society by Blackwood, Pillans, & Wilson, 1986), #60, p. 88); by 1472, his brother Hector is styled constable of Sween instead (#102, p. 104), in which capacity he seems to have been acting as guardian of Niall's son, Malcolm, who achieved his own majority in or before 1478 (#113, p. 182).
130 Watson, *Scottish Verse*, l. 571. Pía Coira observes that, 'quite exceptionally' for poems of this kind, '[Aithbhreac] makes no [direct] allusions to his warrior skills'; *By poetic authority*, p. 195.
131 A eulogy composed for her husband by Cathal MacMhuirich, c. 1595, addresses its final four verses to Màiri, allegedly in the prime of life and a source of praise by many poets; Black, 'Cathal MacMhuirich', p. 328 (text at pp. 344–52, vv. 35–38).
132 Glasgow University Library, Gen 1042, MS 70, v. 1e–f, printed in *The MacDonald Collection*, pp. 26–29; a slightly different version was selected by Margaret Cameron for the appendix of 'sean orain' ('old songs') which followed twenty of her own poems in the first solely female-authored collection of published Gaelic verse: *Òrain Nuadh Ghaidhealach le Marairead Cham'ron* (Edinburgh: D. Mac-Phatraic for the author, 1785), pp. 58–60.
133 Derick S. Thomson, *The MacDiarmid MS Anthology* (Edinburgh: SAP, 1992), pp. 268–69; cf. his discussion of burial imagery in *An Introduction to Gaelic Poetry* (London: Victor Gollancz, 1974), pp. 85–87.
134 'Marbhrann forsair Choire an t-Sithe', printed in Archibald Sinclair, *The Gaelic Songster: An t-Òranaiche, No Òrain ùr agus shean, a' chuid mhòr dhuibh nach robh riamh roimhe ann an clò* (Glasgow: Archibald Sinclair, 1879), pp. 515–17; the subject may have been a soldier in the army of Gilleasbuig Caoch, i.e. Archibald Campbell, eighth Earl and first Marquis of Argyll (d. 1661); cf. C. Ó Baoill, 'Robert Campbell, Forsair Choire an t-Sìth', *SGS* 23 (2007), pp. 57–84.

135 A similar claim for declining appearance is made by Sìleas na Ceapaich (c. 1660–c. 1729) in one of several elegies for her husband and their daughter, Anna: 'ona chaidh sibh an taisgeadh / 'S goirt a chaochail mo chraiceann a shnuadh' ('since you [pl.] have gone to your coffin my skin has altered its complexion terribly'); C. Ó Baoill (ed.), *Bàrdachd Shìlis na Ceapaich: Poems and Songs by Sìleas MacDonald* (Edinburgh: SGTS, 1972), ll. 681–82; cf. Kate L. Mathis, 'Presence, absence, and audience: The elegies of Sìleas na Ceapaich "At Home" and "Abroad"', in Sierra Dye, Elizabeth Ewan, and Alice Glaze (eds), *Gender and Mobility in Scotland and Abroad* (Guelph: Guelph Centre for Scottish Studies, 2018), pp. 185–204.

136 Angela Partridge, 'Wild men and wailing women', *Éigse* 18 (1980–1), pp. 25–37, esp. pp. 29–31.

137 *The MacDonald Collection*, vv. 12–14.

138 Cf. Edward Dwelly, *The Illustrated Gaelic-English Dictionary* (Glasgow: Gairm Publications, 1994), s.v. lom-sguabadh: 'a clean sweep; devastation', perhaps in the sense that she has been drained of emotion by the intensity of her earlier grief.

139 'Marbhrann do Shir Seumas Mac Dhomnaill', in MacKenzie, *Òrain Iain Lom*, ll. 1746–8. Sir James MacDonald, ninth of Sleat, died in December 1678; his predecessor, Alasdair Buidhe, brother to Dòmhnall Glas, twelfth MacDonald of Keppoch (d. c. 1651), drowned in the river Spean c. 1670 (ibid., pp. 289–90). Two of Alasdair's sons had been executed on suspicion of the murder of his nephews, Alasdair and Raghnall, whom Iain Lom had also mourned in 1663 (as note 101, above).

140 MacGregor, 'Lament', p. 143, v. 12; cf. Heather Larson, 'Keening, crooning and casting spells: Women, sleep and folk genres in medieval Irish poetry', *Proceedings of the Harvard Celtic Colloquium* 18/19 (1998), pp. 134–50, esp. p. 144.

141 E.g. 'Marbhrann do Fhearchar Bàn MacRath, Fear Inbhir-ìonaid, 1711, le Donnchadh Mòr MacRath', ed. Nancy McGuire, *The Dornie Manuscripts* (PhD thesis, University of Aberdeen, 2001), pp. 45–47 (vv. 2, 6).

142 Explored in K. Simms, 'Women in Gaelic Society during the age of transition', in Margaret Mac Curtain and M. O'Dowd (eds), *Women in Early Modern Ireland* (Edinburgh: EUP, 1991), pp. 32–42; Dòmhnall Uilleam Stiùbhart, 'Women and Gender in the Early Modern Western Gàidhealtachd', in Elizabeth Ewan and Margaret M. Meikle (eds), *Women in Scotland c. 1100–c. 1750* (East Linton: Tuckwell Press, 1999), pp. 233–49, esp. pp. 241–46.

143 E.g. 'Gaoir nam Ban Muileach', Mairghread's impassioned lament for Sir Iain Maclean of Duart (d. 1716); C. Ó Baoill, *Mairghread nighean Lachlainn: Song-maker of Mull* SGTS (2009), pp. 72–86. Màiri mourned several Macleod and MacKenzie noblemen, beginning perhaps c. 1646 with the death of Ruairidh MacKenzie of Applecross (Ó Baoill, *Màiri nighean Alasdair Ruaidh*, pp. 26–35).

144 William Gillies, 'Traditional Gaelic women's songs', in Marco Fazzini (ed.), *Alba Literaria* (Venice: Amos Edizioni, 2005), pp. 165–78; Anne Frater 'The Gaelic tradition up to 1750', in D. Gifford and D. McMillan (eds), *A History of Scottish Women's Writing* (Edinburgh: EUP, 1997), pp. 1–15.

145 Gillies, 'Clan Donald bards', p. 108.

146 *The MacDonald Collection*, pp. 172–73.

147 Ó Baoill and Bateman, *Gàir nan Clàrsach*, pp. 74–77.

148 Thomson, *MacDiarmid MS*, pp. 273–75. The subject of this poem has become confused in transmission with the elegy, discussed above, for the MacCallum buried in Kingussie, but they are clearly laments for two different men (cf. Ó Baoill, 'Robert Campbell').

149 Margaret Cameron's (fl. 1780s–1810s) lament for Dòmhnall MacPhàrlain of Àth a' Chrathaidh (Achray, near Stirling) suggests that Gilleaspuig's favoured method of catching fish – in darkness, shining a torch upon the water's surface – remained in use at the close of eighteenth century: 'Cumhadh Dhomhnul Mac-Pharlain Choillechratha', in *Òrain Nuadh Ghaidhealach*, v. 14. I am grateful to Ruairidh Maciver for this reference; for Margaret Cameron's corpus, see Maciver, 'Concentric loyalties: Responses to the military in Gaelic women's poetry', *Proceedings of the Harvard Celtic Colloquium* 36 (2016), pp. 105–26.

150 The author of the Killiecrankie lament, for example, compares her grief to his, alongside Deirdre's (Kennedy, 'MacLagan MSS', v. 2); cf. Coira, *By Poetic Authority*, pp. 112, 180.

151 Thomas Owen Clancy, 'Mourning Fearchar Ó Maoilchiaráin: texts, transmission and transformation', in Wilson Mcleod, Anja Gunderloch, and James E. Fraser (eds), *Cànan & Culture/Language and Culture: Rannsachadh na Gàidhlig* 3 (Edinburgh: Dunedin Academic Press, 2006), pp. 57–73, esp. p. 57.

152 Stiùbhart, 'Women and Gender', esp. p. 241.

153 Black, 'Cathal MacMhuirich', p. 333; William J. Watson, 'Classic Gaelic poetry of panegyric in Scotland', *TGSI* 29 (1914–1919), pp. 194–235, at pp. 225–26 (vv. 2, 12).

154 Black, 'Cathal MacMhuirich', pp. 334–35 (text in Ó Baoill and Bateman, *Gàir nan Clàrsach*, pp. 94–99).
155 Michael Newton, 'Early poetry in the MacGregor papers', *SGS* 21 (2003), pp. 47–59, esp. pp. 49–54; cf. Alasdair Duncan, 'Some MacGregor songs', (M.Litt. dissertation, University of Edinburgh, 1979).
156 Maclean, 'Obscure and anonymous', p. 95 (text in Ó Baoill and Bateman, *Gàir nan Clàrsach*, pp. 54–58).
157 MacGregor, 'The view from Fortingall', pp. 68, 74.
158 John Bannerman, 'The Maclachlans of Kilbride and their manuscripts', *ScotStud* 21 (1977), pp. 1–35, esp. pp. 10–11; the poem is printed as 'Le Fear Chillebhride air bas Chrombail, 1658' in *The MacDonald collection*, p. 152.
159 Ó Baoill and Bateman, *Gàir nan Clàrsach*, pp. 130–35; printed also in MacKenzie, *Òrain Iain Lom*, pp. 56–59, as 'Cumha Mhontrois'.
160 Ó Baoill and Bateman, *Gàir nan Clàrsach*, p. 132. Given the skill in verse and obvious devotion to her subject displayed by Diorbhail Nic a' Bhruthainn (Dorothy Brown) in her panegyric to Mac Colla c. 1644, it is possible that she also lamented his death, but no such poems have survived. Her panegyric was printed in 1813 (Paruig Mac-an-Tuairneir, *Comhchruinneacha do dh'orain taghta Ghaidhealach* (Edinburgh: T. Stiubhard, 1813), pp. 86–89; cf. John MacKenzie, *Sar Obair nam Bard Gaelach: the Beauties of Gaelic Poetry and Lives of the Highland Bards* (Glasgow: MacGregor, Polson & Co., 1841), p. 63).
161 Ó Baoill, *Bàrdachd Shìlis na Ceapaich*, pp. 64–69; cf. Mathis, 'Presence'.

9. Satire

1 Ruben Quintero (ed.), *A Companion to Satire* (Oxford: Blackwell, 2007), p. 9. Other helpful discussions of satire include: Brian A. Connery and Kirk Combe (eds), *Theorizing Satire: Essays in Literary Criticism* (New York: St Martin's Press, 1995); Robert C. Elliott, *The Power of Satire: Magic, Ritual, Art* (Princeton: Princeton University Press, 1960); Northrop Frye, *Anatomy of Criticism* (Princeton: Princeton University Press, 1957); Dustin Griffin, *Satire: A Critical Reintroduction* (Lexington, KY: University Press of Kentucky, 1994); Matthew Hodgart, *Satire* (New York: McGraw-Hill, 1969); Laura Kendrick, 'Medieval Satire', in William T. H. Jackson (ed.), *European Writers: The Middle Ages and the Renaissance, Vol. 1* (New York: Scribner's, 1983), pp. 337–75; Alvin P. Kernan, *The Cankered Muse* (New Haven, CT: Yale University Press, 1959).

2   Kendrick, 'Medieval Satire', p. 52.
3   Roderick Lyall, 'Complaint, Satire, and Invective in Middle Scots Literature', in Norman Macdougall (ed.), *Church, Politics and Society: Scotland 1408-1929* (Edinburgh: John Donald, 1983), pp. 44-64 (p. 47).
4   Quintero, *Companion*, pp. 5-6.
5   Several scholars contend that satire had its roots in magic, see Fred Norris Robinson, 'Satirists and Enchanters in Early Irish Literature', D. G. Lyon and G. F. Moor (eds), *Studies in the History of Religion presented to C. H. Toy* (New York: Macmillan, 1912), pp. 95-130 and Robert C. Elliott, *The Power of Satire: Magic, Ritual, Art* (Princeton: Princeton UP, 1960).
6   In Richard Holland's *The Buke of the Howlat* (ed. R. Hanna, STS (2014), l. 811), the rook-bard from Ireland is also associated with spell-winding: 'The barde worth brane-wod and bitterly couth ban'.
7   Roisin McLaughlin, *Early Irish Satire*, (Dublin: Institute for Advanced Studies, 2008) p. 5.
8   See Gillies in chapter on Purpose, above.
9   See Whitley Stokes (ed. and trans.), 'The Siege of Howth', *Revue Celtique* 8 (1887), pp. 47-64.
10 See Whitley Stokes (ed. and trans.), 'The Second Battle of Moytura', *Revue Celtique* 12 (1891), pp. 52-130, 306-08.
11 William Gillies, 'Gaelic: The Classical Tradition', in *AHSL*, p. 245.
12 Gillies, 'Purpose', above.
13 Gillies, 'Classical Tradition', p. 247.
14 Gillies, 'Classical Tradition', p. 257.
15 Howard Meroney, 'Studies in Early Irish Satire', *Journal of Celtic Studies* 1 (1950), pp. 199-226, lists three types of satire: aisnéis (*declaration in prose, without rhyme*), ail (*insult*), and aircetal aíre, (*incantation, verse*) of which ten sub-types exist.
16 Watson, *Scottish Verse*, number xvi. This mock elegy is discussed in William Gillies, 'Gun ann ach an ceò: "Nothing left but their Mist" Farewell and Elegy in Gaelic Poetry', Mapstone, *Older Scots Literature*, pp. 370-96. See Martin and Mathis, Chapter 8, above.
17 William Gillies, 'Courtly and Satiric Poems in the Book of the Dean of Lismore', *ScotStud* 21 (1977), pp. 35-53, esp. p. 39.
18 See Ó Mainnín, above.
19 See Edmund Leach, 'Anthropological Aspects of Language: Animal Categories and Verbal Abuse', in E. H. Lenneberg (ed.), *New Directions in the Study of Language* (Cambridge, MA: MIT. Press, 1964), pp. 23-63.

20 "Manner" is Jonathan Glenn's terminology, who subdivides Dunbar's poetry into modes (types of discourse) and manners (approach taken to a particular matter), see Jonathan Glenn, 'Classifying Dunbar: Modes, Manners and Styles', in S. Mapstone (ed.), *William Dunbar, 'The Nobill Poyet'*, (East Linton: Tuckwell, 2001), pp. 167–82. Conlee, in the introduction to his edition of Dunbar's works, contends that 'above all else Dunbar is a satirist' and maintains that a 'large number of his [=Dunbar's] poems are undoubtedly satiric': John Conlee, *William Dunbar, The Complete Works*, (Kalamazoo MI: MIP, 2004).

21 Bawcutt, *Dunbar*, B 67.

22 A negative portrayal of the owl can also be found in Holland's *Buke of the Howlat* (c. 1450) in which the owl's pride and ambition are punished when the gift of feathers she has received is revoked.

23 Dunbar uses similar stereotypical denominations of Highlanders/Gaels in his *Flyting* ('commoun theif', 'crop and rute of traitouris tressonable', etc.).

24 Bawcutt, *Dunbar*, B 4.

25 Glenn, 'Classifying Dunbar', p. 175.

26 Bawcutt. *Dunbar*, B 72.

27 Bawcutt, *Dunbar*, B 67.

28 The satire classified as 'mac bronn' ('*son of a womb*') in the Book of Ballymote is a good example of this. In the Book of the Dean of Lismore, Donnchadh Óg Albanach describes satire as burning under his skin when he cannot communicate it, but, as it is ripe, he will not spare its victims, but let the poison out. For a transcription and translation of the text see David Greene's article 'Mac Bronn', *Éigse* 5 (1945–47), pp. 232–35.

29 This notion was particularly strong in fifteenth- and sixteenth-century English satirical theory and also discussed by writers such as George Puttenham, *The Art of English Poesy*, ed. F. Whigham and W. A. Rebhorn (Ithaca NY: Cornell University Press, 2007), pp. 120–21.

30 Bawcutt, *Dunbar*, B 9.

31 Bawcutt, *Dunbar*, B 43 and B 75.

32 Bawcutt, *Dunbar*, B 73.

33 Bawcutt, *Dunbar*, B 2.

34 Bawcutt, *Dunbar*, B 3.

35 Poem number I in Nicole Meier (ed.), *The Poems of Walter Kennedy*, STS (2008).

36 Priscilla Bawcutt, *Dunbar the Makar* (Oxford: Clarendon Press, 1992), p. 346.

37 Fox, *Henryson*, pp. 9–19.
38 Fox, *Henryson*, pp. 92–97.
39 Fox, *Henryson*, pp. 47–54.
40 Fox, *Henryson*, pp. 97–103.
41 See J. H. Burns, *The True Law of Kingship* (Oxford: Clarendon Press, 1996), p. 95. See also Lyall's definitions in 'Complaint, Satire and Invective'.
42 See Lyall, 'Complaint, Satire and Invective', 60.
43 For an overview of Lyndsay and his works, see Hadley Williams *Lyndsay*; line citations from Lyndsay's poetry are from this edition. For an in-depth study of Lyndsay in his political and religious context, see Carol Edington, *Court and Culture in Renaissance Scotland: Sir David Lindsay of the Mount* (Amherst: University of Massachusetts Press, 1995).
44 Burns, *True Law of Kingship*, p. 98.
45 See also Royan, above.
46 Greg Walker wisely cautions about applying this equation too strictly in Lyndsay's works. He argues that in *Ane Satyre of the Thrie Estaitis*, the body politic is *not* 'coterminous with the body natural (or allegorical) of the prince': if Scotland is to be revitalised, 'If morality is to triumph it must be through parliamentary legislation and reform, and the re-integration of excluded underclasses into the political community' (223). 'Flytyng in the Face of Convention: Protest and Innovation in Lindsay's *Satyre of the Thrie Estaitis*', in Peter Happé and Wim Hüsken (eds), *Interludes and Early Modern Society* (Amsterdam and New York: Rodopi, 2007), pp. 211–38.
47 Hadley Williams, *Lyndsay*, p. xviii.
48 The most accessible modern edition, with an excellent introduction, is Roderick Lyall (ed.), *Ane Satyre of the Thrie Estaitis* (Edinburgh: Canongate, 1989). Line citations are from this edition.
49 See Lyall, *Ane Satyre*, pp. vii–xiv, for an account of early performances.
50 Walker, 'Flyting', p. 213.
51 See Lyall, *Ane Satyre*, p. xxxi, for a discussion of why Lyndsay might have chosen to end the play with the disorder of Foly's appearance.
52 Ibid., p. 216.
53 T. Thomson and C. Innes (eds), *Acts of the Parliaments of Scotland, 1424–1707*, 12 vols. (Edinburgh: Record Commission, 1814–75), vol. 2, p. 552.

54 James Cranstoun (ed.), *Satirical Poems of the Time of the Reformation*, 2 vols. STS (1891–93), I, p. xi. Hereafter, poems are cited parenthetically using Cranstoun's Roman numeral and line number (e.g., IV.23–24).

55 With important exceptions: work has certainly been begun, though not exhausted, by Priscilla Bawcutt, 'Crossing the Border: Scottish Poetry and English Readers in the Sixteenth Century', in Sally Mapstone and Juliette Wood (eds), *The Rose and the Thistle* (East Linton: Tuckwell Press, 1998), pp. 59–76; Gregory Kratzmann, 'Political Satire and the Scottish Reformation', *SSL* 26 (1991), pp. 423–37; Kratzmann, 'Sixteenth-Century Secular Poetry', in *AHSL* pp. 105–23; Roderick Lyall, 'Complaint, Satire and Invective'; David Parkinson, '"The Legend of the Bischop of St. Androis Lyfe" and the Survival of Scottish Poetry', *Early Modern Literary Studies* 9.1 (May 2003), pp. 1–24; and Tricia A. McElroy, 'Imagining the "Scottis Natioun": Populism and Propaganda in Scottish Satirical Broadsides', *Texas Studies in Literature and Language* 49.4 (Winter 2007), pp. 319–39.

56 Sir William Drury, Elizabeth's border marshal, sent the surviving copy of this poem to William Cecil. In a note, Drury indicated that 'Robert Symple ys the dooer hereoff', while Cecil endorsed the poem as 'An answer to the Bills sett upp against the Regent of Scotland', James Stewart, the Earl of Moray. National Archives, State Papers 52/14/74.

57 Lyall, 'Complaint, Satire and Invective', p. 47.

58 Griffin, *Satire*, p. 132.

59 For discussion of Maddie's appearance in the poems, see Lyall, 'Complaint, Satire and Invective' and McElroy, 'Populism and Propaganda'.

60 For remarks on the transformation of literary models during the Scottish Reformation, see Lyall, 'Complaint, Satire and Invective'; A. A. MacDonald, 'Scottish Poetry of the Reign of Mary Stewart', in Caie et al, *European Sun*, pp. 44–61; and David Parkinson, '"A Lamentable Storie": Mary Queen of Scots and the Inescapable *Querelle des Femmes*', in Houwen et al, *Palace in the Wild*, pp. 141–60

61 P. Hume Brown (ed.), *Vernacular Writings of Buchanan* STS (1892), p. 46.

62 Hume Brown, *Buchanan*, pp. 39–40.

63 The 'Pretended Conference' survives in three manuscript copies and may be found most easily in *The Bannatyne Miscellany*, vol. 1 (Edinburgh, 1827), pp. 33–50; and in Richard Bannatyne's *Memorials*

of Transactions in Scotland, 1569–1573 (Edinburgh: Bannatyne Club, 1836), pp. 5–13. Quotations are from *The Bannatyne Miscellany*, noted parenthetically. 'The Dialogue of the Twa Wyfeis' survives in only one manuscript copy, National Archives, State Papers 52/17/70. 'The Dialogue' has never been printed; quotations are from my own transcription, noted by manuscript page.

64 Mark Loughlin, '"The Dialogue of the Twa Wyfeis": Maitland, Machiavelli and the Propaganda of the Scottish Civil War', in A. A. MacDonald et al, *Renaissance in Scotland*, pp. 226–45, at p. 237. Loughlin provides the most thorough discussion of the 'Dialogue'. Roger Mason provides another valuable perspective on both the 'Dialogue' and the 'Pretended Conference' in 'George Buchanan's vernacular polemics, 1570–1572', *IR* 54.1 (Spring 2003), 47–68.

65 Richard Bannatyne, *Memorials*, p. 5.

66 *The Bannatyne Miscellany*, p. 36, quoting David Calderwood.

67 Important Scottish examples include William Lamb's *Ane resonyng of ane Scottis and Inglis merchand* (1549) and, more splendidly, George Buchanan's *De Iure Regni apud Scotos Dialogus* (1579), written shortly before the wives 'Dialogue'. For Loughlin's speculation about Buchanan's authorship of the 'Dialogue', see his '"The Dialogue"', pp. 235–36. On the gossips' meeting, see Linda Woodbridge, *Women and the English Renaissance* (Urbana: University of Illinois Press, 1981); Susan E. Phillips, *Transforming Talk: The Problem with Gossip in Late Medieval England* (University Park: Pennsylvania State University Press, 2007.)

68 Numerous fifteenth-century English examples similarly satirise women for their idleness, wantonness, and loose tongues. John Skelton drew his celebrated portrait of gossips and booze in *The Tunning of Elynor Rummyng*. Two other examples include *A Talk of Ten Wives on Their Husbands' Ware* and *How Gossips Myne* (Utley, numbers 172 and 107).

69 See David Reid's illuminating introduction to his edition of *Rob Stene's Dream* (Stirling: University of Stirling Bibliographical Society, 1989).

70 See Sally Mapstone, 'Invective as Poetic: The Cultural Context of Polwarth and Montgomerie's *Flyting*', *SLJ* 26.2 (1999), pp. 18–40.

71 Montgomerie, according to Polwarth, flies with wings not his own, with 'sum of simpillis thingis' (l. 59). David J. Parkinson (ed.), *Alexander Montgomerie Poems*, 2 vols. STS (2000), I.170.

72 Robert Pitcairn (ed.), *The Autobiography and Diary of Mr James Melvill* (Edinburgh: Wodrow Society, 1842), p. 22.

10. Performance

1 For a regional study of this range of activity, see Eila Williamson and John J. McGavin, 'Crossing the Border: the Provincial Records of South-East Scotland', in Sally-Beth MacLean and Audrey Douglas (eds), *REED in Review*, Studies in Early English Drama (Toronto: University of Toronto Press, 2006), pp. 157–77. For the theatrical potential of early horse racing, see Eila Williamson, 'Horse-racing in Scotland in the Sixteenth and earlier Seventeenth Centuries: Peebles and Beyond', *RoSC* 14 (2001–02), pp. 31–42.

2 A more developed account of performance in this sense can be found in John J. McGavin, *Theatricality and Narrative in Medieval and Early-Modern Scotland* (Aldershot: Ashgate, 2007).

3 See Pons-Sanz and MacCoinnich, Chapter 1, above.

4 For discussion, see Virginia Blankenhorn, 'Observations on the Performance of Irish Syllabic Verse', *Studia Celtica* 44 (2010), 135–54; William Gillies, 'Music and Gaelic Strict-metre Poetry', ibid., pp. 111–34.

5 National Library of Scotland Adv. MS 73.1.6, fol.24^v; James Logan, *The Scottish Gaël*, 2 vols. (London: Smith, Elder, & Co., 1831), vol. II, pp. 143, 247–48; Thomas Pennant, *A Tour in Scotland and Voyage to the Hebrides MDCCLXXII* (London: B. White, 1776), vol. I, p. 263.

6 Bawcutt, *Dunbar*, B65, and Nicole Meier (ed.), *The Poems of Walter Kennedy*, STS (2008). A selection can be found in Priscilla Bawcutt (ed.), *William Dunbar: Selected Poems* (London and New York: Longman, 1996), pp. 262–76.

7 Alan Harrison, *The Irish Trickster* (Sheffield: Sheffield Academic Press, 1987), pp. 35–70; Ronald Black (ed.), *An Lasair: Anthology of 18th-century Gaelic Verse* (Edinburgh: Birlinn, 2001), pp. 408–12, and 'A Bawdy New Year's Rhyme from Gaelic Scotland', *Scottish Studies* 35 (2007–10), pp. 1–35; also John Shaw, 'Scottish Gaelic Traditions of the *Cliar Sheanchain*' in Cyril J. Byrne, Margaret Harry and Pádraig Ó Siadhail (eds), *Celtic Languages and Celtic Peoples* (Halifax, NS: St Mary's University, 1992), pp. 141–58.

8 Anna Jean Mill, *Mediæval Plays in Scotland*, St Andrews University Publications, no. XXIV (Edinburgh and London, Blackwood & Sons, 1927; reissued New York and London: Benjamin Blom, 1969), p. 300. Until the data collected by the *Records of Early Drama: Scotland* project is published, this remains the best collection of primary records on early Scottish performance. For the post-1650 establishment of

Scottish theatres see Ian Brown (ed.), *The Edinburgh Companion to Scottish Drama* (Edinburgh: EUP, 2011), especially Brown's Chapter 2, 'Public and Private Performance: 1650–1800'.

9 The most recent readily available play text, and information relating to the 1540 'Interlude' version, can be found in Greg Walker (ed.), *Medieval Drama: An Anthology* (Oxford: Blackwell, 2000), pp. 535–623.

10 Priscilla Bawcutt (ed.), *The Shorter Poems of Gavin Douglas*, rev. edn, STS (2003), pp. 1–133.

11 Martin MacGregor, 'Gaelic Barbarity and Scottish Identity in the Later Middle Ages', in Dauvit Broun and Martin MacGregor (eds), *Mìorun Mòr nan Gall, 'The Great Ill-Will of the Lowlander'?: Lowland Perceptions of the Highlands, Medieval and Modern* (Glasgow: University of Glasgow, Centre for Scottish and Celtic Studies, 2009), p. 47.

12 For the royal inauguration, see John Bannerman, 'The King's Poet and the Inauguration of Alexander III', *SHR* 68 (1989), 120–49; Dauvit Broun, *Scottish Independence and the Idea of Britain from the Picts to Alexander III* (Edinburgh: EUP, 2007), Chapter 6. For the Battle of North Inch, see Graeme M. Mackenzie, 'The Rarest Decision Recorded in History: The Battle of the Clans in 1396', *TGSI* 54 (1994–96), pp. 420–87; also George Neilson, *Trial by Combat* (Glasgow: William Hodge & Co., 1890), pp. 239–55; Peter T. Leeson, 'Trial by Battle', *Journal of Legal Analysis* 3 (2011), 341–75; Michael J. Russell, 'Trial by Battle and the Writ of Right', *Journal of Legal History* 1 (1980), 111–34, and 'Trial by Battle in the Court of Chivalry', *Journal of Legal History* 29 (2008), pp. 335–57. See also Purdie and Stevenson, Chapter 7, above,

13 For a study of Scottish performative culture which includes tournament, see Louise Olga Fradenburg, *City, Marriage, Tournament: Arts of Rule in Late Medieval Scotland* (Madison: University of Wisconsin Press, 1991).

14 Mill, *Mediæval Plays*, p. 216.

15 Hugh Macdonald, 'History of the MacDonalds' in J. R. N. Macphail (ed.), *Highland Papers, vol i*, SHS (1914), pp. 45–46.

16 Revs Angus & Archibald MacDonald (eds), *The Clan Donald*, 3 vols (Inverness: Northern Counties Publishing Co., 1896–1904), III: p. 226.

17 John Dewar MS 6, n.f., Argyll Papers, Inveraray Castle (copies in School of Scottish Studies, University of Edinburgh), vol. vii, p. 1 (author's translation).

18 David Calderwood, *The History of the Kirk of Scotland*, 8 vols., ed. Thomas Thomson (Edinburgh: The Wodrow Society, 1842–49), IV, pp. 613–14.

19 *Haddington Court Book 1530-55*, National Records of Scotland B30/9/2, fol. 29ᵛ (27 May).
20 Sir James Balfour, *The Historical Works*, 4 vols. (Edinburgh: W. Aitchison, 1824–25), vol. 1, p. 384.
21 Martin Martin, *A Description of the Western Islands of Scotland* (London: Andrew Bell, 1703), pp. 30, 52, 79, 89, 100, 213, 270, 271, 295; Dòmhnall Uilleam Stiùbhart, 'Leisure and Recreation in an Age of Clearance: The Case of the Hebridean Michaelmas', in J. Borsje, A. Dooley, S. Mac Mathúna and G. Toner (eds), *Celtic Cosmology: Perspectives from Ireland and Scotland* (Turnhout: Brepols, 2014), pp. 207–48.
22 See John Gregorson Campbell, *The Gaelic Otherworld*, ed. Ronald Black (Edinburgh: Birlinn, 2005), pp. 532–35, 575–80; also Black, 'A Bawdy New Year's Rhyme'.
23 Joan F. Flett & Thomas M. Flett, 'Some Hebridean folk dances', *Journal of the English Folk Dance and Song Society* 7 (1952–55), pp. 112–27; T. M. Flett, 'Addenda et Corrigenda: Some Hebridean folk dances', ibid., pp. 182–84; Michael Newton, *Warriors of the Word: The World of the Scottish Highlanders* (Edinburgh: Birlinn, 2009), pp. 245–47, 274–76, and 'Folk Drama in Gaelic Scotland' in Brown, *Edinburgh Companion to Scottish Drama*, pp. 41–46.
24 'A relation of the Imprisonment and Examination of James Cathkin, bookseller, June MDCXIX', in *The Bannatyne Miscellany, I* (Edinburgh: Bannatyne Club, 1827), pp. 197–215 (p. 206).
25 Calderwood, *History of the Kirk*, vol. V, p. 346.
26 See Margo Todd, *The Culture of Protestantism in Early Modern Scotland* (New Haven and London: Yale University Press, 2002), especially Chapter 3, 'Performing Repentance', pp. 127–82.
27 Ninian Winzet, 'Certane Articlis Twechinge doctrine Ordour and maneris, Proponit to the precheowris of the protestantis in scotland, be the catholikis of ye inferior ordour of cleirgye, and layit men crwallie afflictit and dispersit Be the Sadis precheouris', Edinburgh University Library MS, Dd.7.57/3, np.
28 For discussion of religious practice, see Reid and Innes, Chapter 3, above.
29 'Extract Commission and Visitation of Diocese of Dunblane', Edinburgh University Library MS, La.II. 14, p. 37 (15 October 1587); James Kirk (ed.), *Stirling Presbytery Records 1581–1587*, Scottish Church History Society, Edinburgh, 1981.

30 Ibid., p. 39.
31 'The Paradox of Medieval Scotland: 1093–1286 – Social Relationships and Identities before the Wars of Independence', www.poms.ac.uk, accessed 28 July 2012.
32 For a closely worked study of comparative pageantry, see Sarah Carpenter & Graham Runnalls, 'The Entertainments at the Marriage of Mary Queen of Scots and the French Dauphin François, 1558: Paris and Edinburgh', *Medieval English Theatre* 22 (2000), 145–61.
33 P. Sharratt and P. G. Walsh (eds), *George Buchanan Tragedies* (Edinburgh: SAP, 1983); Philip J. Ford and W. S. Watt (eds), *George Buchanan: Prince of Poets* (Aberdeen: AUP, 1982), pp. 152–53, line 3.
34 Jamie Reid Baxter, '*Philotus*: The Transmission of a Delectable Treatise', in van Heijnsbergen and Royan, *Literature, Letters and the Canonical*, pp. 52–68.
35 These extensive records, which are currently being edited for the *Records of Early Drama Scotland* project, can be found in National Records of Scotland, mostly at GD 156/31/1–6.
36 Elphinstone family of Carberry, *Discharges 1616–19*, National Records of Scotland GD156/31/1/5, fol. 114^v (14 April 1618).

11. Translation

1 I will be referring to forms of the language as spoken in Ireland and Scotland generally as 'Gaelic' throughout, suitably modified as necessary. In hibernocentric scholarship, the term 'Classical' is generally reserved to indicate the language as regulated in the various grammatical tracts of the Early Modern Irish period and as employed in the bardic poetry of the same. 'Early Modern' is used to refer to the language of the period more generally, particularly with reference to the language employed in prose texts. In scottocentric scholarship, the term 'Classical' is used more broadly, to indicate all high-register non-vernacular writing, whether in poetry or prose. In this chapter, I have employed 'Classical' in this broader sense.
2 Although one might intellectually distinguish between language, orthography, and type, they are often experienced as a unity. As a teacher of Irish, I have encountered older people who refer to the post-spelling reform Irish they encounter in roman type in contemporary books as a different 'Irish' to that which they learned in school, with an accompanying sense of disenfranchisement or alienation from the language.

3 R. I. M. Black, 'The Gaelic manuscripts of Scotland', in W. Gillies (ed.), *Gaelic and Scotland: Alba agus a' Ghàidhlig* (Edinburgh: EUP, 1989), pp. 146–74, p. 167.
4 Máire Ní Mhaonaigh, 'The literature of medieval Ireland, 800–1200: From the Vikings to the Normans', in M. Kelleher and P. O'Leary (eds), *The Cambridge History of Irish Literature*, Vol. 1, (Cambridge: CUP, 2006), pp. 32–73, p. 41.
5 W. B. Stanford, 'Towards a history of classical influences in Ireland', *Proceedings of the Royal Irish Academy* 70C (1970), pp. 13–91, p. 37. See also Kevin Murray (ed.), *Translations from Classical Literature: Imtheachta Aeniasa and Stair Ercuil ocus a Bás Irish Texts Society Seminar Series* (London: Irish Texts Society, 2006).
6 Kaarina Hollo, 'The literature of later medieval Ireland, 1200–1600: from the Normans to the Tudors. Part II: Prose literature', in Kelleher and O'Leary (eds), *Cambridge History*, Vol. 1, pp. 110–39 (p. 125).
7 See MacConnich and Pons-Sanz, above.
8 Aoibheann Nic Dhonnchadha, 'Medical writing in Irish', *Irish Journal of Medical Science* 169.3 (2000), 217–20, p. 217.
9 Black, 'The Gaelic manuscripts', p. 164.
10 These he defines as those written in 'Common Gaelic' and traditional script prior to 1745 (Black, p. 149), with some important caveats: the Book of the Dean of Lismore (non-Gaelic script and strong influence of vernacular Gaelic), and the Gaelic portion of the Murthly Hours (vernacular Gaelic) are included. He states 'I would say quite arbitrarily that anything earlier than 1600 is to be called classical' (Black, 'The Gaelic manuscripts', p. 150).
11 Nic Dhonnchadha, 'Medical writing', p. 218.
12 Ibid.
13 Francis Shaw, 'Medieval medico-philosophical treatises in the Irish language', in John Ryan (ed.), *Féil-sgríbhinn Éoin Mhic Néill* (Dublin: At the Sign of the Three Candles, 1940, repr. Four Courts Press 1995), pp. 144–57 (p. 156).
14 www.isos.dias.ie/libraries/NLS/NLS_Adv_MS_72_1_4/english/index.html.
15 Shaw, 'Medieval medico-philosophical treatises', p. 157.
16 Nic Dhonnchadha, 'Medical writing', p. 217.
17 www.isos.dias.ie/libraries/NLS/NLS_Adv_MS_72_1_2/irish/?ref=. Black notes here that Donnchadh Albanach's father was also in the habit of travelling between Scotland and Ireland.

18 Nic Dhonnchadha, 'Medical writing', p. 217.
19 Carswell also consulted either the Latin or English version of the Geneva 'Form of Prayers' of which the Book of Common Order is a revised version (Jane Dawson, 'Calvinism and the Gaidhealtachd in Scotland', in Andrew Pettegree, Alastair Duke and Gillian Lewis (eds), *Calvinism in Europe 1540–1620* (Cambridge: CUP, 1994), pp. 231–53, esp. p. 238, R. L. Thomson (ed.), *Foirm na n-Urrnuidheadh: John Carswell's translation of the Book of Common Order* SGTS (1970), lxviii). See also Innes and Reid, above.
20 Thomson, *Foirm*, p. xv.
21 Carswell interestingly uses the plural here (not reflected in Thomson's translation). The term 'canamhain' was used in the Gaelic grammatical tracts to indicate a form that was neither unacceptable nor fully approved – Ó Cuív suggests the definition 'anomalous form which has the sanction of usage' (Brian Ó Cuív, *The Linguistic Training of the Medieval Irish Poet* (Dublin: Dublin Institute for Advanced Studies1973), p. 24). It is used here in a sense approaching that of the modern *canúint*, 'dialect'. This is an interesting acknowledgement of the plurality of the various forms of Gaelic.
22 Thomson, *Foirm*, pp. 10–11.
23 Felicity Heal, 'Mediating the Word: Language and dialects in the British and Irish Reformations', *Journal of Ecclesiastical History* 36.2, (2005), pp. 261–86 (p. 275).
24 Marc Caball, 'Gaelic and Protestant: a case study in Early Modern self-fashioning, 1567–1608', *Proceedings of the Royal Irish Academy* 110C (2010), pp. 191–215 (p. 202).
25 CSP Scotland v, p. 34, cited in John Bannerman, 'Literacy in the Highlands', in Ian B. Cowan and Duncan Shaw (eds), *The Renaissance and Reformation in Scotland: Essays in honour of Gordon Donaldson* (Edinburgh: SAP, 1983), pp. 214–35 (p. 228).
26 Caball, 'Gaelic and Protestant', p. 196.
27 Dawson 'Calvinism and the Gaidhealtachd', p. 238.
28 Thomson, *Foirm*, p. lxxii.
29 Ibid., p. xvii.
30 Tomás de Bhaldraithe, 'Leabhar Charswell in Éirinn', *Éigse* 9 (1958–61), pp. 61–67, cited in Brian Ó Cuív, *Aibidil Gaoidheilge & Caiticiosma: Seaán Ó Cearnaigh's Irish Primer of Religion published in 1571* (Dublin: Dublin Institute for Advanced Studies, 1994), p. 15.
31 Caball, 'Gaelic and Protestant', pp. 204–05.

32 Ibid., p. 205, citing Nicholas Williams, *I bPrionta i Leabhar: na Protastúin agus Prós na Gaeilge 1567–1724* (Dublin: Clóchomhar, 1986), p. 21.
33 Ó Cuív, *Aibidil*, p. 16.
34 Caball, 'Gaelic and Protestant', p. 207.
35 Mícheal Mac Craith, 'Literature in Irish, 1550–1690: From the Elizabethan settlement to the Battle of the Boyne', in Kelleher and O'Leary (eds), *Cambridge History*, Vol. 1, pp. 191–231, p. 194.
36 Ó Cuív, *Aibidil*, p. 8.
37 Matthew Staunton, 'Trojan Horses and friendly faces: Irish Gaelic typography as propaganda', *Revue LISA/LISA e-journal* (2005) [Online], Vol. III/1, pp. 85–98. Online since 27 October 2009, connection on 26 July 2012. lisa.revues.org/2546; DOI: 10.4000/lisa.2546.
38 Ibid.
39 See Chapter 2 for discussion of Latin and Older Scots transmission.
40 Jane Dawson, 'Calvinism and the Gaidhealtachd', p. 239.
41 Ibid.
42 Ibid, p. 242.
43 Ibid, p. 241.
44 Kenneth D. MacDonald, 'Munro, Alexander, of Strathnaver', in Derick S. Thomson (ed.), *The Companion to Gaelic Scotland* (Glasgow: Gairm, 1994), p. 205.
45 Bannerman, 'Literacy in the Highlands', p. 219.
46 Ibid, p. 222.
47 Ibid, p. 233.
48 Ibid, p. 233–34.
49 Extempore oral translation in certain contexts, as discussed above, leaves little trace in the written record, but no doubt represented the greatest part of translation activity during this period.
50 G. Chaucer, *The Riverside Chaucer*, ed. L Benson *et al.* (Oxford and New York: OUP, 1987), *The Parliament of Fowls*, ll. 22–25.
51 E. Pound, *Literary Essays of Ezra Pound Edited with an Introduction by T. S. Eliot* (London: Faber and Faber, 1960), p. 245.
52 R. G. Austin, *Some English Translations of Virgil* (Liverpool: University Press, 1956), pp. 16–17.
53 L. Brewer Hall, 'An Aspect of the Renaissance in Gavin Douglas' *Eneados*,' *Studies in the Renaissance* 7 (1960), pp. 184–92, at p. 192.
54 J. Corbett, *Written in the Language of the Scottish Nation: A History of Literary Translation into Scots* (Clevedon: Multilingual Matters, 1999), p. 28.

55 Gilbert Hay, *The Prose Works of Sir Gilbert Hay*, ed. J. Glenn, 2 vols. STS (2005), vol. 2, p. 2.
56 Cf. R. J. Lyall, 'Vernacular Prose before the Reformation,' in *AHSL*, pp. 163–82 (pp. 167–68).
57 Lyall, 'Vernacular Prose before the Reformation,' p. 168. For further discussion of these texts, see Purdie and Stevenson, above.
58 R. Mason, *Kingship and the Commonweal: Political Thought in Renaissance and Reformation Scotland* (East Linton: Tuckwell Press, 1998), p. 14.
59 W. Whitman, *The Complete Poems*, ed. F. Murphy (London: Penguin, 1986), 'Song of Myself,' ll. 1324–26.
60 T. Rutledge, 'Gavin Douglas and John Bellenden: Poetic Relations and Political Affiliations', in Royan, *Langage Cleir Illumynate*, pp. 93–116.
61 The quality of Bellenden's prose has been briefly addressed by Lyall, 'Vernacular Prose', pp. 172–74.
62 C. Baswell, *Virgil in Medieval England: Figuring the Aeneid from the Twelfth Century to Chaucer* (Cambridge: CUP, 1995), pp. 9–13.
63 Priscilla Bawcutt, *Gavin Douglas: A Critical Study* (Edinburgh: EUP, 1976), p. 130.
64 J. MacQueen, 'Aspects of Humanism in Sixteenth- and Seventeenth-Century Literature', in J. MacQueen (ed.), *Humanism in Renaissance Scotland* (Edinburgh: EUP, 1990), pp. 10–31 (pp. 11–19).
65 Ibid., pp. 11–12.
66 See, for instance, Mason, *Kingship and Commonwealth*, pp. 93–99, or C. Edington, *Court and Culture in Renaissance Scotland: Sir David Lindsay of the Mount* (Amherst, MA: University of Massachusetts, 1994), pp. 101–07.
67 Edington, *Court and Culture*, pp. 101–103.
68 Ibid., p. 107.
69 See Hogg and Macgregor, above.
70 G. Douglas, *The Shorter Poems of Gavin Douglas*, ed. P. Bawcutt, rev. edn, STS (2003); the quotation has been taken here from the London print.
71 J. Derrick McClure, 'Translation and Transcreation in the Castalian Period', *SSL* 26 (1991), pp. 185–98, offers an especially suggestive introduction to the questions here; see also R. D. S. Jack, *The Italian Influence on Scottish Literature* (Edinburgh: EUP, 1972), pp. 54–89.
72 So, for instance, McClure, 'Translation and Transcreation', p. 186: '[t]he value of translation as a means of enriching the target language

was clearly recognized; and in this age of strongly-developing national consciousness many translators, including the Scots, wrote from overtly patriotic motives.'

73 For the Scots quality of these works, see Corbett, *Language of the Scottish Nation*, pp. 61–76; see also R. D. S. Jack and P. A. T. Rozendaal, *The Mercat Anthology of Early Scottish Literature, 1375–1707* (Edinburgh: Mercat Press, 2000), pp. vii–xxxix.

74 This is most emphatically articulated in Jack, *Italian Influence*, p. 54, though it is an argument to which he returns in a number of his essays.

75 Most prominently in P. Bawcutt, 'James VI's Castalian Band: A Modern Myth,' *SHR* 80 (2001), pp. 251–59, but see also K. McClune, 'The Scottish Sonnet, James VI, and John Stewart of Baldynneis', in Royan, *Langage Cleir Illumynate*, pp. 165–80 (pp. 173–74), and Alessandra Petrina, *Machiavelli in the British Isles: two early modern translations of the Prince* (Farnham: Ashgate, 2009), p. 97.

76 *King James VI and I: Selected Writings*, ed. N. Rhodes, J. Richards, and J. Marshall (Aldershot: Ashgate Publishing Company, 2003), p. 35.

77 See, however, McClune, 'The Scottish Sonnet', pp. 173–74.

78 Unless otherwise stated, quotation from *Roland Furious* is taken from D. Heddle (ed.), *John Stewart of Baldynneis' Roland Furious: A Scots Poem in its European Context* (Leiden and Boston: Brill, 2008).

79 John Stewart of Baldynneis, *Poems of John Stewart of Baldynneis, from the MS. In the Advocates' Library, Edinburgh*, ed. T. Crockett, vol 2, STS (Edinburgh and London, 1913), p. 3.

80 *John Stewart of Baldynneis' Roland Furious*, pp. 33–45.

81 *King James VI and I: Selected Writings*, p. 32.

82 *Poems of John Stewart of Baldynneis*, vol. 2, p. 1.

83 It is interesting to consider the relation between Stewart's intertextual mix of 'inventioun' and translation (for which one might wish to use a term such as transcreation or *imitatio*) and our earlier opposition of translation and adaptation.

84 *John Stewart of Baldynneis' Roland Furious*, pp. 19–30. Jack, *Italian Influence*, pp. 63–71.

85 So, for instance, in the moral judgements on Orlando and Angelica in Cantos 34 and 19 (Ludovico Ariosto, *Orlando Furioso*, trans. G. Waldman (Oxford: OUP, 2008), pp. 418 and 218).

86 C. Burrow, *Epic Romance: Homer to Milton* (Oxford: OUP, 1993), pp. 52–75, is especially good here, as is J. D. Garrison, *Pietas from Vergil*

to Dryden (University Park, PA: Penn State University Press, 1987), esp. pp. 145–51.
87 Ariosto, *Orlando Furioso*, pp. 1–2.
88 Jack, *Italian Influence*, pp. 86–87.
89 Petrina, *Machiavelli in the British Isles*, pp. 97–100.
90 *King James VI and I: Selected Writings*, p. 35.
91 Petrina, *Machiavelli in the British Isles*, p. 150.
92 Ibid., p. 150.
93 Jack, *Italian Influence*, pp. 90–144, is again an important starting point here; for Drummond, see also Corbett, *Language of the Scottish Nation*, pp. 77–84, and especially M. Spiller, '"Quintessencing in the Finest Substance": the Sonnets of William Drummond,' in Royan, *Langage Cleir Illumynate*, pp. 193–205; in the same volume, D. Atkinson, '*Flowres of Sion*: The Spiritual and Meditative Journey of William Drummond,' pp. 181–91, offers a useful corrective to focus on Drummond as a translator. Note also the attention afforded Urquhart in the essays in A. F. Thomson (ed.), *Sir Thomas Urquhart of Cromarty, 400th Anniversary Conference* (Cromarty: Cromarty Arts Trust, 2011).
94 On Motteux's editorial intrusiveness, see R. J. Craik, *Sir Thomas Urquhart of Cromarty (1611–1660): Adventurer, Polymath and Translator of Rabelais* (Lampeter: Mellen Research University Press, 1993), pp. 117–18.
95 Francois Rabelais, *Gargantua and Pantagruel*, trans. T. Urquhart and P. le Motteux, 3 vols. (London: Henley Tudor Translations, 1900), vol. 1, p. lxxix.
96 Quoted in Rabelais, *Gargantua and Pantagruel* (Ware: Wordsworth Classics of World Literature, 1999), p. xxxiii.
97 Most recently edited as Sir Thomas Urquhart of Cromarty, *The Jewel*, eds. R. D. S. Jack and R. J. Lyall (Edinburgh: SAP, 1983).
98 Urquhart also composed two collections of epigrams, the first of which, *Apollo, and the Muses*, exhibits the comic coarseness that is such a feature of Rabelais and his translation.
99 H. Brown, *Rabelais in English Literature* (New York: Cass, 1967), p. 119; Urquhart, *Jewel*, pp. 115, 125, 135, 227, 229.
100 Robert H. F. Carver, 'Prose Satire', in G. Braden, R. Cummings, and S. Gillespie (eds), *The Oxford History of Literary Translation in English, volume 2: 1550–1660* (Oxford: OUP, 2010), pp. 358–68 (p. 357).
101 E. Auerbach, *Mimesis: The Representation of Reality in Western Literature*, trans. W. Trask (Princeton, NJ: Princeton University Press, 1953), p. 272.

102 M. A. Screech, *Rabelais* (London: Duckworth, 1979) remains a fine introduction to these aspects of Rabelais's work.
103 Easily the most important work on Urquhart's translation is still L. Sainéan, 'Les Interprètes de Rabelais en Angleterre et en Allemagne', *Revue des Etudes Rabelaisiennes* 7 (1909), pp. 137–258 (pp. 175–206). Because Sainéan proceeds by juxtaposing passages from Rabelais and Urquhart, his work may reward even those with little French. The treatment in his book, *L'Influence et la Réputation de Rabelais* (Paris: J. Gamber, 1930), is much more cursory. A summary of his findings is helpfully mediated by Brown, pp. 111–29, while Craik, pp. 115–209, looks to develop and refine Sainéan's insights. I am indebted to Sainéan throughout these paragraphs.
104 For the French, see Rabelais, *Oeuvres Complètes*, ed. P. Jourda (Paris: Garnier Frères, 1962), vol. 1, pp. 58, 33, 20, 109.
105 Note the similar play on *pers et vert* and perverse in *Pantagruel*, Chapter 31.
106 For Cotgrave, see Sainéan, 'Les Interprètes,' pp. 139–74 and Anne Lake Prescott, *Imagining Rabelais in Renaissance England* (New Haven and London: Harvard University Press, 1998), pp. 48–53.
107 Brown, *Rabelais in English Literature*, p. 123.
108 Rabelais, *Oeuvres Complètes*, vol. 1, p. 486; Sainéan, 'Les Interprètes,' p. 178.
109 Jack and Lyall (eds), *The Jewel*, pp. 1–11, offers a good summary account of Urquhart's life; fuller is J. Willcock, *Sir Thomas Urquhart of Cromartie, Knight* (Edinburgh: Oliphant, Anderson and Ferrier, 1899).
110 N. McDowell, 'Urquhart's Rabelais: Translation, Patronage, and Cultural Politics,' *English Literary Renaissance* (2005), pp. 273–303 (pp. 279–86).
111 Ibid., pp. 286-303.
112 G. Wall, 'Rabelais Renewed?', *Cambridge Quarterly* 22 (1993), pp. 291-305 (p. 299).
113 Erich Auerbach, *Mimesis*, p. 281.

Further Reading

Aitken, A. J., Matthew P. McDiarmid and Derick S. Thomson (eds), *Bards and Makars: Scottish Language and Literature, Medieval and Renaissance* (Glasgow: University of Glasgow Press, 1977).

Allan, David, *Philosophy and Politics in Later Stuart Scotland: Neo-Stoicism, Culture and Ideology in an Age of Crisis, 1540–1690* (East Linton: Tuckwell Press, 2000).

Bawcutt, Priscilla, *Gavin Douglas: A Critical Study* (Edinburgh: EUP, 1976).

Bawcutt, Priscilla, *Dunbar the Makar* (Oxford: OUP, 1992).

Bawcutt, Priscilla and Janet Hadley Williams (eds), *A Companion to Medieval Scottish Poetry* (Cambridge: D. S. Brewer, 2006).

Boardman, Steve and Susan Foran (eds) *Barbour's Bruce and its Cultural Contexts: Politics, Chivalry and Literature in Late Medieval Scotland* (Cambridge: D. S. Brewer, 2015).

Broun, Dauvit and Martin MacGregor (eds), *Mìorun Mòr Nan Gall, "The great ill-will of the Lowlander?": Lowland Perceptions of the Highlands, Medieval and Modern* (Glasgow: Centre for Scottish and Celtic Studies, 2009).

Brown, Ian, Thomas Owen Clancy, Susan Manning and Murray Pittock, *Edinburgh History of Scottish Literature*, vol. 1: *From Columba to the Union (1707)* (Edinburgh: EUP, 2007).

Bruce, Mark P., and Katherine Terrell (eds), *The Anglo-Scottish Border and the Shaping of Identity 1300–1600* (Basingstoke: Palgrave Macmillan, 2012).

Caie, Graham, Roderick J. Lyall, Sally Mapstone and Kenneth Simpson (eds), *The European Sun: Proceedings of the Seventh International Conference on Medieval and Renaissance Scottish Language and Literature, University of Strathclyde, 1993* (East Linton: Tuckwell Press, 2001).

Calin, William, *The Lily and the Thistle: the French Tradition and the Older Literature of Scotland: Essays in Criticism* (Toronto: University of Toronto Press, 2014).

Carpenter, Sarah and Sarah Dunnigan (eds), *'Joyous Sweit Imaginatioun': Essays on Scottish literature in honour of R. D. S. Jack* (Amsterdam: Rodopi, 2007).

Coira, M. Pia, *By Poetic Authority: the Rhetoric of Panegyric in Gaelic Poetry of Scotland to c. 1700* (Edinburgh: Dunedin Academic Press, 2012).

Corbett, John, *Language and Scottish Literature* (Edinburgh: EUP, 1997).

Crawford, Robert, *Scotland's Books: The Penguin History of Scottish Literature* (London: Penguin, 2007).

Dunnigan, Sarah, *Eros and Poetry at the Court of Mary, Queen of Scots and James VI* (Basingstoke: Palgrave Macmillan, 2002).

Dunnigan Sarah, C. Marie Harker and Evelyn Newlyn (eds), *Women and the Feminine in Medieval and Early Modern Scottish Writing* (Basingstoke, New York: Palgrave Macmillan, 2004).

Edington, Carol, *Court and Culture in Renaissance Scotland: Sir David Lindsay of the Mount* (Amherst MA: University of Massachusetts Press, 1994).

Fradenburgh, Louise O., *City, Marriage, Tournament: Arts of Rule in Late Medieval Scotland* (Madison WI: University of Wisconsin Press, 1991).

Gifford, Douglas and Dorothy McMillan (eds), *A History of Scottish Women's Writing* (Edinburgh: EUP, 1997).

Goldstein, R. James, *The Matter of Scotland: Historical Narrative in Medieval Scotland* (Lincoln NE: University of Nebraska Press, 1993).

Gray, Douglas, *Robert Henryson* (Leiden: E. J. Brill, 1979).

Hadley Williams, Janet (ed.), *Stewart Style 1513–1542: essays on the court of James V* (East Linton: Tuckwell Press, 1996).

Hadley Williams, Janet and J. Derrick McClure (eds), *Fresche fontanis: Studies in the Culture of Medieval and Early Modern Scotland* (Newcastle-upon-Tyne: Cambridge Scholars Press, 2013).

Hasler, Antony J., *Court Poetry in Late Medieval England and Scotland: Allegories of Authority* (Cambridge: CUP, 2011).

Hewitt, David and Michael Spiller (eds), *Literature of the North* (Aberdeen: AUP, 1983).

Houwen, L. A. R. J, A. A. MacDonald and Sally Mapstone (eds), *A Palace in the Wild: Essays on Vernacular Culture and Humanism in Late Medieval and Renaissance Scotland* (Leuven: Peeters, 2000).

Houwen, Luuk, *Literature and Religion in Late Medieval and Early Modern Scotland: Essays in Honour of A. A. MacDonald* (Leuven: Peeters 2012).

Jack, R. D. S. (ed.), *History of Scottish Literature*, vol. 1: *Origins to 1660* (Aberdeen: AUP, 1988).

Jack, R. D. S., *The Italian Influence on Scottish Literature* (Edinburgh: EUP, 1972).

Kerrigan, John, *Archipelagic English: Literature, History and Politics 1603–1707* (Oxford: OUP, 2008).

Kratzmann, Gregory, *Anglo-Scottish Literary Relations 1430–1550* (Cambridge: CUP, 1980).

Lyall, R. J., in Jeremy Griffiths and Derek Pearsall (eds), *Book Production and Publishing in Britain 1375–1475* (Cambridge: CUP, 1989).

Lyall, R. J., *Alexander Montgomerie: Poetry, Politics and Cultural Change in Jacobean Scotland* (Tempe, AZ: ACMRS, 2005).

McClure, J Derrick, and Michael R. G. Spiller (eds), *Bryght Lanternis: Essays on the Language and Literature of Medieval and Renaissance Scotland* (Aberdeen: AUP, 1989).

MacDonald, A. A., Michael Lynch and Ian B. Cowan (eds), *The Renaissance in Scotland: Studies in Literature, Religion, History and Culture offered to John Durkan* (Leiden: E. J. Brill, 1994).

MacDonald, A. A. and Kees Dekker, *Rhetoric, Royalty and Reality: Essays on the Literary Culture of Medieval and Early Modern Scotland* (Leuven: Peeters, 2005).

MacDonald, A. A., 'The Scottish Renaissance: A Rough Beast Slouching to be Born?' *European Journal of English Studies* 18.1 (2014), pp. 11–20.

MacGavin, John, *Theatricality and Narrative in Medieval and Early Modern Scotland* (Aldershot: Ashgate, 2007).

McGinley, K. J., and Nicola Royan (eds), *The Apparelling of Truth: Literature and Literary Culture in the Reign of James VI – a Festschrift for Roderick J. Lyall* (Newcastle: Cambridge Scholars Press, 2010).

McLeod, Wilson, *Divided Gaels: Gaelic Cultural Identity in Scotland and Ireland c. 1200–c. 1650* (Oxford: OUP, 2004).

McLeod, Wilson, Abigail Burnyeat, Domhnall Uilleam Stiùbhart, Thomas Owen Clancy and Roibeard Ó Maolalaigh (eds), *Bile ós chrannaibh: a Festschrift for William Gillies* (Perth: Clann Tuirc, 2010).

Mann, Alastair J., *Scottish Book Trade, 1500–1720: Print Commerce and Print Control in Early Modern Scotland*, (East Linton: Tuckwell Press, 2000).

Mapstone, Sally, and Juliette Wood (eds), *The Rose and the Thistle: Essays on the Culture of Late Medieval and Renaissance Scotland* (East Linton: Tuckwell Press, 1998).

Mapstone, Sally (ed.), *William Dunbar, 'the nobill poyet': Essays in honour of Priscilla Bawcutt* (East Linton: Tuckwell Press, 2001).

Mapstone, Sally (ed.), *Older Scots Literature* (Edinburgh: John Donald, 2005).

Martin, Joanna, *Kingship and Love in Scottish Poetry 1424–1540* (Aldershot: Ashgate, 2008).

Martin, Joanna, and Emily Wingfield (eds), *Premodern Scotland: Literature and Governance 1420–1587* (Oxford: OUP, 2017).

Mullan, David George, and Crawford Gribben (eds), *Literature and the Scottish Reformation* (London: Routledge, 2009).

Parkinson, David J. (ed.), *James VI and I, Literature and Scotland: Tides of Change 1567–1625* (Leeuven: Peeters, 2013).

Purdie, Rhiannon, and Nicola Royan (eds), *The Scots and Medieval Arthurian Legend* (Cambridge: D. S. Brewer, 2005).

Reid, Steven J., and David McOmish (eds), *Neo-Latin Literature and Literary Culture in Early Modern Scotland* (Leiden: E. J. Brill, 2017).

Rickard, Jane, *Authorship and Authority: The Writings of James VI and I* (Manchester: MUP, 2012).

Roy, G. Ross and Patrick Scott (eds), 'The Language and Literature of Early Scotland', *Studies in Scottish Literature* 26 (1991), scholarcommons.sc.edu/ssl/vol26/iss1/.

Royan, Nicola (ed.), *Langage Cleir Illumynate: Scottish Poetry from Barbour to Drummond 1375–1630* (Amsterdam: Rodopi, 2006).

Sassi, Carla (ed.), *The International Companion to Scottish Poetry* (Glasgow: Scottish Literature International, 2016).

Thomas, Andrea, *Glory and Honour: The Renaissance in Scotland* (Edinburgh: Birlinn, 2012).

Thomson, Derick S., *Introduction to Gaelic Poetry* (Edinburgh: EUP, 1989).

Van Heijnsbergen, Theo, and Nicola Royan (eds), *Literature, Letters and the Canonical in Early Modern Scotland* (East Linton: Tuckwell Press, 2002).

Von Contzen, Eva, *The Scots Legendary: Towards a Poetics of Hagiographic Narration* (Manchester: MUP, 2016).

Von Contzen, Eva, and Luuk Houwen (eds), *Medievalia and Humanistica: Studies in Medieval and Renaissance Culture – Special Issue* N.S. 41 (2015).

Verweij, Sebastiaan, *The Literary Culture of Early Modern Scotland, Manuscript Production and Transmission, 1560–1625* (Oxford: OUP, 2016).

Walker, Greg, Tom Betteridge, Sally Rush, Eleanor Rycroft, *Staging the Scottish Renaissance*, stagingthescottishcourt.brunel.ac.uk/index.html 2014.

Wingfield, Emily, *The Trojan Legend in Medieval Scottish Literature* (Cambridge: D. S. Brewer, 2014).

Notes on Contributors

William Gillies is Emeritus Professor of Celtic and a Professorial Honorary Research Fellow at the University of Edinburgh. He has published widely on Gaelic language and literature in the late medieval period and has a particular interest in the Book of the Dean of Lismore. He is currently a Vice-president of the Scottish Gaelic Texts Society.

Ulrike Hogg works in the Manuscripts Division of the National Library of Scotland, where she is curator for Gaelic, early modern and music manuscripts. She has published on aspects of medieval and Renaissance Scottish historiography, and on Scottish Gaelic manuscripts and their collectors and scribes.

Sìm Innes is Lecturer in Celtic and Gaelic at the University of Glasgow. He works on Scottish Gaelic literature and has a particular interest in transmission, borrowing and translation of culture and ideas. He has published on a wide range of periods and topics: from late-medieval Gaelic religious poetry to twentieth-century Gaelic drama.

Kate McClune is Lecturer in English at the University of Bristol. She has published widely on Older Scots literary, manuscript and print culture, and on Scots and English Arthurian literature. She is currently editing the work of John Stewart of Baldynneis for the Scottish Text Society.

Aonghas MacCoinnich is a lecturer in Celtic History at the University of Glasgow. He has previously published (in both English and Gaelic) on themes such as clanship, plantation and language-use in the early modern Scottish Gàidhealtachd.

John J. McGavin is Emeritus Professor of Medieval Literature and Culture at the University of Southampton. He is editing with Dr Eila Williamson the South-East Scotland volume of the *Records of Early Drama: Scotland*. He has various publications in the area of medieval and early-modern literature including, with Professor Greg Walker, *Imagining Spectatorship: from the Mysteries to the Shakespearean Stage* (OUP 2016).

Martin MacGregor is Senior Lecturer in Scottish History at the University of Glasgow. His main research interest is Gaelic-speaking Scotland in the period from the fourteenth to the early seventeenth centuries, with particular reference to the historical utility of Gaelic and Gaelic-orientated sources such as poetry and clan histories.

Tricia A. McElroy serves as Associate Dean for Humanities and Fine Arts in the College of Arts and Sciences at the University of Alabama. She is also an Associate Professor of English and member of faculty in the Hudson Strode Program in Renaissance Studies. She has published essays on Scottish Reformation poetry, memoir and life writing, and the uses of literary genre in sixteenth-century histories. She is currently working on a two-volume edition of Reformation satire, *Scottish Satirical Literature, 1567–1584*, which will be published by the Scottish Text Society.

Mícheál B. Ó Mainnín is Professor of Irish and Celtic Studies in the School of Arts, English and Languages at Queen's University Belfast. He has a particular interest in connections between Gaelic Scotland and Ireland, and has published widely in the areas of literature and language. He is director of the Northern Ireland Place-Name Project and a co-investigator on 'Multilingualism: Empowering Individuals and Transforming Societies' funded by the AHRC.

Sally Mapstone is Principal and Vice-Chancellor of the University of St Andrews. She is Honorary President of the Scottish Text Society and an Honorary Fellow of the Association for Scottish Literary Studies. She has published widely on Older Scots literature, and on Scottish book history.

Kate Louise Mathis received her doctorate from the University of Edinburgh, and has taught in the Celtic departments of Aberdeen, Edinburgh, and Glasgow. From 2013 to 2016 she was research assistant for 'Women's Poetry in Ireland, Scotland, and Wales, 1400–1800' (funded by the Leverhulme Trust). Her research interests include grief and violence in medieval Gaelic literature, and the reception of the Ulster Cycle in later-medieval Scotland. She is preparing a monograph on the development of Deirdre from the early medieval period to the Celtic Revival.

Nicole Meier lectures in Medieval Studies at the Department of English, American and Celtic Studies, University of Bonn. She is joint co-ordinator of the Medieval Studies Forum Bonn and has published on Walter Kennedy, Margery Kempe and Old English literature. Her research interests include Middle Scots poetry, the interface between the written and the oral, historical linguistics, manuscript studies, and paleography.

Sara M. Pons-Sanz is Senior Lecturer in Language and Communication at Cardiff University's School of English, Communication and Philosophy. Her work focuses on the impact of multilingualism on medieval English, particularly the Anglo-Scandinavian linguistic contact. Beyond her work in historical linguistics, she has also published in the related field of historical stylistics.

Rhiannon Purdie is Reader in Medieval Literature in the School of English at the University of St Andrews. She has published extensively on Older Scots literature and on the medieval genre of romance, including scholarly editions of Scottish and Middle English romances and related texts.

Steven J. Reid is Senior Lecturer in History at the University of Glasgow. Between 2012 and 2015 he was Principal Investigator on the AHRC-funded project, 'Bridging the Continental divide: neo-Latin and its cultural role in Jacobean Scotland, as seen in the *Delitiae Poetarum Scotorum* (1637)'. He has published widely on intellectual, political and religious culture in Reformation and Jacobean Scotland.

Nicola Royan is Associate Professor of Older Scots in the School of English at the University of Nottingham. She has published widely on fifteenth- and sixteenth-century Scottish literature, in Latin, Scots and English, and has a particular interest in Scottish humanism. She is also president of the Scottish Text Society.

Thomas Rutledge is a Senior Lecturer in Medieval and Early Modern Literature in the School of Literature, Drama, and Creative Writing at the University of East Anglia. His work concentrates on the reception of classical and Italian literature in early-Renaissance Scotland, with a particular focus on the classical 'translations' of Robert Henryson, Gavin Douglas, and John Bellenden.

Katie Stevenson is a medieval historian and Assistant Vice-Principal (Collections) at the University of St Andrews. She has published widely on late medieval Scottish history and has particular interests in chivalric culture.

Index

Abbots of Unreason, 229–30, 231
Aberdeen, 19, 24, 36, 54–55, 56, 70, 76, 104, 107, 155, 164, 229
Adthimchiol an Chreidimh (Calvin's Larger Catechism), 242–43
advice to princes, 9–10, 17, 70, 80–83, 89–93, 120–22, 149, 174, 202, 208–10, 249, 254–55
áer, 201–02
Agallamh na Seanóireach (The Colloquy of the Ancients), 86–87
Ailéin mac Dhubhghaill Bháin, 135–37
Ais-eiridh nan Seann Chánoin Albannaich, 23
Aithbreac inghean Coirceadail, 133, 193–94
Aithirne, 201
Alasdair mac Mhaighistir Alasdair (see MacDonald)
Alexander III, 98, 103, 104, 118, 146, 222
Alexander romances, 158, 160, 162, 177–78, 249
Alexander, Sir William, 154, 234, 260
Monarchike Tragedies, 234

An Clàrsair Dall (see Morrison, Ruairidh)
Annals, 3
Ane Account of a Pretended Conference held by the Regent, the Earl of Murray, 213–14
Angus Og, 186, 187–88, 192, 193
Anti-feminism, 14, 124–25, 129–30, 139, 142, 144, 145, 206
Aonghais, Màiri nighean, 194–95
Arbuthnot, Alexander, 155
Ariosto, Ludovico, *Orlando Furioso*, 97, 160, 256–59
Arundel MS (London, British Library Arundel 285), 49, 65
Ascensius, Jodocus Badius, 39, 54–55, 57, 141
Navicula stultarum mulierum, 141
Asloan Manuscript (Edinburgh, NLS MS 16500), 42–45, 47, 142, 167, 204
Asloan, John, 2, 42, 58, 142, 167, 169
Ayton, Robert, 154–55, 179, 260
'On the Tweed', 154–55

Balfour of Denmilne, James, 172
The Ballettis of the Nine Nobles, 162, 163

Bannatyne MS (Edinburgh, NLS, Adv. 1.1.6), 41, 42–43, 45–46, 49, 51, 66, 146, 151, 153
Bannatyne, George, 2, 41, 46, 47, 49, 51, 66, 169
Barbour, John, 13, 24, 30, 31, 32, 104–05, 109, 146, 157, 158, 162, 163–65
   Bruce, vii, 30–32, 104–06, 109, 121, 158, 163–65
Bassandyne, Thomas, 42–43, 47, 53, 77
bardic schools, 173, 201
'Battle on the North Inch', 222
Bawcutt, Priscilla, xi, 40, 48, 50, 51, 53, 177, 253, 270
Beaton family, 25
Beaton scribes, 239–40
Beaton, David, Archbishop of St Andrews and Cardinal, 14, 72–73
Beaton, John, 26
Beaton, Niall, 63
Beatons, medical compendium (Edinburgh, NLS MS 71.1.2), 63
Bellenden, John, 109, 110, 148, 251, 259, 262
   The Chronicles of Scotland, 98, 109, 110–11, 121, 142, 251–52, 254
   Livy's Ab Urbe Condita, 109, 142, 251–55
Bible, 4, 17, 26, 37, 72, 75, 77, 84, 122, 135, 241, 243–44, 245
   Bedell's, 25
   Gaelic, 25–27, 28, 243–44, 245
   King James, 28
   Old Testament, 69, 161, 186
   translation into Scots, 247–48
   Vulgate translation, 4

'The Bird in the Cage', 213
Black Book of Taymouth, 116–17,
Bochanan, Dúghall, 245
Boece, Hector, 3, 37, 47, 54, 76, 98, 101, 107–09, 110, 112, 121–22, 142, 251, 255
   Scotorum historia a prima gentis origine, 54, 98, 103, 107–08, 111–12, 142, 251
Boethius, *Consolation of Philosophy*, 40, 70, 91–93
book lending, 37
Book of Ballymote (Royal Irish Academy MS23 P 12), 201
Book of Common Order, 239–42
Book of Deer, 24
Book of Fermoy, 312, n. 87
Book of the Dean of Lismore, 2, 7, 11, 16, 24, 28, 29, 44–45, 63–64, 80, 82, 113, 115, 120, 124–46, 148, 184, 185, 187, 188, 192, 193, 198, 202–03, 246–47
Books of Clanranald, 24, 83, 85, 125
Bothwell, Richard, 40
Bousie, David (aka David Alexander), 52, 58
   protocol book (Edinburgh, NRS MS B 21/1/1), 52, 58
Bower, Walter, 1, 102, 103, 105, 162
   Scotichronicon, 41, 53, 70, 103, 105, 162, 179
   Scotichronicon MS, Cambridge, Corpus Christi College, MS 171, 162
Bowie, William, 116–17
Brant, Sebastian, *Das Narrenschiff (The Ship of Fools)*, 141
Brighid, daughter of the Earl of Kildare, 133

Bruce, Robert, see, Robert I
Buchanan, George, 3, 10, 65, 76, 100, 111–12, 122, 149, 152, 173, 174, 178, 213
  Alcestis, 247
  Baptistes, 233
  The Chamaeleon, 213
  Jepthes, 233
  Medea, 247
  Rerum Scoticarum Historia, 111–12
Buke of Alexander, 158, 160, 162, 249
Burne, Nicol, 77

Cairbre mac Étaíne, 201
Cadiou, Andrew, 58
Calderwood, David, 74, 112, 225, 230
calender customs, 228–31
Campbell clan, 2, 22, 24, 28, 29, 124, 133, 141, 143, 145
Campbell, Donnchadh/Sir Duncan, 124, 134–39, 140, 143, 145, 192, 201
Campbell, Archibald, 2nd Earl of Argyll, 185
Campbell, Archibald, 5th Earl of Argyll, 25, 242
Campbell, Cailéan/Colin, first Earl of Argyll, 124, 140, 143
Campbell, Colin, 6th Earl of Argyll, 242
Campbell, Fionnghal, 191–92, 333 n. 109
Campbell, Gilleasbuig, 4th or 5th Earl of Argyll, 80
Campbell, Iseabal Ní Mheic Cailéin, 131, 133, 308, n. 94
Campbell, Iseabal, Countess of Argyll, 130–34, 140, 308, 311, n. 30, n. 72

Campbell, John, Bishop of the Isles, 313, n. 93
Campbells of Argyll, 158
Campbells of Glenorchy, 116–17
Carrick, 19, 21
Carswell, John, Bishop of Argyll, 8, 25, 26, 67–68, 115, 122, 240–42
  Foirm na n-Urrnuidheadh (*Book of the Common Order*), 25, 239–42
'Cath Maige Tuired', 201
Catholicism, 52, 60, 64–65, 67, 70, 72–76, 77, 123
Caxton, William, 39, 166, 168, 239, 248, 249
Castalian Band, 154
Chaimbeul, Mór, 190, 195, 197
Chaucer, Geoffrey, 30–34, 37, 38–39, 40, 45, 46, 51, 90, 93, 141, 247
  'The Reeve's Tale', 31
  Book of the Duchess, 91
  Complaint of Anelida, 34
  Knight's Tale, 92
  Legend of Good Women, 31, 39, 45
  The Parliament of Fowls, 97, 247
  Troilus and Criseyde, 38–39, 45, 91–92
Charteris, Henry, 42–43, 46–47, 52, 53
Charles I, 1–2, 223, 228
chanson de mal mariee, 148, 206
Chepman, Walter, 39, 44, 45, 51, 48–49, 50, 52, 54, 58, 59, 105–06, 169, 181
chivalry, 12–13, 16, 157–72, 222, 254
chivalric literature, 157–72, 252–53
chivalric manuals, 164–69

Clan manuscript histories, 24, 113–19
Clanranald, 192–93
Clappertoun, George, 146–47, 148, 149
Clariodus, 158, 159, 161
Clarsair, 218
Commonweal, 3, 149, 210, 211, 213
Commonwealth, 3, 264
Corpus Christi, 226, 228, 229
Cotgrave, Randle, *Dictionary of the English and French Tongues*, 153, 263
counter-reformation, 66–67
The Crafte of Deying, 176
Craig of Rosecraig, Alexander, 155, 260
Craigie, Sir William, 48, 252
Cranstoun, David, 53
Cresseid Caledonia, 40, 182, 212
Cromwell, Oliver, vii, 198
'The Cruikit iedis the blinde', 213
Cú Chulainn, 67, 118, 120, 187–88
Culloden, vii

dance-dramas, 229
Davidson, Thomas, 47, 52
Dempster, Thomas, *Historia Ecclesiastica Gentis Scotorum*, 112
The Dialogue of the Twa Wyfeis, 213–15
Diggens, Edward (teacher), 36
Donnchadh Óg, 64
Douglas family, 2, 110, 169, 251
Douglas, Gavin, 6–7, 15, 38–39, 42, 49, 51, 52, 53–54, 96–98, 170, 253, 256
  Eneados, 39–40, 52–53, 98, 248–52, 255–56, 262, 265
  The Palice of Honoure, 34, 52–53, 89, 96–97, 220–21, 227, 231, 234, 255
Douglas, Sir James, 164, 169
dream-vision, 8, 64, 200, 204, 205, 213
Drummond, William, 155–56, 228, 234, 260
  Flowres of Sion, 66, 156
  Poems, 155
  Teares on the Death of Meoliades, 180
Drurye, Erasmus, 36
Du Bartas, Guillaume de Salluste, 255–56
  Judith, 256
  L'Uranie, 255
Du Bellay, Joachim, 34, 256
  The Defence and Illustration of the French Language, 34
Duanaire(an), 29, 82, 173, 185, 201
Dumfries, 36
Dunbar, Elizabeth, Countess of Moray, 169
Dunbar, George, Earl of March, 20
Dunbar, William, vii, 7, 12, 13, 14, 17, 18, 32–34, 35, 38–40, 43–45, 46–51, 52, 58–59, 64–65, 121, 141, 146, 147–48, 149, 153–54, 158, 167, 169, 170, 174, 179, 181–82, 201, 203–05, 206, 212, 215, 218, 221
  'Ane murelandis man of uplandis mak', 205–06
  'Apon the Midsummer Evin, mirriest of nichts' (*The Tretis of the Twa Mariit Wemen and the Wedo*), 38, 48, 148, 206, 215

'As yung Awrora with cristall haile', 204
'Complane I wald, wist I quhome till', 205
'I that in heill wes and gladnes', 179
'Illuster Ludovick, of France most cristin king', 181–82
'Invice most vicious he excellis', 203–04
'Off benefice, sir, at everie feist', 205
'Off Februar the fyiftene nycht', 170
'Quhen Merche wes with variand windis past', 151
'Renownit ryall right reuerend and serene' (*The Ballade of Lord Bernard Stewart*), 49
'Ryght as the stern of day begouth to schyne' (*The Goldyn Targe*), 39, 48
'Schir Johine the Ros, ane thing thair is compild' (*The Flyting of Dumbar and Kennedie*) 17, 33, 34, 121, 174, 203, 205, 212, 215–16, 218–19, 221
'Schir, I complane of Injuris', 203
'Schir, ye have mony servitouris', 205
'The waidrapper of Wenus bour', 204
'This hinder nycht, half sleeping as I lay', 205
'This nycht befoir the dawing cleir', 205
'To thee, O Marcifull Salviour myn, Jhesus' (*The Tabill of Confessioun*), 49

Dunfermline, 40, 49
Dunkeld, 142
Eachann Bacach, 61–62 (see also Maclean)

Edinburgh, 4, 23, 36, 42–43, 46, 47, 51, 52, 54, 59, 69, 77–78, 109, 112, 125, 146, 148, 172, 179–80, 181, 192, 210–11, 213, 214, 219–20, 223, 225–26, 231, 234–35, 244, 253
Edinburgh, National Library of Scotland MS 72.1.4, 239–40
Edinburgh, National Library of Scotland MS 73.1.22, 240
education, 17, 22–23, 35, 88, 110, 229, 234
  and Gaelic, 6, 9, 22, 27
  Curriculum, 23
  Englishmen hired as teachers, 36
  Greek, in, 23
  Highlands & Islands, in, 21–22, 88
  Latin in, 3, 4–5, 19, 23
Eger and Grime, 158, 159–60
elegy, 5, 11–12, 14, 61, 83, 120, 139, 173–99, 202
Elizabeth I, 243–44, 246
Elphinstone, Alexander, 4th Lord, 233–36
Elphinstone, Robert, 3rd Lord, 233–36
Elphinstone, William, Bishop of Aberdeen, 4, 70, 101, 107
English language, 4, 20, 22–24, 28–31, 33–36, 37, 76, 113, 246
epic, 104–06, 109, 121, 158, 163–65, 258
Erasmus, Desiderius, 37, 56, 107, 110

Estienne, Henry, 54
euhemerism, 250–51
eulogy, 10, 59, 80–82, 129, 202

female characters, 159–60
Fernaig Manuscript (Glasgow, Glasgow University Library, MS Gen. 85/1 & 85/2), 24, 28, 29, 66
file, 201
Fionnlagh, am Bard Ruadh (Red Bard Finlay), 82, 192–93, 202
    'Theast aon diabhal na nGaoidheal', 82, 201–02
Flodden, 52, 110, 185, 248
Florimond of Albany, 158
flyting, 11, 17, 33, 34, 121, 148, 174, 200, 203, 205, 208–09, 212, 215–16, 218, 221
Fordun, John, 9, 32, 100, 113
    Scotus montanus, 222–23
    Chronica gentis Scotorum, 102–03
Forrester, Robert, 58–59
Fortune, 9, 14, 91–93, 94–95, 148, 185, 209
Fowler, William, 17, 154, 182–83, 185, 256, 259–60
    Il Principe (*The Prince*), 259–60, 265
    Of Death, 178–79
    Tarantula of Love, 260
    Triumphs, 256, 260
Fraser, James, 37
French language, 5, 16, 17, 20, 32, 33, 63, 157, 262, 263
French literature, 16, 40, 104–05, 146, 152, 154, 159, 160, 166, 167, 176–77, 249, 256, 260–61

Gaelic, classical, 24–29, 67–70, 83, 185, 237–38, 241
Gaelic, expansion of, 21
Gaelic, Scottish, 24–30, 32–37, 65–69, 237
    Bible, 22, 25, 26, 27, 67, 241, 244–45
    declining Status, 20, 21, 22, 33, 62, 84, 100, 193
    demographic extent of, 19, 21, 62, 79, 246
    Fenian Tales, 29
    hands, 237
    literature, 79, 86–87, 173, 201
    Lord's Prayer, 26–27
    medical manuscripts, 239–40
    oral tradition, 29, 69, 88, 115–16, 122, 237
    orthography, 23, 24, 28–29, 126, 237, 244–55
    performance, 217–18, 228–29
    Privy Council rulings (1616), 23
    publishing, 23, 62, 69, 240
    song collectors, 29–30, 88
    translations of Classical Latin, 238–39
    type, 237, 243–44
Galloway, 19, 21
Gathelos and Scota, 9, 102
Gau, John, 71
Genealogy, 83–84, 85, 86, 100, 104, 112, 113, 115, 117–20, 123, 168, 186–87, 261
Geoffrey of Monmouth, *Historia Regum Britanniae*, 9, 103
Gesta Romanorum, 64
Gillies, William, 9, 10, 11, 79, 126, 127, 130, 134, 140, 141, 143, 144

Giolla Críost Brúilingeach, 'Dá urradh i n-iath Éireann', 201
Giolla Pádraig Albanach, 239
Golagros and Gawane, 12, 17, 58–59, 158, 159, 160, 161, 170
Gordon of Ruthven, Patrick, 106
  Famous Historie of the Renouned and Valiant Prince Robert surnamed the Bruce, 161
  Pernardo and Laissa, 160–61
Gordon, Sir Robert, 22, 123
  Genealogical History of the Earldom of Sutherland, 123
Gourlay, Robert, 46
Gower, John, 35
  Confessio Amantis, 89, 90, 91, 93
Graham, James, Marquis of Montrose, 85, 156, 191
Gray, James, 43
  Gray MS (Edinburgh, NLS MS 34.7.3), 43
Gray, Robert, 55
Gray, Sir Thomas, 32
  Scalacronica, 32, 43
Gude and Godlie Ballatis, 66, 153
Guthrie, Tyrone, 3
guild plays, 219, 226, 229–30

Haddington, 103, 182, 226, 233
Hamilton family, 36, 212
Hamilton, John, Archbishop of St Andrews, 73
Hamilton, John, 75–76
Hamilton, Patrick, 71
Hannay, Patrick,
  Sheretine and Mariana, 160
Hary, 2, 158, 164, 165
  Wallace, 105, 158, 163–65

Hay, John, 77–78
Hay, Sir Gilbert, 157, 166–67, 184, 251
  Buik of King Alexander the Conqueror, 158, 160, 162, 167, 177–78, 249
  Buke of the Gouernaunce of Princis, 166–67, 249, 251, 255, 260, 265
  Buke of the Law of Armys, 166–67
  Buke of the Ordre of the Knychthede, 166–67, 249
Hays of Errol, 165–66
health, 195, 201, 209, 220, 231
Henry, Prince of Wales, 180–81, 230
Henryson, Robert, 6, 7, 9, 13, 18, 38–46, 89–90, 142, 146, 147, 203, 215
  'The Bludy Serk', 64
  Moral Fabillis, 38, 40–43, 47, 93–95, 206–08
    'The Sheep and the Dog', 207
    'The Two Mice', 206–07
    'The Wolf and the Lamb', 207
    'The Wolf and the Wedder', 207
  Orphius and Eurydice, 44, 177–78
  Testament of Cresseid, 38, 44–47, 95–96, 141–42
Hepburn, Patrick, Earl of Bothwell, 211
heraldry, 167–68
historiography, 5, 8–9, 17, 78, 84–85, 100–23, 184, 251–54
history, 80, 83–87, 100–23, 150, 173, 183, 186–87, 209, 223, 241, 252–53, 254–55, 258, 261

Hogmanay, 229
Holland, Richard, 17, 58, 61, 121, 146, 172
  The Buke of the Howlat, 17, 61, 121, 146, 168–69
Howard, Henry, Earl of Surrey, 149
Hudson, Robert, 154, 183–84, 255–56
Hudson, Thomas, 183–84
  Judith, 255–56
humanism, 3–4, 11, 17, 39–40, 57, 70–71, 97–98, 106–07, 111–12, 122, 213, 233–34, 248, 251
Hume, Alexander, 155
  'Of the Day Estivall', 155
Hume, Anna, 152–53, 156
Hume of Polwarth, Patrick, 155, 215
  Flyting, 215

Iain Lom (see MacDonald, Iain Lom)
Incipit Lamentatio domini Dalphini Franciae pro morte uxoris suae, dictae Margareta, 176–77
Ireland, 7–8, 10, 16–17, 24–26, 29, 60–63, 67–68, 79, 83–88, 96, 102, 110, 113–14, 118–20, 122–23, 125–26, 133, 143–45, 162, 185, 197, 201–02, 237–38, 239, 241–42, 243–44, 246
Ireland, John, 70–71, 249, 251
  Meroure of Wyssdome, 70–71, 249, 251
Irish translations of English texts, 239

Jack, R. D. S, 257
Jacobite rising (1745-1746), 29–30
James I, 37, 58, 89, 103, 110, 165–66, 179, 182
  Kingis Quair, 3, 9, 35–37, 89–93, 94, 96, 146, 260
James II, 177, 219
James III, 1, 70, 107, 138, 164–65, 251
James IV, 1, 12, 35, 70–71, 90, 139, 146, 154, 164, 171, 203–05, 220, 251, 255–57
James V, 1, 76, 107–09, 149, 154, 171, 179–80, 208–09, 210, 220, 229, 252, 253–54
James VI, 1, 4, 10–11, 15, 17, 18, 20, 28, 34, 36, 62, 64, 75–77, 79, 90, 98–99, 111, 146, 153, 154–55, 160–61, 182, 211–15, 219, 225–27, 230–35, 255–57, 259, 260
  Basilicon Doron, 36, 62, 259
  Reulis and Cautelis, or Ane Schort Treatise Conteining Some Reulis and Cautelis to be Observit and Eschewit in Scots poesie, 34, 98, 153, 216, 230, 234, 256–57, 259
  Urania, 255–56
Johnston, Arthur, 3, 155
  Delitiae Poetarum Scotorum, 155
Juvenal, 142

Keating, Geoffrey, 85–86
Kennedie, John, *Calanthrop and Lucilla*, 160–61
Kennedy, Quintin, 73
Kennedy, Walter, 13, 33, 65, 203, 206, 212, 214, 218–19
  'Ane aigit man, twyss fourty yeiris', 206
  'Schir Johine the Ros' (*The Flyting of Dumbar and*

Kennedie) 13, 121, 212, 214, 218, 221
'The Passioun of Christ', 65
King, Adam, 77
King Orphius, 158–59
Kirk, Robert, 25, 26
Knox, John, 8, 60, 72–75, 76, 78, 111, 214
    History of the Reformation in Scotland, 60, 72–75, 112

Lancelot of the Laik, 17, 35, 158–61, 249
Landino, Cristoforo, 39
Langtoft, Peter
    Vita Edwardi Secundi, 31–32
Latin language, 2, 5, 7–8, 19, 20–24, 27, 32, 43, 61, 74, 102–03, 107, 237, 245–46
Latin literature, 2, 3, 9, 14–15, 16, 23, 40, 41, 44, 54, 55, 57, 63–67, 69, 70, 77, 85, 100–03, 113, 116, 122, 124, 130, 141, 143, 146, 152, 155, 167, 173–75, 179, 182, 204, 233, 239, 149, 262
Lebor Gabála Érenn, 84
Lekpreuick, Robert, 43, 53, 57, 211, 213
Lesley, John, *De Origine, Moribus, et Rebus Gestis Scotorum, libri decem*, 76–77, 111
Lhuyd, Edward, 26
Liber Pluscardensis, 103–04, 176–77
libraries, 37, 39, 167, 168
Liddell, James, 54
Lindsay of Pitscottie, Robert, *The historie and chronicles of Scotland*, 110–11, 121
literacy, 4, 8, 23, 63, 244, 246

Little John, 229
Livy, *Ab Urbe Condita*, 3, 16, 251–55
Llull, Ramon, 166, 249
Lockert, George, 54
Lombard, Peter, 53–54
London, King's Inn Library MS 15, 240
Lordship of the Isles, 1, 24, 79–80, 87, 185, 193, 203
Loutfut, Adam, 167
Loutfut MS (London, British Library, Harley MS 6149) 167–68
Lyall, R. J., 40, 182, 212
Lydgate, John, 41, 141
    The Fall of Princes, 141
    Troy Book, 158
Lyndsay, Sir David, 2, 3, 4, 6, 148, 158, 167, 169–70, 185, 208–11, 228
    Ane Satyre of the Thrie Estaitis, 210–11, 219–21, 226–27
    Armorial, 162, 168
    Squyer Meldrum, 12, 158, 169
    The Answer to the Kingis Flyting, 148, 208–09
    'The Deploratioun of the Deith of Quene Magdalene', 148, 179–80
    The Justing Betwix James Watsoun and Jhone Barbour, 170
    The Testament and Complaynt of our Souerane Lordis Papyngo, 209
Lyric, 124–56

Mac an Aba, Domhnall, 137
Mac an Aba, Fionnlagh, 137

Mac an Bhaird, Conchobhair (Cornelius Ward), 68
Mac an Bhaird, Fearghal Óg, 62, 125
Mac an Breatnaigh, Lachlann, 138
Mac an Leagha, Uilleam, 239
Mac an Ollaimh, Giolla-Coluim, 82–83, 186, 187–88, 189–90, 193
Mac an tSaoir, An Bard, 139, 141, 310, n. 63
Mac Bruaideadha, Tadhg mac Daire, 80
Mac Con-Midhe, Giolla-Brighde, 81
MacCulloch of Park, Strathpeffer (Fear na Pàirce), 66
Mac Diarmaid, Sir Donnchadh, 140
Mac Domhnaill (MacDonald), Aonghus Óg, son of the Lord of the Isles, 131
Mac Domhnaill, Captain Somhairle, 69
MacDonald, Alasdair mac Mhaighistir Alasdair, 23
MacDonald, Dòmhnall Gorm of Sleat, 37
MacDonald, Hugh, *History of the Macdonalds*, 223–24
MacDonald, Iain Lom, poet, 30, 185, 187, 190, 192, 198, 199
  'Là Inbhir Lochaidh', 192
  'Òran cumhaidh air cor na Rioghachd', 198
MacDonald, Sìleas 'na Ceapaich', 23, 198–99
MacDonalds of Clanranald, 25, 26
MacDonalds, 24, 185
Mac Fir-Bhisigh, Dubhaltach, 85–86
Mac Gilleasbaig, Ailean, 197–98
MacGill'Eathain (MacLean), Eachann Mòr, eleventh chief of Duart, 125

MacGille-Chonaill, Donnchadh Riabhach, 138
MacGregor, Duncan (Mac Griogóir, Donnchadh), 144
MacGregor, James (Mac Griogóir, Séamas), 64, 140, 144
MacGregors, 185, 197–98
Mac Griogóir, Domhnall Liath, 309, n. 47
Mac Griogóir, Eóin Dubh (d. 1519), 310, n. 59
MacKenzie, Alasdair, 4th of Achilty (Alasdair mac Mhurchaidh, Fear Àicheallaidh), 66
MacKenzies, 36
MacLachan, prob. John, of Kilbride, 198
Mac Laghmainn, Roibéard, 64
Maclean, Eachann Bacach, 30
Maclean, Mairghread nighean Lachlainn, 23, 88, 195
MacLeod, Iain Mòr of Dunvagan, 25
MacLeod, Màiri nighean Alasdair Ruaidh (Mary MacLeod), 23, 88, 191, 196
MacLeod, Sir Ruairidh Mòr of Dunvegan, 25
MacLeods, 185
Mac Mhághnais Mhuileadhaigh, Maol-Domhnaigh, 64
MacMhuirich family, 25
MacMhuirich, Cathal, 184, 186–87, 189, 192, 197, 283
MacMhuirich, Eoin, 122, 188–89, 192
Mac Mhuirich, Niall, 83, 85
MacMhuirich, Nìall Mór, 125
Mac Muireadhaigh, (Mac Mhuirich), Eóin, 122, 127–29, 135, 188–89, 192

MacNèill, Nìall of Gigha, 61
MacNeils of Barra, 26
MacQueen, John, 253
MacRae, Duncan of Inverinate (Donnchadh nam Pìos), 66
MacRaoiridh, Donnchadh, 186–87
Machiavelli, Niccolò di Bernardo dei, 256, 259
Mág Uidhir (Maguire), Cú Chonnacht Óg, lord of Fermanagh, 133
Mair, John, 101, 106–09, 255
  Historia Maioris Britanniae tam Angliae quam Scotiae, 106–07
Maitland, Marie, 152
Maitland, Sir Richard, 2, 146, 149–50, 151–52, 183–84
  Off the Quenis Arryvale in Scotland, 150
Maitland, Thomas, 182, 213–14
Maitland, William, of Lethington, 213–14
Maitland Folio (Cambridge, Magdalene College Pepys Library, MS 2553), 45–48, 49–50, 146, 148, 149
Maitland Quarto (Cambridge, Magdalene College, Pepys Library MS1408), 146, 149
Makculloch MS (Edinburgh, Edinburgh University MS 205, formerly La. III.49), 40–41, 42, 146
Malkculloch, Magnus, 40–41, 43
Margaret, Princess of Scotland, daughter of James I, 176–77
Margaret of Denmark, wife of James III, 1

Martin, Florentine, 58, 59
Martin, Martin, 23, 26, 228
Mary of Guise, Queen Regent, 72–73, 227
Mary, Queen of Scots, 2, 12, 72, 76–77, 89–90, 110–11, 122, 149, 150–52, 208, 211, 215, 229, 230, 234
  Casket Sonnets, 12, 151–52
May Day, 229, 234
Masselin, Robert, 58
Melville, Andrew, 4, 75, 77
Melville, Elizabeth, *Ane Godlie Dreame*, 64
Melville, James, 74–75, 155
  Autobiography and Diary, 65, 74–75, 216
Michaelmas, 228
Middle English, 7, 30–31, 34, 146, 158, 168
Montgomerie, Alexander, 11, 64–65, 90, 127, 153–55, 160, 176, 183, 215, 256
  'Come my children deir drau neir me', 154
  In praise of Maister John Maitland, 153–54
  The Cherrie and the Slae, 89
  The Flyting of Montgomerie and Polwarth, 215–16
  The Ladyis Lamentatioune, 154
  To His Majestie for his Pensioun, 154
  To Robert Hudsone, 154
Mòr Nic Phàidein, 196–97
Moral judgement, 190–91
Morrison, Ruairidh (An Clàrsair Dall), 30, 88
Mull, Isle of, 26

Munro, Alexander, 66, 245
Murray, David, 260
Murthly Hours (Edinburgh NLS, MS 21000), 63
music, 11, 15–16, 80–81, 89, 146–47, 217, 218, 220, 221, 234–36
Myllar, Andrew, 39, 43–45, 48–49, 50, 52, 54, 56–59, 80–81, 89, 105–06, 146–47, 169, 181, 217, 218, 220, 221, 234–36

National Covenant, 78, 233
Nine Worthies, 161–63, 170, 171
NLS Advocates MS 72.1.34, 125
NLS Advocates MS 72.1.36, 125
NLS MS 72.1.4, 239
NLS MS 73.1.22, 240
Norn, 20
notaries public, 40, 42, 43, 52, 58, 61, 64, 142, 167, 169, 207

Ó Cearnaigh, Seaan, 68, 243–44
Ó Conchubhair, Donnchadh Albanach, 240
Ó Conchubhair, Donnchadh Ó, 240
Ó Dálaigh, Cearbhall Óg, 309, n. 45
Ó Dálaigh, Gofraidh Fionn, 61
Ó hEoghusa, Eochaidh, 133
Ó Maoilchiarain, Fearchar, 197
Ó Néill, Seán, 246
O'Rahilly, T. F., *Dánta Grádha*, 142
Oidhche Challainn, 229
Older Scots, 2–5, 8–10, 12, 16–18, 21–23, 30–36, 61, 64–66, 73–74, 75–76, 89–99, 247
    Anglicising influences in, 35, 36
    Burghs, 21
    Expansion of, 19
    Influenced by other languages, 32
    Inglis becomes known as Scots, 21
    Morphology, 31
    Orthography, 30
    Phonology, 30–31
    Poetry, 33–34
    Pronunciation, 35–36
    Status, 20, 32
Omey, Duncan, 246
Òran na Comhachaig (*The Song of the Owl*), 87
Order of Combats for Life in Scotland, 165–6
origin myths, 9, 80, 84, 86, 100–03, 107–08, 112–13, 118–19, 122
Orkney, 1, 20, 166
Osborn manuscript (New Haven CT, Yale University, Beinecke, Music MS 13), 51
Ovid, 23, 37, 91, 260

patronage, 1, 4, 10, 16, 58, 62, 80–89, 116–17, 122, 140, 164, 166–67, 169, 174, 182, 185–86, 215–16, 218–19, 232–36
performance, 2, 3, 11, 12, 15, 16, 122, 171, 210, 217–36
Petrarch, Francesco, 16, 152, 153, 156, 256, 260
Plato, 3, 70
Symposium, 260
political performance, 223–28
Pont, Robert, 77
print culture, 4, 8, 20, 37, 38–59, 62, 67–69, 73–74, 105–06, 153, 169, 208–09, 211–13, 234, 240–45

Protestantism, 3, 4, 8–9, 22, 25, 60–61, 64–65, 66, 69–78, 111–12, 115, 122, 152, 155, 211–12, 230, 234, 243–45
    Calvinist, 64, 69, 178, 241–45
    Lutheran, 66, 71, 153
Purde, John, 41–42
Puttenham, George,
    The Arte of English Poesie, 34

Rabelais, François, 18, 260–65
    Gargantua and Pantagruel, 18, 261–65
Ramsay, Allan, *The Evergreen*, 51, 156
Ramsay, John, of Ochtertyre, 184
Rauf Coilȝear, The Taill of, 158, 160, 170
reacaire, 218
Reidpeth MS (Cambridge, CUL MS Ll.5.10), 47
Reformation, vii, 3, 4, 19, 60, 66–73, 229–32
rituals, 231–32
Robert I, 105, 161, 162–63, 164, 169
Robert II, 104, 164
Robert III, 222
Robin Hood, 229
romance, 12–13, 16–17, 20, 35, 80, 87, 88–89, 104–05, 158–65, 169–71, 175, 200, 249, 258, 261
The Romance of Fergus, 20
Ross, John, 52
Roswall and Liliane, 159
Ruddiman, Thomas, 51, 53

satire, 8, 65–66, 81–82, 87–88, 200–16
Scheves, William, 41, 43
Scot, John, 53

Scott, Alexander, 127, 146–47, 150–51
    'Ane New Year's Gift to the Quene Marie', 150–51
    'Justing and Debait up at the Drum', 170
Scottish Privy Council, 22, 36, 62, 78
Scottish Troy Book, 158
Selden Manuscript (Oxford Bodleian Library, Arch Selden. B. 24), 37, 39, 51, 58, 90
Sempill, Robert, 153–54, 156, 211–12, 213, 214, 215–16
    'Ane Answer maid to the Sklanderis', 212
    'Rob Stene's Dream', 215
Shetland, 1, 20, 23
Sìleas na Ceapaich (see MacDonald)
Sinclair, Henry, 2
Sinclair, Sir William, Earl of Orkney, 166, 167, 249, 255
Sinclairs of Ravenscraig, 58
Sir Colling the Knycht, 158, 159
Skeyne, Gilbert
    Ane Breve Descriptioun of the Pest, 35
    Ane Breif Descriptioun of the Qualiteis and Effectis of the Well of the Woman Hill besyde Abirdene, 35
sonnets, 11, 12, 64, 152, 154, 155, 182, 183, 256
Spence, Alan, 3
SSPCK (Scottish Society for Propagation of Christian Knowledge), 22
St Andrews, 39, 41, 42, 71, 73, 75, 76, 77

Stewart of Baldynneis, John, 9, 64, 89–90, 97, 154, 160, 256, 260
   Roland Furious, 17, 89, 97, 160, 256–59
Stewart, Charles, earl of Lennox, 160
Stewart, Henry, Lord Darnley, 152, 211–12, 213
Stewart, James, Earl of Moray, 211, 212, 213–14
Stewart, William, 109, 148
Stiúbhairt (Stewart), Janet, daughter of John Stewart, Lord of Lorn, 140, 311, n. 72
Stiúbhairt (Stewart), Máire, 133
Stornoway, 23
Stranraer, 23
Sutherland, 21–22, 24, 218
Synod of Argyll, 25, 26, 69, 242–43, 244
Tacitus, *Agricola*, 108–09
   Annales, 3
   Germania, 108–09
'Talland Étair', 201
Táilléar, Giolla-Críost, 64
Thynne, William, 45, 46
Tottel's Miscellany, 153
translation, 3, 4, 5, 8, 11, 16–18, 22, 25, 27, 29, 47, 52–53, 63, 65–69, 71, 77, 87, 98, 109–10, 121, 142, 151–53, 160, 167–68, 176–77, 237–65

Trevet, Nicholas, 40
Tudor, Mary, 52

Ua Briain, Donnchadh, 4th Earl of Thormond, 80
Ua Catháin, Seán, 313, n. 93

Ulster, 25, 187, 242, 244
Ulster Plantation, 83
Union of the Crowns, 4, 15, 18, 20, 36, 79, 106, 154–55, 160
Union of the Parliaments, 1707, vii, 53
Urquhart, Sir Thomas, 4, 18, 259–65
   Ekskubalauron, 264
   Gargantua and Pantagruel, 4, 260–26
   Logopandecteison, 264
   Pantachronochanon, 264
   The Jewel, 4

Valla, Lorenzo, 39
Vaus, John, 7, 54–57, 58
   Rudimenta puerorum in artem grammaticam, 55–57
   Doctrinale, 55–57
   fragments of work, 55
Vegius, Maphaeus, 198, 250
Verse Forms, 63, 66
Virgil, *Aeneid*, 3, 38, 84, 248, 250, 253
Virgin Mary, 8, 41, 61, 63–65, 70, 71, 81, 105, 146–47

Wallace, William, 53, 164–65
Wars of the Three Kingdoms, 4, 79, 184, 198
Watson, James, *Choice Collection*, 156
Watson, William J., 28, 127, 187, 192, 193
Wedderburn, David, 37
Western Isles, 1, 24, 79, 235
Whibley, Charles, 261
William of Touris, 65
Winzet, Ninian, 8, 73–75, 231

Wishart, George, 71
women writers, 88, 174–75, 184, 189, 190–92, 193–96

Wyatt, Sir Thomas, 149
Wyntoun, Andrew, 146
    Original Chronicle, 2, 103–04

www.ingramcontent.com/pod-product-compliance
Lightning Source LLC
Chambersburg PA
CBHW052048230426
43671CB00011B/1829